FOURTH EDITION

Comprehensive Multicultural Education

THEORY AND PRACTICE

Christine I. Bennett
Indiana University at Bloomington

Allyn and Bacon
Boston   London   Toronto   Sydney   Tokyo   Singapore

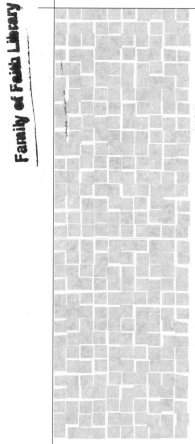

Vice President, Publisher, Education: Sean W. Wakely
Series Editor: Frances Helland
Editorial Assistant: Bridget Keane
Marketing Managers: Ellen Dolberg and Brad Parkins
Editorial Production Service: Chestnut Hill Enterprises, Inc.
Manufacturing Buyer: Suzanne Lareau
Cover Administrator: Linda Knowles
Text Design: Carol Somberg/Omegatype Typography, Inc.

Internet: www.abacon.com

Between the time Website information is gathered and published, it is not unusual for some
sites to have closed. Also, the transcription of URLs can result in typographical errors. The
publisher would appreciate notification where these occur so that they may be corrected.
Thank you.

Library of Congress Cataloging-in-Publication Data
Bennett, Christine I.
    Comprehensive multicultural education : theory and practice /
    Christine I. Bennett. —4th ed.
        p.   cm.
    Includes bibliographical references (p.   ) and index.
    ISBN 0-205-28324-1
    1. Multicultural education—United States.   2. International
education–United States.   3. Global method of teaching.   I. Title.
    LC1099.3.B46   1999
370'19'34'0973–dc21   98-16160
                                                           CIP

Printed in the United States of America

10   9   8   7   6   5   4   RRD-VA   03   02   01   00

Photo Credits: Photo credits can be found on page 436, which should be considered an extension of the copyright page.

Contents

2

The Nature of Culture and the Contexts for Multicultural Teaching

3

Race Relations and the Nature of Prejudice

4

Conflicting Themes of Assimilation and Pluralism among European Americans, Jewish Americans, and African Americans   101

5

Conflicting Themes of Assimilation and Pluralism among American Indians, Hispanics, Asians, Muslims, and Arabs in the United States 130

part II Individual Differences That Affect Teaching and Learning 167

6

Theories of Learning Style and Multiple Intelligence: Interactions between Culture and the Individual   177

7

Beyond Learning Style: An Overview of Other Key Individual Differences   211

Strengthening Multicultural Perspectives in Curriculum and Instruction   *part* **III**   243

8

Multicultural Curriculum Development: A Decision-Making Model and Lesson Plans   247

9

Educational Concepts and Teaching Strategies for Multicultural Classrooms

366

Preface

Comprehensive Multicultural Education was first written for my students and others new to the field of multicultural education. My goal was to create a framework that would help them make sense out of a complex, ambiguous, multidisciplinary field that asks teachers to take risks and deal with controversial topics such as prejudice, racism, social justice, and cultural pluralism. I wanted to provide some of the historical background, basic terminology, and social science concepts that many students have not yet encountered when they enter the field. I hoped to engage readers on an emotional level, move them to take action in their classrooms, and encourage them to pursue academic inquiry and self-reflection after the book had been read. Although the book's basic philosophy and approach remain the same, changes in the third and fourth editions have grown out of more than a decade of conversations with my own students as well as other students and instructors who are engaged in multicultural teacher education. These conversations have provided a steady barometer of the book's strengths and limitations, and they indicate that the book stimulates thinking and dialogue about critical issues in multicultural education in ways that I had only hoped would be possible.

The book deals with questions students continually ask that too often are left unanswered. Doesn't multicultural education lead to lower academic standards? Won't cultural pluralism lead to the Balkanization of our society? Aren't we really stereotyping when we talk about cultural differences? Isn't it racist? Are you saying I can't set up my own standards for acceptable behavior in my classroom? How can I add multicultural content when I don't have time to cover the basic curriculum? What does multicultural education have to do with math and science, or with physical education? Doesn't it really boil down to indoctrination?

My approach to multicultural education focuses on ethnic diversity and community in the United States, diversity rooted in racial, cultural, and individual differences as well as basic human similarities and global connections. Given that we live in a multicultural world, multicultural education is for everyone. Few of our nation's schools, however, have become multicultural in their vision or practice. They are hampered by societal policies and practices, often beyond their control, that impede reform of formal and hidden curricula. Shortage of funds and lack of understanding, for example, make it difficult for schools to replace or supplement biased or outdated books and films, to hire new personnel who can provide positive role models from a variety of ethnic groups, or to study alternatives to discriminatory school practices in areas such as co-curricular activities or student discipline. Teachers and administrators who are uninformed about cultural diversity, whose knowledge of history and current events is monocultural in scope, and who are unaware of their own prejudices are likely to hinder the academic success and personal development of many students, however unintentional this may be. How we might meet challenges such as these through multicultural education is what *Comprehensive Multicultural Education* is about.

The book's approach is unique in several ways. First, its content is comprehensive and interdisciplinary in scope and practical in focus. Key concepts from education and the social sciences are often explained with primary source material, and the implications for teaching and learning are developed through vignettes of teachers and students I have known through the years. A primary goal is to assist practicing and prospective teachers to bridge the gap between multicultural concepts or theories and practices in our schools, such as classroom management, instructional strategies, and curriculum development.

Second, the book develops an interaction between cultural and individual differences. Teachers often fear that tuning into students' cultural differences is an indication of being prejudiced or racist. This fear is related to the misconception that equates color consciousness with racism. It also stems from feelings that differences are bad or inferior, and from the mistaken notion that recognition of differences means we must imitate or adopt these differences. Many cultural awareness and human relations workshops have failed because these basic concerns of the participants were not dealt with. On the other hand, most teachers do believe in individualizing or personalizing their instruction. Most would agree that our ultimate goal as teachers is to foster the intellectual, social, and personal development of all students to each one's fullest potential. This book shows that the ability to reach this goal can be strengthened by an understanding of both cultural and individual differences.

A primary feature of the book's later editions is the development of closer connections between multicultural and global education. These connections were influenced by my experiences in China as director of Indiana University's exchange program with Hangzhou University. The multicultural concepts and strategies I had previously used to help prepare teachers for working in a multiethnic society in the United States proved to be equally powerful in developing the exchange students' readiness for immersion into Chinese society and culture. They were also valuable tools for preparing visiting scholars from China, whom I also taught, for their upcoming experiences in the United States. Several years later these insights were reinforced when I had the opportunity to work with teacher educators at Al Ain University in the United Arab Emirates.

Changes in the book's fourth edition reflect suggestions from my own students as well as colleagues and reviewers who use the book. This edition includes a new chapter on race relations, a fuller (and hopefully clearer) explanation of key concepts, as well as the addition of new concepts such as culturally relevant teaching. A careful review of Part I by Bradley Levinson, my colleague at Indiana University, as well as the reactions of my students who used it during fall of 1997, have helped me refine many areas of the text.

The third and fourth editions are enriched by Salman Al-Ani's writings on Muslims in the United States and Arab Americans, and I deeply appreciate his contributions. I am also grateful to John Kornfeld for his creative and compassionate unit on studies of World War II through multicultural literature for children, and to my former students and the Teacher as Decision Maker Program teachers who have contributed many of the sample lessons found in Chapters 8 and 9. I feel certain that readers will share my enthusiasm for their work.

Several outside reviewers provided excellent suggestions that guided my revisions. Sincere thanks go to Russell Young, San Diego State University; Davie Tate, Jr., Clarion University of Pennsylvania; Johnnie Thompson, Wichita State University; and Lynda J. Earring, Wayne State College.

Finally, I want to thank David Blair, a partner who brings love and energy to my lifework.

CIB

The Case for Multicultural Education

A student who was preparing to become a public school teacher recently wrote the following comments in his journal for an education class.

> Why be concerned about culture? After all, we all live in the same country. Most of us speak the same language, and those who don't have the chance to learn English in school. Most of us dress the same, bathe every day, and enjoy the same foods and entertainment and comforts. If you don't think so, just spend some time in a really foreign country. Then you'll see just how American you are. . . . Sure, I plan to be a teacher . . . and I see it as my responsibility to help everyone learn to the best of their ability and to fit into the American society. When we start to look at differences between the races and other groups, we tend to develop stronger stereotypes. . . . Besides, I think it's prejudiced to look at a person's race or cultural differences especially in the classroom where we're supposed to treat everyone equally.

This book is based on the assumption that our major goal as teachers is to foster the intellectual, social, and personal development of our students to their highest potential. The goal is to provide each student with an equal opportunity to learn. The education major quoted above seems to agree. However, he expresses some serious misconceptions. His sentiments are typical of many prospective and experienced teachers and help explain the difficulties faced by students such as the ones you are about to meet: Fred Young, Sarah Stein, Marcia Patton, Jimmy Miller, Isaac Washington, and Jesús Martinez. What are the misconceptions?

First, there is no awareness that the cultural expectations of students' homes and schools may differ, causing academic difficulties related to transitional trauma in the classroom. Second, there is confusion between equal and equitable learning conditions. Third, there are misconceptions about racism. And fourth, there is a false impression of what it means to be an American. One can also detect in the education major's statement an ethnocentrism that is strikingly similar to the students' science reports described below in Sam Johnson's classroom. In short, the writer lacks a multicultural perspective.

Part I builds the case for multicultural schools. It begins with the stories of six students. Although the names have been changed, each example is based on actual incidents that have recently taken place.

■ THE CASE OF FRED YOUNG

Fred Young grew up in the traditional world of the Navajo. Today, after having earned a doctorate in nuclear physics, Fred works at the Los Alamos scientific labs, where the United States's best scientists seek to understand the universe.

As a child, Fred lived in desperate poverty. He helped support his family at a very young age by hunting game, and sometimes he dug for food in the garbage cans outside Gallup, New Mexico, homes. During these early years, Fred also developed a deep curiosity about the world of nature, wondering what it was made of.

Fred's parents sent him to a boarding school at Ignacio, Colorado, so that he could eat regularly. His curiosity and love of nature continued, and he wondered whether clocks could tell the time of day because they were controlled by the sun. His years at the boarding school were filled with hurt and resentment. "In the White world the basic assumptions are so different that something that would be taken for granted by all my classmates wasn't obvious to me at all," Fred says. "So they thought I was scared or dumb or both. It was embarrassing at times, and it made me angry." The daily insults and arrogance Fred experienced in school built up feelings of resentment and hostility, and he sometimes ran off from school and returned to his family in Monument Valley. His intense curiosity and desire to know always brought him back to school where he put up with the hurt in order to satisfy his quest for knowledge. When Fred attended the University of New Mexico on a tribal scholarship, a textbook explanation of how the rainbow works so excited him that he decided to become a physicist.

Today, despite his accomplishments in the world of White America, Fred is still bewildered about how Anglo society works. And there is still hurt. "Even now strangers will sometimes treat me like a dumb Indian," Fred says.[1]

THE CASE OF SARAH STEIN

Sarah Stein grew up in New York City, where she was close to her maternal grandmother, an Orthodox Jew. Although some members of Sarah's extended family consider themselves to be Reform Jews, her parents are Conservative. They observe the Jewish Sabbath and holidays, and Sarah has attended Hebrew schools twice a week throughout her school years. The family also follows many of the traditional dietary rules.

Sarah has moved to the Midwest, where her parents took new jobs at a large university in a city that has retained its small-town flavor. Sarah attends one of the two high schools in the community where she excels in all of her classes. Nevertheless, like Fred Young, Sarah is experiencing pressures in school and at home.

A bright and eager student who is accustomed to a learning environment where students are continually encouraged to ask questions and discuss while new learning is going on, Sarah has begun to turn off many of her new teachers and classmates. She frequently interrupts lecturers with questions of clarification, violating school expectations that students should be quietly attentive until the teacher's presentation is over. She is often perceived as rude, obnoxious, and pushy.

For the first time, Sarah feels embarrassment over missing school during special holidays. She worries about missing important schoolwork during her absences, and this year she missed two days of the Iowa Tests because they were scheduled during Rosh Hashanah.

In her desire to make new friends, Sarah wants to participate in Friday evening activities, such as school parties and football games. However, this conflicts with her parents' demands that she share the Sabbath meal before going to the synagogue. Other conflicts have caused her to drop out of the school band, although she still continues private clarinet lessons.

Sarah is becoming aware of being an exception, if not in conflict with the way of life in her new school and community. She feels set apart when she wants to feel accepted.

THE CASE OF JIMMY MILLER

Jimmy Miller spent his earliest years in the verdant mountains of Kentucky. He moved to a large industrial city in the Midwest when his father was forced to give up the family farm and found work in an automobile factory.

When Jimmy lived in Kentucky there was no kindergarten, and he started school in the first grade. When his family moved north he was placed in kindergarten rather than moving up to the second grade. Jimmy was a shy child who was large for his age, and the notable size difference between him and his classmates became a source of taunting.

Jimmy remembers the first day in his new school. He and his mother were called hillbillies by some of the children; his mother, confused and fearful, was unable to complete all the required forms. The teacher told him the first day that he had better learn to "talk right" and punished him thereafter when he spoke in his dialect, the only language he had known until that time. The school tested his IQ and placed him in the low-ability classes. Jimmy was unfamiliar with many of the items on the test. His family didn't "fly planes," "go on vacations," "have company," "take lessons," or "pack luggage." The common, everyday middle-class world was strange and frightening to him.

Today Jimmy is in the ninth grade, waiting to drop out of school. He rarely, if ever, speaks out in class and does poorly in all his academic subjects except math, where, much to the school's amazement, he excels. His general science teacher might be surprised to know that when Jimmy was in the first grade he saw his mother save his sister's life by performing a tracheotomy when medical assistance was unavailable. Jimmy learned much about breeding and raising animals and managing crops from his grandfather, and at age five he grafted his first apple tree. The chorus teacher at school has no idea that Jimmy comes from a family of skilled dulcimer crafters. Jimmy is a gifted performer on the dulcimer, but he thinks no one at school cares about this talent.

As in the cases of Fred Young and Sarah Stein, Jimmy Miller feels alienated in school. He feels a *dichotomy* between school and home.

Students like Fred Young, Sarah Stein, and Jimmy Miller often find themselves to be an exception to, if not in conflict with, "the American way of life." They feel the pressures of a dual identity as a result of living within two cultures. Consider that Fred, Sarah, and Jimmy are just three examples of what millions of students experience to some degree in our schools every day. How do we proceed?

A primary purpose of this book is to show how multicultural education can help teachers better achieve their major goal: the intellectual, social, and personal development of all students' highest potentials. If we are going to equalize the opportunities we provide, we must consider culture. We must be aware of our own cultural expectations and the expectations of our students, which may be different from our own.

It is essential to develop deeper insights into society's core culture and the ways it shapes our schools and into the cultural differences that exist in most classrooms. Many students feel alienated in public schools because they experience conflict between the cultural expectations of the home and school. The greater the difference between home and school expectations, the more likely a student will experience transitional trauma in the classroom.

Equity is as important as culture in the educational achievement of children and youth. The equity issue is clearly seen in the following vignette.

THE CASE OF ISAAC WASHINGTON

Isaac Washington is a junior at Jefferson Davis High School, a school located near a burgeoning metropolis in Texas that is known for its academic excellence. Having entered Davis High as a freshman, Isaac is among the first group of Black students to attend the school in response to a school desegregation court order.

Isaac had attended elementary and junior high schools in the African American community. He and his friends had expected to enroll in George Washington High School, an all-Black, outstanding educational facility with a national reputation. For decades, Washington High School had provided a nurturing learning environment that encouraged academic excellence and fostered personal ambition and self-confidence among the student population, many of whom became successful in business, the arts, and the professions. The school was shut down three years ago, despite pleading and protest from the African American community, and its student body was distributed throughout the previously all-White schools. This was done so that the in-coming Black students would not exceed 10 to 15 percent of the host school student population. Most of these students face a lengthy bus ride at the beginning and end of each school day, and most can remember the anger and resentment expressed by members of the White community who opposed their presence in the school. Sports and other extracurricular activities scheduled after school have become impossible because of the long bus ride home.

In contrast to most of his former classmates from Washington High School who were placed in the low-ability tracks, Isaac's classes are in the advanced placement and honors sections. Although he excels in all of his classes, his new school experience weighs heavily on him. Most of his close friends have dropped out of school, even the ones who had thrived in elementary and junior high school, and he is experiencing tensions with old friends in the neighborhood.

At school he is uncomfortable being the only African American in most of his classes. The phenomenon of all-eyes-upon-him whenever a Black writer is studied, for example, or a civil rights issue is discussed is a daily occurrence that he feels he will never get used to. And then there are the insults and racial slurs that constantly occur and seem incurable.

The case of Isaac Washington portrays the unfair burden African American school children and their families have borne in the struggle to desegregate U.S. schools. Typically, though not always, it is the Black children who are bused farthest from home into areas that are unfamiliar and sometimes hostile: it is the Black children who have to adjust to new school expectations, sometimes numerous times in a single school career; it is the Black community that is forced to give up its schools, and all of the history, symbols, and traditions these schools represent.

White children from middle- and upper-income backgrounds can also find it difficult to adjust to new schools. Thrust into a desegregated setting, they often misinterpret and are misunderstood, and they are sometimes fearful and vulnerable.

THE CASE OF MARCIA PATTON

Marcia Patton is the 12-year-old daughter of Mavis and Lew Patton, two politically active lawyers who practice law in a large midwestern city. Marcia is in the first group of White children to attend Jefferson Junior High School, traditionally a school for inner-city Blacks. Although most of the children in her neighborhood attend a high-powered prep school, Marcia's parents are sending her to Jefferson on principle.

On her second day at Jefferson, Marcia clutched her books tightly to her chest as she entered Ms. Samson's language arts class. The teacher smiled as she greeted Marcia. She stepped into the hall to speak with several noisy students who were scrambling around the drinking fountain.

At that moment five classmates burst into the room. They slammed their books down on the desk and crowded around Marcia.

Most of the students were very friendly to her. Several offered to take her to the cafeteria at lunch. Marcia became uncomfortable with the attention when one classmate handled her braids and another swatted them out of the offending student's hands shouting, "Let her hair alone!"

That evening Marcia wrote a letter to Ms. Bryant, her teacher last year, in the secrecy of her bedroom.

"When I first walked in, I saw all these dark faces and for the first time I felt so White. There was nothing but laughing, noisy, dark-skinned faces. My heart was beating so fast I thought I would drop dead for sure. I guess a lot of them won't like me. Still, most of the kids are real nice to me. But even so, I'm scared. Everyone is so loud and sometimes they get so close I can hardly breathe.

"The teachers are real nice to me but I wish Ms. Samson wouldn't call on me so much. We use the book we used in your class last year, and lots of the kids in the class can't read it.

"I've been there over a week now and was feeling better until today. A horrible thing happened and I can't tell anybody but you.

"I went to the bathroom after lunch, and two girls I don't know told me to give them all my money or they would hurt me. I gave them twelve dollars, all I had. They said they'd slash my face if I told anybody. I'm afraid to go back."

Marcia's situation, that of being one of a few White students in a predominantly African American urban school, is a reversal of what many Black, Hispanic, Asian, and Native American children often face. Marcia's situation is complicated by the fact that her parents are using her to act in accordance with their belief in school desegregation. Liberal White parents are frequently criticized for not sending their children to inner-city schools.

Students in this school situation may require a good deal of emotional support. Marcia is afraid of disappointing her parents; she confuses her fears and anxieties about her classmates with being racist and thus is unable to confide in her parents.

Although most of the African American students are willing to accept Marcia and try to make her feel welcome, there are some students who will take out their anger and frustration on her. Because she is a symbol of what they believe to be White oppression, her safety is threatened.

Millions of children enter our schools each year with little or no proficiency in the English language. The story of Jesús Martinez, a highly intelligent Puerto Rican child, is echoed in the school experiences of many language minority children in schools across the country.

THE CASE OF JESÚS MARTINEZ[2]

Jesús Martinez was a bright, fine-looking six-year old when he migrated with his family from Puerto Rico to New York City. At a time when he was ready to learn to read and write his mother tongue, Jesús was instead suddenly thrust into an English-only classroom where the only tool he possessed for oral communication (the Spanish language) was completely useless to him. Jesús and his teacher could not communicate with each other because each spoke a different language and neither spoke the language of the other. Jesús felt stupid, or retarded; his teacher perceived him to be culturally disadvantaged and beyond her help. However, she and the school officials agreed to allow him to "sit there" because the law required that he be in school.

For the next two years Jesús "vegetated" in classes he did not understand—praying that the teacher would not call on him. She rarely did and seldom collected his papers since she felt Jesús was not capable of what "more fortunate" children could do. Jesús' self-concept began to deteriorate.

Another Puerto Rican boy in the classroom who spoke English was asked to teach Jesús English and help him in the process of adjustment. They were not permitted, however, to speak Spanish to each other because the teacher believed it would "confuse Jesús and prolong the period of transition" into English; also, it annoyed other people who could not understand what they were saying. The other boy, then, could not translate academic subject matter for him. Jesús was expected to "break the code," to learn English before learning his other subjects. By the time he began to understand English, he was so far behind in all his coursework that it was impossible to catch up. He was labeled "handicapped" by his teachers and taunted by his schoolmates. In fact, each time he would attempt to use his English, some of the other children would ridicule him for his imperfect grasp of the language. The teacher thought the teasing was all right because it would force Jesús to check his mistakes and provide him an incentive to learn proper English. School had become a battlefield for Jesús and he began to find excuses to skip his classes. The situation became unbearable when, as a result of a test administered in English, Jesús was found to be academically retarded and was put in a class for the mentally retarded.

When Jesús finally dropped out of school, he had not learned English well. Today, although he is fluent in Spanish, he has never learned how to read and write his mother tongue. He is functionally illiterate in both languages.

The school dropout rates among language minority students have remained at close to 40 percent. Bilingual education has continued to be controversial since Congress passed the Bilingual Education Act in 1968, despite strong research evidence that appropriate bilingual programs are effective means of helping children like Jesús become literate. To reverse this trend, there is an urgent need for multicultural schools that are multilingual. The challenge is particularly severe in the United States because bilingual teachers are a scarcity.

Some critics of multicultural education argue that bilingual programs are unnecessary. The fact that many non-native speakers thrive in our schools, particularly immigrants from Europe and parts of Asia and Latin America, is seen as evidence that students who try can succeed. These critics overlook the different histories language-minority students have experienced. Children from immigrant families who choose to live in the United States are likely to be highly motivated to learn English in order to participate fully in society. Children from families who entered the United States involuntarily through slavery, as was the case for most African Americans, or through colonialism and conquest, as was true for most Mexican Americans and American Indians, are often less motivated to learn English, especially if it means they must deny their own language and culture or weaken their connections with family and community.

THE CASE OF SAM JOHNSON

Sam Johnson, general science teacher in Oak Grove Middle School, leaned back in his chair and sighed. The student reports had been a disaster. It's true that technically they were terrific. The students had dutifully done extensive research, and the classroom was decorated with the results of their labor: an elaborate bulletin board on world hunger; large poster displays on nuclear weapons, the expense of toxic waste control, American technological superiority, and genetic differences among races; a pictorial essay of famous scientists; an audiovisual show of how the U.S. government disposes of nuclear wastes; and another bulletin board on the AIDS epidemic throughout the world.

What bothered Johnson were the subtle (and not so subtle) expressions of attitudes, values, and beliefs that permeated the student reports. It was clear that the students felt culturally, and even biologically, superior to people from other nations, especially those from the Third World, the "undeveloped countries" as Stacey had referred to them or the "primitive people" according to John. Johnson had been chilled by Steve's remark that AIDS had originated among African Negroes, showing "a weakness among these people that makes it dangerous for us to associate with them." Margaret and Mark were concerned that nuclear wastes are indeed damaging to human health, as evident by the high rate of leukemia, sterility, and birth defects found in people who drink water from rivers that flow near the deposit sites; they were relieved that these deposits are located on barren lands where few people live, mainly Indians. One of the bulletin board panels on world hunger explained how the infant death rate climbed in "undeveloped countries" after the United States sent huge supplies of canned formula because the sanitary conditions were inadequate to keep the baby bottles clean. One would also conclude from this display that all the world's starving people are dark skinned and have naked children; there was no indication that several million North American children suffer from malnutrition and poverty. Rachael's research on famous scientists showed the "superiority of modern Western Civilization"; all of her selections were White and male (with the exception of Madame Curie), and there was no recognition of the scientific developments in earlier civilizations across the globe.

Johnson was appalled, and actually a bit scared, by Steve and Peter's brilliant but uncompassionate report on nuclear weapons. The boys had glowed over the fact that "today nuclear weapons are over one million times more destructive than the bombs that were dropped on Hiroshima and Nagasaki," and they went on with statistics about the nuclear weapons various nations have stockpiled. Without questioning, they accepted the assumptions that these stockpiles are necessary to prevent a future nuclear holocaust.

What happened to these kids? Sam wondered. How had he failed them? Could anything be done? As he thought back over the school year, he remembered the students' reactions when the Japanese plant for Honda parts was set up in the county. The students reflected their parents' outrage and concern that this was unfair competition for the General Motors factory that provided a major source of employment for the townspeople. Sammy Nakamura, Johnson's only non-Caucasian student and one of a handful of Japanese Americans in a town that is over 99 percent White, was beaten on the way home from school and his family received hate mail and taunts of "Japs go home." Then there was the time Vicki Miller was struck by a car and killed. Joshua had remarked, "That's one less mouth for the government to feed. That whole family has been on welfare for years."

Sam had let these occasions (and others) slip by without any class discussion. So much needed to be covered in the eighth-grade curriculum, but he wondered, isn't there a way to do both? Couldn't he teach science in a way that would lessen his students' ethnocentrism and prejudices, and deepen their awareness of human similarities and the increasing global interdependence?

The case of Johnson's science class illustrates the importance of multicultural education for students in mainstream schools and classrooms, in this case White, middle-income students from a small town that is ethnically encapsulated. Students from monocultural backgrounds must learn about multiple perspectives and world views in order to live harmoniously in a multicultural world. Whether a school's student population is multiethnic of monoethnic, it is essential that students become knowledgeable about increasing global interdependence and the world views associated with different nations, as well as attaining an awareness of the state of the planet.[3]

Multicultural education provides a rationale for lessening the transitional trauma for students like Fred Young, Sarah Stein, Jimmy Miller, and Jesús Martinez. And it provides a way to establish equitable learning environments for students like Isaac Washington, his friends, and Marcia Patton, who find themselves caught up in a societal tragedy wherein desegregated schools per se have supplanted the goal of equity in education.

OVERVIEW

Chapters 1, 2, and 3 are designed to clarify the meanings of some important multicultural concepts from anthropology, sociology, and psychology that are frequently misused and misunderstood. Chapter 1 begins by defining multicultural education and presenting some of the reasons we need it. This includes a discussion of core values that provide a foundation for multicultural education. Chapter 1 continues with an explanation of some of the necessary conditions for multicultural schools and concludes with an overview of the multicultural curriculum model that is more fully developed in Chapter 8.

Chapter 2 introduces the concepts of culture, race, and ethnicity. It then focuses on the development of intercultural competence among teachers and students in culturally diverse classrooms. Chapter 3 introduces key concepts needed to understand and discuss race relations in the United States, such as the nature of prejudice and racism, theories of ethnic identity, and the nature of stereotyping. It concludes with an illustration of racism, seen in misconceptions about Africa, and the need for curriculum reform. Chapters 4 and 5 present historical sketches of some of the major ethnic groups that coexist within United States society.

NOTES

1. Based on "The Long Walk of Fred Young" (television documentary). NOVA. Reproduced by permission of the British Broadcasting Corporation.
2. Based on F. Cordasco and D. Castellanos, "Teaching the Puerto Rican Experience," in Teaching Ethnic Studies, J. A. Banks, ed. (Washington, DC: National Council for the Social Studies, 1973), 227–228.
3. Robert Hanvey, An Attainable Global Perspective (New York: Center for War/Peace Studies, 1975).

chapter 1

Multicultural Schools: What, Why, and How

What Is Multicultural Education?

Multicultural education in the United States is an approach to teaching and learning that is based upon democratic values and beliefs, and affirms cultural pluralism within culturally diverse societies and an interdependent world. It is based on the assumption that the primary goal of public education is to foster the intellectual, social, and personal development of virtually *all* students to their highest potential. Multicultural education is comprised of four interactive dimensions: the movement toward equity, curriculum reform, the process of becoming interculturally competent, and the commitment to combat prejudice and discrimination, especially racism. Cultural pluralism, which is defined more fully in Chapter 2, is an ideal state of societal conditions characterized by equity and mutual respect among existing cultural groups. It contrasts sharply with cultural assimilation, or "melting pot" images, where ethnic minorities are expected to give up their traditions and blend in or be absorbed by the mainstream society or predominant culture. In a pluralistic society members of ethnic minority groups are free to retain many of their cultural ways, as long as they conform to those practices deemed necessary for harmonious coexistence within the society as a whole.

Until recently, multicultural education focused primarily on ethnic groups within one society. But rapidly increasing interconnections among all the nations on Earth, particularly as they face global issues related to the ecosystem, nuclear weapons, human rights, and scarce natural resources, have broadened the scope of multicultural education to include global perspectives.

The movement toward equity aims at achieving fair and equal educational opportunities for all of the nation's children and youth, particularly ethnic minorities and the economically disadvantaged. It attempts to transform the total school environment, especially the hidden curriculum that is expressed in teacher expectations for student learning, grouping of students and instructional strategies, school disciplinary policies and practices, school and community relations, and classroom climates. Greater equity would thus help reverse the problems many ethnic minorities and low-income students face in school and ensure that they attain the highest standards of academic excellence.

The curriculum reform strives to expand traditional course contents that are primarily monoethnic and (in the United States) Anglo-European through inclusion of multiethnic and global perspectives. For most of us, this reform requires active inquiry and the development of new knowledge and understanding about cultural differences and the history and contributions of contemporary ethnic groups and nations, as well as of various civilizations in the past. This aspect of multicultural education focuses on both minority and nonminority children and youth, in contrast to the equity movement that targets primarily ethnic minorities and the poor.

The process of becoming multicultural is one whereby a person develops competencies in multiple ways of perceiving, evaluating, believing, and doing.[1] The focus is on understanding and learning to negotiate cultural diversity among nations as well as within a single nation. In their book *Communicating with Strangers,* for example, Gudykunst and Kim describe the multicultural person as "one who has achieved an advanced level in the process of becoming intercultural and whose cognitive, affective, and behavioral characteristics are not limited but are open to growth beyond the psychological parameters of any one culture. . . . The intercultural person possesses an intellectual and emotional commitment to the fundamental unity of all humans and, at the same time, accepts and appreciates the differences that lie between people of different cultures."[2] According to the authors, intercultural people

- have encountered experiences that challenge their own cultural assumptions (e.g., culture shock or "dynamic disequilibrium") and that provide insight into how their view of the world has been shaped by their culture;
- can serve as facilitators and catalysts for contacts between cultures;
- come to terms with the roots of their own ethnocentrism and achieve an objectivity in viewing other cultures;
- develop a Third-World perspective "which enables them to interpret and evaluate intercultural encounters more accurately and thus to act as a communication link between two cultures";[3]
- show cultural empathy and "imaginatively participate in the other's world view."[4]

This process dimension of multicultural education clarifies the fact that individuals can be multicultural. They need not reject their cultural identities to function in a different cultural milieu, for example, the school. Furthermore, this dimension avoids divisive dichotomies between native and mainstream culture, and brings about an increased awareness of multiculturalism as "the normal human experience."[5]

The commitment is to combat racism, sexism, and all forms of prejudice and discrimination through the development of appropriate understandings, attitudes, and social action skills. This essential ingredient of multicultural education addresses the fact that when people acquire ethnic literacy and an appreciation of cultural diversity they will not necessarily be moved to help put an end to prejudice and discrimination or to solve basic problems of inequity.

Emphasis is on clearing up myths and stereotypes associated with gender and different races and ethnic groups, on stressing basic human similarities, and on developing an awareness of the historical roots and current evidence of individual, institutional, and cultural racism and sexism in the United States and elsewhere in the world. The ultimate goal is to develop antiracist, antisexist behavior in basic everyday life.

Core Values in Multicultural Education and Curriculum

A multicultural curriculum has ideological overtones based on democratic ideals that are lacking in less controversial content areas of the curriculum, such as mathematics, reading, or spelling. Arguments may take place over what methods are most appropriate in these other areas, but there is little disagreement about what knowledge is true. In multicultural education on the other hand, where there are no hard and fast rules about truth, there is disagreement about not only what the curriculum entails but whether it should exist at all.

Four core values provide a philosophical framework for the multicultural curriculum model described briefly at the end of this chapter and developed more fully in Chapter 8: (1) acceptance and appreciation of cultural diversity, (2) respect for human dignity and universal human rights, (3) responsibility to the world community, and (4) reverence for the earth.[6] These core values are rooted in democratic theory and Native American philosophy; together they illustrate the strong ethical foundations of multicultural education.

Although democratic principles are set forth in such documents as the Declaration of Independence, the Bill of Rights, and the U.S. Constitution, democracy in the United States falls short of democracy as an ideal. Still the ideal provides an inspiration for change and reform, as was evident in the Civil Rights movement of the 1960s, when nonviolent civil disobedience was a tactic used to change *unjust* discriminatory laws and practices. As a form of government, a way of life, and a goal or ideal, democracy is based on principles of justice and the recognition of the equality and dignity of all persons regardless of race, religion, sex, or lifestyle. It is also based on procedural justice that assures all citizens equal protection under the law and establishes the principle of majority rule with minority rights. Democratic society protects basic liberties such as freedom of speech, conscience, expression, and association, provided that the human dignity and liberty of others are not violated. A democratic society fosters a "free marketplace of ideas" and depends on an informed, participatory citizenry. Thus it is opposed to indoctrination and censorship and encourages dissent, a free press, free elections, and diverse political parties. Democratic societies attempt to provide equal educational opportunities to help all citizens develop their full potential.

The fourth value, reverence for the earth, originates in the belief that "all things in the universe are interdependent." This philosophy develops an understanding of "the balances that exist in all natural systems, or *ecology* . . . All beings are related and therefore human beings must be constantly aware of how our actions will affect other beings, whether these are plants, animals, people, or streams."[7]

The possibility that these core values might be widely acceptable is evident in the Universal Declaration of Human Rights that was adopted by the United Nations General Assembly in 1948 and reaffirmed in 1993 at the international human rights conference in Vienna. The declaration, which is designed to serve "as a common standard of achievement for all peoples and all nations," states that all persons are born free and equal in dignity and expresses basic civil, economic, political, and social rights of all humans.

These values are brought to life in the following Human Manifesto, a document prepared by the Planetary Citizens Registry in Ottawa, Canada:

Human life on our planet is in jeopardy.

It is in jeopardy from war that could pulverize the human habitat. It is in jeopardy from preparations for war that destroy or diminish the prospects of decent existence.

It is in jeopardy because of the denial of human rights.

It is in jeopardy because the air is being fouled and the waters and soil are being poisoned.

If these dangers are to be removed and if human development is to be assured, we the peoples of this planet must accept obligations to each other and to the generations of human beings to come.

We have the obligation to free our world of war by creating an enduring basis for worldwide peace.

We have the obligation to safeguard the delicate balance of the natural environment and to develop the world's resources for the human good.

We have the obligation to make human rights the primary concern of society.

We have the obligation to create a world order in which man neither has to kill or be killed.

In order to carry out these obligations, we the people of this world assert our primary allegiance to each other in the family of man. We declare our individual citizenship in the world community and our support for a United Nations capable of governing our planet in the common human interest.

Life in the universe is unimaginably rare. It must be protected, respected, cherished.

We pledge our energies and resources of spirit to the preservation of the human habitat and to the infinite possibilities of human betterment in our time.[8]

The core values enable teachers to clarify basic goals about teaching and learning that is multicultural. This clarification is essential in protecting, improving, and building the case for multicultural education, and points the way to needed changes should presently held goals be found inappropriate in the future. The core values can also enable teachers to deal more effectively with controversial issues that are an integral part of multicultural education, such as violations of human rights and destruction of the environment.

Why Is Multicultural Education Essential?

The Need for Academic Excellence and Equity

Demand for the reform of schooling in the United States has been a continuing theme throughout the twentieth century. The educational reform movement gained new momentum in the mid-1980s, beginning with the Reagan administration's report "A Nation at Risk." Nearly a dozen additional major reports on U.S. schools appeared in 1983 alone. The common thread throughout these reports is the demand for a national commitment to true excellence in education.

What many of these reports did not acknowledge, however, is that educational excellence in our schools cannot be achieved without educational equity. Equity in education means equal opportunities for all students to develop to their fullest potential. Equity in education must not be confused with equality or sameness of result or even identical experiences. Potentials may differ, and at times equity requires different treatment according to relevant differences. For example, the case of Jesús Martinez on page 7 shows how the exclusive use of English in the classroom provided "equal treatment" without equity. The common language of instruction was unfair for Jesús since he could not understand English as well as his classmates and was at a disadvantage because all the subjects, such as mathematics, science, and social studies, were taught in English only.

Other evidence of inequity in education exists in the nation's school dropout rates which are disproportionately high among African American, American Indian, and Hispanic youth (see Table 1.1), and the poor. In many schools across the nation, racial and language minority students are overrepresented in special education and experience disproportionately high rates of suspension and expulsion. The majority of African American and Latino students attend schools with large concentrations of economically disadvantaged and/or lower-achieving students due to outdated texts, poor facilities, and underprepared teachers.[9] These are schools where teachers often de-emphasize higher-order thinking skills because of the misconception that low-achieving students must master the basic skills before they can develop higher-level skills.[10] Other studies suggest that there is differential treatment and lower teacher expectations of racial and language minority students, compared with their nonminority peers.[11] If these trends are to be reversed, drastic steps are needed to enhance the achievement and academic success of students labeled "at risk" in the nation's schools. Achieving educational excellence requires an impartial, just educational system. Consider the following statistics on the nations dropout rate:[12]

■ TABLE 1.1

	1980 Census (%)	1990 Census (%)
American Indian/Alaska natives	42.0	44.5
Hispanics	39.9	35.3
Blacks	24.7	13.6
Whites	14.3	8.9
Asian/Pacific Islanders	9.6	9.6

Again, the major goal of multicultural education is the development of the intellectual, social, and personal growth of all students to their highest potential. This goal is no different than the educational excellence goal. It depends, however, upon the teacher's knowledge, attitudes, and behavior and whether he or she provides equitable opportunities for learning, changes the monocultural curriculum, and helps all students become more multicultural (i.e., helps them develop or at least appreciate multiple systems of perceiving, evaluating, believing, and doing). This goal includes those students in monocultural classes and schools. Although one's ethnic group is just one of a number of identity sources available, ethnicity is at the heart of the equity problem in this society. Therefore, discussions about achieving educational excellence require concern about those ethnic groups that have been consistently cut off from equal access to a good education.

There is a lot of rhetoric in education about the human potential and the need for equality of opportunity. Multicultural education moves beyond the rhetoric and recognizes that the potential for brilliance is sprinkled evenly across all ethnic groups. When social conditions and school practices hinder the development of this brilliance among students outside the predominant culture, as is the case within this society, the waste of human potential affects us all. The cumulative loss of talented scientists, artists, writers, doctors, teachers, spiritual leaders, and financial and business experts is staggering. The concern for developing human potential goes beyond individuals with special talents and gifts, however. High levels of development and achievement are believed possible for nearly everyone. Only those who are known to have limited mental capacity or to have severe psychological problems might be considered to be beyond the reach of most schools. (And this is only because most teachers must work with

By the year A.D. 2020, children of color will exceed one-third of the school-age population in the United States.

large groups of students and often lack the resources or skills required for learners with special needs.)

Multicultural education contributes to excellence in a second important way: It builds knowledge about various ethnic groups and national perspectives into the curriculum. The traditional curriculum is filled with inaccuracies and omissions concerning the contributions and life conditions of major ethnic groups within our society and for nations across the globe.[13] Obviously, the attainment of any degree of excellence is stunted by curriculum content that is untrue or incomplete. Given that we live in an interdependent world that is rapidly shrinking, ignorance of global issues and national perspectives is foolish and even dangerous.

The Existence of a Multiethnic Society

Today approximately 25 percent of this society's school-age children are ethnic minorities. Current patterns of immigration, particularly with the influx of people from Southeast Asia, Latin America, and the Caribbean, ensure that ethnic pluralism will continue to be the American way in the foreseeable future. It is estimated that by the year 2020 over 30 percent of our school-age population will be children of color. It is also estimated that over 20 percent of this nation's school-age children live in economic poverty, over half of them White.[14] Given the extensive research indicating that disproportionately high numbers of ethnic minority students and the economically poor are dropping out of school or are being suspended or expelled, and that disproportionately high numbers of those who do remain in school are achieving far below their potential, teachers today face a tremendous challenge. If these patterns are to be reversed, schools must affirm cultural pluralism. Multicultural schools would obviously be better equipped to deal with the complexities of a pluralistic society than are the traditional monocultural schools. Schools based on the philosophy of cultural pluralism represent a compromise between cultural assimilation on the one hand and cultural separatism or segregation on the other.

Cultural pluralism is considered dangerous to society by those who believe it heightens ethnic group identity and leads to separatism, intergroup antagonism, and fragmentation. As will be noted in Chapter 2, this misconception overlooks a crucial ingredient of pluralism. All ethnic groups are expected to conform to those elements of the predominant culture that are necessary for societal well-being. Cultural pluralism seems possible in a nation such as the United States since it is, from a non-Native American perspective, a nation of (voluntary and involuntary) immigrants.[15] With the exception of American Indians and certain segments of the Hispanic population, land is not an issue in ethnic identity for most groups. In contrast to those areas of the world where cultural pluralism has resulted in fragmentation, for example, portions of Europe and the former Soviet Union, many ethnic groups in the United States contributed to the development of the predominant culture or were immersed in an already existing dominant culture when they arrived.[16]

Clearly, our schools are faced with educating a culturally pluralistic population. Pluralistic schools can identify baseline expectations for learning and behavior that are expected of all students. Every attempt must be made to lessen the cultural conflict that may result from cultural bias at this baseline. Some groups may perceive certain rules as culturally biased, for example, the prohibition of hats (a Yarmulke) in a school serving Orthodox Jews or unexcused absences during religious holidays. The scheduling of extracurricular activities after school discourages students who travel to school by bus; certain school traditions may also symbolize the preeminence of a particular group, such as team names and colors, school emblems, and yearbook titles.

The Existence of an Interconnected World

There is a certain urgency about the need to foster global awareness among today's children and youth. The human race faces a number of critical concerns that if left unresolved are likely to result in the destruction of life as we know it: destruction of the ozone layer, environmental pollution, poverty, overpopulation, nuclear arms, famine and world hunger, the spread of AIDS and other diseases. The resolution of these problems as well as participation in global trade and economic development require global cooperation. This cooperation requires human beings who possess some degree of crosscultural understanding.

The urgency of teaching about the state of the planet and of developing responsible world citizens was expressed by Robert Muller, assistant secretary general of the United Nations, on the occasion of the fortieth anniversary of the United Nations and International Youth Year (1985):

> A child born today will be faced as an adult, almost daily, with problems of a global interdependent nature, be it peace, food, the quality of life, inflation, or scarcity of resources. He will be both an actor and a beneficiary or a victim in the total word fabric, and he may rightly ask: "Why was I not warned? Why was I not better educated? Why did my teachers not tell me about these problems and indicate my behavior as a member of an interdependent human race?" It is, therefore, the duty and the self-enlightened interest of governments to educate their children properly about the type of world in which they are going to live.[17]

All of us are participants in the global arena. It is unavoidable. The question is the degree to which this participation is informed and enlightened.

Equity and Democratic Values

Finally, equity is not only a matter of bettering our country's educational system. It is required if we value this nation's democratic ideals: basic human rights, social justice, respect for alternative life choices, and equal opportunity for all. Making reality fit these ideals, however, is not always easy. It is ideally un-American to be racist or sexist, for example, but because many teachers fear teaching about values or changing attitudes, they ignore the issues of prejudice and discrimination. Multicultural education, on the other hand, confronts the fact that this is a racist society with a history of White supremacy. An effective curriculum would point out that White racism has greatly influenced how people perceive, evaluate, believe, and act—and that this legacy persists. Because its aim is to reduce the ignorance that breeds racism and to develop the understanding and actions people need to become antiracist, multicultural education can help overcome barriers to achieving our ideals.

Democratic principles are at the heart of many issues addressed by multicultural education such as the struggle for minority rights in a society based on majority rule, the right to dissent, and the limits of free speech. Multicultural classrooms nurture freedom of expression, the search for truth, and fairminded critical thinking, but they are not value free.

■ Conditions for Multicultural Schools

The Example of Effective School Desegregation in Urban Settings

Under what conditions do students benefit from desegregated schooling? Most desegregated schools were forced to do so before this question was answered. The assumption over the past quarter century seems to have been that segregated schools are inherently bad and desegregated schools inherently good.

To the degree that segregated schools foster unwarranted fears, misconceptions, and negative stereotypes between isolated groups, in addition to unequal educational opportunities, this assumption is correct. It is false, however, to assume that simply desegregating a school will eliminate these inherent problems. Both research and casual observation in the vast majority of desegregated schools document the existence of resegregation through formal practices such as tracking, grouping, and scheduling of extracurricular activities, and through informal practices such as student seating preferences in classrooms and cafeterias. Many desegregated schools face the problems of racial tension, apathy, and absenteeism as a reaction to forced busing and desegregation. All these conditions militate against personal growth and achievement among students.

Unfortunately, there has rarely been time for thoughtful consideration of the question, Under what conditions do students benefit from desegregated schooling? In most U.S. schools, teachers, students, and administrators have been forced to desegregate without the help of guidelines to establish good race relations and academic achievement among minority and majority students alike. Nevertheless, answers to the question do exist. The purpose of this section of the chapter is to provide a synthesis of important, but not widely used, concepts and theories that hold promise for school desegregation, and to suggest guidelines for effective desegregation in a variety of settings.

The focus will be on the urban setting, which typically has involved racial desegregation. Urban desegregation highlights the process that occurs unrecognized in many other school settings where race may not be a factor. Numerous possibilities come to mind: rural versus urban, labor versus management, wealthy versus poor, military versus civilian, Christian versus non-Christian, Polish American versus Italian American, and American Indian versus non-Indian.

How the Host School Responds

There are at least four possible ways schools can respond to school desegregation: business-as-usual, assimilation, pluralistic coexistence, and integrated pluralism. These possible responses have been identified and described by H. A. Sagar and J. W. Schofield, as a result of their research in desegregated schools.[18]

Business-as-usual may be characterized as follows:

> Insofar as possible, these interracial schools tried to maintain the same basic curriculum, the same academic standards, and the same teaching methods that prevailed under segregation. . . . Furthermore, they strove to enforce the same behavioral standards, to espouse the same values, and to apply the same sanctions to student offenses. In short, the schools did not perceive themselves as having to adjust their traditional practices in order to handle the new student body. Rather, the students were expected to adjust to the school.[19]

This type of response does not consider whether old rules or procedures are desirable when the nature of the student population has changed.

Compatible with the business-as-usual approach to desegregation is the *assimilationist* response.

> The assimilationist ideology holds that integration will have been achieved when the minority group can no longer be differentiated from the white majority in

terms of economic status, education, or access to social institutions and their benefits. This will be accomplished by fostering a "color-blind" attitude where prejudice once reigned . . . and by imparting to minority persons the skills and value orientations which will enable them to take their place in the currently white-dominated social structure. . . . No significant change is anticipated since the newly assimilated minority individuals will be attitudinally and behaviorally indistinguishable from the majority. Stated in its baldest form, the assimilationist charge to the schools is to make minority children more like white children.[20]

Those who do not assimilate are resegregated, drop out, or are suspended or expelled. The fact that students' race and culture may make a difference, say in students' and teachers' perceptions of each other and expectations about appropriate classroom behavior, is not considered. The assimilationist response is often based on an erroneous assumption that to recognize race is to be racist.

Schools that desegregate with the business-as-usual or assimilation response appear similar. The subtle difference is that under the assimilation response a conscious decision has been made by the host school about expectations for new students. Business-as-usual schools proceed as they have in the past and, perhaps unconsciously, expect all new students to fit in.

Like the business-as-usual and assimilation response, the *pluralistic coexistence* response also involves resegregation. But in contrast to the assimilation response, where only those students who do not fit in are resegregated, pluralistic coexistence is based on separation of different racial or ethnic groups. Students are allowed to maintain different styles and values, but within a school environment comprised of separate turfs for different racial groups. Typically, there are different schools within a school, and little or no attempt is made to encourage students to mix. Describing one such school, Sagar and Schofield write,

> The principal tolerated almost complete informal resegregation of the students, to the point where there were considered to be "two schools within a school." The school's annex, for example, became known as a black area, or the "recreational study hall," while the library served as a white area, or "non-recreational study hall."[21]

In this formerly all-White school, the African American principal tried to appease White parents by maintaining advanced academic programs to prevent them from withdrawing their children, who had become the minority. In this school situation, separate was clearly unequal.

In contrast with these three responses to school desegregation, *integrated pluralism* actively seeks to avoid resegregation of students.

> [It] is pluralistic in the sense that it recognizes the diverse racial and ethnic groups in our society and does not denigrate them just because they deviate from the white middle class patterns of behavior. Integrated pluralism affirms the equal value of the school's various ethnic groups, encouraging their participation, not on majority-defined terms, but in an evolving system which reflects the contributions of all groups. However, integrated pluralism goes beyond mere support for the side-by-side coexistence of different group values and styles. It is integra-

tionist in the sense that it affirms the educational value inherent in exposing all students to a diversity of perspectives and behavioral repertoires and the social value of structuring the school so that students from previously isolated and even hostile groups can come to know each other under conditions conducive to the development of positive intergroup relations. . . .

Integrated pluralism takes an activist stance in trying to foster interaction between different groups of students rather than accepting resegregation as either desirable or inevitable.[22]

The first three responses above are obviously unacceptable. Integrated pluralism, the last response, is the goal to strive for. Desegregation per se, or merely mixing formerly isolated ethnic groups in the same school, does not go far enough. Integration, on the other hand, recognizes and accommodates all the groups that were formerly segregated—in other words, it creates the conditions for cultural pluralism.

More than half a century ago, noted Black sociologist W. E. B. DuBois wrote about the issues of segregated versus desegregated schools:

A mixed school with poor and unsympathetic teachers, with hostile public opinion, and no teaching of truth concerning black folk, is bad. A segregated school with ignorant placeholders, inadequate equipment, poor salaries, and wretched housing, is equally bad. Other things being equal, the mixed school is the broader, more natural basis for the education of all youth. It gives wider contacts; it inspires greater self-confidence; and suppresses the inferiority complex. But other things seldom are equal, and in that case, Sympathy, Knowledge, and Truth, outweigh all that the mixed school can offer.[23]

The philosophy of DuBois lends powerful support to the case for multicultural schools. Teachers must be free of racial prejudice and ethnocentrism (the belief that one's own culture is superior to all others) if they are to be effective with students of diverse cultural, racial, and socioeconomic backgrounds. Although prejudice and ethnocentrism seem to be part of the human condition, teachers should be less prejudiced and ethnocentric than the average person.

Research on the characteristics of effectively integrated schools shows that a policy consistent with integrated pluralism has the best potential for encouraging good race relations, academic achievement, and personal development among students. Three necessary conditions underlie cultural pluralism in the school, or the integrated pluralism response: positive teacher expectations, a learning environment that encourages positive intergroup contact, and a multicultural curriculum.[24]

◼ *Multicultural School Conditions*

Positive Teacher Expectations

Teachers often make snap judgments, based on their perceptions, about students and thus treat them differently. Many teachers interact with students differently according to the student's race and socioeconomic status. Barbara Lightfoot has aptly referred to teachers as "judges of deviance."

Much has been written about the power of teacher expectations. Research also supports the basic assumption that teacher attitudes influence student achievement. One of the first studies, and probably best known, is the controversial study by Rosenthal and Jacobson, who reported their success in influencing student achievement by giving teachers phony data about their students.[25] Approximately 20 percent of the student population, selected at random, were identified as "bloomers" on an intelligence test. Teachers were given the names of these supposedly high-potential students, to be held in confidence, and these students did indeed achieve at significantly higher levels than their classmates. Although the methodology used in this study has been questioned by some, even its critics accept the notion that teacher expectations often affect student achievement.

Two decades of research since this study "leads to a consensus that teachers' expectations can and sometimes do affect teacher-student interaction and student outcomes; however, the processes are much more complex than originally believed."[26] One conclusion, for example, is that teacher beliefs and expectations interact with student beliefs and behaviors. To the extent that ethnicity influences behaviors and beliefs, it is a factor in teacher expectations. Only a few recent studies have focused on ethnicity, however, although several researchers in the 1970s and early 1980s did so.

In one follow-up to Rosenthal and Jacobson's "Pygmalion" study, social studies student teachers were asked by their university supervisors to rank their students from high to low in terms of academic ability after two days in the classroom.[27] The student teachers did so without expressing uncertainty or difficulty. During the semester, their interactions with the high and low students were coded by their university supervisors. Results showed that lows were less frequently encouraged to participate in class discussion or to interact with the teacher, either directly by being called on or indirectly by receiving extended teacher feedback when they volunteered. Teachers tended to neglect the students they rated low.

In another study involving student teachers, all White females, the women were asked to teach a comparable current events lesson to a biracial group of students.[28] Each was given a class roster that contained phony IQ data for each student. High and low IQs were distributed at random, but evenly for Black and White students. Classroom observers recorded no significant difference in student behavior during the lesson, but the student teachers perceived the bright Black students as more hostile and disruptive. A likely explanation is that these student teachers felt threatened by students who did not fit their expectations (that is, they were not expecting a group of Black students who were also bright).

A growing body of evidence indicates that many White teachers have lower expectations for their non-White students. In one midwestern study of high school student discipline in two large urban school corporations, for example, teachers who responded to an anonymous questionnaire felt Black students had less innate potential than White students on every variable, except basketball, where Blacks were perceived as having equal potential. Other variables included band, orchestra, drama, and scholastics.[29]

Another study of classroom interaction in forty-one middle school classrooms showed that when teachers have equal achievement expectations for Black and White students there is more interracial friendship and interaction among the students. A classroom climate of acceptance among students was more likely to exist when teachers did not distinguish between the learning potential of Black and White students.[30] Other studies have shown that a classroom climate of acceptance is related to increased student achievement, especially among minorities in the classroom.

Studies by Gay, Rist, and the U.S. Civil Rights Commission have shown that many teachers have lower expectations for African American and Mexican American students.[31] In the Rist study, which involved Black teachers and students, the teacher had lower expectations for the darker-skinned children. All three studies showed that teachers interacted with low-expectation students in intellectually limiting ways and were more supportive and stimulating with their White or light-skinned students.

Given the fact that teacher expectations strongly influence student achievement, and given the fact that many teachers hold lower expectations for African American and Hispanic students, is integrated education possible? I believe it is. Not all administrators, teachers, and students are racially prejudiced and not all have low expectations. Therefore racial prejudice is not necessary to the human condition. Many teachers, administrators, and students who are racially prejudiced can develop the kinds of understanding required to become less so. This is a major goal of multicultural education among adults.

Lower teacher expectations for particular racial or ethnic groups are based on negative racial or ethnic prejudice. Teachers, like all people, often are not aware of their prejudices; thus they may not be aware of their lower expectations for some students.

A major theme in this book is the belief that if teachers are to have equally positive expectations for students of all races, they must understand the cultural differences that often exist in the desegregated classroom. The fact that cultural differences frequently are associated with racial differences often confirms myths and stereotypes associated with race. Teachers need guidelines, such as the Aspects of Ethnicity discussed in Chapter 2, to help them observe and interpret culturally different behavior. Such guidelines can help prevent blanket assumptions that certain behaviors and values go with certain racial groups.

A Learning Environment That Supports Positive Interracial Contact

Too often, we simply bring together groups of students who share different histories and hope for the best. The best rarely happens. Casual contact between different ethnic groups may reinforce existing negative stereotypes or generate new ones. This fact was exemplified recently in a kindergarten classroom in a Florida school district during its initial attempts at desegregation. As the school year began, White students, most of whom had already had several years of nursery school, could be found busily working in one of the higher ability achievement groups. Their African American classmates, who had been bused from across town and had not had preparatory nursery school experience, ran wildly around the room until they could be settled into one of the remedial or lower achievement groups. White parents who advocated school desegregation were dismayed by their children's negative reports. For many of these White kindergartners, initial contact with Black children appeared to be creating negative racial prejudices. For most of the Black kindergartners, the vicious cycle of low expectations and low academic achievement was beginning.

Scenes like this can be avoided when school policies and practices are guided by social contact theory. In 1954, the year of the landmark school desegregation decision, Gordon Allport first published his theory of positive intergroup contact. He summarized his theory as follows:

> Given a population of ordinary people, with a normal degree of prejudice, we are safe in making the following general prediction: Prejudice (unless deeply rooted in the character structure of the individual) may be reduced by equal status contact between majority and minority groups in the pursuit of common goals. The effect is greatly enhanced if this contact is sanctioned by institutional supports (i.e., by law, custom or local atmosphere), and if it is of a sort that leads to the perception of common interests and common humanity between members of the two groups.[32]

It is unlikely that the young children described in this scene harbored deep-seated racial prejudice. If this is also true for the teacher, classroom practices can be implemented to encourage academic achievement and good race relations. Social contact theory provides a framework that can help educators identify policy guidelines for effective school desegregation, as well as promising practices that have been uncovered by recent research in desegregated schools.

According to contact theorists, at least four basic conditions are necessary if social contact between groups is to lessen negative prejudice and lead to friendly attitudes and behaviors:

1. Contact should be sufficiently intimate to produce reciprocal knowledge and understanding between groups.
2. Members of various groups must share equal status.
3. The contact situation should lead people to do things together. It should require intergroup cooperation to achieve a common goal.
4. There must be institutional support—an authority and/or social climate that encourages intergroup contact.[33]

These four conditions of positive social contact can be used as guidelines for observing desegregated schools and for detecting problem areas. One of the most difficult conditions for most schools to establish is an equal status environment for the different racial groups within the student body. Often there are sharp socioeconomic differences, as well as differences in the initial achievement

How the host school responds to court order desegregation is critical in the development of equitable, effective learning environments.

levels of Black and White classmates. Tracking and grouping practices may be viewed as necessary, but they may also lead to resegregation. A history of racial discrimination in education and hiring practices means schools often face a limited pool of available Black and Hispanic administrators and teachers who can serve as high-status role models.

Other potential violations of the conditions of positive intergroup contact stem from school rules, discipline practices, extracurricular activities, and symbols and traditions. Some rules are perceived as inequitable (for example, prohibition of "bad language" and hats). Scheduling extracurricular activities after school excludes students who travel by bus and limits opportunities for intergroup contact in cocurricular activities. School traditions often become a problem during initial stages of desegregation and act as symbolic indicators of where the school's authority stands on integrated pluralism.

> If "new" students come to an "old" school, there is a frequent tendency for both racial groups to perceive the school as "belonging" to the "old" group. The school name, team nicknames, school songs, and titles of school publications are a few of the many symbols that may symbolize preeminence of a particular racial group. There are other, more subtle, customs that may symbolize segregation in ways not anticipated. If editors have always been college preparatory students, and there are few college preparatory students in the "new" group, continuation of the tradition will symbolize unequal status. . . . "Preserving traditions" can be an euphemism for "putting minorities in their place." Opposition to integration may focus on defense of symbols. When this happens, school personnel need to realize what is happening and deal with reality.[34]

Underlying these relatively visible concerns is a hidden problem; a mutual lack of knowledge about communication modes, values, and perceptions among culturally different students and teachers, which often leads to misunderstanding and conflict. For example, many White teachers and students are unknowingly ignorant about the structures and meanings of Black vernacular. The double negative "ain't got no" may signify a "low-class," uneducated person, while use of the term "nigger" among Blacks may be viewed by Whites as insulting or threatening. Black students, on the other hand, might regard all Whites as racist and interpret the behaviors of White teachers and classmates from that perspective. As long as students and teachers are left to their own devices, there is little opportunity for the kind of intimate contact between culturally different students that could foster mutual understanding. Informal segregation is typically the rule throughout the school.

Social contact theory can be used as a guide to alleviate obstacles to school integration. Although visions of integrated schools may differ, there are at least two necessary observable characteristics. First, there is a relaxed interracial mixing among the majority of students and teachers in casual and informal settings at school. Second, there is real academic achievement and personal growth among all students, as seen in formal course work and extracurricular activities. These two characteristics appear to be interactive. Where good race relations exist student achievement is higher, and the reverse is also true.

There is no standard recipe for integrating the desegregated school. Neither are there specific requisite practices. There are, however, necessary conditions for positive intergroup contact (equal status, knowledge, cooperation, and institutional support) that schools can use as a guide in making decisions about specific desegregation practices. For example, some form of ability grouping might be appropriate in creating an equal-status environment in one school but not in another What is important is that ability groups do not produce racially visible differences.

Research by scholars such as Elizabeth Cohen suggests ways of creating equal status among racially different students who bring differing entry-level skills to the classroom.[35] In one study Cohen provided special instruction to lower achievers prior to their participation in small-group cooperative learning. The lower achievers could then make unique contributions to their group, which helped equalize their classroom status. Furthermore, achievement and interracial friendship were enhanced.

A study conducted by Garlie Forehand and Marjorie Ragosta focused on school characteristics of effectively desegregated schools.[36] They defined effectiveness in terms of student achievement and race relations. Data were collected from tests, questionnaires, and interviews in nearly 200 schools. All the schools were racially mixed and represented a wide range of socioeconomic, demographic, and geographic conditions.

The results identified school conditions under which benefits in integrated education were maximized in a wide variety of settings, sometimes even where large socioeconomic differences existed within the student population. In their *Handbook for Integrated Schooling,* which developed from their findings, the

TABLE 1.2
Strategies for School Integration: Summary of Research Findings

School Practice	Conditions of Positive Intergroup Contact			
	Equal Status	Knowledge/ Acquaintance	Common Goal	Institutional Support
Multiethnic curriculum	✓	✓		✓
Extracurricular activities scheduled during school day	✓	✓	✓	✓
Open discussion of race and racial issues in classroom		✓		✓
Biracial work and play teams among students	✓	✓	✓	✓
Biracial seating patterns		✓		✓
Rules and discipline: equal punishment for equal offense	✓			✓
Equitable rules (If punishment for the infraction of a rule appears to be associated with race, determine whether the rule is equitable.)	✓			✓
Academic achievement and good race relations established as explicit goals				✓
Biracial staffing that reflects school's racial composition	✓			✓
Biracial staffing in high-status positions				✓
Student-focused human relations activities	✓	✓	✓	✓
Class and program assignments that do not result in racially identifiable groups	✓	✓		✓
Individualized instruction that rewards improvement as well as academic absolutes	✓			✓

researchers have presented a number of practices that characterize effectively desegregated schools. Table 1.2 presents an overview of these and other research findings and shows their relationship with the conditions of positive intergroup contact.

Other research shows that biracial work and play teams among students are one of the most powerful ways to improve race relations. As seen in Table 1.2, this practice meets the four conditions of positive intergroup contact. One promising strategy that builds on this fact is *team learning,* an approach developed by Robert Slavin and his associates at the Center for Social Organization of Schools at the Johns Hopkins University. Team learning can help establish an equal-status environment among students who bring different entry skills to the classroom because the tasks can be designed to fit student strengths. (Team learning is examined in Chapter 9.)

A Multicultural Curriculum

Curriculum can be viewed as the experiences, both official and unofficial, that learners have under the auspices of the school. Following this definition, a multicultural curriculum is one that attends to the school's hidden curriculum—for example, teachers' values and expectations, student cliques and peer groupings, and school regulations. It also attends to the values, cultural styles, knowledge, and perceptions that all students bring to the school. A multicultural curriculum, in its broadest sense, influences the total school environment.

Here, however, the focus will be limited to those planned experiences in school that are intended to develop student understandings, values, attitudes, and behaviors related to the goals of multicultural education shown in Figure 1.1.

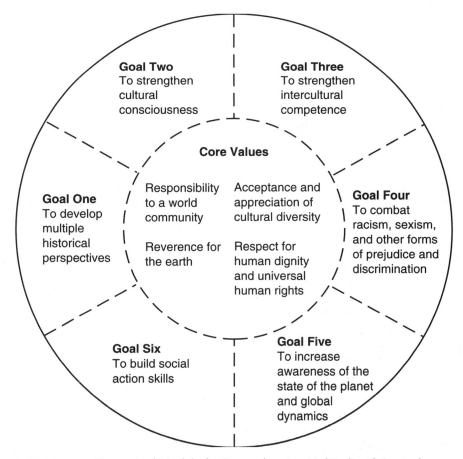

FIGURE 1.1 *Conceptual Model of a Comprehensive Multicultural Curriculum*

Understanding Multiple Historical Perspectives

Most of us tend to be ahistorical when it comes to knowledge about Third World nations as well as ethnic minorities within our own society. It is difficult to be otherwise, given the nature of the traditional curriculum that emphasizes the political development of Euro-American civilization. An important goal of a multicultural curriculum, therefore, is the development of multiple historical perspectives that will correct this Anglo-Western European bias. Past and current world events must be understood from multiple national perspectives, and both minority and nonminority points of view must be considered in interpreting local and national events.

Developing Cultural Consciousness

Cultural consciousness is the recognition or awareness on the part of an individual that she or he has a view of the world that is not universally shared and differs profoundly from that held by many members of different nations and ethnic groups. It includes an awareness of the diversity of ideas and practices found in human societies around the world and some recognition of how one's own thoughts and behaviors might be perceived by members of differing nations and ethnic groups.[37]

Developing Intercultural Competence

Intercultural competence is the ability to interpret intentional communications (language, signs, gestures), some unconscious cues (such as body language), and customs in cultural styles different from one's own. Emphasis is on empathy and communication. The goal is to develop self-awareness of the culturally conditioned assumptions people of different cultural backgrounds make about each others' behaviors and cognitions.

Combating Racism, Sexism, Prejudice, and All Forms of Discrimination

Combating racism, sexism, prejudice, and discrimination means lessening negative attitudes and behaviors based on gender bias and misconceptions about the inferiority of races and cultures different from one's own. Emphasis is on clearing up myths and stereotypes associated with gender, different races, and ethnic groups. Basic human similarities are stressed. The goal is to develop antiracist, antisexist behavior based on awareness of historical and contemporary evidence of individual, institutional, and cultural racism and sexism in the United States and elsewhere in the world.

Raising Awareness of the State of the Planet and Global Dynamics

Awareness of the state of the planet and global dynamics is knowledge about prevailing world conditions, trends, and developments. It is also knowledge of the world as a hugely interrelated ecosystem subject to surprise effects and dramatic ramifications of simple events, such the introduction of new technologies, or health and nutrition practices into a society.[38]

Developing Social Action Skills

Social action skills include the knowledge, attitudes, and behaviors needed to help resolve major problems that threaten the future of the planet and the well-being of humanity. One emphasis is on thinking globally and acting locally; the goal is to develop a sense of personal and political efficacy and global responsibility resulting in a participatory orientation among adult members of society. Another emphasis is enabling minorities and nonminorities to become change agents through democratic processes.

The six goals contained in the curriculum model overlap; each individually represents a necessary but insufficient focus for multicultural education. For example, to increase cultural consciousness without also developing the understanding, skills, and attitudes that cluster around intercultural competence might lead to greater ethnocentrism and polarization. It would be impossible to develop people's intercultural competence (such as empathy) without also developing their senses of personal identity and security, which come with cultural consciousness. Furthermore, both these goals should foster an appreciation of both human similarities and ethnic diversity and an awareness of how racism and negative prejudices originate and subjugate. The sixth goal, enabling people to become change agents, goes beyond study and discussion and deals with the skills and behaviors needed to eradicate discriminatory practices as well as to bring about other desired changes.

The cluster of goals in the curriculum model does not require that teachers stress each goal equally. Rather, these six goals should be woven into an overall curriculum design that allows separate subject areas and courses to emphasize those goals that are most compatible with the subject matter boundaries and age groupings of a particular school system. In some school settings, for example, historical perspectives and cultural consciousness might be emphasized in literature and the arts; intercultural competence in language and communications; reduction of racial/ethnic prejudice and discrimination in biology and world and U.S. history; and social action skills in government, business, or economics.

Furthermore, a careful sequence of learning experiences designed to foster social action skills could begin in kindergarten with simple decision-making activities and culminate in the final year of high school with a community action project. Ideally, teams of teachers within a school, school system, college, or university would collaborate on the sequencing and articulation of multicultural perspectives in curriculum objectives, strategies, and materials. With clarification of multicultural goals, it becomes possible to build them into the curriculum, as will be illustrated in Chapter 9.

A multicultural curriculum cannot come to life unless fair-minded critical thinking is at the heart of teaching and learning. Both teachers and their students must became critical thinkers who can "gather, analyze, synthesize, and assess information, enter sympathetically into the thinking of others, . . . [and] deal rationally with conflicting points of view."[39] Furthermore, a multicultural curriculum requires that teachers and students are moved to care about human welfare beyond themselves, their family, and their friends. And, finally, it requires a focus on community action so that teachers and students can become agents of change. But without critical thinking and teaching at the center, multicultural education is likely to result in indoctrination rather than ethical insights based on core values.

CONCLUSIONS

The case for multicultural education presented in this chapter takes a position that may not be widely accepted. It could be viewed as overly idealistic and based upon unrealistic assumptions about the possibilities for human altruism.

It would be possible to develop an alternative, perhaps more negative, approach, one based on fear of human annihilation and concerns about the survival, health, and future of one's grandchildren. People become concerned about multicultural and global issues when the focus is on economic competition in the world arena, unsafe storage of nuclear wastes, the greenhouse effect, and futile military or diplomatic efforts based on ignorance of history and culture. Even the goal of combating racism, one that has never been a national policy, could be viewed positively by perpetrators of racism once it is realized that economic and political gains in (or cooperation with) Third World nations cannot be taken seriously as long as we practice racism at home and abroad.

The fact is, however, that the multicultural education movement is idealistic. It means learning to think through a "language of hope and possibility."[40] Multicultural education is based on visions of humans living in greater harmony with each other and with the earth. It asks that we develop citizens who are able to consider alternative viewpoints, are able to examine values and assumptions (one's own as well as those of others), and are willing to learn to think critically. It requires a degree of open-mindedness that may be impossible to develop in people with a highly rigid belief structure. This does not mean that the visions of multicultural education should be abandoned.

By clearly stating the goals and core values of multicultural education, it becomes possible to articulate reasons for disagreement. This can lead to a healthy dialogue, even among strong supporters, that can move us beyond theory and rhetoric into practice.

The concept of radical cultural relativism, or the notion that anything goes, is a frequently voiced concern. Many adults who have school-age children, for example, see multicultural education as requiring students to accept abhorrent sociopolitical practices. These objectionable practices may include news-making events such as the stifling of political dissenters within ethnic communities, and physical violence such as female infanticide, or the mutilation of the genitalia of young women. The goals and core values proposed in this chapter can help us deal with cultural relativism in at least three ways. First, if we accept respect for human dignity and universal human rights as a basic value, then we cannot be neutral about injury to or destruction of human life. Ultimately, the goal is for these practices to end. Second, if we consider *multiple* historical perspectives we can at least understand why such practices do occur. And third, if we develop cultural consciousness and intercultural competence we may be able to understand that we might very well accept and even participate in such behaviors had we been born and raised in that society.

Another important concern is that many nations, ethnic minorities, and economically disadvantaged people will not participate in multicultural education efforts. We know, for example, that the global aspects of multicultural education are often viewed with suspicion by Third World people who fear it is a continuation of Western racism and imperialism. This is a sobering limitation. If we were to take seriously our own national creed of justice and equality for all and if combating racism were to become a national policy, this suspicion might be lessened.

COMPARE AND CONTRAST

1. Monocultural and multicultural education
2. Equity and equality
3. Core values and dimensions of multicultural education
4. School desegregation and school integration
5. Social contact theory and resegregation
6. Cultural relativism and core values of multicultural education

ACTIVITIES AND QUESTIONS

1. You have been asked to present a major address at the annual meeting of the Society for Intercultural Education, Training, and Research (SIETAR). This year's meeting is in Paris during the month of July. All your expenses are paid, including a three-week European study tour with educators from around the world. Choose your topic: "The Case against Multicultural Education" or "The Case for Multicultural Education." Plan a rigorous and inspiring speech. (For an excellent review of the critics of multicultural education, see Christine Sleeter, "An Analysis of the Critiques of Multicultural Education," in James A. Banks and Cherry M. Banks, Editors, *The Handbook of Research on Multicultural Education*, New York: Macmillan; 1995, pp. 81–94. This chapter includes references to the major critiques as well as Sleeter's commentary on the strengths and weaknesses of each.)

2. What are the advantages and disadvantages of the core values suggested in this chapter? As you think about your own multicultural teaching, how might you revise them? Why?

3. *Interracial Contact: A Personal History.* Consider your earliest memory of an interracial incident and also your most recent experience. Results can be shared in small and large groups.

4. Under what conditions can school desegregation lead to positive race relations among students and staff? According to contact theorists, at least four

basic conditions are necessary if social contact between different isolated groups is to lessen negative prejudice and lead to friendly attitudes and behaviors. These conditions are listed below. As you read each one, note current practices in your school or classroom that would impede the development of that condition (negative practice) as well as practices that would help establish it (positive practices). Finally, note practices not in use that could be implemented to help build this condition in your school or classroom (possibilities).

A. Contact should be sufficiently intimate to engender knowledge and mutual understanding between different ethnic or racial groups that have been isolated from each other.

Negative Practices	Positive Practices	Possibilities
1. _____	1. _____	1. _____
2. _____	2. _____	2. _____
3. _____	3. _____	3. _____

B. Members of the various ethnic groups should share equal status.

Negative Practices	Positive Practices	Possibilities
1. _____	1. _____	1. _____
2. _____	2. _____	2. _____
3. _____	3. _____	3. _____

C. The contact situation leads people to do things together; it requires intergroup cooperation to achieve a common goal.

Negative Practices	Positive Practices	Possibilities
1. _____	1. _____	1. _____
2. _____	2. _____	2. _____
3. _____	3. _____	3. _____

D. There is institutional support—an authority and/or social climate that encourages intergroup contact.

Negative Practices	Positive Practices	Possibilities
1. _____	1. _____	1. _____
2. _____	2. _____	2. _____
3. _____	3. _____	3. _____

5. When might racially segregated schools be better than integrated schools?

6. Imagine that you are teaching in a culturally pluralistic classroom where student groups are strangers to each other due to de facto segregation and/or rural-urban distinctions. Show how you can use Allport's social contact theory as guidelines for your instructional decisions. Be specific.

NOTES

1. M. Gibson, "Approaches to Multicultural Education in the United States: Some Concepts and Assumptions," *Anthropology and Education Quarterly* 7, no. 4 (November 1976):7–18. Reprinted in *Anthropology and Education Quarterly 15,* no. 1 (Spring 1984):99–120.

2. W. B. Gudykunst and Y. Y. Kim, *Communicating with Strangers: An Approach to Intercultural Communications* (New York: Addison-Wesley, 1984), 230.

3. Ibid., 231.

4. Ibid.

5. Gibson, "Approaches to Multicultural Education," 176.

6. See acknowledgments in Chapter 8.

7. P. V. Beck, Anna Lee Walters, and Nia Francisco, *The Sacred: Ways of Knowledge, Sources of Life* (Tsaile, AZ: Navajo Community College Press, 1977),12.

8. This quote is taken from the Planetary Citizens Registry (P.O. Box 2777, San Anselmo, CA 94960) and was quoted in D. Dufty, S. Sawkins, N. Pickard, J. Power, and A. Bowe, *Seeing It Their Way: Ideas, Activities and Resources for Intercultural Studies* (London, England: Reed Education, 1976), 29. Reprinted by permission.

9. See for example, Jonathan Kozol, *Savage Inequalities* (New York: Crown, 1991).

10. Foster, 1998

11. Padron, 1994

12. B. N. Kunisawa, "A Nation in Crisis: The Dropout Dilemma," *NEA Today* 6, no. 6 (January 1988):61–66. And William Celis III. "Hispanic Rate for Dropouts Remains High," *New York Times,* Wed, Oct. 14, 1992, pp. 1 and B8.

13. See, for example, *Asia in American Textbooks: An Evaluation* (New York: Asia Society,1976); J. Friedlander, *The Middle East: The Image and the Reality* (Los Angeles: University of California Press, 1980); S. J. Hall, *Africa in U.S. Schools, K–12: A Survey* (New York: African Institute, 1978); and *In Search of Mutual Understanding,* Japan/United States Textbook Study Project, Joint Report (Washington, DC: National Council of the Social Studies, January 1981).

14. M. Harrington, "Who Are the Poor? A Profile of the Changing Faces of Poverty in the United States in 1987" (Washington, DC: Justice for All National Office.) U.S. Bureau of the Census, Current Population Reports, Series P-23, No. 173, Population Profile of the United States: 1991. U.S. Government Printing Office, Washington, D.C.

15. M. Walzer, E. T. Kantowicz, J. Higham, and M. Harrington. *The Politics of Ethnicity* (Cambridge, MA: Belknap Press of Harvard University Press, 1982).

16. Ibid.

17. R. Muller, "The Need for Global Education" (from a speech presented by World Federalists of Canada, available from Sally Curry, 25 Dundana Avenue, Dundas Ontario, Canada L9H 4ES). See also "Can Man Save This Fragile Earth?" *National Geographic* 174, no. 6 (December 1988).

18. H. A. Sagar and J. W. Schofield, "Integrating the Desegregated School: Problems and Possibilities," in *Advances in Motivation and Achievement: The Effects of School Desegregation on Motivation and Achievement,* vol. 1, D. E. Bartz and M. L. Maehr, eds. (Greenwich, CT: JAI Press, 1984), 203–242. Following quotation is reprinted by permission of the publisher. Copyright © 1984 by JAI Press.

19. Sagar and Schofield, "Integrating the Desegregated School," 208.

20. Ibid., 212.

21. Ibid., 220–221.

22. Ibid., 231–232.

23. W. E. B. DuBois, "Does the Negro Need Separate Schools?" *Journal of Negro Education* 4 (103S):326, as quoted in Derrick Bell, *And We Are Not Saved: The Elusive Quest for Racial Justice* (New York: Basic Books, 1987), 120–121. For a discussion of some exemplary schools serving African American children and youth today, see *EBONY Special Issue on Save the Children,* XLIII, no. 10 (August 1988).

24. T. Pettigrew, "The Case for the Racial Integration of the Schools," in *Report on the Future of School Desegregation in the United States,* O. Duff, ed. (Pittsburgh: University of Pittsburgh, Consultative Resource Center on School Desegregation and Conflict, 1973).

25. R. Rosenthal and L. Jacobson, *Pygmalion in the Classroom: Teacher Expectation and Pupils' Intellectual Development* (New York: Holt, Rinehart and Winston. 1968).

26. T. L. Good, "Two Decades of Research on Teacher Expectations: Findings and Future Directions," *Journal of Teacher Education,* July–August, 1987:33. See also H. Cooper and T. Good, *Pygmalion Grows Up: Studies in the Expectation Process* (New York: Longman, 1983) and J. Dusek (ed.), *Teacher Expectancies* (Hillsdale, NJ: Erlbaum, 1985). For a discussion of the disproportionately high numbers of ethnic minorities among the nation's school dropouts due to "a dysfunctional education system that produces dropouts," see B. N. Kunisawa, "A Nation in Crisis: The Drop Out Dilemma," *NEA Today* 6, no. 6 (January 1988):61–65.

27. C. Cornbleth, O. L. Davis, Jr., and C. Bennett Button. "Expectations for Pupil Achievement and Teacher-Pupil Interaction," *Social Education* 38 (January 1974):54–58.

28. Described in G. Gay, "Differential Dyadic Interactions of Black and White Teachers with Black and White Pupils in Recently Desegregated Social Studies Classrooms: A Function of Teacher and Pupil Ethnicity," Office of Education, Project no. 2F113 (January 1974).

29. C. Bennett and J. J. Harris, III, "Suspensions and Expulsions of Male and Black Students: A Study of the Causes of Disproportionality," *Urban Education* 16, no. 4 (January 1982):399–423..

30. C. Bennett, "A Study of Classroom Climate in Desegregated Schools," *Urban Review* 13, no. 3 (1981):161–179.

31. Gay, "Differential Dyadic Interactions"; also see R. Rist, "Student Social Class and Teacher Expectations: The Self-Fulfilling Prophecy in Ghetto Education," *Harvard Education Review* 40 (August 1970); U.S. Civil Rights Commission, *Teachers and Students. Report V: Mexican-American Education Study. Differences in Teacher Interaction with Mexican-American and Anglo Students* (Washington, DC: Government Printing Office, March 1973).

32. Allport, *The Nature of Prejudice,* 281.

33. Ibid.

34. G. A. Forehand and M. Ragosta, *A Handbook for Integrated Schooling* (Princeton, NJ: Educational Testing Service, 1976), 79.

35. E. Cohen, "Status Equalization in the Desegregated School" (paper presented at the annual meeting of the American Educational Research Association, San Francisco, April 1979); and idem., "Student Influence in the Classroom (paper presented at the annual meeting of the American Educational Research Association, Toronto, 1978).

36. G. Forehand and M. Ragosta, *Handbook for Integrated Schooling* (Princeton, NJ: Educational Testing Service, 1976). In 1994, on the fortieth anniversary of the Supreme Court's school desegregation ruling, we find that nearly 70% of the nation's African American students attend segregated schools. See the *New York Times,* May 18, 1994, for a series of articles on the nation's struggle to desegregate schools.

37. R. Hanvey, *An Attainable Global Perspective* (New York: Center for War/Peace Studies, 1975), 4.

38. Ibid, 6.

39. Richard Paul, *Critical Thinking: What Every Person Needs to Survive in a Rapidly Changing World,* Revised Third Edition (Santa Rosa, CA: Foundation for Critical Thinking, 1993), 123.

40. I am grateful to Bradley Levinson for bringing this phrase to my attention.

chapter 2

The Nature of Culture and the Contexts for Multicultural Teaching

*T*he case for multicultural education began with a look at the nation's children and youth, their teachers, and the schools that serve them. The stories of Fred Young, Sara Stein, Jimmy Miller, Isaac Washington, Marcia Patton, Jesús Martinez, and the students in Sam Johnson's science classes on pages 2–9 highlight the tremendous cultural and individual diversity of the nation's school-age population. These stories illustrate that even well-intentioned teachers sometimes do not connect with their students, especially ethnic and language minority students like Jesús and Fred, low-income or rural youth like Jimmy, or culturally encapsulated mainstream students like Sam Johnson. This book is about how we can do better through multicultural teaching.

Most teachers would agree that our major goal is to foster the intellectual, social, and personal development of *all* students to their highest potential. Virtually all of us would agree that each student should be provided an equal opportunity to learn. These views are rooted in the deep cultural values of mainstream society in the United States which emphasize individualism, personal uniqueness, self-actualization, self-sufficiency, and equality of opportunity. Multicultural teaching goes beyond this goal to focus on principles of social justice, compassion for humanity, and social responsibility which are also rooted in the deep cultural values of our democratic society, even though they are not yet a social reality. Multicultural teachers seek to foster feelings of compassion, fair-minded critical thinking, and a spirit of social responsibility and participa-

Many classrooms provide an opportunity for students from various ethnic backgrounds to meet for the first time.

tion within themselves and their students. They are caring advocates for students from all cultural, racial, linguistic, and socioeconomic backgrounds.

Multicultural teachers seek intercultural competence—the knowledge and understanding of their students' cultural styles. They feel comfortable and at ease with their students. Interculturally competent teachers are aware of the diversity within racial, cultural, and socioeconomic groups, they know that culture is ever changing, and they are aware of the dangers of stereotyping. At the same time, they know that if they ignore their students' cultural attributes they are likely to be guided by their own cultural lenses, unaware of how their culturally conditioned expectations and assumptions might cause learning difficulties for some children and youth.

■*What Is Culture?*

Culture is a complex concept that anthropologists and sociologists have defined in a variety of ways. Prior to the late 1950s, it was typically defined in terms of patterns of behavior and customs. As early as 1871, for example, Tylor defined culture as "that complex whole which includes knowledge, belief, art, morals, law, custom, and any other capabilities and habits acquired by man as a member of society."[1]

This definition contrasts with more recent definitions of culture that focus on shared knowledge and belief systems, or symbols and meanings, rather than on habits and behavior. Geertz defines culture as "an historically transmitted pattern of meanings employed in symbols, a system of inherited conceptions expressed in symbolic form by means of which men communicate, perpetuate and develop their knowledge about and attitudes towards life."[2] Spradley and Mc-Curdy define culture as "the acquired knowledge that people use to interpret experience and to generate social behavior."[3] They also assert that *cultural knowledge* "is like a recipe for producing behavior and artifacts." Goodenough explains further:

> A society's culture consists of whatever it is one has to know or believe in order to operate in a manner acceptable to its members, and do so in any role that they accept for any one of themselves. Culture, being what people have to learn as distinct from their biological heritage, must consist of the end product of learning knowledge, in a most general, if relative, sense of the term. By this definition, we should note that culture is not a material phenomenon—it does not consist of things, people, behavior, or emotions. It is rather an organization of these things. It is the forms of things that people have in mind, their models for perceiving, relating and otherwise interpreting them. As such, the things people say and do, their social arrangements and events, are products or by-products of their culture as they apply it to the task of perceiving and dealing with their circumstances.[4]

According to LeVine, culture is "a shared organization of ideas that includes the intellectual, moral, and aesthetic standards prevalent in a community and the meanings of communicative actions."[5] Triandis makes a distinction between subjective culture, the "world view or the way a cultural group perceives its environment, including stereotypes, role perceptions, norms, attitudes, values, ideals, and perceived relationships between events and behaviors, and . . . material or concrete culture which includes the objects and artifacts of a culture."[6]

There exists a great deal of cultural diversity within any society since few individuals know or have access to all of the cultural heritage of their group. Some individuals have access to multiple cultures and may develop multiple standards for perceiving, believing, doing, and evaluating.[7] Where we happen to be born and when, may influence the culture, or cultures, we acquire. The family, the neighborhood, the region, the nation, and the era or decade can all make a difference. Initially, we have little control over the language we learn to speak, the concepts and stereotypes we acquire, the religion we accept, the gestures and expressions that amuse or reassure us, or the behavior that offends or pleases us. Furthermore, if we have been exposed to just one culture, we tend to assume that our way is the best way, the only way, and are likely to be unaware that we even have a culture. One way to develop cultural consciousness is to see how someone from another culture perceives or *misperceives* us. The views of international visitors and students in the United States can trigger deeper insights into our own culture. For example, some regard dating and romantic love as a source of severe psychological strain and are thankful that their families select their mate. Some are offended by the chemical odor of antiperspirants and soaps or body odor associated with eating beef. Many become sick after eating food to which they are unaccustomed. Many perceive the nursing home phenomenon as evidence that older family members are not loved or valued. Some are appalled by the material comforts we lavish on our pets. And some are uncomfortable in the typical American classroom where students are encouraged to question and challenge the teacher.

Understanding our own and other cultures clarifies why we behave in certain ways, how we perceive reality, what we believe to be true, what we build and create, what we accept as good and desirable, and so on. In a complex society that combines peoples of diverse national and indigenous origins, such as the United States, a variety of cultures coexist, along with the Anglo-Western European dominant culture. Avoiding ethnocentric explanations of students' behavior—that is, not interpreting their behavior from our own culturally biased viewpoint—requires awareness of our own cultural expectations.

The Importance of a World View

Worldview refers to "the way people characteristically look out on the universe."[8] It consists of values, beliefs, and assumptions, or the way a cultural group perceives people and events. Individual idiosyncrasies do exist, but it is also true that people who share a culture develop similar styles of cognition; similar processes of perceiving, recognizing, conceiving, judging, and reasoning; and similar values, assumptions, ideas, beliefs, and modes of thought.[9] What we see as good or bad depends on whether or not it supports our view of reality. Saral points out that

> it is thus apparent that there is no absolute reality, nor is there a universally valid way of perceiving, cognizing, and/or thinking. Each world view has different underlying assumptions. Our normal state of consciousness is not something natural or given, nor is it universal across cultures. It is simply a specialized tool, a complex structure for coping with our environment.[10]

Because schools are patterned after the predominant culture, it is essential to understand the dominant world view that originated primarily in Britain and Western Europe. This is not an easy task for those who happen to share this view of the world and take it for granted. Lessening the transitional trauma many students face in our classrooms, however, requires an awareness of our expectations or of our worldview. Let's consider one example of Mexican Americans.

According to Ramos and Ramos, many educators are influenced by ethnocentric sociological researchers from the mainstream who have generated erroneous concepts and conclusions about Mexican Americans. There are many misconceptions about Mexican Americans:

- Present-time oriented and desire immediate gratification.
- Nonintellectual, that is, formal education is not valued.
- Nongoal, nonsuccess oriented.
- Fatalistic and superstitious.
- Prefer living within the extended family group.
- Believe in machismo and a male-dominated society.[11]

The Ramoses challenge the validity of these long-held generalizations and suggest that each may be based on ethnocentric interpretations of evidence.

They use an example of a migrant family (migrants comprise about 10 percent of the Mexican American population) to make the point.

Consider the Ortiz family, who followed the crops from Texas to Michigan. Every fall they arrived in Colorado to pick sugar beets. Although they lived there only for the picking season, the children enrolled in school and were signed up for the government-subsidized hot lunch program. The Ortiz family felt that there was some reluctance on the part of the school personnel to give the children free lunches. After all, the school personnel observed, the parents drove the children to school in a new car and had probably bought it with no thought for the children's future.

Why does the Ortiz family own, or at least have a down payment on, a new car when they cannot buy lunches? It is simply because it is impossible to be a migrant worker without dependable transportation, and when one car breaks down, another must replace it. Actually, the car represents the future rather than the present. If the Ortiz family can forego some essentials today, the chances are that with the aid of a new car, they can travel faster and pick more crops to get ahead in the future. As Mr. Ortiz once told me, his hope is that the car will get his family to the jobs before the other pickers arrive and thus enable him to get the better jobs. On the surface the Ortiz family's actions appear to confirm the present-time orientation, but upon considering the circumstances we find the opposite to be true.[12]

How can misinterpretations such as this be avoided? How can we gain insights into our unconsciously held assumptions and world view? Kluckhohn writes that "studying [other cultures] enables us to see ourselves better. Ordinarily we are unaware of the specialized lens through which we look at life."[13] The comparison in Box 2.1 is an example of how we can understand the macrocultural world view by learning about a microculture.

The Navajo Way

BOX 2.1

To a Navajo, time is ever flowing; can't be broken. Exactness of time is of little importance.

To a non-Indian, time is of the utmost importance and must be used to its fullest extent.

To a Navajo, the future is uncertain. Nature, which is more important than man, may change anything. This life is what counts—there is no sense that life on earth is a preparation for another life.

Non-Indians prepare for the future. Such items as insurance, savings, and plans for trips and vacations show to what extent non-Indians hold this value.

Patience: Navajo. To have patience and to wait is considered a good quality.

Non-Indian. The man who is admired is the one who is quick to act.

Age: Navajo. Respect is for the elders. Experience is felt to bring knowledge. Age has priority though increasing power is going to those who speak English well. Knowledge is power.

BOX 2.1

(Continued)

Non-Indian. The great desire to look younger and live longer. Much money is spent to pursue these efforts.

Family: Navajo. The Indian cultures consider many more individuals to be relatives than do non-Indians. Clan relationships are strong. The Navajo is wary of nonrelatives and foreigners.

Non-Indian. Biological family is of utmost importance, and relationships are limited within this group.

Wealth: Navajo. Wealth is to be consumed and used as security—always to be shared. Many Indians are suspicious of individuals who collect material possessions. Some tribes give love gifts and enjoy this practice.

Non-Indian. Non-Indian cultures have measured wealth in terms of material things. Many such possessions often constitute status symbols and are considered highly desirable.

Nature: Navajo. Humanity lives in perfect balance with nature. The earth is here to enjoy. Heed signals from nature—learn from animals. People are an integral part of this universe and must do their part to maintain harmony and balance among the parts of the cosmos.

Non-Indian. Culture here is a constant search for new ways for control and mastery of the elements around. Artificial lakes are made; natural waters are controlled; electricity is generated and controlled. Such accomplishments are looked upon with pride.

Cultural premises among the Navajos may be summarized as follows:

1. The Universe is orderly.
2. There is a basic quest for harmony.
3. The universe, though personalized, is full of dangers.
4. Evil and good are complementary and both are present in all things, thus human nature is neither basically good nor evil.
5. Everything exists in two parts, male and female, which belong together and complete each other.
6. The future is uncertain—nature (which is more powerful than people) might change anything.
7. This life is what counts—there is no sense that life on earth is a preparation for another existence.
8. Time and place are symbols of recapitulation.
9. Events, not actors or quality, are primary.
10. Time is ever flowing, can't be broken.
11. Concept of life as one whole—Navajos have a hard time thinking in terms of social, economic, and political distinctions.
12. Like produces like . . . the part stands for the whole.

Source: "Teacher-Aide Guide for Navajo Area," product of a conference at the Dzilth-na-o-dith-hle Community School, Bloomfield, NM, June 8–12, 1970. Reprinted by permission of the Bureau of Indian Affairs, Eastern Navajo Agency—OIEP.

It is easy to identify ways in which our schools are consistent with the non-Indian way. School days are organized into strict time schedules punctuated by the bell. The competitive learning environment rewards individual excellence. Students learn ways to control disease, and they dissect frogs in the science lab. They debate the rightness or wrongness of public policies such as nuclear arms control, school prayers, and school desegregation. Many questions are asked; quick answers are associated with intelligence, slow ones with dullness. The list could go on.

Different world views often lead to mutual misperceptions, hostility, or conflict. For example, an American professor and his wife visiting Thailand for the first time were greeted with inquiries about their weights and salaries. A Japanese businessman terminated dealings with an American because the latter, not wishing to waste time or pry, initiated business discussions without the customary inquiries about family and other personal matters.

Evidence indicates that the same process of misperception that operates between members of different nations who are unaware of each other's world view also operates in many schools and classrooms. The Panther Prowl, an annual homecoming celebration at a high school in central Florida, illustrates this misperception and cultural conflict. The Black and White students experienced little interracial contact outside of school. Two different musical groups, one Black and one White, had been hired to perform at the assembly. When the Black musicians began to perform, Blacks in the audience responded by clapping, stomping, singing, and dancing. The Black performers kept cool, interacted with the Black audience, and were clearly enjoying it. A group of White students became very upset, demanded quiet, and finally walked out. Black students, in turn, felt the Whites were being purposefully rude and unresponsive to the Black performers. Later that evening, several interracial fights broke out on campus.

According to anthropologist Roger Abrahams, what happened at the Panther Prowl is an example of the different performance traditions in Black and White cultures. The Anglo-European tradition places a virtuoso performer on a pedestal. The audience is passive recipient, and appreciation is expressed with applause at acceptable times. For many Black Americans, however, the essence of the performance is an active interchange between performer and audience. Great performers, including public speakers and ministers, are those who keep their "cool" while getting their audience "hot."[14] Many Blacks and Whites have, of course, learned to appreciate and enjoy each other's music and performance traditions. Where this mutual understanding has not occurred, however, conflicts such as at the Panther Prowl can be expected.

High- and Low-context Cultures

One promising way to conceptualize culture and avoid crosscultural misunderstanding has been developed by Edward T. Hall. *Beyond Culture, The Silent Language,* and *The Hidden Dimension* are classics in the area of intercultural study and vividly describe how humans can be unknowingly influenced by their culture. People from different cultures may perceive the world differently, often unaware that there are alternative ways of perceiving, believing, behaving, and judging. Hall argues that most of us hold unconscious assumptions about what is appropriate in terms of personal space, time, interpersonal relations, and ways of seeking truth (e.g. scientific inquiry, meditation, revelation, etc.) These cultural differences exist to varying degrees among Anglo-Europeans and ethnic minorities within our society (for example, certain American Indian nations such as the Hopi and Navajo, African Americans, Mexican Americans, Puerto Ricans, Jews, Chinese Americans, and rural Appalachians), as well as among different nations.

Cultural differences and misunderstandings often become evident when people from different cultures try to communicate. Often they assume erroneously that they are communicating. This is why Hall's simple but elegant theory of culture can be helpful to us, provided that it is used as a framework for observing and understanding behaviors, while avoiding stereotypes and guarding against a reified and static view of culture.

Hall envisions a continuum of *sociocultural tightness* to distinguish between high-context cultures at one end and low-context cultures at the other; specific cultures may be described according to where they lie on the continuum.[15] Hall focuses on interpersonal communication styles as a key for illuminating basic cultural differences and similarities. In low-context cultures, such as much of the United States, Germany, and Scandinavia, meaning is gleaned from the verbal message itself, for example, a spoken explanation, a memo, or computer program. What is said is more important than who said it, and often we don't even know the author. Members of the university community, for example, often communicate by phone or memo over a period of years or decades without ever meeting each other in person. High-context cultures, such as East Asian, Arab, southern European, Native American, Mexican, and portions of the rural United States, are generally the opposite. Meaning must be understood in terms of the situation or setting in which communication takes place. A classic example is the written Chinese language, in which many characters may be pronounced in several different ways, depending on the context within which they are used. Thus it is necessary to avoid reification of the categories and to keep in mind the diversity within nations and ethnic groups that is related to regional, gender, and socioeconomic differences.

With these limitations in mind, consider the overview of key characteristics of high- and low-context cultures in Table 2.1.[16] In theory, high- and low-context cultures differ according to orientations toward time and space, reasoning, verbal messages, social roles, interpersonal relations, and law and authority in social organizations. Initially, it might appear that high-context cultures are more humanistic and low-context cultures more mechanistic. This interpretation is too simplistic. It is true that members of high-context cultures tend to live in tune with nature and with other humans who are part of their social network, and that people in low-context cultures are often at odds with nature and tend to have more fragmented social relationships. It is also true that individuals in high-context cultures tend to gain their identity through group associations

■ **TABLE 2.1**
Summary of Hall's Conception of Culture According to Context

	High Context	*Low Context*
Time	*Polychronic* Loose schedules, flux, multiple simultaneous activities. Last-minute changes of important plans. Time is less tangible.	*Monochronic* Tight schedules, one event at a time, linear. Importance of being on time. Time is more tangible (e.g., is spent, wasted, is "money").
Space & Tempo	*High-Sync* Synchrony, moving in harmony with others and with nature, is consciously valued. Social rhythm has meaning.	*Low-Sync* Synchrony is less noticeable. Social rhythm is underdeveloped.
Reasoning	*Comprehensive Logic* Knowledge is gained through intuition, spiral logic, and contemplation. Importance of feelings.	*Linear Logic* Knowledge is gained through analytical reasoning (e.g., the Socratic method). Importance of words.
Verbal Messages	*Restricted Codes* "Shorthand speech," reliance on nonverbal and contextual clues. Overall emotional quality more important than meaning of particular words. Economical, fast, efficient communication that is satisfying, slow to change; fosters interpersonal cohesiveness and provides for human need for social stability. Stress on social integration and harmony; being polite.	*Elaborate Codes* Verbal amplification through extended talk or writing. Little reliance on nonverbal or contextual cues. Doesn't foster cohesiveness but can change rapidly. Provides for human need to adapt and change. Stress on argument and persuasion; being direct.
Social Roles	*Tight Social Structure* Individual's behavior is predictable; conformity to role expectations.	*Loose Social Structure* Behavior is unpredictable; role behavior expectations are less clear.
Interpersonal Relations	*Group Is Paramount* Clear status distinctions (e.g., age, rank, position), strong distinctions between insiders and outsiders. Human interactions are emotionally based, person oriented. Stronger personal bonds, bending of individual interests for sake of relationships. Cohesive, highly interrelated human relationships, completed action chains. Members of group are first and foremost.	*Individual Is Paramount* Status is more subtle, distinctions between insiders and outsiders less important. Human interactions are functionally based, approach is specialized. Fragile interpersonal bonds due to geographic mobility. Fragmented, short term human relationships, broken action chains when relationship is not satisfying. Individuals are first, groups come second.

Continued

TABLE 2.1
Summary of Hall's Conception of Culture According to Context (*continued*)

	High Context	Low Context
Social Organization	*Personalized Law and Authority* Customary procedures and whom one knows are important. Oral agreements are binding. In face of unresponsive bureaucracies, must be an insider or have a "friend" to make things happen (e.g., going through the "back door"). People in authority are personally and truly responsible for actions of every subordinate.	*Procedural Law and Authority* Procedures, laws and policies are more important than whom one knows. Written contracts are binding. Policy rules, unresponsive bureaucracy. People in authority try to pass the buck. Impersonal Legal procedures

(e.g., place of work, neighborhood organizations, family or lineage), while individuals in low-context cultures usually develop an identity based on their personal efforts and achievements. On the other hand, members of high-context cultures are less open to strangers (although they are often known for their warm hospitality toward foreigners who are "guests"), make stronger distinctions between insiders and outsiders, and are more likely to follow rigid role expectations and bureaucratic traditions that have become outdated and inefficient. In comparison, the greater personal freedom, openness, and individual choice found in low-context cultures might be seen as more humanistic than mechanistic. It is important to realize that both high- and low-context cultures possess positive ingredients that are necessary for human survival. For example, high-context cultures provide a strong human support network that helps guard against the alienation of a technological society; and low-context cultures provide ways of adapting, changing, and using new knowledge that can help resolve human problems such as starvation and disease.

What does this theory have to do with schools in the United States? First, the vast majority of schools in this society are modeled after the low-context dominant culture. Academic and social events operate according to tight schedules, often printed months in advance. Competition, individual excellence, and personal responsibility are stressed. Interpersonal relations, nonverbal communication, and cooperation are de-emphasized. Consider again the Navajo and non-Indian cultural premises in Box 2.1. These can be understood in terms of high- and low-context culture in that time orientations tend to be polychronic, harmony with nature is highly valued, clan relationships are strong, and there is a wariness of nonrelatives and foreigners.

Second, in contrast to the low-context culture at school, many students have grown up in high-context microcultures. Without an understanding of the different assumptions and expectations of their home and classroom culture,

Cultural emersion experiences in China provide Westerners with insight into their own world view.

they are likely to experience some degree of psychological discomfort, or transitional trauma, as they attempt to adjust to school.

Third, Hall's theory of high- and low-context culture can be included in the school curriculum as a means of helping students become more multicultural. Students can learn to use Hall's theory as a tool for understanding human conflicts that are rooted in deep culture.

■*Differences between Culture and Race*

All humans share a common ancestry, believed to have originated in Africa, and belong to the species *Homo Sapiens* (Latin for human being and wise). The concept of race is a social construction used to group humans according to observable traits such as size, skin color, and hair texture. In contrast to culture, which is learned and can be modified (even rejected) over time, race refers to immutable physical characteristics. Scientists estimate that only a tiny fraction of our genetic makeup is associated with racial features. As surgeons and pathologists know, under the skin it is difficult to distinguish among us.

Still, following a trend among eighteenth-century European scientists to classify all living things, the term *race* was used to describe the human diversity that developed over the eons in response to geographic differences. Many scientists argue that only the fittest survived extreme climatic conditions, high altitudes, intensity of the sun, and life-threatening pests such as the Malaria mosquito. Where people were relatively isolated due to geographic barriers like mountains and the oceans, breeding in isolation led to more distinct phenotypes. The commonly identified but misconstrued racial types today were developed by Blumenback from the racial classification created by Carolus Linnaeus, the eminent nineteenth-century Swedish biologist. These racial categories are Mongoloid, Negroid, and Caucasoid, and sometimes Malayan and Native American.[17]

Darwin attacked the scientific use of race, and many social scientists have abandoned the concept because it has not provided useful knowledge in understanding human nature and cannot be easily defined.[18] Montagu called race man's most dangerous myth. He warns, "It is not possible to make the sort of racial classifications which anthropologists and others have attempted. The fact is that all human beings are so mixed with regard to origin that between different groups of individuals . . . 'overlapping' of physical traits is the rule."[19] Typically there are greater physical differences among individuals within a given race than there are between people of different races. Nevertheless, the concept of race persists and remains a primary basis for categorizing self and others within U.S. society.[20] Despite the irrelevancy of race as a concept for defining humanity, the United States is a race-conscious society, as are some other nations, such as South Africa, Brazil, and Japan.

It should be clear that culture is in no way determined by skin color, or other physical attributes associated with race. Individuals from any so-called racial group can become multicultural, or competent in any cultural milieu they have access to, if they so choose. For example, there are Whites who act Black and vice versa; many Hispanic communities contain tremendous racial diversity (e.g., Puerto Ricans include people who are Black, Indian, Latino, or White); and there are Black Africans in Ethiopia who are Orthodox Jews, as well as African Americans who identify with Judaism. It is also true, however, that racial isolation and segregation have been a fact of history for large segments of the population; as a result, cultural differences that can be *associated* with race have survived. The fact that cultural differences are sometimes linked with racial differences confirms myths and stereotypes associated with race. African Americans, for example, are often perceived as having more rhythm and as being natural athletes. Jews are often perceived as being miserly and more intelligent. These perceptions are usually based on the erroneous belief that genetic biological factors, rather than cultural factors, explain what is perceived.

◼ *What Do We Mean by Ethnic Groups?*

An ethnic group is a community of people within a larger society that is socially distinguished or set apart, by others and/or by itself, primarily on the basis of racial and/or cultural characteristics, such as religion, language, and tradition.

TABLE 2.2

Estimated Population of Ethnic Groups in the United States, According to Race, Hispanic Origin, Jewish and Muslim, 1990

Race	1990 Total	1990 Percentage
All Persons	248,709,873	100.0
White Americans	199,686,070	80.3
African Americans	29,986,060	12.1
American Indian, Eskimo, or Aleut	1,959,234	0.8
American Indians	1,878,285	0.8
Eskimos	57,152	0.0
Aleuts	23,797	0.0
Asian or Pacific Islander	7,273,662	2.9
Chinese Americans	1,645,472	0.7
Filipino Americans	1,406,770	0.6
Japanese Americans	847,562	0.3
Asian Indian	815,447	0.3
Korean Americans	798,849	0.3
Vietnamese	614,547	0.2
Native Hawaiians	211,014	0.1
Samoans	62,964	0.0
Guamanians	49,345	0.0
Other Asian or Pacific Islander	821,692	0.3
Other Race	9,804,847	3.9

Hispanic Origin	1990 Total	1990 Percentage
All Persons	248,709,873	100.0
Hispanic origin	22,354,059	9.0
Mexican	13,495,938	5.4
Puerto Rican	2,727,754	1.1
Cuban	1,043,932	0.4
Other Hispanic	5,086,435	2.0
Not of Hispanic origin	226,355,814	91.0

Jewish and Muslim	1990 Total	1990 Percentage
All Persons	248,709,873	100.0
Jewish	6,800,000	2.8
Muslim	5,000,000	2.1

An ethnic group may be distinguished "by race, religion, or national origin."[21] The central factor is the notion of being set apart from the larger society; the distinctiveness may be based on either physical or cultural attributes, or both. As is explained on page 50, an ethnic group may also be an ethnic minority, but not always (see Table 2.2).

Some people in the United States identify primarily with the Anglo-Western European core culture, frequently labeled White Anglo-Saxon Protestant (WASP). This ethnic group comprises the predominant society, or dominant culture, which was established prior to the arrival of diverse nationality and religious groups that have immigrated to this country since about 1820. Examples of ethnic groups based on these nationality and religious groups are the Germans, Irish, Italians, Jews, Greeks, Chinese, Japanese, Mennonites, and Poles. Other ethnic groups are people whose ancestors were indigenous or who inhabited the land before the westward expansion of the Anglo-Western European core culture. These groups include the Native Americans and the Mexican Americans, whose Spanish and Mestizo ancestors had settled large portions of the West and controlled what now consists of eight states in the Southwest. Still another ethnic group is the African American group, whose ancestors were brought here as slaves. Also recognized as an ethnic group are the geographically isolated mountain people of Appalachia, who have maintained many traditions related to their Scottish Irish roots.

Diversity within Ethnic Groups

It is important to think of ethnic groups as imprecise and arbitrary social constructions, not absolute categories of people. Even within relatively well-defined ethnic groups, such as African Americans or Jewish Americans, there exists tremendous heterogeneity. When we consider factors such as income, level of education, geographical region, generation of immigration or entry (and whether it was voluntary, involuntary, or a product of colonialism), family structure, size and composition of the ethnic community, and biological features such as skin color, we see greater variation *within* ethnic groups than between them.

Individuals also differ in their sense of ethnic identity. They differ in the extent to which they adhere to traditional attitudes, values, beliefs, and behaviors, and their sense of identity may be strong even when there is little involvement in the traditional culture, such as language use and dress. For example, some third- or fourth-generation Irish or Italian Americans might retain little of their traditional culture of origin but still maintain a symbolic ethnicity, or strong sense of loyalty to their ethnic group. Sometimes individuals who are perceived and labeled by others as members of an ethnic group reject their ethnic group and feel totally assimilated into mainstream society.

When Is an Ethnic Group a Minority Group?

The label *minority group* is confusing; today, many individuals prefer not to be labeled a "minority" because the term connotes inferior or lesser status vis-à-vis the majority. Furthermore, minority is often confused with numerical minority, when in fact a numerical minority may control a numerical majority. White slave owners, for example, were a numerical minority on the large southern plantations, and today in many small towns throughout the South and

Southwest, White minorities hold political and economic control despite the larger numbers of African American or Mexican American citizens. A numerical minority of White South Africans controlled the South African government and society from 1910 until the end of apartheid in the 1990s.

From a sociological perspective, whether or not an ethnic group is also a minority group depends on the degree to which it holds a subordinate status in the society. Wirth defines minority group, in terms of subordinate position, as "a group of people who, because of their physical or cultural characteristics, are singled out from others in the society in which they live for differential and unequal treatment and who therefore regard themselves as objects of collective discrimination."[22] Most social scientists view ethnic groups as minority groups when they:

- suffer discrimination and subordination within a society;
- are set apart in terms of physical or cultural traits disapproved of by the dominant group;
- share a sense of collective identity and common burdens;
- inherit their group membership at birth; and
- marry primarily within their groups.[23]

A review of U.S. history reveals that most, if not all, ethnic groups have experienced minority group status, usually during the early stages of immigration or colonization. From the above definition, it is clear that some ethnic groups have remained minority groups for many generations and others have not. It has been easier for White ethnics to shed their minority status because discrimination against them has not been based on racial classification.

The degree to which an ethnic group retains minority group status depends on how it is received by and/or receives the predominant society. Does it experience long-term segregation? Is it quickly absorbed into the mainstream? Does it wish to retain its own cultural traditions? It is important to realize, however, that individuals in the same ethnic group differ in their experiences associated with minority status, including prejudice, discrimination, and feelings of powerlessness.

Cultural Assimilation and Pluralism

Cultural assimilation, sometimes referred to as the effect of the American "melting pot," is often mistakenly equated with multicultural education. *Cultural assimilation* is "a process in which people of diverse ethnic and racial backgrounds come to interact, free of constraints, in the life of the larger community. It is a one-way process through which members of an ethnic group give up their original culture and are absorbed into the core culture, which predominates in the host society."[24] Cultural assimilation has been a strong theme throughout the history of the United States.

Between 1820 and 1970, more than 45 million immigrants, mostly from European nations, entered the United States. The prevalent view was that the newly arrived ethnic groups would give up their unique cultural attributes and accept the Anglo-American way of life. The school was expected to play the major role in this forced assimilation. Education historian Cubberly vividly describes the process:

> Everywhere these people (immigrants) tend to settle in groups or settlements and to set up their own national manners, customs, and observances. Our task is to break up their groups and settlements, to assimilate or amalgamate these people as part of the American race, and to implant in their children, so far as can be done, the Anglo-Saxon conception of righteousness, law, order, and popular government, and to awaken in them reverence for our democratic institutions and for those things which we as a people hold to be of abiding worth.[25]

The melting-pot theory is still widely accepted, especially by classroom teachers. In an attempt to educate students in "the American way," many teachers view cultural differences as deficits and disadvantages. They are blind to their students' personal and cultural strengths. As an example, many Spanish-speaking students like Jesús Martinez, who could not read English, were placed in classes for the mentally retarded after scoring low on IQ tests that were written in English. Students like Fred Young were perceived as "dumb."

In recent years the theory of cultural pluralism has emerged as an alternative to the melting pot. *Cultural pluralism,* in its ideal form, is a process of compromise characterized by mutual appreciation and respect between two or more cultural groups.[26] In a culturally pluralistic society, members of different ethnic groups are permitted to retain many of their cultural traditions such as language, religion, and food preferences, so long as they conform to those practices deemed necessary for social harmony and the survival of society as a whole. The stained-glass window, tapestry, and mosaic are images frequently associated with cultural pluralism. Each part retains some of its uniqueness while contributing to the beauty and strength of the whole composition.

The concept of cultural pluralism fits well with the democratic ideals of the United States, such as majority rule with minority rights, and the concept of *E Pluribus Unum.* It was developed in the early twentieth century by democratic philosopher Kallen, who wrote that each ethnic group had the democratic right to retain its own heritage.[27] Kallen immigrated to this country from Poland and argued vehemently against forced Americanization of immigrants. His views, however, were not given much credence until after the civil rights movement in the United States during the 1960s and 1970s.

Gay described the psychological and political effects of this civil rights movement in our society:

> Newly formed student activist organizations, as well as the older established civil rights groups, began to demand restitution for generations of oppression, racism, and cultural imperialism. The shifting ideological focus of the movement was captured in such slogans as "Black is beautiful," "Yellow is mellow," "Black power," and "Power to the people." Moreover, as the slogans suggest, the civil rights movement for Afro-Americans gradually became a movement for recogni-

tion of all minority groups, including Mexican-Americans, Native Americans, Asian-Americans, and Puerto Ricans.[28]

What began as a Black Power movement spread to include many other minority groups, including women. It also helped inspire and rekindle ethnic consciousness among numerous White ethnic groups, particularly among the third and fourth generations of southern and eastern European immigrants. As a result, today's society is much more aware, and even appreciative, of its cultural diversity.

A common misconception is that cultural pluralism is dangerous to society because it heightens ethnic group identity and leads to separatism, polarization, and intergroup antagonism. This view overlooks a critical ingredient of cultural pluralism: All groups must conform to certain rules that are necessary for the survival of the society as a whole. The question of what is good and necessary for the survival of a society is a difficult one, and the processes maintaining social boundaries between different ethnic groups are complex. The Amish provide a good example of the struggle for cultural pluralism in this society. In some regions they are allowed to maintain their own communities, schools, and traditions, but are expected to abide by the rules of the larger society. Another example is Chasidic Jews, who maintain their orthodox religion in a society that is highly secular and primarily Christian in religious outlook. Other examples include the Cherokee, Navajo, and Chippewa nations, as well as other Indian tribes that have treaty rights to land, fishing rights, and other special relationships with the federal government.

Cultural pluralism is an ideal state of societal conditions characterized by equity and mutual respect among existing culture groups. How we can envision and work toward cultural pluralism in multicultural classrooms is the focus of the next section.

■ *Guidelines for Understanding Cultural Differences in the Classroom: Aspects of Ethnicity*

Longstreet has developed a clear and useful scheme (based in part on Hall's theory) for understanding differences in culturally pluralistic classrooms.[29] Originally conceived for desegregated classrooms, it can be used as a guideline for observing and interpreting human behavior in any setting.

Longstreet defines ethnicity as "that portion of cultural development that occurs before the individual is in complete command of his or her abstract intellectual powers and that is formed primarily through the individual's early contacts with family, neighbors, friends, teachers, and others, as well as with his or her immediate environment of the home and neighborhood."[30] Most older students will have gained some intellectual control over these learned behaviors and are to some degree bicultural, but even among bicultural adults that control is likely to remain incomplete.

Longstreet goes on to identify five aspects of ethnicity that provide teachers with guidelines for pinpointing potential sources of misunderstanding in multicultural classrooms. These aspects of ethnicity can be used to illuminate cultural differences among nations as well as among ethnic groups within a society. The following outline is based on Longstreet's aspects of ethnicity.[31]

Guidelines for Understanding Cultural Differences

Verbal Communication

Grammar
Semantics—meanings of words
Phonology—sound, pitch, rhythm, and tempo of words
Discussion modes—patterns of participating and listening

Nonverbal Communication

Kinesics—body language
Proxemics—personal space
Haptics—frequency, quality, and location of touch
Signs and symbols—meanings associated with artifacts, such as clothing, jewelry, emblems, flags, and traffic lights

Orientation Modes

Body positions—unconscious movements and relaxation
Spatial architectural patterns
Attention modes
Time modes

Social Values

Ideal behaviors (beliefs about how one ought or ought not to behave, such as seeking truth and beauty, being sincere, fair, compassionate, rational, loyal, and orderly.)[32]
Ideal goals (beliefs about some end-state of existence that is worth or not worth attaining, such as "security, happiness, freedom, equality, ecstasy, fame, power, and states of grace and salvation.")[33]

Intellectual Modes

Preferred ways of learning
Knowledge most valued
Skills emphasized

Longstreet distinguishes between an individual's ethnic heritage and the culture of the school. She regards *scholastic ethnicity* (i.e., school culture) as a national phenomenon because the public school bureaucracy and traditions are similar throughout the nation and across several generations. The form and uses of grading, the content of study, the "uniform number of periods per day, bells, hall monitors, and even required notes for absences" are all examples of turn-of-the-century school practices that still predominate.[34] The greater the distinction between scholastic ethnicity and the student's ethnic heritage or home culture, the greater the alienation that student is likely to experience. Let's consider these aspects of ethnicity in greater depth.

Verbal Communication

The almost exclusive use of standard American English in U.S. schools is a striking example of the macrocultural orientation. Whether or not all schoolchildren should develop enough skill in standard English to make its use a functional option is not being debated. (All students should be expected to attain some degree of proficiency in standard American English.) What should be examined, however, is the cultural conflict many children experience in schools that ignore or repress the language they have known since birth. According to Mario Benitez,

> . . . all the pre-primers available on the market assume a level of development in oral languages that the Mexican American child has not reached at the beginning of first grade. Phonologically speaking he neither hears nor discriminates certain sounds. Accustomed as he is to hearing Spanish mostly at home, he hears Spanish in the classroom instead of English and tries to decode accordingly. The result is frustration and awareness that he is failing at something [while] the other children are succeeding.[35]

The truth of Benitez's remarks is usually accepted when referring to Latino, American Indian, and East Asian American children—those whose first language often is not English. It is recognized as well that standard American English may create similar learning problems for African American children. Recently, a group of elementary teachers in a rural school in central Florida noted that, as early as first grade, White students surpassed Blacks in reading. Until they listened to tapes of Black students speaking, they were oblivious to the distinct Black dialect. They then realized that asking many of these children to learn to read available materials was like asking Whites to begin reading Old English.

Areas of potential conflict related to verbal communication are dialect differences, especially grammar and semantics, and discussion modes. Students who speak "country," African American vernacular, or any nonstandard dialect are often perceived as uneducated or less intelligent. Many White students and some upper- and middle-income Black students who have grown up in ethnically encapsulated environments cannot understand their Black or Latino peers, or incorrectly assume they do understand. Use of the term "nigger" among some African Americans, for example, is distressing to some teachers even when students use the term with affection.

Abrahams and Gay have clearly identified some important classroom implications of language differences.

> To understand the relationship that exists between [the teacher and] students, and the students' classroom behavior, the middle-class teacher needs to realize that older Black students use a variety of verbal techniques, and that they use these techniques to discover [the teacher's] strengths and weaknesses, to find out where [the teachers] stand on issues ranging from how "hip" [they are] to racial attitudes, and to locate [their] breaking point. Once these are discovered they help the student to exert some control over the situation.
>
> Because [Black] street culture is an oral culture, and is dependent largely upon the spoken word for its perpetuation and transmission, its language is very colorful, creative, and adaptive. It is in a constant state of flux and new words are al-

ways being invented. Further, new slang words are constantly created as a way of maintaining an in-group relationship and of excluding outsiders. Thus, there emerges something of a secret code that only in-group members completely understand. It is used by students and others in street culture to convey messages to each other about the "enemy," even in his presence. Of course, some of these terms have been picked up by White "hipsters," but often the meaning is changed because of the different cultural perspective.[36]

Discussion modes, or the way members of the same ethnic group "engage in discussion when they are among themselves, at parties, at home with their families, or at meetings of committees,"[37] are also a frequent source of intercultural misunderstanding. Longstreet offers a vivid illustration:

> I had invited five black students in an economic opportunity program to my graduate workshop [Inner Detroit, Michigan]. The ostensible purpose was to discuss the inadequacies of university programs for diverse ethnic minorities. The discussion was, to begin with, quite orderly, that is, first one person spoke, then another, and so forth. However, as the discussion turned to more heated topics, the black Americans literally took it over. The whites in the group (more than half) sat as though they were an audience invited to observe an extraordinary event. The blacks seemed to all talk at once, becoming progressively louder and more shrill in pitch. Even as teacher, I did not feel there was any opportunity for me to interject an opinion or comment. There was a lull, and most unexpectedly one of the black girls turned to the whites who were gathered on one side of the circle: "And you," she asked pointing her finger at them, "why aren't you joining in? Do you think you're too good to tell us how you feel?" The whites seemed to find no way to respond to her accusation, and 1, myself, was stunned. Vaguely in my mind I had decided that the black group was determined to take over the discussion and make those "whiteys" listen. There really had been, as far as I could remember, no pause that would have let any of the whites enter the animated discussion. Furthermore, so many people seemed to be talking at once that I had trouble following what was being said.[38]

Longstreet and the White students in her seminar obviously assumed that the best way to conduct a discussion was to follow the "you-take-a-turn-then another-takes-a-turn" model. This is, in fact, the accepted mode in most classrooms. While some African American students might find this mode too restrictive, many Asian American students, even those considered to be culturally assimilated, are also uncomfortable with the mode but for different reasons. Accustomed to thinking through a position and verbalizing only after careful reflection, they are often frustrated by not having an opportunity to express their thoughts in the midst of a spontaneous, heated, seemingly loud discussion. And they are perceived negatively by non-Asian classmates, as were the Whites in Longstreet's seminar.

The typical mainstream mode is for the teacher to talk and students to listen. Students are passive recipients. Indeed, research indicates that teachers do over 75 percent of the talking in classrooms. The cardinal rule is that students must raise their hands and may not speak until given permission. One must never interrupt another who is speaking, especially the teacher.

This may sound like good classroom management, and often it is, especially for middle-class children. In mainstream society, adult questioning of children is common practice. Parents enjoy that kind of interaction and often use it to develop the child's ability to speak; thus the child is not confused when adults in school continue the process. For many inner-city African American children, however, question-and-answer elicitation may be wrongly interpreted as hostile because it occurs most frequently in their homes when the adult is angry at the child. And among language-minority students, the strategy may trigger feelings of embarrassment and inadequacy.

Several scholars note that the "passive" and "indirect" language many White middle-class teachers use creates confusion and misunderstanding between themselves and many low-income children and children of color.[39] Based upon their view of politeness and showing respect, these teachers often speak in soft tones, offer choices, and use questions rather than commands. For example, they may say "Johnny, don't you want to sit down?" Or, "Tishanna, what did I ask you to do?" rather than telling the students to behave or get to work. The students often misinterpret this style as indications that the teacher is incompetent and uncaring.

What about students who learn best in a more informal setting that encourages an active interchange between the speaker and the audience? Think back to the Panther Prowl and the different participation styles of the Blacks and Whites in that audience. Daniels and colleagues show how for many Blacks communication and participation involve the whole self in a simultaneous interaction of intellect, intuition, and sensuality.[40] Because communication and participation are central to learning, students with an African American world view apparently learn best in settings that encourage a simultaneous response of thought, feeling, and movement. Silence and sitting still are often signs that the Black child is bored.[41]

In the low-context dominant culture, on the other hand, intellectual, emotional, and physical responses are easily separated. Messages become distinct from people in the form of memos, and ideas are analyzed in their written form, without the benefit of nonverbal cues. Society assumes that individuals, such as lawyers, sometimes argue viewpoints they do not believe, and in school teachers often ask students to sharpen their thinking by arguing a position they cannot accept. In some cultures, these are impossibilities.[42] Children from White middle-class families are often comfortable in the classroom role of passive recipient. They can learn to be rational and to remove emotions and feelings from decisions. Many are unable to concentrate in a more active, noisy environment. These generalizations are supported by the extensive ethnographic research of Kochman in Chicago. Kochman, who is White, writes that "Black culture has given me a powerful appreciation of qualities and concerns that my own middle-class culture tends to downgrade: individual self-assertion and self-expression, spiritual well being, spontaneity and emotional expressiveness, personal (as opposed to status) orientation, individual distinctiveness, forthrightness, camaraderie, and community."[43]

Nonverbal Communication

It is estimated that 50 to 90 percent of what humans communicate is nonverbal. That is, most of the messages we send are through unconscious body movements, expressions, and gestures (kinesics); our unconscious use and organization of personal space (proxemics); and when, where, and how often we unconsciously physically touch others (haptics).

The literature is filled with fascinating examples of cultural differences in nonverbal communication. Much of this research was conducted over two decades ago. If misunderstood, it could foster racial stereotypes. It is included in this chapter because it illuminates cultural differences that sometimes do exist among members of a culturally pluralistic society. Ignorance of cultural differences allows us to mistakenly assume that everyone is operating according to the same verbal and nonverbal speech patterns and cultural norms. Acknowledging differences within foreign cultures can alert us to more subtle differences at home. Greetings are one example and illustrate how the accepted behaviors of one culture may be seriously misunderstood in another.

> The Copper Eskimo welcome strangers with a buffet on the head or shoulders with the fist, while the northwest Amazonians slap one another on the back in greeting. Polynesian men greet one another by embracing and rubbing each others back; Spanish-American males greet one another by a stereotyped embrace, head over the right shoulder of the partner, three pats on the back, head over reciprocal left shoulder, three more pats. In the Torres Straits, the old form of greeting was to bend the right hand into a hook, then mutually scratching palms by drawing away the right hand, repeating this several times. An Ainu, meeting his sister, grasped her hands in his for a few seconds, suddenly released his hold, grasped her by both ears and gave the peculiar Ainu greeting cry; then they stroked one another down the face and shoulders. Kayan males in Borneo grasp each other by the forearm, while a host throws his arm over the shoulder of a guest and strokes him endearingly with the palm of his hand. When two Kurd males meet, they grasp one another's right hand, raise them both, and alternately kiss the other's hand. Andamanese greet one another by one sitting down in the lap of the other, arms around each other's necks and weeping for a while; two brothers, father and son, mother and daughter, and husband and wife, or even two friends may do this; the husband sits in the lap of the wife. Friends' "goodbye" consists in raising the hand of the other to the mouth and gently blowing on it, reciprocally. At Matavai a full-dress greeting after long absence requires scratching the head and temples with a shark's tooth, violently and with much bleeding. This brief list could be easily enlarged by other anthropologists.[44]

Imagine how public hugging and kissing, customary behaviors during greetings and departures among many Westerners, is often perceived by non-Westerners. "Kissing is in the Orient an act of private lovemaking, and arouses only disgust when performed publicly: thus, in Japan, it is necessary to censor out the major portion of love scenes in American-made movies."[45]

Eye aversion (looking down or away) is another potential source of intercultural misunderstanding. Within the dominant culture, "good" direct eye contact signifies that one is listening to the speaker, is honest, and is telling the truth. Within some African American communities (particularly when survival often depends on showing deference to Whites), as well as among the Navajo and many Asian nations, eye aversion is a sign of deference and respect accorded to another. Imagine how a teacher raised within the White dominant culture is likely to perceive a student who looks down or away when questioned about some stolen lunch money or cheating on an exam. On the other hand, many students are bicultural and may give mixed messages.

In general, it appears that people from high-context cultures require less personal space and do more touching. Americans in the United States attempt to preserve a layer of personal space around themselves even in crowded conditions and are careful to ask for pardon should personal belongings touch another person. Libraries are perfect places to observe proxemics in the United States. Most library patrons set up their own territory at the study table and feel irritated or uncomfortable when someone else's pencil, paper, books, or foot invades the space. In China, a relatively high-context culture, bumping or stepping on another's foot seems to pass unrecognized and certainly requires no apology.

Variations in proxemics within a high- or low-context culture do exist, however. In China, for example, gender makes a difference. It is common to see males walking hand in hand (or even intertwined) with males, and females with females. This does not signify being gay or lesbian, as it would in some cultures. Traditionally, heterosexual touching was strictly private in China, although today this is changing in most urban areas. Despite these changes, deeply rooted cultural expectations related to dating and courtship are likely to cause misunderstandings between Chinese and Americans.

Orientation Modes

Differences between *Black time* and *White time* in this society are common knowledge. White time is monochronic time during which things are accomplished one at a time in a linear fashion familiar to low-context Anglo-Western Europeans. Events occur "on time" according to a clearly stated schedule. Black time, polychronic time, is the opposite. The notion of Black time should be expanded to include people from polychronic cultures more generally, for example, southern Europeans and American Indians. In high-context cultures, time is polychronic. Many activities take place simultaneously, and schedules are invisible. In fact, these activities each seem to operate on a schedule of their own. A party or pow-wow takes place when people get there and ends when people leave. Business deals are closed only after preliminary exchanges concerning family, friends, and personal niceties that may take days or weeks. Hall states that "polychronic cultures are by their very nature oriented to people. Any human being who is naturally drawn to other human beings and who lives in a world dominated by human relationships will be either pushed or pulled toward the polychronic end of the time spectrum. If you value people, you must hear them out and cannot cut them off simply because of a schedule.[46]

School life operates according to monochronic time. Schedules and procedures "take on a life of their own without reference to either logic or human needs."[47] Classes end at a specified time, it does not matter if an exciting discussion is still going on. Such attitudes as the following are implicit: People who know how to organize their time do not "waste" time. People who can meet deadlines are more successful than those who do not.

Architectural arrangements in schools and classrooms are another important consideration in orientation modes. Room arrangements may range from very formal—students' desks arranged in straight rows and the teacher located behind a desk or lectern—to very informal—pupils roam freely or read lying on carpet scraps or comfortable furniture. Some students will associate serious learning with a formal environment and be confused or feel discomfited by an open-concept classroom, but other students will feel stifled in a formal setting. Central to Hall's cross-cultural research is the way humans use and organize space:

> My own interest in space as a cultural phenomenon stemmed from the observation that Americans overseas were confronted with a variety of difficulties because of cultural differences in the handling of space. People stood "too close" during conversations, and when the Americans backed away to a comfortable conversational distance, this was taken to mean that Americans were cold, aloof, withdrawn and disinterested in the people of the country. U.S. housewives muttered about wasted space in houses in the Middle East. In England, Americans, who were used to neighborliness, were hurt when they discovered that their neighbors were no more accessible or friendly than other people, and in Latin America, ex-suburbanites, accustomed to unfenced yards, found that the high walls there made them feel "shut out." Even in Germany, where so many of our countrymen felt at home, radically different patterns in the use of space led to unexpected tensions.[48]

Social Values

Social values are an important aspect of world view. Values are beliefs about how one ought or ought not to behave or about some end state of existence worth or not worth attaining. Values are abstract ideas, positive or negative, that represent a person's beliefs about ideal modes of conduct and ideal terminal goals.[49] Core values refer to the most general beliefs about desirable and undesirable goals and behaviors and are especially important for the selection of cultural behavior from among alternatives.[50] Values are like a yardstick used to judge and compare the attitudes and behaviors of ourselves and others.

Consider some of the mainstream values that are predominant in U.S. society, although they vary tremendously by region and social class: cleanliness, hard work, material comforts and material wealth, private property, health and youth, promptness, problem solving and progress, formal education, being direct, and the right to dissent.

These values are reflected in many of our folk expressions:

Cleanliness is next to godliness.
It's better to have tried and failed than never to have tried at all.
Time is money.

Never put off until tomorrow what you can do today.
Early to bed and early to rise make a man healthy, wealthy, and wise.
If at first you don't succeed, try, try again.

Anthropologist Francis Hsu describes a series of postulates about U.S. society, based on his experience in both the United States and China. His observations may provide insight into mainstream values in the United States. Hsu's Blueprint (see Box 2.2) can also guide reflections about our own personal social values that may or may not be consistent with the dominant culture. To what extent do you agree with Hsu's perceptions?

Most academic activities are based on competition and individual achievement. Many macrocultural children, therefore, learn best when working on their own, sometimes with the help of an adult. Most learn to expect and accept this

---

A Blueprint of United States Culture   Francis L. K. Hsu

BOX 2.2

Postulate I. An individual's most important concern is his self-interest: self-expression, self-development, self-gratification, and independence. This takes precedence over all group interests.

Postulate II. The privacy of the individual is the individual's inalienable right. Intrusion into it by others is permitted only by his invitation.

Postulate III. Because the government exists for the benefit of the individual and not vice versa, all forms of authority, including government, are suspect. But the government and its symbols should be respected. Patriotism is good.

Postulate IV. An individual's success in life depends upon his acceptance among his peers.

Postulate V. An individual should believe or acknowledge God and should belong to an organized church or other religious institution. Religion is good. Any religion is better than no religion.

Postulate VI. Men and women are equal.

Postulate VII. All human beings are equal.

Postulate VIII. Progress is good and inevitable. An individual must improve himself (minimize his efforts and maximize his returns); the government must be more efficient to tackle new problems; institutions such as churches must modernize to make themselves more attractive.

Postulate IX. Being American is synonymous with being progressive, and America is the utmost symbol of progress.

Source: Francis L. K. Hsu, *The Study of Literate Civilizations* (New York: Holt, Rinehart and Winston, 1969), pp. 78–82. Reprinted by permission of author and copyright holder.

competitive structure, and some need and thrive on it. Tests in school are nearly always individual rather than group exercises. Whole systems of instruction are individualized (programmed texts, learning labs, computer-assisted instruction, and independent study projects). Educators motivate students with classroom games modeled after competitive sports and quiz shows (for example, baseball and "Jeopardy"). They reward individual achievement with gold stars, "happy face" stamps, and privileges.

Within high-context cultures, these preferences are often reversed: competition and individual excellence in play and cooperation in work situations. Gay and Abrahams focus on inner-city African American youth and suggest that the preference for cooperation in work may develop "because so much of the transmission of knowledge and the customs of street culture takes place within peer groups (and thus) the Black student is prone to seek the aid and assistance of his classmates at least as frequently as he does the teacher's."[51] We also find this among most Mexican school children.[52] What is nearly always interpreted by teachers as cheating, copying, or frivolous socializing may in fact be the child's natural inclination to seek help from a peer (borrowing a pencil or talking after a test has begun).

In a powerful ethnographic study of ten Mexican-origin families living in border communities, Guadalupe Valdes uncovers cultural conflicts and misunderstandings between the parents and teachers that are based upon differing values and assumptions.[53] For example, what appears to be a lack of interest in education by Mexican-origin parents is in fact a strong commitment to family values. Valdes is critical of school interventions that are designed to promote school success without consideration and respect for these familial values. In Chapter 9 we will examine some promising approaches that address this concern: culturally relevant teaching and teaching that makes strategic connections between household cultures (funds of knowledge) and classroom culture.

Intellectual Modes

Intellectual modes refer both to what types of knowledge are valued most and to learning styles, or how learning takes place within an individual. Students who value spiritual or religious knowledge may experience transitional trauma when religious beliefs are challenged or when courses seem to overemphasize science and technology. Students who seek knowledge related to practical living may feel frustrated when their course work seems too theoretical. As important as the types of knowledge offered is the way students are *expected* to learn. In the average classroom those students learn best who are competitive, work well independently, use linear logic rather than intuition, emphasize rational thought over feeling (and can separate these), prefer abstract thinking over the senses, and require little physical mobility.

The dominant culture emphasizes visual learning through the written word. In Euro-American tradition, seeing is believing, and it is commonly accepted that the highest levels of thinking are possible only for humans who can reflect on thoughts recorded on the written page. No equivalent to the West African *griots,* musicians who served as living/singing encyclopedias, exists in the Euro-American core culture (although they are often compared to bards). Griots serve as professional oral historians who continue the "ancient traditions of praise-singing, story-telling, and genealogy in contemporary African culture."[54]

Many African Americans have grown up in an oral tradition, which, Herskovitz claims, is a carry-over from Africa. Traditional African societies, for example, had elaborate communication systems using drums, singing, and dance rituals. From the time African Americans first arrived in the United States, music and the spoken word have been at the heart of the Black experience.[55] Their oral/aural tradition thrives in the New World. Classroom examples of the oral/aural tradition are easily illustrated. My students, mostly Black or Latino males labeled remedial, scored considerably higher on tests when I *read* the questions to them. Working with Black and Mexican American eighth graders in Texas, I found that their comprehension of a U.S. history text was better if they listened to a tape of the text while reading it. Many of my Anglo pupils preferred to read without hearing the tape. Similar examples are abundant, and helpful, provided that they do not lead to racial stereotypes and assumptions that all Blacks learn aurally and all Whites learn visually.

Current research suggests that certain learning styles are associated with specific ethnic groups in this society. For example, Shade, in her article "African American Cognitive Style: A Variable in School Success?" makes a strong case that many African Americans have learning styles that conflict with our low-context schools.[56] And, according to Hilliard, who has written widely on race and intelligence, African Americans who have grown up outside the dominant culture process information differently from what is expected in our schools.[57] Other research suggests that many Hispanics and Native Americans, indeed anyone from a high-context culture, face comparable cultural conflicts related to intellectual modes. (This research is examined more closely in Chapter 6.)

The notion that certain learning styles are associated with different ethnic groups is both promising and dangerous. Promise lies in the realization that low academic achievement among some ethnic minorities may sometimes be attributed to conflicts between styles of teaching and learning, not low intelligence. This leads to the possibility that teachers will alter their own instructional styles to be more responsive to the learning needs of students. Danger lies in the possibility that new ethnic stereotypes will develop while old ones are reinforced, as in "Blacks learn aurally," "Asians excel in math," "Mexican American males can't learn from female peer tutors," and "Navajos won't ask a question or participate in a discussion."

In summary, Longstreet's aspects of ethnicity provide useful guidelines for observing and understanding human behavior. Although it is impossible to fully understand the cultural orientations of all students, the five aspects of ethnicity are common components of any cultural orientation that teachers can cue into: verbal communication, nonverbal communication, orientation modes, social values, and intellectual modes. The greater the differences between the deep culture of teachers and students, the more likely it is that students' and teachers' preferred ways of communicating and participating are different. Those teachers who are unaware of their pupils' needs and preferences force the learner to do most of the adjusting. Those pupils, like Jesús Martinez, who cannot make the adjustment cannot learn much in the classroom. Unless the teacher is knowledgeable about students' cultural identity, pupils whose ethnic group differs from the teacher's and/or classmates' are more likely to experience cultural conflict in the classroom than pupils who share the same ethnicity as the teacher.

CONCLUSIONS

This chapter has emphasized understanding human diversity as it relates to culture. (Later in this book we will consider additional aspects of diversity, including students' personal attributes.) If we limit our focus to culture, we run the risk of stereotyping. If, on the other hand, we ignore students' cultural attributes and rely totally on our own culturally biased lenses, we are likely to limit the chances for successful learning to those who are most "like us."

Differences in modes of communication, participation, and world view enter the classroom when students and teachers represent different ethnic groups and/or different nationalities. Equalizing the learning opportunities for students becomes more difficult to achieve when teachers and students have alternative world views. It is a challenge to find out how learners can be taught when we do not understand their language, when we misinterpret their behavior, when our tried and true methods of diagnosing and motivating fail. Most of us expect cultural differences when meeting recent immigrants or visitors from another country, such as Vietnam, Saudi Arabia, or France. Fewer of us are aware that cultural differences can also occur between ethnic groups that comprise our own society, as well as among individuals within these groups.

Even as we enter the twenty-first century, despite the fact that we live in a polycultural society, most of our schools remain monocultural. Students from different ethnic groups often bring with them cultures that are to some degree distinct from the schools of the predominant culture. To teach effectively in pluralistic classrooms, which characterize most schools in the United States, teachers must recognize the validity of the cultures present.

COMPARE AND CONTRAST

1. Culture and race
2. Cultural assimilation and cultural pluralism
3. Ethnic group and minority group
4. High-context and low-context culture
5. World view and ethnicity
6. Scholastic ethnicity and cultural pluralism

ACTIVITIES AND QUESTIONS

1. Experience *Bafá Bafá*, a cross-cultural simulation. (In general, sixteen to forty participants are required.) The simulation creates a situation that al-

lows participants to explore the idea of culture, creates feelings similar to those one would encounter when exposed to a different culture, gives participants experience in observing and interacting with a different culture, and provides numerous insights that can be applied to culturally pluralistic classrooms.

2. Conduct international interviews on perceptions of the dominant culture. Work with another class member, or partner, to interview an international student on campus or a visitor in the community. Each partner should interview a different individual, preferably from different families, to discover their perceptions of the dominant culture. Overall, an attempt should be made to interview people from different world regions as well as several from the same nation. The interviews can be discussed in small groups organized by geographic areas of the world, and results compiled prior to reporting these data to the large group as a whole. Comparisons of perceptions about the dominant culture can be displayed and discussed.

3. Complete the following chart:

Perspectives of Major Social Values in the Dominant Culture

Hsu's Perceptions	Your Perceptions	Navajo Perceptions
1.	1.	1.
2.	2.	2.
3.	3.	3.
4.	4.	4.
5.	5.	5.

What similarities and differences do you see in these three different sources? Can you find evidence of how the perceptions of each were shaped by the person or group's original culture (Chinese, Navajo, and your own)?

4. Using the examples of Fred Young, Sarah Stein, Jimmy Miller, and any other students you know about, including yourself, give one or more examples of transitional trauma due to cultural conflict between home and school for each category.

Type of Transitional Trauma

Students	Language	Nonverbal Communication	Social Values	Other?
Fred Young				
Sarah Stein				
Jimmy Miller				
Jesús Martinez				
Yourself				

5. Reconsider the student's journal entry that opens this section, "Why Study Culture?" What are some of the points you agree with (if any)? List as many as you can. What major assumptions does the student make? What points do you disagree with (if any)? List as many as you can and briefly explain why.

6. Read the book *Black Elk Speaks* by John G. Neihardt. What inferences can you make about Lakota culture based on Black Elk's story? (For example, significance of the circle; how historical events are noted; the naming of people, places, events, and celebrations; and the concept of private property.) What contrast do you see between the Lakota world view (especially social values) and that of the dominant culture? What similarities? How might North American history be written differently from the Lakota perspective?

7. Read *The Doll Maker,* a novel by Harriet Arnow, which portrays the life of an Appalachian family that migrates to Detroit after World War II. What does the book reveal about the cultures of many of the geographically isolated Appalachian families? Specifically, what did you learn about verbal and nonverbal communication, social values, and approaches to learning? What are some of the cultural strengths, which many teachers might overlook, that Gertie's children bring to the classroom? What are some possible sources of transitional trauma her children could face when they enter an urban school?

NOTES

1. E. B. Tylor, *Primitive Culture* (1871; reprint, New York: Harper Torchbooks, 1958).
2. Geertz, *Interpretation of Culture* (New York: Basic Books, 1973) 89.
3. J. P. Spradley and D. W. McCurdy, *Anthropology: The Cultural Perspective* (New York: John Wiley & Sons, 1975), 5.
4. W. H. Goodenough, *Cultural Anthropology and Linguistics,* Georgetown University Monograph Series on Language and Linguistics, no. 9, 1957, 167.
5. R. A. LeVine, "Properties of Culture: An Ethnographic View," in *Culture Theory: Essays on Mind; Self and Emotion,* R. A. Sweder and R. A. LeVine, eds. (Cambridge, England: Cambridge University Press, 1986).
6. H. C. Triandis, "Cultural Training, Cognitive Complexity and Interpersonal Attitudes," in *Cross-cultural Perspectives on Learning,* R. W. Brislin, Stephen Bachner, and Walter J. Lonner, eds. (New York: John Wiley & Sons, 1975).

7. M. Gibson, "Approaches to Multicultural Education in the United States." *Anthropology and Education Quarterly,* 15, no. 1 (Spring 1984).
8. J. P. Spradley and D. W. McCurdy, *Conformity and Conflict* (Glenview, IL: Scott, Foresman, 1990), 480.
9. A. J. Kraemer, "A Cultural Self-Awareness Approach to Improving Intercultural Communication Skills," ERIC ED 079 213 (April 1973).
10. T. B. Saral, "Consciousness Theory and Intercultural Communication" (paper presented at the International Communication Association, Portland, Oregon, April 14–17, 1976).
11. R. Ramos and M. Ramos, "The Mexican American: Am I Who They Say I Am?" in *Chicanos: As We See Ourselves,* D. T. Arnulfo, ed. (Tucson, AZ. University of Arizona Press, © 1979), 1. This list and the following extract from the same source are reprinted by permission. Copyright ©1979.
12. Ibid., 55–56.

13. C. Kluckhohn, *Mirror for Man* (Greenwich, CT: Fawcett, 1965), 19.

14. R. D. Abrahams, "Cultural Conflict in the Classroom" (videotape from symposium sponsored by the Alachna County Teacher Center, Gainesville, Florida, January 30, 1975).

15. E. T. Hall, *The Silent Language* (New York: Doubleday, 1959). See also by Hall, *The Hidden Dimension* (New York: Doubleday, 1966), *Beyond Culture* (New York: Doubleday, 1976); *The Dance of Life* (New York: Doubleday, 1983); and "Proxemics: The Study of Man's Spatial Relations," in *Intercultural Communication: A Reader,* Larry A. Samouar and R. E. Porter, eds. (Belmont, CA: Wadsworth, 1972), 172–180.

16. C. Bennett, "Teaching Intercultural Competence and Informed Citizenship." (The table was developed for the paper presented at the Annual Conference of the National Council of the Social Studies in New York, November 1986.)

17. J. Kelso, "The Concept of Race," *Improving College and University Teaching 15,* no. 95 (Spring 1967):7.

18. Ibid.

19. A. Montagu, *Man's Most Dangerous Myth: The Fallacy of Race,* 5th ed. (New York: Oxford University Press, 1974), 7.

20. H. J. Ehrlich, *The Social Psychology of Prejudice* (New York: John Wiley & Sons, 1973).

21. M. M. Gordon, *Assimilation in American Life* (New York: Oxford University Press, 1966).

22. L. Wirth, "The Problem of Minority Groups," in *The Science of Man in the World Crisis,* R. Linton, ed. (New York: Columbia University Press, 1945).

23. As discussed in J. R. Feagin and C. B. Feagin, *Racial and Ethnic Relations* (Englewood Cliffs, NJ: Prentice Hall, 1993), 10.

24. D. L. Sills (ed.), "Assimilation," in *International Encyclopedia of the Social Sciences,* vol. 1 (New York: Macmillan/Free Press, 1968), 438.

25. E. P. Cubberly, *Changing Conceptions of Education* (Boston: Houghton Mifflin, 1909), 16.

26. D. L. Sills (ed.), "Pluralism," in *International Encyclopedia of the Social Sciences,* vol. 12 (New York: Macmillan/Free Press, 1968).

27. H. M. Kallen, *Culture and Democracy in the United States* (New York: Boni and Liveright, 1924); see also M. R. Konvitz, "Horace Meyer Kallen (1882–1974): Philosopher of the Hebraic American Idea," in *American Jewish Yearbook, 1974–1975,* M. Fine and M. Himmelfarb, eds. (Philadelphia: Jewish Publication Society of America, 1974), 65–67.

28. G. Gay, "Multiethnic Education Historical Development and Future Prospects," *Phi Delta Kappan* 64, no. 8 (April 1983):560–561.

29. W. Longstreet, *Aspects of Ethnicity: Understanding Differences in Pluralistic Classrooms* (New York: Teachers College Press, 1978). These excerpts have been reprinted with the permission of the author.

30. Ibid., 19.

31. Ibid.

32. Milton Rokeach, *Beliefs, Attitudes, and Values* (San Francisco: Jossey-Bass, 1969), 124.

33. Ibid.

34. Longstreet, *op. cit.,* 22.

35. M. Benitez, "A Blueprint for the Education of the Mexican American," ERIC ED 076 294 (March 1973):7. Also see B. Perez and Maria E. Torres-Guzman, *Learning in Two Worlds* (New York: Longman, 1992).

36. R. D. Abrahams and G. Gay, "Talking Black in the Classroom," in *Language and Culture Diversity in American Education,* R. D. Abrahams and R. C. Troike, eds. (Englewood Cliffs, NJ: Prentice Hall, 1972). 201–202.

37. Longstreet, *Aspects of Ethnicity,* 50.

38. Ibid., 51–52.

39. S. B. Heath (1983) *Ways with Words: Language, Life, and Work in Communities and Classrooms* (Cambridge England: Cambridge University Press); L. Delpit (1995) *Other People's Children: Cultural Conflict in the Classroom* (New York: The New Press).

40. J. Daniels, I. Hines, G. Ross, and G. Walker, "Teaching Afro-American Commu-

nication," ERIC ED 082 247 (November 1972). See also G. Gay and W. Barber, *Expressively Black* (New York: Praeger, 1988).

41. See for example, B. Shade, ed., *Culture, Style, and the Educative Process* (Springfield, IL: Charles C. Thomas, 1989).

42. M. Bennett, "Culture and Changing Realities" (Society of Intercultural Education Training and Research [SIETAR], preconference workshop, Third Annual SIETAR Conference (Chicago: February 25, 1977).

43. T. Kochman, *Black and White Styles in Conflict* (Chicago: University of Chicago, 1981), 4–5.

44. W. LaBarre, "Paralinguistics, Kinesics, and Cultural Anthropology," in *Intercultural Communication: A Reader,* Larry A. Samouar and Richard E. Porter, eds. (Belmont, CA: Wadsworth, 1972), 172–180.

45. Ibid., 173.

46. Hall, *Beyond Culture,* 58.

47. Ibid.

48. Ibid.

49. M. Rokeach, *Attitudes, Values and Beliefs* (San Francisco: Jossey-Bass, 1969).

50. Spradley and McCurdy, *Anthropology,* 495.

51. G. Gay and R. D. Abrahams, "Black Culture in the Classroom," in *Language and Culture Diversity in American Education,* R. D. Abrahams and R. C. Troike, eds. (Englewood Cliffs, NJ: Prentice Hall, 1976), 80.

52. Bradley Levinson, personal communication, July 1997.

53. Guadalupe Valdes, *Con Respeto: Bridging the Distance Between Culturally Diverse Families and Schools: An Ethnographic Portrait* (New York: Teachers College Press, 1996).

54. K. A. Appiah and H. L. Gates, *The Dictionary of Global Culture* (New York: Knopf, 1997), 262.

55. M. I. Herskovitz, *The Myth of the Negro Past* (Boston: Beacon Press, 1969). See also C. Keil, *Urban Blues* (Chicago: University of Chicago Press, 1966); and L. Jones, *Blues People: The Negro Experience in White America and the Music That Developed from It* (New York: William Morrow, 1963). "African Perspectives," panel at the annual meeting of the National Council for the Social Studies, NCSS, Orlando, Florida, November 19, 1988.

56. B. J. Shade, "Afro-American Cognitive Style: A Variable in School Success?" *Review of Educational Research* 52, no. 2 (Summer 1982): 219–238. See also J. Hale Benson, *Black Children: Their Roots, Culture, and Learning Styles,* rev. ed. (Baltimore: Johns Hopkins Press, 1986).

57. A. Hilliard, "Alternatives to IQ Testing: An Approach to the Identification of Gifted Minority Children." (Final Report to the California State Department of Education, 1976).

chapter 3

Race Relations and the Nature of Prejudice

*T*he improvement of race relations through the reduction of prejudice and racism is a central goal of multicultural education. Teachers, along with parents and other important family members, can make a significant difference in how children and youth perceive themselves and others. In my work with beginning and experienced teachers over the years, I have seen many examples of teachers working through the hidden curriculum as well as the formal curriculum to reduce prejudice. There is the physical education teacher who uses interracial teams and peer coaching to develop technical skills; mathematics and science teachers who use partner learning and cooperative learning teams to teach concepts within a classroom climate of acceptance; and English teachers who use multicultural literature and peer editing in cooperative teams to enhance writing skills, as well as positive intergroup relationships. In my own teaching in a newly desegregated high school serving Black, Latino and White students, I remember the positive impact on virtually all the students when they discovered the distinctions between individual and institutional racism, and developed insights into their own socialization concerning racial attitudes and beliefs. There are teachers like Sam Johnson (on page 245) who work to reduce racial prejudice in schools where most of the students are White.

Teaching aimed at reducing prejudice and discrimination can be difficult as well as rewarding. It requires an understanding of the prevalence and nature of prejudice, as well as clarity about key concepts such as prejudice, stereotype, discrimination, racism, and sense of racial or ethnic identity. This chapter provides an introduction to these concepts and contemporary race relations as a context for multicultural teaching.

The Prevalence of Prejudice and Racism

In March of 1968 the Kerner Commission released its report on civil disorders and warned that the United States was becoming dangerously divided into two societies, unequal and separated by race. Now, as we enter the twenty-first century, many social scientists believe that racial tensions have worsened. For example, sociologists Feagin and Vera write, "At some time in the not-too-distant future a racial war between the haves and have-nots in the United States is not inconceivable. The hour is already late to take action to prevent such a racial war."[1] Yet other scholars and government officials argue that race relations have improved dramatically. For example, according to a recent Gallup poll, the number of surveyed White Americans who would vote for a Black presidential candidate increased from 35 percent in 1972 to 93 percent in 1997, surpassing the 91 percent of African Americans who would vote for a Black presidential candidate; and the approval of interracial marriages rose between 1972 and 1997, from 25 percent to 61 percent among Whites and from 61 percent to 77 percent among Blacks.[2] Federal and state legislation outlaws discrimination in employment, elections, and public housing; and "figures like Colin Powell, Oprah Winfrey, Michael Jordan and Tiger Woods are idolized by whites, blacks, Hispanics, and Asians alike."[3]

Some argue that although there are still racial tensions in the United States, they are not as bad as in other countries. For example, an immigrant of Indian ancestry from Singapore, whose husband is White, believes "race relations are much better in this country that in her native Singapore, whose population is three-quarters ethnic Chinese."[4] Others point out the numbers of refugees seeking asylum in the United States, as among Haitians in the 1990s and Chinese college students and professionals after Tiananmen Square in 1989, as evidence of freedoms and the higher quality of life here.

Let us consider some indicators of the nation's racial climate in the 1990s. Think of other examples you could add to the list.

■ In April of 1992, the acquittal of four White Los Angeles police officers in the beating of an African American motorist, Rodney King, triggered violent riots in south-central Los Angeles. Approximately 50 people were killed, 1,600 business were destroyed or severely damaged, and financial losses were nearly $800 million.[5]

■ A Harvard University study of the nation's schools stated that desegregation is being dismantled, with schools becoming more isolated by race, poverty, and lack of connection to the outside world. It reported that Hispanic students are even more likely than African Americans to "be isolated in schools that are largely minority and poor."[6]

- The O. J. Simpson case fueled discussions and disagreements within families, communities, college classrooms, and the workplace. Reactions to the not-guilty verdict were deeply divided along racial lines. Differing racial perceptions of our criminal justice system and of the trustworthiness of local law enforcement became visible, but the roots of these different views often remain misunderstood.

- Incidents of ethnoviolence on college campuses and elsewhere in society have increased, with more than a hundred incidents reported each year. These "hate crimes" are directed primarily at people of color and Jews, as well as gays and lesbians. The Southern Poverty Law Center alone reported a "sampling" of 90 violent acts during the summer of 1994, just a portion of the year's total incidents.[7]

- The number of "Web Hate Sites" on the Internet has increased dramatically in the 1990s, with over 250 hate sites available in 1997. From a Web site on the Internet called Nazism Now, it is only a mouse click to reach I Hate Jews—The Anti-Semitic Homepage, Knights of the Ku Klux Klan and the White Nationalism Resource Page. (These sites) "celebrate white supremacy, anti-Semitism, anti-Government fervor and denial of the Holocaust."[8]

- Henry Louis Gates, renowned Harvard Scholar and expert in African American Studies, argues that well-educated and economically strong African Americans are becoming more discouraged about race relations. Gates writes that the percent of surveyed middle-class African Americans who believe Whites want to see greater opportunities for Blacks declined from 70 percent in 1964, to 20 percent in 1992. Further, he argues, "Blacks with a college education are especially likely to seriously entertain claims that AIDS was concocted to infect Blacks, or that the government conspired to make drugs available in poor neighborhoods in an effort to harm Blacks."[9]

The number of White Americans who perceive "reversed racism" in affirmative action programs is increasing. Feelings of alienation are especially strong among White males. This view is expressed by one White college student as follows:

> As a white male, I feel like I'm the only subsection of the population that hasn't jumped on the victim bandwagon. And I feel from a racial perspective, as a white man, I have been targeted as the oppressor, and frankly I'm getting a little tired of it, because I haven't done a whole lot of oppressing in my life. . . . I feel like I'm branded with this bad guy label. . . . Supposedly, as we study gender and race, as white men we run the world; I never knew that. . . . I haven't oppressed anybody, but I've experienced feeling oppressed.[10]

Racial and ethnic tensions are also widespread across the world. Some examples include: Indians in Brazil who are estranged from their land and suffer an epidemic of suicide; "Ethnic cleansing" in Bosnia-Herzegovina; persistent Arab-Israeli conflict and violence in the Middle East; neo-Nazi attacks on immigrants in German cities; genocide massacres in Rwanda of Tutsi by Hutu, followed by Tutsi reprisals in Congo (formerly Zaire); cruel treatment of Mbutu, commonly named Pygmies, by Bantu throughout central Africa; and discrimination against the Ainu in Japan. Our focus in this chapter, however, is on prejudice and race relations in the United States. While it is unlikely that prejudice can ever be completely eradicated, Allport writes "the situation is not without hopeful features. Chief among these is the simple fact that human nature seems, on the whole, to prefer the sight of kindness and friendliness to the sight of cruelty."[11]

Most race relations experts have studied racism in terms of the costs of racism to the victims, especially the denial of equal access to educational, economic, and political power. Other deleterious effects include loss of role models and knowledge of the past, physical and mental suffering, and even loss of life. Scholars have begun to recognize that racism victimizes Whites as well. Forbes, for example, in his studies of Native American and Chicano peoples, wrote that "Anglo American young people grow up in a never-never land of mythology as regards non-whites, and it is crucial for our society's future that damaging myths be exposed and eliminated."[12]

Rutledge Dennis is a sociologist who studies the effects of racism on White children. In a discussion of these effects, Dennis stresses ignorance of other people, development of a double social psychological consciousness, group conformity, and moral confusion and social ambivalence.[13] A dual consciousness develops within White children who are taught to hate and fear others and to conform to racial etiquette on the one hand, while being taught Christian love on the other. Because racism deprives Whites of getting to know Blacks (and other people of color), it fosters "their ignorance of the many-sidedness of the Black population" and thus reinforces stereotypes.[14] Given the interdependency of the human race and the great variety of cultures on earth, this ignorance is not only senseless but dangerous.

Among adults, Dennis sees three effects of racism on the White population: irrationality, inhibition of intellectual growth, and negation of democracy. He argues that feelings of White superiority contribute to the basic immaturity of the many Whites and their inability "to grow up, to accept the judgments of civilization."[15] Dennis also reminds us of the words Booker T. Washington spoke in 1911:

> It is a grave mistake for the vast majority of Whites to assume that they can remain free and enjoy democracy while they are denying it to Blacks. The anti-democratic not only wants to ensure that Blacks do not enjoy certain rights, he also wants to ensure that no White is free to question or challenge this denial.[16]

The Nature of Prejudice

Prejudice is an attitude based on preconceived judgments or beliefs (usually negative) that develops from unsubstantiated or faulty information. These attitudes are learned from people who have significant influence in our lives, such as parents and peers; experiences in school; and societal messages in films, television, and the news media. Prejudice can be directed toward an entire group or an individual because he or she is a member of the group. It can be race-based, gender-based, age-based, ethnicity-based, class-based, etc. It can also be based on religion. For example, prejudice against Jews is called anti-Semitism.

An attitude is a relatively enduring organization of interrelated beliefs centered on an object or situation that includes a predisposition to take action.[17] Thus, while prejudice is an attitude, it is likely that action will result. A common expression of prejudice is telling ethnic jokes or "talking about" certain groups, among like-minded people and sometimes with strangers. Some prejudiced individuals make a conscious effort to avoid people from the group, such as taking a longer route home to avoid certain neighborhoods, or frequenting restaurants and taking vacations where members of the group are unlikely to be present. Prejudice becomes *discrimination* when the individual actively excludes members of the group, or denies them participation in a desired activity. In it most extreme form discrimination causes physical harm, or even death, to members of the group.[18] Thus, discrimination is the overt expression of prejudice in behavior that does harm to members of the group, ranging from exclusion to violent action. While discrimination usually stems from prejudice, sometimes nonprejudiced people discriminate unintentionally because they are unaware of unfair societal practices and policies.

Gordon Allport, national authority on prejudice and the personality, visualizes social relationships among groups along a continuum from most friendly (cooperation) to hostile (scapegoating), with respect, tolerance, predilection, prejudice, and discrimination in between (see Figure 3.1). Mildly hostile relationships begin with predilections, the most normal form of group exclusion, where people prefer to associate with others with whom they feel most comfortable and familiar. Allport argues that humans prefer the familiar because of

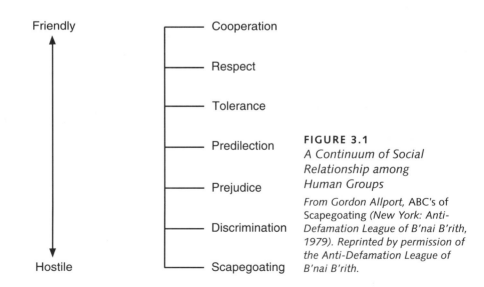

Friendly

Hostile

- Cooperation
- Respect
- Tolerance
- Predilection
- Prejudice
- Discrimination
- Scapegoating

FIGURE 3.1
A Continuum of Social Relationship among Human Groups

From Gordon Allport, ABC's of Scapegoating *(New York: Anti-Defamation League of B'nai B'rith, 1979). Reprinted by permission of the Anti-Defamation League of B'nai B'rith.*

FIGURE 3.2

Hypothetical Lessening of In-group Potency as Membership Becomes More Inclusive

From Gordon Allport, The Nature of Prejudice, © 1979, Addison-Wesley, Reading, Massachusetts. Reprinted with permission of the publisher.

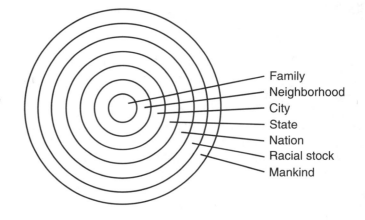

Family
Neighborhood
City
State
Nation
Racial stock
Mankind

"the principles of ease, least effort, congeniality, and pride in one's own culture," not prejudice.[19] Many of my students say they become aware of their predilections when they attend churches or places of worship different from their own. They also sense their predilections when entering a crowded cafeteria filled with strangers; there is a strong desire to sit with friends. It is natural to prefer one's own family, religion, or ethnic group. But if a person *exaggerates* the virtues of one's own group and also develops a dislike for another group (as often happens when there is no opportunity to get to know members of the group), then it is easy to develop prejudices.

Although prejudice takes many forms, *racial* prejudice is our emphasis in this chapter. Racial prejudice often leads to racial discrimination, but not necessarily. Since the Holocaust of World War II and the Civil Rights Movement of the 1960s, discrimination is viewed as unfair by most people and many acts of discrimination are illegal. Thus racial prejudice takes much more subtle forms than in the past.

We cannot assume that it is mainly White people who are racially prejudiced. There are racially prejudiced people in every ethnic group, and many people of color are quick to point out that feelings of racial prejudice exist within their communities. Anthropologist John Gwaltney's study of African Americans in the Northeast, *Drylongso, A Portrait of Black America*, illustrates racial prejudice held by Blacks in interviews such as the following:

> My uncle is a preacher and he says that white people are born evil. He'll tell you in a minute that the Bible says that the wicked are estranged from the womb. Now, as far as he is concerned, when you say "the wicked," you have said "the white race." He cannot stand white people, and although he is a man with good common sense most of the time, you cannot make him see reason about this race thing. He looks as white as any white person, but you'd better not tell him that unless you are ready to go to war. He won't even call them men. He says, "The beni did this" or "The beni have said so-and-so."

His daughter married a white boy about five years ago. They have two nice kids and are getting along fine, but Uncle Joshua acts like they're dead. She was— I mean she is—his only girl and they were very close, so it's hard for everybody. It's been five years now, and you could count the weeks on the fingers of your hands that Felicity has come to see him. He just won't have anything to do with her. She said that she'd keep coming to see him, and I guess she will because she's just as stubborn as he is.[20]

African Americans and other minorities may hold racial prejudices, and may act upon them by discriminating against Whites. Such forms of prejudice among oppressed groups often develop *in response* to their condition in society, in an attempt to recover a sense of dignity. Thus efforts to end the nation's racial tensions and to work toward the eradication of racial prejudice require the involvement of *everyone,* minority and nonminority alike, if we are to succeed.

The Nature of Racism

Racism involves systematic oppression through persistent behavior that is the result of personal racial prejudice and racial discrimination within societal structures. Racism is a complex concept that includes attitudes of racial superiority, institutional power that suppresses members of the supposedly inferior race, and a broadly based ideology of ethnocentrism or cultural superiority. Racism is an action or policy that harms or suppresses members of a racial group. It "results from the transformation of race prejudice and/or ethnocentrism through the exercise of power against a racial group defined as inferior, by individuals and institutions with the intentional or unintentional support of the entire culture."[21] However, most social scientists argue that ethnic minorities do not hold sufficient power to be actively racist. It is *not* possible for minorities in the United States to systematically deny Whites access to opportunities and privileges, or to maintain privileges for themselves at the expense of nonminorities. According to this argument, while anyone can be racially prejudiced and can discriminate on the basis of race, in the United States only White people can be racist. They can also become anti-racist.

Some people mistakenly believe that simply recognizing a person's race is racist. Sometimes teachers say, "I love *all* of my children. I don't even know what color they are." Given the social reality, to be unaware of a student's race is being dishonest. Don't we notice whether a student is male or female, has blue eyes or brown? Granted, we cannot always know if a student is ethnically Black or White or Native American, but where race is obvious, why not recognize the fact? It is only when we lower our expectations, accept stereotypes, or discriminate that racial identity can conjure up negative attitudes and behaviors. The recognition of physical racial differences does not mean racial prejudice or racism. Many people of color regard race as an essential aspect of their personal identity and may be offended by teachers and others who claim to be color-blind.

Distinguishing Individual, Institutional, and Cultural Racism

Racism operates on three interrelated levels: individual, institutional, and cultural. It is important to understand the distinctions and similarities among these types of racism if it is to be eradicated on all levels.

Individual racism is the belief that one's own race is superior to another (racial prejudice) and behavior that suppresses members of the so-called inferior race (racial discrimination). The racist believes that members of another race are inferior, and assumes that the physical attributes of a racial group determine the social behavior of its members, as well as their psychological and intellectual characteristics. These racist beliefs might remain submerged as hidden racial prejudice, but usually the racist believes this inferiority is a legitimate basis for inferior social treatment.

Let's consider some examples and nonexamples of individual racism.[22] Alice is a White elementary school teacher who believes minority students are less motivated than her White students and, therefore, she intentionally assigns them to the less desirable and less challenging classroom activities. Gregg is a White high school assistant principal who assigns a majority of the African American and Mexican American students to unchallenging classes taught by the most disliked or inexperienced teachers because he believes these students cannot be taught,

Taking a stand against racism: a middle-school poster.

anyway. Kevin, the newly hired mathematics teacher, who is also White, finds that most of his students in his basic math classes are African Americans and Latinos, many more than a random selection of the student population should produce. Raised in a racially diverse neighborhood, he feels comfortable with his students, but he has had no experience or preparation for the basic math curriculum. Sue is a middle school teacher who misinterprets a minority student's nonassertiveness and lack of eye contact as an indication that the student is disinterested in school. She devotes her attention to the students who are active participants or who show their interest with direct eye contact.

Both Alice and Gregg depict individual racism that is intentional. Alice's behavior is overt and easily observable, but Gregg's covert behavior may go unnoticed. Kevin and the other teachers who are assigned most of the African American and Mexican American students may not question or even wonder about the silent resegregation of the student population by Gregg. While Kevin is not acting in a racist manner per se, unless he questions the system that places most minority students in an unchallenging class with inexperienced teachers, he is (however unwittingly) participating in a system that perpetuates inequities in education (institutional racism). Like Alice and Gregg, Sue conveys individual racism even though it is unintentional. Her lack of understanding of the student's background leads her to misjudge the student through her own cultural lens; as a result, the student does poorly in her class.

Institutional racism consists of "those established laws, customs, and practices which systematically reflect and produce racial inequalities in American society . . . whether or not the individuals maintaining those practices have racist intentions."[23] In contrast to individual racism where perpetrators can be identified, institutional racism is imbedded in policies that have generally become accepted as natural or normal over time. When racism is not challenged by oppressed groups or by nonminorities who are anti-racist, people may be unaware of the impact of discriminatory policies and how they benefit from or are hurt by them, while others are aware that a change in policy would result in a loss of power and prestige.

Consider some examples of institutional racism from the past. Article 1, section 2 of the U.S. Constitution provided that three-fifths of the slave population would be counted for purposes of representation, and slavery was not abolished until the 13th Amendment was passed in 1865. White abolitionists who may not have been individually racist, that is, they may not have believed in the racial inferiority of African Americans in slavery, were nonetheless part of a society whose institutions were racist. They benefited from the national wealth generated by enslaved African Americans. Until recently, there were laws on the books in many states that prevented African Americans from voting. For example, anyone whose father or grandfather had not voted in a given year (say 1866) was denied the right to vote. Interracial marriages were illegal in many states, and in Louisiana citizens with any African American ancestry could be denied passports. Even the Supreme Court has, at times, upheld racial segregation laws, the most famous case being *Plessy v. Ferguson* in 1896, which ruled that separate facilities were legal as long as they were equal.

After the Civil War and up until World War II, lynching became a major means of keeping Blacks in their place. Between 1892 and 1921, nearly 2,400 African Americans were lynched. Most of the perpetrators were never punished for their actions; in some cases local police officers were involved in these crimes.[24] (Many Whites, particularly Jews and Italians, were also lynched, but Blacks made up the greatest proportion.)

Mexican American citizens have been the victims of racism as well. The outrageous Sleepy Lagoon incident and the zootsuit riots in Los Angeles during World War II are just two egregious examples. Today, disproportionately higher numbers of Black and Latino soldiers are given the most dangerous combat duties, as in Vietnam; are overrepresented in prisons and on death row; and are overrepresented among students who are suspended, expelled, or placed in classes for the retarded. Inequitable access to highly skilled lawyers is another prevalent example of institutional bias, as were many of the draft deferments in the past.

Other examples of institutional racism include formal and informal real estate practices that prohibit some races from buying or renting in particular sections of town, and practices that deny certain races access to clubs and organizations such as fraternities and sororities. Textbooks and educational materials that present erroneous information about certain racial groups or omit their contributions are other examples of institutional racism in our schools, although they could also result from "personal" racial prejudice of the author.

Carmichael and Hamilton were among the first to distinguish between individual and institutional racism:

> Racism is both overt and covert. It takes two, closely related forms: individual whites acting against individual blacks, and acts by the total white community against the black community. We call these individual racism and institutional racism. The first consists of overt acts by individuals, which cause death, injury or the violent destruction of property. This type can be recorded by television cameras; it can frequently be observed in the process of commission. The second type is less overt, far more subtle, less identifiable in terms of specific individuals committing the acts. But it is no less destructive of human life. The second type originates in the operation of established and respected forces in the society, and thus receives far less public condemnation than the first. When white terrorists bomb a black church and kill five black children, that is an act of individual racism, widely deplored by most segments of society. But when in that same city—Birmingham, Alabama—five hundred black babies die each year because of the lack of proper food, clothing, shelter and proper medical facilities, and thousands more are destroyed or maimed physically, emotionally, and intellectually because of conditions of poverty and discrimination in the black community, that is a function of institutional racism.[25]

In another pioneering book that distinguishes between individual and institutional racism, Knowles and Prewitt wrote that individual acts of racism as well as racist institutional policies can

> occur without the presence of conscious bigotry, and both may be masked intentionally or innocently. . . . Institutions have great power to reward and penalize.

They reward by providing career opportunities for some people and foreclosing them for others. They reward as well by the way social goods are distributed—by deciding who receives training and skills, medical care, formal education, political influence, moral support and self-respect, productive employment, fair treatment by the law, decent housing, self-confidence and the promise of a secure future for self and children.[26]

Feagin extends these early works in his writings about institutionalized racism and sexism in terms of direct discrimination and indirect discrimination.[27] Examples of direct and indirect institutional racism in education illustrate the difference. Direct institutional racism includes laws and informal practices that result in ethnic minority children being segregated into inferior public schools. Direct institutional discrimination leads to indirect institutional discrimination when these poorly educated minorities cannot compete with nonminorities and do not qualify for advanced education and/or employment even though school officials and employers may be eager to recruit ethnic minorities. As a result of unemployment or low-paying jobs, most also cannot afford adequate health care, nutrition, or housing.

The doctrine of White racism was also institutionalized in national immigration legislation. In 1793 George Washington proclaimed that the "bosom of America is open to receive not only the Opulent and respectable Stranger, but the oppressed and persecuted of all Nations and Religions whom we shall welcome to a participation of all our rights and privileges."[28] Obviously, slaves and free people of color were not to be included in this policy, nor were native peoples or Mexicans of the Southwest. In 1882 Chinese people were excluded, and in 1908 the exclusion was extended to Japanese immigrants. The National Origins Acts passed in 1924 and 1929 restricted the number of immigrants to 150,000 annually and set up quotas that favored people from Northern and Western Europe. About 70 percent of those allowed to enter were from Britain, Ireland, Scandinavia, and Germany. The remaining 30 percent came from Southern and Eastern Europe. The Walter-McCarran Act, passed in 1952, did little to change these discriminatory quotas. And, in fact, this law was aimed at keeping so-called undesirables out of the United States.

In 1965 the quota system was abolished. Each year, 170,000 immigrants can now enter the United States from Africa, Asia, Australia, and Europe, and another 120,000 can enter from North and South America. Referring to the immigration law of 1965, President Lyndon Johnson announced:

It does repair a very deep and painful flaw in the fabric of American Justice. It corrects a cruel and enduring wrong in the conduct of the American nation. The days of unlimited immigration are past, but those who come will come because of what they are and not because of the land from which they sprung.

Cultural racism includes both individual and institutional expressions of racial superiority and suppression. It refers to the subtle and pervasive uses of power by Whites "to perpetuate their cultural heritage and impose it upon others, while at the same time destroying the culture of ethnic minorities."[29] Cultural racism combines ethnocentrism, the view that other cultures are inferior to the Anglo-European, and the power to suppress or eradicate manifestations of non-Anglo-European cultures. The legacy of cultural racism can be found in the formal curriculum—in tests, media, and course offerings. It can also be detected in the hidden, informal curriculum, as in low expectations for minority student achievement held by nonminority teachers, ethnic/racial myths and stereotypes held by students and teachers, and an unfamiliar, nonsupportive, unfriendly, or hostile school environment.

Cultural racism within the United States is the belief in the inferiority of the implements, handicrafts, agriculture, economics, music, art, religious beliefs, traditions, language, and story of non-Anglo-European peoples and the belief that these people have *no distinctive culture* apart from that of mainstream White America.[30] As an example of the cultural racism that pervades Western society, consider the following racial classification of humankind developed by Carl von Linné (Carolus Linnaeus), the eminent eighteenth-century Swedish biologist.

1. HOMO. Sapiens. Diurnal; varying by education and situation.
2. Four-footed, mute, hairy. WILD MAN
3. Copper-coloured, choleric, erect. AMERICAN
   Hair black, straight, thick; nostrils wide, face harsh; beard scanty; obstinate, content, free. Paints himself with fine red lines. Regulated by customs.
4. Fair, sanguine, brawny. EUROPEAN
   Hair yellow, brown, flowing; eyes blue, gentle, acute; inventive. Covered with close vestments. Governed by law.
5. Sooty, melancholy, rigid. ASIATIC
   Hair black, eyes dark; severe, haughty, covetous. Covered with loose garments. Governed by opinions.
6. Black, phlegmatic, relaxed. AFRICAN
   Hair black, frizzled; skin silky; nose flat, lips tumid; crafty; indolent, negligent. Anoints himself with grease. Governed by caprice.[31]

Linné's list has three major problems. First, he links physical attributes such as skin color, hair texture, and facial features to personality, mental abilities, and behavior. Second, he classifies large segments of humanity into categories according to a few visible traits. And, third, he makes value judgments based on his own ethnocentric view of the world. Native Americans have wide nostrils and harsh faces and are "obstinate, content, free . . . [and] regulated by customs." Europeans are "gentle, acute, inventive . . . [and] governed by law"; Asiatics have black hair and dark eyes, and are "severe, haughty, covetous . . . [and] governed by opinions"; and Africans have black, frizzled hair and are "crafty, indolent, negligent . . . [and] governed by caprice." Western society has tended to accept the logic behind this classification of Homo *Sapiens,* along with the erroneous assumption that mental, behavioral, and sociocultural tendencies are determined by a few visible biological traits and the belief that Western Europeans are superior to all others.

As noted in Chapter 2, social scientists like Montagu have called race man's most dangerous myth. They warn that it is impossible to categorize people according to their physical traits."[32] Nevertheless, the concept of race persists and remains a primary basis for categorizing self and others within U.S. society.[33] The eighteenth-century conception of race has had a powerful influence on our cognition, and we find that in this society race is often an important basis for ethnic identity.

Theories of Ethnic Identity

Counselors and psychologists who are working to improve race relations and reduce prejudice agree that "race appreciation is a lifelong developmental process that begins with a healthy sense of one's own racial/ethnic identity."[34] People must feel good about themselves before they can respect and feel good about others. Several theories of ethnic identity have recently been developed to understand this developmental process. Beginning in the 1960s, the original focus was on ethnic identity development among African Americans. The sense of ethnic identity often developed in response to racism or oppression. Since the early 1980s theories have also been developed for Chicanos, Asian Americans, and Whites.[35] These theories can help us understand increasing racial tensions in the United States.

Mapping one's sense of cultural identity.

"The Negro-to-Black Conversion Experience"

One of the earliest theories of ethnic identity was created several decades ago by William Cross, who has continued to develop and refine his work over the years.[36] Cross originally focused on the "Negro to Black conversion experience," which occurred as African Americans lived through the civil rights movement of the 1960s. Although his theory focuses on Nigrescence, the "process of becoming Black," it is applicable to any group that has experienced oppression and is moving toward liberation, for example other ethnic minority groups and women. Cross describes five developmental stages: Pre-Encounter, Encounter, Immersion-Emersion, Internalization, and Internalization-Commitment.

Black people who are in stage one, or *pre-encounter,* accept the dominant world view. They seek to be assimilated into White mainstream society and could be described as anti-Black and anti-African. The second stage, *encounter,* is triggered by a shattering experience that destroys the person's previous ethnic self-image and changes his or her interpretation of the conditions of Black people in the United States. For many Black Americans the murder of Martin Luther King, Jr., was such an experience. White violence and outrage over the busing of Black school children to historically White schools is another *encounter* experience for African Americans.

A person who enters stage three, *immersion-emersion,* desires to live totally in the world of Blackness. The individual feels Black rage and Black pride and may engage in a "kill Whitey" fantasy. Cross describes the stage-three person as having a pseudo-Black identity because it is based on hatred and negation of Whites rather than on the affirmation of a pro-Black perspective. Stage-three Blacks often engage in "Blacker than thou" antics and view those Blacks who are accepting of Whites as Uncle Toms. In Stage four, *internalization,* the individual internalizes his or her ethnic identity and achieves greater inner security and self-satisfaction and may be characterized as the "nice Black person" with an Afro hair style and an attachment to Black things. There is a healthy sense of Black identity and pride and less hostility toward Whites.

The individual who moves into stage five, *internalization-commitment,* differs from the one who remains in stage four by becoming actively involved in plans to bring about social changes. The uncontrolled rage toward Whites is transformed into a conscious anger toward oppressive and racist institutions, from symbolic rhetoric to dedicated long-term commitment. Stage-five individuals feel compassion toward those who have not completed the process. They watch over new recruits, helping them conquer hatred of Whites and the "pitfalls of Black pride" without Black skills. The super-Black revolutionary of stage three gives way to the Black humanist in stage five.[37]

More recently, Cross has made distinctions between the development of personal identity (PI) and the development of a reference group orientation (RGO). *Personal identity* refers to "variables, traits, or dynamics that are in evidence, to one degree or another, in all human beings, regardless of social class, gender, race or culture."[38] These are "universal components of behavior" such as "high or low anxiety, self-esteem, introversion-extroversion, depression-happiness, concern for others, and so on."[39] *Reference group orientation,* on the other hand, refers to "those aspects of 'self' that are culture, class, and gender specific"[40] and focuses on "values, perspective taking, group identity, life styles, and world views" that are associated with these various groups.[41] Cross points out that to date most of the research and discussion of ethnic identity development among people-of-color living in the United States has focused on African Americans. However, he believes that the important distinctions between personal identity and reference group identity are generic to the analysis of identity development in most minority groups. It is possible, therefore, for members of ethnic minorities who have a healthy sense of personal identity and a sense of well being to range along a continuum of strong-to-weak identification with their ethnic group. In other words, two individuals from the same ethnic group (for example, Black, Mexican American, or Chinese American) might have very similar personality types but hold extremely different world views. The opposite is also possible. Black people in the United States, for example, have created a strong sense of community among a group of individuals who represent a broad range of personalities.[42]

To explain the crucial distinctions between PI and RGO,

> any plausible theory on minority-identity development should be capable of distinguishing between the psychological consequences of oppression and the psychological triumphs of an oppressed group. The exploitation of a minority group does not presuppose the dehumanization of that group. If an oppressor can control the reference group orientation of a minority, it does not matter that the exploited group has members who, individually speaking, present healthy profiles on various measures of personal identity (PI). In the early 1950s the Negro community turned its back on (opera singer) Paul Robeson and (sociologist) W. E. B. DuBois, not out of a sense of personal self-hatred, but rather because their White-oriented world view dictated that certain kinds of Negroes should be condemned and others, like Booker T. Washington, deified. That today such figures as DuBois, Robeson, Garvey, and Malcolm X, as well as Washington, are held in considerable esteem is hardly a symptom of personality change, but it does reflect a dramatic reorganization of the reference groups to which the world view of many Blacks is anchored.[43]

The Banks Typology of Ethnic Identity Development

Another theory of ethnic identity, developed by James A. Banks, is particularly helpful because of its well-developed implications for the classroom and its applicability to all ethnic groups, including Whites. Banks's six-stage typology is based on "existing and emerging theory and research" and on his own "observations and study of ethnic behaviors."[44]

In stage one, *ethnic psychological captivity,* "the individual has internalized the negative ideologies and beliefs about his or her ethnic group that are institutionalized within the society."[45] The stage-one person feels ethnic self-rejection and low self-esteem and is ashamed of his or her ethnic group identity.

Typically, such a person tries to avoid situations that lead to contact with other ethnic groups or strives aggressively to become highly culturally assimilated. Examples would be the Black person who passes for White, the guilt-ridden White liberal who tries too hard to be accepted in the Black community, the Mexican American who is afraid to leave the barrio, or the Polish American who anglicizes his or her name out of embarrassment.

Stage two, *ethnic encapsulation, is* characterized by ethnic exclusiveness and separatism.

> The individual participates primarily within his or her own ethnic community and believes that his or her ethnic group is superior to that of others. Many stage-two individuals, such as many Anglo-Saxon Protestants, have internalized the dominant societal myths about the superiority of their ethnic or racial group and the innate inferiority of other ethnic groups and races. Many individuals who are socialized within all-White suburban communities and who live highly ethnocentric and encapsulated lives may be described as stage-two individuals.[46]

Members of the Ku Klux Klan are ethnically encapsulated, as were Black Muslim followers of Elijah Muhammad. Both groups appealed to stage-one individuals who feel the pain of low self-esteem and are thus susceptible to groups that preach the supremacy of their special group.

In stage three, *ethnic identity clarification,* the individual is able to clarify personal attitudes and develops a healthy sense of self and ethnic identity. Once the individual learns to accept self, it is possible to accept and respond more positively to outside ethnic groups. According to theories of human development, such as Abraham Maslow's hierarchy of needs, until a person has met basic human needs (i.e. physiological, safety, love, and esteem) and is becoming self-actualized, ethnic identity clarification is not likely. The individual in stage three feels ethnic pride, but at the same time feels respect for different ethnic groups.

Stage four is *biethnicity.* "Individuals within this stage have a healthy sense of ethnic identity and the psychological characteristics and skills needed to participate in their own ethnic culture, as well as in another ethnic culture. The individual also has a strong desire to function effectively in two ethnic cultures," and may thus be described as biethnic.[47] According to Banks, levels of biethnicity vary greatly. Many African Americans, for example, "learn to function effectively in Anglo-American culture during the formal working day" to attain social and economic gains. In private, however, their lives "may be highly black and monocultural."[48] All ethnic minorities, White and non-White alike, who wish to make social and economic advances are forced to become biethnic to some degree. This is not the case for members of the dominant culture who "can and often do live almost exclusive monocultural and highly ethnocentric lives."[49] Recent research on children and adolescents show that African American and Mexican American families raise their children to be bicultural far more than do White families."[50]

Stage five is *multiethnicity.* "The individual at this stage is able to function, at least at minimal levels, within several ethnic sociocultural environments and to understand, appreciate, and share the values, symbols, and institutions of several ethnic cultures. Such multi-ethnic perspectives and feelings . . . help the individual to live a more enriched and fulfilling life and to formulate more creative and novel solutions to personal and public problems."[51]

Stage six is one of *globalism and global competency.* "Individuals within stage six have clarified, reflective, and positive ethnic, national, and global identifications and the knowledge, skills, attitudes, and abilities needed to function in ethnic cultures within their own nation as well as in cultures within other nations. These individuals have the ideal delicate balance of ethnic, national, and global identifications, commitments, literacy, and behaviors. They have internalized the universalistic ethical values and principles of humankind and have the skills, competencies, and commitments needed to act on these values."[52]

Although Banks stresses the "tentative and hypothetical" nature of his typology, even in its rough form it helps illuminate important sociopsychological differences between individual members of an ethnic group. Inside any particular school, we may find the entire array of stages within each ethnic group on campus. An awareness of this ethnic group diversity helps destroy ethnic stereotypes. Individuals do not become open to different ethnic groups until and unless they develop a positive sense of self, including an awareness and acceptance of their own ethnic group. This is an extension of the basic psychological principle that self-acceptance is a necessary condition for accepting others. The typology should not be viewed as a hierarchy; people do not necessarily begin at stage one and progress to stage six. Individuals can move from one stage to another, and depending upon personal experiences could become less open-minded as they go through life. Stages five and six are ideals that help us describe and visualize the goals of multicultural education.

White Racial Identity Development

Several theories of White identity development are available, notably Hardiman's White Identity Development Model (WID), Helm's Model of White Racial Identity Development, and Ponterotto's White Racial Consciousness Development Model.[53] There models share common themes and have been integrated by Sabnani, Ponterotto, and Borodovsky into "an all inclusive model of White identity development" comprised of five stages: Pre-Exposure/Pre-Contact, Conflict, Pro-Minority/Antiracism, Retreat Into White Culture, and Redefinition and Integration.[54]

Individuals in stage one, *Pre-Encounter/Pre-Contact,* lack awareness of themselves as racial beings. They are unaware of societal exploitation of people of color, and oblivious to racial tensions and issues. They are unaware of the role of Whites in an oppressive society, unaware of White privilege, and are unaware of their worldview that includes minority group stereotypes. Some Whites remain in this stage for life.

Whites who enter stage two, *Conflict,* encounter and internalize new information about race relations. For example, knowledge could come from interactions with people of color, readings, the media, or a course on race relations. As a result of their discovery, these individuals feel torn between loyalty to their White peers, family, and friends, and their desire to uphold non-racist values and (frequently) their religious values and beliefs in equality. For the first time they acknowledge their Whiteness; they commonly feel confusion, guilt, anger, or depression. To escape these feelings, individuals in *Conflict* move on into stage three or four.

Stage three, *Pro-Minority/Anti-Racism,* describes White people who begin to resist racism and identify with minority groups. Sometimes they overidentify with people of color or act in paternalistic ways; these responses are likely to be ridiculed or rejected by people of color as well as other Whites, creating greater confusion, alienation, despair, or withdrawal into White culture (stage 4). People who remain in this stage maintain a strong pro-minority position, and feel tremendous guilt and anger toward White society.

Individuals who *Retreat Into White Culture,* stage four, avoid further racial conflict by withdrawing from situations that are emotionally or physically threatening. "White flight" into White schools and neighborhoods is an example of this, resulting from deep fear and/or anger directed at another racial group. Individuals seek comfort and security in same-race settings, and develop a strong pro-White mentality.

Whites who reach *Redefinition and Integration,* stage five, come to terms with what it means to be White in a racist society. They develop a balanced and healthy sense of racial identity that enables them to "acknowledge their responsibility for maintaining racism while at the same time identifying with a White identity that is non racist (or anti-racist). . . . They see the good and bad in their own group as they do in other groups."[55] Individuals in this stage now devote their energies to nonracial issues and desire the end of all forms of oppression.

The Nature of Stereotypes and Multicultural Teaching

A major goal of multicultural education is the elimination of stereotypes. Although some stereotypes are positive, for example, the overgeneralization that all Jews are highly intelligent, they are still harmful in that they lead to inaccurate perceptions and judgments. Furthermore, many positive stereotypes refer to those who dominate a society and give justification for their preeminent position, as happened with stereotypes about Aryan superiority prior to World War II. When these erroneous beliefs, either favorable or unfavorable, are applied universally and without exception to all members of a group they become stereotypes.

A stereotype is a mental category based on exaggerated and inaccurate generalizations used to describe *all* members of a group. Some common stereotypes are athletes are dumb; Jews are stingy; Japanese Americans are highly intelligent; African Americans are violent; fat people are lazy and lack self-discipline; sorority girls are superficial; Whites are racially prejudiced; African Americans are sexually promiscuous; and Hispanics speak Spanish. Often there is just enough fact to make a stereotype seem true. For example, there *are* some dumb blondes, interfering mothers-in-law, cruel stepmothers, and Asian whiz kids, and these kernels of truth work to keep the stereotypes alive.

As psychologists have pointed out, stereotyping is a natural phenomenon in that all humans develop mental categories to help make sense of their environment.[56] According to Triandis,

> We stereotype because it is impossible for the human brain to employ all the information present in man's environment. Furthermore, there is a natural tendency to simplify our problems and to solve them as easily as possible. A "pet formula" such as "Mexicans are lazy" makes it possible for an Anglo employer to eliminate much of his mental effort by simply not considering Mexicans for jobs in his firm. If he were to check on each applicant and to understand the causes of his behavior he would have to work much harder. Furthermore, categorization helps perception. When somebody tells us, "Careful, a drunken driver!" our driving instantly becomes more defensive. The category "drunken" implies many behaviors on the part of the other driver, and we adjust to them quickly and usefully.
>
> But categorization also has a penalty. The broader the categories, the more inaccurate they are likely to be. The more they help us, in that they allow us to simplify our problems, the more likely they are to cause us to perceive the world incorrectly.[57]

In addition to developing stereotypes about others, we can accept social stereotypes about ourselves. Positive stereotypes can give us an exaggerated sense of superiority, while negative stereotypes can cause self-doubt and anxiety. In several recent studies of outstanding African American and White undergraduates at Stanford, for example, psychologist Claude Steele discovered a "stereotype vulnerability" phenomenon that may explain why many bright students of color score lower than their nonminority peers on standardized tests.[58] He administered the most difficult verbal-skills questions from the Graduate Record Exam to all the Black and White students in his studies. Before the test, half the students were told that the purpose of the research was to measure "psychological factors involved in solving verbal problems," while the other group was told that the exam "was a test of your verbal abilities and limitations." [59] Black students in the first group performed as well as their White classmates (who performed equally in both settings), but Black students who were told the test measured their intellectual potential scored significantly lower than all the other students. Why did this occur?

Steele argues that lower test scores among bright African American students result not from a conscious or unconscious acceptance of negative stereotypes about Black intelligence, but rather, "that they have to *contend* with this whisper of inferiority at the moment when their mental abilities are most taxed. In trying not to give credence to the stereotype . . . the students may redouble their efforts only to work too quickly or inefficiently."[60] He also suggests that "much of what is mistaken for racial animosity in America today is really 'stereotype vulnerability.' "[61] When people from different races meet for the first time, they are aware of the stereotypes about their own group; they use up so much psychic energy trying to deflect these stereotypes that they show discomfort and confirm the stereotypes by acting, for example, "racist" or "incompetent."

It is sometimes argued that stereotypes help develop strong in-group feelings and are necessary if cherished ethnic traditions and beliefs are to be preserved. The individual holds positive stereotypes about his or her own group and negative stereotypes about out-groups. From this point of view, multicultural education may seem undesirable. However, based on the theory of cultural pluralism, a basic assumption of multicultural education is that different ethnic groups can retain much of their original culture if they so choose yet be multicultural at the same time. In other words, it is believed that people can learn about multiple ways of perceiving, believing, doing, and evaluating so that they can conform to those aspects of the dominant culture that are necessary for positive societal interaction, without eroding identification with their original ethnicity. It is assumed that ethnic traditions and beliefs can be preserved under conditions of intercultural contact that will reduce myths and stereotypes associated with previously unknown groups. These are big assumptions. Is it possible to destroy ethnic stereotypes and still maintain a sense of ethnic identity in a cultural pluralistic society? In other words, are multiple loyalties possible?

Those who believe in the feasibility of cultural pluralism will find support in the work of Gordon Allport. Allport has written that group loyalty does not necessarily mean one feels hostile toward out-groups. "Hostility toward out-groups helps strengthen our sense of belonging, but it is not required."[62] To illustrate his point, Allport diagrammed some of the in-groups to which one might belong, with the central core being most potent and the outermost circle being the weakest (see Figure 3.2 on page 74). There is no intrinsic reason, however, why loyalty to humanity ("mankind"—the outermost circle) must be weakest. Allport writes:

> Race itself has become the dominant loyalty among many people, especially among fanatic advocates of "Aryanism" and among certain members of oppressed races. It seems today that the clash between the idea of race and of One World (the two outermost circles) is shaping into an issue that may well be the most decisive in human history. The important question is, Can a loyalty to mankind be fashioned before interracial warfare breaks out?
>
> Theoretically it can, for there is a saving psychological principle that may be invoked if we can learn how to do so in time. The principle states that concentric loyalties need not clash. To be devoted to a large circle does not imply the destruction of one's attachment to a smaller circle. The loyalties that clash are almost invariably those of identical scope. A bigamist who has founded two families of procreation is in fatal trouble with himself and with society. A traitor who serves two nations (one nominally and one actually) is mentally a mess and socially a felon. Few people can acknowledge more than one alma mater, one religion, or one fraternity. On the other hand, a world-federalist can be a devoted family man, an ardent alumnus, and a sincere patriot. The fact that some fanatic nationalists would challenge the compatibility of world-loyalty with patriotism does not change the psychological law. Wendell Willkie and Franklin Roosevelt were no less patriots because they envisioned a United Nations in One World.[63]

If we accept Allport's reasoning, it is clear that loyalty to an ethnic group need not preclude loyalty to the nation and vice versa. Respect and cooperation among different groups can replace prejudice, discrimination, and scapegoating.

The assumption that everyone is prejudiced is neither helpful nor accurate. There are individual differences in the extent to which we reject outsiders. Furthermore, it has been established that the person who rejects one out-group is likely to reject any out-group.[64] Although no single theory adequately explains the development of prejudice, it appears that less prejudiced people feel less aggression toward others, hold a generally favorable view of their parents, and perceive their environment as friendly and nonthreatening. No child is born prejudiced. Prejudices are learned within a context influenced by personal needs and social influence.

Pate suggests that some people reject prejudiced thinking because of intellectual and psychological strengths.[65] He identifies four areas of defense against prejudice: positive view of self, positive view of society (for example, belief in democratic values of equality and justice), positive view of other people, and logical thinking. An individual with low self-esteem is more likely to be prejudiced than one with high self-esteem. A positive view of society means

> a person should have basically democratic views with a belief in equality and a sense of justice. A positive view of other people includes a degree of empathy, a feeling that people are basically worthwhile, and an aversion to manipulating people for selfish reasons. Logical thinking is just that—a quality of reasoning ability which does not jump to conclusions, see only the superficial, reach faulty conclusions, confuse cause and effect, or overgeneralize.[66]

Obviously teachers are limited in what they can do to modify the deeply prejudiced personality. We should remember, however, that not everyone who accepts stereotypes is deeply prejudiced. Furthermore, there is no known reason why we cannot or should not attempt to reduce ethnic group stereotypes and at the same time foster within our students a healthy sense of ethnic pride and respect. Those who feel genuine pride (not superiority) in their own ethnic group are most apt to accept other ethnic groups. Stereotypes impede that acceptance.

Avoiding Stereotypes

It is important to remember that we run the risk of stereotyping when we seek the perspective of a particular nation or ethnic group. People within every national or ethnic group differ from each other in important ways. Not all White Anglo-Saxon Protestants are racially prejudiced. Not all Mexican Americans identify with their native heritage. Not all African Americans are knowledgeable about life in the Black ghetto or can speak for the Black community on race-relations issues. Not everyone who speaks Spanish is from Mexico.

Within any one nation or ethnic group, social conflicts and different viewpoints emerge due to such factors as geographic origins, social class, and gender. Personal qualities such as aptitude, personality, and appearance also make a difference. All these factors interact with the individual's sense of national or ethnic identity; some individuals tend to be assimilated into the dominant culture, others are more ethnically encapsulated, and still others are bicultural or even global in perspective. Geographic origins, social class, and sense of ethnic identity are especially helpful in explaining ethnic diversity.

The following suggestions illustrate how an awareness of diversity within ethnic groups and nations can be developed, along with an understanding of the group's perspective.

- Select a nation or ethnic group and plan ways of portraying the diversity within it. Include male and female viewpoints, different generations and age groups, dissimilar occupations, geographical regions, socioeconomic backgrounds, neighborhoods, and intergroup experiences.
- When social issues are debated, or when students are asked to play roles, include a realistic mix of opinions that portray the different viewpoints within many ethnic groups and nations.
- Help students identify diversity within their own ethnic group and nation, including physical features associated with different races, attitudes, opinions, and socioeconomic factors.
- Provide a variety of role models from each ethnic group present in the school.
- When tracking of students and ability grouping is used, avoid ethnically identifiable groups.

An Illustration of Racism and the Need for Curriculum Reform

The traditional curriculum in most schools in the United States is a classic example of institutional and cultural racism. From elementary school, where uncounted numbers of children have been taught to "sit like an Indian" (which in itself is a racial stereotype), to colleges and universities, where thousands more have learned the misconception that IQ differences are related to race, schools have fostered the belief in White supremacy. The traditional monoethnic curriculum has presented one way of perceiving, believing, behaving, and evaluating: the Anglo-Western European way. School texts and educational media have presented negative myths and stereotypes about most of our ethnic minorities, have overlooked important contributions, and have presented a distorted view of past and current history that reinforces the doctrine of White supremacy. The case of Africa and the cultural roots of African Americans provides one example.

Africa: Common Misconceptions

The truth about Africa has been so distorted among non-Africans that with the emergence of Africa on the world scene in 1960 (the year most contemporary African nations achieved independence and sent representatives to the United

Nations), most Westerners were almost totally ignorant about the earth's second largest continent. For centuries perceptions of the "Dark Continent" had been clouded over with myths and stereotypes, and Africa was greeted then as now with all the myths and stereotypes intact. Some of the simplest myths are most common: lions in the jungles, the isolated Dark Continent, inferior savages, a race of Negroes—heathens developed only by the grace of God and the White man—and land of turmoil, incapable of self-government. Because these myths and stereotypes are alive today in the school's curriculum (however unintentional the distortions and omissions may be), in the hands of unaware and unskilled teachers the curriculum continues to feed the racist doctrines and practices of White supremacy.

Raised on a diet of Westernized history, Tarzan books and films, and sensationalized news media, many in the United States believe Africa to be a primitive land of hot, steamy jungles inhabited by wild animals and savages. In truth, less than 10 percent of the African continent is jungle. (And of course, lions live in grasslands, not jungles.) Nearly half of the African continent consists of grassy savannah, and approximately one-third is searing desert.[67]

The idea that Africa has been isolated until recently is also false. Ancient Africans had contact with the Greeks, Romans, Chinese, and early Indonesians, and there is evidence that they may have entered the western hemisphere long before the Spaniards. Archaeological evidence reveals active trade with Arabs and Indians via the Indian Ocean and the Sahara, which was at one time a lush fertile nursery of African civilizations. For example, cave paintings and chariot tracks preserved in rock attest to a lively commerce that began before the Sahara dried up and became a desert. Europeans traded with the Moroccans, probably without knowing that many goods (primarily gold, salt, and ivory) originated south of the Sahara. Davidson describes the bustling port of Kilwa from the twelfth to the fifteenth centuries as the chief trading center of East Africa and one of the liveliest in the entire world. "On any given day . . . workers could be seen loading their masters' dhows with African gold, iron, ivory and coconuts, and unloading textiles and jewelry from India and exquisite porcelain from China."[68]

Related to the misconception that Africa was an isolated dark continent prior to the arrival of the Europeans is the belief that Africans were uncivilized savages. Early writings of Muslim scholars who traveled throughout Africa in the tenth and eleventh centuries provide evidence that African civilization was as advanced, or more so, than that of Europe, even according to the material standards typically used by Westerners. The Arab geographer alBakri, for example, wrote in 1067 (one year after 20,000 Normans conquered England) that "the king of Ghana . . . can raise 200,000 warriors, 40,000 of them being armed with bows and arrows."[69] When Mali's king, Mansa Musa, made his pilgrimage to Mecca in 1324, his "entourage was composed of 60,000 persons, a large portion of which constituted a military escort. No less than 12,000 were servants, 500 of whom marched ahead of their king, each bearing a staff of pure gold. Books, baggage men, and royal secretaries there were in abundance. To finance the pilgrimage, the king carried 80 camels to bear his more than 24,000 pounds of gold."[70] Because King Musa spent so much money in the Middle East, the value of gold in the great commercial center of Cairo was depressed for at least twelve years.[71]

Yet few people have learned about the achievements of the early West African kingdoms of Ghana, Mali, and Songhai, the forest kingdom of Benin, or KanemBomu in the interior. The prosperity and power of the great West African empires, which covered an area almost as large as the United States, arose from the agricultural base of the Niger River Valley; their control of the gold and salt trade between North African Arabs; the existence of the open savannah that foot and horse soldiers could quickly traverse; and their rulers' adoption of Islam, which brought them aid, allies, and smoother trade among Muslims of North Africa and the Middle East.[72]

Although ancient Egypt is a staple of world history and art history courses and a source of fascination for young children and youth, the Black African influences on Egyptian civilization, and therefore Anglo-European civilization, has been hidden. Few people have heard that the ancient kingdom of Kush, which thrived during the Ptolemaic era, was a center of extensive iron smelting, and developed the Meroitic alphabet.

Africa's record of achievement is not limited to the large kingdoms, however. Elaborate social and political systems, complex religions (frequently dismissed as animism), effective health care practices (for example, the herbal-psychological services of the traditional healer), and advanced expressions of music and art all developed in African villages as well as in large empires. Some scholars assert that the greatest genius of the African peoples was their capacity for social organization, a talent that operated at the village level and in the complex kingdoms.[73] In community attitude that "joined man to man in a brotherhood of equals, in moral attitudes that guided social behavior, in beliefs that exalted the spiritual aspects of life above the material," many Africans achieved a kind of social harmony that could exist without the power of a centralized authority.[74] This is not to overlook the fact that prior to European invasions nearly all ethnic groups in Africa practiced some form of slavery. It is important to recognize, however, that although they suffered great liabilities African slaves were guaranteed extensive rights, had a relatively stable family life, and often experienced a great deal of social mobility. In fact, eventual freedom was often presumed.[75]

Ibn Battuta, a Berber scholar and theologian from Tangiers who crossed the Sahara in 1352 and spent a year in Mali, found some of his hosts' customs unpleasant, but he wrote about the high sense of justice among the people. "Of all peoples, the Negroes are those who most abhor injustice. The Sultan pardons no one who is guilty of it. There is complete and general safety throughout the land. The traveler here has no more reason than the man who stays at home to fear brigands, thieves or ravishers."[76] Furthermore, "the blacks do not confiscate the goods of any North Africans who may die in their country, not even when these consist of large treasures. On the contrary, they deposit these goods with a man of confidence . . . until those who have a right to the goods present themselves and take possession."[77]

In the late fifteenth century, Europeans did not need to rely on the travelogues of Muslim scholars and could see for themselves that Africa was not a primeval wilderness inhabited by savages. Instead, these visitors discovered

> prosperous, self-contained cities linked to each other by a busy, carefully ordered trade. Their inhabitants—merchants, artisans, laborers, clerks—lived comfortable lives. Their pleasures were the familiar ones cherished by all people—feasting and family gatherings. Africa was in many ways no more savage than Europe—at the time just concluding the Hundred Years' War and only recently occupied with burning Joan of Arc.[78]

Nevertheless, myths about Africa continued to flourish in Europe and eventually were transported to the colonies in North America. These myths conjured visions of the great White hunter facing primitive tribes with their cannibalism, depraved customs, loincloths, and spears. Early slave-ship records promoted the view that it was only through the grace of God and the White man that these heathen savages would be Christianized and civilized. Sensationalized news stories and films have helped keep the Tarzan image alive, as well as images of the noble savage unspoiled by the evils of industrialized society.

How and why did these myths develop? First, competition among the emerging European nations and houses of commerce led to practices of secrecy lest rivals benefit from knowledge gained through the early explorations of lands unknown to Europe. Second was the blatant "dishonesty of literary hacks who concocted all sorts of nonsense for a gullible public."[79] Third was the need to justify slave trade in the minds of Christians and the enlightened. Assurances that slaves were heathen savages who would benefit by becoming Christianized and civilized became a basic rationalization. It should also be noted, however, that Spanish colonists distinguished between Blacks and Indians, thinking the former were sub-human and therefore unworthy of conversion.[80] Related to the desire to expand Christianity is the fact that Europeans launched into an era of imperialism and the quest for new lands and natural resources. To control new colonies, in this case the African colonies, traditional history, culture, and sources of group identity had to be suppressed and were replaced (at least temporarily) by the colonialists' culture, history, and doctrines of White supremacy. Today, many textbooks contain outdated information about African nations. Rapidly changing events on that continent make maps and other content obsolete even in relatively new texts. Furthermore, news media and periodicals, which could be used to supplement outdated materials, are often inadequate sources for understanding current and past events in Africa.

> The *Washington Post,* probably the most important news source of American political decision makers, covers Africa's fifty-two nations and 350,000,000 people with one reporter, who within a few days was ordered to cover the independence of Mozambique, the coup against the Emperor of Ethiopia, and the Ali-Foreman fight in Zaire. This is an impossible assignment! (As one Madison, Wisconsin, newspaper editor noted, there is more and better reporting on Africa in one weekly airmail issue edition of the British *Manchester Guardian* than in all the American national press combined.) Those who know Africa and read the U.S.

press' political reporting frequently find that the stories are shallow, and stereo-typical, overemphasizing the importance of ethnicity and tribe, fixated on the bizarre and exotic, primarily dependent on white expatriates for information and sometimes covertly allied with white racialist interests.[81]

In addition to outdated content, most current textbooks that attempt to present Africans to elementary and secondary school students emphasize exotic and irrelevant information about race and overemphasize small groups of people such as the Mbuti, San, and Khoi peoples, commonly referred to as Pygmies, Bushmen, and Hottentots. The combined population of these three groups is estimated to be between 25,000 and 250,000, or approximately 0.007 to 0.07 percent of the total population of Africa (over 350 million).[82]

> The names chosen to describe these people—"Bushmen," "Pygmies" and "Hottentots"—are not names which are used by the people themselves; rather, they are deprecating and unflattering terms given to them by Europeans who . . . did not learn or use the appropriate names. Pygmy comes from a Greek word meaning short or dwarf. The name Bushman was given to the San people by South African whites who exterminated many of them and drove others from their fertile lands into the desert bush areas. . . . Many young Americans come to believe that many or most African people live like these exotic, small atypical groups because so much of the curriculum is devoted to their study.[83]

Given the vast reservoir of African history and cultures available and yet unknown by most people in the United States, the textbook emphasis on Pygmies and Bushmen is telling. These peoples exemplify survival in an inhospitable environment and may be more spiritually developed than many humans who live in higher technological societies, but the texts neither point this out nor establish the array of humanity found on the African continent. Thus the unsophisticated non-African reader who comes across illustrations and texts that only show Africans in the bush perceives emotionally and physically uncomfortable conditions and "improper behavior" (scanty clothes, scarification, dipping food from a common bowl) and evaluates the people as inferior. American children and youth need to understand the basic human characteristics they share with the various peoples of Africa. This is not achieved by emphasizing exoticism and cultural differences associated with so-called primitive humanity.

Some Effects of Misconceptions about Africa

One result of this deformed view of past and present Africa is that it promotes ignorance and disdain of Africans. These are dangerous outcomes in a world whose peoples are growing closer and more interdependent. Another obvious result of ignorance about Africa is that it feeds the doctrine of White supremacy and the belief that African Americans as a group are inferior because they are genetically related to Africans. Myths and theories from the past that were used to justify slavery continue to serve as a rationalization for inferior schools, substandard homes, low-paying jobs, and segregated restaurants, rest rooms, and transportation. The Council on Interracial Books for Children concludes the following:

> To justify the treatment of the African slave, and later of the Afro-American citizen, white society encouraged an army of propagandists to "scientifically" prove the inferiority of Black people. While this ideology of racism was applied to all people of color with whom Euro-American society came into contact, its severest application was against Afro-Americans. Because they were the most physically different from whites, because their numbers were the second largest to whites, and because of their geographical and social proximity to whites, Black people have been perceived as the greatest threat.
>
> White supremacist ideology has infected every level of national life. Government officials, social scientists, ministers, teachers, journalists and doctors have all played a part, as new and more sophisticated revisions of the myths and rationalizations of white supremacy keep reappearing. Whether it is religious leaders in colonial days pointing to Biblical passages damning Ham; biologists of a hundred years ago "studying" cranial structures; Social Darwinists utilizing theories of evolution and survival of the fittest; geneticists of the 1920s "proving" inborn moral inferiority; Moynihan-like theories of Black "pathology"; recent genetic pronouncements of Shockley and Jensen about Black IQ—all serve as pseudo-scientific apologies for the ongoing oppression directed against Black people.[84]

Another effect of these deformed images of Africa is the misconceptions about Black African people that crop up in textbooks and other educational materials. These misconceptions are then transferred to African Americans. According to Beryle Banfield, president of the Council on Interracial Books for Children,

> Racism in textbooks is usually most evident in five important areas: the historical perspective from which the material is presented; the characterization of Third World peoples; the manner in which their customs and traditions are depicted; the terminology used to describe the peoples and their culture and the type of language ascribed to them; and the nature of the illustrations.[85]

■ CONCLUSIONS

Although both cultural and racial differences might be an important source of transitional trauma, misunderstanding, and conflict in the classroom, race is often the more serious factor. White American culture rooted in Anglo-European traditions predominates in most schools, most of which are controlled by White people. We find evidence of this in the growing body of literature that shows alarmingly high rates of dropping out among Latino and American Indian students and the declining enrollments of African American students on the college campuses—the result of our society's pervasive legacy of racism. A major goal of multicultural education is to help us understand this legacy and move toward a more just society.

This chapter's discussion of racism has emphasized Africa and African Americans. We must be careful, however, not to regard racism strictly as a Black-White issue. There are parallels to the case of Africa all over the world.

The results of ignorance and misunderstanding have been seen in Southeast Asia during the Vietnamese war and its aftermath—and again in Central America, an area many perceive simplistically as the Banana Republics.

Likewise, not only are non-White ethnic groups in United States society affected by racism; many White immigrants, such as the Irish, Italians, and Jews from Eastern Europe also have experienced cruel discrimination. Today, for example, immigration officials in California sometimes violate the civil rights of Mexican Americans who are assumed to be illegal aliens by stopping them and asking them for identification. Immigrants from Asia—the Vietnamese and Chinese—now face resentment and racial prejudices in many aspects of their lives.

Because space does not permit all-inclusive illustrations, the focus on Africa and African Americans is appropriate. In terms of numbers, African Americans represent the largest ethnic minority. More important, however, is the fact that no other group entered this society primarily as slaves. The experience of slavery and its justification firmly entrenched the doctrine of White supremacy in the minds and institutions that shaped U.S. history and led to the overall suppression of dark-skinned citizens.

Obviously, schools do not exist in a vacuum. They are only one aspect of a broader social context that, despite many changes that help encourage social justice for everyone, is still racist in many ways because it supports White privilege. How do we proceed in the face of this? First, we must accept that schools can and should make a difference. Those who would equate a stand against racism with preaching values can be told that it is un-American, undemocratic, and antihuman to be racist. We can then proceed as follows:

- Recognize racist history and its impact on oppressors and victims.
- Examine our own attitudes, experiences, and behaviors concerning racism.
- Understand the origins of racism and why people hold racial prejudices and stereotypes.
- Understand the differences among individual, institutional, and cultural racism.
- Be able to identify racist images in the language and illustration of books, films, television, news media, and advertising.
- Be able to identify current examples of racism in our immediate community and society as a whole.
- Identify specific ways of combating racism.
- Become antiracist in our own behavior.

In Chapters 4 and 5 the case for multicultural education is further developed through a discussion of the roots of cultural diversity in the United States. They provide a comparative analysis of important ethnic groups in terms of their origins and responses to various forms of oppression.

COMPARE AND CONTRAST

1. Predilection, prejudice, and discrimination
2. Individual and institutional racism

3. Racial prejudice and racism
4. Stage of ethnic identity and stereotype vulnerability
5. Theory of multiple loyalties and ethnic encapsulation
6. Positive and negative perceptions of Africa

ACTIVITIES AND QUESTIONS

1. Given the fact that approximately 90 percent of our genetic makeup is identical to that of other humans, and less than 3 percent determines biological characteristics associated with race, why is race so important in our society today?

2. How have distortions of African history contributed to racism? Which came first, racism or distortion? Explain.

3. Consider the characteristics Glen Pate has identified as defenses to prejudice: highly positive view of self, strong belief in equality and justice, highly positive view of other people, and ability to think logically and critically. How do you rate yourself on each category? Teachers you know? Students? Assuming Pate's theory is valid, how can schools help strengthen defenses to prejudice among teachers, administrators, and students? What could be done in your specific teaching area?

4. In what ways have White Americans been harmed by White racism in the United States? What can/should elementary, middle, and secondary school teachers in your area do to lessen the problem?

5. Divide into small groups of approximately six. Have each member share his or her earliest memory of race or ethnicity and most recent memory. Share the results with the large group and if possible develop comparisons and contrasts by race and gender.

6. Read the *Autobiography of Malcolm X* and analyze the extent to which Banks's typology of ethnicity stages accurately describes the life of Malcolm X. What stage or stages of ethnicity are reflected in his life experiences? Use specific examples from the autobiography to support your arguments. Note those experiences that you believe produced a change to a different stage of ethnicity (in either direction) for Malcolm X.

7. Apply Banks's typology to yourself. Choose the stage that best describes you at your present level of ethnicity. Describe those important life experiences and circumstances that help explain where you are in terms of your ethnicity. If you have experienced more than one stage, explain why.

8. Select one of the ethnic identity theories presented in this chapter and use it as a lens to analyze main characters in books such as the following: *The Color Purple*, by Alice Walker, *Lakota Woman*, by Mary Crow Dog, *Maggie's American Dream*, by James Comer, *The Rice Room: Growing Up Chinese American from Number Two Son to Rock 'n Roll*, by Ben Fong-Torres, *Rabbi Rabbi*, by Abraham Kane, *The Education of a WASP*, by Lois

Stalvey, *Always Running: La Vida Loca, Gang Days in LA,* by Luis Rodriguez, *Hunger of Memory,* by Richard Rodriguez, *No-No Boy,* by John Okada, *The Joy Luck Club,* by Amy Tan, *The Women of Brewster Place,* by Gloria Naylor, or *The Autobiography of Malcolm X.*

9. Read the short story, *High Yaller,* by Rudolph Fisher. (This story takes place in New York shortly after World War I. It focuses on the social and romantic conflicts experienced by Evelyn Brown, an African American woman with light complexion.) Find out the extent to which conflicts over skin color are still important among African Americans today. Find out whether similar conflicts are present within other ethnic minority groups.

10. Imagine that a racial incident occurs in the school or community where you are teaching. (Members of your class or groups can come up with authentic examples!) Explain how you would use this as a "teachable moment" with the students in your classes. (Specify your grade level, i.e., early childhood, primary grades, upper elementary, middle or secondary school, or adult.)

NOTES

1. J. R. Feagin and H. Vera, *White Racism* (New York: Routledge, 1995), 193.

2. S. A. Holmes, "A Rose-Colored View of Race," *New York Times,* Sunday June 15, 1997, p. 4.

3. Ibid.

4. S. A. Holmes, "Many Uncertain about President's Racial Effort," *New York Times,* Monday, June 16 1997, p. B–10.

5. S. Mydans, "Los Angeles Policemen Acquitted in Taped Beating," *New York Times,* April 30, 1992, p. A1, B8.

6. P. Applebome, "Opponents' Moves Refueling Debate on School Busing," *New York Times,* Tuesday, September 26, 1995, p 1.

7. Intelligence Report, October 1994, Southern Poverty Law Center, pp. 9–12.

8. M. Janofsky, "Anti-Defamation Leagues Tells of Rise in Web Hate Sites," *New York Times,* October 22, 1997, p. A17.

9. H. L. Gates, Jr., and C. West, *The Future of the Race* (New York: Vintage Books, 1996), 20–21.

10. Feagin and Vera, *op. cit.,* p 146.

11. G. Allport, *The Nature of Prejudice* (Reading, MA: Addison Wesley, 1954), xiii–xiv.

12. J. Forbes, *Education of the Culturally Different: A Multi-Cultural Approach* (San

Francisco: Far West Laboratory for Educational Research and Development, 1969), 50.

13. M. Dennis, "Socialization and Racism: The White Experience," in *Impacts of Racism on White Americans,* B. P. Bowser and R. G. Hunt, eds. (Beverly Hills, CA: Sage, 1981), 71–85.

14. Ibid.

15. Ibid., 82.

16. Ibid.

17. M. Rokeach, *Beliefs, Attitudes, and Values* (SanFrancisco, CA: Jossey-Bass, Inc., 1968).

18. J. G. Ponteratto and P. B. Pedersen, *Preventing Prejudice: A Guide for Counselor and Educators* (Newbury Park, CA: Sage, 1993).

19. G. Allport, *ABC's of Scapegoating* (New York: Anti-Defamation League of B'nai B'rith, 1979). The quotations on the following pages are from Gordon Allport, *The Nature of Prejudice,* ©1979, Addison-Wesley, Reading, Massachusetts. Reprinted with permission of the publisher

20. J. L. Gwaltney, *Drylongso: A Self-portrait of Black America* (New York: Random House, 1980), 73–74. The following quotations are reprinted by permission Random House,

Inc., and John Brockman Associates, Copyright ©1980 by John Langston Gwaltney.

21. J. M. Jones, "The Concept of Racism and Its Changing Reality," in *Impacts of Racism on White Americans*, B. D. Bowser and R. G. Hunt, eds. (Beverly Hills, CA: Sage, 1981), 118.

22. See Ridley, C. R. (1989). "Racism in Counseling as an Adverse Behavioral Process," in P. B. Pederson, J. G. Draguns, W. J. Lonner, & J. E. Trimble (Eds.), *Counseling Across Cultures* (3rd. ed) (pp. 55–77) Honolulu: University of Hawaii Press.

23. Jones, *op. cit.,* 131.

24. J. R. Feagin and C. B. Feagin, *Racial and Ethnic Relations* (Englewood Cliffs, NJ: Prentice Hall, 1993), 224.

25. S. Carmichael and C. V. Hamilton, *Black Power: The Politics of Liberation in America* (New York: Random House, 1967).

26. L. L. Knowles and K. Prewitt, *Institutional Racism in America* (Englewood Cliffs, NJ: Prentice Hall, 1969).

27. J. R. Feagin and C. B. Feagin. *Discrimination American Style: Institutional Racism and Sexism* (Englewood Cliffs, NJ: Prentice Hall, 1978), 30.

28. M. A. Jones, *American Immigration* (Chicago: University of Chicago Press, 1960), 79.

29. G. Gay, *Racism in America: Imperatives for Teaching Ethnic Studies* (Washington, DC: National Council for the Social Studies), 27–49.

30. Jones, "The Concept of Racism," 148.

31. Ibid., 18.

32. A. Montagu, *Man's Most Dangerous Myth: The Fallacy of Race,* 5th ed. (New York: Oxford University Press, 1974), 7.

33. H. J. Ehrlich, *The Social Psychology of Prejudice* (New York: John Wiley & Sons, 1973).

34. Ponteratto and Pedersen, *Preventing Prejudice,* 39.

35. Ibid.

36. W. E. Cross, Jr., "The Negro to Black Conversion Experience: Toward a Psychology of Black Liberation," *Black World* 20 (July 1979). Synopsis used by permission of the author.

37. Ibid.

38. W. E. Cross, Jr., "A Two-Factor Theory of Black Identity: Implications for the Study of Identity Development in Minority Children," in *Children's Ethnic Socialization: Pluralism and Development,* J. S. Phinney and M. J. Rotheram, eds. (Newbury Park, CA: Sage, 1987), 121.

39. Ibid.

40. Ibid., 123.

41. Ibid.

42. Ibid., 126.

43. Ibid., 128–129.

44. J. A. Banks, *Teaching Strategies for Ethnic Studies,* 3rd ed. (Boston: Allyn and Bacon, 1984). Synopsis and quotations from this work are used by permission of Allyn and Bacon, Inc., and J. A. Banks. Copyright © 1984 by Allyn and Bacon, Inc.

45. Ibid., 55–56.

46. Ibid., 56.

47. Ibid.

48. J. A. Banks, *Multiethnic Education: Theory and Practice* (Boston: Allyn and Bacon, 1981), 132.

49. Ibid.

50. D. A. Rosenthal, "Ethnic Identity Development in Adolescence," in *Children's Ethnic Socialization: Pluralism and Development,* J. S. Phinney and M. J. Rotheram, eds. (Newbury Park, CA: Sage, 1987), 156–179.

51. Banks, *Teaching Strategies,* 56.

52. Ibid.

53. Ponteratto and Pedersen, *Preventing Prejudice: A Guide for Counselors and Educators* (Newbury Part, CA: Sage, 1993), 63–83.

54. Ibid.

55. Ibid., 78.

56. H. C. Triandis, *Attitude and Attitude Change* (New York: John Wiley and Sons, 1971), 102–103. Quotation reprinted by permission of the publisher Copyright © 1971 by John Wiley & Sons, Inc.

57. Ibid.

58. E. Watters, "Claude Steele Has Scores to Settle," *The New York Times Magazine,* September 17, 1995, 45–47.

59. Ibid., 45.

60. Ibid., 46.

61. Ibid., 47.
62. G. Allport, *The Nature of Prejudice*(Reading, MA: Addison-Wesley, 1979), 42. The quotation on the following pages are from Gordon Allport. *The Nature of Prejudice,* © 1979, Addison-Wesley, Reading, Massachusetts. Reprinted with permission of the publisher.
63. Ibid., 44.
64. Ibid.
65. G. S. Pate, "The Ingredients of Prejudice" (Paper presented at the College and University Faculty Assembly of the National Council for the Social Studies, Boston. 24 November 1982).
66. Ibid.
67. B. Davidson, *African Kingdoms* (New York: Time-Life Books, 1966).
68. Ibid., 29.
69. E. A. Toppin, "The Forgotten People," *Christian Science Monitor,* March 6, 1969 (special insert).
70. J. H. Franklin, *From Slavery to Freedom* (New York: Alfred A. Knopf, 1967), 15.
71. Davidson, *African Kingdoms,* 83–84.
72. Toppin, "Forgotten People."
73. Davidson, *African Kingdoms,* 22.
74. Ibid.
75. M. F. Berry and J. W. Blassingame, *Long Memory: The Black Experience in America* (New York: Oxford University Press, 1982), 1–6.
76. Davidson, *African Kingdoms,* 82
77. Ibid.
78. Ibid., 21.
79. Ibid.
80. I am again indebted to Bradley Levinson for this observation.
81. D. Wiley, "The African Connection," *Wisconsin Alumnus* 77, no. 2 (January 1976): 7–11.
82. A. Zikiros and M. Wiley, *Africa in Social Studies Textbooks* (East Lansing: African Studies Center, Michigan State University, 1978), 15.
83. Ibid.
84. *Stereotypes, Distortions and Omissions in U.S. History Textbooks* (New York: Council on Interracial Books for Children, 1977), 16.
85. B. Banfield, "How Racism Takes Root," *UNESCO Courier,* March 1979, 31.

Conflicting Themes of Assimilation and Pluralism among European Americans, Jewish Americans, and African Americans

*T*he next two chapters further the case for multicultural education by providing brief overviews of the histories of major ethnic groups in the United States. Why is this history important? First, we often overlook the different histories of ethnic minority children and youth as a factor in their contemporary school experiences. For example, some people wonder why many Mexican Americans want to maintain fluency in Spanish or have difficulty learning English when immigrants from Western European countries mastered English within a generation. How do we explain the disproportionately high poverty rates among African Americans, American Indians, Puerto Ricans, and Appalachian Whites? Why do language-minority children and low-income students drop out of school at higher rates than students fluent in Standard English and students from middle- and upper-income families? Second, we tend to lump students into broad ethnic categories such as Asian Americans, who are often viewed as the "model minority" and academic whiz kids, and thus overlook the tremendous diversity and learning needs of students within the group. And third, these brief histories illustrate the ethnic pluralism in our contemporary society that is better served by multicultural schools than by monocultural schools.

Sources of Cultural Diversity in the United States: An Overview

Those who accept the myth of the melting pot overlook the fact that assimilation was never intended for everyone. Various nonassimilationist strategies were used to deal with indigenous people, Americans Indians. These included policies of genocide, resettlement on reservations, and subordination through forced labor or slavery. African Americans were suppressed under slavery and later under the Jim Crow laws, which legalized the separation of Blacks and Whites. With the 1896 U.S. Supreme Court decision in *Plessy v. Ferguson,* separate but equal facilities for Blacks became the law of the land. Gerrymandering is still used to divide Black neighborhoods to dilute their voting power. Many Latinos have experienced segregation and oppression similar to African Americans, particularly those with darker skin.

During the late 1800s and early 1900s, nativist prejudice and stereotyping were directed at European immigrants, particularly those from southern Europe. There was fear that the "American race" would become mongrelized. One prominent journalist wrote

> Races cannot be cross-bred without mongrelization, any more than breeds of dogs can be cross-bred without mongrelization. The American nation was founded and developed by the Nordic race, but if a few more million members of the Alpine, Mediterranean and Semitic races are poured among us, the result must inevitably be a hybrid race of people as worthless and futile as the good-for-nothing mongrels of Central America and Southeast Europe.[1]

Such sentiments are found in our nation's congressional record and in the major scholarly textbooks of that time.

The second and third generations of White ethnic groups who did not appear racially different from the Caucasian core could, if they so chose, give up their language and traditions, change their names, and assimilate. However, this was not possible for African Americans, East Asian Americans, Native Americans, or darker-skinned Mexican Americans. Members of these racially identifiable ethnic groups who wanted to melt in were prevented from doing so. Thus a society that perceived itself as being based on the so-called American way actually fostered the development of diverse cultures within its national boundaries. Policies of segregation meant that isolated groups would retain aspects of their original culture and create a new culture that was distinct from the Anglo-Western European core.

African American culture exemplifies this process of creating a culture within a culture in the United States.

> The millions of enslaved Africans could only bring with them certain parts or aspects of their ancestral cultures—whatever they could carry in their minds. One includes here speech characteristics (pitch, intonation, timbre), folklore heroes and motifs, religious beliefs or values, artistic skills and preferences, and the like.

But the slaves had only harshly limited opportunities to maintain anything like the full content of their original cultures[2]

Social organizations could not be transmitted, for example, the priesthood associated with a religion, a guild of smiths associated with ironworking, and a royal lineage associated with a regal tradition. Therefore, the new setting required that they "innovate, fabricate, synthesize, and adapt whole new patterns of and for existence."[3] While the material aspects of African cultures—the technology of ironworking, wood carving, and weaving—died out or were greatly transformed, nonmaterial aspects survived. Jones has written that music, dance, and religion are the most significant legacies of the African past, even to the contemporary African American.[4] In the past it was believed that slaves were stripped of their original culture, but most scholars today would agree that African cultural origins have helped shape the African American cultures that have been created throughout the Western Hemisphere.[5]

A brief history of some of the major ethnic groups in the United States helps illuminate cultural pluralism in contemporary society. These different histories also help explain their differing successes in U.S. American schools today. We begin with the story of European Americans.

European Americans

According to the U.S. census in 1990, 80 percent of the population is White, non-Hispanic.[6] This figure embraces a diverse group of citizens in terms of religion, social values, political perspectives, wealth, educational attainment, and openness to the ethnic diversity that has characterized our society for nearly 400 years. Diversity among European Americans is rooted in how they have evolved through their relations with other ethnic groups and the larger society.

Origins: The Roots of Diversity and Community

The first Europeans to settle in North America in large numbers were the English and Welsh. Their migration differed from later European immigration in that it involved the subordination of native people and the take-over of their homeland. The early settlers were supported by the king of England, who viewed the colonies as a source of new raw materials and a marketplace for English manufactured goods.

Although colonial society was ethnically diverse in terms of race (20 percent of the population was African American), religion, and language, an Anglo Protestant core culture was established. English became the dominant language and English common law became the basis for the U.S. legal system. Later, public education became a way of socializing non-British immigrants.

With the public school movement which began in earnest in the first decades of the nineteenth century, British dominance of public schools became a fact of life. Urban schools were seen as a means of socializing non-British immigrants into

Anglo-Protestant values and the values of the U.S. industrial system. British American industrialists and educators established most public schools, shaped curricula and teaching, and supervised operations. Although some, such as John Dewey, believed education gave greater opportunity to poor immigrants, many educators emphasized the social-control aspects of schools. Americanization pressures on immigrant children were often intense. Whether children were Irish, Jewish, or Italian, Anglicizaton was designed to ferret out non-Anglo-Protestant ways, to assimilate the children in terms of Anglo-Protestant manners, work habits, and values.[7]

Until recently, influence from American Indian cultures on the Anglo Protestant core culture has been overlooked. Some scholars argued that the unique form of democracy that emerged in the United States was influenced as much by native people as by the British, the eighteenth-century French, and the Romans and Greeks.

When Americans try to trace their democratic heritage back through the writings of French and English political thinkers of the Enlightenment, they often forget that these people's thoughts were heavily shaped by the democratic traditions and the state of nature of the American Indians.[8]

Native peoples, particularly those who lived in the northeastern part of the continent, provided the models for some aspects of American democracy that differed from what was known in Europe: a federal system of government, the separation of civil from military authorities, the concept of impeachment, admission of new territories as states (partners rather than colonies), political debate that allowed one person to speak at a time, group authority (councils) rather than individual authority, the caucus, an egalitarianism that disallowed slavery (compared with Greek democracy that was based on massive slavery), and a political voice for women.[9] Most of this has been left out of the history books, which is typical of the fate of a colonized people. In his discussion of early Anglo-Saxon cultural dominance, Banks writes:

Early in American colonial life, non-English groups began to be evaluated negatively. The New England colonies, which were predominantly English, took steps to bar the settlements of Roman Catholics. The French Huguenots became the focal point of English hostility. Later, the Scots-Irish and the German immigrants were the victims of English antagonism. An English mob prevented a group of Irish immigrants from landing in Boston in 1729. Several years later, another mob destroyed a new Scots-Irish Presbyterian church in Worcester . . . As early as 1727, nativistic feeling toward the Germans in Pennsylvania ran high. (Nativism was a movement designed to restrict immigration to America and to protect the interest of the native-born. It was an extreme form of nationalism and ethnocentrism.) To discourage further foreign settlement in the colony, Pennsylvania passed a statute in 1729 increasing the head tax on foreigners, allegedly to prevent persons likely to become public charges from entering the colony. Other antiforeign legislation emerged in the eighteenth century. In 1798, Congress, dominated by the Federalists, passed the Alien and Sedition Acts to crush the Republican party by destroying its large base of immigrant support. . . . The Alien and Sedition Acts lengthened the time required to become an American citizen from five to fourteen years and gave the president almost unlimited control over the behavior of immigrants. They virtually nullified the freedoms of speech and the press.[10]

Over 34.5 million Europeans immigrated into the United States between 1820, when the government began to record immigration, and 1960. Europeans represent 82 percent of the total immigration during this time period.[11] Between 1820 and 1921, when Congress passed the first quota act to restrict immigration, the European immigrants "came in a series of gigantic waves, each more powerful than the last and separated one from another only by short periods of time."[12]

The first wave began soon after the end of the Napoleonic Wars and peaked just before the Civil War and at the time was described as "one of the wonders of the age."[13] Over 5 million immigrants arrived, numbering more than "the entire population of the United States at the time of the first census in 1790."[14] The overwhelming majority were from western and northern Europe. Over half were from the British Isles; 2 million were from Ireland and another three-quarter million were from England and Wales. Germany contributed another million and a half immigrants, including 200,000 German-speaking people from Alsace and Lorraine who were listed as French citizens. Switzerland, Norway and Sweden each contributed 40,000 people, and another 20,000 arrived from the Netherlands.[15]

The underlying reasons for this massive movement of people are complex and differ in the various parts of Europe. For example, economic change was a factor in Ireland, while religious factors were important in Norway, Holland, and Prussia and among Mormon converts from Great Britain and Scandinavia. In addition to contrasting factors among groups and personal idiosyncrasies among individuals, there are also a number of social and economic factors that underlay the movement as a whole and that gave it most of its impetus:

1. A population explosion in Europe due to better health practices and an increased food supply
2. The growth of the factory system in Europe that displaced artisans and made workers vulnerable to unemployment cycles
3. The shift from a medieval communal system of agriculture to large-scale production that freed serfs and peasants from the land
4. Political and religious discontent
5. A heightened awareness of America as a land of opportunity
6. The removal of legal restrictions on emigration and the development of inexpensive ocean transportation.[16]

As a whole, immigrants into the United States have been characterized as individuals or families who relied on their own strength and resources. They were self-directed, unassisted, and therefore free to determine their own destiny within the constraints most would face in the "New World." The types of people varied greatly over time and country of origin. The Irish immigrant experience illustrates this diversity and corrects a common misconception of the wholly impoverished immigrant. (It would be more accurate to see them as people who feared a future loss of security or status.)[17] Prior to 1830, the majority of Irish immigrants were small farmers burdened by intolerable rents, tithes, and taxes. After 1830 there was a steady flow of laborers and evicted tenant farmers; typically, the younger and most able-bodied family members were sent to the United States "in the confident hope, which only rarely was disappointed," that money would be sent back to Ireland to finance the voyage of remaining family members to the United States.[18]

> While the number of departures steadily increased throughout the 1830s and early 1840s, it was not until the Great Famine that the floodgates finally opened and the exodus attained epic proportions. The successive potato blights of 1845–49, leading as they did to untold deaths from starvation and fever and to appalling physical suffering even for those who survived, were a catastrophe which finally broke the Irish peasant's tenacious attachment to the soil and convinced many of the futility of further struggle against hopeless odds. . . . the famine had reversed the peasant's former attitude to emigration; hitherto considered a banishment, it now came to be regarded as a happy release. The prevailing mood of despair gripped not only the laborer and the [tenant farmer] but even those who [were] substantial farmers. Thus all classes were represented in the million and a half people who left Ireland in the decade that followed.[19]

The second wave of European immigrants entered the United States during the decades of industrialization following the Civil War. They continued to come primarily from northern and western Europe. Beginning in the 1880s, the number of immigrants from southern and eastern Europe began to increase. The third wave lasted from 1890 until 1914, when 15 million new immigrants entered the United States, primarily from Austria-Hungary, Italy, Russia (including Poland), Greece, Rumania, and Turkey.[20] Over 2.5 million were Jews from Russia and Eastern Europe and nearly 4 million were from southern Italy.[21]

The "new" immigrant group was as diverse in terms of motivations and socioeconomic background as the previous groups of "old" immigrants, although their "great variety of contrasting types" has been overlooked.[22] However, the vast majority of immigrants from southern and eastern Europe were culturally very different from the English and Scots who had established the English colonies and from the first two waves of immigrants from northern and western Europe. Indeed, their arrival triggered legislation to restrict immigration on "racial grounds." People from southern and eastern Europe were described by the U.S. Immigration Commission to be "incapable of assimilation and were even biologically inferior to the Nordic stock out of western and Northern Europe."[23]

Distinct geographic patterns of settlement emerged among European immigrants, sometimes in an attempt to preserve ethnic distinctions, and to some degree will persist into the twenty-first century. Typically, immigrants would settle in areas where they could use the skills they brought with them from Europe.

The Irish were an exception; although most had been country dwellers, they rejected farming and country life and settled overwhelmingly in the cities. Nearly two-thirds of the Irish settled in New York, Pennsylvania, New Jersey, and New England. Few Germans settled in New England and over half settled in "the upper Mississippi and Ohio valleys, especially in the states of Ohio, Illinois, Wisconsin, and Missouri,"[24] but there were also large numbers in New York, New Jersey, and Pennsylvania. Norwegians, Swedes, and Danes were heavily concentrated in Minnesota, Illinois, Wisconsin, the Dakotas, and the state of Washington.[25] Nearly two-thirds of the Dutch settled in Michigan, New York, Wisconsin, and Iowa, while the Finnish were concentrated in Michigan, Minnesota, and Massachusetts.[26]

Ethnic pluralism characterized U.S. society throughout this period of massive immigration and the first generations of settlement. Many ethnic communities were named after European towns, and their schools, churches, and newspapers were patterned after European models. The German communities of the Midwest in the latter half of the nineteenth century illustrate this healthy state of ethnic pluralism as it was manifested in bilingual education.

> The Germans were afforded the most extensive programs of bilingual education in the history of the country. The public school districts in cities within the so-called German Triangle, Cincinnati, St. Louis, Milwaukee, Chicago, Indianapolis, and others, also developed formal offices of German instruction to supervise the programs. . . . In some school districts, as much as 70 percent of the school population took some of their instruction in German as late as 1916. This situation persisted until the beginning of World War I, when anti-German sentiment made German study unpopular.[27]

With the rise of anti-German sentiment in the twentieth century, German community support for separate schools, churches, and civic organizations declined. In the face of heightened prejudice, threats of violence, and discrimination, many German Americans made the choice to disappear through greater cultural assimilation.

Assimilation in the Face of Prejudice and Discrimination

Of all the European immigrants to the United States, the 3 million English immigrants assimilated most swiftly. Job mobility was easy for skilled workers from textile, mining, and manufacturing industries. Eventually displaced by machines or later immigrant groups, many English American workers moved up into managerial and technical positions. As a group they were spared the poverty, language differences, hostility, and discrimination experienced by most other European immigrants.

With the exception of the British immigrants, virtually all the immigrants from Europe experienced harsh prejudice and discrimination after settling in the United States. The Irish and Italians provide examples from the "old" and "new" immigrants, respectively.

The school has been an agent of assimilation for the children of many European immigrant families in the United States.

Irish Americans suffered verbal abuse, stereotyping, intentional discrimination and violent attacks from the time of their arrival in North America.[28] Much of the violence has been directed at Irish Catholics, and

> By 1850 most large cities had seen anti-Catholic demonstrations and riots. Philadelphia became a center for anti-Irish Catholic violence. There, in 1844, two major riots "resulted in the burning of two Catholic churches . . . ; the destruction of dozens of Catholic homes; and sixteen deaths." In the 1850s Protestant nativist groups such as the Know-Nothings played a major role in attacks on Irish Americans.[29]

Resistance to Irish immigration is also evident in nineteenth-century literature, cartoons, and theater. The Irish were stereotyped as immoral, lazy, violent, and mentally inferior. Influential journals such as *Harpers' Weekly* dehumanized the Irish through apelike images that portrayed the poor Irish as the "missing link" between humans and the gorilla.[30]

By the end of the nineteenth century, immigrants from eastern and southern Europe, such as the Italians and Slavs, were the new targets of stereotypes and violence. There were myths about disease, illiteracy, and intellectual inferiority. "Popular writers, scholars, and members of congress warned of the peril of allowing inferior stocks from Europe into the United States."[31]

As early as the 1870s, Italians had been stereotyped as criminals, and the Mafia myth has persisted into the 1990s.[32] Films and prime-time television often reinforce the image of Italians as gangsters and hoods. Like all stereotypes, there is a grain of truth to these images, for example, the increased involvement of Italians in organized crime during prohibition. Yet crime-rate statistics among the Italian-born were lower than for English and Welsh foreign-born in 1910 and were about the same as for all native-born Americans in the 1920s and 1930s. Only a very small percentage of Italians are currently involved in organized crime, which is being taken over by more recent groups from Asia, Latin America, and Russia.[33]

Like the Irish before them, the Italians have also been the victims of violence. For example, they have been lynched at the hands of vigilante mobs for violating racial taboos in the South and they have been executed in "the midst of hysteria over left-wing un-American activities."[34]

Advocates of the melting-pot theory often use examples of White ethnic groups, such as the Irish, to support their assimilationist position. Indeed, the Irish have moved up the socioeconomic ladder and are strong influences in our nation's political and economic spheres. While assimilationists would argue that Irish ethnic identity among Irish Americans is fading, pluralists would look for signs of cultural retention and a spirit of ethnic identity.

Feagin offers valuable insights into the assimilation of the Irish, along with evidence that there is still an Irish ethnic group to be recognized.[35]

> While Irish Protestants seemed to have begun blending in relatively early, for Irish Catholics, because of nativistic attacks and discrimination, ethnic identity was less voluntary in the first few decades than it was to become later. In the beginning the Irish Catholic group, concentrated in the cities, had a cultural heritage which was distinctly different from that of the British-dominated host culture; yet there were some modest similarities in language and customs. Over several generations of sometimes conflictual interaction the Irish adapted substantially to the host society. Yet in this interaction process was created a distinctive Irish ethnic group which reflected elements both of its nationality background and of the host culture revised to fit the subordinate situation of the Irish.
>
> This Irish Catholic group changed over several generations of contact with the public school system and mass media, but it also retained enough distinctiveness from its nationality heritage and its experience as a subordinate group in the nineteenth century to persist as a distinctive ethnic group for many decades, even into the last third of the twentieth century. With future assimilation it may be that this distinctiveness will come to be more in the area of behavior and less in the areas of ethnic identity and sense of one's ethnic heritage. Thus the Irish seem to be moving at cultural, structural, and marital levels in the direction of the core society. But the Irish remain. It is useful to distinguish here between ethnic identity and ethnic impact. Ethnic identity for the Irish, the sense of the past, may be weakening, while the impact of the Irish background on Irish behavior is still obviously strong.
>
> Indeed, an example of the persistence of Irish ethnicity, even of distinctive ethnic communities, and its positive and negative functions, can be seen in the desegregation struggle which took place in Boston in the mid-1970s. There a working-class and lower-middle-class Irish community, South Boston, was involved in a judge's school desegregation plan; the plan was vigorously, even vio-

lently, opposed by the Irish. As one reporter noted: "Antibusing demonstrators, wearing tam-oshanter hats in the neighborhood high school colors, have broken up rallies of women's groups and dogged Senator Edward M. Kennedy's appearances. The usually jovial St. Patrick's Day parade was a procession of antibusing floats." This is more than a legal desegregation struggle. Different views of schooling and of urban communities are reflected in the controversy; the South Boston Irish see the schools as a socializing force, reinforcing traditional family and community values, whereas frequently blacks and suburban, Protestant whites now view them as avenues of upward mobility for nonwhite minorities. Irish resistance to the racial desegregation of central city neighborhoods is based in part on protecting one's own ethnic community against all intruders, whoever they may be.[36]

Italian Americans are another example of a White ethnic group that has overcome initial prejudice, discrimination, and violence and has moved upward into the higher economic and political spheres of the host society. Even though the social mobility of Italian Americans over the past few generations makes them an American "success story," they have not been completely assimilated into the dominant culture. Many "have remained enmeshed in kinship-friendship networks predominantly composed of other Italian Americans,"[37] and most prefer Italian American neighborhoods and marry within the Italian American community. Non-Italian marriage partners tend to be from other Catholic groups—Irish, German, or Eastern European. According to Feagin,

> Italians came to the United States with significant differences from the dominant British group, but they at least shared some European historical background and a Christian tradition with that group. By virtue of interaction in the public schools and the influence of the mass media, the linguistic and custom gap narrowed substantially, but by no means completely. Nationality characteristics, the immigrant heritage, have had a persistent impact. Italian Americans became in some ways similar to members of the host culture, but in other ways they retained their distinctiveness. Over time, because of their heritage, together with segregation and strong community and kinship networks, a distinctive American ethnic group was spawned. In the complex adaptation process an Italian American group was formed, distinctive in terms of both certain persisting nationality characteristics and unique experiences in the United States. No longer an Italy-centered group dominated by its heritage, neither has it simply become British Protestant American or simply American. Substantial adaptation without complete assimilation at a number of levels characterizes Italian Americans. The third and fourth generations appear to retain a great deal of Italian Americanness, in their commitment to the family and Italian community. Particularly for working-class Italian Americans there is still a rich family community life in the 1970s.[38]

Feagin and Feagin's most recent work indicates that this sense of an Italian American community persists in the 1990s.[39]

Jewish Americans

Jewish Americans are unique among European American immigrants in that their sense of peoplehood was not linked to a nationality. The Jews are unified by religion and tradition rather than by national origins. Jews are descendants of the Hebrews, a people who in ancient times lived in what is now Israel and its immediate environs. After the Roman Empire conquered their homeland in A.D. 70, Jews were eventually scattered all over the world (although mainly across Europe and the Mediterranean), where they remained a minority wherever they lived.

Origins: Roots of Diversity and Community

Individual Jews were among the earliest settlers who came to the Atlantic coast colonies in the 1600s. The first group of Jewish immigrants who came to America were Sephardic, coming primarily from Spain and Portugal in the 1700s. Prior to the Spanish Inquisition, Sephardic Jews in Spain enjoyed more freedom and attained greater positions of wealth and power than Jews anywhere else in Europe. Many owned large landed estates and were important political figures, bankers, and industrialists. Jewish wealth, in fact, was used to help finance the explorations of Columbus. Conditions changed suddenly in 1492 when Ferdinand and Isabella decreed that Jews either convert to Christianity or be expelled. Some Jews pretended to convert, remained in Spain, and practiced their faith in secret. Others fled to the eastern Mediterranean, and still others came to the American colonies, which were known for greater religious freedom.

The stream of German Jews began soon after the arrival of Sephardic Jews. Quickly, the German Jews came to predominate within the Jewish American population, which grew from approximately 3,000 at the time of the American Revolution to over a half million by 1880.[40] Differences existed between Sephardic and German Jews, and those differences are still evident today. According to Thomas Sowell, Sephardic Jews tended to emphasize business over scholarship. Drawing upon their expertise developed in Spain, most recovered from their earlier financial losses and were economically prosperous by the time the war broke out. Furthermore, they tended to look down on other Jews who were not of Sephardic origins, particularly the German Jewish immigrants.[41]

German Jews differed from later Jewish immigrants in that they did not settle in concentrated Jewish communities. Instead they spread out across the nation, working as "small tradesmen and professionals scattered among their non-Jewish clientele."[42] By the time the third wave of Jewish immigrants began in the 1880s (escapees from persecution in Russia), German Jews had become well established.

> The German Jews were active, not only in their own communities but also in American society at large as businessmen and bankers. . . . Many Jews were destined to play important roles in developing such major American institutions as Macy's Department Store chain, Sears Roebuck, and the *New York Times*. As of 1880, 40 percent of all German-Jewish families had at least one servant. Only 1 percent of the heads of Jewish families were still peddlers, and fewer than 1 percent worked as laborers or domestic servants.[43]

The third (and largest) group of Jewish immigrants came from Eastern Europe, particularly from Russia, where Jews were the victims of Russification and of peasant massacres called *pogroms*. Between 1880 and World War I, approximately 2 million Jews fled to the United States. Sowell writes that their arrival was an acute embarrassment to the German Jews in America.

> The size of the eastern European Jewish immigration swamped the existing American Jewish community of largely German origin. The eastern European Jews were also heavily concentrated in New York City and, in fact, were even more localized on the lower east side of Manhattan, which contained the largest number of Jews ever assembled in one place on earth in thousands of years. The German Jews already established in America were appalled not only by the numbers but also by the way of life of the eastern European Jews. The eastern Jews were not only poorer—most arrived destitute, with less money than any other immigrant group—but were also far less educated (a 50 percent illiteracy rate), and with rougher manners than the more sophisticated and Americanized German Jews. Eastern European Jews had lived a provincial life, outside the mainstream of the general European culture in which German Jews were immersed. Eastern Europeans even looked different—earlocks, skull caps, beards, old-fashioned Russian-style clothing, scarves about the women's heads, and a general demeanor reminiscent of a painful past that German Jews had long ago left behind. The Orthodox Jewish religious services were full of traditions and practices long abandoned by the modern Reform Judaism of Germans. The very language of the eastern European Jews—Yiddish—was a folk dialect disdained by more educated Jews, who used either the language of the country or classical Hebrew.[44]

At times the Jewish philanthropic tradition overcame these negative attitudes, however. "German Jewish organizations made strenuous efforts to aid, and especially to Americanize, the eastern Jewish immigrants. Schools, libraries, hospitals, and community centers were established to serve 'downtown' Jews, financed by 'uptown' Jews."[45] However, the lines of distinction between German Jews and Eastern European Jews remained visible.

Most Eastern European Jewish immigrants did manual work, particularly in the garment industries, where they met the demands for cheap labor in the notorious sweatshops. These Jews lived in crowded, filthy slums that averaged more than 700 people per acre and were infected with tuberculosis and other diseases. Because of their religious orthodoxy, Jews from Eastern Europe lived and worked in close proximity with other Jews to satisfy their need for kosher food, a synagogue, and recognition of the Sabbath (many non-Jewish businesses and factories operated on Saturdays). Thus there were large concentrations of Jews in New York, Chicago, and Philadelphia.

The Jewish American community today reflects both the unity and diversity of its origins in Europe and the Mediterranean. As a group, Jewish Americans have a tradition of humanitarianism, commitment to civil rights issues for all peoples, and political support for most liberal candidates. In contrast to some other groups, most Jewish Americans have not become more conservative as they moved up the socioeconomic ladder. Many Jews were active in the civil rights movement of the 1960s and in protests against the Vietnam War. Jews are noted for their support of the Anti-Defamation League and numerous other civil rights organizations. On the other hand, friction has recently developed between portions of the Jewish and African American communities over issues such as Israel and Zionism, inner-city reforms, and affirmative-action programs. Jews also differ among themselves on the issue of Zionism (support of modern Israel) and Arab-Israeli relations.

The Jewish religion remains a major source of diversity among Jews, as well as the major source of identity for Jews as a distinct ethnic group. The major religious movements (Orthodox, Conservative, and Reform) differ sharply in their degree of adaptation to the non-Jewish dominant culture, and there are secular Jews who maintain their Jewish identity even though they do not accept any form of religious Judaism. This becomes a more complex issue because, for many Jews, Judaism is the essence of being Jewish.

Although differences exist within each response, retention of the original Jewish faith and tradition is strongest among the Orthodox Jews and weakest among Reform Jews. Conservative Judaism developed in the nineteenth century as an attempt to balance the Reform movement, which many Jews thought had become too secular. The numerical strength of these different responses is difficult to establish, but it seems that Orthodox Judaism is the smallest group in the United States.

Among Orthodox Jews the Sabbath is kept from sundown on Friday until sundown on Saturday. Religious services are in Hebrew and daily prayers are said in the morning, late afternoon, and after sunset. Dietary rules are strictly observed; for example, neither pork nor shellfish is eaten, and milk and meat are not consumed at the same meal. Only kosher food, that prepared in accordance with Jewish law, may be eaten. For example, meat may be eaten only if it comes from a healthy animal that has been killed quickly and painlessly.

Religious services among Reform and Conservative Jews contain much more English than do traditional Orthodox services. Men and women worship together, and organ music may be part of the service. Conservative Jews generally observe Jewish dietary laws in all public functions of the synagogue, while they may or may not keep a kosher kitchen at home. Reform Jews are least likely to keep kosher, are more likely to attend a synagogue or "temple" only on high holidays (Rosh Hashanah and Yom Kippur), and are more likely to marry non-Jews than are Orthodox or Conservative Jews.

Although Jewish Americans represent an economically prosperous group and although Judaism has become partially Americanized, Jewish Americans have not been accepted into the Anglo-Saxon core. Writing in the late 1970s, Feagin stated that anti-Semitism, or discrimination against Jews, was still a factor in the United States.

> From the late nineteenth century onward Jewish Americans have been excluded from hotels, restaurants, social clubs, voluntary associations, and housing. Such discrimination has persisted into the 1960s and 1970s. Thus the social ties of Jewish Americans have been firmly cemented together, at least partially, for defensive reasons. The Jewish community and the extended Jewish family—one can underscore this point—have provided the critical defensive context for survival in the face of anti-Semitism. The "Jewish mother" stereotypes have a nucleus of truth in the vigorous protective actions taken by Jewish mothers—and fathers—in

defending their children from the onslaughts of non-Jews. Even in recent decades Jewish families have remained cohesive bastions of defense for their members.

Consequently, in recent decades the intermarriage rate has not been as high as some analysts have predicted, given the high level of acculturation of Jewish Americans.[46]

In the 1990s, Feagin and Feagin found persisting anti-Semitism in the United States and a strong sense of ethnic identity among Jewish Americans.[47]

Accommodation in the Face of Anti-Semitism

Despite long centuries of political fragmentation and persecution, Jews have kept alive their religion and cultural traditions. Judaism is one of the world's oldest religions and was the first to teach the existence of one God, giving birth to both Christianity and Islam. Jews were persecuted along with the early Christians prior to the Christianization of the Roman Empire. During the Middle Ages, Renaissance, and Enlightenment, they were attacked as heretics by Christians and have been the victims of scapegoating and discrimination up to the present. Of the estimated 14 to 20 million people killed by the Nazis in World War II concentration camps, at least 6 million were Jews. The Holocaust exterminated three-fifths of the Jewish population in Europe; approximately 1.5 million of the victims were Jewish children. Because Jews maintained their own religion, language, and traditions and lived in segregated communities or ghettos, they became "a marked people—natural targets for whatever passions or fears might sweep over an ignorant and superstitious population."[48] Furthermore, because Jews were typically barred from owning land, they often worked as middlemen, particularly money lenders, tax collectors, and small businessmen, performing the economic functions that "are almost universally unpopular around the world," as seen in the case of the Chinese in Southeast Asia, the East Indians in Uganda, and the Ibos in Nigeria.[49]

Restrictions on Jews were most relaxed in Western Europe, and many Jews began to assimilate to some degree into their host society. In Western Europe Jews could retain the Jewish religion and still be perceived as French, German, or English. What became Germany was one of the most liberal areas toward Jews, and it was there in the early 1800s that Reform Judaism originated. National policies toward Jews were more restrictive in Russia and Eastern Europe, and most Jews there remained Orthodox.

Contrary to popular myths and stereotypes of wealthy Jews in control of U.S. finance, business, and industry, the Jewish community contains sharp socioeconomic differences. It is true that as a group Jewish Americans show the highest family income index of any major ethnic group in this society.[50] However, it is also estimated that out of a population of about 6 million, over half a million Jewish Americans are below the nation's poverty level. While the percentage of Jews on college and university faculties and in other professions is much higher than their 2.6+ percent of the U.S. population, very few occupy top executive positions or positions of political power. The widely held belief that Jews control the nation's business, banking, and finance is a misconception.

Most Jewish Americans fall into middle-income categories that include middle-management jobs and small business.[51]

According to annual reports published by the Anti-Defamation League (ADL), blatant acts of anti-Semitism, such as arson attempts and vandalism of Jewish tombstones or synagogues, are on the increase. "A record 1,897 incidents were reported for 1991—up 11 percent over 1990. The 1991 incidents included 950 attacks on individuals and 49 acts of vandalism against Jewish-owned property (arson, bombings, and cemetery desecrations). Among these incidents, 101 occurred at sixty college campuses."[52] According to a 1996 Audit of Anti-Semitic Incidents,

- In 1996, the total number of anti-Semitic incidents reported to the Anti-Defamation League—including acts against both property and persons—was 1,722. This total, comprising reports from 41 states (9 states reported none), the District of Columbia and the U.S. Virgin Islands, represents a decrease of 121 incidents, or 7 percent, from the 1995 total of 1,843. The 1995 total, in turn, represented an 11 percent decline from 1994. This two-year drop is the first multi-year decline in 10 years. Since the all-time high of 2,066 recorded in 1994, anti-Semitic incidents are down 17 percent.

- Unlike previous years, when the number of harassment and vandalism incidents essentially moved in tandem (both would rise or fall), there was a rise in incidents of anti-Semitic vandalism and a decline in acts of harassment in 1996. This decline in harassment incidents accounts for the overall drop in anti-Semitic acts. The 781 incidents of anti-Semitic vandalism occurring in 1996 represent an increase of 54 incidents, or a 7 percent increase. In contrast, only 941 incidents of harassment occurred, a decline of 175, or 16 percent.

- For the sixth straight year, acts of anti-Semitic harassment outnumber incidents of vandalism. The 941 incidents of harassment, threat or assault represent 55 percent of the total number of incidents. Of these, 733 incidents were directed against individuals, as opposed to institutions, continuing the troubling predominance of such "in your face" attacks. (The remaining 208 harassment incidents were directed against institutions, e.g., threatening phone calls to a Jewish community center or hate mail sent to a synagogue.)[52a]

A Jewish American perspective emerges out of this array of past experiences, beliefs, and opinions. All Jewish Americans are influenced by the challenge of living within a culture that is predominantly Christian. As part of a worldwide Jewish community, Jewish Americans are influenced by a long history of discrimination, which was experienced most recently in the horror of the Holocaust. They are influenced by the existence of Jewish communities in the modern state of Israel and elsewhere, such as the former Soviet Union. These influences help to unify Jewish Americans despite their individual and group differences.

■ *African Americans*

Today, African Americans comprise 12 percent of the population of the United States. Prior to the massive emigration of peoples from Europe, they made up one-fifth of the population. Throughout nearly four centuries of U.S. history,

African Americans have been critically important to the nation's commercial and industrial growth. While all immigrants groups have contributed hard labor to build the nation, African Americans, involuntary immigrants who arrived in chains, are an exception in that they could not reap the benefits of their labor for themselves and their families.

Opposition and Liberation Amidst the Legacy of Slavery

African American history and the national experience can be visualized according to three watersheds: First was slavery, beginning with capture and forced migration from Africa, followed by nearly 150 years of bondage; next was emancipation, followed by another 50 years of tenant farming and economic exploitation under the conditions of sharecropping; and thrid was the great migration north in the first half of the twentieth century that created contemporary Black urban communities and a second emancipation, the Civil Rights Movement of the 1950s and 1960s.[53] The themes of opposition and liberation provide a lens for the following brief overviews of these three periods.

Phase One: Enslavement

It is estimated that over 100 million Black Africans were either killed or transported to the Americas between 1502 when the slave trade began and its actual end in the 1860s.[54] When the legal slave trade ended in 1801, over 400,000 Africans had been forced into slavery in North America and another 10 to 50 million were forcibly transported to South America and the Caribbean.[55] By 1860 the African American population in the United States had grown from 400,000 to more than 4 million, with the majority being born into slavery.[56]

Slaves in the United States were the personal property of their masters. They were in absolute bondage for life and were denied the rights of property and all other civil and legal rights and could hold property only at the will and pleasure of the master.[57] Slaves could neither give nor receive gifts; could make no will, nor, by will, inherit anything. They could not enter contracts for work or for matrimony and "could buy or sell nothing at all, except as (the) master's agent, could keep no cattle, horses, hogs, or sheep and (in some states) could raise no cotton."[58] They were also denied the civic privileges of education and worship. "Every Southern State except Maryland and Kentucky had stringent laws forbidding anyone to teach slaves reading and writing, and in some states the penalties applied to the educating of free Negroes and mulattos as well."[59]

Most historians agree that the earliest Africans who came to the English colonies were indentured servants and, like indentured servants from Europe, gained their freedom after a fixed number of years.[60] (It is also widely agreed that Africans explored and settled in other regions of the Americas prior to the slave trade.) Children of these Black servants were automatically free from birth. The number of free persons of color who acquired this status because they were never slaves was strengthened by African Americans who were freed or escaped slavery prior to the Civil War. Once the concept of chattel slavery evolved in the late 1600s, slaves became property for life and passed the legacy on to their children. Freedom could be attained, however, through voluntary manumission by slave owners, escape, self-purchase, purchase by already free relatives or philanthropic Whites, or through special legislation as a reward for unusual service to the community.[61] Mulatto children of White mothers were also automatically free from birth. Between 10 and 14 percent of the African American population in the United States was free prior to the Civil War.

The status of free African Americans during colonial days and the early 1800s was precarious at best, particularly in the South. Free Blacks could be kidnapped and sold into slavery, especially after the Fugitive Slave law was passed in 1850. Free people of color were denied voting rights, were excluded from the militia and from carrying U.S. mail, and were permitted to bear arms only if they could obtain a permit. Free Blacks could, however, own real estate and some attained great wealth. A Black elite developed in the lower South, for example, where African Americans (formerly subjects of France and Spain) had more legal and customary rights than elsewhere in the South. In the state of Louisiana there developed a large group of prosperous free Black planters, as well as a highly educated free Black elite.[62] Furthermore, in Louisiana free Blacks traveled freely and could testify in court.

Slave life has been revealed in slave autobiographies, numerous history texts, and recent films such as Alex Haley's *Roots, Queen,* and *Amistad.*[63] Scholars have argued about the degree to which slavery was a "paternalistic" system (wherein White masters rationalized slavery in terms of "Christianizing" and caring for the slaves), the degree to which slaves resisted their oppressors, and the degree to which carry-overs from African cultures have survived and influenced African American culture today. The most widely accepted view among scholars today is:

> [In] the face of physical torture and white attempts to eradicate their cultures, the many peoples of Africa among the slaves . . . became a single African American people and forged their own oppositional culture, an African American culture. Drawing on deep African spiritual roots, these new Americans shaped their own religion, their own art and music, their distinctive versions of Afro-English, and their own philosophical and political thinking about racial oppression, liberation and social justice. In the colonies and later in the United States the pressures on black Americans to conform to the white core culture forced them to become bi-cultural, to know both the dominant Euro-American culture and their own culture as well. Since the days of slavery there has been a centuries-long struggle for the maintenance of this oppositional culture, a culture part African and part an African American adaptation to the concrete history of white oppression. This culture has provided the foundation of active black resistance to oppression since the seventeenth century.[64]

The struggle to maintain an African American oppositional culture is described by Roger D. Abrahams, a preeminent scholar of African American culture, in his study of the corn-shucking celebrations throughout the South prior to the Civil War.[65] Originating in the English custom of harvest home, the corn-shucking harvest ceremony became an important autumn event. "It was regarded as a slaves' holiday, one which called for the field workers to enter freely into a work party as a prelude to a feast and a dance."[66] The master would have immense quantities of corn hauled up to the crib, often heaped as high as a house. Slaves would gather from miles around, select two leaders or generals, and choose up two sides. The teams would then compete to see who could shuck the most corn the fastest, amid singing and shouting. An extravagant feast was provided by the master, followed up with dancing that lasted most of the night.

In his study of this particular event, Abrahams sees the corn-shucking ceremony as being

> characteristic of a dynamic process taking place on the plantation in which the slaves neither divested themselves of their African cultural heritage nor acculturated to the behaviors and performance pattern of their masters. To the contrary, the hands were encouraged to act and perform differently. The practices emerged as forms of active resistance, not in the sense that they attacked the system but rather in the ways in which they maintained alternative perspectives toward time, work, and status.[67]

The owners and their families and guests observed the slave dances from the big house verandah. Over time these events became an important source of enjoyment for the White ruling elite. As the slave dancers engaged in the performance and self-expression, they transformed the event into one of social and moral mockery. Meanwhile their masters were oblivious to the hidden meanings and ridicule directed at them. Abrahams explains how later the dances developed into the minstrel and vaudeville shows and influenced White culture as well as African American performance style today (e.g., the subversive treatment of authority and interplay with the audience).

Phase Two: Emancipation, Sharecropping, and Tenancy

The decade of Reconstruction following the civil war was a period of hope for African Americans. The former slaves, nearly 200,000 of whom had fought for the union military (37,000 died), held high expectations for their freedom. They sought independence from White control.[68] A top priority was ownership of land, and the right to determine the use of their own labor, as a basis for control over their family life. Some made Herculean efforts to be reunited with family members, with thousands advertising in the Black press for lost loved ones.[69] They consolidated the network of churches, schools, and mutual aid societies that had been forged during slavery, a "semi autonomous culture centered on family and church."[70] They withdrew from White-controlled churches and developed independent Black Churches, especially Methodist and Baptist.

> The church played a central role in the Black community; a place of worship, it also housed schools, social events, and political gatherings, and sponsored many of the fraternal and benevolent societies that sprang up during Reconstruction. Inevitably, black ministers came to play a major role in politics. More than 200 held public office during Reconstruction.[71]

Self sufficiency and community improvement were also evident in their "thirst for education."

> Before the war, every Southern state except Tennessee had prohibited the instruction of slaves. Now, adults as well as children thronged the schools established during and after the Civil War. Northern benevolent societies, the Freedman's Bureau, and, after 1868, state governments, provided most of the funding for black education during Reconstruction but the initiative often lay with African-Americans, who pooled their meager resources and voluntarily taxed themselves to purchase land, construct buildings, and hire teachers."[72]

The Reconstruction Act of 1867 gave Black men in the South the right to vote; three years later the 15th Amendment was ratified, outlawing voter discrimination based on race (gender discrimination was outlawed in 1920). Over 1,500 African Americans were elected to political office in the Reconstruction South, although nowhere was their political representation proportionate with the total population.[73] For the first time in American history there was a biracial government, and it

> functioned effectively in many parts of the South. Public facilities were rebuilt and expanded, school systems established, and legal codes purged of racism. The conservative oligarchy that had dominated Southern governments from colonial times to 1867 found itself largely excluded from political power, while those who had previously been outsiders—poorer white Southerners, men from the North, and especially former slaves—cast ballots, sat on juries, and enacted and administered laws. (One Northern correspondent reported in 1873) "One hardly realizes the fact that the many Negroes one sees here . . . have been slaves a few short years ago, at least as far as their demeanor goes as individuals newly invested with all the rights and privileges of an American citizen."[74]

What went wrong? Most historians agree that the failure of Reconstruction lies in the lack of land distribution reform. African Americans gained civil rights and political rights through the 14th and 15th Amendments, but proposals for land distribution legislation were rejected by Congress. Although they were no longer slaves, they became sharecroppers, "working the land of their former master in exchange for part of the crop. Forced to buy goods from the planter's store, they were trapped in a vicious economic cycle, making barely enough to pay off their debts."[75] Thomas Fortune, an editor of the New York *Globe*, testified before a Senate committee in 1883 about "widespread poverty" and government betrayal.[76] A Negro farm laborer in the South was usually

> paid in "orders," not money, which he could only use at a store controlled by the planter, "a system of fraud." The Negro farmer, to get the wherewithal to plant his crop, had to promise it to the store, and when everything was added up at the end of the year he was in debt, so his crop was constantly owed to someone, and he was tied to the land, with the records kept by the planter and storekeeper so that the Negroes "are swindled and kept forever in debt."[77]

Sharecropping and tenancy became firmly entrenched during the post–Civil War years, trapping both Blacks and many Whites in a system that lasted until pressures initiated by two world wars and the New Deal initiated its demise.

The long post-emancipation period of sharecropping and tenancy was a time of lynching, race riots, Jim Crow legislation, and the rise of terrorist groups such as the Ku Klux Klan. Lynching became a way for vigilante mobs to keep African Americans (as well as sympathetic Whites) "in their place" after the Civil War and Reconstruction. Recorded lynchings show that nearly 3,500 African Americans were lynched between 1882 and 1951, but actual lynchings are believed to be over 6,000.[78] Most of the lynchings were carried out in southern states, but in the North there were race riots, led by Whites against Blacks, at the end of World War I, as well as other forms of White violence and oppression. The 1920s saw a rebirth of the Ku Klux Klan. Its focus was Christian morality versus sin.

> The enemies of America, the Klan proclaimed, were booze, loose women, Jews, Negroes, Roman Catholics (whose "dago pope was bent on taking over the U.S."), and anybody else who was not a native-born white Protestant Anglo-Saxon. Many churchmen across the nation acclaimed the Klan's program, and in the south especially, Methodist and Baptist clergymen lent the K.K.K. massive support. It was not long before it blossomed into a mighty nationwide organization that claimed to number in its hooded ranks about 4,000,000 members.[79]

Some of the most blatant evidence against the melting-pot myth is the oppression of African Americans under slavery and later under the Jim Crow laws, which legalized the separation of Blacks and Whites. Separate but equal facilities for Blacks became the law of the land, although separate facilities were rarely (if ever) equal. An extreme dual system pervaded all aspects of life in the American South. Jim Crow laws were passed to keep "coloreds" separate from Whites in schools, public transportation, restaurants, theaters, baseball fields, public bathrooms, swimming pools, doctors' offices, and so on. Many courtrooms had separate Bibles for giving oaths. Intermarriage was illegal in thirty-eight of the forty-eight states until the mid-twentieth century, and Blacks were denied their right to vote through grandfather clauses, poll taxes, and outrageous literacy tests until voting rights legislation was passed between 1964 and 1970.

Phase Three: Northern Migration and a Second Emancipation

Most historians agree that the civil rights movement of the 1950s and 1960s is rooted in political and cultural changes that began with the migration north of African Americans during the first half of the twentieth century.[80] At the end of the Civil War, about 90 percent of the African American population lived in the southern states, primarily on farms. By the mid-twentieth century millions of African Americans had migrated north in search of a "promised land," and by 1960 only half of the Black population lived in rural areas, with only a tenth still working on farms.[81]

According to the historian, Thomas C. Holt,

> These demographic and economic changes laid the basis for the greatest political mobilization of black Americans since Reconstruction. Freed from the constraints

of the rural South, blacks began to organize in both formal and informal political arenas. In the North during the 1920s and in southern cities by the 1940s and 1950s, blacks organized once again to protest segregation, Jim Crow, and job discrimination. With the advent of the New Deal, blacks became an important factor in national politics, and federal executive and judicial policies reflected the change. These political changes, together with a greatly augmented black intelligentsia and the revival of racial liberalism in the aftermath of Nazism, were essential precursors to the southern civil rights movement that seemingly exploded full-blown in the 1950s. Before that movement had run its course, the face of southern institutions had been radically transformed: voting and holding office in unprecedented numbers, blacks decisively influenced presidential politics and enticed erstwhile foes, among them Governor George Wallace of Alabama, to recant their earlier racist views.[82]

While it is generally agreed that the urbanization of African Americans in the twentieth century was critical to the destruction of racial segregation in the South, scholars disagree on the personal impact of urbanization on African Americans. Some social scientists emphasize the negative impact on "Black peasants" who were ill prepared for urban life.[83] The author Richard Wright, in *12 Million Black Voices,* shares a perspective that could support the view that African Americans became victims in Northern Ghettos. Wright, who ran away from home in the delta country of Mississippi at age fifteen and worked his way up to Chicago, described the feelings of many African Americans who were part of the Great Migration—and their experiences once they arrived.[84]

> We see white men and women get on the train, dressed in expensive clothes. We look at them guardedly and wonder will they bother us. Will they ask us to sit down while they sit down? Will they tell us to go to the back of the coach? Even though we have been told that we need not be afraid, we have lived so long in fear of all white faces that we cannot help but sit and wait. We look around the train and we do not see the old familiar signs: FOR COLORED and FOR WHITE. . . .

Wright describes the mixed feelings of freedom and fear experienced by the migrants as they disembark in Chicago, Indianapolis, New York, Cleveland, Buffalo, Detroit, Toledo, Philadelphia, Pittsburgh, and Milwaukee. Encountering thousands and thousands of strangers, people in the North at first seem indifferent and distant, especially the "Bosses of the Buildings" who helped African Americans find jobs in the factories and foundries, as well as places to live in crowded and noisy apartments. The migrants soon discover that, far from feeling indifferent, these Bosses

> are deeply concerned about us but in a different way. It seems as if we are now living inside of a machine; days and events move with a hard reasoning of their own. We live amid swarms of people, yet there is a vast difference between people, a distance that words cannot bridge. No longer do our lives depend upon the soil, the sun, the rain, or the wind; we live by the grace of jobs and the brutal logic of jobs. In the South, life was different; men spoke to you, yelled at you, or killed you. The world moved by signs you knew. But here in the North cold forces hit you and push you. It is a world of things.[85]

In Chicago, for example, both Black and White migrants experienced a bewildering shortage of housing, which led to competition for available apartments. Wright describes the process of White fright and flight to the suburbs, followed by the conversion of vacated houses into apartments (called "kitchenettes") by the Bosses of the Buildings. As many as five or six persons would live in a one-room kitchenette.[86]

The kitchenette, with its "filth and foul air, with its one toilet for 30 or more tenants," is at the root of the high infant death rate; it is a seed bed for malnutrition and diseases such as scarlet fever, dysentery, typhoid, tuberculosis, and pneumonia; and is an arena for crimes against women and children, while bringing wealth to the Bosses of the Buildings.[87]

While perspectives such as Wright's provides insights into the origins of poverty and injustice in many of the nation's urban centers today, it is unfair to view African American migrants as mere victims. Many African American family histories include people and events connected with the Great Migration, histories laden with courageous individuals and fascinating events, as well as harrowing experiences with discrimination. Like other educators who use personal and family narratives in teaching, I have encountered numerous students with family migration stories worthy of becoming a novel or film, that focus on themes of love, escape, bravery, justice, and mystery, as well as experiences of incredible cruelty and meanness.

These family stories resonate in a recent study of the African American migration to Chicago, *Land of Hope* (1989).[88]

> Black southern migrants were bearers of a deeply ingrained and distinctive culture; from their southern experience a race-conscious world view emerged that informed both their choice to migrate and their responses to the urban environment-responses necessarily different from those of both northern-born blacks and white ethnic immigrants.[89]

Settlement and adjustment in the north was influenced by the migrants' southern communal and kinship networks, as in the "transfer almost intact of churches, barber shops, and other social institutions from specific southern communities;" and, "from the black perspective, class difference shaped social relations within the black community . . . while outside that community, race was the dominant variable."[90]

Throughout these decades, African Americans resisted postslavery oppression through political organizations, such as the National Association for the Advancement of Colored People (NAACP) and the Urban League, which were both organized in the first decade of the twentieth century. They have resisted with nonviolent civil disobedience, as in the bus boycotts, freedom rides, lunch counter sit-ins, and peaceful protest marches to end segregation during the civil rights movement of the 1960s. Dr. Martin Luther King, Jr., epitomized the hope of African Americans in his famous "I have a dream" speech before tens of thousands of demonstrators—both Black and White—during the March on Washington in August 1963. African Americans have also resisted oppression with violence, as in the riots in Los Angeles (Watts in 1965 and South Central Los Angeles in 1992), in Detroit (1967), and in Newark (1967). The 1960s

Mapping the roots of ethnic diversity in the United States.

were years of growing Black pride and Black community consciousness. The Black Power movement and the Nation of Islam ("Black Muslims") pressed for Black identity and Black self-help enterprises. A group of young African American men formed the Black Panthers, an organization to provide breakfast programs for school children and protection for the Black community against White police brutality, and a variety of other militant organizations aimed at Black nationalism and Black community support emerged.[91]

Themes of opposition and liberation are also expressed in African American literature, art, music, and film. The Harlem Renaissance was a period of vibrant creativity among African American writers and musicians during the 1920s.[92] Artists such as Romare Bearden and Jacob Lawrence have chronicled African American history, and Black film directors such as Spike Lee portray contemporary African American perspectives.[93]

Yet, despite decades of effort to end oppression, and despite genuine progress in the second half of the twentieth century, we still feel the sting of the nation's legacy of slavery.

> The spectacle of "slavery unwilling to die" can be seen today: informal barriers to voting continue in the South; most black children still attend de facto segregated schools; most black families live in segregated residential areas; most blacks in all income classes face informal discrimination by banks, real estate people, landlords, and homeowners; most black defendants are tried by juries in which black citizens are underrepresented if not absent; and most black workers face some discrimination in employment.[94]

Despite significant individual and cultural differences among African Americans, most are influenced by a "double-consciousness," an expression first used by W. E. B. DuBois in his pioneering sociological study, *Souls of Black Folk* to describe the experience of being Black in a White society. Most are influenced by feelings of Black solidarity born out of abhorrence of slavery and a hatred of subordination by White society that is passed from one generation to the next.

■ *Who Has Assimilated?*

Cultural pluralism can be visualized along a continuum with cultural assimilation at one end and cultural suppression at the other. There are degrees of assimilation and suppression, with cultural pluralism falling somewhere between the extremes. Figure 4.1 illustrates the continuum between theoretical extremes of total assimilation and total segregation. Box 4.1 lists characteristic responses among ethnic minority groups under conditions of assimilation, pluralism, and suppression in contrast with macrocultural responses.

The true test of assimilation is when members of an ethnic group experience the following conditions:

- Change of cultural patterns to those of the predominant society
- Large-scale entrance into cliques, clubs, and institutions of the predominant society on the primary group level
- Large-scale intermarriage
- Development of a sense of peoplehood based exclusively on the predominant society
- Absence of prejudice
- Absence of discrimination
- Absence of value and power conflict [95]

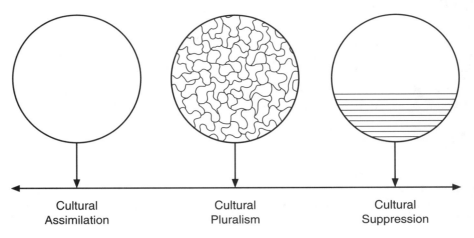

FIGURE 4.1
What Happens When Cultures Meet?

BOX 4.1

Assimilation

The ethnic minority group:

- Gives up its original culture
- Identifies with and is absorbed into the predominant Anglo-Western European culture
- Is no longer identifiable as distinct from the predominant Anglo-Western European culture

Pluralism

The ethnic minority group:

- Retains many of its traditions, such as language, religion, artistic expression, and social customs
- Adopts many aspects of the predominant Anglo-Western European culture such as language; monogamy; military service; local, state, and federal laws; and full rights of citizenship
- Develops an ethnic perspective and also identifies with the nation as a whole
- Respects and appreciates different ethnic traditions that it may or may not choose to experience

Suppression

The ethnic minority group:

- Is segregated from the rest of society, including schools, churches, jobs, housing, restaurants, and clubs
- Develops a unique culture, retains its original culture, or a combination of both
- May develop a "dual consciousness" in order to survive

The macroculture:

- Accepts members of other ethnic groups once they give up their original identity
- Views other cultures as unacceptable, inferior, or a threat to social harmony and national unity
- Suppresses the culture and contributions of other groups

The macroculture:

- Respects and appreciates ethnic diversity
- Encourages ethnic minorities to keep many of their traditions alive
- May or may not adopt some of society's different ethnic traditions and current way of life

The macroculture

- Regards the ethnic minority as inferior
- Control's society's economy, government, schools, churches, news and other media
- Accepts the doctrine of White supremacy and sets up policies to preserve it
- Suppresses the culture and contributions of other groups

CONCLUSIONS

Today, people who trace their roots back to northern and western Europe are more fully assimilated into U.S. society than are those whose roots are from southern and eastern Europe. The ethnic pluralism movement that peaked in the 1970s was strongest among white ethnic groups that were part of the third wave of European immigrants. Michael Novak, author of *The Rise of the Unmeltable Ethnics,* described the pain and alienation many immigrants from eastern southern Europe experienced under pressure to give up their cultural identities and assimilate. Of Slavic background himself, Novak explained why many Slavs, Poles, Greeks, and Italians (the "Unmeltable ethnics") felt alienated in the 1970s, due to continuing prejudice, discrimination, and an aura of Anglo-Protestant cultural arrogance.[96] In *Further Reflections on Ethnicity* he wrote that, especially in the United States,

> the new ethnicity demands extraordinary efforts to find alliances between white ethnics and blacks. Alex Haley's *Roots* showed how powerful is the human thirst to have a history. As long ago as blacks in America were slaves, the ancestors of many of us were serfs. . . . To learn one's own history in America is to learn the analogous histories of all the others. We each contribute to each other's identity and to each other's future possibilities.[97]

The search for an understanding of the multicultural roots of culture and society in the United States continues in the next chapter with the brief histories of four more ethnic groups: American Indians; Hispanics (Cuban Americans, Mexican Americans, and Puerto Ricans); Asian Americans; and Muslim and Arab Americans.

COMPARE AND CONTRAST

1. Cultural assimilation and cultural pluralism
2. Jim Crow laws and the "melting pot" theory
3. English and Irish immigrant experience
4. German and Italian immigrant experience
5. Second and third wave of European immigration to the United States
6. Jewish American perspectives and African American perspectives
7. Orthodox, Conservative, and Reform Jews
8. Liberation in the Three Watersheds of African American History

ACTIVITIES AND QUESTIONS

1. Anti-immigration sentiment in the United States has increased dramatically in the 1990s. How is this trend similar to past periods of anti-immigrant feeling? How is it different?

2. Do you see any connection between current immigration trends and the criticism of multicultural education being voiced in the news media? Explain.

3. View "The Distorted Image: Stereotype and Caricature in Popular American Graphics, 1850–1922" or another source of trade cards, cartoons, and labels from the past. How are African Americans, Chinese, Jews, Irish, Germans, Italians, and others portrayed? How are these images different or the same as the images found in contemporary film, television, and advertising?

4. Interview family members or others who have immigrated to the United States themselves or who remember the stories of others who have immigrated. What did they expect people and life in the United States to be like? To what extent have their prior expectations been confirmed? What do they like best about life in the United States? What do they find most difficult?

5. Read about the "hidden origins of slavery" in Chapter 3 of Ronald Takaki's book, *A Different Mirror: History of Multicultural America*. What is the significance of Bacon's rebellion, "the largest rebellion known in any American colony before the (American) Revolution" (p. 65)? How might our national history be different if Black and White laborers had become unified?

6. Based on the brief histories provided in this chapter, prepare a case in favor of affirmative action. Or, prepare a case against it.

NOTES

1. K. L. Roberts, Why Europe Leaves Home, reprinted in "Kenneth L. Roberts and the Threat of Mongrelization in America, 1922," in *In Their Place,* L. H. Carlson and G. A. Colbum, eds. (New York: John Wiley & Sons, 1972), 120.
2. S. W. Mintz, "Creating Culture in the Americas," in *Readings in Anthropology 75/76* (Guilford, CT: Dushkin, 1974), 202.
3. Ibid.
4. L. Jones, *Blues People: The Negro Experience in White America and the Music That Developed from It* (New York William Morrow, 1963), 21.
5. S. Elkins, *Slavery: A Problem in American and Institutional Intellectual Life* (Chicago: University of Chicago Press, Universal Library Ed., 1963). See also L. Foner and E. Genovese (eds.), *Slavery in the New World* (Englewood Cliffs, NJ: Prentice Hall, 1969) and M. L. Herskovitz, *The Myth of the Negro Past* (Boston: Beacon Press, 1969).
6. U.S. Census.
7. J. R. Feagin and C. B. Feagin, *Racial and Ethnic Relations,* 4th ed. (Englewood Cliffs, NJ: Prentice Hall, 1993), 73.
8. J. Weatherford, *Indian Givers* (New York: Fawcett Columbine, 1988), 129.
9. Ibid., 117–149.
10. James A. Banks, *Teaching Strategies for Ethnic Studies* (Boston: Allyn and Bacon, 1991), 247, 249.
11. J. Hraba, *American Ethnicity* (Itasca, IL: F. E. Peacock, 1979), 9.
12. M. A. Jones, *American Immigration* (Chicago: University of Chicago Press, 1960), 93.
13. Ibid., 92.
14. Ibid., 94.
15. Ibid.
16. Ibid., 94–101.
17. Ibid., 107.
18. Ibid., 109.
19. Ibid.
20. Ibid., 179.
21. Hraba, *American Ethnicity,* 10.
22. Jones, *American Immigration,* 180.
23. Hraba, *American Ethnicity,* 8.
24. Jones, *American Immigration,* 118.
25. Ibid., 209.
26. Ibid., 118 and 209.
27. R. Ruiz in C. Sleeter, *Empowerment Through Multicultural Education* (Albany, NY: SUNY Press, 1991), 225
28. Feagin and Feagin, *Racial and Ethnic Relations,* 92.
29. Ibid., 93.
30. Ibid., 91.
31. Ibid., 119.
32. Feagin and Feagin, *Racial and Ethnic Relations,* 120–121.
33. Ibid., 121.
34. Ibid., 123.
35. Feagin, *Racial and Ethnic Relations* (Englewood Cliffs, NJ: Prentice Hall, 1978). The

following ethnic capsules and other quotes are from this work and are reprinted by permission of the publisher.

36. Ibid., 108–109.

37. Ibid., 140.

38. Ibid., 141–142.

39. Feagin and Feagin, *op. cit.,* 133.

40. T. Sowell, *Ethnic America: A History* (New York: Basic Books, 1980), 77. The quotations from this source are reprinted by permission of the publisher. Copyright © 1981 by Basic Books.

41. Ibid., 76.

42. Ibid., 77.

43. Ibid., 78.

44. Ibid., 80.

45. Ibid., 81.

46. J. R. Feagin, *Racial and Ethnic Relations* (Englewood Cliffs, NJ: Prentice Hall, 1978), 179–180.

47. J. R. Feagin and C. B. Feagin, *Racial and Ethnic Relations,* 4th ed. (Englewood Cliffs, NJ: Prentice Hall, 1993), 146–149.

48. T. Sowell, *Ethnic America: A History,* 71–72.

49. Ibid., 73.

50. Ibid., income index, appendix.

51. Feagin and Feagin, *Racial and Ethnic Relations,* 170.

52. Ibid., 149.

52a. 1996 Audit of Anti-Semitic Incidents, 1997, 44 pages. (http://www.adl.org)

53. T. C. Holt, "African-American History," in *The New American History,* E. Foner, ed. (Philadelphia, PA: Temple University Press, 1990), 212.

54. M. F. Berry and J. W. Blassingame, *Long Memory: The Black Experience in America* (New York: Oxford University Press, 1982), 7. Quotations reprinted with permission from Oxford University Press, copyright © 1982.

55. Ibid., 7.

56. E. D. Genovese, *Roll Jordan Roll: The World the Slaves Made* (New York: Random House, 1976), 5.

57. S. M. Elkins, *Slavery* (New York: Grosset and Dunlap, 1963), 59.

58. Ibid.

59. Ibid., 60.

60. H. Zinn, *A People's History of the United States* (New York: Harper Perennial, 1992).

61. T. Sowell (ed.), *Essays and Data on American Ethnic Groups* (Washington, DC: Urban Institute, 1978), 7–64.

62. Berry and Blassingame, *Long Memory,* 37. Quotations reprinted with permission from Oxford University Press, copyright © 1982.

63. Alex Haley, *Roots: The Saga of an American Family* (New York: Doubleday & Company, Inc., 1977).

64. Feagin and Feagin, *Racial and Ethnic Relations,* 217.

65. R. D. Abrahams, *Singing the Master: The Emergence of African American Culture in the Plantation South* (New York: Pantheon Books, 1992).

66. Ibid., 3.

67. Ibid., xxii.

68. E. Foner and O. Mahoney, *America's Reconstruction: People and Politics After the Civil War* (New York: Harper Perennial, 1995).

69. Ibid.

70. Ibid.

71. Ibid., 38.

72. Ibid., 41.

73. Ibid., 44.

74. Ibid., 112.

75. R. Takaki, *A Different Mirror: A History of Multicultural America* (Boston: Little, Brown and Company, 1993), 134.

76. Zinn, *A People's History of the United States,* 204.

77. Ibid.

78. J. H. Franklin and I. S Starr, eds., *The Negro in 20th Century America: A Reader on the Struggle for Civil Rights* (New York: Random House, 1967).

79. Ibid., 189.

80. Holt, in *The New American History,* 224.

81. Ibid.

82. Ibid., 225.

83. Ibid.

84. R. Wright, "We are leaving!" from *12 Million Black Voices,* 1939, quoted in *The Negro in American History,* Vol.2: Which Way to Equality? by Stanley Seaberg. The Scholastic Great Issue Series (New York:

Scholastic Book Services, 1969, pp. 48–53) 48.

85. Ibid., 50.

86. Ibid., 51.

87. Ibid., 52.

88. Holt, in *The New American History,* 228.

89. Ibid.

90. Ibid.

91. Feagin and Feagin, *Racial and Ethnic Relations,* 225.

92. N. I. Huggins, *Harlem Renaissance* (London: Oxford University Press, 1971); D. L. Lewis, *When Harlem Was in Vogue* (New York: Alfred A. Knopf, 1981).

93. M. Schwartzman, *Romare Bearden: His Life and Art* (New York: Harry N. Abrams, Inc., 1990); E. H. Wheat, *Jacob Lawrence: The Frederick Douglas and Harriet Tub-*

man Series of 1938–40 (Hampton, VA: Hampton Museum Press, 1991); P. K. Maultsby, "Africanisms in African-American Music," in Joseph E. Holloway, ed., *Africanisms in American Culture* (Bloomington, IN: Indiana University Press, 1991), 185–210.

94. Feagin and Feagin, *Racial and Ethnic Relations,* 253.

95. D. L. Sills, ed., "Assimilation," in *International Encyclopedia of the Social Sciences,* vol. 1 (New York: Macmillan/Free Press, 1968), 438.

96. J. A. Banks, *Teaching Strategies for Ethnic Studies.* Fifth Edition. 254

97. M. Novak, *Further Reflections on Ethnicity* (Middletown, Pennsylvania: Jednota Press, 1977), v.

chapter **5**

Conflicting Themes of Assimilation and Pluralism among American Indians, Hispanics, Asians, Muslims, and Arabs in the United States

Chapter 4 clarified the distinction between cultural assimilation and cultural pluralism and visualized them along a continuum. Cultural pluralism was pictured as a compromise, a state of accommodation, between total assimilation at one end of the continuum and total suppression or conflict at the other. The examples of immigrants from Europe, Jewish Americans, and African Americans were used to illustrate the tensions between pluralism and assimilation, even among those who eventually became part of the mainstream culture.

In this chapter we examine historical and cultural sketches of some additional ethnic minority groups that have not been assimilated but are part of the national kaleidoscope. These histories and cultural tendencies are important because they illustrate that the United States is a culturally pluralistic society, thus supporting the case for multicultural education.

Some critics of multicultural education fear that cultural pluralism will lead to the disintegration of the nation, as happened in the former Soviet Union and Yugoslavia. This criticism overlooks the fact that from its infancy the United States has sought to create national unity amid ethnic diversity. The case for cultural pluralism can be strengthened by an understanding of this history. With this goal in mind, the chapter continues Chapter 4's comparative analysis with five additional ethnic groups: American Indians, Hispanics, Asian Americans, Muslims, and Arab Americans. The analysis focuses on two common themes:

A multicultural classroom in action.

(1) origins, with emphasis on the roots of diversity within the group, as well as the sense of community, and (2) the group's response to forces of suppression and pressures to assimilate.

Teaching and learning in an ethnically diverse society.

American Indians

Who is an American Indian? The answer varies. Some full-blooded native people do not regard a person with one-quarter native heritage to qualify, while others accept 1/128. The majority of native peoples accept a person with at least one-fourth tribal heritage as a member. The U.S. Census Bureau lists anyone who claims native identity as a native. According to Hirschfelder, one Native American law center has identified fifty-two legal definitions of Native Americans.[1] The 1990 Census identified about 500 tribes and bands of various sizes. Largest, with populations of over 100,000 each, are the Cherokee, Navajo, Chipppewa, and Sioux.[2] Approximately 5 percent of U.S. territory is currently held by Native Americans and Alaskan Natives, or 94 million acres of land. This may be compared to the 2 billion acres of land used by native people in 1492.[3]

Origins: Roots of Diversity within the Native American Community

Ten primary culture areas have been identified in North America, beginning with the Arctic, home of the Inuit people, and stretching to Mesoamerica, the southernmost culture area. The ten culture areas are described by Herman Viola in *After Columbus: The Smithsonian Chronicle of the North American Indians* as follows:[4]

- *Arctic*   The last Siberian wanderers to reach America: ancestors of the Aleuts and Inuits probably arrived starting 5,000 years ago and ranged from Alaska to Greenland.
- *Sub Arctic*   Nomadic hunters of the taiga or northern forests: Carriers, Crees, Dogribs, and Kutchins pursued such big game as caribou and moose and small fur-bearing animals.
- *Northwest Coast*   Premier woodworkers: the sea-faring Haidas, Kwaki-utls, and Tlingits crafted totem poles, boats, and elaborate dwellings from the region's giant evergreens.
- *Plateau*   Fishermen, foragers, and hunters: the Nez Perce, Spokane, and Yakima Plateau tribes lived in underground, pit-house villages in Columbia River country.
- *Plains*   The horse and the gun transformed the Arapaho, Cheyenne, Sioux, and other plains tribes from farmers into nomadic buffalo hunters.
- *Northeast*   Three great confederacies—Powhatan, Iroquois, and Miami—occupied settlements on the coast and in forested uplands, where they farmed, hunted, and fished.
- *Southeast*   Skilled farmers; the Creeks, Chickasaws, Choctaws, Cherokees, Yamasees, and Seminoles built their villages in river valleys.
- *Southwest*   Pueblo-dwelling Hopi and Zuni lived on rugged mesas and, along with such desert-dwelling agricultural tribes as the Pima, fought Apache and Navajo hunter-raiders.

■ *Great Basin*   Making the most of scarce, seasonal resources, bands of Paiutes, Utes, Shoshones, and Bannocks roamed a land of arid basin and snowy range.

■ *California*   In a bountiful area smaller than today's state, a dense but diverse population of hunter-gatherers lived in tribal bands and spoke hundreds of different languages.

In their culture, language, and physical appearance, native peoples of North America are as dissimilar as are the peoples of Europe.[5] At the time of the European invasion there were hundreds of different Native American societies. Over 200 different languages were spoken, and political, social, and economic systems differed dramatically. And yet there is a shared cultural perspective, a world view that reflects basic spiritual values and reverence for the earth. When the European settlers and adventurers explored North America, they were oblivious to the history and culture of the native peoples that had developed over the previous 20,000 years. "They did not find monuments of antiquity awaiting them such as existed in the old world (paintings, sculpture and architecture) . . . the continent seemed silent."[6]

> The continent did not speak to the newcomers because the civilizations of North America did not always speak in loud stone. They spoke in earth and wood, in fiber and textile, in bead and shell. Even when they did choose to speak in stone, they selected small images that could be carved from softer stone, such as the carved animal pipes of the ancient Hopewell people, or the polished red pipe stone of the Plains. Even the stone buildings at Chaco Canyon in New Mexico or Mesa Verde in Colorado spoke in a softer tone, without triumphant arches, expansive domes, soaring pillars, or other modes of imperial adornment and ostentation.[7]

At one time, North America was among the most wooded places on earth. Except for the Great Plains and southwestern desert areas, the American Indians were a forest people, living

> in a virtually eternal "wooden age." . . . The Indians had lived in and around forests for millennia, and had carefully managed and shaped the forests through these years. They consciously followed practices that maximized the growth of trees and plants that they found useful and minimized those that obstructed them.[8]

Through controlled burning, for example, American Indians kept the forests open and allowed large trees to flourish. The trees were harvested for building dugout canoes and making roof beams for homes and community buildings. Controlled fires had additional benefits, such as killing parasitic plants, irritating insects and pests, and poisonous snakes. It also stimulated new growth that attracted large game. In the Plains area the Indians burned tall prairie grasses to lure buffalo closer to their villages, and after centuries of land management that kept the forests open and attractive to large animals, buffalo had adapted to the forest and moved east to provide "the Indians of the Eastern forest with new sources of food and raw materials."[9] The Indians also developed practices to maintain the wildlife populations of birds, fish, and large animals on which they depended for survival.

American Indians were among the best hunters in the world. In addition to their incredible speed and accuracy, "their genius lay in their intimate knowledge of animal habits and in their sophisticated approach to hunting, which stressed tactics over technology."[10] For example, Native American hunters could reproduce the calls of birds and animals and camouflaged themselves in animal skins, horns, or antlers and used a variety of traps and strategies to ambush their prey. The "universal tool kit" for the entire continent was the bow and arrow, the spear, and (in some areas) the sling shot.[11]

Conflict, Accommodation, and the Legacy of Genocide

Estimates of the Native American population size at the time of the European invasion of North America vary greatly. Early analysts have estimated the indigenous population in North America at between 500,000 and 1,150,000, but more recently the figure has been estimated at nearly 10 million.[12] Current scholars believe that the early estimates did not consider factors such as European diseases, especially smallpox, measles, and syphilis, which wiped out large portions of the Native American population during early years of contact. Furthermore, lower estimates had helped legitimize European takeover of unsettled territories.

The first 250 years of European contact with Native Americans included accommodation as well as conflict. In the eastern portions of the continent, American, British, Dutch, French, and Spanish powers fought each other and Native Americans for control of the land. As long as the natives controlled the balance of power in North America, the European and U.S. governments recognized them (at least on paper) as the "rightful owners of land in the Americas. Land was not to be taken from Indians except in fair exchange. Indians were needed not only as military allies, but also as producers and suppliers."[13] This philosophy was reflected in words from Article 111 in the Northwest Ordinance.

> The utmost good faith shall always be observed towards the Indians; their land property shall never be taken from them without their consent; and in their property, rights, and liberty, they never shall be invaded or disturbed, unless in just and lawful wars authorized by Congress; but laws founded in justice and humanity shall from time to time be made, for preventing wrongs being done to them and for preserving peace and friendship with them.[14]

With the era of westward expansion came the image of a native savage race attacking helpless settlers as they resisted the pressures of farmers and missionaries on the frontiers. Although the Indian Removal Act, passed in 1830, stipulated that natives could be relocated only on condition of their consent, the end result was that the federal government forcibly removed those native people living east of the Mississippi to reservations in the West. On the "trail of tears," for example, 4,000 Cherokees died during the forced march out of the

South to the native territory in present-day Oklahoma. "Oklahoma, already the home of the Five Civilized Tribes of the Southeast, was soon to become a vast concentration camp into which Indians from tribes as far apart as the New York Seneca and the West Coast Modace were to be squeezed."[15]

According to Hraba, ethnocentrism and cultural conflict played a large role in the bitter land conflict between the European American and the Native American:

> It was the permanent settler who transplanted the European market economy and brought the legacy of private property. Sizable investments of labor and capital were made by settlers, for land had to be cleared, homes and whole towns built, and a system of transportation constructed on the frontier. . . . [It is] estimated that each homestead site required an initial investment of $1,000 to bring it into production. Private ownership of the land gave a settler some sense of security that he would realize a return on his investments, for he had legal title to the land, and the land and the improvements he made on it could not be capriciously taken from him.[16]

Many European settlers had experienced the oppression of serfdom and found security in the ownership of private property. The Anglo-European world view concerning land, private property, and exclusive ownership was incompatible with the Native American world view, which stressed egalitarianism, nonmaterialism, and opposition to the unnecessary alteration of nature or destruction of any part of the earth. Given these divergent perspectives, the era of treaties would seem to have been doomed by misunderstanding if not deceit. The impact of the Dawes Act passed by Congress in 1887 further illustrates these conflicting world views. The act provided each Native American family with 160 acres of reservation land, with the titles held in trust by the federal government for 25 years. Furthermore, every attempt was made to suppress native traditions, especially religions and education. The native boarding schools that were established required elementary school-age children to leave their families for the academic year. "Reservation Indians were expected to emulate white settlers . . . by becoming farmers and tilling allotments of privately owned land . . . [and] would eventually assimilate into American society."[17] These expectations clearly violated Native American cultural values, and the results were disastrous for the native people, whose numbers shrank drastically and who lost over 90 million acres of land to the Whites.

American Indians were declared citizens of the United States in 1924, and since the 1930s native nations have been recognized as legally autonomous self-governing territories, separate from any state. The Indian Reorganization Act of 1934, which established current policies, can be viewed from several angles. In one sense, the act indicates a return to the early principle that native peoples have a right to self-determination: Reservation lands have been returned to tribal management, community day schools have replaced distant boarding schools, and traditional cultures, including religions, are encouraged.

On the other hand, the illegally seized lands have not been restored, many treaty agreements are still ignored, and the reservations are in a sense colonies subjected to the political and economic policies of a foreign ruler in Washington, DC. Most reservations are located on barren land; compared to all other ethnic groups in the United States, the Native American population suffers the poorest health, the shortest life span, and the greatest economic impoverishment. According to Forbes, noted authority on Native American affairs,

> It must be openly acknowledged that Indians are poor because white people are rich, that the land, timber and minerals which white people use to produce their wealth were virtually all taken by force or deception. It must be recognized that Indian reservations usually exist in marginal land, not originally of value from the perspective of white economic development.[18]

Many American Indians feel torn between their native culture and that of the surrounding American society. This was illustrated recently at the Wind River Reservation (population 6,000) in Wyoming, where nine young men committed suicide during a two-month period. They ranged in age from 14 to 25. As a result of the tragedy, tribal elders have revived traditional medicine practices not used since a flu epidemic in 1918 and are introducing the school-age population to traditional spiritual practices to help them recover some of their cultural identity.[19]

American Indians have gone through centuries of efforts to Christianize and "civilize" them.[20] Throughout this history of miseducation, American Indians have resisted the pressure to give up their cultural identity. The twenty-four tribal colleges that have developed since the 1970s as a response to the unsuccessful experience of Indian students on mainstream campuses are a symbol of a revitalized ethnic identity among native peoples in the United States.

Today, many Native American leaders openly criticize the Anglo-European core culture and its religion. Christianity is sometimes criticized "as a crude religion stressing blood, crucifixion, and bureaucratized charity rather than practicing sharing and compassion for people."[21] Other criticisms of White Europeans are that they are newcomers to the continent, sharply accelerated war, killed off many animal species, betrayed the Native Americans who had aided them in establishing settlements, destroyed the ecosystem, polluted the environment, and became slaves to technology.[22]

> They had what the world has lost. They have it now. What the world has lost, the world must have again lest it die. Not many years are left to have or have not, to recapture the lost ingredient. . . . What, in our human world, is this power to live? It is the ancient, lost reverence and passion for human personality, joined with the ancient, lost reverence and passion for the earth and its web of life. This indivisible reverence and passion is what the [Native] American . . . almost universally had; and representative groups of them have it still.
>
> If our modern world should be able to recapture this power, the earth's natural resources and web of life would not be irrevocably wasted within the twentieth century, which is the prospect now.
>
> True democracy, founded in the neighborhoods and reaching over the world, would become the realized heaven on earth. And living peace—not just an interlude between wars—would be born and would last through ages.[23]

The ideas expressed in this passage are important because they illustrate how an ethnic minority that comprises only about 2 percent of the population can contribute to the thinking and policies of the dominant culture. The idea of ecology does not belong exclusively to American Indian cultures, nor do all Native Americans subscribe to it. However, American Indians have provided our nation with a strong voice in thinking about environmental issues such as overdevelopment of the land, loss of natural resources, and storage of toxic wastes. More Americans are becoming aware of the connections between the health of the earth, their own personal physical and spiritual well-being, and the wholesomeness of their communities.

Hispanics

The term *Hispanic* embraces a diverse group of peoples ranging from recent immigrants to those who have been living in the southwestern United States for over 300 years. Their numbers are over 22 million (9 percent of the total population), with "roughly 60 percent tracing their ancestry to Mexico, and the rest to Puerto Rico, Cuba, El Salvador, the Dominican Republic, Colombia, Venezuela, and about two dozen other countries of Central and South America."[24]

Five regions of the United States are most affected by increased Hispanic populations due to high birthrates or immigration. In the Southwest, where the majority live, schools are most affected by changing demographics, levels of poverty are highest, and levels of literacy and school achievement are lowest. In the Northeast, where the Puerto Rican population has received an influx of Dominicans, Central Americans, and South Americans, there exists a large professional class of Hispanics as well as some of the highest rates of poverty. South Florida, comprised mainly of Cubans, is characterized by high levels of educational attainment. The Chicago Metropolitan Area is a cross section of the Hispanic population and, although socioeconomic levels are low, educational attainment has been above average. Finally, in the Pacific Northwest, the Hispanic population is numerically small but growing rapidly, and due to the high proportion of migrant farm workers, the levels of education are low.[25]

Origins: Roots of Diversity and Community

Mexican Americans, Cubans, and Puerto Ricans have become part of the United States through dramatically different experiences. Mexicans were taken over through territorial conquests or immigrated to this country, Cubans entered as political refugees, and Puerto Ricans were turned over to the United States by Spain at the end of the Spanish American War in 1898.

Mexican American history begins prior to 1500 B.C. with the development of Mayan civilizations, one of the most advanced societies in the so-called New World. "During the years of Mayan ascendancy, Mesoamerica stood with the Near East, West Africa, and the Indus River Valley as a cradle of civilization,"[26] with major achievements in math, science, art, architecture, mining, agriculture, and textiles. Mexican American history continues with the rise and fall of Toltec civilization and the creation of the Aztec empire, which, during the rule of Montezuma II in the early sixteenth century, has been considered among the most advanced civilizations in the world. The military conquest of Mexico at the hands of Hernan Cortez and his soldiers in 1521 marks the beginning of 300 years of Spanish rule. The Spanish conquerors of Mexico cohabited with the indigenous peoples and African American slaves, although the Spanish distinguished between Indians and Blacks—the latter being even more vilified than the former.[27] Under the Spanish system, Blacks could be slaves, Indians could be only peons. Together these groups formed a Mestizo population known as *La Raza,* the race. Also important are the many "pure" or ethnically identified Indians who still live in Mexico and migrate to the United States, and who attempt to preserve their ethnic autonomy from mainstream Mexican culture.[28]

The historical issues of territory are essential in understanding Mexican American perspectives. The U.S. government's annexation of Texas in 1845 triggered war with Mexico and resulted in the U.S. takeover of nearly half of Mexico's territory. As McWilliams points out, Mexican Americans differ from European immigrant groups in that initially "Mexicans were annexed by conquest, along with the territory they occupied, and, in effect, their cultural autonomy was guaranteed by a treaty."[29] This was the Treaty of Guadalupe Hidalgo, a treaty that was ultimately not honored.

Most **Cubans** arrived in the United States after Fidel Castro overthrew the Cuban dictatorship of Fulgencio Batista in 1959. Today there are over a million Cuban Americans in the United States, making them the nation's third largest Spanish-speaking ethnic group. More than half the Cuban population has settled in the greater Miami area, and there are also large settlements in New York City and Los Angeles.

The Cuban immigrant experience is unique in several ways, although there are similarities with the experience of Vietnamese Americans, as will be evident in the next section. First, most Cubans came to the United States as political refugees. They felt threatened and sought freedom and security, rather than the economic prosperity sought by most immigrant groups. Second, Cubans who entered during the U.S. government airlift between 1965 and 1973 tended to be from upper- and middle-income groups. Caucasians and Chinese Cubans were overrepresented, and there were few Black Cubans among them.[30] Most were admitted to the United States without waiting for visas or having to worry about immigration quota restrictions. Of all the Spanish-speaking ethnic groups in this society, Cuban Americans are the most economically prosperous and the most highly educated.

The most recent wave of Cuban immigrants arrived in 1980 via the Mariel boat lift. Strongly supported by Cubans who had previously settled in the United States, a flotilla of private boats transported close to 125,000 Cuban refugees to Key West, Florida, between April and June of 1980.

Puerto Rican origins in the United States are both unique and similar to the origins of other ethnic groups in this society. Two unique aspects are the two-way flow of people between the island and the mainland and the question of statehood or national independence for Puerto Rico.

Puerto Ricans have been U.S. citizens since 1917 and have traveled freely and easily back and forth, lately, thanks to convenient and inexpensive air travel. In contrast to most immigrant groups, Puerto Ricans have not been subjected to restrictive quotas and are U.S. citizens when they arrive.

Over one-third of the total Puerto Rican population (2,727,754 out of 6,250,000 in 1990) resides on the mainland, primarily in New York City, Chicago, and cities in New Jersey, California, and Florida. The population is more mobile than most ethnic groups in the United States, returning frequently to the homeland, often for Christmas or family events. Movement between the island and mainland is affected largely by economic conditions, but also by political and social factors related to the independence question and the desire to maintain cultural traditions. Maintenance of the Spanish language, for example, is essential.

The Puerto Rican experience is also unique among immigrant groups in the United States in that Puerto Ricans are divided over the issue of national independence, statehood, or maintaining its commonwealth status. As a commonwealth, Puerto Rico is a U.S. possession subject to most federal laws. Puerto Ricans are subject to military conscription and have fought with the U.S. military in all wars since World War I. Although U.S. citizens, Puerto Ricans cannot vote in U.S. elections and are represented only by an elected resident commissioner who is a nonvoting member of Congress. They pay no federal taxes. The status question has not yet been settled and sometimes divides members of the same family as some actively seek national independence while others advocate statehood.

Despite the major differences in their history and culture, Puerto Ricans, Cuban Americans, and Mexican Americans share a common heritage and world view that stems from the cultural fusion of Spanish and Native American values. Both Cuba and Puerto Rico were colonies of Spain for over 300 years, ending with the Spanish-American War in 1898. Mexico was ruled by Spain from the arrival of Cortez in 1519 until the end of the struggle for Mexican Independence in 1821. They also share a history of cultural conflicts related to the pressures of Americanization and race relations that are problematic.

Accommodation and the Legacy of Colonialism

It is estimated that nearly 40,000 Taino Indians inhabited Puerto Rico when Christopher Columbus arrived in 1493. During the Spanish takeover, indigenous people revolted; many were killed. Others escaped from the island or died from diseases. Black slaves were brought from Africa, beginning in 1511, to replace the native laborers. Slavery was maintained in Puerto Rico until it was abolished in 1873.[31]

Spain ruled Puerto Rico for nearly 400 years, using the island primarily as a military outpost. The governance was oppressive and inept, controlled primarily by a small, upper-class elite who were descendants of the original Spanish colonizers. Although the people suffered from illiteracy, poverty, and poor health, they were filled with the spirit of independence and self-government, particularly after Spain turned Puerto Rico over to the United States at the end of the Spanish-American War in 1898. The Puerto Ricans' hopes for a plebiscite to determine their political destiny were quickly shattered. During the next half a century, Puerto Rico was headed by a series of governors appointed by the U.S. government, and during this time conditions in Puerto Rico changed little from what they had been at the end of Spanish rule.[32] In 1948, Puerto Ricans elected their own governor for the first time, Luis Munoz Marin. Dramatic changes occurred during the sixteen years of his leadership. He helped establish Puerto Rico as a commonwealth (a result that satisfied neither the statehood nor independence advocates) and created new economic programs such as Operation Bootstrap, a plan that attracted U.S. investments to build up industry in Puerto Rico. Although the yearly per capita income jumped from $188 in 1940 to $1,234 in 1969, Operation Bootstrap critics point out that the upper class and U.S. industrialists have benefited most from the program.[33]

The legacy of colonialism is still evident in Puerto Rico's high level of unemployment and the impoverished living conditions of the urban poor. It is also evident in the Americanization of Puerto Rican schools that stress the English language over Spanish, and historical figures, events, and achievements from the United States rather than Puerto Rican history.

Among Mexican Americans the legacy of colonialism relates to the "imperialistic expansion resulting in the colonization of communal people who already lived in the area" (what is now the southwestern United States).[34] The Texas revolt and the annexation of Texas by the United States in 1845 triggered the Mexican War, which eventually forced Mexico to cede the southwestern territory to the United States for $15 million.[35] Given the choice to remain on their lands or move south, most Mexicans stayed, guaranteed by the Treaty of Guadalupe Hidalgo the full rights of citizenship and protection of property. In the end, however, most Mexican landowners lost their lands to Anglo Americans. The methods of take-over ranged from "lynching, to armed theft, to quasi-legal and legal means such as forcing expensive litigation in American courts to prove land titles."[36] McWilliams explains the situation this way:

> Many of the villagers neglected to bring their papers into court and often had lost evidences of title. Most of them lacked funds to defend titles; or, if they retained an Anglo-American lawyer, a large part of the land went in payment of court costs and fees. . . . Litigation over land titles was highly technical and involved; cases dragged on in the courts for years; and . . . control of resources shifted to the Anglo-Americans.[37]

One of the more popular techniques for expropriating land from the Mexicans was taxation. "American politicians would levy property tax rates at levels that only the largest of Spanish landholders could afford, thereby forcing small Hispanic entrepreneurs off their land and into wage labor."[38]

Without knowledge of this aspect of history, one cannot understand the border phenomenon of Mexico and contemporary society in the Southwest, where "Mexican migrants have moved within one broad geographical area, a of which was at one time controlled by their own people."[39] The stretch of 1,936 miles between Mexico and the United States has been described as "the world's most extraordinary border. Nowhere, with the possible exception of East and West Berlin, Germany [prior to the end of the Berlin Wall in 1990], is the contrast so stark. On one side of the blurry line stands an economic super-power, on the other a nation burdened with widespread poverty . . . (a place where) you can jump from the First World to the Third World in five minutes."[40]

According to Feagin, there remains a strong sense of cultural identity among Mexican Americans, whether they have experienced the traditional life of rural villages or the faster-paced life of the urban barrios. The Spanish language is the most notable example and has persisted as a primary language or as part of a bilingual pattern.

> The relative isolation of many Mexican Americans in the Southwest, their close-ness to Mexico, and the constant movement across the border are important rea-sons for the persistence of loyalty to the Spanish language. Most parents in the southwest wish their children to retain ties to their Mexican culture, particularly language, customs, and religion. Commitment to Catholicism remains strong even in later generations. The legacy of prejudice and discrimination still encour-ages a bicultural pattern of adaptation [that] resists full acculturation.
>
> Widespread prejudice and severe discrimination faced the Mexicans who were conquered in the aggressive expansion of the United States, as well as the waves of first-generation migrants entering the United States since 1900. However, as time passed, some lighter-skinned Mexican Americans in larger cities were treated with much less prejudice and discrimination. Darker-skinned persons have often been treated just as black Americans. There still remains considerable prejudice and discrimination directed against Mexican Americans, the great bulk of whom are in the working-class and lower-class groups.[41]

Feagin explains that there has been little absorption of Mexican Americans into the North American culture's primary group structures and few marriages outside the community. He reports that most marriages are within the Mexican American group, ranging from about 75 to 95 percent, depending on the geo-graphical area. He also writes that most Mexican Americans maintain their identity as persons of Mexican descent.

> Pressures brought by outside oppression forced many, particularly in earlier decades, to try to hide their Mexican origin under the euphemism of "Spanish," "Latin," or "Hispanic" Americans, but this cannot necessarily be taken as a sign of identification assimilation. It was the middle- and upper-class Mexican Ameri-can who in the 1920s began to use such terms as these in an attempt to overcome prejudice. In recent years there has been a shift back to "Mexican" and "Mexican American." In a mid-1960s survey the overwhelming preference was for "Mexi-can" or "Mexican American" in Los Angeles, while in San Antonio the prefer-ence of a majority was still for "Latin American." Given the great stigma still attached to "Mexican" in Texas, this latter result is not too surprising. However, few in either city wanted to be called just "American." In the last decade, "Chi-

no" has come to be used by activists and has spread widely throughout the
xican American population, particularly among the young persons, as a sign
.. accented group pride.[42]

Mexican Americans are not like European immigrant groups whose level
of segregation has declined over the generations. Despite the growth of a prosperous middle class that is largely assimilated into mainstream society, many
Mexican Americans still experience intentional discrimination at many levels.[43]
Commenting on the colonial perspective, Feagin writes:

> The rise of a Mexican American middle class, and the mobility obvious therein,
> can be seen as a way of maintaining the subordination of most Mexican Ameri-
> cans rather than as a vanguard phenomenon leading to assimilation of the ma-
> jority. From this viewpoint equal-opportunity advocates have distorted the
> meaning of this economic upgrading. A small segment of the Chicano popula-
> tion is dramatically moving upward, but as a token elite used to control the rest
> of the population.[44]

Farm workers in the United States are a vivid example of the lasting legacy
of colonialism among Mexican Americans and other minorities. Although the
vast majority of Mexican Americans live in urban areas, approximately 10 percent are farm workers. Of this 10 percent, a majority are migrant workers.
Based primarily in Texas, California, and Florida, the migrant workforce travels throughout the country, following the harvest season in the nation's fields
and orchards. Ashabranner writes,

> The course of these human streams is always north, following the ripening crops.
> After they harvest the vegetables and fruits in Washington, Minnesota, New York,
> and other states along the Canadian border, the migrant streams turn south to-
> ward the places they started from. For some, there will be late crops and second
> plantings to harvest along the road back. The growing of food in America never
> stops.[45]

No one knows the total number of migrant workers in the United States,
but it is estimated at close to a million, plus uncounted numbers of children.
(The state of Texas estimated a need for 21,434 migrant workers in 1985; Indiana estimated a need for 7,395 workers.)[46]

Child labor is outlawed in every U.S. industry except agriculture. From the
age of 14, any child can work in the fields without restriction. Any 12- or 13-
year-old can work with his or her parents' consent. A child of any age can labor
on farms that are not covered by the minimum-wage law, and many are not. A
study made for the U.S. Department of Health and Human Services states:
"Child labor is an economic necessity for the migrant family due to the low level
of income. By the age of four, most children work in the fields at least part of
the day. And most older children drop out of school well before high school to
work full-time in the fields."[47]

Today, Hispanic peoples—Mexican Americans, Mexican nationals, Puerto
Ricans, and Central Americans—comprise over 70 percent of the migrant workforce. African Americans now comprise about 15 percent of the migrant work-

force nationally. Whites comprise less than 10 percent, and workers from the Caribbean Islands approximately 5 percent.[48] The plight of migrant farm workers in North America worsened during the 1980s. The average annual income remains well below the poverty line ($13,294 for a family of four in 1991); 90 percent drop out before completing high school; 50 percent leave school before finishing the ninth grade; and they are twenty-six times more likely than the national population to contract parasitic diseases because of heavy exposure to pesticides and insecticides.[49] Other preventable diseases such as tuberculosis, influenza, pneumonia, and tooth and gum deterioration occur at a rate 200 to 500 percent higher than among the national population.[50] The rate of infant and maternal mortality is two-and-a-half times higher than the national average contributing to an average life expectancy of 49 years among migrants, compared to the average North American life expectancy of 74 years.[51]

How does the life of migrant farm workers compare with life in urban areas where approximately 87 percent of Mexican Americans live? The quality of life varies greatly, but Acuna and others reported a grim picture in the late 1980s. Research showed that nearly one-third of Mexican American families live in poverty, lack home ownership, and dwell in substandard (unsanitary and unsafe) rental housing.[52]

Cuban Americans are more assimilated into U.S. society than Puerto Ricans and Mexican Americans. However, they have suffered hardships, particularly those who fled Cuba after Castro took over. The first group of Cuban refugees who entered the United States received a warm welcome from Anglo society. This is not the case for Cuban immigrants who arrived in 1980 via the Mariel boat lift. In contrast to the upper-income professionals and technicians who had arrived in the 1960s, the Mariel Cubans were generally of humble origins and their reception ranged from warm to hostile. "A Gallup poll conducted nationally in late May 1980 found that 59 percent of respondents felt that Cuban emigration was bad for the United States. In the Miami area, a similar survey conducted by the *Miami Herald* in May 1980 found that 68 percent of the non-Latin White population and 57 percent of the Black population surveyed felt that the new wave of Cuban refugees would have a large negative impact."[53] Describing the Mariel immigrants of 1980, Diaz writes,

> The characteristics of the Cubans who emigrated via the Mariel boat lift showed that there was a higher proportion of Black Cubans, single males, and blue-collar workers than found among previous groups of Cuban immigrants. Much has been written about the "undesirable" or "criminal" element that came to the United States during the boat lift. The Cuban government seized the opportunity to rid itself of people who had committed serious crimes or suffered mental or physical problems; but people in these categories constituted less than 5% of the 125,000 entrants. Also, the fact that a person spent time in a Cuban jail could be due either to criminal or political activity. Consequently, not all "criminals" would have had that label if they had been living in the United States. Most of the Mariel Cubans originally detained were eventually released. However, about 1,200 Mariel Cubans have remained in jail since their arrival in the United States. The bulk of these prisoners have been detained at the Atlanta Federal Penitentiary.[54]

As is true among Puerto Ricans and Mexican Americans, most Cuban Americans express a strong desire to maintain their language and other aspects of their cultural heritage. This has important implications for schools that serve the Cuban American community such as Dade County, where Cubans comprise one-third of the school-age population. At the same time, many Cuban Americans are "unashamedly patriotic, grateful to the United States for their freedom."[55]

Asian Americans

Asian Americans number over 7 million, or 2.9 percent of the population.[56] This is a dramatic jump from 3.5 million in 1980. As the nation's fastest growing racial group on a percentage basis, it is estimated that Asian Americans will reach 6.4 percent of the population by the mid-twenty-first century.[57]

Origins: Roots of Diversity and Community

The dramatic increases in the numbers of Asian Americans have been accompanied by equally dramatic shifts in the nation of origin. Prior to 1970, two thirds of all Asian Americans were of Japanese or Chinese origin. In 1970, Japanese formed the largest group, but were surpassed by Chinese in 1980. Since the end of the war in Vietnam, Laos, and Cambodia in 1975, 750,000 Southeast Asians and even larger numbers of Koreans and Filipinos have immigrated to the United States.[58]

> There are . . . profound differences among Asians in their reasons for coming to America and their experiences just before arrival. The early Chinese, Japanese, and Filipino immigrants were primarily healthy young men with families waiting for them to return with a share of America's wealth. Few got rich. like gold seekers from our eastern states, many returned poor and embarrassed at their failure. Those who stayed, however, found in the United States an economy eager for muscle power and placing no premium on formal education. Compare that experience to refugees from nations decimated by war. Strong young men have been killed by the thousands, leaving their widows, children, and elderly parents to migrate to safety. No extended families farm ancestral lands, assuring a haven in case of failure in the new world. In the United States they find few jobs not requiring skill in English and extensive formal education. For many refugee families, only the children can hope to share fully in the American promise.[59]

This discussion of origins will focus on the experiences of Chinese Americans, Japanese Americans, and the recent refugees from Southeast Asia.

The first Asians were from China, entering not as immigrants but as sojourners who intended to return to their families in China. When China opened up to outside trade in the mid 1800s, family elders sent their youngest sons to work temporarily under labor contracts in other countries. "Permanent emigration of families was not really an option because Chinese believed in living close to their ancestral grounds."[60] Between 1840 and 1900, 2.5 million Chinese left China for temporary work in other countries such as Cuba, Peru,

Hawaii, Sumatra, Malaya, Australia, New Zealand, and Vietnam. Three hundred thousand came to the United States to work first in the gold mines and mining communities and then later on the railroads.[61]

> The Chinese were first hired to work on the transcontinental railroad because the owners could not attract enough white workers. At the time the lure of gold in the mountains was still greater than the pay of a railroad job. The railroad owners at first did not think the Chinese had the stamina for such difficult work but the Chinese proved themselves excellent workers. Charles Crocker, one of the Big Four, said, "They worked themselves to our favor to such an extent that if we were in a hurry . . . it was better to put the Chinese on at once." In time, workers were recruited directly from China, as the Chinese labor force swelled to nearly 14,000 men.[62]

Next came the Japanese. When they first entered the United States in the late 1800s, the Japanese inherited a climate of anti-Asian feeling directed previously at the Chinese. However, there were important differences as well as similarities in the early Japanese and Chinese experiences.

In 1868, Japan sent 148 contract laborers to work in the sugar-cane fields of Hawaii. These laborers were city folk, unskilled in farm work. The experiment ended in an embarrassing failure, and the laborers were sent home. However, the incident led to deeper involvement of the Japanese government in the lives of Japanese workers abroad than was the case for Chinese and greater protection of Japanese citizens living in other countries. Japanese emigration proceeded slowly and was legalized in 1885. As was true for the Chinese and many other immigrant groups, the Japanese came to the United States to gain wealth.

The most recent Asian immigrants are from Southeast Asia. In contrast to the early groups of Chinese and Japanese laborers who arrived over a century ago, today's Southeast Asian immigrants are a heterogeneous group that includes large numbers of well-educated families and leaders from South Vietnam, "destitute boat people, who are in large part ethnic Chinese from Vietnam, and largely nonliterate mountain tribesmen, like the Hmong and Mieu from Laos and Vietnam."[63]

Prior to 1975, there were approximately 10,000 Southeast Asians living in the United States, mostly from Vietnam. With the fall of Saigon in 1975, there occurred a mass exodus of Vietnamese citizens to the United States. It began with the "baby lift," which brought nearly 3,000 children to the United States, most of them orphans, and continued with the evacuation of approximately 145,000 Southeast Asian refugees. Most of these individuals had been associated with the war effort in Vietnam. Approximately 40 percent of them were school-age children.[64]

In contrast to the second wave of refugees that began in 1976 and continues to the present, this first group was relatively homogeneous in terms of nationality, socioeconomic background, education, and familiarity with Western societies. Thuy states,

> Before their arrival in the United States, a good number of them were not only already well-educated and from well-to-do families by Vietnamese standards, they

also had been exposed to Western culture and the English language, due to the French occupation and American involvement in Vietnam. Many were professionals and/or members of the educational and social elite, and, generally speaking, they had occupied relatively high economic statuses in their native country.[65]

The second wave of refugees was much more diverse and, in general, could be characterized as suffering from poorer health, being from lower educational and socioeconomic backgrounds, and having less exposure to Western cultures. For the most part, this second group included "the Laotian refugees and the Hmong tribes people of Laos who crossed the Mekong River to Thailand; the Cambodian refugees who escaped famine and the war in Cambodia to enter Thailand; and the Vietnamese and Chinese Vietnamese who set sail from their homeland to seek asylum in refugee camps and who have been known as 'the boat people.' "[66]

It is estimated that over 40 percent of those fleeing perished during the escape. Many of the children and adults who arrived in the United States, as well as in other host societies (such as Australia, Canada, China, and France), experienced traumatic ordeals and harrowing escapes. Those who fled and left family members behind, often because of the desire to spare wives and children the physical dangers, suffer from guilt, depression, and loneliness.

Although the U.S. government passed emergency legislation that provided over $400 million for assistance in the resettling process, the sudden arrival of 150,000 refugees between 1975 and 1976 caught the U.S. public and refugee service providers off guard. This state of unpreparedness added to the culture shock that accompanied resettlement in a new country where the language and way of life, as well as the legal, economic, and transportation systems, were all foreign. Although the U.S. government's original plan was to disperse the refugee population evenly across the fifty states, after a short period of resettlement many of the refugees have moved to ethnic clusters located in Florida, Louisiana, Texas, Washington, DC, and California. These secondary and tertiary migrations are often inspired by a desire to live among their own people with whom they feel more comfortable, as well as a desire for warmer weather, jobs, and better educational opportunities. In some cases, ugly hostility in the larger community has forced many of the refugees to withdraw into ethnic enclaves for protection and comfort.[67] However, the refugees from Southeast Asia have not faced the severe discrimination and prejudice experienced by their predecessors from China and Japan. In fact, many communities and individual family sponsors have provided warm welcomes.

Accommodation in the Face of Prejudice and Discrimination

With the completion of the railroads in the 1870s, anti-Chinese feeling intensified as cheap Chinese laborers flooded markets where non-Chinese workers had been employed. After more than a decade of anti-Chinese journalism, violence, and active struggle on the part of the Chinese for civil rights and equality, Congress passed the Chinese Exclusion Act in 1882. This law prohibited Chinese laborers from entering the United States and denied those Chinese already here the right to become naturalized citizens. Implying that they were undesirable solely on the basis of their ethnicity, the Exclusion Act had a devastating impact on the Chinese American community, and their numbers shrank to only 60,000 in 1920.[68] The population was predominantly men since only the very wealthy Chinese had been able to bring their wives and families with them.

Despite these strong anti-Asian feelings directed initially at the Chinese, the number of Japanese immigrants jumped from 25,000 in 1900 to 70,000 by 1910, triggering headlines in California newspapers that protested the "Yellow Invasion of California." Wishing to avoid the embarrassment of another exclusion act, in 1907 President Theodore Roosevelt negotiated the Gentlemen's Agreement between the United States and Japan. The agreement meant that Japan would stop issuing passports to Japanese laborers. However, the wives, children, and parents of laborers already in the United States, as well as professionals, were allowed to immigrate. Although the agreement drastically reduced the number of Japanese immigrants to the United States, it avoided the bachelor-oriented society the exclusion acts had created for the Chinese. As Japanese men saved enough money to start families, their families in Japan would arrange a marriage between the son and a daughter of good family background. Usually, the son would not return to Japan to be present at the ceremony and was represented by proxy. The bride would then sail to America where her husband would meet her, using her picture as a means to identify her, creating what was called the "picture bride" phenomenon.

Most Japanese immigrants, known as *Issei*, settled in Hawaii and California. Many worked in agriculture, beginning as tenant farmers and then saving money to buy their own land. Through the use of muscle power rather than machines, the *Issei* converted lands never previously farmed, and by 1920 they worked over 50 percent of the California acreage dedicated to hand-labor crops. These successes triggered action such as California's alien land law that made it illegal for individuals ineligible for citizenship, that is, the *Issei*, to own land. By 1920, fourteen states passed such legislation. To circumvent these acts, the *Issei* purchased land in the names of their children, for the *Nisei* (the second generation) were U.S. citizens by birth and could own land even as infants.[69]

By far the most tragic example of prejudice and discrimination directed at Asian Americans occurred after the Japanese bombed Pearl Harbor. On February 19,1942, President Franklin D. Roosevelt signed Executive Order 9066, which mandated the relocation of Japanese people living on the West Coast. More than 110,000 of the 126,000 Japanese in the United States were affected, two-thirds of whom were native-born U.S. citizens.[70] Initially, the evacuees were housed in temporary centers that had been hurriedly converted from fairgrounds, racetracks, and livestock exposition halls. Mine Okubo, an evacuee, describes the conditions:

> The guide left us at the door of Stall 50. We walked in and dropped our things inside the entrance. The place was in semidarkness; light barely came through the

dirty window on either side of the entrance. A swinging half-door divided the 20 by 9 foot stall into two rooms. . . . The rear room had housed the horse and the front room the fodder. Both rooms showed signs of a hurried whitewashing. Spider webs, horse hair, and hay had been whitewashed with the walls. A two-inch layer of dust covered the floor, but on removing it we discovered that linoleum . . . had been placed over the rough manure-covered boards. We opened the folded cots lying on the floor of the rear room and sat on them in the semi-darkness. We heard someone crying in the next stall.[71]

Later, the Japanese Americans were moved to one of ten permanent camps that sometimes housed as many as 20,000 people. Germans, Italians, and Japanese in Hawaii were also threatened, and some Japanese were relocated into concentration camps. The camps were bordered with barbed wire, guarded by the military, and offered little privacy. Some object to the label *concentration camp* because it associates the Japanese American relocation experiences with the Holocaust in Germany, where 6 million Jews were annihilated. There are, of course, significant differences in the two experiences: Few Japanese were killed, and many who could prove their loyalty were released to fight in the war, participate in work-release programs, or move east. Nevertheless, the experience represents a massive violation of the civil rights of over 100,000 people and brought unjustifiable personal tragedy and financial ruin to many of them. Even though the War Relocation Authority (WRA) was established to supervise the evacuations and the Federal Reserve Bank was ordered to protect their property, most evacuated Japanese Americans suffered great financial losses, ultimately mounting to over $400 million. President Ronald Reagan signed a reparation bill in 1988 that provided $20,000 to be paid to each surviving Japanese American who had been interned, but these people's personal and financial losses can never be fully recovered.

Why did it happen? The forced imprisonment of Japanese Americans had traditionally been explained from a military viewpoint. Japan had attacked the United States and the West Coast was particularly vulnerable to sabotage because of the military facilities concentrated along the coastline. It was feared that the Japanese (as well as Germans and Italians) were engaged in spy activities. Others have emphasized strong racist anti-Japanese prejudice that had long infected California as well as the federal government. (See anti-Japanese legislation at both the federal and state levels.[72]) Still others emphasize the role of farm and business elites eager to eliminate Japanese competition. Little understood by non-Japanese Americans is the impact of the relocation experience on the Japanese American community. The loosening of family ties between *issei* and *nisei* is only one example. Also little known is the fact that Japanese Americans did protest and resist their imprisonment, that many Japanese soldiers fought with great valor during the war, and that returning home after 1945, many Japanese Americans could not regain their farms and businesses and faced violence and discrimination in their communities. As a result of this history, many Japanese American adults still feel an anxiety about the security of their daily lives in U.S. society.

Japanese Americans are often regarded as a classic example of the U.S. success story. Stereotyped earlier as the "yellow peril," now they are often stereotyped as the model minority. Japanese Americans have the highest literacy rate of any ethnic group in our society, tend to be financially well off, and have been assimilated into the predominant language and religion. The similarity between traditional Japanese values and attitudes and the dominant culture may be a superficial mask hiding some deep cultural differences.

> Acculturation for the Japanese has in some ways been less difficult, because of a rough similarity in certain Japanese and core culture values. Certain traditional Japanese values such as *enryo,* the deferential or self-denying behavior in a variety of situations, and the ancient Buddhist–Confucian ethic of hard work aimed at individual honor and the success of the group have been useful for the Japanese operating in the United States context. *Enryo* was useful in coping with oppression and bears some similarity to the Protestant Ethic. As a result, Japanese Americans have sometimes been viewed in recent years as "just like whites." Yet the basic values are, in a number of ways, still fundamentally Japanese. In this sense, then, complete acculturation has not been fully attained. What appears to be Angloconformity acculturation may not always be so.[73]

The success of Japanese Americans in U.S. society is often used as an example of what other non-Whites, particularly African Americans and Mexican Americans, could also accomplish. However, Feagin points out a number of factors that contributed to the success of Japanese Americans and Jewish Americans, which were not available to larger oppressed groups, such as African Americans.

> The success of Japanese Americans, seen as rooted in their values and family styles, has been cited by numerous writers as a paramount "bootstraps" example of what other nonwhites, particularly blacks and Mexicans, could be if they would only conform to these patterns. Stereotyping that sees the Japanese as an Asian Horatio Alger story and as paragons of hard-working, docile, not-rocking-the-boat virtues has been noted as carrying a clearly negative undercurrent. Critics of this cultural background interpretation have noted a number of other factors at least as important in shaping Japanese economic success—the role of the Japanese government in supporting immigrants, the availability of a ghettoized, small business niche on the West Coast, and the effect of intense racial discrimination in the surrounding environment in forging group solidarity. . . . Japanese Americans created small businesses to serve one another and the basic economic needs of a frontier economy. This hostile situation fostered a situation where both Japanese employers and employees saw themselves as a single racial "class" versus the outside world. Out of dire economic necessity, employers and employees, often with kinship or regional ties, worked together against white competitors. Success came at the price of being ghettoized in the small business economy and, later, in certain professions. As with Jewish Americans, Japanese Americans have "made it" as a group in American society in a distinctive way, a process (and result) of adaptation not in line with certain idealistic assimilation or inclusion models. Thus the long-term effects of past discrimination are still reflected in the concentration of Japanese Americans in the small business economy or in certain

professional/technical occupations. Smaller oppressed groups, it seems, have a better chance of establishing an economic niche, where they go because of widespread prejudice and discrimination, but where they can also attain some measure of success, particularly in an expanding economy. It appears that such niches are not as readily available to larger oppressed groups such as black Americans.[74]

It is possible that the Japanese American experience will provide a model for the new immigrants from Southeast Asia, the Vietnamese, Cambodians, and Laotians. Butterfield reports that among the children of 6,800 Indochinese who have arrived in the United States since 1978, "one-quarter . . . earned straight A's and 44 percent got an A average in math, though two-thirds of them arrived in the United States knowing no English."[75] These successes are attributed to a belief in the efficacy of hard work and the malleability of human nature, part of the Confucian ethic. "The belief that people can always be improved by proper effort and instruction is a basic tenet of Confucianism. This philosophy, propounded by the Chinese sage in the fifth century B.C., in time became a dynamic force not only in China but also in Korea, Japan, and Vietnam, sanctifying the family and glorifying education."[76]

A top priority among Southeast Asians is acquisition of the English language. Learning English can be frustrating for both students and teachers, particularly among second-wave refugees who have had little or no previous exposure to Western languages, because English and the various Southeast Asian languages share little in common linguistically. Nevertheless, as noted previously, many U.S. schoolchildren from Southeast Asian families are successful. On the other hand, because they are Asians, many are also victims of the "model minority myth" associated with Japanese Americans. Stereotypes about Asian "whiz kids" and jealousy over the relatively high percentages of Asian Americans in the nation's colleges and universities may blind some non-Asian parents, fellow students, and teachers to the deep cultural conflict many Southeast Asian Americans face in our schools. Thuy describes the kind of clashes that occur in Asian families and within schools.

> Practices which are quite acceptable in American culture, and the values which are taught and observed in American schools, sometimes collide head-on with those which are taught and observed in Indochinese families. American cultural practices such as dating and reverence of individuality are two possible sources of conflict between Indochinese school children and their parents. This often leads to family disturbances and discord, and, in turn, strains the parent-child relationship and widens the generation gap. In addition, the practice of placement by age rather than academic preparation makes education irrelevant, inappropriate, and inequitable for a significant number of refugee children who are older and/or have received limited or no education in their homelands. Placement problems have led to a high dropout rate among illiterate and semiliterate children, older children, or children with limited past education because, in addition to the tremendous language barrier and unfamiliarity with the American educational system, these children are unable to live up to the academic expectations of the teacher.[77]

■*Muslims in America and Arab Americans, by Salman H. Al Ani*

Muslims in the United States

Muslims in the United States derive a sense of community and identity from religion rather than from race or national origin. They fall under two categories—indigenous ones and immigrants. The majority of the former are African Americans, while only about 70,000 are Caucasian (white). The immigrants come from diverse parts of the world, including the Middle East and North Africa, Eastern Europe, sub-Saharan Africa, South Asia, and some Southeast Asian countries, such as Malaysia. Muslims constitute about one fifth of the world's population. Following a substantial increase in their numbers during the past decade, there are now approximately 5 million Muslims in the United States,[78] about one-third of whom are native-born Americans. However, the exact number is not known, because the census that is conducted every ten years does not inquire into religious affiliation.

Community and Diversity: Immigrant and Indigenous Origins

Immigrant Muslims come from a variety of ethnic, linguistic, and cultural backgrounds. They came to the United States in basically three different waves, the first of which started at the end of the nineteenth century and continued to 1925. Most Muslims who came during this period were poor and uneducated and were from Bilad ash-Sham (Greater Syria), the area that after World War I became known as Jordan, Lebanon, Palestine, and Syria. They also came from Turkey, Albania, India, and a few other countries. In the majority of cases they settled in Dearborn, Michigan; Toledo, Ohio; Cedar Rapids, Iowa; Michigan City, Indiana; and other midwestern cities and towns. These groups form the core of the early immigrant Muslims in the United States. Cedar Rapids is unique inasmuch as one of the first mosques in North America, referred to as the Mother Mosque in North America, was built there in 1934.[79]

The second major group began to arrive after World War II, as political and social unrest in the Middle East and North Africa drove many Muslims to immigrate to America. The partition of Palestine and the establishment of the state of Israel in the late 1940s, as well as the creation of Pakistan, also resulted in the migration of Muslims to the United States. Unlike the first wave, the majority this time were educated professionals. A substantial number of students who came to the United States to study eventually settled here. The third wave, which continues to the present day, came as a result of the liberalization of the immigration regulations in the late 1960s. Many of the Muslims in this group emigrated from Egypt, North Africa, Pakistan, India, and from several other Muslim countries, including Albania and what was then Yugoslavia.

The oil-rich Middle Eastern countries have sent a large number of Muslim students to study at U.S. universities and colleges, especially since the 1970s. These students have played active and sometimes leadership roles in Muslim communities and have influenced Muslim Student Association (MSA) branches all over the United States.

The first generation of Muslim immigrants experienced difficulties in adjusting to the U.S. environment. As a result they tend to live in groups formed on the basis of ethnic, cultural, and social origins. Therefore, they do not integrate easily either with indigenous American Muslims or with other Muslims of different ethnic backgrounds. This state of affairs makes it difficult for them to establish a national political base that could give them the sort of influence enjoyed by other ethnic or religious groups.

Muslims in the United States enjoy the freedom to practice their religion, both as individuals and as groups. They have managed to establish communities in almost every city in this country. Also, they have built or purchased over 600 mosques and Islamic centers, where they worship, celebrate holidays (*Eids*), hold social gatherings, and organize schools that teach Islam and Arabic to adults and children. In addition, American Muslims have established national organizations such as the Islamic Society of North America (ISNA), whose headquarters in Plainfield, Indiana, include a beautiful mosque and adjoining buildings that sit on over 100 acres of land, with a small lake. ISNA holds an annual national convention on Labor Day weekend in various major cities and is attended by Muslims from all over the United States and Canada, as well as from many other countries.[80]

Originally called the Muslim Student's Association (MSA), ISNA was founded in 1963. Local MSAs are still found on virtually every major college and university campus in the United States. The MSA in Bloomington, Indiana, built a beautiful mosque in 1993 where students and other Muslims gather to pray (especially for the Friday, jumah, prayers), to celebrate festivals, weddings, and other social occasions, and to study Islam and Arabic. (Mosques were traditionally used just for worship and the study of Islam and Arabic, but use as multipurpose community social centers has caught on in MSA mosques throughout the United States.) The Muslim community of Bloomington is truly universal. At the jumah prayers on Fridays people of every linguistic, social, and cultural background come together as one group. The one element that brings them together, even with the diversity of their backgrounds, is the universality of the message of Islam.

Muslims believe in one God (Allah) and that Muhammad is His Prophet and Messenger. In the seventh century A.D. when Muhammad was forty years old and living in Makkah, the Qur'an (Holy Book) was revealed to him in the Arabic language. It was revealed from God through the Angel Gabriel over the period of twenty-three years leading up to the Prophet's death at the age of sixty-three. Muslims all over the world, including Americans, regardless of their linguistic or ethnic backgrounds, are supposed to recite the Qur'an in Arabic, especially during their prayers. This means that it is important for all Muslims to learn Arabic, at least enough for this purpose. Although the Qur'an has been translated into almost all languages of the world, Muslims still rely on the Arabic text and consider the translations as mere interpretations. Muslims in the United States feel strongly about teaching the Qur'an, the Arabic language, and basic Islamic beliefs to members of their communities, especially to their children. Therefore, wherever there is a large concentration of Muslims, Arabic-Islamic schools have been developed. In smaller areas, the teaching is done in mosques, Islamic centers, or homes.

The Qur'an is the last revealed word of God and is the prime source of every Muslim's faith. The teachings of the Qur'an and the Hadiths (sayings and deeds of Prophet Muhammad) form the foundation for Islamic law (Shariah) and regulate the daily lives of Muslims. For example, drinking alcohol and eating pork and pork products are prohibited.

There are Five Pillars that form the framework of the Muslim faith. These are (l) the Declaration of Faith or the **Shahadah,** which is a simple formula that all the faithful pronounce. It simply states that "I bear witness that there is no one worthy of worship except God (Allah) and that Muhammad is His Servant and Messenger"; (2) prayer or **Salat:** Prayers in Islam are obligatory and are performed five times a day—at dawn, noon, mid-afternoon, sunset, and nightfall. (3) Fasting: Every year in the month of **Ramadhan** all Muslims fast from first light until sunset. Those who are sick, elderly, or on a journey and women who are pregnant or nursing are permitted to break the fast and make up an equal number of days later in the year. During the fasting periods no food, drink, or intercourse is allowed; (4) Alms giving or **Zakat:** In Islam it is believed that all things belong to God and that wealth held by men is held in trust. Zakat means purification and it is a contribution that is collected and distributed to the poor and needy. Zakat usually amounts to two and a half percent of one's capital; and (5) Pilgrimage or **Hajj:** an annual pilgrimage to the Ka'bah, the holy sanctuary in Makkah, is performed at least once in a lifetime provided one has the means and health to undertake the journey. About 2 million Muslims, from every corner of the globe, go to Makkah each year. The Hajj begins in the twelfth month of the Islamic year, which is based on a lunar rather than a solar calendar. For Muslims in the United States, charter flights and group trips are arranged.

African American Muslims

The major movement of African American Muslims today can be traced back to a man named W. D. Fard, who was of Middle East origin. In 1930, Fard founded the first African American movement and named it "The Lost-Found Nation of Islam in the Wilderness of North America," which later became known as the Nation of Islam (NOI) or the Black Muslims. Fard proclaimed himself to be "supreme ruler, Allah or God in Person." He disappeared mysteriously in 1934, but before this he proclaimed his disciple, Elijah (Poole) Muhammad, to be the Messenger of God. The latter assumed leadership of the NOI from the mid-1930s until his death in 1975.[81]

Elijah Muhammad attracted many followers, especially in Detroit and Chicago. The program for his followers was freedom, justice, and equality. He also advocated the establishment of a separate state and the prohibition of al-coholic beverages and of eating of pork and pork products. In addition, he pro-hibited intermarriage and mixing with the White race. The sources of his teachings were his own interpretations of the Bible, the Qur'an, and the man-uals of W. D. Fard. Under his leadership the movement became nationwide. He made Hajj (pilgrimage to Makkah) in 1960 and his book *The Message to the Black Man in America*[82] was published in 1965. This book embodies his basic teachings and philosophy. It is considered the basic source for the movement. The NOI continued to grow under the leadership of Elijah Muhammad and spread to almost all major U.S. cities and acquired an international reputation.

At the death of Elijah Muhammad in 1975, the NOI joined the mainstream of Islam and became a true Islamic organization under the leadership of Elijah's son, Warith Deen Muhammad,[83] who changed the name to American Muslim Mission. This reorganization of the NOI is known as "the change." Warith Deen's brother wrote:

> Elijah Muhammad's doctrine and policies underwent basic modifications and outright reversals with the accession in 1975 of his son, now known as Warith Deen Muhammad. Referring to himself as the "Mujaddid" (Renewer) he dis-carded the belief in the divinity of Fard, the messengerhood of his father, the evil nature of European-Americans and the superiority of one people over another.[84]

Imam Warith Deen rejected the doctrine of his father and directed the move-ment in line with the principles of orthodox Islam. He studied Arabic, the Qur'an, and Islamic jurisprudence. He preached an entirely different message than that of his father. He debunked all forms of racism and abandoned his fa-ther's idea of a separate state. Most importantly, he rejected his father's claim to be the Messenger of Allah and the doctrine that Fard was Allah. Imam Warith Deen preached the orthodox Islamic doctrine that there is only one God and that Muhammad (Peace Be Upon Him) is His Messenger. He changed the name of temples to masjids or mosques and ministers to imams. In addition, he taught that the Qur'an is the revealed word of Allah. In February 1990 he headed a delegation to Makkah for the Council of Mosques, and in 1992 he became the first Muslim imam or leader to give an invocation before the U.S. Senate. He is the most highly respected Muslim leader in the United States today. Lately, he has been actively engaged in trying to bring harmony between indigenous Amer-ican and immigrant Muslims.

In 1985 Imam Warith Deen officially dissolved the American Muslim Mis-sion and integrated its members into the mainstream of the Muslim community in the United States. This move enhanced his own leadership and position among the Muslims in North America and throughout the Muslim world. The NOI movement did not die completely. In 1978 one of the disciples of Elijah Muhammad, Louis Farrakhan, who disagreed with "the change" that Warith Deen had instituted, revived the NOI. Farrakhan has about 20,000 followers, with headquarters in Chicago, who adhere faithfully to the teachings and phi-losophy of Elijah Muhammad.

An interesting phenomenon in the history of Muslims in the United States was the emergence of al-Hajj Malik Shabazz, commonly known as Malcolm X. Both his life and untimely death left a mark on the American scene, for he not only was a distinguished Muslim leader but also proved to be an important African American leader. He was born as Malcolm Little in 1925 in Omaha, Nebraska, the son of a Baptist minister. Prior to joining the NOI movement he was involved in drugs, criminal activities, promiscuity, and wild parties. This led to his being arrested and imprisoned. While he was in prison in the late 1940s, he joined the NOI and began preaching the teachings of Elijah Muhammad to his fellow prisoners. He became one of the close disciples and a strong supporter of Elijah Muhammad.

Malcolm X made a few trips to Africa and the Middle East, after which he abandoned the teachings of the NOI and its leader. Instead, he then began preaching orthodox Islam and founded the Muslim Mosque, Inc. After performing Hajj, he became known as al-Hajj Malik Shabazz. (The Muslim honorific title al-Hajj is added to any Muslim's name who performs Hajj to Makkah.) In December 1963, Malcolm X's relationship with NOI deteriorated due to his well-known statement concerning President John F. Kennedy's assassination, that "The chickens are coming home to roost." This statement and his popularity as a leader eventually led to a break between him and the NOI.

While Malcolm was performing Hajj in August 1964, he wrote an article in which he expressed the following thought:

> At Makkah I saw the spirit of unity and true brotherhood displayed by tens of thousands of people from all over the world, from blue-eyed blondes to black-skinned Africans. My religious pilgrimage (Hajj) to Makkah has given me a new insight into the true brotherhood of Islam, which encompasses all the races of mankind.[85]

It is interesting that the recently released FBI file on Malcolm X runs to about 2,000 pages.[86] The bureau opened his file shortly after his release from prison in 1953 and continued collecting information on him even after his death. He was assassinated in New York City in February 1965. A film titled *Malcolm X* that was released in 1993 portrays the various aspects of his life.

Muslim Concerns

Muslims, while they enjoy freedom of religion and the relaxed atmosphere of a pluralistic environment that tolerates various ideologies and religious practices, feel some prejudices against their way of life. Yvonne Haddad writes on this issue:

> [They] American Muslims are concerned over insensitive and racist statements on radio, television and in the press. They see media coverage of terrorists attacks by Muslims abroad, and particularly what is identified as "fanatic Muslim fundamentalism," as unbalanced and prejudicial, increasingly causing other Americans to equate Islam with terrorism.[87]

As a result of indiscriminate reporting of some criminal acts committed by individuals who happen to be Muslims, it becomes ingrained in the minds of people that all Muslims are fanatics and criminals. This is not the case; the majority of Muslims are peaceful, law-abiding citizens just as in other ethnic groups. It is the style of the media's reporting of events, such as the Gulf War, that leaves a negative and prejudicial impression of the Muslim community in the United States.

One myth that Muslims feel uneasy about is their religion being referred to as "Muhammadism" instead of Islam. Muslims are not followers of Muhammad in the sense that Christians are followers of Jesus Christ. They follow the teachings of the Qur'an as revealed to Muhammad. The term "Muhammadism" has a negative connotation and is a misconception of the religion of Islam. Muslims, not only in the United States but all over the world, are insulted when this term is used to refer to their religion.

Another myth regarding Muslims is that all Muslims are Arabs. This is not true. In fact the Arabs account for only about one-fifth of the population of Muslims worldwide. The largest Muslim countries are not even in the Arab world. Among these are Indonesia and Pakistan. Furthermore, there is a wide misconception that Iran is an Arab country. Iran is a Muslim country, and the people speak a language called Farsi that belongs to a branch of the Indo-European language family; its lexicon is heavily influenced by Arabic loan words.

Although religious pluralism in the United States gives Muslim Americans religious freedom, they often feel restricted in many ways. For instance, it is difficult for them to leave their jobs to attend Friday prayers. Also, Islam forbids interest on loans and this makes it difficult for strict Muslims to function financially within the Western banking system. Another concern is for Muslim women who adhere to the Islamic dress code. Their religion requires them to cover their heads with a hijab or scarf. This makes it almost impossible for them to obtain jobs, as most businesses in the United States do not accept this mode of dress. Some social customs that are taken for granted in U.S. society, but that are anathema to strict Muslims, such as dating and free mixing between the sexes, also present problems.

Islam is part of the Abrahamic tradition, as are Christianity and Judaism. Muslims feel strongly about their religion being part of this tradition. When religion is discussed and reference is made to the Judeo-Christian tradition, Muslims feel that they are not directly included, on the national scene, as active participants and members of this major religious group. They would like to see active involvement and participation concerning their faith and fate in U.S. religious, cultural, educational and even political dialogues taking place in the United States.

Arab Americans

The Arab community in the United States shares a common ethnic background with the Arab world that encompasses the Middle East and North Africa. Arabs first immigrated to the United States primarily from what is now Syria and

Lebanon in the latter part of the nineteenth century, and this trend continued until shortly before World War II. The majority were Christians, merchants, farmers, and even some intellectuals such as Gubran Khalil Gubran, a noted author and artist. Most of them are now in the second and third generation and have assimilated into the American way of life. Although they have retained some of their cultural heritage and have discouraged intermarriage, language and ethnic identity gave way to new realities.[88]

Early Arab immigrants to the United States, in contrast to later immigrants, did not have a direct association or link to specific Arab countries. Most of the Arab countries that exist today were not in existence during this period because, until the beginning of the World War I, the greater part of the Middle East was under the rule of the Ottoman Empire. Therefore, in the majority of cases the early immigrants identified themselves as Syrians since they came from the region of Greater Syria. In fact they established churches and clubs in which the name "Syrian" plays a prominent part.

> The Syrians' acceptance of America as their permanent home was signaled by establishment of such institutions as Eastern-rite churches, an Arabic-language press, and several educational and charitable associations, mainly in the more populous East Coast urban colonies.[89]

It is interesting that a number of politicians, film stars, and well-known businessmen trace their ancestry to Syria and Lebanon. Some of these are Danny Thomas; Casey Kasem; consumer advocate Ralph Nader; former senator and founder in 1980 of the national organization called the American Arab Anti-Discrimination Committee (ADC), James Abourezk; clothing magnate Farah; Dr. James Zogby, a writer and politician and founder and head of the Arab American Institute; former White House Chief of Staff and former governor of New Hampshire John Sununu; and Donna Shalala, secretary of health and human services with the Clinton Administration. This is a brief list. Many other professional Americans of Arab descent, such as doctors, engineers, professors and scientists, contribute greatly to the American way of life.

The period between the first and second world wars did not witness any substantial wave of Arab immigrants. This is partially due to the restrictions of U.S. laws, especially the quota law of 1924 that severely limited the number of Arabs immigrating to the United States. After World War II, many of the present-day Arab countries were established and the majority of the immigrants at this time, in contrast to those in the earlier period, were Muslims. Political events in the middle East, such as the establishment of Israel in 1948, contributed to an increase of Arab immigrants to the United States. These new Arab immigrants were generally better off economically than the earlier group. They were educated professionals and a substantial number of students who did not return to their country of origin after studying in the United States. The exact number of Arab Americans in the United States today is not known. However, the available estimates are 2.5 to 3 million or approximately 1 percent of the U.S. population.[90] Arab Americans are considered one of the fastest growing groups of immigrants, settling all over the United States, especially in large cities such as Chicago, New York, Detroit, and Los Angeles. Even though they are Arabic-speaking people, there exists no real feeling of Arab solidarity among them.

Former Congressman Paul Findley writes about the weak and almost nonexistent political stand of Arab Americans when compared with the Jewish-Israeli lobby that is visible, powerful, and influential, especially in Washington, DC. He states that, "Arab American lobbies, fledgling forces even today, were nonexistent." He further states, "Even if a congressman had wanted to hear the Arab viewpoint, he would have had difficulty finding an Arab spokesman to explain it."[91] This state of affairs continues, although there is a growing trend for Arab Americans to become more politically organized.

Arab American Origins

Arab Americans are linked ethnically and historically to the Arab people of the Middle East. The Arab people today number approximately 220 million and inhabit the Middle East and African regions that consist of over 20 countries. An Arab can be Muslim, Christian, Jew, or of some other belief. The Arab people are Semites and their original homeland is the Arabian Peninsula. In the pre-Islamic period, seventh century A.D., the Arabs lived in tribal communities and some established small kingdoms. There was no clear national consciousness among the various communities in Arabia even though they shared the same language and, to some extent, the same cultural heritage.

The Arabs pride themselves with having an expressive, eloquent, and poetic language. They honor their poets and celebrated the occasions when a poet became recognized as a defender of the tribe. In the pre-Islamic period, annual festivals were held in Makkah where some poets recited their works. Seven of the poets became so famous that some of their poems were written in gold and hung on the walls of the Ka'bah, the religious sanctuary in Makkah. These poems are memorized by many members of the tribes, and this tradition has endured throughout the history of the Arabs even to today.

With the advent of Islam in the seventh century, the Arabs and the Arabic language acquired a new status. The Qur'an was revealed in Arabic and gave the Arabic language a status of glory that it never had before. Arabic became the language of the Islamic civilization and the lingua franca of the entire Islamic empire that extended from the eastern shore of the Mediterranean to the western region of China. Today the Arabic language (including various regional dialects) is still the medium of expression for all Arab countries. The Arabic alphabet is used with many of the Islamic languages, including Farsi (Persian), Urdu, and several other languages of the region. Also, the Arabic language is recognized as one of the six official languages at the United Nations.

Images and Challenges

Both positive images and negative stereotypes surround Arab Americans. Positive images include the strong ties among nuclear and extended families, care and respect for elders, and the generosity and hospitality that are well known by those entertained or hosted by an Arab. But it is the negative images and stereotypes of the Arab world in general and Arab Americans specifically that are the most prevalent. As one author states:

> The Arab-American community, now estimated to be over two million, has suffered and continues to suffer in many ways the curse of negative stereotyping of Arabs. Thus, Arab Americans are made to feel ashamed of their ancestors and their former homeland. As a result, some have avoided reference to their Arab heritage, for instance, often describing themselves in terms of geographic region from which they came or the religious sect to which they belong.[92]

The negative image of Arab Americans, particularly of Palestinian Arabs, is more widespread and intense because of the Arab-Israeli conflict. Palestinians are often viewed by the media as Arab refugees or terrorists. Many Arab Americans perceive that they are an easy target for insults and slurs. Whenever major events take place in the Middle East, such as the Gulf War, the Arab American community often becomes the focus of investigation and interrogation.

The U.S. movie industry has always had a fascination with the Arab character, either real or mythical. A study reviewing a century of Arabs portrayed in U.S. movies states:

> Over the past century the movies have recorded changes, invariably for the worse, in an Arab image that was tinged with negative elements to begin with. For Americans, the Arab has long been the quintessential Other—fundamentally different from us, both fascinating and repugnant, enacting the taboos of our society. Brought to life on the screen from our collective imagination, the Arab does terrible deeds and receives appropriate punishments.[93]

Arab Americans are often erroneously perceived as a unified single ethnic group. Their complexity is frequently overlooked. In reality, Arabs in the United States, especially the first generation who in turn influence their offspring, come from different countries with different allegiances and interests. For example, Lebanese Arabs tend to congregate and rally around the specific interests of their origin, as do Egyptians, Palestinians, and Iraqis. However, cultural, linguistic, and possibly religious affiliations play a role in uniting them with a common perspective. In the United States today, the Arab community, especially in large metropolitan areas, has managed to publish Arabic newspapers and to produce its own television and radio shows. The persistent Arab-Israel conflict contributes to this growing sense of common identity among Arab Americans. The establishment of Israel in 1948 and the war of 1967 resulted in a large number of Palestinian refugees, who were scattered throughout many Arab countries and other parts of the world, including the United States. An estimated 80,000 to 100,000 Palestinians are now living in the United States. Former President Jimmy Carter wrote concerning this conflict:

> In simplest terms, the Arab-Israeli conflict is a struggle between two national identities for control of territory, but there are also historic, religious, strategic, political, and psychological issues that color the confrontation and retard its amicable solution. What each wants is no less than recognition, acceptance, inde-

pendence, sovereignty, and territorial identity. Neither officially recognizes the other's existence, so any testing of intentions must be done through uncertain intermediaries.[94]

President Carter, who orchestrated a peace treaty between Egypt and Israel in 1979, envisioned a day when the Palestinians and Israelis would settle their conflict peacefully. His dream was partially fulfilled when on September 13, 1993, at the White House in Washington, DC, official representatives of the Palestinians and the Israelis met to sign a peace agreement. While this treaty signifies the possibility of a new era in Arab-Israeli relations, the long history of conflict continues to influence the Arab American world view.

CONCLUSIONS

The history of immigration to the United States is marked by openness during periods of economic prosperity and hostility during times of economic decline and political insecurity. Hostility and xenophobia increased again in the 1990s because the influx of immigration is at its highest point since the first decade of this century. Critics of immigration argue that newcomers are taking jobs away from the native-born population and are a drain on the nation's public welfare resources, health services, and the public schools. These assertions are not backed up by most of the recent research conducted by academics and government officials.[95] Most studies show "that immigrants, legal and illegal, are more of a boon than a bane in this country."[96] They indicate that, on the average, immigrants actually help create more jobs and are more likely to be self-employed, start their own businesses, and pay higher tax rates than do natives. Furthermore, they indicate that immigrants do not make higher use of welfare or unemployment benefits than natives. Nevertheless, the fears and negative images of immigrants persist. Thus many classroom teachers face difficult challenges as the nation's school-age population becomes ever more diverse and the social climate becomes more xenophobic.

In *Preparing for the Twenty-First Century,* Paul Kennedy identifies global demographic imbalances between richer and poorer nations as the major issue underlying all the other important forces we will face in the next century.[97] Poorer nations are experiencing population explosions along with shrinking natural resources, while the rich nations (who account for about one-sixth of the world's population and control five-sixths of its wealth) are experiencing problems of stagnant or negative population growth. One result of these changing demographics is massive emigration from "have-not" nations to wealthier nations such as the United States. If we are to benefit from these changing demographics, the massive educational reforms advocated by multiculturalists must be implemented. Multiculturalists argue that if we establish an equitable society based on the ideal of cultural pluralism, we can accommodate the predicted influx of immigrants from poorer nations. Economic, cultural, and spiritual growth will then benefit society as a whole.

COMPARE AND CONTRAST

1. Accommodation and liberation
2. Racism and anti-Semitism
3. Minority group perspective and ethnic group diversity
4. Ethnic group diversity and stereotype
5. Chinese, Japanese, and Southeast Asian immigrant experiences
6. African American perspectives and Native American perspectives
7. Cuban American, Mexican American, and Puerto Rican perspectives
8. Muslim and Arab American perspectives

ACTIVITIES AND QUESTIONS

1. *Ethnic Roots Essay.* Your analysis may take weeks or months and could be shared with other members of your class or workshop. A photo essay could be an alternative. Describe your ethnic background in terms of

   a. Where your ancestors came from, when they arrived in this country, and where they settled.
   b. The immigrating ancestor or family member who has had the strongest influence on your own development. Tell why this person immigrated and when he or she settled. Describe the most difficult problem(s) this person faced upon arrival, and how he or she (or later family members) dealt with the problem(s).
   c. Description of your family in terms of cultural assimilation, accommodation, segregation or separatism, and amalgamation.

2. Using Longstreet's definition of ethnicity on pages 53–63, describe your own ethnicity in terms of your

   a. verbal communication
   b. nonverbal communication
   c. orientation modes
   d. values
   e. intellectual modes
   f. other. Be specific and explain how your early experiences shaped each of these aspects of your ethnicity. Briefly explain the degree to which your own ethnicity helped you meet school expectations (grades K–12). If you have experienced any areas of mismatch, be specific.

3. Is it always necessary that members of an ethnic group "trade off" some aspects of their traditional culture?

4. Consider the current statistics on school dropouts, suspensions, and expulsions. Based on the different histories and world views of Jewish Americans, Japanese Americans, African Americans, Mexican Americans, and Native Americans, how do you explain their differing successes in North American schools today? Which of these experiences do you predict will

provide us with a model for the Southeast Asian refugee experience? Explain your reasoning.

5. Read *Black Elk Speaks* by John G. Neihardt. How would you describe the great Sioux leaders? How did they become powerful? In your opinion, how did the sacred hoop become broken? Could it ever be restored?

6. Read *Further Reflections on Ethnicity,* a collection of essays by Michael Novak, author of *Rise of the Unmeltable Ethnics.* Describe the White ethnic perspective. To what degree is this perspective compatible with non-White ethnic perspectives in this society?

7. A common misconception is that pride in one's own culture and ethnic group breeds intolerance and ethnocentrism toward other cultures and ethnic groups. How would you clear up this misinterpretation about interethnic relations?

8. How do you respond to Jack Forbes's statement on the usurpation of native peoples' lands and resources? As quoted earlier, Forbes wrote: "It must be openly acknowledged that Indians are poor because white people are rich, that the land, timber and minerals which white people use to produce their wealth were virtually all taken by force or deception. It must be recognized that Indian reservations usually exist in marginal land, not originally of value from the perspective of white economic development."[98] Is there any way of resolving this conflict? Explain.

9. The diversity of religious holidays celebrated in many communities presents teachers with potential problems and possibilities. What are some of the potential problems? What are some of the alternative ways teachers can prevent these problems and build on the possibilities? What will you do as a teacher around such national holidays as Thanksgiving, Christmas, and Easter?

NOTES

1. A. Hirschfelder, *Happily May I Walk: American Indians and Alaska Natives Today* (New York: Charles Scribner, 1982).
2. J. A. Banks, *Teaching Strategies for Ethnic Studies,* 5th ed. (Boston: Allyn and Bacon, 1991), 151.
3. A. Hirschfelder, *Happily May I Walk,* 4.
4. Herman J. Viola. *After Columbus: The Smithsonian Chronicle of the North American Indians* (New York: Orion Books, 1990), page 18.
5. Viola, *After Columbus,* 27.
6. J. Weatherford, *Native Roots: How the Indians Enriched America* (New York: Crown Publishers, Inc., 1991), 27.
7. Ibid., 16–17.

8. Ibid., 41.
9. Ibid., 42.
10. Ibid., 67.
11. Ibid.
12. Hraba, *American Ethnicity,* 212; and Feagin and Feagin, *Racial and Ethnic Relations,* 120.
13. Ibid., 212–213.
14. D. McNickle, "Indian and European: Indian-White Relations from Discovery to 1887," in *The Emergent Native Americans,* D. E. Walker, Jr., ed. (Boston: Little Brown, 1972), 75–86.
15. V. J. Vogel, *This Country Was Ours* (New York: Harper & Row, 1972), 70.
16. Hraba, *American Ethnicity,* 214.

17. Ibid., 225.
18. J. D. Forbes, "Teaching Native American Values and Cultures," in *Teaching Ethnic Studies: Concepts and Strategies,* J. A. Banks, ed. (Washington, DC: National Council for the Social Studies, 1973), 217. Reprinted from the NCSS 43rd yearbook, *Teaching Ethnic Studies,* edited by James Banks, with permission of the National Council for the Social Studies.
19. "Wind River's Last Generation," *Time,* October 21, 1985:40. For a compelling discussion of land issues and the reservation, see W. La Duke and W. Churchill, "Native America: The Political Economy of Radioactive Colonialism," *Journal of Ethnic Studies* 13, no. 3 (Fall 1985):107–132.
20. W. G. Tierney, "Native Voices in Academe: Strategies for Empowerment," *Change,* 23(2), 1992: 36–39.
21. Feagin and Feagin, *Racial and Ethnic Relations,* 219.
22. Ibid.
23. J. Collier, *Indians of the Americas* (New York: New American Library, 1947), 4.
24. Hispanics: A Melding of Cultures," *Time* (Special issue on "Immigrants: The Changing Face of America"), July 8,1985:36, and 1990 Census.
25. L. F. Estrada, "Anticipating the Demographic Future," *Change,* 20(3), 16–17.
26. C. McWilliams, *North from Mexico: The Spanish-speaking People of the United States* (New York: Greenwood Press, 1968), 207.
27. This point was brought to my attention by Bradley Levinson, personal communication, July 1997.
28. Ibid.
29. McWilliams, op. cit., 207.
30. C. Diaz, "Puerto Ricans in the United States: Concepts, Strategies, and Materials," in *Teaching Strategies for Ethnic Studies,* 4th ed. J. A. Banks, ed. (Boston: Allyn and Bacon, 1987).
31. J. P. Fitzpatrick, "Puerto Ricans," in *Harvard Encyclopedia of American Ethnic Groups* 4th ed., S. Thernstrum, A. Arlov, and O. Handlin, eds. (Cambridge, MA: Harvard University Press, 1980), 859, and

Banks, ed., *Teaching Strategies for Ethnic Studies,* 358.
32. Ibid.
33. Ibid., and Banks, ed., *Teaching Strategies for Ethnic Studies,* 358.
34. Feagin and Feagin, *Racial and Ethnic Relations,* 289.
35. Ibid., 288.
36. Ibid., 288–289.
37. McWilliams, *North from Mexico,* 77.
38. J. Hraba, *American Ethnicity* (Itasca, IL: F. E. Peacock, 1979), 241.
39. "Symbiosis along 1,936 Miles," *Time* (special issue on "Immigrants: The Changing Face of America"), July 8, 1985: 36.
40. Ibid.
41. Feagin and Feagin, *Racial and Ethnic Relations,* 318–319.
42. Ibid., 320.
43. Ibid.
44. Ibid., 322.
45. B. Ashabranner, *Dark Harvest* (Dodd, Mead, 1985), 19.
46. HCR, Migrant and Seasonal Agricultural Areas, 2021 L Street, N.W., Washington, D.C., June 28, 1985.
47. Ibid., 45.
48. Ibid., 20.
49. R. Acuna, *Occupied America: A History of Chicanos,* 3rd ed. (New York: Harper & Row, 1988), 438.
50. Ashabranner, *Dark Harvest,* 44.
51. Ibid.
52. Acuna, *Occupied America,* 450.
53. Diaz, "Puerto Ricans in the United States," 394.
54. Ibid., 395.
55. J. S. Olson, *The Ethnic Dimension in American History,* vol. 2 (New York: St. Martin's Press, 1979), 379.
56. *1990 Census.
57. "Asians: To America with Skills," *Time* (Special issue on "Immigrants: The Changing Face of America"), July 8, 1985: 44–46, and 1990 Census.
58. Ibid.
59. T. Knoll, *Becoming Americans: Asian Sojourners, Immigrants, and Refugees in the Western United States* (Portland, OR: Coast to Coast Books, 1982), 5–6.

60. Ibid., 14.

61. Ibid.

62. "Chinese Americans: Realities and Myths," in *Teacher's Guide* (San Francisco: Association of Chinese Teachers, n.d.), 11.

63. Knoll, *Becoming Americans,* Foreword.

64. V. G. Thuy, "The Indochinese in America: Who Are They and How Are They Doing," in *The Education of Asian and Pacific Americans: Historical Perspective and Prescriptions for the Future,* D. T. Nakanishi and M. Hirano-Nakanishi, eds. (Phoenix, AZ: Oryx Press, 1983).

65. Ibid., 107.

66. Ibid., 103.

67. Ibid.

68. "Chinese Americans: Realities and Myths," 11.

69. Knoll, *Becoming Americans,* 62.

70. Feagin and Feagin, *Racial and Ethnic Relations,* 338.

71. B. Hosokawa, *Nisei: The Quiet Americans* (New York: William Morrow, 1969), 329–330.

72. M. B. Carrott, "Prejudice Goes to Court: The Japanese and the Supreme Court of the 1920s," *California History* (Summer 1983):122–139.

73. Feagin and Feagin, *Racial and Ethnic Relations,* 356.

74. Ibid., 359–360.

75. F. Butterfield, "Why Asians Are Going to the Head of the Class," *New York Times,* "Education Section," August 3, 1986:18–19.

76. Ibid., 21.

77. Thuy, "The Indochinese," 103.

78. For further discussion on this issue see C. L. Stone's "Estimate of Muslims Living in America," in *The Muslims of America,* Yvonne Yazbeck Haddad, ed. (New York: Oxford University Press, 1991), 25–36.

79. Yahya, Aossey, Jr., *Fifty Years of Islam in Iowa 1925–1975* (Cedar Rapids, IA: Unity Publishing Co., n.d.), p. 2.

80. For further information on Muslim organizations, see Gutbi Mahdi Ahmed's article "Muslim Organizations in the United States," in Haddad, ed., *The Muslims of America,* 11–24.

81. For further information regarding the NOI movement and Elijah Muhammad, see the chapter entitled "Muslims in the United States: An Overview of Organizations, Doctrines and Problems" by Elijah's son, Akbar Muhammad, in *Islamic Impact,* Yvonne Haddad et al., eds. (Syracuse, NY: Syracuse University Press, 1984), 195–217.

82. This 355-page book was published by Muhammad's Temple No. 2, 7351 Stony Island Avenue, Chicago, IL, 1965.

83. The name Warith Deen is an Arabic name that means "the inheritor of the religion."

84. "Muslims in the United States: An Overview of Organizations, Doctrines and Problems," in *Islamic Impact,* Yvonne Haddad et al., eds. (Syracuse, NY: Syracuse University Press, 1984), p. 208.

85. This quote appeared in an article Malcolm X wrote for an Egyptian newspaper, August 1964.

86. A summary of the FBI file on Malcolm X was published in Clayborne Carson, *Malcolm X: The FBI File* (New York: Carroll & Graf Publishers, 1991).

87. Yvonne Y. Haddad, "A Century of Islam in America," Occasional Paper (Washington, DC: American Institute for Islamic Affairs, 1986).

88. John Zogby, *Arab America Today* (Washington, DC: Arab American Institute, 1990), v.

89. Alixa Naff, *Becoming American: The Early Arab Immigrant Experience* (Carbondale, IL: Southern Illinois University Press, 1985),12–13.

90. Baha Abu-Laban, *Social and Political Attitudes of Arab-Americans,* ADC Issue Paper No. 24. (Washington, DC: ADC Research Institute, 1990), vi.

91. Paul Findley, *They Dare to Speak Out* (Westport, CT: Amana Books, Lawrence Hill & Company, 1985), 1–2.

92. Michael W. Suleiman, *The Arabs in the Mind of America* (Brattleboro, VT: Amana Books, 1988), 150–151.

93. Laurence Michalek, "The Arab in American Cinema: A Century of Otherness," *The Arab Image in American Film and Televi-*

sion (Washington, DC: ADC Research Institute, n.d.), 2.

94. Jimmy Carter, *The Blood of Abraham* (Boston: Houghton Mifflin Company, 1985), 112.

95. "Immigrants: A Cost or a Benefit?" *New York Times* OP-ED Friday, September 3, 1993, A11.

96. Larry Rohter, "Revisiting Immigration and the Open-Door Policy," *New York Times,* Sunday, September 19, 1991, 4.

97. P. Kennedy, *Preparing for the Twenty-First Century* (New York: Random House, 1993).

98. Forbes, "Teaching Native Americans Values and Cultures," 217.

part II

Individual Differences That Affect Teaching and Learning

*A*s with our previous case studies, the schools you are about to visit are real. Although their names have been changed, the teachers and students you will meet are actual people, and the incidents described have recently taken place.

There is nothing unique or unusual about these schools, teachers, or students. Some of the people and events will seem familiar, which is partly why they are included. Other people and events may seem exaggerated or unrealistic. These examples serve to illustrate that efforts to develop individual and cultural perspectives in teaching and learning must be broad in scope. Concern should not be limited to inner-city schools or settings where most students are ethnic minorities, but should include any classroom where students are not achieving because of personal and cultural characteristics that conflict with what predominates in a classroom. Is there a classroom in existence that does not merit this concern?

WARREN BENSON'S CLASSROOM

It is 2:00 P.M., beginning of the sixth-period class, and Warren Benson, a young teacher, looks around the room. Only eight students out of a possible thirty are present.

"Where is everybody?" he demands. "They don't like your class," a girl volunteers. Three girls saunter in. Cora, who is playing a cassette recorder, bumps over to her desk in tune with the music. She lowers the volume. "Don't mark us down late," she shouts. "We was right here."

Benson, a first-year teacher who spent four years in the navy between high school and college, had requested this school. Here he found students from poverty homes, students who couldn't read, students who hated school and teachers, students with drug problems, students waiting to drop out. Almost one-third of the students came from homes where one or both parents speak only Spanish.

For years Benson's dream was to teach on a Native American reservation. He believed this school would be good preparation. Now, after two months in the classroom he has real doubts. Doubts about these kids. Doubts about himself.

Benson tells everyone to take out today's vocabulary words. "Aw, come on man, give us a break," a student called Spark moans. Cora turns up the volume and croons, "Hey-ey-ey, bay-bee . . . ah wants ya to know-o-o-o. . . ." Then, lowering the volume, she asks, "Mr. Benson, you got a pencil?" Another straggler walks in. "You late, boy," one student says. "So what, boy," the straggler answers. Benson asks for a definition of the first word, *tariff*.

No response. "Ricardo?" "What?" Ricardo asks, tuning in briefly. A few students busily leaf through the text, trying to locate the glossary.

Spark tells some nearby students his ancestors are Aztec Indians. "You an Indian?" Ricardo asks. "You got a tomahawk and all?" Benson defines *tariff* for Ricardo, who listens for a second, then throws a paper airplane over Benson's head and hits a girl in the neck. Benson continues. "Number two is Treaty of Guadalupe. Who can tell us what the Treaty of Guadalupe is?"

"ML Benson," Cora interrupts, "I got to go to the bathroom." Benson tells her no. "Goddammit, motherf—, I got to go to the bathroom," she yells. "I'll give you a pass today," says Benson, "but this is the last time."

Benson tries to get back into the lesson. "Who can tell us what the Treaty of Guadalupe is?" "Ain't no word Treaty of Ha-wa-da-loop in here," shouts Spark. A blonde student sits silently in a corner chair; everyone else is talking.

Cora returns to the classroom. She grabs Benson's hand and pats it. "You ain't mad, is you?" Benson ignores her. Then he shouts to make himself heard above the din of conversation. "Get quiet!" Benson slams his fist on the lectern. Then he glares at the students until he has their attention. "Okay. It's obvious that you haven't learned these words. Everybody take out a paper. I'm going to give you a vocabulary test."

It is evident that Warren Benson's class typifies one of the most difficult and challenging teaching situations imaginable. The problems Benson faces—problems of poorly skilled students, high absenteeism, and unruly classes—are faced by teachers throughout the nation.

A theme that runs through the next two chapters is that we must learn to teach others as they would be taught (that is, learn), rather than necessarily as we would teach or have others teach us. We must be able to cue into the critical characteristics of learners in our classroom (critical meaning those characteristics that strongly affect the way a person learns). Some of these characteristics are accurately labeled individual differences. Others stem from cultural differences and alternatives.

Read the following incident, which took place recently in the Midwest. The case of Kevin Armstrong illustrates that it is often difficult to distinguish between individual and cultural characteristics, unless a teacher knows what to look for.

THE CASE OF KEVIN ARMSTRONG

It is the second day of a new school year, 2:15 P.M. The phone rings and Ms. Armstrong answers it.

"Hello, Ms. Armstrong?" a voice inquires. "This is Ms. Dixon over at Wildwood Elementary School. Kevin's teacher. I—"

Ms. Armstrong, a striking Black woman in her early thirties, interrupts, "What's wrong?"

"Nothing is wrong," answers Ms. Dixon. "I'm just calling to let you know that we've decided to put Kevin back in second grade. He just isn't ready for third-grade work."

Ms. Armstrong is stunned. Prior to their move from Denver to a midwestern university town, Kevin had done superior work in a desegregated school that was considered good. Over half the students were White. "What do you mean he isn't ready for third grade?" she asks coldly. "Teacher last year didn't say nothin' about him having problems."

"Ms. Armstrong, what I'm suggesting is for Kevin's own good. He's way behind the other children in my class. He'll feel like a failure if he stays."

"How you think he'll feel if you put him back?" she snaps. "He been lookin' to third grade all summer long."

"I hoped you would understand that we want to do what's best for Kevin," responds Ms. Dixon. "Would you like to come to the school and talk this over with the principal?"

"We comin'." Ms. Armstrong hangs up and turns to face her husband.

Wildwood is considered by many to be the best elementary school in town. Standardized achievement test scores are among the highest in the state and the school boasts many innovative academic programs. Except for a few who, like Kevin, live in a string of apartment buildings bordering the school district, most of the children come from wealthy homes. The community is largely professional. A handful of Black and Latino children attend the school, and most have been adopted by Anglo parents.

Mr. Peters, the principal, explains to Mr. and Mrs. Armstrong why he and Ms. Dixon believe Kevin would be better off in second grade. Ms. Dixon, also present, remains silent.

"Kevin is too immature for third grade. Ms. Dixon picked this up immediately. Physically he is small for his age, and his attention span is very short. During music class he is unable to sit still. In class he can't wait for his turn to speak and in general it's clear that he hasn't learned to control himself the way our other third graders do. Ms. Dixon has already given the children some pretests to see how much they remember. And, of course, Kevin's reading, writing, and math skills are way below grade level."

"Can't you give him a chance? This is just the second day. Can't we get him some tutoring or something? I read somewhere about some special programs for kids in the district who have problems," Ms. Armstrong asks.

"Some schools in the city do, but not us. We don't have enough students who need them to justify the expense. If we keep Kevin in third grade, he'll be isolated from his classmates, working by himself. That doesn't seem fair to Kevin."

"But still that's better than puttin' him back," counters Ms. Armstrong. "We'll be goin' back to Denver in a year and a half."

Stating that it is against their best judgment, Ms. Dixon and Mr. Peters agree to keep Kevin in the third grade on a trial basis.

Ms. Dixon's conclusion that Kevin was not capable of third-grade work after less than two days of observation warrants questioning. She was aware of his geographical move. The adjustment to a new home, new school, and new friends can be difficult for any child. The additional adjustments an African American child must make to a setting such as Wildwood can be traumatic. Many children like Kevin are raised in a cultural environment that is significantly different from what predominates at school. For these children, the school's expectation of appropriate behavior requires so much energy that little remains for the business of learning.

Reconsider the case of Kevin Armstrong and meet one of his schoolmates, Rachael Jones. Their teachers perceive them strictly as failing individuals. These teachers like *all* their children and believe in treating each one the same. Ironically, by treating Kevin and Rachael the same as their classmates, teachers are probably stacking the deck against them. In order to provide equal opportunity for all students, it is sometimes necessary to offer unequal treatment, according to relevant (though not frivolous) differences.

Ms. Dixon is fearful of probing into Kevin's blackness and dismisses that fact as irrelevant. She is unable to entertain the thought that Kevin might have special needs because deep inside she fears this may be a racist notion. Ms. Dixon has had a Black student before, the adopted daughter of a prominent physician in town. The girl performed beautifully in class, was a top student, and confirmed Ms. Dixon's view that there are smart Blacks and dumb Blacks, and Kevin falls into the second category.

Rachael is White. The conditions of her life are largely unknown to her teacher who, thus, has no reason to believe that there is any possible explanation for her failure other than her lack of ability to learn. Her whiteness masks the possibility that she might need unequal treatment in order to attain success in school.

KEVIN RECONSIDERED

Anyone who knows Kevin around the apartment complex is struck by his clever wit, his mischievous nature, and the way he gets other kids of all ages to do just what he wants. Whether it is an after-school snack, a bicycle, or a toy sale (other kids' toys, of course), Kevin somehow manages to outsmart the other children and many of their parents as well. The apartment children often get into a lot of trouble, though usually it's not too serious. Kevin is always there, but somehow he always escapes blame. Physically, he is tough. Although he is very small for his age, he can get the better of kids almost twice his size.

One day, close to Mother's Day, a newspaper reporter came around asking all the youngest kids what was special about their mothers. Most of the children mentioned their mothers' good cooking and things their mothers buy them. Kevin, however, said his mother is special because she collects frogs—all kinds, all sizes. Fully enjoying the reporter's surprise, Kevin later added that most of the frogs weren't real ones.

On rainy days Kevin usually plays in a friend's apartment. He often builds complicated structures with a borrowed Erector set. He seems to know all the television programs, channels, and times by heart, but can read the *TV Guide* if necessary (as well as *Jaws* and Captain Marvel comics).

Kevin was the organizer of a week-long toy sale and earned a commission as manager. He kept all the financial records and supervised the cash flow for an entire week. To the casual observer, Kevin is a bright and lively eight-year-old.

It is a different story inside Ms. Dixon's classroom, where Kevin is far behind everyone else in class. He works by himself in a cubby much of the time. Kevin sits in his desk a lot better than he did at the first of the year. But he still hams it up any chance he gets. The other kids love that and see Kevin as a kind of class clown.

Ms. Dixon is concerned about Kevin. His progress this year is very slow, slower than any child she has known in her three years of teaching (all at Wildwood). Kevin does not concentrate on one activity long enough to finish anything, and he is easily distracted by his classmates. Often he does not listen to her directions and, thus, cannot do the assignments, or does them incorrectly. Although she is often amazed at his creative and unusual ideas, Ms. Dixon is distressed by his sloppy and careless writing habits and his lack of effort in math.

THE CASE OF RACHAEL JONES

Rachael lives in Kevin's apartment complex and is a second grader at Wildwood. This is her first year there, too. Rachael's mother, a hardworking and good-hearted woman in her thirties, cleans apartments in the complex. Her work has become so steady that she is off Aid to Dependent Children (ADC) for the first time in six years. Although Rachael's stepfather has a college degree, he has been unable to find work in his field and works as a city bus driver. Rachael's natural father (and her eldest brother as well) is a man who is continually in and out of prison and pays no support for any of his five children. While money is a continual problem for the family, the remarriage of Rachael's mother has brought a degree of stability and security.

Like Kevin, Rachael is at the bottom of her class. She is often sick and is frequently absent from school. Rachael complains to her mother that her schoolwork is too hard. Homework assignments are usually put off until 9:30 or 10:00 P.M., and Rachael's mother is unable to help her. On occasion she will ask one of the women she works for to help Rachael. Unlike Kevin, Rachael fears adventure, even the three-quarter-mile walk to school, and has few friends. Her long blonde hair hangs limply and her clothes seldom fit properly, a fact that sometimes elicits cruel remarks from schoolmates.

Ms. Bryant, Rachael's second-grade teacher, sees Rachael as a shy, quiet little girl who is doing the best she can. She has placed Rachael in her slowest reading and math group, where Rachael's progress is so slow that it is doubtful she will be able to go on to third grade next year.

THE CASE OF MAX BRITTEN

There had always been something different about Max that his teachers couldn't quite understand. As early as kindergarten his teachers sensed something. He tuned out a lot during class, and his work was inconsistent, ranging from very high to very low. The teacher suspected he was capable of doing better, although a learning disability was also a strong possibility. At the school's request Max was completely tested by the head of the Children's Neurology Clinic. The physician reported that Max was a bright, exceptionally independent child who could learn anything he wanted to learn. But that would be the key: his interest. Max also suffered from a severe case of sibling rivalry regarding his younger brother that might require future attention.

After kindergarten, Max's parents (both college professors) were divorced, and he moved with his mother and brother to the Midwest, where he attended the same school as Rachael and Kevin. Max became quite shy and had a difficult time making friends. At school he was often teased and scapegoated in subtle ways unobservable by his teachers. At home he was continually taunted by his peers with the exception of one friend who suffered similar rejection.

Max's schoolwork deteriorated. His teacher felt he was immature, easily distracted, and did not listen well. He was in the lowest reading and math groups. In contrast, Max's younger brother was a top student at Wildwood. He was liked by teachers and classmates and was involved in sports and music. As one teacher said to Max's mother, "Your sons are like night and day, salt and pepper." In the third grade, for some unknown reason, the school did not receive the results of Max's Iowa Tests. There was no record of his past test scores, and the fourth-grade teacher wondered if Max were mildly retarded or perhaps suffered from some sort of learning disability.

Despite his parent's divorce, Max's home environment was highly supportive, and during summer vacations with his maternal grandparents Max was a different person. He was an avid stamp collector and through stamps had come to know more about geography than most adults. He read *Time* and *National Geographic* regularly, and frequently consulted his *World Book* encyclopedias, a gift from his grandparents. Yet it became clear that Max was becoming increasingly miserable at school. One day he cut school and hid at home. When his mother returned from work he told her he just couldn't go back. The school decided to test Max to see if he was eligible for special education.

The confidential psychological evaluation of Max in the fourth grade stated that "Max is a handsome, blond-haired, blue-eyed boy. He is somewhat quiet but friendly. Max reportedly gets along well with his classmates although the teacher notes that he tends to keep to himself. . . . Max frequently does not attend to critical instructions regarding assignments that often results in missed work and/or poor performance on assignments. When singled out for individual attention Max's work tends to improve; his work also improves when he is specifically requested to redo an unsatisfactory assignment."

On the day Max was given a variety of IQ tests, his teacher excitedly told him to tell his mother that he had done a fantastic job on the tests. He had done so well in fact, that none of the socioemotional tests were administered.

The written report stated that "The results of the current psychological evaluation show Max to be a child of superior intellectual ability. . . . Interviews with Max's teacher suggest that Max can perform academically when he is given large amounts of individual attention or when required to redo unsatisfactory assignments. However, there is only a limited amount of individual attention that can be afforded to any individual child in a typical classroom."

"There is some suggestion that Max finds the individual attention he receives very soothing and rewarding and therefore sees little incentive in performing well consistently. This is not unusual in view of Max's family situation. . . . It is recommended that Max be reassured about his academic ability but, also, it should be explained that he must satisfy certain criteria in order to complete the fourth grade successfully. Max is not eligible for special services at the present time."

Later, during the case conference Ms. Johnson stated that Max became a different person as a result of doing well on the tests, and the schoolwork began to improve. Max's mother reported that he was beginning to make new friends in the neighborhood and that he seemed happier at home.

Suppose Max, for emotional reasons, was unable to perform well on the test. What would have happened? The case of Max illustrates that factors related to school success are very complex and not necessarily linked to cultural conflicts or racial differences. Both Max and his teacher were from White, economically advantaged backgrounds.

It is possible that problems faced by children like Kevin and Rachael and the students in Warren Benson's classroom grow out of conflict between their world view and that which predominates in school, or to negative prejudices on the part of teachers and classmates. It is also possible that, like Max, their failure is due to a mismatch between teaching and learning styles, or to some special personal qualities that need to be understood. Teachers must be sensitive to all the possibilities, which is not an easy task.

When we observe what goes on in most classrooms, the assumption seems to be that students are basically the same. The fact that there are important individual differences along with the obvious similarities seems to be overlooked.

On the other hand, there are classrooms where teachers value diversity and use it to create classroom climates that encourage both academic achievement and friendship. Consider Ms. Lindsey, the third-grade teacher in the case of Maria Chacón.

THE CASE OF MARIA CHACÓN

Maria Chacón entered Harmony Hills elementary school last fall, just a few days after she and her family moved to Texas. Orally proficient in Spanish, Maria did not speak English and seemed to comprehend little when she first arrived. Now, at the end of the school year, she speaks fluently with her English-speaking classmates along with those who speak Spanish. Her reading comprehension and writing skills in Spanish have grown well above grade level, and she is beginning to read and write in English as well. Even more impressive is her academic progress in math and science.

Maria's teacher has only limited proficiency in Spanish, but is attempting to improve her own language competency since many of her students are monolingual in either Spanish or English. Some of Maria's classmates entered third grade proficiently bilingual, but many have had little access to formal education and had not yet acquired basic academic skills. And some, like Maria, entered with very limited proficiency in English but could read and write in their mother tongue. Once settled in, Maria became part of a linguistically and academically diverse cooperative team, the Dream Makers. Each day the Dream Makers worked for an hour on activities designed to develop conceptual learning and language proficiency. Jack was the team facilitator who made sure everyone contributed ideas and listened to the others. Carlotta, who is proficiently bilingual, served as the interpreter. Tony, the team checker, made sure students completed their work, and Heather was the team harmonizer who made sure the team members were helpful and respectful to each other. Maria started out as the team's "setup officer" who was in charge of getting all the supplies needed for team activities. By March she had moved into the role of team reporter, writing primarily in Spanish. Carlotta helped with the English translations. The Dream Makers also spent an hour each day working at one of the math/science learning centers.

Maria, like most of her classmates, has thrived in third grade. She has made many new friends and excellent academic progress this year. Everything in Maria's classroom is labeled or written in both Spanish and English, bilingual pictographs are used wherever possible, and bilingual parents are nearly always present to work with Ms. Lindsey and the children.

Linguistic diversity interacts with a range of individual differences. The next two chapters analyze individual differences that are known to affect learning. These characteristics are complex and interrelated and must not be regarded as mutually exclusive categories. The list that follows could be conceptualized in a variety of ways, but experience has shown that it is helpful in guiding and clarifying teachers' observations of students.

Learning styles (including a need for structure)
Learning skills
Aptitudes and achievements
Motivation
Self-concept
Gender
Interests
Physical attributes
Peer relationships
Family conditions
Values, attitudes, and beliefs
Sense of ethnic identity

These characteristics should be examined and understood on two levels: a personal level, focusing on the student as an individual, and a group level, focusing on the student's ethnicity and cultural background. There is a layer of personal identity that is universal to all students. For example, all students have learning styles, interests, strengths, self-concepts, physical attributes, and so on. The specific manifestations of these universal characteristics, however, are shaped to some degree by differing cultural experiences. Aural and kinesthetic modes of learning, for example, are found among individuals in all cultures. They tend to be important, or "the primary mode of information processing for the majority" of African Americans.[1] Both males and females can excel in math. In the United States males tend to be more successful at it than females, however.

To provide equitable learning environments, teachers must be aware of both individual and cultural differences. There is a necessary interaction here. If teachers are unaware of cultural differences when they exist, they may perceive a student as being unacceptably deviant or deficient. On the other hand, they must also be aware of the individual diversity that exists within any one ethnic group and guard against stereotypes. And, finally, they must see the similarities among individuals across the range of groups found in their classrooms.

Chapter 6 provides an introduction to students' learning styles, a key variable that often affects school success. Chapter 7 provides an overview of eleven additional characteristics and discusses the importance of how teachers perceive individual and cultural differences. In Part III, Chapter 9 explains how teachers can create flexible learning environments that will help them manage student diversity in multicultural classrooms while maintaining high levels of achievement and personal development among all learners present.

NOTES

1. Barbara J. Robinson Shade, 1989, "Afro-American Cognitive Patterns: A Review of the Research," in B. J. R. Shade (ed.) *Culture, Style, and the Educative Process* (Springfield, IL: Charles C. Thomas), 99.

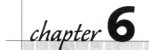
Theories of Learning Style and Multiple Intelligence: Interactions between Culture and the Individual

*T*his chapter provides an introduction to two theories that have important implications for multicultural teaching: learning styles and multiple intelligences. These theories represent distinct fields of study that are beginning to be integrated by educators who believe that the combination forms a powerful model of human intelligence and learning.[1]

An Introduction to Learning Style

Students differ in the way they approach learning. Some work well in groups; others prefer to work alone. Some need absolute quiet in order to concentrate; others do well with noise and movement. Some need a great deal of structure and support; others are more independent and self-motivated. Some students grasp oral instructions quickly; others need to see the instructions in writing. Some require a warm personal rapport with the teacher, while others do not. Some are intuitive; others prefer inductive or deductive reasoning. Some learn best in a formal environment, while others prefer a more relaxed atmosphere. The list of differences could go on.

Psychologists have been researching the nature of learning styles for a number of decades. Only recently has the utility of this research been made known to educators. Typically, we look for emotional reasons to explain why a child is not learning; we look for an emotional block or conflict, or a learning disability. Many teachers ignore the possibility that children are not learning because they are not given an opportunity to use their own style of learning in the classroom.

Take, for example, a child like Max (page 172) who has a slow warm-up period of twenty to thirty minutes. He does not easily get into something new, but once involved he may show a good deal of perseverance. He may be a physical learner who needs to become involved in the learning process. This takes time.

Once immersed, he may go deeper than his classmates. The quick changes of learning activity typical in most elementary classrooms can make it impossible for the slow-to-warm-up learner to get past the point of warming up. Thus, he is rarely able to complete work expected by the teacher. The frequent change of activity may also be frustrating and discouraging because once into an activity he has difficulty shifting to a new one. If he makes it past the eighth grade, the slow-to-warm-up learner will also find it difficult to learn within the rigid time schedules of most secondary schools. Unless helped, the slow-to-warm-up student gets caught in a vicious cycle of anxiety, inability to concentrate, and failure.

The idea that we must gear our teaching to students' learning style needs is revolutionary and, perhaps, unsettling. It triggers the fear that we sometimes create the conditions of failure for some students. Fortunately, the movement has progressed far enough to provide some of the tools we need to discover the important differences that affect learning and to design appropriate instructional strategies and materials.

As previously noted in Chapter 2, the notion that certain learning styles are related to certain ethnic groups is both dangerous and promising. It is dangerous because it can foster stereotypes. It is promising to the degree it illuminates cultural variables that influence the way children learn and helps teachers discover ways of strengthening academic achievement among learners of diverse cultural backgrounds. Recall that intellectual modes, meaning both styles of learning and the types of knowledge most valued, are one of the five aspects of ethnicity Longstreet uses to mediate cultural differences in the classroom.

■*What Is Learning Style?*

The National Task Force on Learning Style and Brain Behavior adopted the following definition of *learning style* with the understanding that it would be revised if necessary:

> Learning style is that consistent pattern of behavior and performance by which an individual approaches educational experiences. It is the composite of characteristic cognitive, affective, and physiological behaviors that serve as relatively stable indicators of how a learner perceives, interacts with, and responds to the learning environment. It is formed in the deep structure of neural organization and personality [that] molds and is molded by human development and the cultural experiences of home, school, and society.[2]

The fact that this definition is offered as tentative should alert us to the fact that learning style is an emerging concept. Despite decades of research, there are more questions than answers about learning styles. Nevertheless, knowledge about learning styles has become one of the most promising avenues to improving education. We must be careful, however, not to view learning styles as the panacea that will eliminate failure in the schools. To address learning styles is often a necessary, but never sufficient, condition for effective teaching.

■*Why Be Concerned about Learning Styles?*

The rationale behind learning styles is similar to the broader rationale for multicultural education. Knowledge about learning styles provides insights that move us beyond the rhetoric associated with "individual differences," "human potential," and "creating the independent learner."[3] First of all, when a student is having difficulty learning, it is now possible to pinpoint which of the many individual differences affect his or her learning. Understanding individual differences has been especially challenging for junior high and high school teachers. Gerald Kusler, a specialist on learning style theory, wrote:

> Most secondary teachers want to know the students they teach. But, two factors tend to block even the most committed. First, teachers don't really know what they need to know about learners. . . . Second, the typical secondary teacher spends about 90 hours in class with between 125 and 150 youngsters. "Getting to know you" can become "putting the name with the face (or the seat)."[4]

Recent developments in learning style research have produced a variety of efficient ways to gather information about students. Thus, if a student has a strong modality preference, a teacher can provide visual, auditory, or kinesthetic experiences that will enhance the student's learning. Teachers can provide more structure for those who need it, or assist reflective thinkers in developing skills needed for standardized tests. The possibilities are endless.

Second, by focusing on how students learn we assume that they can learn. This is basic to the humanists' view that all of us have the capacity to grow and develop to our fullest potential. Third, when students are taught *how* they learn they become involved in a teaching-learning partnership. In schools where learning styles are assessed and shared with learners, students become involved in structuring how they will learn what is taught. This is an important step in creating the independent learner.[5]

The concept of learning style can also provide some of the teeth needed to move us beyond the rhetoric of educational equity for those ethnic groups who have not yet been well served by our nation's schools. This notion warrants some discussion.

One can assume that teachers, unless they learn to do otherwise, expect their students to learn the same way that they themselves do. Teachers who dislike group work rarely use it with their students. Teachers who require the written word remember to write the assignment on the board, but they may not think of taping the text for their auditory learners. Teachers who are incremental learners tend to spell out short-term objectives, while the intuitive teachers may seem less organized. A teacher's learning style does not have to become a teaching style straitjacket; teachers can learn to be flexible and teach in a variety of ways. Being flexible is important because research shows that students do better in classes taught by teachers with the same learning style as their own. Students also tend to like these teachers better.[6]

The concept of learning styles offers a value-neutral approach for understanding individual differences among ethnically diverse students. Many learning styles are bipolar, representing a continuum from one extreme of a trait to another. Usually, no value judgment is made about where one falls on the continuum. "It is acceptable for example, to be a kinesthetic or an audio visual learner, to reason abstractly or concretely."[7] The assumption is that everyone can learn if teachers respond appropriately to individual learning needs.

Learning style is believed to be a combination of both heredity and environment. While it is to some degree rooted in the individual's neurological structure, learning styles do change with age and experience. Young children, for example, seem to be more kinesthetic and tend to develop a visual or auditory preference as they mature. In highly technical societies, such as the United States, cognitive styles tend to move in the direction of analytical thought.

Numerous instruments now exist for discovering student learning style. In her selected bibliography of learning-style assessment instruments, for example, Cornett lists thirty.[8] Keefe and others have organized the available measures into four categories: cognitive style instruments, affective style instruments, physiological style instruments, and comprehensive or multidimensional instruments.[9] Cognitive style instruments are those that measure the learner's typical mode of perceiving, thinking, problem solving, and remembering.[10] Affective style instruments are those that measure personality traits related to attention, motivation, and need for structure. Physiological style instruments are those that measure biologically based responses, such as personal nutrition and health, and perception of aural or visual stimuli. Comprehensive or multidimensional instruments are those that assess more than one of the three categories of learning style and several dimensions within these categories.[11] Because comprehensive instruments that can measure all three aspects of learning style (cognitive, affective, and physiological dimensions) do not yet exist, it is wise to select instruments from two or more categories to better understand a student's learning style.

The four learning style approaches to be described in this chapter represent a cross section of these categories. Each strategy has been extensively researched and is used successfully by classroom teachers across the country. Assessment instruments and instructions for each may be obtained by writing to individuals noted at the end of this chapter, where a selected annotated list of other learning style instruments is also included.

Four Strategies for Discovering Learning Styles

Field Independence–Dependence

Imagine yourself in a psychology laboratory, seated on a chair in a tilted room. The experimenter asks you to adjust the chair and your body to the true upright position. Can you do it?

Now imagine that you are seated in a darkened room with a luminous rod in a luminous picture frame, which is set aslant. You are instructed to set the rod to the true vertical position. Are you able to do so?

These two experiments were part of the dramatic research begun by Herman Witkin and his associates in 1954. The research illustrates the field independence–dependence dimensions of learning style. Those participants labeled field dependent consistently aligned themselves to the tilt of the room, leaning perhaps as much as thirty degrees but perceiving themselves to be sitting upright. They also tended to be influenced by the slant of the picture frame and were unable to place the rod in its true upright position. Other participants, those labeled field independent, ignored their immediate surroundings. In the tilted room test they used internal cues to adjust their bodies to an upright position. In the luminous rod test, they tended to ignore the frame and set the rod in its true upright position.[12]

Diagnosis of field independence–dependence is now greatly simplified through use of a simple embedded figures test. Figure 6.1 illustrates the task as it appears in the Hidden Figures Test.[13] If we visualize people along a contin-

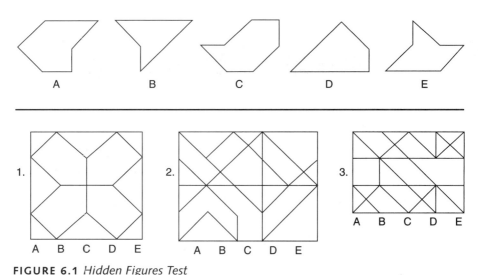

FIGURE 6.1 *Hidden Figures Test*

Adapted from Hidden Figures Test (Cf-1), Kit of Factor-Referenced Cognitive Tests. (Ans. 1, A; 2, B; 3, E.) Copyright © 1962 by Educational Testing Service. Reprinted by permission.

uum from extreme field dependence to extreme field independence, we find that people at the field-dependent end are unable to locate simple figures embedded in the complex pattern. Field-independent people, on the other hand, can quickly separate the simple figure from the background.

For years, knowledge generated about learning styles by Witkin and others has been unavailable to teachers and counselors. Only recently have classroom implications been discussed. When trying to identify relatively field independent–dependent students, think in terms of clusters of personality and intellectual characteristics. These clusters include the following characteristics.[14]

TABLE 6.1

Field–independent Learner	Field–dependent Learner
1. Perception of discrete parts	1. Global perception
2. Good at abstract analytical thought	2. Poor at analytical problem solving
3. Individualistic and insensitive to others, poorly developed social skills	3. Highly sensitive and attuned to social environment, highly developed social skills
4. Favors "inquiry" and independent study, provides own structure to learning	4. Favors a "spectator approach" to learning, adopts organization of information to be learned as given
5. Intrinsically motivated, unresponsive to social reinforcement	5. Extrinsically motivated, responsive to social reinforcement

Field independence–dependence does not appear to be correlated with intelligence, with the exception of analytical intelligence, which requires the separation of component parts from the whole. It is not related to other aspects of intelligence, such as verbal comprehension. However, most schools and tests tend to be geared to the highly analytical learner who can think abstractly (field-independent learners). Some psychologists suggest that people can be helped to develop cognitive strategies, that people can be taught to make conscious choices about which cognitive process to use in certain situations. Thus, field independents might learn to be more sensitive to other people, and field dependents might increase their analytical skill.

Research by Ramirez and Castañeda suggests that learning style is related to world view, that certain learning styles tend to be predominant in certain cultures.[15] They indicate that Mexican Americans tend to be relatively field dependent or global in orientation. Furthermore, their research suggests that bilingual individuals tend to be bicognitive; that is, fluent speakers of Spanish and English tend to have greater cognitive flexibility than monolinguists, being able to move back and forth between global and analytical orientations as needed.

The field independence–dependence approach to learning styles is the most widely researched, with over two thousand studies completed to date.[16] There are some problems, however. The Embedded Figures Test (EFT) makes field dependents, now more frequently known as "field-sensitive learners," feel like failures. The more field sensitive the individual, the less likely he or she will be successful in locating a simple figure within a complex whole. Given a school's emphasis on testing, it becomes difficult to convince the student who scores between zero and eight out of thirty-two possible points that the test reveals little about learning potential. Another problem is that the terms *field sensitive* and *field independent* tend to label students and can lead to stereotyping. Therefore, the EFT should be administered with care and with a full discussion of the insights it offers into how the individual approaches learning.

Castañeda and Gray have developed observation guidelines based on field independence-dependence research that can help teachers discover where a student falls on the continuum without testing. They also describe the teacher characteristics and curriculum approach that are most compatible with each learning style. These are summarized in Boxes 6.1, 6.2, and 6.3.[17]

Field Sensitivity   *Alfredo Castañeda and Tracy Gray*

BOX 6.1

Field-sensitive Behaviors

Relationship to Peers

1. Likes to work with others to achieve a common goal
2. Likes to assist others
3. Is sensitive to feelings and opinions of others

Personal Relationship to Teacher

1. Openly expresses positive feelings for teacher
2. Asks questions about teacher's tastes and personal experiences; seeks to become like teacher

Instructional Relationship to Teacher

1. Openly expresses positive feelings for teacher
2. Seeks rewards which strengthen relationship with teacher
3. Is highly motivated when working individually with teacher

Characteristics of Curriculum That Facilitate Learning

1. Performance objectives and global aspects of curriculum are carefully explained
2. Concepts are presented in humanized or story format
3. Concepts are related to personal interests and experiences of children

BOX 6.1

(Continued)

Field-sensitive Teaching Style

Personal Behaviors

1. Displays physical and verbal expressions of approval and warmth
2. Uses personalized rewards which strengthen the relationship with students

Instructional Behaviors

1. Expresses confidence in child's ability to succeed, is sensitive to children who are having difficulty and need help
2. Gives guidance to students; makes purpose and main principles of lesson obvious; presentation of lesson is clear with steps toward "solution" clearly delineated
3. Encourages learning through modeling; asks children to imitate
4. Encourages cooperation and development of group feelings, encourages class to think and work as a unit.
5. Holds informal class discussions; provides opportunities for students to see how concepts being learned are related to students' personal experiences

Curriculum-related Behaviors

1. Emphasizes global aspects of concepts; before beginning lesson ensures that students understand the performance objectives; identifies generalizations and helps children apply them to particular instances
2. Personalizes curriculum; teacher relates curriculum materials to the interests and experiences of students, as well to her or his own interests
3. Humanizes curriculum; attributes human characteristics to concepts and principles
4. Uses teaching materials to elicit expression of feelings from students; helps students apply concepts for labeling their personal experiences

Source: Alfredo Castañeda and Tracy Gray, "Bicognitive Processes in Multiracial Education, *Educational Leadership* 32 (December 1974). Reprinted with permission of the Association for Supervision and Curriculum Development. Copyright © 1974 by the Association for Supervision and Curriculum Development. All rights reserved.

Field Independence   Alfredo Castañeda and Tracy Gray

BOX 6.2

Field-independent Behaviors

Relationship to Peers

1. Prefers to work independently
2. Likes to compare and gain individual recognition
3. Task oriented; is inattentive to social environment when working

BOX 6.2

(Continued)

Personal Relationship to Teacher

1. Rarely seeks physical contact with teacher
2. Formal; interactions with teacher are restricted to tasks at hand

Instructional Relationship to Teacher

1. Likes to try new Tasks without teacher's help
2. Impatient to begin tasks; likes to finish first
3. Seeks nonsocial rewards

Characteristics of Curriculum That Facilitate Learning

1. Details of concepts are emphasized; parts have meaning of their own
2. Deals with math and science concepts
3. Based on discovery approach

Field-independent Teaching Style

Personal Behaviors

1. Is formal in relationship with students; acts the part of an authority figure
2. Centers attention on instructional objectives; gives social atmosphere secondary importance

Instructional Behaviors

1. Encourages independent achievement; emphasizes the importance of individual effort
2. Encourages competition between individual students
3. Adopts a consultant role; teacher encourages students to seek help only when they experience difficulty
4. Encourages learning through trial and error
5. Encourages task orientation; focuses student attention on assigned tasks

Curriculum-related Behaviors

1. Focuses on details of curriculum materials
2. Focuses on facts and principles; teaches students how to solve problems using shortcuts and novel approaches
3. Emphasizes math and science abstractions; teacher tends to use graphs, charts, and formulas in teaching, even when presenting social studies curriculum
4. Emphasizes inductive learning and the discovery approach; starts with isolated parts and slowly puts them together to construct rules or generalizations

Curricula for Field Sensitivity and Field Independence
Alfredo Castañeda and Tracy Gray

BOX 6.3

Field-sensitive Curriculum

Content

1. Social abstractions: Field-sensitive curriculum is humanized through use of narration, humor, drama, and fantasy. Characterized by social words and human characteristics. Focuses on lives of persons who occupy central roles in the topic of study, such as history or scientific discovery.
2. Personalized: The ethnic background of students, as well as their homes and neighborhoods, is reflected. The teacher is given the opportunity to express personal experiences and interests.

Structure

1. Global: Emphasis is on description of wholes and generalities; the overall view or general topic is presented first. The purpose or use of the concept or skill is clearly stated using practical examples.
2. Rules explicit: Rules and principles are salient. (Children who prefer to learn in the field-sensitive mode are more comfortable given the rules than when asked to discover the underlying principles for themselves.)
3. Requires cooperation with others: The curriculum is structured in such a way that children work cooperatively with peers or with the teacher in a variety of activities.

Field-independent Curriculum

Content

1. Math and science abstractions: Field-independent curriculum uses many graphs and formulae.
2. Impersonal: Field-independent curriculum focuses on events, places, and facts in social studies rather than personal histories.

Structure

1. Focus on details: The details of a concept are explored, followed by the global concept.
2. Discovery: Rules and principles are discovered from the study of details; the general is discovered from the understanding of the particulars.
3. Requires independent activity: The curriculum requires children to work individually, minimizing interaction with others.

Students' Need for Structure

Students in any classroom may differ greatly in their ability to rely on themselves, to take on new assignments, to make choices, and to organize themselves and their materials. Some need frequent reassurance from the teacher and continually ask if what they are doing is right and what they should do next.

Students also differ in their need for an explanation of the instructions before beginning a test or assignment. Teachers often give instructions to a group of thirty to forty students, expecting all of them to understand the first or second time. A teacher may become irritated at students who never seem to listen or pay attention. In many cases, perhaps the student is not paying attention, but students can differ in their need for directions from the teacher. Students at all age levels differ from one another in their ability to carry out independent projects and activities. Some can handle long-term assignments while others can work independently only for short periods of time.

Need for structure is sometimes regarded as a manifestation of learning style. David Hunt, of the Ontario Institute for Studies in Education, conceptualizes learning style on the basis of the amount of external structure needed by the student. He identifies the characteristics of students who require much,

Self-motivated students who require little structure can pursue independent projects with relative ease.

some, and little structure and teaching approaches that are most desirable for students who require a certain degree of structure.

The paragraph completion method has been used since the 1960s by Hunt and his associates to assess a student's conceptual level.[18] This method, which requires special training to administer, asks the learner to complete six to eight open-ended statements by writing two or three sentences about his or her feelings for each one (*What I think about rules . . . , When I am . . . , What I think about parents . . . , When someone does not agree with me . . . , When I am not sure . . . , When I am told what to do . . .* , and so on).[19] Learner responses are then coded and scored according to the structure of the response, not the content. The result is a general indication of the amount of structure the student needs at the time. He also emphasizes that there are many high-ability students who require structure and warns that many teachers confuse learning style with ability. This confusion is particularly likely with younger (i.e., grade six) students because "teachers tend to equate high level verbal ability with a learning style that requires little structure."[20] While many high achievers do require structure, it is less likely that students who are at lower achievement levels will need less structure. Hunt writes, therefore, that "learning style and ability show a low, but significant relation, yet they are distinct from one another . . . [furthermore] the relation decreases as students grow older."[21]

Hunt's approach to learning style is practical for teachers, most of whom know that certain students are more independent than others, and that others need more guidance and support. Hunt makes it possible for teachers to sharpen these observations by providing specific behaviors to look for. Box 6.4 summarizes some of these behaviors and can be used as a guideline for identifying a student's need for structure. Suggestions about teaching strategies that best meet a student's need for structure are summarized in Box 6.5.

Learning Styles and Students' Needs   David Hunt

BOX 6.4

Characteristics of Students Who Require Much Structure

1. They have a short attention span, cannot sit still for the period—in constant movement.
2. They have no inner control as individuals, do not know how to function in group situations (many physical and verbal fights).
3. They (usually boys) are physical with each other and try the rules often.
4. They ask for direction often. (They do not rely on themselves or want to think.)
5. They are literal and unable to make inferences or interpretations.
6. They lack self-confidence, generally have a poor self-image.
7. They have difficulty organizing themselves and their materials.

BOX 6.4

(Continued)

8. They do not reveal anything of themselves or express personal opinions—everything is very objective. They are afraid to get emotionally involved with a story or film.
9. They have a wide range of abilities.
10. They see things in black and white with no gray in between.
11. They want to know the basic information or process and are not interested in the sidelights.
12. They are incapable of handling general questions or thinking through a problem; they guess and let it go at that.
13. They do not assume responsibility for their own actions.
14. They work only because the teacher tells them to work and look to peers for approval.
15. They are laconic; they give brief answers with little elaboration.

Characteristics of Students Who Require Some Structure

1. They are oriented to the role of the good student (one who gets the right answers, has neat work, and good work habits).
2. They seek teacher approval and strive to please the teacher; they go along with what the teacher says.
3. They want to work alone at their own desks.
4. They are reluctant to try anything new; they do not like to appear wrong or dumb.
5. They do not express personal opinions.
6. They do not ask questions.
7. They are confused by choices.
8. They are incapable of adjusting to a different teacher; they are upset by visitors or alterations of the schedule.
9. They look for reassurance and frequently ask, "Is this right?" "What should I do now?" "What should I write?"
10. They are not particularly imaginative.
11. They participate well in the class as a whole but do not work well in small groups.
12. They are grade conscious.

Characteristics of Students Who Require Little Structure

1. They like to discuss and argue; everybody wants to talk at once with few listening; therefore the noise level is high and progress somewhat slower.
2. They will question and volunteer additional information.
3. They want to solve things themselves; they don't want the teacher's help until they have exhausted all resources.
4. They are averse to detail and dislike going step by step, are able to see the entire picture and tend to ignore the steps required to get there, are creative and

BOX 6.4

(Continued)

like to formulate and act on their own ideas, and often get so involved that they do not hear the teacher.

5. They are capable of abstract thinking; they do not require concrete objects.
6. They are less afraid of making mistakes than other students, are more imaginative, go off on sidetracks, and are able to see alternatives.
7. They can stay at one thing for a longer time and can work by themselves with little or no supervision.
8. They have a greater depth of emotions and are more open about themselves than other students.
9. They display greater ability in making interpretations and drawing inferences than other students do.
10. They are somewhat self-centered and not very concerned with others.

Source: Adapted from David E. Hunt, "Learning Style and Students needs: An Introduction to Conceptual Level," in *Student Learning Styles: Diagnosing and Prescribing Programs* (Reston, VA: National Association of Secondary School Principals, 1979). By permission of the author.

Structure Requirements
David Hunt

BOX 6.5

Teaching Approaches for Students Who Require Much Structure

1. Have definite and consistent rules—let them know what is expected of them.
2. Give specific guidelines and instructions (step by step); even make a chart of the steps.
3. Make goals and deadlines short and definite—give them the topic, how many lines/pages, how it is to be done and the exact date it is due.
4. Provide a variety of activities during the period, incorporating some physical movement whenever possible.
5. Make positive comments about their attempts; give immediate feedback on each step; give much assurance and attention; praise often.
6. Use visuals and objects they can see, feel, and touch.
7. Get them to work immediately and change pace often.
8. Display their work—it is a form of reinforcement to which they respond.
9. Capitalize on their interest to assist them in learning the various skills (for example, stories or projects dealing with cars with grade nine boys).
10. Begin with factual material before discussion.
11. Move gradually from seat work to discussion; provide more group work as they are able to handle it.
12. Leave them at the end of each period with the satisfaction of having learned new material and having success in what they have been studying—almost a

BOX 6.5

(Continued)

complete lesson each period with minor carry-over to the next period with the mention of something interesting to come.

13. Give short quizzes and objective tests initially.
14. Provide opportunities for choice and decision making as they appear ready for them.

Teaching Approaches for Students Who Require Some Structure

1. Arrange students initially in rows and gradually get them working in pairs, then in small groups.
2. Have definite and consistent rules—let them know what is expected of them.
3. Use creative skits to encourage spontaneity, self-awareness, and cooperation.
4. Tell them what to do each day. Some teachers find that initialing the students' work daily provides the contact they desire and the impetus to continue—they can see how much they have accomplished.
5. Provide nonthreatening situations where they have to risk an opinion.
6. Provide a lot of praise and success-oriented situations.
7. Give them group problems to encourage sharing.
8. Provide opportunities for choice and decision making as students appear ready for them. Push them gently into situations where they have to make decisions and take responsibility.

Teaching Approaches for Students Who Require Little Structure

1. Allow them to select their own seats.
2. Give them many topics from which to choose.
3. Set weekly or longer assignments and allow students to make up their own timetables.
4. Encourage them to use each other as resources.
5. Allow more mobility and give them more opportunities to take part in planning and decision making.
6. Give them freedom to pursue projects on their own.
7. Have them work in groups with the teacher serving as a resource person.
8. Train them to listen to instructions (and to listen in general) as they tend to go off on their own.
9. Remind and encourage them to take an interest in others.

Source: Adapted from David E. Hunt, "Learning Style and Students Needs: An Introduction to Conceptual Level," in *Student Learning Styles: Diagnosing and Prescribing Programs* (Reston, VA: National Association of Secondary School Principals, 1979). By permission of the author.

Many of these suggestions may seem like common sense. The point is, however, that most teachers do not act on them; instead, they insist on the same amount of structure for all students. Hunt provides guidelines for flexibility as educators match their teaching with the amount of structure a student requires.

Perceptual Modalities

The Edmonds Learning Style Identification Exercise (ELSIE) is an effective technique for discovering perceptual modes. Classroom teachers can administer, score, and roughly evaluate the ELSIE in less than a half-hour of class time. The ELSIE can be used in grades seven to adult, and possibly as early as fourth grade.

The ELSIE provides a profile of modality strengths, based on the individual's response to a selected list of fifty common English words that are read once at ten-second intervals. Students are asked, as they hear each word, to indicate on their answer sheet which of the following responses is their "own immediate and instantaneous reaction to the word itself."[22]

1. Visualization: a mental picture of some object or activity
2. Written word: a mental picture of the word spelled out
3. Listening: the sound of the word with no mental picture
4. Activity: a "physical or emotional feeling about the word, such as a tightening of a muscle or a feeling such as warmth, sorrow, etc."[23]

Students can tally the number of responses in each response category and then plot their own profiles to discover their own perceptual strengths and weaknesses. The learner's scores in all four categories are charted on a stanine scale displayed as bands above and below the mean. A sample profile is shown in Figure 6.2. These profiles are interpreted such that "the further the individual varies from the mean in any one of the four categories, the stronger or weaker will be that mode of learning for that individual, that is, the more (or less) easily the individual is able to learn by using that approach. Scores at the extremes (either in the ±3 or ±4 band) may be considered indicative of a strongly dominant influence—positively or negatively—of that mode."[24]

Students who score high on visualization learn best when they can actually see objects and activities. Visual media such as films, pictures, demonstrations, and models would enhance their learning.

Learners who score high on the written word portion learn best by reading about what is to be learned. "Persons scoring very high in this category have a great dependency on the written word. . . . Persons scoring very low in this category may read quite well, but they tend to translate written words into another category (visual images or sounds) rather than being able to get meaning from the words immediately."[25]

Learners with a modality strength in listening are auditory learners. The higher the score for listening, the better the individual can learn from hearing the spoken language without recourse to some other mode. Listening labs and tapes are usually very effective with auditory learners.

Learners who score high on activity require some manner of physical activity in order to facilitate learning. Many activity or kinesthetic learners are compulsive underliners or notetakers "in class or at lectures (and even films), but they will seldom need to refer to their notes at a later time, for the activity of writing seems to impress the information on their memory."[26]

(Profile Sheet)
Total Responses: 1 — 28   2 — 5   3 — 16   4 — 1

Band	Visualization 1	Written Word 1	Listening 3	Activity 4
+4				
	38	20	22	26
+3				
	34	17	17	20
+2				
	29	15	15	16
+1				
	19	13	13	12
0				
0	17	11	11	10
	12	9	9	6
−1				
	7	7	7	3
−2				
	4	5	5	2
−3				
	2	3	3	1
−4				

Bands: 1: +1   2: −2   3: +2   4: −3

FIGURE 6.2
Edmonds School District, Learning Style Identification Exercise

*From Harry Reinert, "One Picture Is Worth a Thousand Words? Not Necessarily!" The Modern
Language Journal 60 (April 1976): 164. Reprinted by permission of the author.*

Reinert reports finding far greater diversity between individual learning profiles than he had originally anticipated and suspects that "many slow learners are
'slow' only because they have never had a chance to learn in the way they could
have learned."[27] The ELSIE provides teachers with specific information about
students' learning strengths and weaknesses, making it possible for teachers to
give individual students the kind of help they need. For some students, drills, out-
lining, or copying definitions is helpful; for others it is a waste of time. Some students benefit from listening to a tape of the text as they read; some even require
it if they are to comprehend. For others, auditory stimuli are a hindrance.

The ELSIE can also be valuable for understanding the overall learning style
makeup of a particular class. Reinert suggests that each class has a unique profile. Once teachers know what it is, they can plan instruction that should be
most effective for the class as a whole. For example, Reinert gives evidence that

casts doubt on the overall effectiveness of films with some groups. One picture is not always worth a thousand words.

Learning Style Inventory

The *Learning Style Inventory* (LSI) developed by Rita Dunn, Kenneth Dunn, and Gary Price is a multidimensional approach to learning styles. Oriented to the classroom teacher, the LSI is currently the approach most widely used. Its validity and reliability are backed up by extensive research. The Dunns define learning style as "the way *each* learner begins to concentrate on, process, and retain new and difficult information."[28] If teachers are to identify a student's learning style, "it is necessary to examine each individual's multidimensional characteristics to determine what is most likely to trigger each student's concentration, maintain it, respond to his or her natural processing style, and cause long-term memory."[29]

By 1990, after two decades of research, Dunn and Dunn had developed a conceptual framework for the LSI that included twenty-one elements within five categories of stimuli (see Figure 6.3). The stimuli are (1) the *immediate en-*

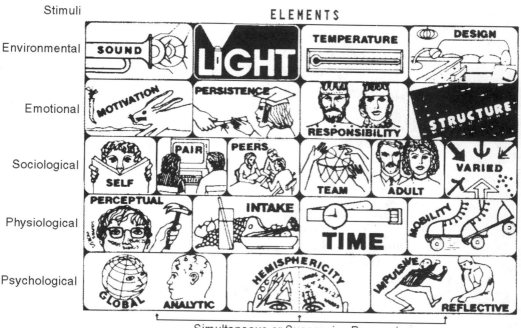

FIGURE 6.3
Diagnosing Learning Style

From Rita Dunn and Kenneth Dunn, *Teaching Secondary Students Through Their Individual Learning Styles, p. 4.* Copyright © 1993 by Allyn and Bacon.

Young children can develop understanding of abstract concepts, such as cooperation, through concrete experiences that use all of the learning modalities.

vironment (sound, light, temperature, and furniture/seating designs); (2) the learner's *own emotionality* (motivation, persistence, sense of responsibility, and need for structure); (3) the *learner's sociological preference* (learning best alone, with a partner, in small groups, or with an adult, and preferring variety over patterns and routines); (4) the learner's *physiological characteristics* (perceptual strengths, time-of-day energy levels, and need for intake and/or mobility while learning); and (5) the learner's *cognitive processing inclinations* (global/analytic, right/left, and impulsive/reflective).

Two versions exist, one for the primary grades and one for grade four to adult. The LSI consists of a 104-item, self-report questionnaire, which may be scored and analyzed by computer. If computerized scoring is used, each student receives a printout that includes a profile and narrative describing the learner's preferences related to classroom environmental conditions and his or her own emotional, sociological, and physical needs. The LSI identifies needs such as peak learning times, informal or formal classroom arrangements, perceptual modality, structure, and motivation.

The Dunns' definition of learning style has been criticized for overlooking cognitive processes and overemphasizing how four basic stimuli (environmental, emotional, sociological, and physical) affect a person's ability to absorb and retain information. According to some critics, their definition is unclear, seriously flawed, and raises more questions than it answers. "How did these educators decide on these eighteen elements and four types of stimuli? How do

Nurturing musical intelligence in young children.

these eighteen elements interact? Is there a synergistic effect that any one element has when it interacts with two or three others analogous to the way certain drugs react differently in continuation than when alone? . . . Where is the element of intelligence?"[30] Others within the learning style movement give LSI more favorable reviews. Keefe, for example, writes that the LSI "is a practitioner-oriented instrument with commendable validation and widespread application, particularly in elementary and middle-level schools."[31]

The most recent model developed by the Dunns has been expanded to include cognitive processes most specifically in terms of global or analytic processing inclinations. Five elements (sound, light, design, persistence, and intake) are highly correlated with processing style.[32]

> Global learners tend to prefer learning with what conventional teachers think of as distractions—sound (music, tapping, or conversation), soft illumination (covering their eyes or wearing sunglasses indoors), an informal design (lounging comfortably), peer orientation (wanting to work with a friend), and a need for intake (snacks) *while* studying. Furthermore, globals tend not to be persistent; they begin working with a burst of energy which lasts for a relatively short period, and then they want a "break." Globals return to their task and work again for another short interval; then they want another break. Globals also dislike working on one thing at a time; they often become engaged in multiple tasks simultaneously and concentrate on several in varying sequences. Thus, globals may begin an assignment in the middle or at the end.

Analytics, on the other hand, tend to prefer learning in silence, with bright lighting, and a formal design—a conventional classroom. They rarely eat, chew, drink, or smoke *while* learning; instead, they eat afterward. Analytics tend to be persistent; they may not always start an assignment immediately, but once they *do* begin, they have a strong emotional urge to continue until the task is done or until they come to a place where they feel they can stop.[33]

The Dunns have developed comprehensive guidelines and illustrations to help teachers translate their learning style model into classroom practice, grades K–12.

In summary, *learning style theory* emphasizes the different processes people use to absorb information, solve problems, and create objects. It also emphasizes the thoughts and feelings associated with these processes[34] and thus helps us understand the distinct *styles* of our students. In contrast, the theory of multiple intelligences, to be considered next, attempts to understand how human potential for learning is shaped by cultures and different kinds of *contents and disciplines in* the world, such as mathematics, language, music, and interpersonal relations.[35] It provides a concrete context for understanding learning styles.

■ *The Theory of Multiple Intelligences*

The theory of multiple intelligences is based on the work of Howard Gardner, a cognitive and developmental psychologist at Harvard who has greatly influenced our view of how children learn and how they should be taught. When his theory of multiple intelligences was first published in *Frames of Mind* (1983), he wrote that "the idea of multiple intelligences is an old one, and I can scarcely claim any great originality for attempting to revive it once more."[36] Yet his ideas have become an inspiration for educators who believe in the human potential for learning. Indeed, Gardner has "sparked a revolution of sorts in classrooms around the world, a mutiny against the notion that human beings have a single, fixed intelligence."[37]

Gardner defines intelligence as "the human ability to solve problems or to make something that is valued in one or more cultures. As long as we can find a culture that values an ability to solve a problem or create a product in a particular way, then I would strongly consider whether that ability should be considered an intelligence."[38] Originally Gardner identified seven intelligences: Logical-mathematical and Linguistic intelligences, which have been emphasized in our schools and intelligence tests, as well as Musical, Spatial, Bodily-kinesthetic, Interpersonal, and Intrapersonal intelligences, which have been de-emphasized or ignored in most instruction and intelligence tests. More recently he has added the naturalist intelligence to his collection of intelligences described below.

Gardner also sets four criteria for what counts as a human intelligence. First, it must be connected with a portion of the brain, as has been discovered with brain-injured people or stroke victims who might lose their musical abilities but not their ability to speak or write, or who lose their linguistic ability but can still sing.[39] Second, it must exist in "special populations" that excel or

BOX 6.6

The Intelligences, in Gardner's Words

- Linguistic intelligence is the capacity to use language, your native language, and perhaps other languages, to express what's on your mind and to understand other people. Poets really specialize in linguistic intelligence, but any kind of writer, orator, speaker, lawyer, or a person for whom language is an important stock in trade highlights linguistic intelligence.

- People with a highly developed logical-mathematical intelligence understand the underlying principles of some kind of a causal system, the way a scientist or a logician does; or can manipulate numbers, quantities, and operations, the way a mathematician does.

- Spatial intelligence refers to the ability to represent the spatial world internally in your mind—the way a sailor or airplane pilot navigates the large spatial world, or the way a chess player or sculptor represents a more circumscribed spatial world. Spatial intelligence can be used in the arts or in the sciences. If you are spatially intelligent and oriented toward the arts, you are more likely to become a painter or a sculptor or an architect than, say, a musician or a writer. Similarly, certain sciences like anatomy or topology emphasize spatial intelligence.

- Bodily kinesthetic intelligence is the capacity to use your whole body or parts of your body—your hand, your fingers, your arms—to solve a problem, make something or put on some kind of a production. The most evident examples are people in athletics or the performing arts, particularly dance or acting.

- Musical intelligence is the capacity to think in music, to be able to hear patterns, recognize them, remember them, and perhaps manipulate them. People who have a strong musical intelligence don't just remember music easily—they can't get it out of their minds, it's so omnipresent. Now, some people will say, "Yes, music is important, but it's a talent, not an intelligence." And I say, "Fine, let's call it a talent." But then we have to leave the word *intelligent* out of *all* discussions of human abilities. You know, Mozart was damned smart!

- Interpersonal intelligence is understanding other people. It's an ability we all need, but is at a premium if you are a teacher, clinician, salesperson, or politician. Anybody who deals with other people has to be skilled in the interpersonal sphere.

- Intrapersonal intelligence refers to having an understanding of yourself, of knowing who you are, what you can do, what you want to do, how you react to things, which things to avoid, and which things to gravitate toward. We are drawn to people who have a good understanding of themselves because those people tend not to screw up. They tend to know what they can do. They tend to know what they can't do. And they tend to know where to go if they need help.

BOX 6.6

(Continued)

- Naturalist intelligence designates the human ability to discriminate among living things (plants, animals) as well as sensitivity to other features of the natural world (clouds, rock configurations). This ability was clearly of value in our evolutionary past as hunters, gatherers, and farmers; it continues to be central in such roles as botanist or chef. I also speculate that much of our consumer society exploits the naturalist intelligences, which can be mobilized in the discrimination among cars, sneakers, kinds of makeup, and the like. The kind of pattern recognition valued in certain of the sciences may also draw upon naturalist intelligence.

are impaired in the ability, such as "prodigies, autistic individuals, idiot savants, and learning-disabled children."[40] And third, it must have an "identifiable developmental history, through which normal as well as gifted individuals pass in the course of (human evolution toward expert 'end-state' performances)."[41] Thomas Armstrong, author of *Multiple Intelligences in the Classroom,* explains Gardner's third criterion for an intelligence.

Gardner suggests that intelligences are galvanized by participation in some culturally valued activity and that the individual's growth in such an activity follows a developmental pattern. Each intelligence-based activity has its own developmental trajectory: That is, each activity has its own time of arising in early childhood, its own time of peaking during one's lifetime, and its own pattern of either rapidly or gradually declining as one gets older.[42]

For example, musical intelligence seems to appear in early childhood and "remains relatively robust until old age," higher mathematical intelligence peaks in young adulthood and declines after age forty, while linguistic and spatial intelligences (writing novels or becoming a painter) often blossom in old age.[43]

Individuals may have strengths in one or more areas of intelligence. Despite this, our schools tend to emphasize linguistic and logical mathematical intelligence and have overlooked the others. Gardner's theory has strong implications for multicultural education in that it illustrates how different cultures tend to value and develop the different areas of intelligence. He recommends that teachers develop "intellectual profiles" of individual students as a basis for emphasizing students' strengths and bolstering their weaknesses.

Culture is integral to Gardner's theory of multiple intelligence in that by definition, "intelligence refers to the ability to solve problems or to make something that is valued in one or more cultures." (When we consider that some of the tasks required to score high on many "intelligence tests" are not valued in many cultures, for example repetition of random digits backwards and forwards, it is understandable why some tests are culturally biased.[44]) However, it is crucial to guard against stereotyping by thinking some cultures emphasize musical intelligence, others emphasize linguistic intelligence, and still others emphasize logic. Although the specific manifestations often differ tremendously, Gardner argues that all of the world's cultures value the eight intelligences he has identified. In every culture the elders pass on to their younger members the stories, myths, great art and music, social mores, political institutions, and number systems of the society—among many other "end-states" of accomplishments.[45] Thus, there are powerful implications for multicultural education in multiple intelligences theory. The research base and connections between learning style theory and multicultural education are much weaker. However, there is the potential to understand important interactions between cultural differences and individual differences by focusing on cultural and learning styles.

Relationships between Culture and Learning Style

How does culture influence the way individuals learn to know and understand the world? How does it influence the way they think, perceive, remember, and solve problems? In her research into relationships between culture and individual learning styles, Worthley has identified five cultural factors that appear to have an effect on learning styles.[46] One is the socialization process, particularly where a society's child-rearing practices fall along a continuum from authoritative to laissez-faire. The more control a society exercises over its children the more field dependent they become. A second factor is sociocultural tightness. The more the established social structures exert pressure to conform, as in high-context cultures, the more field dependent are its people. Third is the factor of ecological adaptation. In some societies survival depends upon keen observations of the environment, for example, accurate reading of the snow conditions of the arctic region or wave patterns of the sea or facial expressions of an oppressor. These environments produce people with highly developed perceptual skills, as with the Alaskan Natives, the Trukee of the South Pacific, and African Americans in a community of hostile Whites. A fourth factor is the biological effect, particularly nutrition and physical development. Some research has shown, for example, that children who lack protein tend to be more field dependent. (This relationship is not necessarily causative, however.) Finally, language exerts an important influence on learning style, especially the degree to which a society is literate. Contemporary literate societies emphasize written language while traditional preliterate societies emphasize direct experience observation and modeling.[47]

In discussing her findings, Worthley writes that

> while diversity among individuals within any culture is the norm, research has shown that these individuals tend to exhibit a common pattern of perception when the members of that culture are compared to the members of another culture. A "cultural personality" is more than a myth or stereotype. In addition, individuals from relatively pluralistic cultures such as that of the United States (actually a polyglot of many sub-cultures) tend to exhibit greater diversity in learning style than individuals from relatively singular cultures such as that of the African Kpelle tribe.[48]

Asa Hilliard, noted scholar of African American culture and history, argues that learning styles are a component of cultural behavioral styles—the habits, values, predisposition, and preferences that develop during the child's cultural socialization process.[49] Children of equivalent intellectual potential who grow up in different cultural milieus learn "to manifest their mental power in somewhat different ways."[50] Hilliard's research, which contrasted African and African American culture with European and European American culture, for example, identified "a unique African American core culture that could be empirically described."[51] Realizing that there are multiple individual differences within each group, he focused on "central tendencies" and reported that "a given individual in many ways may be very much like most of the members of his or her historical groups of reference."[52] Hilliard wrote that "most individual African Americans are very much a part of core African American culture," even though some may operate on the behavioral margins of their historical group of reference . . . [and] others may operate in ways that are quite outside the norms of [the African American community]."[53] He concluded that "most African Americans, and even a few European Americans, shared in this core culture to a greater or lesser degree."[54]

When teachers misunderstand their students' cultural behavioral styles, they may underestimate their intellectual potential and unknowingly misplace, mislabel, and mistreat them. They may underestimate their students' cognitive abilities, academic achievement, and language skills. Hilliard finds that when teachers have low expectations for student learning they will simplify, concretize, fragment, and slow the pace of instruction, or fail to offer abstract, conceptually oriented instruction to the child. "Thus, we see that it is not the learning style of the child that prevents the child from learning; it is the perception by the teacher of the child's style as a sign of incapacity that causes the teacher to reduce the quality of instruction offered."[55]

There has been a great deal of study focused on the learning styles of African American children and youth.[56] A number of Black scholars report that the schools take a "White Studies" approach in both subject matter and teaching strategies.[57] Black children and youth who are not bicultural, having grown up outside the dominant culture, tend to process information differently from the predominant way it is processed in schools. Their learning styles are often described as relational, as opposed to the analytical style rewarded in schools.[58] Hilliard observes learning style tendencies among African Americans that are very compatible with high-context culture (discussed in Chapter 2) and with the core of African American cultural style. He argues that African American people who identify with the African American core culture tend to:

1. Respond to things in terms of the whole picture instead of its parts.
2. Prefer inferential reasoning to deductive or inductive reasoning.
3. Approximate space, numbers, and time rather than stick to accuracy.
4. Focus on people and their activities more than on things.
5. Have a keen sense of justice and are quick to analyze and perceive injustice.
6. Lean toward altruism, a concern for one's fellow man.
7. Prefer novelty, freedom, and personal distinctiveness.
8. Be very proficient in nonverbal communications and not "word" dependent.[59]

Although all researchers might not agree with Hilliard, a growing body of research tends to confirm his conclusions.[60] Learning styles have been identified as an important variable in the school success (or failure) of ethnic minorities in the United States. The fact that our schools tend to be monoethnic, despite the array of diverse learning styles associated with different ethnic groups, may help explain the high drop-out rates among African Americans, Latinos, and Native Americans. Further, consideration of learning style characteristics of several ethnic minorities will illustrate how they are often incongruent with learning styles accepted in our schools.

Recent studies on the learning styles of some Native American and Alaskan Native youth have established the importance of visualization in learning. Children learn to learn through careful observation, for example, the behavior and expressions of adults, changing weather conditions, the terrain, and wildlife. Overall, the research on Native American students presents a common pattern in the way they "come to know or understand the world. They approach tasks visually, seem to prefer to learn by careful observation which precedes performance, and seem to learn in their natural settings experientially."[61] This is in contrast to African Americans who tend to be relational and field dependent. Where Native Americans fit on the continuum of relational/analytical or field dependent/field independent is not clear. What is clear, however, is that the learning style of many American Indian students is different from that of mainstream students.[62] Phillips describes how this difference can cause problems in school:

> [Native] American students customarily acquire the various skills of their culture (i.e., hunting, tanning, beadwork) in a sequence of three steps. First, the child over a period of time watches and listens to a competent adult who is performing the skill. Secondly, the child takes over small portions of the task and completes them in cooperation with and under the supervision of the adult, in this way gradually learning all of the component skills involved. Finally, the child goes off and privately tests himself or herself to see whether the skill has been fully learned: a failure is not seen by others and causes no embarrassment, but a success is brought back and exhibited to the teachers and others. The use of speech in this three-step process is minimal. When these same children go to school they find themselves in a situation where the high value placed on verbal performance is only the first of their cross-cultural hurdles. . . .Acquisition and demonstration of knowledge are no longer separate steps but are expected to occur simultaneously. Furthermore, this single-step process takes place via public recitations, the assumption apparently being that one learns best by making verbal mistakes in front of one's peers and teachers. Finally, the children have little opportunity to observe skilled performers carrying out these tasks, for the other children who perform are as ignorant and unskilled as they. Under these circumstances, it is small wonder that these [Native] American students demonstrate a propensity for silence.[63]

In contrast to the mainstream adage, "If at first you don't succeed, try, try, again," the Native American view is likely to be, "If at first you don't think, and think again, don't bother trying."[64]

Compared to the research on learning styles of other U.S. ethnic groups, there is a paucity of research on Asian American learners.[65] The education research that does exist on Asian Americans, particularly on Japanese American students, has indicated that many are hardworking, high achieving, relatively nonverbal, and seek careers in math and science.[66] As a result,

> many teachers stereotype Asian and Pacific American students as quiet, hardworking, and docile, which tends to reinforce conformity and stifle creativity. Asian and Pacific American students, therefore, frequently do not develop the ability to assert and express themselves verbally and are channeled in disproportionate numbers into the technical/scientific fields. As a consequence, many Asian and Pacific American students undergo traumatic family/school discontinuities, suffer from low self-esteem, are overly conforming, and have their academic and social development narrowly circumscribed.[67]

Perhaps the successful "model minority" myth associated with Asian Americans explains why there has been little study of their educational problems and learning styles. Particularly needed is insight into the learning styles of the most recent immigrants from Southeast Asia, many of whom face major difficulties in our schools.

A recent study of the learning styles of Hmong refugees, hill people from northern Laos who have settled in the Midwest, offers valuable insights into learning style characteristics that may be applicable to recent Southeast Asian refugees in general.[68] The Hmong students studied tend to be primarily field dependent and to use global rather than analytical problem-solving techniques. They are also reported to be passive and receptive, rather than active; unaccustomed to dealing with abstractions; and dependent upon mimesis (memorization), close identification with the teacher, peer influence, group support, and cooperation.

Learning Styles and Teaching Styles

As teachers we tend to teach the way we learn best, unless we make a conscious effort to do otherwise. We can, therefore, discover a great deal about our teaching style by analyzing our learning style. Indeed, this is important, for just as students may be negatively affected by learning style mismatches, teachers are often negatively affected by teaching style mismatches.

Gregorc writes, "Teachers whose teaching styles closely approximate their *major learning preferences* report comfort, ease, and authenticity."[69] Teachers who consistently mismatch their learning and teaching styles "report feelings of awkwardness, lack of efficiency and authenticity, and pain—mental and physical."[70] Many teachers are not aware of their teaching style and learning style preference and view pain and fatigue as natural results of hard work and study—"not as possible indicators of disease." Many teachers attempt to conform to a distinct image of what a teacher should be, even if the image is unnatural for them. Others are influenced by traditional or required practice.

"There are teachers, for example, who tell us that 'poetry *must* be taught this way,' and that 'we can't individualize and still meet mandated behavioral objectives,' or that 'students are not permitted to move around my room.' "[71]

Stress and teacher burnout can result from extended periods of mismatch. Thus, educators' understanding of their own learning and teaching styles benefits them as much as their students. Fortunately, it is not difficult to attain this self-awareness.

Teachers find the ELSIE and the GEFT useful approaches for assessing their own perceptual modality preferences and their tendency toward field insensitivity–sensitivity or field independence–dependence. Most often these teachers agree that they expect their students to learn the same way they do. They also report that this self-awareness gives them insight into some of the "disease" they experience when trying to be more flexible in their teaching. The insight itself often leads to feeling greater ease as they add new teaching styles to the old.

The idea of teaching style must not be confused with a teacher's method of instruction, such as the lecture, small group work, or oral reports. Teaching style refers to the teacher's pervasive personal behaviors and media used during interaction with learners. It is the teacher's characteristic approach, whatever the method used.[72]

In one recent review of learning style research, Dunn and Dunn examined a large number of "well-designed and carefully conducted research"[73] studies. They reported that when students are taught through their individual learning styles, their academic achievement increases significantly, their attitudes toward school improve significantly, and school discipline problems are significantly reduced.[74] Furthermore, "students have significantly more positive attitudes toward a subject when their learning styles are similar to their teachers' teaching styles."[75] Other research has documented that students perform better in classes taught by teachers with learning styles similar to the student.[76] This makes sense if one assumes that most teachers teach in ways that match their own learning styles. Only recently have demands been made that teachers become more flexible and use a variety of reaching styles in order to respond to the diversity of learning styles among their students.

■ Learning Styles and Effective Teaching

When a majority of students fail to learn, teachers are thought to have taught incompetently; the learning style movement, therefore, represents a tremendous challenge to teachers. It rejects the notion that good intentions are enough. Competence is required and is measured in terms of student growth and development.

Competence among teachers is often compared to competence in other professions. A well-intentioned doctor whose patients do not recover may still be called a doctor, and a well-intentioned architect whose buildings crumble may still be called an architect; neither, however, could be labeled competent in his or her profession. Similarly, a teacher who attends class every day with the intention of teaching is referred to as a teacher, even if no one learns. A competent teacher, however, is one who facilitates high levels of learning. The overall implication is that learning failure is due to teaching failure.

On the other hand, the learning style movement is more conducive to attaining higher levels of teacher competence than other philosophies in the past. Defining effective teaching has been difficult because judgments have been based on one teacher's effect on a large group of learners doing the same activity. This is misleading; few teaching strategies are appropriate for all or even a majority of students; thus the results of studies to determine teaching strategies and successful programs are disappointing. Nothing seems to make a significant difference; however, if researchers could examine the potential impact of specific strategies on individual students, research might be much more valuable.

Consider three first-grade teachers in one midwestern elementary school as an example. Hoping to evaluate the relative effectiveness of the phonetic, visual, and kinesthetic approaches to reading, each teacher chose one approach. Their comparisons of student growth in reading at the end of the year showed no significant differences; thus they concluded that the three approaches were equally effective and that it made little difference which one was selected. These teachers accepted the belief that every class should have some students progressing below, at, and above grade level. Had they examined the program's effect on individual students (especially on the failures) rather than on the class as a whole, they may well have found that the approach does make a difference. Many failing or below-grade-level readers within each class might have progressed with one or more of the other approaches. In these, as in all first-grade classrooms, different students would have benefited from different kinds of teaching.

To equalize opportunities for success, it is imperative to use unequal teaching methods that respond to relevant differences among students. Torrence writes that

> alert teachers have always been intuitively aware of the fact that when they change their method of teaching certain children who had appeared to be slow learners or even non-learners became outstanding achievers and some of their former star learners became slow learners. They have also learned that when they change the nature of the test used for assessing achievement, such as from a multiple choice test to one requiring creative applications of knowledge and decision making, the star learners may change position in class ranking markedly.[77]

The goal is to maximize the number of stars who can exist simultaneously in the classroom—to formulate a plan that can work even with the most diverse group of students. Research documents the fact that a wide range of learning styles exists among students in every classroom.[78] Add to this the list of individual differences that will be considered in the next chapter. Equity in the classroom will require alternative ways of learning, often simultaneously. Yet many of us are uncomfortable with what feels like creeping chaos in the classroom, which seems easier to manage when students are all doing the same activity. Although individuals or small groups often are allowed to progress at their own rate or read at their own level, we rarely let students learn in different ways. Those who continue to teach diverse groups of learners in nonflexible class-rooms must not be lulled into complacency by the fact that some students are learning. Perhaps many are. If they can adjust, teachers ask, why can't every-one else?

It is essential that teachers provide students with a variety of ways to learn so that the students' learning is in harmony with their cultural backgrounds. Some Native American children, for example, tend to be uncomfortable with large- and small-group recitations led by the teacher. They often prefer work-ing individually at their desks, or in small cooperative groups where the teacher acts as facilitator and supervisor.[79] Individual competition is to be avoided, es-pecially when individual excellence at the expense of others is stressed because it violates the value of personal humility. Writing about competition among Native American youth and their peer society, Wax states that

> it has frequently been observed that Indian children hesitate to engage in an in-dividual performance before the public gaze, especially where they sense compe-titive assessment against their peers and equally do not wish to demonstrate by their individual superiority the inferiority of their peers. On the other hand, where performance is socially defined as benefiting the peer society, Indians become excellent competitors (witness their success in team athletics).[80]

An effective learning environment for Native Americans is one that does not single out the individual but provides frequent opportunities for the teacher to interact privately with individual children and with small groups, as well as op-portunities for quiet, persistent exploration.

CONCLUSIONS

In her anthology *Culture, Style and the Educative Process,* Shade reviews a wide range of literature and research on the cultural styles of African Ameri-cans, Asian Americans, American Indians, Latinos, and European Americans. Her contributors wrote at different times and in different geophysical environ-ments, yet their "suggestions for promoting the academic success of culturally different children are remarkably similar."[81] Four major suggestions emerged to help teachers use culture and cognitive style in their teaching:

1. Inclusion of "multisensory presentations to open all pathways to the brain."[82]
2. Acceptance and understanding of different behavioral styles that other-wise could lead to unwarranted discipline problems.
3. Restructuring of the classroom social environment to make it more in-clusive and less exclusive.
4. Inclusion of a variety of communication and thinking styles to strengthen information processing by *all* students.[83]

Without alternative paths to success, we will continue to thwart the learn-ing of some, and often many. If classroom expectations are limited by our own cultural orientations, we impede success for learners guided by another cultural orientation. If we teach only according to the ways we ourselves learn best, we are also likely to thwart success for learners who may share our cultural background but whose learning style deviates from our own.

Everyone knows of gifted teachers, whose awareness and human sensitivity enable them to bridge cultural and individual gaps. They manage to provide each student with what he or she needs to be successful. But to what extent this flexibility and openness depend on basic personality traits may never be known. In any case, every teacher who wants to can take steps that will open the channels of success to all learners, regardless of their cultural or individual ways. To do this, we should adopt the following guidelines:

- Become familiar with multiple intelligence theory and its classroom applications.
- Know our own teaching and learning styles.
- Determine how far we can stray from these strengths and preferences and still be comfortable.
- Begin with a few students, those who are having difficulty in our classes.
- Know the learning style patterns that seem to characterize various ethnic groups.
- Build classroom flexibility slowly, adding one new strategy at a time.
- Use all modes (visual, auditory, tactile, and kinesthetic) when teaching concepts and skills.

COMPARE AND CONTRAST

1. Learning style theory and multiple intelligence theory
2. Field-sensitive and field-independent learning
3. Cognitive, affective, and physiological dimensions of learning style
4. Learning style and teaching style
5. Need for structure and modality strengths
6. Cultural style and learning style

ACTIVITIES AND QUESTIONS

1. Consult *Multiple Intelligences in the Classroom* (ASCD, 1994) written by Thomas Armstrong. Develop a plan for incorporating multiple intelligence theory in your own teaching.

2. When might it be best for teachers to mismatch their teaching styles with students' learning styles? Are there times when a match is absolutely necessary? Explain.

3. The idea that certain learning styles are related to certain ethnic groups is both dangerous and promising. Explain.

4. Analyze your own learning style. (Instructors and workshop leaders can obtain permission to use many of the learning style measures currently available.) What insights did you gain about the way you teach or are likely to teach?

5. The following list describes four students according to one or more aspects of learning style. Consider each student; based on the limited information provided, write what you believe would be the most effective instructional and evaluation strategies you could use in a subject area of your choice. Be specific and refer to actual materials and/or resources available to you. For each student, fill in a description under each of the following headings:

   a. Grade level, skill, or concept to be taught

   b. Appropriate teaching strategy/materials

   c. Appropriate evaluation strategy

   Description of the students:

   • Peggy Joyce—requires structure and has visual preferences

   • George—requires a quiet learning environment, is teacher motivated, prefers learning alone, is a factual and kinesthetic learner, and requires mobility

   • Moses—lacks persistence, is a peer-oriented learner, has auditory preferences, requires food intake, and learns best in the morning

   • Doris—requires a formal learning environment, is persistent, responsible, peer oriented, adult and teacher motivated, and can learn in several ways

6. Identify a concept or skill you are likely to teach and create a lesson that allows you to develop it both inductively (for field-independent learners) and deductively (for field-sensitive learners).

7. Select one or more learning style measures and administer it to one or more groups of students, or individuals. Which approach to learning styles did you select, and why? How effective did the approach appear to be? What are its advantages/disadvantages? What problems, if any, did you encounter? Did you discover any new insights or teaching implications for your classroom? If yes, explain fully. If not, was the exercise a waste of time? Explain.

8. Read further about learning styles. What is your current assessment of the learning style movement as an approach for enhancing student achievement? Is it another educational fad, or is there real potential here? Explain.

NOTES

1. See, for example, Harvey Silver, Richard String, and Matthew Perini, "Integrating Learning Styles and Multiple Intelligences," *Education Leadership,* Vol. 55, No.1, 1997, 22–27.

2. J. W. Keefe and M. Languis (untitled article), *Learning Stages Network Newsletter* 4, no. 2 (Summer 1983):1.

3. G. E. Kusler, "Getting to Know You," in *Student Learning Styles and Brain Behavior* (Reston, VA: National Association of Secondary School Principals, 1983),13.

4. Ibid., 11–12.

5. Ibid.

6. H. A. Witkin, C. Moore, and F. J. McDonald, "Cognitive Style and the Teaching/

Learning Processes" (American Educational Research Association Cassette Series 3F, 1974).

7. J. W. Keefe, "Assessing Student Learning Styles: An Overview," in *Student Learning Styles and Brain Behavior* (Reston, VA: National Association of Secondary School Principals, 1983), 44.

8. C. E. Cornett, "What You Should Know about Teaching and Learning Styles," *Fastback* 191 (Bloomington, IN: Phi Delta Kappa Educational Foundation, 1983), 32–37.

9. Keefe, "Assessing Student Learning Styles."

10. S. Messick (ed.), *Individuality in Learning* (San Francisco: Jossey-Bass, 1976).

11. Keefe, "Assessing Student Learning Styles."

12. Witkin, Moore, and McDonald, "Cognitive Style."

13. Hidden Figures Test (Cf-l), from the *Kit of Factor-Referenced Cognitive Tests* (Princeton, NJ: Educational Testing Service, 1962).

14. Witkin, Moore, and McDonald, "Cognitive Style."

15. M. Ramirez and A. Castañeda, *Cultural Democracy: Bicognitive Development, and Education* (New York: Academic Press, 1974).

16. P. Cross, *Accent on Learning* (San Francisco. Jossey-Bass, 1976),116.

17. A. Castañeda and T. Gray, "Bicognitive Processes in Multicultural Education," *Educational Leadership* 32 (December 1974):203–207, Tables 1–3.

18. D. E. Hunt, "Learning Style and Student Needs: An Introduction to Conceptual Level," in *Student Learning Styles: Diagnosing and Prescribing Programs* (Reston, VA: National Association of Secondary School Principals, 1979).

19. D. E. Hunt, quoted in Cornett, *What You Should Know About Teaching and Learning Styles,* 36.

20. Ibid., 31.

21. Ibid.

22. H. Reinert, "One Picture Is Worth a Thousand Words? Not Necessarily!" *Modern Language Journal* 60 (April 1976):163. Reinert's article is summarized and quoted here by permission of the author. The *Modern Language Journal* is published by the National Federation of Modern Language Teachers Associations (Madison, WI: University of Wisconsin Press).

23. Ibid., 162.

24. Ibid., 165.

25. Ibid., 169.

26. Ibid., 166.

27. Ibid., 161.

28. R. Dunn and K. Dunn, *Teaching Secondary Students through Their Individual Learning Styles: Practical Approaches for Grades 7–12* (Boston: Allyn and Bacon, 1993), 2.

29. Ibid., 2.

30. R. Hyman and B. Rosoff, "Matching Learning and Teaching Styles: The Jug and What's in It," *Theory into Practice* 23 (Winter 1984):36.

31. Keefe, "Assessing Student Learning Styles," 52–53.

32. Dunn and Dunn, 48.

33. Dunn and Dunn, 47–48.

34. Silver, Strong, and Pirini, op. cit. p. 22.

35. Howard Gardner, *Multiple Intelligences: Theory and Practice* (New York: Basic Books, 1993), 45.

36. Howard Gardner, *Frames of Mind: The Theory of Multiple Intelligences* (New York: Basic Books, 1985), 11.

37. Kathy Checkley, "The First Seven . . . and the Eighth," *Educational Leadership,* Vol. 55, No. 1. 1997, 8.

38. Howard Gardner, quoted in Checkley, ibid.

39. Ibid, 13.

40. H. G. and Thomas Hatch, "Multiple Intelligences Go to School: Educational Implications of the Theory of Multiple Intelligences," *Educational Researcher,* November 1989, 4.

41. Gardner, *Frames of Mind,* 64.

42. T. Armstrong, *Multiple Intelligences in the Classroom* (Alexandria, VA: ASCD, 1994), 5.

43. Ibid.

44. Ibid., 161.

45. Ibid.

46. K. M. Evenson Worthley, "Learning Style Factor of Field Dependence/Independence and Problem Solving Strategies of Hmong

Refugee Students" (Master Thesis, University of Wisconsin—Stout, July 1987).

47. Ibid., 45.

48. Ibid., 34.

49. Asa G. Hilliard, III, "Behavioral Style, Culture, and Teaching and Learning," *Journal of Negro Education,* 61:3 (Summer 1992), 370–371.

50. Ibid., 370.

51. Ibid.

52. Ibid., 371.

53. Ibid.

54. Ibid.

55. Ibid., 373.

56. B. J. Shade, "Afro-American Cognitive Style: A Variable in School Success?" *Review of Educational Research* 52, no. 2 (Summer 1982):220.

57. J. E. Hale-Benson, *Black Children: Their Roots, Culture, and Learning Styles,* rev. ed. (Baltimore: Johns Hopkins University Press, 1986).

58. R. Cohen, "Conceptual Styles, Culture Conflict and Nonverbal Tests of Intelligence," *American Anthropologist,* 71:828–856.

59. A. Hilliard, "Alternatives to IQ Testing: An Approach to the Identification of Gifted Minority Children" (Final report to the California State Department of Education, 1976).

60. G. Gay, "Culturally Diverse Students and Social Studies," in J. P. Shaver, ed., *Handbook of Research on Social Studies Teaching and Learning* (New York: Macmillan, 1991).

61. K. Swisher and D. Deyhle, "Styles of Learning and Learning Styles: Educational Conflicts for American Indian/Alaskan Native Youth," *Journal of Multilingual and Multicultural Development* 8, no. 4 (1987):350.

62. Ibid.

63. J. C. Phillips, "College of, by and for Navajo Indians," *Chronicle of Higher Education,* 15 (January 16, 1978):10–12.

64. Swisher and Deyhle, "Styles of Learning and Learning Styles," 348.

65. Worthley, "Learning Style Factor," 18.

66. F. M. Yoshiwara, "Shattering Myths: Japanese American Educational Issues," in *Education of Asian and Pacific Americans: Historical Perspectives and Prescriptions for the Future,* Don T. Nakanski and Marsha Hirano-Nakanski, eds. (Phoenix, AZ: Oryx Press, 1983), 23.

67. B. H. Suzuki, "The Education of Asian and Pacific Americans: In Introductory Overview," *Education of Asian and Pacific Americans: Historical Perspectives and Prescriptions for the Future,* Don T. Nakanishi and Marsha Hirano-Nakanishi, eds. (Phoenix, AZ: Oryx Press, 1983), 9.

68. Worthley, "Learning Style Factor."

69. A. F. Gregorc, "Learning/Teaching Styles," in *Student Learning Styles: Diagnosing and Prescribing Programs* (Reston, VA: National Association of Secondary School Principals, 1979), 24.

70. Ibid.

71. Ibid.

72. B. Bree Fischer and L. Fischer, "Styles in Teaching and Learning," *Educational Leadership* 36 (January 1979):245–254; see also Gregorc, "Learning/Teaching Styles."

73. Dunn and Dunn, "Learning Styles/Teaching Styles," 142.

74. Ibid.

75. Ibid., 145.

76. Witkin, Moore, and McDonald, "Cognitive Style."

77. P. Torrence, "Cultural Discontinuities and the Development of Originality of Thinking," *Exceptional Children* 29 (September 1962):2–3.

78. Dunn and Dunn, "Learning Styles/Teaching Styles," 145.

79. Swisher and Deyhle, "Styles of Learning and Learning Styles," 351.

80. M. L. Wax, *Indian Americans: Unity and Diversity* (Englewood Cliffs, NJ: Prentice Hall,1971), 85.

81. B. J. R. Shade, ed. *Culture, Style and the Educative Process* (Springfield, IL: Charles C. Thomas, 1989), 33.

82. Ibid., 337.

83. Ibid.

chapter 7

Beyond Learning Style: An Overview of Other Key Individual Differences

*A*n appropriate response to students' learning styles is often a necessary condition for success in the classroom, but it is rarely sufficient. Learning style is only one of a cluster of characteristics that may need to be considered. A student may be so interested in a particular subject, for example, that he or she will learn it regardless of the teacher's style. On the other hand, students who lack confidence, or who experience severe problems outside the classroom, may be unable to learn under even the best classroom conditions. This chapter explains eleven individual characteristics that, along with learning styles, often make a difference in how students learn. The chapter concludes with a discussion of teacher perceptions of individual differences as being either culturally disadvantaged or culturally different.

Learning Skills

Learning skills refer to a student's abilities to change or attain new capabilities. They include a child's ability to accurately receive aural and visual stimuli, to control large and small muscles, and to coordinate eye–hand activities. Other examples are decision-making skills and critical thinking, such as the ability to distinguish fact from opinion and the ability to generate alternative solutions to a problem and understand the consequences of each.

Schools can strengthen learning skills, in this case, the bodily kinesthetic.

Why do students of the same age often differ in their learning skill? How we answer this question is influenced by our conception of intelligence (an individual's ability to learn from experience, or to acquire and retain knowledge). Those who believe that intelligence is predetermined at birth would also believe that it is only natural for the brightest students to have the strongest learning skills. Others believe that intelligence develops primarily through environmental experiences. According to this view, students could not be expected to possess specific learning skills unless they had been taught or had had an opportunity to develop them through experience.

Probably the best response to the old nature–nurture controversy surrounding intelligence is that the individual's highest potential is determined at conception, and that the degree to which this potential is fulfilled depends largely on what the individual experiences during the formative years. The mother's emotional and physical health during pregnancy, as well as the nutrition provided the infant and young child, can influence how this potential is developed. It can be assumed that, barring cases of extreme nutritional and emotional deprivation, the vast majority of students have the capacity to develop the learning skills necessary to succeed in school. What must be remembered, however, is that they are not all ready to do so at the same time. Just as children mature physically at different rates, so do they mature mentally at different rates. Because mental development is more difficult to observe, we often do not know what the child is ready for.

Students who experience conflict between their home and school culture, such as Fred Young and Jimmy Miller, and students from low-income families, such as Rachael Jones, are often perceived as being culturally disadvantaged, "deficient," and lacking in ability to develop learning skills. Later in this chapter, teacher perceptions will be explained more fully.

Piaget and his associates at the Geneva Institute have generated the theory that all humans in all cultures move through a hierarchy of four stages as they develop intellectually.[1] Although everyone moves through the same stages, and in the same order, how quickly one moves through these stages depends on the combination of maturation (growth of brain tissues and development of the endocrine system), physical experiences, social interactions, and ego balance or a general progression of equilibrium through assimilation or accommodation of new learnings.

The first of these stages, the *sensorimotor intelligence stage,* usually operates during the first two years of life. During this period the infant's behavior is primarily motor, and the basic intellectual processes are developed through physical interaction with the environment. Objects exist for the child only if they can be seen, touched, or heard.

The second stage, *preoperational thought,* usually extends from ages two to seven. Verbal and conceptual abilities expand during this stage, and the child is capable of intuitive thought, though it tends to be illogical and ethnocentric.

The third stage, *concrete operations,* is entered at about age seven. Here the child shows striking new abilities to think in a logical way and to solve concrete problems. Thought processes such as ordering, classification, seriation, and mathematics are possible, provided concrete objects are involved. The ability to think abstractly has not yet begun to appear.

Between eleven and fifteen years of age, the individual enters the stage of *formal operations.* In this stage students come to understand highly abstract concepts, such as justice, love, and prejudice. Their thoughts are no longer tied to actual objects and experience; they can think about ideas and use logic. Until the child fully develops stage-four thought processes, therefore, he or she is incapable of certain intellectual activities that require abstract reasoning.

Cognitive anthropologists have begun to question Piaget's conclusions, particularly because he overlooks the connection between the individual and his or her culture.[2] Whether or not one accepts Piaget's theory of cognitive development, it is crucially important to know where students are in terms of their intellectual growth and development. Students who may have the same potential for high achievement may be approaching it at different rates, or may differ in their past opportunities to learn. A suburban child, for example, may not know as much about animals and nature as a child who has grown up on a farm. An inner-city child may know little about raking leaves or fishing. A rural child may never have flown in an airplane or visited a large city. Although these children's horizons may be broadened through vicarious experiences on television, much remains to be learned about the impact of that medium on their cognitive development.

When teachers ask students to perform tasks they are not ready for—due to slower rates of maturation or absence of necessary experiences—they may create the conditions of failure and make it less likely that the individual's intelligence will be developed to its fullest potential. The challenge is to ask students to perform mental tasks that match their intellectual development. If we aim too high, we can trigger feelings of frustration, self-doubt, and failure. If we aim too low, the student may become frustrated, bored, and alienated.

Levels of Achievement and Aptitudes

Achievement level is defined as the knowledge a student has previously acquired that relates to what is being taught. Although this knowledge could include learning skills such as critical thinking and decision making, the emphasis here is on content, which consists of the concepts and generalizations within the subject matter.

What students already know about what we plan to teach is of obvious importance to their success in the classroom. Do they have the basic knowledge—the building blocks—needed to understand new material? Can they read musical notes? Can they comprehend the textbook? Have they mastered their multiplication facts? Do they already know most of what we plan to teach this year? Perhaps a student is obsessed with reading about space or dinosaurs, has had years of experience helping in a parent's store, is already an expert mechanic, is an authority on Beethoven, or has a hobby collecting fossils. Perhaps a student has grown up in a world of crime and injustice or has developed more insight into the problems of alcohol and drug abuse than could be provided in any college text.

Aptitudes refer to special abilities, talents, or natural tendencies that enable a person to learn or understand quickly. When students show a special aptitude for what is being taught, they will probably learn at a rapid rate. Students who show little aptitude for a subject will require more time to learn it. Teachers must be careful not to assume, however, that a slow rate of learning means a low aptitude. There may be other explanations. The student may lack more basic knowledge; one cannot learn division, for example, until multiplication is mastered. The learner may not be ready to handle abstractions or may lack self-confidence. Students may be reflective rather than impulsive learners or may experience transitional trauma due to cultural conflict between home and school.

Teachers must recognize that students' learning rates may differ. If we assume that a slow rate of learning indicates low aptitude, however, we are lowering our expectations and probably the student's self-expectations for success. The challenge is knowing when it is necessary and fair to expect more, and when it is not.

Current research on gifted and talented children and youth can make teachers more alert to the special talents and aptitudes that many students possess. Current research indicates that gifted students are evenly distributed across all racial groups and socioeconomic levels.[3] The traditional conception that gifted students are those who score very high on intelligence tests has given way to a much broader view. Today, many kinds of giftedness are recognized: intellectual, academic (one or more specific subjects), creative thinking, leadership, visual and performing arts, athletic, and mechanical. Students in all these categories would score above average on an intelligence test, but not necessarily in the highest ranges. For example, a highly creative student with excellent critical thinking skills could score 115 on an IQ test (generally believed to be the lowest level possible for the gifted). Traditional intelligence tests "do not measure other critical characteristics such as artistic excellence, superior moral attitudes and behaviors, creative or divergent production behaviors, superior psychomotor abilities, or superior leadership abilities."[4]

In the last chapter we learned that Gardner's theory of multiple intelligence identifies a range of intelligences: linguistic, musical, logical, mathematical, spatial, bodily kinesthetic, and personal.[5] Sternberg, author of *Beyond IQ: A Triarchic Theory of Human Intelligence,* also challenges the traditional conceptions of intelligence. In a theory that is compatible with Gardner's, Sternberg identifies three equally important aspects of intelligence: the analytic, the practical, and the synthetic (or creative intelligence). He argues that the school focuses on analytic intelligence through the emphasis on the ability to absorb and recite facts and neglects the practical and creative aspects of the mind.[6]

When considering the levels of achievement and aptitudes of students whose cultural background differs from the Anglo-European dominant culture that predominates in school, it is important to remember the following factors.

- The past experiences and opportunities of ethnically different students are often not the ones teachers recognize and value.
- Measures of achievement and aptitude have traditionally been most appropriate for White, middle-income groups.
- Instructional content and strategies have also been developed primarily for White, middle-income students.
- Teachers often lack understanding of cultural difference and have lower expectations for student success.
- The student may not be fluent in standard English or may speak a dialect the teacher regards as slang.
- The student may have a learning style preference that is not accommodated by the teacher.
- The student may not be accepted by a majority of classmates, a factor that has been found to lower achievement levels among children in the minority.

Motivation

Motivation refers to the inner drive, the feeling of intent or desire, that causes the student to learn. There exists within students a natural reservoir of motivation.[7] Provided that children feel respected and cared for by their teachers, there are no racial or cultural differences in their basic love of learning in the early grades. Natural excitement, the love of learning, and the desire to know are seen most clearly among children in kindergarten and the primary grades.

As students move through school, however, the excitement often dims and teachers typically have to do something to motivate students to learn.

In our efforts to motivate students, we find there are differences in what works. Some students respond to competition, for example; turn any learning activity into a competitive game and they thrive. For competition types, the boredom of a history review or spelling list disappears when the class plays "Double Jeopardy" or baseball; the chance to play Quiz Bowl can make the weekly reading of *Time* part of their routine. Other students, however, dislike competition and feel anxious and less able to learn or perform in a competitive situation. Even high-achieving students, who theoretically could survive the competition, sometimes do better in a cooperative setting.

Peer approval is another prime motivation for some students. Whether or not a student achieves in a given class may depend on how a clique or peer reference group feels about the teacher and subject. It is common for high-ability students to suppress their school achievements in order to be accepted by their peers. Those students who are moved by adult or teacher approval may be easier to motivate, though in some cases pressure from parents can cause undue tension and anxiety.

Younger students may be motivated by consumable rewards such as candy or other treats. Older students can often be motivated by opportunities for making choices, experiencing greater independence, or assuming new responsibilities, particularly if the options have real meaning for them.

Many of these strategies may sound like manipulation, especially if we accept the view of Maslow and other humanists who believe that all humans by nature continually search for growth and self-expansion. The question for teachers is: How can we act to utilize the natural motivation that exists within the students we teach?

Maslow states that human needs are organized into a "hierarchy of relative prepotency; physical needs, safety needs, belongingness and love needs, esteem needs, and the need for self-actualization."[8] Ordinarily, the needs at one level must be partially satisfied before the individual seeks to satisfy needs at the next level. Once the basic "lower" needs are met (food and water, protection, love, and self-esteem), there exists within everyone the compelling desire to grow and expand to his or her fullest potential, to be what Maslow refers to as self-actualized. A self-actualized person is one who is self-directed and grows by using all of his or her natural abilities. Self-actualized people search to fulfill their highest needs through aesthetic experiences and a concern for ethics.

This theory has important implications for teaching. Only when students' basic needs are met are they ready to learn at their fullest potential. Their needs for food, water, shelter, clothing, and protection from harm must be satisfied before they can be concerned above love and belonging. The sense of belonging is necessary for building the self-esteem that is, in turn, necessary for self-actualization. As the individual begins to become self-actualized, the desire for knowledge, understanding, and aesthetic experiences intensifies.

Teachers obviously cannot control the student's world outside the classroom. We cannot solve problems such as poverty and hunger, family conflicts, child abuse, or a child's inability to make friends. Neither a hungry child nor a rejected child is likely to place a high priority on learning. Teachers, neverthe-less, are in a prime position for helping students meet needs at all levels. We must do what we can to work toward the goal of helping all students reach their fullest potential. Some of the strategies known to maximize motivation, devel-opment, and achievement among students are suggested in Box 7.1. These sug-gestions are arranged in four categories: instructional qualities, personal qualities, content, and classroom climate.

Teaching Strategies

BOX 7.1

Instructional Qualities

- Provide each student with an opportunity to make an important contribution to class activities.
- Provide each student with an opportunity to experience success.
- Provide students with effective feedback or helpful information about their pro-gress; be prompt; be clear about the criteria for success.
- Shift patterns of instruction; use a variety of strategies and sensory channels.
- Alter the physical learning environment when necessary to make it compatible with the purpose of the lesson. (For example, desks in a circle facilitate equal communication, rows may be more effective for a film, and opposing blocks of chairs can enhance a classroom debate.)

Suggestions about Content

- Begin with clear objectives that are challenging but unattainable.
- Make clear why the objectives are important and worth attaining.
- Cultivate curiosity and creativity.
- Invite students to participate in planning and evaluating their curriculum.
- Build on students' existing interests while trying to create new ones.
- Organize at least part of the curriculum around real-life problems.

Suggestions about Personal Qualities

- Search for ways to express care for each student.
- Never belittle or ridicule a student.
- Project enthusiasm.
- Avoid distracting behaviors and overuse of terms such as "uh" and "you know."
- Use movement—don't stay behind the desk.
- Be genuine.

Suggestions about Climate

- Get to know the students. Learn their names right away.
- Find ways to help students know each other.
- Insist that students show respect for each other; create a classroom climate of trust and acceptance.

■*Self-Concept*

Self-concept, or self-image, is a complex set of beliefs that an individual holds true about himself or herself. This set of beliefs may be viewed globally or may be broken down into components. For example, we have beliefs about our achievement abilities, both overall and in specific areas. We have beliefs about our character, such as our integrity or compassion. We have beliefs about our physical attractiveness, strength, and coordination.

How we see ourselves develops out of our interactions with others, the way we feel others perceive us and treat us. This self-image influences our behaviors, which, in turn, affect the way others see us and treat us, and the cycle (be it benevolent or vicious) is complete.

It appears that a positive self-image is a necessary though not sufficient condition for school success. Students with negative self-images seldom achieve at above-average levels. On the other hand, many students with positive self-concepts do not achieve at high or above-average levels, as we might expect. Feeling good about oneself does not guarantee being a top student, but feeling bad nearly guarantees doing poorly.

When a student with low self-esteem enters a classroom, self-concept becomes one of the most challenging individual differences in how he or she will learn. Because students with a negative self-image are not fully able to learn, school becomes an arena for failure that prevents them from achieving the success needed for high self-esteem. A vicious cycle develops whereby the school itself, by providing experiences of failure, helps keep the student's self-image deflated.

> Once a child is convinced he cannot learn in school, the task of educators becomes almost impossible. He may well make trouble for his classmates, his teachers, and himself. A negative self-concept is just as crippling and just as hard to overcome as any physical handicap. In fact, a negative self-image may be even more crippling, because it is often hidden from the view of the naive or untrained observer. Most children who hate themselves act out this self-hatred by kicking the world around them. They are abusive, aggressive, hard to control, and full of anger and hostility at a world which has told them that they are not valued, are not good, and are not going to be given a chance. Such attitudes often continue to cripple an adult life.[9]

Do the children and youth of ethnic-minority backgrounds tend to have less positive self-images than those of nonminorities? The answer to this question is debatable. Research findings to date are contradictory and inconclusive.[10] Some have assumed, for example, that Black self-concepts would be lower because of the history of slavery and oppression Blacks have experienced in this society.[11] Although some research tends to support this view, other researchers have discovered that Black students' self-concepts are as high or higher than their White counterparts.[12]

A number of researchers have studied the impact of school desegregation on the self-concepts of minority students. In his extensive review of research on minority student self-concepts, Weinberg sees evidence supporting the proposition that attendance at an interracial school benefits Black students' self-conceptions.[13] However, he cautions against artificial self-esteem programs that do not offer minority students the opportunities to acquire the knowledge and skills needed for school and occupational successes.

Others assert that Black students benefit more from schools that have been historically Black, where Black teachers are more caring and supportive of Black students, have high academic expectations, and provide Black students with positive role models as well as a knowledge of Black history and achievements. Since such schools are unavailable to the majority of Black students today, Weinberg seems justified in his conclusions.

In his book *Inviting School Success: A Self-concept Approach to Teaching*,[14] Purkey develops the conception of teaching as inviting. Teachers have the capacity to invite or disinvite, to encourage or discourage, student development and achievement. Purkey explains that invitations are the verbal and nonverbal, formal and informal, messages that make students feel responsible, able, and valuable. (Conversely, a disinvitation is a message that makes students feel that they are irresponsible, incapable, and worthless.) Even a child with a very low sense of self-esteem can be invited to learn by a caring teacher. No matter how bad the overall school situation is, the teacher always has the power to invite and disinvite students.

The authors of *Perceiving, Behaving, and Becoming* agree that a positive self is teachable and that self-knowledge and growth as education goals are as important as the acquisition of subject matter.[15] They call for classroom climates that are free from destructive competition, prejudice, bigotry, and vicious conflict between opposing interest groups; for teachers who behave as friendly representatives of society; and for social experiences that make students feel acceptable, liked, wanted, able, respected, worthy, and important.[16]

Gender

A student's gender affects learning in many ways. Several gender-related differences and assumptions that influence learning come to mind immediately, such as the old belief that boys are more adept at math and science while girls excel in English and the humanities.[17] The Project on Equal Education Rights of the Legal Defense and Education Fund of the National Organization of Women has found that schools still discourage girls from taking math, science, computer, and vocational classes.[18] Another example of gender-related differences is the fact that girls mature physically and emotionally at an earlier age than boys. However, recent research in moral development and epistemology points to even more important, although less understood, differences in the ways that girls and boys learn and understand the world. These differences have important implications for student learning.

Some of the most important and useful work in the area of gender differences has been done by Carol Gilligan in her work *In a Different Voice*.[19] Gilligan undertook her study in an attempt to include a female perspective in the male-dominated field of psychology and moral development. She found that when measured against a male standard, women were often ranked at "lower" stages of moral development than men. However, when Gilligan listened to women themselves, what she heard was not an inferior or superior voice but simply a different voice. The two different voices or ethics that she heard she named the "ethic of care" and the "ethic of justice." Although these two ethics are not gender-specific, they are gender-related in that the ethic of care is more commonly a female ethic and the ethic of justice a male ethic.

The ethic of care, according to Gilligan, has to do with connection and responsibility. Those who are rooted in this ethic are more concerned with nurturing relationships than with securing rights. Theirs is a world grounded in personal experience, and moral judgments are made based on concrete circumstances and the need to take care of others. The ethic of justice, on the other hand, relies on a more abstract notion of individual rights and the application of universal principals in making moral decisions. These differences in moral perspectives have been found to be related to identity development. For those operating within an ethic of care, *self* is understood in connection and relatedness to others, while those whose ethic is one of justice understand themselves more in terms of autonomy and separation.

These differences have important implications in the classroom. Because the Western intellectual heritage upon which our educational system is based relies heavily on abstract, objective reasoning and an atomistic understanding of the world, those who operate under the ethic of care—usually girls—are at a definite disadvantage. Although Gilligan has asserted that this voice is merely different, in the classroom it is often heard as inferior, or worse, it is not heard at all—in both a metaphorical and a literal sense.

Belenky and her associates in their work *Women's Ways of Knowing* found the metaphors of "silence" and "finding a voice" to be very important in the development of women's selves, minds, and ways of learning.[20] In extensive interviews of 135 women from varying ethnic, socioeconomic, and educational backgrounds, they found that a great many women had gone or were still going through a period of feeling "deaf and dumb." Said one woman, looking back on her educational experiences, "'I could never understand what they were talking about. My schooling was very limited. I didn't learn anything, I would just sit there and let people ramble on about something I didn't understand and would say Yup, yup. I would be too embarrassed to ask, 'What do you mean?' "[21] Although this woman's experience was somewhat extreme, a surprisingly large number of women surveyed reported having felt similarly about their abilities to communicate and understand through language. Although not literally deaf and dumb, these women felt incapable of hearing and learning from the words of others and unable to speak and have a voice themselves.

Metaphors of "silence" and "finding a voice" are important in the development of young girls' sense of self, their minds, and their ways of learning.

This metaphor of silence can actually be substantiated by literal examples of female voicelessness. Contrary to the myth that women and girls talk in excess, studies have found that men interrupt women far more than other men, and more than women interrupt men or other women.[22] Furthermore, in naturally occurring conversation between women and men who describe themselves as sexually liberated, it was found that although women initiated 62 percent of conversations, only 36 percent of their topics succeeded in fostering conversation, while men had a 96 percent success rate.[23] It appears that in the classroom, boys have dominant voices as well. Sadker found that teachers praise—and criticize—boys far more than girls. She also found that boys call out for the teacher's attention eight times more than girls do, and that teachers accept boys' unsolicited remarks as contributions. When girls do the same, they are told to raise their hands.[24]

This voicelessness—both metaphorical and literal—which girls experience in the classroom is only reinforced by the silence of female voices in the curriculum. Literature courses still focus largely on a White male canon; history and social studies continue to lean toward the male-dominated world of politics rather than the more female-oriented social realm; and the fact that math and science are still heavily dominated by males is seldom questioned or criticized in the classroom. Voicelessness, whether literal or metaphorical, not only restricts the student's ability to contribute in the learning experience but it also restricts all of us from a vital portion of the curriculum.

Special Interests

Students' special interests refer to the hobbies and recreational activities they enjoy most and pursue whenever they can. Interests may also refer to personal concerns and problems the student faces. Wise teachers attempt to discover their students' special interests because outside interests can become a catalyst for student learning in the classroom.

Experienced teachers can supply numerous examples of reaching the unreachable by relating course content and activities to the student's special interest. Fractions can be taught through musical rhythms, history through sports, science through the outdoors, reading through motorcycle manuals, personal accounting through part-time jobs such as paper routes or child care, and civics through community issues and problems.

A classic case of building on student interest is described by Daniel Fader and Elton McNeil in *Hooked on Books*.[25] By instituting an extensive reading program based on paperbacks, magazines, and newspapers that most teachers would frown upon but that are related to the students' lives, Fader and McNeil were able to motivate even the most bored and apathetic students.

Physical Characteristics

Physical characteristics (the body itself) are closely related to the other individual differences being considered. Physical health and maturation, for example, affect intellectual and emotional growth and development; attractiveness, health and vitality, size, age, strength, agility, coordination, and gender can all affect self-perception, peer acceptance, and readiness for learning. When the individual is perceived as being different from what is believed to be normal, physical differences must be considered.

During the years of emerging adolescence, typically between ages ten and fourteen, physical differences are especially important. Tremendous physical changes take place with the onset of puberty among males and females. Bones lengthen, muscles enlarge, the endocrine glands produce hormones, and the individual develops sexually. Curtis and Bidwell write,

> This interrelationship between the hormonal balance of the body and the nervous system of the brain has certain implications for the development of the educational system for emerging adolescents. The possibility of extreme changes in mood and volatility found in many emerging adolescents becomes much more easily explained when the possibility of temporary chemical imbalance due to temporarily uneven hormonal secretions is noted. The concerns of the emerging adolescent about his or her physical body may create psychosomatic problems which, while not noted by adult observers, may have great impact upon the emotions of the emerging adolescent. Last, since the emotions are affected to some extent by the hypothalamus, it is not unreasonable to expect that the emotions of the emerging adolescent might be less predictable than in childhood or in later adolescence when hormonal secretions become less of a factor in the physical development of the youngster.[26]

Physical differences are also often associated with various ethnic groups. Research on prejudice shows that in United States society skin color is the most salient characteristic that influences people's perceptions and judgments of each other.[27] Historically, lighter-skinned individuals have been favored over those with dark skin, sometimes even among African Americans and Hispanics. Even though the civil rights movement of the 1960s helped to expand social recognition that Black is beautiful, skin color often makes a difference in the classroom. Studies of classroom interaction show that many teachers have higher expectations for the achievement of their White or lighter-skinned students than for Black, Hispanic, or darker-skinned students, and they interact with White students in more positive ways.[28]

Although they may be unaware of their prejudices, these teachers have accepted the racist view that a student's physical traits associated with race determine that student's social behavior, character, and intellectual abilities. This view leads to actions that subordinate students of another race.

■ *Peer Relations*

The social structure of the classroom and the social status of the individual student with respect to classmates can have an impact on student learning. In the vignette of Max Britten in the opening section of Part II, rejection and scapegoating by his peers had a negative impact on his school achievement. His schoolwork improved during those periods when he was accepted by the neighborhood clique. A single student in Warren Benson's class who decided to get serious about learning might face the rejection of peers. Warren would have to find a way to motivate certain cliques and make class attendance and learning socially acceptable.

Some researchers have discovered a positive relationship between a student's popularity among classmates and social interactions; others have found that social acceptability is also related to achievement.[29] School desegregation research has shown that school and classroom climates of acceptance have a significant impact on the academic achievement of minority students.[30] Students who represent a numerical minority tend to achieve better in classroom climates of acceptance.

One study of classroom climate in over 40 desegregated seventh- and eighth-grade classrooms in Indianapolis showed that in classroom climates of acceptance, both Black and White students selected many friends of their own and different races.[31] Students also frequently initiated conversations with students of both races. In the low-acceptance classrooms, both Black and White students tended to limit their conversations and friendship choices to their own race. This study did not analyze the relationship between student interracial popularity (that is, interracial friendship choices and conversations) and achievement, but teachers in the high-acceptance classrooms felt there were no important racial differences in student achievement or aptitude. Teachers in the low-acceptance classrooms reported that White students were higher achievers than Black students. The study suggests that teachers themselves have a lot to do with the type of climate that is established. When compared with their peers, teachers in high-acceptance classrooms tended to be strong and directing, fair, warm, spontaneous, and involved in the teaching profession.

Fordham and Ogbu argue that peer pressure not to act White, that is, not to strive for academic achievement, is one major reason Black students do poorly in school.[32] Based on their research in Washington, DC, Fordham and Ogbu write that many Black adolescents identify attitudes and behaviors such as the following as acting White and therefore unacceptable:

- Speaking standard English
- Listening to White music and White radio stations
- Going to the opera or ballet
- Spending a lot of time in the library studying
- Working hard to get good grades in school
- Getting good grades in school (those who get good grades are labeled "brainiacs")
- Going to the Smithsonian
- Going to a Rolling Stones concert at the Capital Center
- Doing volunteer work
- Going camping, hiking, or mountain climbing
- Having cocktails or a cocktail party
- Going to a symphony orchestra concert
- Having a party with no music
- Listening to classical music
- Being on time
- Reading and writing poetry
- Putting on airs

They argue that this view of acting White is shared by many Black adolescents in other areas of the nation, as well as by other minorities such as those "American Indians and Mexican Americans [who] perceive the public schools as an agent of assimilation into the white American or Anglo frame of reference . . . [and as] detrimental to the integrity of their cultures, languages, and identities."[33]

Their research with academically successful and unsuccessful Black high school students reveals that because they fear being labeled a "brainiac," "many academically able black students do not put forth the necessary effort and perseverance in their schoolwork, and consequently, do poorly in school. Even black students who do not fail generally perform well below their potential for the same reasons."[34]

The problem developed partly out of our racist past, where many White Americans refused to acknowledge the intellectual potential of Black Americans, and partly because many Black Americans subsequently learned to doubt their own intellectual ability, began to define academic success as White people's prerogative and began to discourage their peers, perhaps unconsciously, from emulating White people in striving academically, that is, from acting White.[35]

Ogbu and Fordham find that the more successful Black students have developed strategies for coping with their peers and the "burden of acting white." Males are able to obtain good grades without being rejected by their peers through participation in athletics, clowning and "acting crazy," or trading academic assistance for protection. Females tend to maintain a low school profile through strategies such as cutting classes selectively so as not to accumulate enough absences in any one class to fail it, "putting brakes" on their academic performance, and refusing to participate in the school's academic clubs and academic competitions.

Peer pressure related to perceptions that academic achievement means acting White is only one important reason why some Black students do not achieve in school. Some scholars argue that a better explanation for why students of color are not academically motivated is that they feel a lack of respect and a lack of caring from teachers and administrators,[36] or they feel alienated because they live in communities where high rates of poverty and racial segregation are combined.[37] Other important factors are the social and economic barriers many Black Americans face as adults (for example, a job ceiling) and the fact that traditionally many Black Americans have been provided with substandard schooling. Until changes in the opportunity structures occur, many Black adolescents, as well as adolescents in other subordinate minorities, are likely to view academic school success as "a kind of risk which necessitates strategies enabling them to cope with the burden of acting white."[38]

In the face of these barriers, what can teachers do? If school personnel and parents understand these problems, they can help students learn to separate the pursuit of academics from the idea of acting White and can reinforce students' sense of ethnic identity in ways that are compatible with intellectual achievement. The possibilities are noted in the case of E. Sargent, a journalist with the *Washington Post,* who attended public schools in Washington, DC. Sargent describes how his knowledge of African American history, acquired *outside* the schools, strengthened his sense of Black identity and his ability to deal with the burden of acting White.

> While I had always been a good student, I became a better one as a result of my sense of black history. I began to notice that my public school teachers very rarely mentioned black contributions to the sciences, math, and other areas of study. . . . They never talked about ways blacks could collectively use their education to solve the great economic and social problems facing the race.
>
> My mind was undergoing a metamorphosis that made the world change its texture. Everything became relevant because I knew blacks had made an impact on all facets of life. I felt a part of things that most blacks thought only white people had a claim to. . . . Knowing that there is a serious speculation that Beethoven was black—a mullato [sic]—made me enjoy classical music. "Man, why do you listen to that junk? That's white music," my friends would say. "Wrong. Beethoven was a brother." I was now bicultural, a distinction most Americans could not claim. I could switch from boogie to rock, from funk to jazz and from rhythm-and-blues to Beethoven and back. . . . I moved from thinking of myself as disadvantaged to realizing that I was actually "superadvantaged."[39]

■ *Family Conditions*

Family conditions refer to the child's experiences at home and include a wide range of factors such as love and emotional support, sibling relationships, parents' occupations, special learning experiences, economic resources, ethnicity, and so on.

The family's influence on the child's sense of ethnicity is of interest. As noted in Chapter 2, Longstreet points out the strong relationships between family and ethnicity when she defines ethnicity as "that portion of cultural development that occurs before the individual is in complete command of his or her abstract intellectual powers and that is formed primarily through the individual's early contact with family, neighbors, friends, teachers, and others, as well as with his or her immediate environment of the home and neighborhood."[40] Until the time a child can think abstractly, he or she naturally develops certain food and clothing preferences, ways of talking, body language, and values. These cultural ways can change later if a person chooses to do so. But for most of the time a child attends school, ethnic origins have a strong influence. How similar these cultural ways are to the dominant culture is a factor in school success.

Although teachers often have no idea about what their students' home conditions are like, they make assumptions. Marcia comes from a rich family and has all the advantages; the fact that she's not doing well in school must be due to poor aptitude. Rachael lives in the poor section of town, has not been exposed to good books or music, and does not value school, thus little can be expected from her. Max comes from a split home; therefore, he feels rejected and needs extra attention in school, but a teacher with thirty-three other students can't provide it.

Too often, we assume that children and youth from low-income backgrounds or single-parent homes receive insufficient love and support from their families. We tend to assume the opposite for the child from the typical all-American family in suburbia. Although there is some truth to these stereotypes, parents and students are rightfully offended when schools assume that children from low-income backgrounds are deprived of love and emotional support. Divorced parents are also rightly offended at the single-parent stereotypes. Research on the long-term effects of divorce on children shows that divorce is indeed traumatic for children, particularly male children under age six.[41] During their immediate family crisis, many children do not achieve in school. Typically, at least a year is needed to adjust even under the best of conditions. Research also shows that after a period of transition and under supportive conditions some children recover sufficiently to resume progress in school, and that children raised in single-parent homes often develop greater independence, responsibility, and initiative.[42]

Children and adolescents from low-income families and the underclass, a term describing the poorest of the poor and those who are trapped in a vicious cycle of poverty, are the least likely to graduate from high school. In the mid-1980s, for example, the dropout rates for nonpoor Whites were 8.6 percent, compared to 27.1 percent for poor Whites, and 9.3 percent for nonpoor Blacks, compared to 24.6 percent for poor Blacks.[43] Children raised in poverty are likely to suffer from hunger and chronic malnutrition that can stunt their growth and development, and sap their energy for schoolwork. "The Physicians Task Force on Hunger in America estimated that in 1985, about 20 million Americans, including 12 million children, were hungry at some point every month. They also concluded that malnutrition affected almost half a million children in 1985."[44] In 1991, 21.8 percent of the nation's children under 18 years lived in poverty.[45]

Children from poverty homes may experience lower teacher expectations for school success and fall into a cycle of low self-expectations and failure. They may also have few role models who illustrate the value of schooling or encourage them to work hard at their studies. Some sociologists have also identified a suspicion among poor Whites, often from rural areas, of schools and teachers who represent "middle class" values and behaviors. A peer group dynamic can emerge among poor Whites in urban schools that is similar to what Fordham and Ogbu discovered among Black adolescents who experience peer pressure not to work in school (i.e., act White).

It would be impossible to know and fully understand the family conditions of all students. Teachers can realize, however, that sometimes a student is unable to learn in school because of problems at home or because of a conflict between home and school. Teachers can avoid diminished expectations based on erroneous assumptions that a student is simply slow or unmotivated. We can provide encouragement and support in school and better the chances that eventually a child will be resilient and catch up. We can avoid stereotypes and misconceptions by asking ourselves the following questions:

Does the family provide love and emotional support?
Does the family provide adequate food and shelter?
Does the student have unusual family responsibilities?
Are there mutual feelings of respect and ease between family members and
    school personnel?
Is there any cultural conflict between home and school expectations?

Beliefs, Attitudes, and Values

Beliefs, attitudes, and values are at the heart of culture. They are also at the heart of concern about individual differences within cultural similarities. Beliefs, attitudes, and values have developed out of shared and unique past experiences, and they strongly influence (while being influenced by) behavior and perceptions of the world.

A person's beliefs, attitudes, and values may be viewed together as an integrated cognitive system; change in any one of the three parts of the system will affect other parts and is likely to result in a change of behavior.[46] A *belief* refers to an opinion, expectation, or judgment that a person accepts as true. Not all beliefs are equally important to the individual; they vary along a central-peripheral dimension. Central beliefs are most resistant to change, and the more central the belief that is changed, the more widespread the repercussions in the rest of the belief system.[47]

An *attitude* may be defined as a relatively stable organization of interrelated beliefs that describe, evaluate, and advocate action with respect to a person, object, or situation.[48] This definition suggests that attitudes have three components: an idea or thought, a feeling or emotion, and a readiness to respond or predisposition to action.[49] An attitude is thus a package of beliefs about what is true or false, desirable and undesirable.

As stated in Chapter 2, *values* are beliefs about how one ought or ought not to behave, or about some end state of existence worth or not worth attaining. Values are abstract ideals, positive or negative, that represent a person's beliefs about ideal modes of conduct and ideal terminal goals.[50] A value is a standard we use to influence the values, attitudes, and actions of others; it is like a yardstick that we use to guide the actions, attitudes, comparisons, evaluations, and justifications of ourselves and others.[51]

Consider some examples that illustrate the complex cognitive system of beliefs, attitudes, and values. The first situation involves drug usage; the second, racial discrimination in the collegiate Greek system; and the third, cultural conflict between a teacher and a student.

In the first situation, two young high school students attend an unsupervised party where everyone is smoking pot. Neither student has ever used drugs before and for various reasons each feels hesitant about doing so. They are both encouraged to join in the activity, and it appears that they would be excluded from the group if the invitation were refused. What do they decide to do and how are they likely to feel after the decision? (See Box 7.2.)

Cognitive Systems—Drugs

BOX 7.2

Student A	Student B
Beliefs	
• Pot is not harmful; it is neither physically nor psychologically addictive.	• Pot can become psychologically addicting.
• My parents will be angry if I smoke pot.	• Sometimes pot contains lethal additives.
• Almost everybody smokes pot.	• People who use pot suffer from feelings of inadequacy or boredom with life.
• The laws against marijuana are unfair, and they aren't strictly enforced in this town anyway.	• Pot is illegal.
• I will be accepted by this group if I smoke pot.	• It is possible that this party could be busted by the police.
• Pot makes a person feel more relaxed and euphoric.	• I will be accepted by this group if I smoke pot.

BOX 7.2

(Continued)

Attitudes

- The idea of smoking pot with these friends feels good and I want to stay and accept the invitation.

- The idea of smoking pot with these friends feels bad and I want to leave.

Values

- Personal enjoyment and friendship are more important than obeying a foolish law.

- Health and self-respect are more important than social acceptance.

Because each person's beliefs are highly consistent in this example, and no value conflicts were presented, it is easy to infer what each person will do. In reality, however, the relationship between attitudes and behavior is usually not so clear cut.

The next example in Box 7.3 takes place on a college campus during rush. The illustration could also apply to many noncollegiate situations such as housing developments, apartment complexes, fraternal organizations, and social clubs.

Cognitive Systems—Racial Discrimination

BOX 7.3

Student A	**Student B**
Beliefs	
• Blacks are immoral and sexually promiscuous.	• Whites are stupid about life.
• Blacks are dirty.	• Whites are intellectually superior.
• Blacks are lazy and never on time.	• Whites are prejudiced against blacks.
• Blacks are loud and violent.	• Whites are dirty, especially in preparation of foods.
• Blacks are less intelligent.	• Whites are emotionally cold and colorless.
• Blacks are poor.	
• Blacks are not like me.	• Whites are not like me.
• I'm not prejudiced; I can't help the way other people are.	• I'm not prejudiced; I can't help the way other people are.
• If I express my honest beliefs, some people will like me; others will dislike me.	• If I express my honest beliefs, some people will like me; others will dislike me.

BOX 7.3

(Continued)

Student C   ## Student D

Beliefs

Student C	Student D
• Jews are bookworms.	• Humans are basically the same.
• Jews are mercenary and out to get all they can for themselves.	• Nonphysical differences among humans develop from different experiences.
• Jews are loud and obnoxious.	• Cultural differences enrich the human experience.
• Jews are aggressive.	• Cultural differences can lead to conflict and stereotypes if they are not understood.
• Jews can't be trusted.	
• Jews like to stick together.	
• Jews are not like me.	• United States society has a history of White racism, which affects the way different ethnic groups see each other.
• I'm not prejudiced; I can't help the way other people are.	
• If I express my honest beliefs, some people will like me and others will dislike me.	• Humans learn to prejudiced, and they can learn to be antiprejudiced.

Students A,B,C   ## Student D

Attitudes

Students A,B,C	Student D
• I will feel terrible if this person is allowed to join my group.	• I will feel good if this person is allowed to join my group.
• I will feel embarrassed if my friends disagree with me.	• I will feel ashamed if I don't say what I really believe.
• I don't want others to think I'm prejudiced.	• I don't want to lose my friends.

Values

• I have the freedom and right to associate with whomever I choose, especially in the private domain of my life.	• I should always take a stand against human injustice wherever it occurs.
• I want to be liked, accepted, and respected by my friends and associates.	• My own self-respect is more important than the acceptance of those who don't take a stand for social justice.
• My own self-respect is more important than the acceptance of those who won't stand up for the right of individual freedom and choice.	• I want to be liked, accepted, and respected by my friends and associates

The situation takes place in a college fraternity or sorority that has historically been composed of people from one group: Jewish, White, or African American, and so on. A student from a different background has made it to the final selection stage and may be invited to join the organization. The students described in Box 7.3 are in a unique position to influence others. How do you think each will act?

It seems clear that student D would take a stand in favor of inviting the person to join. But what about student A, B, or C? The value conflicts seem stronger with those students who believe in a person's right to associate with whomever they choose, but who do not wish to be seen as prejudiced by close associates. These students seem unaware that the beliefs that underlie their attitudes and possible behavior are based on stereotypes.

The third situation in Box 7.4 takes place in the classroom. Sherri, a third-generation Japanese American whose family has retained many Japanese traditions, attends a school where most of her classmates have grown up within the dominant culture. Once again the teacher is conducting a lively discussion. The students are actively involved and frequently challenge each other's ideas as well as the teacher. Sherri views the situation differently from many of her classmates and the teacher.

The case of Sherri shows how different beliefs based on cultural differences can lead to conflict in the classroom. Had the teacher known something about Japanese culture she might have responded more effectively to Sherri.

Cognitive Systems—Cultural Conflict

BOX 7.4

Sherri	Teacher
Beliefs	
• Teachers possess great knowledge.	• I am not the "fountain of all knowledge."
• The teacher is an authority.	
• It would show disrespect to question a teacher.	• Students learn best when they are actively involved.
• Careful reflection is required before one speaks out publicly.	• By challenging authority, students learn to think critically.
• It is rude and disrespectful to interrupt others.	• Students who don't participate are either shy, bored, or not prepared for class.
	• Students are truly motivated when they initiate comments and questions on their own, without teacher intervention.

BOX 7.4

(Continued)

Sherri	Teacher
Attitudes	
• I feel uncomfortable in this class-room because the students are rude and disrespectful. • I want to be a good student. • I feel frustrated because I never get an opportunity to express my ideas.	• I feel uncomfortable with Sherri's lack of participation. • I must work harder to get her to speak up, to express her views and support them.
Values	
• Being educated is one of life's high-est virtues. • As educators, teachers deserve the highest respect.	• Being educated is one of life's high-est virtues. • My most important role as a teacher is to encourage students to think critically.

Of course, not all teachers in U.S. society stress student involvement to the degree that this teacher does, and not all third-generation Japanese Americans would be as reticent as Sherri about class participation. Much depends on the individual's sense of ethnic identity, or the degree to which a person retains his or her ethnic origins.

Sense of Ethnic Identity

Sense of ethnic identity was discussed in Chapter 3. It refers to the degree to which a member of any particular ethnic group affirms the original culture that was learned from family and closest childhood associates. Original culture may refer to national origins such as Polish or Italian societies or to a culture created within the context of generations of segregation from the U.S. dominant culture, as with African Americans. All people belong to an ethnic group, but we may differ from other members of our group in terms of how closely we follow the original verbal language, body language, social values, and traditions. These differences in ethnic identity lead to the great differences found within any one ethnic group.

Consider again the example of Sherri. Many *Sansei*, or third-generation Japanese Americans, may retain the cultural values of the traditional middle-class agricultural system of Japan. Such values include education, hard work, achievement, patience, and respect for elders. Educational authorities were to be honored, obeyed, and respected without question.[52] Sherri apparently had retained many traditional Japanese values and beliefs. Many other *Sansei*, however, could be expected to be comfortable with the teacher's expectations.

Conceptions of stages of ethnic identity, such as those described in Chapter 3, need further refinement and may not prove to be the most valid approach for understanding sense of ethnic identity. Enough is known, however, to realize that students differ in their psychological readiness to interact with people from different ethnic groups. This is true whether the meeting occurs through actual experience or through texts and media. Students and teachers who are ethnically encapsulated will hold more negative prejudices against different ethnic groups than will others. Individuals who are in psychological captivity may be embarrassed by discussions of their group's contributions and characteristics and may reject or deny evidence of individual and institutional racism. Individuals in the highest stages may, if permitted to voice their views, serve as models for others. However, they could be totally rejected by individuals in stage one or two.

■*Teacher Perceptions of Individual Differences Related to Ethnicity and Poverty*

Teachers tend to regard individual differences based on cultural differences as deficits or disadvantages. The fact that disproportionately large numbers of ethnic minorities are below the U.S. poverty level reinforces the idea that ethnic differences represent cultural disadvantages. Even though more than half of the nation's poverty children are low-income Whites, non-Whites are vastly overrepresented. As shown in Table 7.1, for example, 28.4 percent of all African Americans lived below the poverty level in 1996, compared to 8.6 percent of all Whites and 29.4 percent of Hispanics. In 1991, 27.5 percent of Native Americans, 35.5 percent of Vietnamese, and 36.3 percent of Puerto Ricans lived at or below the poverty level. As emphasized in Chapter 3, and in the ethnic group histories in Chapters 4 and 5, the disproportionately high rates of poverty among people of color is due primarily to societal inequities and the privileges experienced by middle- and upper-income Whites.

The United States has the highest rate of poverty in the industrial world. An analysis of the origins and conditions of poverty in the United States is beyond the scope of this book. What is important is that approximately 35.7 million people are living at or below the poverty level ($13,924 or less for a family of four in 1991), and that this figure represents over 20 percent of U.S. children, including 30 percent of the children who live in large urban areas.[53] What is important is that most of those who are failing in school are from poverty backgrounds. What is important is how the teacher perceives and receives the poverty child. Teachers must ask themselves the following question: "Are we talking about groups of individuals whose backgrounds, attitudes, and general capabilities have failed to equip them adequately for a life of opportunities or are we talking about minority cultures of a country where the attitudes of the majority have inhibited the participation of the minorities in these opportunities?"[54] Do these children fail because their intellectual development is deficient from what is expected at school? Or do they fail because they cannot fit in?

TABLE 7.1
Poverty in the United States, by Ethnic Group

Ethnic Group	PERCENTAGE OF PERSONS BELOW OFFICIAL POVERTY LEVEL		
	1980[a]	1991[b]	1996[c]
American Indian	27.5%	31.2%	
Eskimo	28.8	26.9	
Aleut	19.5	16.8	
Asian and Pacific Island	**13.1**	**13.8**	**14.5**
Japanese	6.5	7.0	
Chinese	13.5	14.0	
Filipino	7.1	6.4	
Korean	11.1	13.7	
Asian Indian	9.9	9.7	
Vietnamese	35.5	25.7	
Hawaiian	15.8	14.3	
Guamanian	13.9	15.3	
Samoan	29.5	25.8	
Spanish Origin	**23.5**	**28.7**	**29.4**
Mexican	23.3	26.3	
Puerto Rican	36.3	31.7	
Cuban	13.2	14.6	
African American	**29.9**	**32.7**	**28.4**
Central city	30.1	38.1	
Urban fringe	20.2	24.8	
Rural	36.4	52.7	
White	**9.4**	**11.3**	**8.6**
Central city	11.1	10.7	
Urban fringe	6.1	5.4	
Rural	11.2	13.5	
White ethnic groups (selected)			
English	11.3	NA	
German	8.1	NA	
French	10.7	NA	
Irish	9.6	NA	
Italian	7.3	NA	
Polish	7.0	NA	

[a]In 1988, the official poverty level was defined by the government as $11,024 or less for a family of four.

[b]U.S. Bureau of the Census, Current Population Reports, Series P-60, No. 181, *Poverty in the United States*, 1991; and 1990 U.S. Census, Social and Economic Characteristics, Tables 94, 95, 98, 112, and 121.

[c]Leatha Lamison-White "Poverty in the United States: 1996" U.S. Department of Commerce, Economics, and Statistics Administration. Table A. "Persons and Families in Poverty by Selected Characteristics: 1995 and 1996" p. vii.

Source: Based on the 1980 U.S. Census Summary Report of General Social and Economic Characteristics, Tables 129, 139, 149, 165, and 171.

Failure, the Deficit Argument

The deficit position argues that the poverty child is failing in school because he or she is unready for school. The poverty home is viewed as an environment that retards children's overall development and leads to their disadvantage in school.

The deficit argument focuses on the developmental lags in cognitive development. The elements within the argument, however, comprise an acceptable explanation for the high rates of school failure among ethnic minorities and the nation's poor. It stands in opposition to the philosophy of multicultural education and the belief that teachers can accommodate cultural and individual diversity in the classroom while maintaining high levels of academic achievement and personal development among their students. Unfortunately, the deficit point of view is still alive today, nurtured by outdated and ill-founded research and related literature published in the 1960s. Quotes from some of these works will illustrate the deficit philosophy.

> More than a million children starting school each fall are disadvantaged, victims of too little too late. The impoverishment of their lives is so severe that failure is a natural consequence. For those caught up in this most vicious of cycles, compensatory education is desperately needed to preclude tragedy.[55]
>
> Perhaps the most serious deficiencies occur in the area of cognitive functioning: in the processes of thinking, in language skills and reading. . . . The consequences of cognitive deficiencies in culturally deprived children are complicated by their pattern of motivation and attitudes. . . . Such children have a feeling of alienation induced by family climate and experience combined with a debilitatingly low self-concept; they tend to question their own worth, to fear being challenged, and to exhibit a desire to cling to their families; they have many feelings of guilt and shame. . . . These children are wary and their trust in adults is limited; they are hyperactive . . . quick to vent their hostility, orally and physically. In other ways they are apathetic, unresponsive, and lack initiative. It is difficult for them to form meaningful relationships.[56]
>
> These are socially disadvantaged children because they are denied the experiences of normal children. They lack toys and challenging objects to play with; they lack conversation models and, thus, develop a poor vocabulary.[57]
>
> Negro scores averaging about fifteen points below the white average on IQ tests must be taken seriously as evidence of genetic differences between the two races in learning patterns. Research suggests that such a difference would tend to work against Negroes and against the "disadvantaged" generally when it comes to "cognitive" learning—abstract reasoning—which forms the basis for intelligence measurements and for the higher mental skills. Conversely, Negroes and other "disadvantaged" children tend to do well in tasks involving rote learning— memorizing mainly through repetition—and some other skills, and these aptitudes can be used to help raise their scholastic achievement and job potential.[58]

Failure, the Difference Argument

This position argues that the United States is a polycultural society with monocultural schools. It accuses the school, rather than the child, of unreadiness. Its proponents claim that the deficit view is based on ethnocentric research; that is, research based on Anglo-middle-class norms and values. Furthermore, they claim that the deficit view damages the learner's self-esteem because school success requires a denial of family and community. They cite as evidence teachers who, operating out of the deficit position, often make statements like, "If only we didn't have to send the children home at night," or "What can we expect of kids with parents like that?" Given a choice of fitting in at home or school, most children choose the former; thus the conflict between home and school expectations must be lessened. Because the child is powerless to change the school, it is the teacher's responsibility to find out where the child is and build from there.

Riessman typifies the difference position, which also emerged in the 1960s. He argues against the cultural deficit point of view in his explanation of the hidden IQ and cultural positives of poverty children and youth.[59] According to Riessman, mainstream schools put a premium on speed and tend to equate slowness with dullness. He claims that the assumption that slow pupils are not bright functions as a self-fulfilling prophecy, and argues that it is important to recognize that there are weaknesses in speed and strengths in slowness. Recognizing that many of these children have serious skill deficiencies and undesirable anti-intellectual attitudes, Riessman urges teachers to build upon the cultural positives that poverty children bring to school. He includes the following in his list of positives:

■ Cooperativeness and mutual aid that mark the extended family
■ Avoidance of the strain accompanying competitiveness and individualism
■ Equalitarianism, informality, and humor
■ Freedom from self-blame and parental overprotection
■ Enjoyment of each other's company and lessened sibling rivalry
■ Security found in the extended family and traditional outlook
■ Enjoyment of music, games, sports, and cards
■ The ability to express anger
■ The freedom from being word-bound
■ An externally oriented rather than an introspective outlook
■ A spatial rather than temporal perspective
■ An expressive orientation in contrast to an instrumental one
■ Content-centered rather than a form-centered mental style
■ A problem-centered rather than an abstract-centered approach
■ The use of physical and visual style in learning[60]

Riessman argues that disadvantaged children often do poorly on tests because they lack meaningful, directed practice; they lack motivation, and they are typically fearful of the examiner. In reviewing a study by Haggard, Riessman writes,

> Haggard decided to control each of these factors [practice, motivation, rapport]. He gave both low-income and middle-class children three one-hour training periods in taking IQ tests. These periods included careful explanations of what was involved in each of the different types of problems found on the IQ tests. The examinations were given in words that were familiar to both groups. Haggard also

offered special rewards for doing well, and he trained his examiners to be responsive to the inner-city children as well as to the middle-class youngsters, thus, greatly enhancing the rapport.

Under these conditions the IQ's of the inner-city children improved sharply. This occurred even on the old IQ tests with the middle-class biased items. Apparently more important than the content of the test items was the attitude of the children toward the test situation and the examiner. . . .

It is noteworthy that the middle-class youngsters improved far less than the inner-city youngsters in the Haggard experiment. This is because they were already working nearer their capacity, and the new environmental input—that is, the equalization of the test environment did not [expand the gap] between the two groups; rather it led to a sharp reduction of the difference.[61]

Typically, proponents of the deficit view propose school reforms that focus on remediation. They suggest a cultural injection as an antidote for poverty—the earlier the better—and advocate compensatory education programs.

Typically, programs based on the deficit view of reform place the burden of change on the child. Preschool programs assume that poverty children lag behind their middle-class counterparts in preparation for school, and propose a preschool compensatory program designed to make them learn at an even greater rate because their problem is essentially one of catching up. Since language development is crucial for school success, some programs recommend preschools that concentrate directly on language (for example, drill and rote memorization activities in standard English) rather than the indirect learning readiness emphasis of Head Start (such as tasting and learning about new foods).[62]

Reforms proposed by the difference advocates, on the other hand, focus on changing the school rather than the child. To date, large-scale programs modeled on this approach are rare. But there are some. Bicultural schools exist in several states where learning a second or third language is expected of everyone. Reading programs designed for the linguistically different begin with primers in the vernacular, and then systematically work toward teaching contrasts between the dialect and standard English.

Who are the disadvantaged in the United States schools? Fantini and Weinstein have written that the disadvantaged are those for whom the curriculum is outdated, inadequate, or irrelevant. They also include anyone who is unable to attain the basic goals of physical comfort and survival; feelings of potency, self-worth, and connection with others; and concern for the common good of humanity.[63]

There is a tendency for many of us to be ethnocentric and see the disadvantaged as being primarily minorities and lower-income people. Anyone who has not had the "normal" advantages of a middle-income home life is a potential candidate for being labeled disadvantaged. This is not a helpful attitude because it focuses on where our students *aren't*, and blinds us to where our students *are*.

A good example of this is a young elementary school teacher in Chicago who was appalled to learn that some of her inner-city children did not know that beds go in a bedroom. What she did not realize is that many of her children's homes had beds in the kitchen, as a matter of course, particularly in the cold of winter. Furthermore, she confused and degraded (however unintentionally) her children with such comments as "Johnny! We don't speak that way!" Johnny is speaking the way all the important people in his life speak.

This does not mean that we can ignore the fact that the achievement levels of students like Kevin and Rachael are deficient. This does not mean that expectations or standards of achievement should be lowered. The question is How can we reverse the existing patterns of failure in schools and equalize the chances of all students to achieve success?

The deficit position breeds insensitivity and blindness to students' strengths, but the difference position isn't free from problems either. The simple notion of differences implies the question, Different from what? The human tendency is to view whatever is different from *me* in less positive terms.

In the attempt to find out how students learn best, it seems more helpful to see them as representing alternatives rather than as beings that are deficient or different. Alternatives connote the coexistence of worthy options, and open us to the various ways our students have learned to perceive, evaluate, believe, and behave. As Benitez states, "Teachers must be helped to understand that the poor and racial or ethnic minorities can and actually have been able to learn at the same level as others when the proper environmental support was provided."[64]

CONCLUSIONS

This and the preceding chapter examined some of the individual differences that exist within the broader pools of culture. These characteristics are common to the human condition. Each student has special interests and aptitudes, preferred ways of learning, levels of skills, personal values, various self-images, a family and peers, and the potential to become self-actualized.

Teachers cannot assume that because students are members of a certain ethnic group they will be a certain way. We cannot, for example, assume that Carmen Hernandez knows Spanish or that Isaac Washington, who lives near Sixty-third and Halsted in Chicago, is not an expert on Beethoven. On the other hand, we know that cultures provide a context within which our lives unfold. The more that is known about culture, therefore, the better we can interpret student differences that *are* linked to cultural ways that differ from what is expected in school. How teachers can accommodate cultural and individual differences in the classroom is the focus of Chapter 9.

COMPARE AND CONTRAST

1. Learning skills and learning styles
2. Concrete and formal operations
3. Achievements and aptitudes and learning skills
4. Self-concept and motivation
5. Attitudes and beliefs

6. Ethnicity and sense of ethnic identity
7. Physical attributes and disabilities
8. The cultural deficit and cultural difference explanations of school failure

ACTIVITIES AND QUESTIONS

1. Consider the following guidelines for understanding individual and cultural differences in the classroom.

TABLE 7.2

Individual Differences That Can Make a Difference in How Students Learn	*Aspects of Ethnicity That Can Lead to Cultural Conflict or "Transitional Trauma" in the Classroom*
• Learning styles • Learning skills • Achievements and aptitudes • Self-concept • Gender • Peer relationships • Motivation • Physical attributes • Special interests • Family backgrounds • Beliefs, attitudes, and values • Sense of ethnic identity	• Verbal communication • Nonverbal communication • Orientation modes (e.g., conception of time, room arrangement, relaxation position) • Social values • Intellectual modes

Reconsider the Armstrong and Benson vignettes and answer the following questions, using the preceding guidelines. Share your ideas in small and large groups.

The Case of Kevin Armstrong

a. Why did Ms. Dixon perceive that Kevin was not ready for third grade? (List as many reasons as you can think of.)

b. Assume that, like Ms. Dixon, you know Kevin only in the school context. To what extent do you agree with her decision? Explain.

c. From Kevin's point of view, what are some possible explanations for his behavior? (List as many as you can think of.)

d. What are some of the strengths or personal positives Kevin brought to the classroom that his teacher was unaware of?

e. How do you suppose Kevin's parents feel about the school's action concerning their son?

f. If you were Kevin's teacher, how would you handle the situation?

Warren Benson's Classroom

a. What two or three student behaviors do you find most disturbing? Briefly, what are some probable reasons for these behaviors?

b. What evidence of possible cultural conflict do you find in this classroom? How have these students probably experienced cultural conflict in their previous schooling? List as many possible examples of intercultural conflict and/or misunderstandings as you can. Be specific.

c. To what degree is it possible for you to analyze Warren Benson's classroom without falling into ethnic stereotypes about the teacher and the students? Do the guidelines help?

2. Read *Other People's Children: Cultural Conflict in the Classroom,* by Lisa Delpit, especially Part I. How does the author address the cultural deficit perspective discussed in this chapter? To what extent do you agree that the cultural deficit mentality of the 60s and 70s has reemerged in the "at risk" label used by many educators today?

3. Read *Savage Inequalities* by Jonathan Kozol. What insights, if any, does the book provide regarding social and educational inequities in society today? How do the schools in your community and state compare with the schools described by Kozol? What can and should be done to provide more equitable schools for all the children and youth in our society?

4. List five individual differences that you see as being important influences in how a student learns. Find out how you could diagnose or assess and respond to each one. Use specific examples in a content area of your choice.

NOTES

1. J. Piaget, "The Genetic Approach to the Psychology of Thought," *Journal of Educational Psychology* 52 (December 1961):277; Piaget, *The Psychology of Intelligence* (Paterson, NJ: Littlefield, Adams, 1963); and John H. Flavell, *The Developmental Psychology of Jean Piaget* (Princeton, NJ: Van Nostrand Reinhold, 1973).

2. R. A. Shweder, "Anthropology's Romantic Rebellion against the Enlightenment, or There's More to Thinking Than Reason and Evidence," in *Culture Theory: Essays on Mind, Self, and Emotion,* Richard A. Shweder and Robert A. LeVine, eds. (Cambridge, England: Cambridge University Press, 1984), 27–66.

3. G. Clark, "Examining Some Myths about Gifted and Talented Students" (faculty

guest editorial, *Herald Telephone,* Bloomington, IN, Summer 1982).

4. Ibid.

5. H. Gardner, *Frames of Mind: The Theory of Multiple Intelligences* (New York: Basic Books, 1983).

6. R. Sternberg, *Beyond IQ: A Triarchic Theory of Human Intelligence* (New York: Cambridge University Press, 1985).

7. A. W. Combs (ed.), *Perceiving, Behaving, Becoming,* ASCD Yearbook, 1962 (Alexandria, VA: Association for Supervision and Curriculum Development, 1962).

8. A. Maslow, *Motivation and Personality* (New York: Harper and Brothers, 1954), 83.

9. F. Patterson, "The Purpose and Trend of the Conference," *in Negro Self-Concept: Implications for School and Citizenship,*

W. C. Kvaraceus et al., eds. (New York: McGraw-Hill, 1965).

10. M. Weinberg, *Minority Students: A Research Appraisal* (Washington, DC: National Institute of Education, 1977).

11. Patterson, "Purpose and Trend of the Conference," 4–5.

12. M. D. Caplin, "The Relationship between Self-Concept and Academic Achievement," *Journal of Experimental Education* 37 (Spring 1969): 13–16. See also P. Zerkel and E. Moser, "Self Concept and Ethnic Group Membership among Public School Students," *American Educational Research Journal* 8 (March 1971):253–65; and A. Soares and L. Soares, "Self-perceptions of Culturally Disadvantaged Children," *American Educational Research Journal* 6, no. 1 (1969):31–45.

13. Weinberg, *Minority Students*.

14. W. Purkey, *Inviting School Success: A Self-Concept Approach to Teaching* (Belmont, CA: Wadsworth, 1978).

15. Combs, *Perceiving, Behaving, Becoming*.

16. Ibid.

17. I am grateful to Marta Rose, 1988–89 Fellow in the Teacher as Decision Maker Program at Indiana University, for writing this section on gender.

18. M. Conroy, "Sexism in Our Schools: Training Girls for Failure?" *Better Homes and Gardens,* 1988:44.

19. C. Gilligan, *In a Different Voice* (Cambridge, MA: Harvard University Press, 1982).

20. M. F. Belenky, B. McVicker Clinchy, N. Rule Goldberger, and J. Martuch Tarule, *Women's Ways of Knowing: The Development of Self, Voice, and Mind* (New York: Basic Books, 1986).

21. Ibid., 23.

22. M. Brown Parlee, "Conversational Politics" in Feminist Frontiers: *Rethinking Sex, Gender, and Society,* L. Richardson and V. Taylor, eds. (New York: Newbury Award Records, 1983), 8.

23. Ibid.

24. Conroy, "Sexism in Our Schools."

25. D. N. Fader and E. B. McNeil, *Hooked on Books: Program and Proof* (New York: Berkley Medallion Edition, 1968).

26. T. E. Curtis and W. W. Bidwell, *Curriculum and Instruction for Emerging Adolescents* (Reading, MA: Addison-Wesley, 1977).

27. H. J. Ehrlich, *The Social Psychology of Prejudice* (New York: John Wiley and Sons, 1973).

28. C. Bennett and J. J. Harris III, "Suspensions and Expulsions of Male and Black Students: A Study of the Causes of Disproportionality," *Urban Education* 16, no. 4 (January 1982):399–423; see also G. Gay, "Differential Dyadic Interactions of Black and White Teachers with Black and White Pupils in Recently Desegregated Social Studies Classrooms: A Function of Teacher and Pupil Ethnicity," OE Project no. 2F113 (January 1974); U. S. Civil Rights Commission, *Teachers and Students. Report V: Mexican-American Education Study. Differences in Teacher Interaction with Mexican-American and Anglo Students* (Washington, DC: Government Printing Office, March 1973); and R. Rist, "Student Social Class and Teacher Expectations: The Self-Fulfilling Prophecy in Ghetto Education," *Harvard Education Review* 40 (August 1970):411–451.

29. W. R. Borg and M. D. Gall, *Educational Research: An Introduction,* 3rd ed. (New York: Longman, 1979).

30. N. St. John, "School Integration, Classroom Climate, and Achievement," ERIC ED 052 269 (January 1971); and idem, *School Desegregation: Outcomes for Children* (New York: John Wiley and Sons, 1975).

31. C. Bennett, "A Study of Classroom Climate in Desegregated Schools," *Urban Review* 13 (Winter 1981); and idem, "Student Initiated Interaction as an Indicator of Interracial Acceptance," *Journal of Classroom Interaction* 15 (Summer 1980).

32. S. Fordham and J. Ogbu, "Black Students' School Success: Coping with the "Burden of 'Acting White' " *Urban Review* 18, no. 3 (1986):176–206.

33. Ibid., 177.

34. Ibid.

35. Ibid.

36. Lisa Delpit, *Other People's Children: Cultural Conflict in the Classroom.* (New York: The New Press, 1995).

37. William Cross, "Oppositional Identity and African American Youth: Issues and Prospects," Chapter 7 in *Toward a Common Destiny,* 1995, p. 190.

38. Fordham and Ogbu, op.cit., 203.

39. E. Sargent, "Freeing Myself. Discoveries That Unshackle the Mind," *Washington Post,* February 10,1985 (Quoted in Fordham and Ogbu, "Black Students' School Success," 198–199.)

40. W. Longstreet, *Aspects of Ethnicity: Understanding Differences in the Pluralistic Classroom* (New York: Teachers College Press, 1978).

41. J. S. Wallerstein, "Children of Divorce: The Psychological Tasks of the Child," *American Journal of Orthopsychiatry* 53 (April 1983):230–243; and M. Hetherington and R. Parke, *Child Psychology: A Contemporary Viewpoint* (New York: McGraw-Hill, 1979), 431–64.

42. Ibid.

43. M. Harrington, *Who Are the Poor?* (Washington, DC: Justice for All, 1987), 18.

44. Ibid., 13.

45. U.S. Bureau of the Census, Current Population Reports, Series P-60, No. 181, *Poverty in the United States,* 1991 p. vii.

46. M. Rokeach, *Beliefs, Attitudes and Values* (San Francisco: Jossey-Bass, 1969).

47. Ibid., 3.

48. Ibid., 132.

49. H. C. Triandis, *Attitude and Attitude Change* (New York; John Wiley and Sons, 1971), 8.

50. Rokeach, *Beliefs, Attitudes, and Values,* 124.

51. Ibid., 160.

52. G. T. Endo and C. Kubo Della-Piana, "Japanese Americans, Pluralism, and the Model Minority Myth," *Theory into Practice* 20 (Winter 1981):45–51.

53. F. Williams (ed.), Language and Poverty (Chicago: Markham, 1970), 2. For other insights into poverty, see M. Harrington, *Who Are the Poor?* (Washington, DC: Justice for All, 1987); L. Silk, "Now, to Figure Why the Poor Get Poorer," *New York Times,* "The Week in Review," December 18,1988:1, 5; and U.S. Bureau of the Census, Current Population Reports, series P-16, No. 181, *Poverty in the U.S.: 1991 and Poverty in the U.S.: 1996.*

54. Ibid.

55. J. L. Frost and G. R. Hawkes, *The Disadvantaged Child* (Boston: Houghton Mifflin, 1966), preface.

56. H. Taba and D. Elkins, *Teaching Strategies for the Culturally Disadvantaged* (Chicago: Rand McNally, 1966).

57. J. M. Beck and R. W. Saxe, *Teaching the Culturally Disadvantaged Pupil* (Springfield, IL: Charles C Thomas, 1969).

58. A. Jensen, quoted in *U.S. News and World Report* 66 (March 10,1969):48–51.

59. F. Riessman, "The Overlooked Positives of Disadvantaged Groups," *Journal of Negro Education* 33 (Summer 1964).

60. Ibid. (List format not in the original.)

61. F. Riessman, *The Inner-City Child* (New York: Harper & Row, 1976).

62. C. Bereiter and S. Engleman, *Teaching Disadvantaged Children in the Pre-School* (New York: Prentice Hall, 1966).

63. M. Fantini and G. Weinstein, *The Disadvantaged: Challenge to Education* (New York: Harper & Row, 1968).

64. M. Benitez, "A Blueprint for the Education of the Mexican American," ERIC ED 076 294 (March 1973).

part III

Strengthening
Multicultural
Perspectives in
Curriculum and
Instruction

*W*hat does it mean to teach in a multicultural manner? It means creating classroom environments where students are respected, cared for, and encouraged to develop their fullest potential. It means creating curricula that include diverse and multiple perspectives. It means helping students develop some degree of intercultural competence. And it means fostering fair-minded critical thinking, compassion, and social action to improve societal conditions. Chapters 8 and 9 provide conceptual frameworks and sample lessons to illustrate the possibilities.

Let's consider two teachers who are striving to teach in a multicultural manner. The first teacher is Lisa Stuart, a first-year social studies teacher at a large suburban high school; next we revisit Sam Johnson, the middle school science teacher introduced in pages 8 to 10.

THE CASE OF LISA STUART

Lisa has just completed her university course work and student teaching. Academically talented, highly creative, and hard working, Lisa was an outstanding student teacher with great promise. She took to heart what was taught at the university about the importance of multicultural education and its special connections with the social studies. But there had been little opportunity to act upon these commitments during student teaching since few materials were readily available, and she was expected to "cover the curriculum." Her social studies methods instructor at the university had assured her that once she had her own classroom it would be possible, especially since she has accepted a position in what is considered an enlightened school.

This September evening, however, Lisa is visibly nervous as she prepares to greet parents at the school open house. Several students and colleagues have alerted her to the fact that a large group will attend and plan to question what is happening in her social studies classes. A number of parents have already complained to the principal. Several question her use of *Huckleberry Finn* as a resource, some because they feel it belongs in an English course and others because they see it as a racist book. Other parents are outraged over her treatment of apartheid and showing the film, *Witness to Apartheid*. Again, their complaints stem from different concerns. Some are angry that the students are encouraged to question U.S. government and corporate policies. Others are upset that Afrikanner perspectives are studied along with the history and viewpoints of the British, Coloreds, and Black South Africans, fearing that students might be led to sympathize with the previous South African government.

The frantic calls to her university mentor, in the face of brewing parental discontent, have helped her better articulate the goals of her curriculum. She feels nervous but confident that she can clearly explain what her goals are and why they are important. The parents from her first period class file into her room. . . .

Lisa finishes her explanation of the curriculum model on the overhead transparency. [This model is presented in Chapter 8.] She explains how *Huckleberry Finn* provides her students an opportunity to examine history through literature. Next week a panel of African American parents will explain their objections to the book, and the chair of the English department will explain why the book is part of the curriculum. Lisa also tells the parents that she will help students examine the book within the historical context at the time it was written. Comparisons will be drawn with social conditions in contemporary United States and South African societies. The perceptions of human rights issues in different periods of history and in different nations will be considered. "If we value respect for human dignity and universal rights," Lisa explains, "we cannot be neutral about apartheid in South Africa or the Ku Klux Klan at home, even though we must be careful to examine the various alternative perspectives and viewpoints related to these issues."

As the session draws to a close, Lisa is not sure how the parents feel. For the moment, they appear thoughtful. If nothing else, Lisa thinks, at least they are clearer about what they are disagreeing with. Some may have been made to feel uncomfortable with their original objections.

Lisa is representative of numerous beginning teachers who are attempting to teach in a multicultural manner. Many experienced teachers, such as in the following case, are also trying to do so by revising their curriculum without sacrificing important course content they have taught over the years.

SAM JOHNSON'S CLASSROOM REVISITED

It is the second week in October. Sam Johnson's classroom is filled with the students' preparations for World Food Day as part of their life science unit on The Causes and Effects of Hunger. The students have brought in collections of pictures and articles on food and hunger across the world and in the United States. There are student-created posters and diagrams showing the biological impact of starvation and malnutrition. Student-made graphs show that approximately one out of every eight people on earth suffers from hunger, and that 40,000 children die of hunger every day, or 15 million a year. Additional posters show that crop failures, floods, and other natural disasters do contribute to hunger, but the most important cause of hunger is poverty. Several world maps have been created to show global facts and trends such as the following:

■ Most of the world's hungry live in Third World nations, located primarily in the Southern Hemisphere, Central America, South America, Africa, the Middle East, and Southeast Asia, but hunger does exist in the so-called First World, North America, Western Europe, Australia, and Japan, and in Second World nations, the Soviet Union and Eastern Europe.
■ The Third World has 74 percent of the world's population, but only 26 percent of the world's wealth.

- The First World has 17 percent of the world's population, and 56 percent of the world's wealth, and in the Second World, the ratio is respectively 9 percent to 18 percent.
- The Third World nations contribute a significant portion of the world's natural resources, or raw materials, from which First and Second World nations generate wealth.

A bulletin board labeled "Working to End World Hunger" lists the addresses of local, national, and worldwide organizations that are working to end world hunger. Sam's students have organized a recycling drive, a community garden project, and a Thanksgiving food drive, and have prepared an educational program for parents and students entitled "Ending World Hunger: Think Globally and Act Locally." Most have written letters to a congressional representative or senator to express their concerns that millions die every year of starvation despite the fact that we produce sufficient food to provide over 3,000 calories per day for every human on earth.

When Sam's principal questioned him about how much life science his students were learning, Sam was able to report that student motivation and achievement were higher than in previous years. Even on the textbook publisher exams, most of Sam's students were well above mastery on core concepts related to the nature and continuity of life, human biology, and ecological relationships.

The transformation of Sam's classroom (compared to what we saw earlier) illustrates that it is possible to incorporate multicultural perspectives into the ongoing curriculum. These changes reflect a rationale based upon Sam's conceptions of his students, his community, his subject matter, and the goals and values of multicultural and global education. In Chapter 8 the curriculum model that guides Sam's revisions will be explained.

Multicultural Curriculum Development: A Decision-Making Model and Lesson Plans

*W*hat does it mean to teach from a multicultural perspective? What are the goals, the intended outcomes? What crucial assumptions are made when these goals are accepted? What evidence, if any, indicates that these goals are attainable? The purpose of this chapter is to provide some answers to these questions.

Once the values and goals of a comprehensive multicultural curriculum have been established, it becomes possible to build them into the curriculum. The model presented in Chapter 1 can be extended into specific plans for student learning. It offers a way to revise the traditional curriculum to include multicultural values, goals, and content without sacrificing the basic skills, concepts, and understandings our students need to develop in the various subject areas. In this chapter we see how teachers can become engaged in this revision process.

Developing a Course Rationale

According to Posner and Rudnitsky, an adequate course rationale must address three value areas: conceptions of the learner, the society, and the subject matter.[1] As shown in Figure 8.1, these valuative considerations influence or determine the educational goals of a particular course. This model provides extremely useful guidelines for teachers who are designing curriculum. It clarifies the values that are related to three essential components, assuring a comprehensive approach rather than one that is society centered, or child centered,

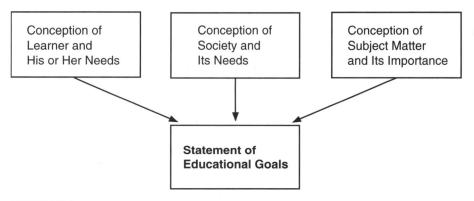

FIGURE 8.1
Components of a Course Rationale

or subject-matter centered.[2] When it comes to designing a *multicultural* curriculum, however, more is needed. The core value concepts must also be articulated because multicultural education has ideological overtones that are lacking in less controversial aspects of the curriculum. These values serve as a perceptual filter through which the conceptions of learner, society, subject matter, and goals are determined. (See Figure 8.2.)

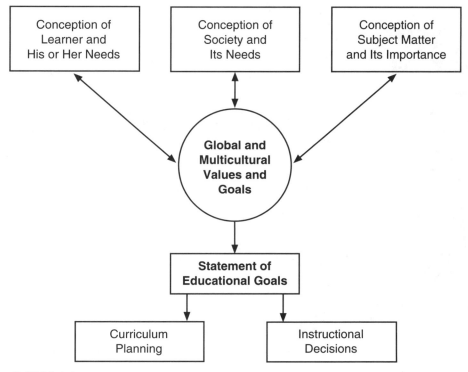

FIGURE 8.2
Instructional Decisions

Sam Johnson illustrates how multicultural perspectives can be built into the curriculum once the core values and goals have been established. (See Sam's original science class on pages 8 to 10 and the dramatic transformation a year later on pages 245 and 246.) Sam used the model in Chapter 1 to clarify his conception of learner needs, society needs, and the nature of his subject area. He viewed his students as being overly ethnocentric, racially prejudiced, uninformed, and lacking compassion for their fellow humans. The same characteristics were reflected in the school's broader community that found itself in a global economy, however unwillingly. Sam valued the traditional science curriculum but wanted to focus it on state-of-the-planet issues. His course goals and objectives, therefore, included knowledge, attitudes, and skills that include multicultural perspectives that fit the proposed curriculum model.

Developing Plans for Instruction

Effective multicultural lessons contain the same ingredients as any effective lesson. (See Figure 8.3.) Plans for instruction are based on decisions about the nature of the learner, the nature of the subject matter, societal needs, and what is known about effective pedagogy. In addition, however, multicultural and global lessons are based upon a special rationale that clarifies the instructor's values and goals. The decision-making worksheet (Figure 8.4 on page 251) is designed to help teachers clarify these values and goals and to select one or more goals as a basis for their own classroom instruction.

The Importance of Fair-Minded Critical Thinking

Fair-minded critical thinking is at the heart of multicultural teaching. If teachers and their students are not continually engaged in critical thought, multicultural education is likely to result in indoctrination rather than ethical insights based on core values such as acceptance and appreciation of cultural diversity, respect for human dignity and universal human rights, responsibility to a world community, and reverence for the earth.

Given the importance of prejudice reduction, perspective taking, and responsible social action in multicultural education, critical-thinking skills are essential. Richard Paul, a major leader in the international critical-thinking movement, provides an eclectic definition of critical thinking that distinguishes between uncritical and critical thinking.[3] The uncritical thinker is one whose thoughts are shaped by egocentric desires, social conditioning, and prejudices. Uncritical thinkers are unaware of assumptions, relevant evidence, and inconsistent reasoning. They tend to be "unclear, imprecise, vague, illogical, unreflective, superficial, inconsistent, inaccurate, or trivial."[4] Critical thinkers, on the other hand, think about their thinking in an attempt to be "more clear, precise, accurate, relevant, consistent, and fair."[5] They attempt to be constructively skeptical and work to remove bias, prejudice, and one-sided thought. To be fair-minded, critical thinkers must show empathy for diverse opposing points of view and seek truth without reference to one's self-interest or the vested interests of one's friends, community, or nation.

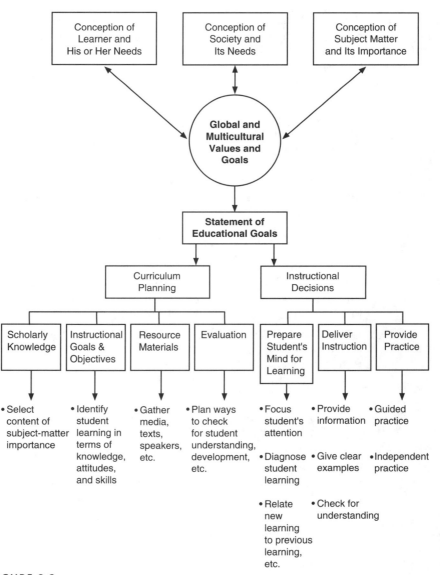

FIGURE 8.3
Extended Guidelines for Instructional Decision

To foster critical-thinking skills, we need to engage students in complex issues or problem-solving situations that are interdisciplinary and contain multiple points of view and possible solutions with differing consequences. One excellent way of strengthening critical thought is to build decision-making activities into the curriculum. Decision-making "trees" help students to see connections among thoughts, values, and actions and provide structure as they work through the stages in the decision-making process.[6]

FIGURE 8.4 *Multicultural Curriculum Planning*

Decision-Making Worksheet

Step One: Clarifying the Goals of a Multicultural Curriculum.

Listed below are six goals of a multicultural approach to teaching. (See Figure 8.1 on page 248.) Considering the courses you plan to teach, rank these goals from 1 to 6, with the first indicating the goal you value most and the sixth the goal you value least.

Work alone first; then discuss your decision with other members of your team and try to reach a consensus as to which goal seems most important. You will choose one member of your group to share your decision and reasons with the larger group.

_____ 1. *To Develop Multiple Historical Perspectives*
Multiple historical perspectives are the knowledge and understanding of the heritage and contributions of diverse nations and ethnic groups, including one's own. The goal is to develop awareness of historical and contemporary experiences among the world's diverse nations and ethnic groups. This awareness includes both minority-group viewpoints and those held by many members of the macroculture or nation, especially the differing interpretations of human events.

_____ 2. *To Strengthen Cultural Consciousness*
Cultural consciousness is the recognition or awareness on the part of an individual that he or she has a view of the world that is not universally shared and differs profoundly from that held by many members of different nations and ethnic groups. It includes an awareness of the diversity of ideas and practices found in human societies around the world and some recognition of how one's own thoughts and behaviors might be perceived by members of differing nations and ethnic groups.[4]

_____ 3. *To Strengthen Intercultural Competence*
Intercultural competence is the ability to interpret intentional communications (language, signs, gestures), some unconscious cues (such as body language), and customs in cultures different from one's own. Emphasis is on empathy and communication. The goal is to develop self-awareness of the culturally conditioned assumptions that people of different cultural backgrounds make about each other's behaviors and cognitions.

(continued)

FIGURE 8.4 *(continued)*

_____ 4. *To Combat Racism, Sexism, and All Forms of Prejudice and Discrimination*

Reduction of racism, sexism, and all forms of prejudice and discrimination is lessening negative attitudes and behaviors based on gender bias and misconceptions about the inferiority of races or cultures different from one's own. Emphasis is on clearing up myths and stereotypes associated with gender, different races, and ethnic groups. Basic human similarities are stressed. The goal is to develop antiracist, antisexist behavior based on awareness of historical and contemporary evidence of individual, institutional, and cultural racism and sexism in U.S. society and elsewhere in the world.

_____ 5. *To Increase Awareness of the State of the Planet and Global Dynamics*

Awareness of the state of the planet and global dynamics is knowledge about prevailing world conditions, trends, and developments. It is also knowledge of the world as a highly interrelated ecosystem subject to surprise effects and dramatic ramifications of simple events.[5]

_____ 6. *To Build Social Action Skills*

Social action skills include the knowledge, attitudes, and behavior needed to help resolve major problems that threaten the future of the planet and well-being of humanity. One emphasis is on thinking globally and acting locally; the goal is to develop a sense of personal and political efficacy and global responsibility resulting in a participatory orientation among adult members of society. Another emphasis is enabling minorities and nonminorities to become change agents through democratic processes.

The statement we believe identifies the most important multicultural education goal is: _____

_____

_____

Our reasons for this are the following:

1. _____

2. _____

3. _____

(continued)

FIGURE 8.4 *(continued)*

The goal we value least is:_____

_____

Our reasons are the following:

1. _____

2. _____

3. _____

Step Two: Identifying Objectives for Student Learning

My teaching area is _____ . I can build multicultural curriculum goals into this area with objectives for student learning such as the following:

1. _____

2. _____

3. _____

Step Three: Writing the Lesson Plan

By yourself or in a small group, write a lesson plan that will help you begin to realize your objectives.

The Curriculum Model: Goals, Assumptions, and Content

Goal One: Understanding Multiple Historical Perspectives

Most of us tend to be ahistorical when it comes to understanding contemporary issues, whether they are local, national, or global in scope. We also tend to view these issues from the viewpoint of the predominant society. It is difficult to be otherwise, given the nature of the traditional curriculum that emphasizes the political development of Euro-American civilization. For example, informed and ethical decisions about Affirmative Action programs in education and employment require an understanding of the nation's history, as well as the perspectives of minorities and nonminorities, that few people possess. An important goal of a multicultural curriculum, therefore, is the development of multiple historical perspectives that will correct this Anglo-Western European bias. Past and current world events must be understood from multiple national perspectives, and both minority and nonminority points of view must be considered in interpreting local and national events.

Among the assumptions underlying this goal are the following:

- People must possess a degree of self- and group-esteem, as well as personal security, before they can be empathetic in their interrelations with others.
- Awareness of the achievements of one's culture group will enhance one's self- and group-esteem.
- Knowledge that corrects misconceptions about certain people (for example, that nonindustrialized people are less civilized than industrialized people) helps destroy the myth of Euro-American superiority.
- People can achieve a psychological balance between cultural pride and identity on the one hand and appreciation of cultures different from their own on the other. (For example, increased group pride does not necessarily increase ethnocentrism.)

Chun-Hoon in "Teaching the Asian-American Experience" expresses the importance of minority perspectives: "The greatest danger to an open society is an education that homogenizes its people into limited and fixed conformity; the greatest danger to a small minority like Asian-Americans is that they will be imprisoned in the images created for them by mass society and that their own personal reality will not be able to transcend the imposed psychological colonization of society-as-a-whole."[7]

Chun-Hoon asserts that schools bear a large responsibility for ensuring that minorities are accurately represented. He believes this can happen only when the majority and the minority perspective is used in teaching the experience of minority groups:

> Unless, for example, we can understand the relocation of Japanese-Americans during World War II, both from the perspective of those who were interned as well as from the perspective of those who interned them, we achieve only a partial understanding of the event itself. For in this instance, the fullness of the historical event is not measured by the inconsequential effects experienced by the overwhelming American majority, but the extreme effects experienced by the Japanese minority. History is not made or experienced impartially, and attempts to report it or teach it neutrally all too often merely neutralize the real significance of events themselves. Accordingly, the major imperative of teaching the Asian-American experience, or any minority's history, is the ability to represent these dual perspectives fairly and completely.[8]

But how are multiple historical perspectives developed? Such perspectives are based upon knowledge and understanding of the world views, heritage, and contributions of diverse nations and ethnic groups, including one's own. Subject matter from the fields of history, literature, and the arts can be used to provide understanding about people's contemporary culture, world view, and differing interpretations of human events. This knowledge builds an awareness of historical and contemporary developments among the world's diverse nations and ethnic groups, awareness of traditional and contemporary attitudes held by the members of the dominant culture with respect to these groups, and knowledge about minority perspectives.

Content that builds within each student a sense of ethnic pride and identity is central, as is content about the achievements of people from other nations and cultures. Therefore, teachers could use subject matter that has traditionally been confined to ethnic studies courses such as Black history, Mexican American literature, Native American cultures, and White ethnics, as well as world culture courses. Teachers could use this content in ways that would encourage students to get at the underlying values and patterns of socialization of a particular culture rather than focusing only on the more superficial cultural trappings (such as foods and holidays), heroes, and historical events.

Every classroom offers opportunities for developing historical perspectives. Students can interview family members about their own ethnic roots and experiences. Bulletin boards can display people of the week or points of view on a variety of topics, or who's who in math, music, science, and so on. A multicultural calendar provides an excellent way to *introduce* students to people from many ethnic groups and nations, and can become a springboard for more in-depth study. Tiedt and Tiedt offer several suggestions of ways the calendar can be used: "Celebrating the birthdays of specific men and women can bring these people to life as students learn about their contributions. Focusing on events significant in the history of various ethnic groups in the United States is an effective way of informing all students about this country's multiethnic heritage. Information about these groups will provide the minority group student special opportunities to identify with his or her history."[9] The multicultural calendar is a helpful teaching aid that can be used for immediate reference and display. The calendar could be modified for junior and senior high school students to highlight people who have contributed to specific fields, such as sports and athletics, science and industry, mathematics, literature, politics, and the arts. Students can help create the calendar by doing research, planning the displays, and doing the artwork.

If multiple historical perspectives are to be understood, textbook distortions, stereotypes, and serious omissions surrounding ethnic minorities and Third World nations must be corrected. Acceptable revisions of the curriculum must be guided by an understanding of ethnic minority and Third World viewpoints, as well as the traditional majority point of view. Consider two phenomena that have traditionally been examined only from the Anglo-European viewpoints: slavery and manifest destiny.

Slavery

Slavery and emancipation are classic examples of how textbooks have excluded the African American point of view. Slavery is often introduced as an economic necessity. Later slavery is treated as a problem for Whites.

The African American perspective on slavery would include African cultural origins and histories of the array of African civilizations (just as England and Europe are discussed prior to colonization by Whites). It would also include evidence of Black people's strength under conditions of extreme oppression (in many cases the strongest and most intelligent Africans were sold into slavery and survived the middle passage), and of the expressions of African American culture that emerged in United States society.

A vivid example of how one's thinking can be dulled by limited frames of reference is the erroneous assumption often made concerning the social status structure among American slaves: House slaves, drivers, artisans, and mulattoes are accorded higher status than field slaves. According to Berry and Blassingame, however, the social structure from the slaves' viewpoint was far more complex.

> Occupations translated into high social standing only if they combined two of the following features: mobility (frequently allowing the slave to leave the plantation); freedom from constant supervision by whites; opportunity to earn money; and provision of service to other blacks. . . . At the bottom of the ladder were those slaves who had the most personal contact or identified most closely with masters (house servants, concubines, drivers, mulattoes). Since conjurors and physicians helped to maintain the slave's mental and physical health, they received more deference than any other black.[10]

Native-born Africans were revered as links to the ancestral home, as were the educated. "Old men and women with great stores of riddles, proverbs, and folktales (creators and preservers of culture) played a crucial role in teaching morality and training youths to solve problems and to develop their memories. Literate slaves had even more status than the sources of racial lore because they could read the Bible, tell the bondsmen what was transpiring in the newspapers, and write letters and passes."[11]

Rebel slaves who resisted floggings, violated racial taboos, or escaped from their masters were held in the highest esteem by the slaves and were preserved as heroes in slave folktales and songs. "Physical strength, skill in outwitting whites, possession of attractive clothes, and ability to read signs and interpret dreams also contributed to a slave's social standing."[12]

Hamilton has described the lack of Black perspectives in the curriculum as part of the reason many Black parents give up on traditionally desegregated schools and prefer Black community control of schools serving Black children and youth. He quotes Killens and Bennett to illustrate how African Americans may view history differently from what is in the textbooks.[13] According to Killens,

> We [black Americans] even have a different historical perspective. Most white Americans, even today, look upon the Reconstruction period as a horrible time of "carpetbagging," and "black politicians," and "black corruption," the absolutely lowest ebb in the Great American Story.
>
> We black folk, however, look upon Reconstruction as the most democratic in the history of this nation; a time when the dream the founders dreamed was almost within reach and right there for the taking; a time of democratic fervor the like of which was never seen before and never since.
>
> For us, Reconstruction was the time when two black men were Senators in the Congress of the United States from the State of Mississippi; when black men served in the legislatures of all the states in Dixie; and when those "corrupt" legislatures gave to the South its first public-school education.[14]

> Even our white hero symbols are different from yours. You give us moody Abe Lincoln, but many of us prefer John Brown, whom most of you hold in contempt as a fanatic; meaning of course, that the firm dedication of any white man to the freedom of the black man is prima-facie evidence of perversion or insanity.[15]

And Bennett challenges the traditional role and image of Abraham Lincoln, who he believes "was not the Great Emancipator. As we shall see, there is abundant evidence to indicate that the Emancipation Proclamation was not what people think it is and that Lincoln issued it with extreme misgivings and reservations."[16]

Manifest Destiny and the Native American and Hispanic Perspectives

One of the most blatant examples of Anglo-European bias in the curriculum is the fact that United States history is traditionally taught as an east-to-west phenomenon. The northward flow of peoples and cultures from central Mexico is largely overlooked. Our legacy from the Spanish colonizers who imposed Catholicism, the Spanish language, and an economic system of mining and agriculture on the native populations, and who helped create Mestizo and Creole populations, is largely ignored. If, on the other hand, history were taught according to a larger frame of reference, alternative perspectives to manifest destiny could be presented, particularly Chicano and Native American perspectives. Our legacy from the native peoples, which is just beginning to be discovered, would be recognized. People would realize that American Indian contributions penetrate all aspects of society, including our form of government, a federation modeled after the Iroquois League.[17]

What is the native perspective that should become part of the revised curriculum? Forbes provides excellent guidelines in the following illustrations of what teachers must do to teach the history of Indian people from their viewpoint.

- The unsubstantiated theories of white anthropologists should be treated as such. For example, Native Americans are not mongoloid because . . . there is not a shred of evidence linking Indians exclusively with any single race.
- The Bering Straits migration theory should be treated with great skepticism since there is absolutely no evidence (except logic) to support it. Indian people generally believe that they evolved or were created in the Americas. This viewpoint should be respected although it is acceptable to discuss the possibility of migration as an alternative explanation. The point is that there is no empirical evidence to support any particular migration theory.
- American Indians should be treated as the original Americans and the first 20,000 years of American history must be discussed prior to any discussion of European, African, or Asian migrations to the Americas. Likewise, in the discussion of the pre-European period, data derived from archaeology should be supplemented by American Indian traditional literature (as found in *The Book of the Hopi, The Sacred Pipe, The Constitution of the Six Nations,* and other available paperback books).

- The ongoing evolution of Indian groups must be dealt with, from 1492 to the present. That is, one must deal with the internal history of native tribes and not merely with European relations. For example, the development of the Iroquois confederation, the Cherokee Constitution of 1824, the Handsome Lake religion, the Comanche-Kiowa-Apache-Cheyenne-Arapaho alliance system, the westward movements of the Otchipwe, Cree, Dakotas and others, the teachings of the Shawnee Prophet, the Kickapoo Prophet, and so on, must be discussed as significant developments in the heartland of the United States at a time when Europeans are only marginal (i.e., along the Atlantic Coast).
- The teacher must deal truthfully with European expansion; native wars of liberation and independence must be dealt with as such and not as acts of aggression carried out against so-called peaceful Whites.
- The teacher will want to try to use accurate names for the American Indian groups in his or her region (such as Otchipwe in place of Chippewa). The correct names can usually be found in Hodge's *Handbook of Indians North of Mexico.*
- Native heroes and resistance leaders of the post-1890 period (such as Carlos Montezuma and Yukioma) must be dealt with—American Indian resistance did not cease with the "last Indian war."
- American history, from a native perspective, is not merely a material success story (bigger and bigger, more and more, better and better), nor does it consist solely in the reverse (that Whites have actually brought about the near-destruction of this land). History is not progressive, but cyclical. That is, the evils of the White man and some Indians and others are a repetition of previous eras wherein other people went astray and contributed to the destruction of a cycle. We are now in the fourth or fifth world from the native perspective.
- This world may be self-destroyed because of man's evil. . . . More inventions . . . may not lead to any great utopia in the future but simply to the end of this epoch. Furthermore, what really matters is the spiritual struggle of all creatures, the struggle for perfect character development, not a great invention.
- White people, for example, may exult over the development of a new type of rocket ship and regard a flight to the moon as an event worth recording in a history book. But from a wholly different perspective the decision of an ordinary man to give up a needed job whose demands run counter to his ethics is more significant because it is a spiritual act directly relevant to man's highest level of aspiration. From the traditional American Indian perspective, at least, the history of America should focus on man's spiritual development and not on his material progress.[18]

Establishing Multiple Historical Perspectives—The Challenge

An accurate representation of multiple historical perspectives is not always possible. Even when one wants a full, unbiased depiction of ethnic minority viewpoints and experiences, for example, lack of available information is a major problem. Political history in the schools has emphasized White males in power positions, and past omissions and inaccuracies make it difficult to establish the experiences and contributions of all groups.[19] Racist and sexist practices of the past make rediscovery of history difficult. Because copyrights and patents were not available to women and non-Whites until relatively recently, many early contributions remain unrecognized. Literature, art, even monuments are all tainted with bias. One example is African American soldiers in World War I. Of the 200,000 African Americans sent to France, nearly 30,000 fought on the front lines and received high accolades from the French. Yet no Black American soldiers were permitted to march in the glorious victory parade up the Champs Elysees. "The ultimate injustice was the U.S. War Department's insistence that African American soldiers not be depicted in the heroic frieze displayed in France's *Pantheon de la Guerre*."[20]

Chinese Americans experienced a similar fate after contributing most of the labor needed to complete the western portion of the transcontinental railroad. Nearly 10,000 Chinese workers had been involved, and much of their labor was high risk, using explosives and working at dangerous heights. Yet not a single Chinese face appears in a famous photograph that captured the first meeting of locomotives from east and west.[21]

Although oral history and folklore are not free of distortions and are often inaccessible to outsiders, oral literature and oral history along with music and the visual arts remain some of the best means of discovering ethnic minority perspectives. The facts that most slaves were barred from learning to read or write and that many immigrant groups such as the Chinese, Japanese, Mexicans, and Eastern European Jews entered initially as illiterate laborers mean that few pieces of literature or documents written by these people for themselves are available. Oral history, including songs, folktales, jokes, proverbs, aphorisms, verbal games, and (among African Americans) toasts offer the richest sources for understanding ethnic perspectives. Levine's exceptionally rich study of Black folklore, for example, has led him to paint a picture of slavery that differs dramatically from the view traditionally accepted by popular culture as well as by many scholars.

> I have only begun to touch upon the reservoir of tales and reminiscences which stress slave courage, self-respect, sacrifice, and boldness. The accuracy of this picture is less important for our purposes than its existence. These stories were told and accepted as true—a fact of crucial importance for any understanding of post-slavery Afro-American consciousness. Once again a vibrant and central body of Black thought has been ignored while learned discussions of the lack of positive reference group figures among Negroes, the absence of any pride in the Afro-American past, the complete ignorance Negroes have concerning their own history, have gone on and on. The concept of Negro history was not invented by modern educators. Black men and women dwelt upon their past and filled their lore with stories of slaves who, regardless of their condition, retained a sense of dignity and group pride. Family legends of slave ancestors were cherished and handed down from generation to generation. Postbellum Negroes told each other of fathers and mothers, relatives and friends who committed sacrifices worth

remembering, who performed deeds worth celebrating, and who endured hardships that have not been forgotten.[22]

It should be clear that minority perspectives are not built only from heroes and success stories, or from an emphasis on foods, fads, and festivals. Cortez cautions against this in "Teaching the Chicano Experience" with words that can be applied to every ethnic group.

> Certainly heroes and success stories comprise part of the Chicano experience. Chicanos can develop greater pride and non-Chicanos can develop greater respect by learning of Chicano lawyers, doctors, educators, athletes, musicians, artists, writers, businessmen, etc., as well as Mexican and Chicano heroes (heroes either to their own culture or to the nation at large). However, the teaching of the Chicano experience often becomes little more than the display of Emiliano ZaPata, Pancho Villa, Benito Juarez, and Miguel Hidalgo posters or an extended exercise in "me too-ism"—the list of Mexican Americans who have "made it"according to Anglo standards.
>
> In falling into these educational clichés, the very essence of the Chicano experience is overlooked. For this essence is neither heroes nor "me too" success stories, but rather the masses of Mexican-American people . . . [The] teacher should focus on these Chicanos, their way of life, their activities, their culture, their joys and sufferings, their conflicts, and their adaptation to an often hostile societal environment. Such an examination of the lives of Mexican Americans—not Chicano heroes or "successes"—can provide new dimensions for the understanding of and sensitivity to this important part of our nation's heritage.[23]

Obviously, people differ in their awareness of alternative ethnic and national perspectives. Most of us are more aware of some minority perspectives than others, particularly if we have lived a minority experience. Each of us, however, needs to become more informed about ethnic and national perspectives beyond our own—especially when we have grown up in a racist society, with an incomplete, biased curriculum.

The challenge to become knowledgeable about new ethnic and national perspectives may seem overwhelming at first, but it is a challenge that teachers are obliged to meet. The following suggestions are offered as possible ways of proceeding; with effective guidance, students can participate in all these steps.

- ■ Start small. Begin by selecting one or two nations and/or ethnic groups, preferably those that hold special meaning for your students, the community, and yourself.
- ■ Become informed about their perspectives regarding current events and the subject areas you teach. Consult global and/or ethnic primary source materials, such as literature, films, art, news media, and music. A list of key questions can help guide the research or you may prefer to avoid preconceptions and let the issues emerge.
- ■ Become acquainted with community resources (both people and organizations) in your area that can provide knowledge about your selected nations or ethnic group(s). Complete a list of local residents who would be willing to visit your school or be interviewed by students.

■ Examine your texts and supplementary materials for bias.

■ Develop a resource file of primary source materials and teaching strategies that will help you present the selected group's perspectives to your students. Everything from news articles containing statistics that can be converted into math problems, to songs, speeches, and cartoons can be collected.

■ Select one or more areas of your course in which the group's contributions and viewpoints have been overlooked. Create and teach a lesson that provides more accurate knowledge by including the group's perspectives.

Lesson Plans That Develop Multiple Historical Perspectives

Three Views of History   David Page

LESSON 8.1

On December 7, 1941, Japanese armed forces attacked Pearl Harbor. That night 600 Japanese immigrants were picked up by the FBI and held in detention centers. Two months later President Roosevelt signed Executive Order 9066 authorizing exclusion of all people with Japanese ancestry from the West Coast, and their relocation into internment camps. One hundred twenty thousand people were forced from their homes and put into these camps. Sixty percent of these people were U.S. citizens. Personal possessions of those evacuated were either confiscated by the government, or sold at a fraction of their real worth. Over 30,000 Japanese and Japanese American families were forced to live in these camps from 1942 until 1945. The ostensible reason for their imprisonment was national security. A closer look reveals that many other forces were at work.

Objectives

1. Students should be able to understand some of the many factors that enable institutionalized racism to exist and the different points of view on why it happened.
2. Students should be able to identify with victims of racism as fellow human beings.
3. Students should be able to see that not all laws are necessarily just, and that in some cases we must work to change laws for the better.

Materials Needed

Copies of Executive Order 9066, which gives the U.S. Military the right to exclude any person from any area during wartime.

Video recording: *The Politics of War: Japanese Americans 1941–1945*, Chelsea House Educational Communications, 1970, ten minutes. Nonethnic narrator portrays situation of U.S. citizens of Japanese ancestry in the wake of Pearl Harbor, explaining war relocation and authority activities, such as *nisei* detention camps, property losses, and abridgment of civil rights.

(Continued)

Sound recording: *They Chose America: Conversations with Japanese Immigrants.* Princeton, NJ: Visual Education 5302–05-p, 1975 (twenty-nine minutes, use side one only). A Japanese American talks about his experiences in the United States, before, during, and after the war.

The three items listed above give three very different views of the same event. All are true, but all are incomplete when viewed alone.

Executive Order 9066 gives the official view for the internment. It bases its reason for enactment on national security and the right of the federal government to enact such a law during wartime.

The video records the events that preceded the enactment of Order 9066; it starts with a description of the social and political position of Japanese and Japanese Americans living on the West Coast before and during the war. This video recording provides an impersonal view of the Japanese internment. It speaks of the Japanese only as a group, not as individual people. The only people who speak are Caucasian historians and a narrator.

The sound recording features an older Japanese American man who was sent to an internment camp as a young adult during the war. He gives his view of what it was like to lose his home and possessions, and the uncertainty he felt about his future.

Each point of view will be presented to a student separately, after which the student will be asked to rate seven statements about the internment of Japanese aliens and Japanese Americans. The statements are as follows:

Strongly agree 1 2 3 4 5 Strongly disagree

1. Japanese and Japanese Americans were interned mainly for national security.
2. Japanese and Japanese Americans were interned mainly for their own safety because Caucasians might think they were the enemy.
3. Japanese and Japanese Americans were interned because of racism.
4. Japanese and Japanese Americans were interned because of scapegoating.
5. Japanese and Japanese Americans were interned because of the economic competition experienced with Caucasians.
6. Americans of Japanese descent were more dangerous than citizens of Italian or German descent.
7. The internment of Japanese Americans during World War II was justified.

Evaluation

After all questions have been answered, students should compare the three ratings to each other. In most cases students will have changed answers for at least a couple of the questions. Ask the students to write a short paper that details how and why their answers changed.

Maps as a Metaphor: The Power of Perspectives

LESSON 8.2

In this lesson, geographical maps are used as a metaphor for understanding cultural perspectives or world view. Maps both shape and are shaped by our views of the world.

> The objectivity of contemporary world maps is so taken for granted that most of us are unaware of their inherent biases. All maps reflect the assumptions and conventions of the society and the individuals who create them. Such biases seem blatantly obvious when one looks at ancient maps but usually become transparent when one examines maps from modern times. Only by being aware of the subjective omissions and distortions inherent in maps can a user make intelligent sense of the information they contain.[24]

Most of us take for granted our own view of the world and are unaware of the basic assumptions that guide our thoughts and perceptions. In the same way, the objectivity of contemporary world maps is so taken for granted that most of us are unaware of their inherent biases. By studying a variety of modern maps of the world we can see how scientific inquiry, as well as our understanding of human events, literature, and arts, is shaped by our limited perspectives. The search for truth is enhanced when we become aware of our biases and erroneous assumptions.

Goals

- Students will understand that all maps contain distortions and that different maps send different messages.
- Students will understand how maps affect our interpretations of the world.
- Students will realize that by gaining insight into basic assumptions, values, and beliefs we can think more critically about human events, creations, and scientific Inquiry.

Lesson Activities

1. Students work in groups of two to four. Each group is given a different type of world map. The students are instructed to locate Africa (or another part of the world) on their map and list on newsprint all the information they can find about Africa. They are to pretend that they know nothing about Africa other than what they can find on their map.
2. All groups report to the class, explaining their map and the information they have garnered. The maps and lists are displayed together to show the different types of information each group discovered.
3. In a follow-up discussion, students identify the strengths and weaknesses of each map, define what a "perspective" is, and develop implications for what they will be studying (e.g., the scientific method; differing points of view in history, or current events; the perspective of an author or character; and perspectives in art or architecture).

LESSON 8.2

(Continued)

Materials Needed

Maps and globes (e.g., Mercator Projection, Peters Projection, McArthur Projection, the Earth Ball, the Endangered Species Ball, National Geographic Map of Africa, and graphic maps).
Newsprint, markers and masking tape, background reading.

Sources

Phil Porter and Phil Voxland. "Distortions in Maps: The Peters Projection and Other Developments." *Focus,* Summer 1986, pp. 22–30.
Denis Wood. "The Power of Maps." *Scientific American*, May 1993, pp. 88–93.

Note: The above is my own Lesson.

The purpose of the following lesson plan for a music listening class is to expand the student's understanding and enjoyment of the art of music through the development of perceptive listening abilities. This lesson, developed by Allison Hoadley, is designed for high school juniors and seniors. There is a fairly even distribution of Blacks and Whites, males and females.

Introduction to the Blues   *Allison Hoadley*

LESSON 8.3

Goals

- Develop historical perspectives and Black and White culture consciousness through the study of a form of music originated by African Americans as an expression of their own emotions and experiences, and through investigating the influence of this musical form on the music of both White and Black Americans.
- Increase intercultural competence through understanding how Blacks and Whites use music as a form of communication to express their attitudes and beliefs.
- Help eradicate racial prejudice through: learning a little of the history of Black people in the United States; recognizing the widespread influence of a Black style of music; working with students of another race to achieve a common goal.

Behavioral Objectives

1. The student will demonstrate his or her knowledge of how the blues style originated in the United States by getting at least 75 percent of the answers correct on a short quiz to be given the following class period.
2. The student will be able to accurately describe the general harmonic structure of a standard twelve-bar blues progression on the above quiz.
3. The student will be able to correctly harmonically analyze a twelve-bar progression in a blues song through listening.

(Continued)

4. The student will be able to describe the characteristics of a blues melody and explain how these characteristics affect the moods of the style.
5. Students will create, with the help of a few fellow students, their own blues with original words and melody, to be performed the next class period.

Motivation

A recording of Black blues music—"That's All Right" (Louis Myers)

Activities

1. Introduce students to the blues and rouse their interest in the topic by playing a recording of Louis Myers singing "That's All Right." Discuss with them in general terms the type of music they just heard, and briefly define the blues as a form of African American folk music that later gave birth to jazz.
2. Play the recording again; instruct the class to listen for a pattern in the harmony. Once they can perceive the repeating harmonic pattern, play part of the recording once more and tell students to listen for the number of measures of the harmonic pattern. Introduce the term twelve-bar blues.
3. Play the chord progression slowly on the piano. Students will listen and write out the chords being played in each bar:

1	2	3	4	5	6	7	8	9	10	11	12
I^7	I^7	I^7	I^7	IV^7	IV^7	I^7	I^7	V^7	IV^7	I^7	V^7

   Discuss the chord progression in a standard twelve-bar blues.

4. Play a recording of "Graveyard Dream Blues" (Bessie Smith). Instruct the students to hold up one, four, or five fingers according to the I, IV, and V chords they hear. Play part of the recording again; instruct students to listen to the melody and determine what mood they think is being conveyed, and how the melody contributes to that mood. Discuss briefly melodic differences between this song and the second movement of Haydn's Symphony no. 94 (*Surprise*). Show them the first few bars of the blues melody written out on a blackboard; have students give the pitch inventory. Show and explain the blues scale (with flatted third and seventh); explain how the use of blues notes contributes to the overall mood.
5. Explain the historical development of the blues, importance of emotion in presentation, development of performance practices.
6. Expose the class to additional recordings:
   "Billie's Blues"—Billie Holiday
   "It Ain't Necessarily So"—*Porgy and Bess,* George Gershwin
   "The South's Gonna Do It Again"—Charlie Daniels Band. Discuss similarities and differences between these and previous examples.
7. Have students team up with one or two other students to create their own blues on a standard progression with words that reflect their own personal feelings and experiences. This will be performed later in the week.

(Continued)

Materials

Recordings:

"That's All Right," Louis Myers, from *Sweet Home Chicago* "Graveyard Dream Blues," Bessie Smith, from *Any Woman's Blues*
"Billie's Blues," Billie Holiday, from *Billie Holiday's Greatest Hits*
"It Ain't Necessarily So," George Gershwin, *Porgy and Bess* (Odyssey Records)
"The South's Gonna Do It Again," Charlie Daniels Band, from *Fire on the Mountain* (Epic Records)

A piano

Evaluation

1. Students' knowledge concerning the origin, historic developments, and structure of the blues will be assessed through a short quiz to be given the next class period.
2. Students' understanding of the terms and concepts presented will be evaluated through their participation or lack of participation in the discussion.
3. Students' harmonic listening ability may be perceived through checking their written analysis of the chords of a blues progression played on the piano and through watching them raise the correct number of fingers when listening to a recording.
4. Students' ultimate understanding of the nature of blues can be observed through experiencing their own original performance in this style.

Reprinted with permission of the author.

Goal Two: Developing Cultural Consciousness

Closely linked to the development of multiple historical perspectives is the second goal, the development of cultural consciousness. This goal makes the following assumptions:

■ An individual must have an understanding of his or her own world view.
■ Humans have the capacity to reduce their ethnocentrism.

Cultural consciousness is defined in terms of two dimensions of Hanvey's "attainable global perspective": perspective consciousness and cross-cultural awareness. Perspective consciousness is "The recognition or awareness on the part of the individual that he or she has a view of the world that is not universally shared, that this view of the world has been and continues to be shaped by influences that often escape conscious detection, and that others have views of the world that are profoundly different from one's own."[25]

Most Japanese, for example, do not see themselves as racist. Yet, their deep assumptions about the inferiority of certain races has recently resulted in statements by Japanese officials about the "inferiority" of American Blacks and Hispanics, as well as discrimination against Japanese citizens of Korean or Chinese parentage. As another example, Westerners have assumed until very recently that human dominance over nature is both attainable and desirable. Teachers can foster the development of perspective consciousness by helping students examine their assumptions, evaluations, and conceptions of time, space, causality, and so forth.

The second aspect of cultural consciousness, Hanvey's cross-cultural awareness, refers to "an awareness of the diversity of ideas and practices to be found in human societies around the world, of how such ideas and practices compare, and including some limited recognition of how the ideas and ways of one's own society might be viewed from other vantage points."[26] Crosscultural awareness, a difficult but attainable goal, is seen by Hanvey as an antidote for the human "practice of naming one's own group 'the people' and by implication relegating all others to not-quite-human status." This human trait of chauvinism "has been documented in nonliterate groups all over the world . . . [and] shows itself in modern populations as well. It is there in the hostile faces of the white parents demonstrating against school busing . . . [it lurks] in the background as Russians and Chinese meet at the negotiating table to work out what is ostensibly a boundary dispute. And it flares into the open during tribal disputes in Kenya."[27]

Hanvey identifies four levels of cross-cultural awareness as follows:[28]

Information	Mode	Interpretation
1. Awareness of superficial or very visible cultural traits: stereotypes	Tourism, textbooks, *National Geographic*	Unbelievable (i.e., exotic, bizarre)
2. Awareness of significant and subtle cultural traits that contrast markedly with one's own	Culture conflict situations	Unbelievable (i.e., frustrating, irrational)
3. Awareness of significant and subtle cultural traits that contrast markedly with one's own	Intellectual analysis	Believable, cognitively
4. Awareness of how another culture feels from the standpoint of the insider	Cultural immersion: living the culture	Believable because of subjective familiarity

According to Hanvey's scheme, believability is achieved only at levels 3 and 4. He argues that believability is a necessary condition "if one group of humans is to accept other members of the biological species as human."[29] The attainment of these higher levels of cross-cultural awareness is an integral part of the third multicultural curriculum goal, development of intercultural competence.

As the world becomes a smaller place, cultural consciousness is an essential ingredient in mediating cultural conflicts along the "fault lines" that separate the world's seven or eight main civilizations.[30] For example, Huntington argues that, with the end of the cold war in Europe, "the Velvet Curtain of culture has replaced the Iron Curtain of ideology as the most significant dividing line in Europe."[31] This cultural division "between Western Christianity on the one hand, and Orthodox Christianity and Islam on the other, has reemerged,"[32] for example, in the former Yugoslavia, in the Persian Gulf, and in Italy, France, and Germany, where violence against Arab and Turkish immigrants increased in the 1990s. Huntington cautions that the Western world view, which is based on "ideas of individualism, liberalism, constitutionalism, human rights, equality, liberty, the rule of law, democracy, free markets, the separation of church and state, often have little resonance in Islamic, Confucian, Japanese, Hindu, Buddhist or Orthodox cultures."[33] It can also be argued that the desire for basic inalienable rights, human dignity, and liberty is universal. But to achieve these conditions on a global scale, foreign policy makers must be conscious of culture.

■ *Lesson Plans That Develop Cultural Consciousness*

The Many Faces (and Shoes) of Cinderella   Patricia A. O'Connor

LESSON 8.4

Rationale

In today's multicultural world, students need to realize that while people from different cultures may look different and may see and experience events in a different way, deep down people all across the world are the same. By utilizing the well-known fairy tale, Cinderella, and its many cultural variations, students will be able to see that each culture experiences and conceptualizes the Cinderella motif in a unique way—the Cinderellas of the world look different, dress differently, have different skills, and live in a different "world." And yet the theme is the same all across the world. In addition, students will utilize the timeless and cross-cultural Cinderella motif to create a modern version of the tale. By doing so, they will be able to relate a very old tale to their world and experience firsthand the influences that a culture has on a piece of literature. This will be good preparation for analysis of future literature—how a culture and a historical period influence literature (both oral and written) and how a piece of literature relates to our world today.

Learning Objectives

1. Students will be able to compare and contrast cross-cultural versions of Cinderella by reading a selected version of the tale, by summarizing and reporting excerpts (both orally and visually) to the class, and by completing the variant analysis guide (see guide below).

LESSON 8.4

(Continued)

2. Students will be able to recognize cultural influences on the Cinderella motif by preparing a written report summarizing the differences between the U.S. version and the version they read and analyzing how the culture influenced each tale.
3. Students will learn firsthand how a culture influences the expression of the tale by creating a modern version of the Cinderella tale which reflects current culture. In doing so, they will utilize past knowledge of setting, character development, and descriptive writing.

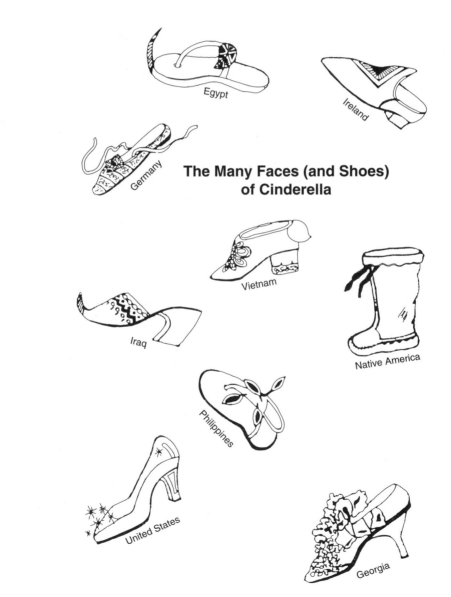

**The Many Faces (and Shoes)
of Cinderella**

(Continued)

Day 1

Teaching Strategies

Opening exercise: Students are asked to recall the fairy tale, Cinderella, and to write a brief description of Cinderella's physical features and the shoe she drops. Discussion of descriptions will follow. Students are shown a poster of the various shoes different cultures envision Cinderella wearing and a few overheads of illustrations from different versions. A brief introduction to the unit will follow, in which students will be given the theme ("The Many Faces of Cinderella"), an outline of the unit, and a brief description of intended projects: analysis of different versions, discussion of different interpretations, creation of a modern version of *Cinderella* (or *Cinder"fella"* as the case may be). We also discuss the importance of being aware of the multicultural variations of the motif and of multicultural influences in general

    Group exercise: Working in small groups of varying abilities (see explanation of group work roles below), students read a selected version of the tale (each group will have a different version—see descriptions below), discuss the differences, prepare an illustration of four scenes from the tale (to be posted on the wall), and give a five-minute oral presentation to the class. A discussion of similarities and differences follows, and students are given a variant analysis guide to be completed on the version they read. We go through the guide in class, discuss the terms, and complete it for the U.S. version.

    Assignment: Complete the variant analysis guide.

Day 2

Teaching Strategies

Review the variant analysis guide and discuss any problems. A copy of a completed variant analysis guide for each version is posted with the illustration prepared on Day 1. A brief lecture on the history of the Cinderella motif, the particular history surrounding the U.S. version, and the various interpretations follows. As a class, students discuss the cultural influences in the U.S. version and some ideas of how the other stories were influenced culturally. A one- to two-page written report summarizing the differences between the U.S. version and the version read by the particular groups is assigned with completed reports due tomorrow.

    Writing project: Students are asked to create—with their subgroup partner—a modern version of the Cinderella tale. A handout of directions and rules is discussed at this time. Prior to breaking into pairs, students briefly review setting, character development, and descriptive writing. The subgroups/pairs begin working on a modern version, with an initial focus on setting and characters.

    Assignment: Work individually (at home) on modern versions. This individual work is turned in the next day to assure that everyone works on the project.

(Continued)

THE MANY FACES OF CINDERELLA: VARIANT ANALYSIS GUIDE

TITLE:

COUNTRY OF ORIGIN:

Opening	
Hero/heroine's (H/H's) innocence/ guilt (with respect to siblings)	
H/H's passivity/activity	
Sibling rivalry	
Father's role	
Midnight prohibition	
Prince/Princess' role in finding H/H	
H/H's treatment of stepsiblings/ stepparent	
Level of violence	
Helpful spirit/being	
Role of animals	
Flight from the event (Why?)	
Presence of dead mother/father	
Type of shoe, clothing, or ring	
Ending	

Days 3~4

Teaching Strategies

Students break into subgroups, review individual work, and compile the information into a complete story by revising and editing on the computer. Then students return to main groups and decide which version to prepare for the dramatic reading. The subgroup whose version is not selected critiques the selected version

(Continued)

and makes suggestions for changes and improvement. (It may be that a compilation of the two versions can be attempted.) Visuals for the presentation are encouraged. If a decision acceptable to all members cannot be reached, the instructor decides by tossing a coin.

Day 5

Projects are turned in, and presentations ensue.

Additional Activities

Additional activities—from collecting marriage divination rituals to examining feminist and historical perspectives—can be found in the *Oryx Multicultural Folktale Series: Cinderella and Writing and Reading across the Curriculum.* Most of the activities can be adapted to the age of the students.

Group Work

Students will be working in preassigned groups of four or five that were selected based on varying abilities and intelligences of the students. Within that group, they have also been assigned to a subgroup partner, with the same selection qualities used for the main group.

Their main group roles are as follows:

The Eye: This person makes sure that everyone in the group has a chance to talk and explain his or her ideas and that the group stays on task.

The Ear: This person listens and participates in the group discussion, takes notes during the group's brainstorming sessions, and provides team members access to these notes.

The Mouth: This is the spokesperson for the group and facilitates the oral reports and presentations for the group.

The Legs: This person listens for group problems and/or questions and acts as a liaison with the teacher.

The Heart: This person is attentive to the feelings of the individual members and helps the group reach compromises when conflict arises.

Our Cinderella: Writing Project Instructions

Objective: Following the Cinderella motif, write a modern version of the tale that reflects the culture, language, and events of today. By "culture," I do not specifically mean U.S. culture; I mean culture as it relates to YOU, in your school, home, and ethnicity.

Note: You do not need to include every element of the motif. Your version should be based on the following theme:

> A young man or woman persecuted by his/her family who receives magical help from unusual sources so that his/her true worth can be known by a potential mate of higher rank.

LESSON 8.4

(Continued)

And it should incorporate at least eight features of the motif (see variant analysis guide).

1. With subgroup partner, decide what culture you wish to represent, your basic setting, characters, and plot. Pay attention to the following questions when working on this section:

    Where is this story taking place? What city/neighborhood? What ethnic group? Who are the main characters?

    What do they look like?

    How do they sound?

2. Each partner should then work individually on development of the story. Then partners will get back together, combine versions, revise story, and add new information. Pay attention to your answers to the above questions when writing.

3. Reconvene with your main group. Exchange and critique versions. Decide which story you will present as a group. Each subgroup will have the opportunity to make suggestions and changes at this point. It may be possible to do a compilation of the two versions.

4. Prepare for presentation of your story. You have a total of ten minutes to present your story to the class. You can act it out or give a dramatic reading. Illustrations of the text are highly encouraged.

5. LET IT ALL HANG LOOSE!! Be creative, use slang, and provide illustrations, but most of all, let your imagination guide the story.

Rules

Completed versions must incorporate three metaphors and three similes.

Only three forms of the verb "to be" can be used in the entire story. (Be descriptive, don't just tell us!)

Evaluation

Oral and Visual Report

Students are graded on understanding of the story and selection of main scenes for illustration.

Written Report

Students are graded on understanding of differences between the versions and the influence of culture on the versions. In addition, reports will be checked for punctuation, grammar, and sentence structure. Revised reports may be requested.

Modern Version

Students will be graded on application of motif to modern times and incorporation of the main theme and elements. While use of slang and colloquialisms will be allowed and encouraged, correct spelling, appropriate punctuation, and grammar of nondialogue writing will be stressed.

(Continued)

Bibliography

Cooper, J. C., *Fairy Tales: Allegories of the Inner Life*. Aquarian Press, Wellingbor-rough, Northamptonshire, England, 1983.

Behrens, Laurence, and Rosen, Leonard J. *Writing and Reading across the Curriculum*. Little, Brown and Company, Boston, 1985.

Luthi, Max. *Once upon a Time: On the Nature of Fairy Tales*. F. Ungar Publishing Co., New York, 1970.

Meyer, Rudolf. *The Wisdom of Fairy Tales*. Floris Books, Edinburgh, Scotland, 1981.

Philip, Neil. *The Cinderella Story*. Penguin Books, New York, 1989.

Sierra, Judy. *The Oryx Multicultural Folktale Series: Cinderella*. Oryx Press, Phoenix, Arizona, 1992.

The Invisible One (Native American/Micmac) Oochigeaskw, a member of the Micmac people of eastern Canada who is mistreated by her sisters, goes forth wearing a dress made of tree bark. Her future husband is no mere human prince; he is an invisible supernatural being. Oochigeaskw passes a different kind of test than the other heroines of Cinderella tales; she passes a test by seeing what other young women do not.

Nomi and the Magic Fish (Africa) Nomi, a girl who is mistreated by her stepmother, is helped by a magical talking fish. Her naughty tattle-tale dog is different from pets in other Cinderella tales who are faithful and helpful even after death. This particular version was recorded by a young woman of the Zulu people of South Africa.

How the Cowherd Found a Bride (India) This male Cinderella story features many of the elements of the Cinderella motif—mistreatment by family, a food-giving cow, magic tree, falling in love through finding a gold object, helpful animals, and marriage of the hero to a person of royal status.

Ashpet (U.S./Appalachian) Ashpet is a servant in the house of a cruel woman and her two daughters. As in many of the Cinderella tales, Ashpet's troubles are not over after her wedding. The two daughters come to see her after her marriage and end up pushing her into a river where she is captured by the Hairy Man.

The Story of Tam and Cam (Vietnam) This story of Cam and her evil stepsister Tam mirrors the other Cinderella tales, but Cam shows higher resilience and adaptability than many of the Cinderellas. While Tam and her mother might win a contest for the cruelest stepmother/sister, they certainly get two of the worst punishments.

Cap o' Rushes (England) This story of Cap o' Rushes is told in the regional dialect of the storyteller. It is a different strain of the Cinderella motif, where the heroine is driven out of the house by her father and is later reconciled with him at her wedding feast. This version is thought to be the source of Shakespeare's *King Lear*.

Five Great Values of the Lakota Sioux — Gayle Reiten

Objectives

- Students will develop some familiarity with the traditional cultural values of the northern Great Plains Sioux that still govern and influence their society today.
- Students will understand how these values shape the world view of the Sioux and influence their response, both individually and as a group, to the dominant culture in the United States.

Introduction

The primary cultural symbol among the Sioux is the circle. It represents Wakan Tanka, the Great Spirit, and is found everywhere within the Lakota world view. The horizon and the four directions form a circle. The traditional dwelling house, the tipi, is a circle. All nature is circular. This circularity means that the Lakota view the world as a whole, not in parts and pieces to be separately analyzed. In this lesson plan the Siorian values will be examined separately, but it is important to remind the class of their interrelatedness.

The First Great Value: Generosity and Sharing

Among the Sioux people the idea of the value of generosity and sharing is very strong. This idea springs from their belief that the earth was the mother from whom they all came. Therefore the land and the food to be found upon it belonged to all; the food that resulted from the hunt or from gathering was shared with all others in the band who needed it.

Generosity and sharing as an ideal led to the custom of the GiveAway, in which any or all of one's possessions are given away in a ceremony to honor someone. The honoree could be a recent college graduate, a young man home from the army, or a dead relative. In this process one honors the Great Spirit, the person to whom one gives, and lastly oneself. However, paradoxical as this may seem, if one gives or shares with the idea of getting honor in return, one destroys the essence of sharing.

For this reason, when someone does something for you unasked, out of kindness, it is very rude to thank the person, for it is as if you were paying for the generosity—a terrible insult among the Sioux. However, if you ask someone to do something for you and the person complies, a thank-you is acceptable.

Another aspect of sharing is that doing and giving of oneself for the benefit of the group is a requirement in Siouan culture. If one has a talent or talents and denies these to one's people, it is wrong. As a result, the Sioux share both praise and shame. For instance. they share in pride for Ben Reifel, one-time congressman from South Dakota, and they share the shame of Siouan drunks lying in the gutter.

Historically: Since the land belonged to all, the Sioux had no concept of property ownership and often believed when they signed treaties that they were ceding use of the land rather than ownership.

(Continued)

Currently: When a Siouan family moves to an urban area from the reservation in order to better their economic well-being, they often "fail" by non-Indian standards. Many family and friends will come to visit, spend time, create an extended family. However, this may lead to crowded housing conditions and financial strain as all are given enough money to function within the urban environment.

Questions: For the Lakota, what are the strengths connected with holding the value of generosity and sharing in the modern world? What are the weaknesses?

Activity: Some members of the class might wish to research the lives of famous Sioux such as Crazy Horse, Red Cloud, Sitting Bull, Spotted Tail, Billy Mills, Ben Reifel, Ella Deloria, and Vine Deloria (both senior and junior).

The Second Great Value: Respect for Old Ones

The Lakota Sioux have always had great respect for their old ones. The Lakota believed one could not speak from ignorance and wisdom came only with age. One would be considered a young man or woman until the age of 45 or 50; then perhaps one might be considered a "wicasa"—a man—and to become "really a man" one needed to be more than 60.

This respect for the old ones has led to respect for anyone in authority—a priest, a teacher, a policeman, a judge. One way respect is shown is through aversion of the eyes. Another consequence of respect for elders is the custom whereby children of hospitalized parents spend much of their time, if not all their time, in the hospital with their parents. This is a matter both of respect and of generosity and sharing—the Lakota seldom leave a sick member of the family alone.

Historically: Early missionaries and teachers were confused by the Sioux. "They seem so shifty and dishonest!" "William Noheart never looks me in the eye." These comments reflected non-Indians' lack of understanding of behavior meant to reflect respect. It is still a problem.

Currently: A few years ago, the federal government gave the tribal government of the Standing Rock Sioux money to build a nursing home for the elderly on the reservation. But the home stood empty for years and was finally converted to government offices.

Questions: Why did the Standing Rock Sioux not make use of the government-built nursing home? In what ways does our dominant culture treat older ones with respect? In what ways does it not? Do others of us have the same respect for the elderly as do the Sioux? Do we express it differently? In what ways do we show respect to authority, and what kinds of body language do we use?

Activity: Demonstrate the difference between a non-Indian greeting a stranger and the way a Sioux would greet a stranger.

The Third Great Value: Getting Along with Nature

For the Sioux, getting along with nature meant more than not misusing the natural world. The Lakota people traditionally believed that Wakan Tanka, the Great Spirit, was in all things, in a rock or tree as much as in a person. And this being,

(Continued)

this existence of the Great Spirit within each thing, was called that entity's "Innermost"—a concept that might be compared to the non-Indian idea of a soul or spirit. Furthermore, the Sioux saw the earth, through the Great Spirit's power, as mother to all—and all therefore are related to each other.

This leads to the Siouan ideas about respect for the Innermost. Since everyone's Innermost should be respected, out of politeness the Sioux will tell others what they want to hear, and never with the feeling that this is untruthful. They will also avoid telling someone what that person doesn't want to hear. The Sioux believe that when the Innermost is not respected, hurt is always the result. From this develops their great desire to get along with one another and to respect each person's Innermost.

Historically: The buffalo was the heart of the Siouan culture in the eighteenth and nineteenth centuries. Every part of the buffalo was used in some way. Nonetheless, because the Sioux people believed they were related to the buffalo, it could not be wantonly slaughtered. The Sioux would pray for understanding and forgiveness on the part of the buffalo before they began the hunt, and the entire process had a sense of sacred ritual about it.

Currently: Because of the belief among the Sioux that they must "get along together," one will often observe group togetherness, especially among children. But the group togetherness ideal, while a strength, can also be a weakness. For example, there is strong peer pressure among the reservation Sioux not to appear "better" or "different." And the ideal is often shattered by problems with drug and alcohol abuse, the biggest Native American health problem.

Questions: Can you think of some other ways the value of getting along with nature is a strength? A weakness? How does the non-Indian react to these ideas?

Activities: Research the buffalo's history and find out why these animals are now so few in number. Art classes might want to research paintings that portray the Sioux and the buffalo.

On the subject of current Sioux life, learn more about Native American problems with substance abuse, or about the adjustments that urban American Indians must make in cities such as Minneapolis, Oakland, Boston, Chicago, and Cleveland.

The Fourth Great Value: Individual Freedom

Individual freedom is strongly related to all the other values, for it involves the essence of choice. No one can ever force anyone else's decision. But this is not freedom to run amok. Individual freedom for the Sioux meant freedom to choose to do the right thing. And the most important thing, the most right thing, was whatever would enable survival of the group. The value of sharing was also involved in choosing to help one's relatives and friends.

Since no Sioux had any right to impose his or her will upon another, the Lakota form of government was the most basic of democracies, with all the men and older women meeting together and making decisions. If any of those within the group did not agree with the decisions made, they were free to go. Many times

(Continued)

this is exactly what happened, and new bands of the Sioux were created out of disagreement over some fundamental decision.

The respect for individual rights and abilities also led to the Siouan style of leadership. The idea of a "chief," one overall leader, really came from the non-Indian. Leadership depended upon the situation. One man might be best at leading raids on other tribes for horses. Another might be called upon to lead and organize the buffalo hunt. The style of making war was also not forced. If a man wanted to get up a raiding party, only those who chose to go went with him.

There were never any jails among the Sioux. They had two primary methods of social control: ridicule and banishment. Ridicule could run the gamut from gentle teasing of an adolescent who had behaved in a socially unacceptable manner to intense ridicule for an adult who had committed a more serious offense. Stealing among the Sioux was practically unknown, and still is to this day, because of the great respect for the individual. Serious crimes, such as murder, were punished by banishment. Survival on the northern Great Plains without the group was difficult at best—therefore banishment could be equivalent to a death sentence.

Historically: Sitting Bull is among the most famous of Sioux leaders, but few non-Indians know that he was not a great warrior leader. Rather, Sitting Bull was a "wicasa wakan," a holy man. Others were the military leaders during the Battle of the Little Big Horn.

Currently: The style of government on Sioux Indian reservations today often leads to a virulent form of reservation politics. Tribal government has democratic forms based on the past; and because of the strong belief in individual freedom, political disagreements can be strong. However, groups who disagree with one another are no longer free to move.

Questions: In what ways are dominant culture beliefs about individual rights the same as the beliefs the Sioux held? In what ways are they different? Does the dominant culture value social freedom more than individual freedom, or vice versa? Give examples.

Activity: Read Marie Sandoz's novel *Crazy Horse* and try to determine how Lakota values functioned in making Crazy Horse one of the greatest Sioux leaders.

The Fifth Great Value: Bravery

For the Sioux, eagle feathers were the mark of bravery, and they had to be earned. Bravery was a matter of individual freedom; one had to choose to do the right thing. One could never boast about one's own exploits in battle; one allowed someone else, a friend or relative, to do so. Training for bravery began young. Little babies were not allowed to cry, for their cry could give away the location of the people in a tight situation.

A famous war cry the Sioux gave at the Battle of the Little Big Horn was: "Today is a good day to die!" This can be understood only within the context of

(Continued)

the Lakota value of bravery. The Sioux believed that if the worst thing one had to fear was death—and if death itself was not really something to be afraid of—then if one died in the process of protecting one's family and people, today was indeed a good day to die. But the Sioux were not fanatic about death, as in some other cultures, and were as afraid of battle as any humans might be. Life itself was the most precious thing the old-time Sioux had, and to give it was the greatest sharing a Sioux warrior could offer.

Historically: The image of the war bonnet with many eagle feathers sweeping down to the ground is basically incorrect. Seldom did any warrior earn enough eagle feathers to create such a bonnet, though headdresses with a number of eagle feathers were possible. Young women could also earn eagle feathers or wear them by inheritance.

Currently: The Sioux people are intensely patriotic, and in the twentieth century have contributed soldiers for U.S. wars out of all proportion to their population. To fight in the U.S. armed forces for them is still the way to protect the people.

Questions: Is our definition of bravery in the dominant culture the same as or different from that of the Sioux? Are some or all of the Siouan values found within the U.S. dominant culture? To what degree are these values visible within the dominant culture's literary and film images of the American Indians?

Activity: Obtain Arthur Kopit's play *Indians* and have the class read, discuss, and/or present it using Sioux values as a basis for the discussion.

Additional Resources

Brown, Dee. *Bury My Heart at Wounded Knee.* New York: Holt, Rinehart and Winston. 1970.

Bryde, John F. *Modern Indian Psychology.* Vermillion: University of South Dakota Press, 1971.

Malan, Vernon D., and Clinton J. Jesse *The Dakota Indian Religion.* Bulletin 473. Brookings: South Dakota State College, 1959.

Reprinted with permission of the author.

The following Lesson 8.6 was developed for freshmen or sophomores in general ability groups. Prior to this lesson, students ask parents and grandparents about the countries of their ancestry. Through this vehicle, with library research if necessary as a supplement, students are to bring to class at least eight facts about one country of their ancestors. Six of these facts should pertain to the physical characteristics of the country and two should be emotional, feelings these families carry about those roots. This plan is designed to develop culture consciousness.

Modeling toward Understanding

Elizabeth Ellis

Objectives

The twofold goal is to let students begin to look into their own cultural backgrounds and to take the first step of writing poetry through imitation. On a larger scale, they will become aware of their classmates' cultural backgrounds.

Strategy

Using the following outline, students will plug in the information indicated to complete the poem. Their role will be to assume the guise of someone who really knows and loves the country in question. Sentences do not have to be complete, and traditional grammar concerns are secondary to creativity. They will be given a copy of my attempt as a guide to show the task does not need to be difficult, and to provide motivation through that reassurance. At the end, copies of Hughes's poem will be distributed for comparison and discussion. Also, each student will later receive copies of the entire class collection of poems.

Outline

I've known _____ (place) _____ .
I've known _____ (physical fact) _____ and _____ (physical fact) _____ .
_____ (emotion—translate feelings about place) _____ .
I _____ (verb) _____ in _____ (physical fact) _____ when.
_____ (time) _____ .
I _____ (verb) _____ and _____ (verb) _____ .
I looked _____ (physical fact) _____ and _____ (verb) _____ .
I heard _____ (physical fact) _____ when _____ (time) _____ .
I've known _____ (place) _____ .
_____ (physical fact) _____ .
_____ (emotion—summarize feelings about place) _____ .

Materials

Copies of outline and of teacher's trial run
Copies of Langston Hughes's "The Negro Speaks of Rivers"

Teacher's Try
I've known Ireland.
I've known the interminable staunch greenness and the endless
    drifting rain.
The pall of its rain echoes the cloud of upheaval Lying over it.
I cry in Ireland when the bombs rip through.

LESSON 8.6

(Continued)

I learned of the desperation and how it destroys the proud history.
I looked at Dublin and saw a girl sobbing as she walked by the Liffey.
I heard the anger and boredom of its young when all seems fruitless
and false.
I've known Ireland.
Poor, sad, endlessly proud in its ballys and knocks.
Does the horror ever end?

The Negro Speaks of Rivers
I've known rivers.
I've known rivers ancient as the world and older than the flow
of human blood in human veins.
My soul has grown deep like the rivers.
I bathed in the Euphrates when dawns were young.
I built my hut near the Congo and it lulled me to sleep.
I looked upon the Nile and raised the pyramids.
I heard the strong of the Mississippi when
Abe Lincoln went down to New Orleans,
and I've seen its muddy bosom turn
all golden in the sunset.
I've known rivers:
Ancient, dusky rivers.
My soul has grown deep like the rivers.[34]
—Langston Hughes

Evaluation

Students will be asked in a writing assignment for their journals or a similar non-graded (nonthreatening) situation to point out any new facts that they learned about themselves through this assignment and what they learned about their class-mates. This would tell me if the poem was worth writing.

Reprinted with permission from the author.

Scrapbook Americana   *Cindy Ort*

LESSON 8.7

This is a semester-long project, initiated at the beginning of the school year. Several weeks prior to this, the American teacher must locate a teacher in Germany (or another country of choice) who is interested in cooperating in the project. If the American teacher does not have personal contacts in Germany, he/she may locate one through the American Association of Teachers of German. However, the specific goals of global education must be clearly explained to the German teacher to ensure success.

(Continued)

Over the course of the semester, the class will produce a scrapbook and a cassette about themselves and their American lives. The following project sheet is suggested as a guide for the students, but they should be encouraged to be creative. Many of their own ideas may be better than those suggested by the teacher. The stated purpose of the scrapbook is to show German teenagers what it is like to be an American. The students should be encouraged to use not only photographs but realia from their day-to-day lives. Near the end of the semester, possibly just before Christmas break, the scrapbook and cassette are to be mailed to the class in Germany. At the same time, the German class will be working on a similar scrapbook about their own lives and will mail it at the designated time. When the students return from Christmas break, they will have the German class's scrapbook to look forward to.

Although most class time will be devoted to language practice, a portion of each week should be set aside for work on the project and to monitor progress—perhaps half the period on Friday. The project will be more fruitful if the students work on the scrapbook cooperatively by tackling topic areas, such as What do Americans do for fun? rather than having students do a set number of pages on themselves.

A cassette will accompany the scrapbook and, again, its content is largely up to the students' discretion and creativity, with the teacher's guidance. Each student will be required to speak for a minimum of one minute, in German, about himself or herself. This can often be quite difficult for a first-year student. To ensure success, they will each keep a section of their class notebook for this project, starting at the very beginning of the semester. With each new vocabulary list or grammar point, they will be encouraged to think of sentences about themselves. The new sentences will be entered in their notebooks as possible items for the recording. Students may also want to record music, skits, a few moments of an athletic event, school cheers, whatever. This will require some planning on their part but can also be a lot of fun. A video recording would be preferable, but at the present time, U.S. and German software are usually not compatible.

Objectives

- Students will begin to view their own lifestyles from a new perspective.
- Students will examine their preconceptions about Germans and Germany.
- Students will begin to learn about the concepts of stereotyping, labeling, and prejudice.

Activities

1. Students will discuss characteristics of Germans and Americans in their groups.
2. Groups will write lists of agreed-upon characteristics.
3. Groups will share their lists with the class at large and will discuss them.

Materials

Pencil and paper
Guidelines for group discussion

(Continued)

Evaluation

Following class discussion, have the students write a paragraph about what they learned from the activity or the discussion concerning our ideas about ourselves and our ideas about other nationalities.

Instructions

Divide the class into two sets of groups, with four or five students in each group. When dividing the class into groups, try to see that each group is a cross section of the whole class.

Each A-group is given a sheet of guidelines and instructed to generate a list of traits for the typical American. Each B-group is given a sheet of guidelines and instructed to generate a list of traits for the typical German. Allow the groups ten minutes to complete this. Then have a discussion with the entire class, discussing first their ideas about typical Germans and then their ideas about typical Americans. Did the groups come up with similar answers? Did the German groups have trouble answering theirs? If so, why? Or did they have quick responses? Were the ideas about typical Germans more negative than the ideas of typical Americans? Why or why not?

Discuss the terms stereotyping, typical, average, labeling, prejudice. Point out how little we know of daily German life (and they of ours). Then note sequencing of textbook, which deals with aspects of German life. Emphasize that one of the main goals of the course is to familiarize yourself with everyday German life and to develop a greater understanding of the German people. Tell students that they will learn tomorrow about a semester-long project for this goal.

Distribute the fact sheet about Germans. Information for the fact sheet came from *These Strange German Ways*. (See Bibliography on Teaching Resources.)

Fact Sheet

Did you know . . . ?

1. Germans drink more coffee than they do beer!
2. There are 200 kinds of bread and 1,500 kinds of sausage (cold cuts) and 5,000 brands of beer in Germany.
3. Germans usually don't drink plain water, nor is it served at restaurants unless requested. Children usually drink juice or milk. Adults prefer beer or wine or mineral water with their meals.
4. Germans seldom eat sweet corn, and most Germans have never heard of eating pumpkin. They consider corn and pumpkin to be suitable for livestock.
5. The government regulates German store hours. Most are closed by 6:30 on weekdays and by 2:00 P.M. on Saturdays.
6. German supermarkets are very much like American, but Germans also often shop for produce, cheese, and eggs at the local outdoor markets that are open once or twice a week.

(Continued)

7. Germans seldom move. Fifty-eight percent would commute and 41 percent would learn a new trade rather than move, according to a recent survey. In the United States, one-fifth of the population moves every year.

8. Germans usually keep the doors inside a building closed, whether it be their private home or the office building. You should always knock.

9. The majority of married German women wear a wedding band—on their right hand. Less than half of the married men do.

10. Germans seldom have bridal showers, but friends often bring gifts on *poltern-abend,* the evening before the wedding, when friends break flower pots and crockery on the doorstep of the bride-to-be. For good luck, the bride must sweep up the broken crockery by herself.

11. Germans must be 18 to get a driver's license and *must* attend driver's training classes. Half of all applicants fail the exam the first time. It is extremely difficult.

12. Drunken driving in Germany is a felony. Children under 12 must sit in the back seat. There is no speed limit on parts of the Autobahn.

13. German television programs are not interrupted by commercials. The ads are all lumped together at the beginning and ending of the day's programming. Germans watch American programs regularly: "Dynasty," "Dallas," and "Bonanza" are favorites.

14. Ninety percent of Germans belong to either the Catholic or Lutheran churches, but the majority do not participate regularly. They are, however, regularly taxed by the government which then gives the money to the churches.

Guidelines for Scrapbook Project

Look around you. What is life like in the United States? What is your life like? How do you live? What would you show people to help them understand if they had never been here before and knew nothing about you?

This semester you will make a scrapbook about yourselves to send to a class in Germany. They have probably read quite a lot about the history and geography of the United States, but they probably don't know very much about how ordinary U.S. citizens live, just as you may not know what it is like to be a German teenager. The class in Germany will also be working on a scrapbook to send to you. By sharing these scrapbooks, you can learn a lot about how German teenagers live and maybe someday you will have the opportunity to visit them. Here are the categories for the sections of the scrapbook: home life, families, school, church, community, entertainment, future plans, jobs, hobbies, and any other ideas you may have. These are the things to include in the scrapbook: list of addresses of all class members; photographs of the class, your home, your room, your car, the school, and pictures of you and your friends or family doing ordinary or extraordinary things. Play candid camera! Realia could include a copy of the school newspaper, a placemat or menu from the restaurant where you work, a copy of a report card or a school lunch ticket. an ad for a rock concert, a funny sticker. What ideas can you come up with?

Each of you must contribute a minimum of ten pictures and/or realia, in at least five different categories. You will work with your group on a different section each week. Some of you will have an opportunity to use the school camera

LESSON 8.7

(Continued)

and darkroom. If you have your own camera, plan now to take pictures so you can get them developed for the project. Arrangements are possible for using school film. See me about this.

We will also be sending an audial message to our German friends. Each of you will be required to talk about yourself in German for a minimum of one minute. You will keep a special page in your notebook to prepare for this: At the end of each book chapter, you will use your new vocabulary and grammar to think up at least two sentences about yourself. You will enter these in your notebook and save them for possible use on the recording. Now comes the fun part! What else could we include on the cassette to make it more interesting? A skit? A school cheer? A song? Sounds from a basketball game? A radio ad?

Materials

Large scrapbook, preferably loose-leaf type with ample supply of refill pages
     scissors, tape, markers, glue
Tape recorder and blank cassettes
Camera and film, optional
Dark room and supplies, optional

Teaching Resources

Arnsdorf, Dieter, and Manfred Heid. *Erzahl doch mal van dir!: Zu Gast bei deutschen Freunden.* New York: Langenscheidt, 1985.
Burmeister, Irmgard, ed. *These Strange German Ways.* Hamburg, Germany: Atlantik-Brucke e.V., 1980.
Moeller, Jack, Helmut Liedloff, and Clifford J. Kent. *German Today 1.* Boston: Houghton Mifflin, 1982.
Weiss, Edda. *Deutsch: Entdecken Wir Es!*, 2nd ed. New York: McGraw-Hill, 1980.

Other Suggested Materials, Resources, and Realia

For contact with German teacher: American Association of Teachers of German, 523 Bldg., Rt. 38, Suite 201, Cherry Hill, New Jersey 08034.
For free slides on daily German life: Inter Nationes, Kennedy-Allee 91–103, D5300 Bonn 2, Germany.
German Youth Hostel travel book and map: Deutsches Jugendherbergswerk Hauptverban, Postfach 220, Bismarckstrasse 8, 4930 Detmold, Germany.
Placemat from McDonald's of Germany
German shopping net
Copies of *Bravo,* a favorite German youth magazine, available from the German Consulate.
Small children's books : *Pixi Bucher* from Carlsen Verlag, Reinbek bet Hamburg, Germany, and *Pevau-Buchlein* from Pestalozzi-Verlag, D8520 Erlangen, Germany.

Reprinted with permission from the author.

Goal Three: Developing Intercultural Competence

Intercultural competence is the ability to interpret intentional communications (language, signs, gestures), some unconscious cues (such as body language), and customs in cultural styles different from one's own. The emphasis is on empathy and communication. This goal recognizes that communication among persons of different cultural backgrounds can be hindered by culturally conditioned assumptions made about each other's behavior and cognitions. It is also based on the fact that, as Kraemer states, "the effects of cultural conditioning are sometimes so pervasive that people whose experience has been limited to the norms of their own culture simply cannot understand a communication based on a different set of norms ... [and] cannot understand why a 'self-evident' communication from them cannot be comprehended by others."[35]

Some of the assumptions underlying this goal are as follows:

- Language is at the heart of culture and cognition.
- People's effectiveness in multicultural communication can be improved by developing their cultural self-awareness (their abilities to recognize cultural influences on their own cognitions).
- There are modes of human communication that can transcend cultural barriers.
- Although cultures are continually changing, some aspects of the diverse cultures within a larger society, such as an African American core culture in the United States, or Navajo culture in the Southwest, can be identified, defined, and taught.
- Persons can achieve a psychological balance between cultural pride and identity on the one hand, and appreciation of cultures very different from their own on the other (that is, increased intercultural contact will not necessarily lead to cultural assimilation).

Although this goal clearly overlaps the goals of developing historical perspectives and cultural consciousness, to teach for intercultural competence means going beyond the study of world views, heritage, and contributions associated with a particular people. It means building an understanding of how one is influenced by the values, priorities, language, and norms of one's culture. This knowledge then can grow into the realization that every person's perception of reality is shaped by experience. Once people understand how their own language, experience, and current modes of cognition relate to their own culture, contrasts may be made with the cultural experience and modes of cognition of culturally different others. Ultimately, they are able to move to a level of *transpection,* what Hanvey refers to as "the capacity to imagine oneself in a role within the context of a foreign culture."[36]

Gudykunst and Kim define intercultural competence in terms of the *intercultural person.* As noted in Chapter 1, "The intercultural person represents one who has achieved an advanced level in the process of becoming intercultural and whose cognitive, affective, and behavioral characteristics are not limited but are open to growth beyond the psychological parameters of any one culture. . . .

The intercultural person possesses an intellectual and emotional commitment to the fundamental unity of all humans and, at the same time, accepts and appreciates the differences that lie between people of different cultures."[37] According to Gudykunst and Kim, intercultural people are individuals who

- Have encountered experiences that challenge their own cultural assumptions (e.g., culture shock, dynamic disequilibrium) and that provide insight into how their view of the world has been shaped by their culture;
- Can serve as facilitators and catalysts for contacts between cultures;
- Come to terms with the roots of their own ethnocentrism and achieve an objectivity in viewing other cultures;
- Develop a "third world" perspective "which enables them to interpret and evaluate intercultural encounters more accurately and thus to act as a communication link between two cultures;"[38] and
- Show cultural empathy and can "imaginatively participate in the other's world view."[39]

It is one thing to develop knowledge and awareness of human similarities and another to develop empathy. Knowledge is a necessary but insufficient ingredient. According to Dufty et al., the goal is informed empathy, or "knowledge plus sensitivity in trying to imagine oneself in another's shoes or bare feet. Empathy varies from trying to understand how other people think and view the world to how other people emote, feel or sense."[40] As an illustration, consider the following three responses made by students who were asked to imagine themselves as someone from another culture, based on pictures of an unfamiliar culture. Responses A and B exemplify informed empathy while response C seems totally lacking in empathy, however informed it may be. Negative empathy or nonempathy, as illustrated in response C, shows "a lack of skill in identifying with others, a lack of cultural imagination, or an inability to think in terms other than those of your own culture."[41]

Student A's response: The holy man came to ward off the spirits which were giving my daughter headaches.

Student B's response: When I die I hope my body will be cremated and my ashes thrown into the sacred Godavari River.

Student C's response: I live in a typical agricultural village in a crude mud hut. I am a New Guinea highlander. Our tribe's religion is animism. My diet is essentially vegetative. The natural vegetation is chopped away with primitive stone axes, the lower story plants are burnt producing nutrient for the soil. After fifty years, the ecology of my area returns to its original state.

The goal of intercultural competence is a major objective of curriculum writers connected with UNESCO's efforts toward international understanding through education.[42] Although these educators have limited the scope of intercultural competence to the international scene, many of the accompanying theories and practices are appropriate for education within a domestic multicultural society.

The work of Triandis and his associates has led to a form of cross-cultural training called culture assimilator, a programmed learning approach designed to increase understanding between members of two cultures.

> As the reader of the assimilator goes through the items, he learns to what features in the episodes he should attend, and which aspects he should ignore [Discrimination learning]. The episodes are selected so that they expose the trainee to situations that emphasize the distinctive features of social situations [that] he must learn to discriminate. The items are also selected to give the trainee contrasting experiences with situations differing sharply on such features. The training, then, emphasizes the distinctive features of events [that] make the situation in the other culture most different from the situations that the trainee has already learned in his own culture. As he receives more and more training with related items, he can abstract features which such items have in common. We call such invariances "cultural principles." After the trainee goes through a half a dozen items featuring the same principle, he is presented with a summary sheet in which the principle is stated as a conclusion. Thus, if he has not abstracted the principle by that point, it is given to him.
>
> As an example . . . consider some recent work on black/white subcultural differences. Black subjects have a tendency to assume that all white persons are prejudiced against blacks. This has major implications for social perception in interracial encounters. Almost any behavior of the white can be misinterpreted, if the context in which it is seen reflects prejudice.[43]

Culture assimilators have been developed for a number of nations, such as Israel and Iran, and for Black and White cultures within the United States. To

A repertoire of multiethnic songs from around the world can strengthen cultural consciousness and intercultural competence.

date, these assimilators have been developed entirely for industrial work settings. Similar approaches to multicultural education, however, can be developed for school settings.

Although the culture assimilator can alert teachers to potential sources of misunderstanding in verbal and nonverbal communication, it typically does not provide instruction in the host language or host dialect. Language, chorus, drama, and speech teachers have multiple opportunities for building intercultural competence by teaching accurate pronunciation, intonation, syntax, and word meanings associated with different languages and dialects. In classrooms where multiple dialects of English are spoken, for example, teachers can draw from each one to teach the parts of speech and rules of grammar. Similarly. they can build up student vocabulary and analytical thinking skills. Speech teachers can develop understandings of culturally different styles of posturing and other nonverbal cues. Business teachers could include instruction on culturally different expectations concerning punctuality, eye contact, and handshaking or bows during job interviews. Physical educators and directors of athletic events can alert students to culturally different rules, notions of fair play, and body moves associated with certain sports.

Language is one of the great barriers to intercultural competence in United States society and to empathy and respect among culturally different people. Writing from a Chicano perspective, Rivera states the following:

> Historically, state and local institutions have insisted that to become "good Americans" all minority and immigrant groups have to abandon their native languages and cultures, give up their group identity, and become absorbed as individuals into the dominant group. If any group has resisted . . . it has been regarded as uncivilized, un-American, and potentially subversive. Furthermore, it is difficult for many people to accept the idea that a native-born Mexican American who happens to speak Spanish and who retains many of the values of his native culture might well be a loyal American. As a result, social and educational institutions in the Southwest and California have directed their activities toward the elimination of both the Spanish language and Mexican culture.[44]

Ironically, millions of dollars are spent to encourage schoolchildren to learn a foreign language.

A multicultural curriculum offers guidelines for moving beyond these contradictions. When teachers accept the goal of developing competencies in multiple systems of standards for perceiving, evaluating, believing, and doing, it becomes obvious that knowledge about multiple dialects and languages is part of becoming educated. A society and a world comprised of linguistically different peoples require the ability to interpret an array of verbal and nonverbal communication modes to at least minimal degrees, and accurate interpretation requires some degree of empathy. Of course, it is unrealistic to expect that most people could ever become proficient in more than a few languages. Most North Americans thrive with only one language, provided that language is English, so there is often little motivation to become bilingual or multilingual. The opportunity exists, however. Consider Table 8.1, which gives some indication of the language diversity within the United States.

TABLE 8.1
Language Diversity in the United States: Percentage of School-age Population Speaking Language other than English at Home

Location	Language
15% and Over	
California	German, Italian, Spanish, Polish, Yiddish, French, Russian, Hungarian, Swedish, Greek, Norwegian, Dutch, Japanese, Chinese, Serbo-Croation, Portuguese, Danish, Arabic, Tagalog, Armenian, Turkish, Persian, Malay (Indonesian), Scandinavian, Basque, Mandarin, Gypsy (Romani)
Arizona	Spanish, Uto-Aztecan
New Mexico	Spanish
Texas	Spanish
Alaska	South Alaskan, Eskimo, North Mexican
Florida	Spanish
New York	German, Italian, Spanish, Polish, Yiddish, French, Russian, Hungarian, Swedish, Greek, Norwegian, Slovak, Dutch, Ukranian, Lithuanian, Czech, Chinese, Portugese, Danish, Finnish, Arabic, Rumanian, Balto-Slavic, Celtic, Hebrew, Armenian, Near Eastern Arabic dialects, Turkish, Uralic, Albanian, Persian, Scandinavian, Amerindian, Dalmatian, Breton, Mandarin, Egyptian, Georgian, Gypsy (Romani), Athabascan
Hawaii	Japanese, Tagalog, Polynesian
10.0–14.9%	
Nevada	Spanish
Colorado	Spanish
Illinois	German, Italian, Spanish, Polish, Yiddish, Russian, Swedish, Greek, Norwegian, Slovak, Dutch, Ukranian, Lithuanian, Czech, Serbo-Croatian, Danish, Balto-Slavic
New Jersey	German, Italian, Polish, Yiddish, Russian, Hungarian, Slovak, Dutch, Ukrainian
Connecticut	Italian, Polish, French

Sources: Theodore Andersson and Mildred Boyer, *Bilingual Schooling in the United States* (Washington, DC: U.S. Office of Education, 1970), pp. 2627; and U.S. Bureau of the Census, *General Social and Economic Characteristics* (Washington, DC, 1980), Figure 7, p. 10g.

At the very least, it is possible and imperative that we become proficient with one or more of the most prevalent dialects or languages that coexist with our native tongue, be it English, Spanish, Chinese, or Appalachian dialect. The process of adding even one new dialect or language to our repertoire strengthens awareness of cultural conflicts and misconceptions that emerge from verbal and nonverbal cues associated with different languages. It becomes easier to understand how others misperceive and are misperceived. The important role of language instruction in developing intercultural competence is discussed in the next chapter where the concept of bilingual education is dealt with more fully.

Literature and the arts provide other rich sources for developing informed student empathy. Short stories, poems, song lyrics, drama, and pieces of visual art often hold messages about universal human experiences and emotions such as love, grief, anger, protest, and death. Affirmations of the human spirit, which thrives under even the most oppressive conditions, are found in spirituals created by African American people during slavery in the American South and in poems and drawings created by young Japanese American children and Jewish children who were imprisoned in concentration camps during World War II. A story such as *Annie and the Old One* can help young non-Indian children relate to humans who live in a culture that differs from their own.[45] Annie is a young Navajo girl who tries to halt time to delay the death of her beloved grandmother, whose time to die is drawing near. Each night Annie unravels the rug her grandmother is weaving in order to delay her grandmother's death, which will come when the rug is completed. Although Annie is unable to prevent the inevitable, her grandmother teaches her how to face life and accept death. The experience or fear of losing a loved one is something with which most children can empathize.

Literature and artistic achievements by one's own people provide sources of identity and pride within the individual, and sources of respect from others.

Multicultural dances can help children feel connections with children from different cultures.

They can help expand students' readiness for empathy. Self-knowledge, self-acceptance, and security are necessary before people can understand and accept others with whom they may disagree. Furthermore, literature and the arts provide numerous opportunities for asking students to imagine themselves as someone else. What is a certain character feeling? What is the artist or composer expressing?

The selection and interpretation of appropriate materials from literature can be problematic, however. In an excellent publication by the National Council of Teachers of English, *Black Literature for High School Students,* authors Dodds Stanford and Amin state that most teachers agree that Black literature can help foster interracial understanding. However, teachers differ in their interpretations of literature and in their views about what literature is appropriate.

> Whites tend to react favorably to books in which white people behave generously and kindly, and often do not notice when behavior is somewhat patronizing and fails to bring about meaningful change for black people. *To Kill a Mockingbird* . . . is probably the best example of a book which many white teachers feel promotes positive interracial attitudes by showing Atticus' courage. Most black teachers, however, point out that Atticus, in fact, compromised and survived in a destructive social system, and that for the blacks in the novel, Atticus' "heroism" was a paternalistic insult. In a just system, Tom Robinson would never have needed defending—and Atticus would not have been a hero.[46]

These caveats are not limited to Black literature. They apply to all literature, where racist or sexist themes are evident.

On the other hand, in books that avoid White paternalism and provide the realities of barrio, reservation, or ghetto life—such as *The Autobiography of Malcolm X* and Dick Gregory's *Nigger*—four-letter words and dialect are often objected to. Some teachers, minority and nonminority alike, fear these works will reinforce negative stereotypes about the ethnic groups portrayed. They also find that White students are sometimes so disturbed by Black, Chicano, or Native American hatred of Whites that they cannot get beyond feelings of anger, grief, or guilt. Such reactions are understandable and need to be expressed, provided the environment is caring and supportive. However, there is often a danger that students will remain in a state of either nonempathy or overempathizing.

These risks can be minimized with careful instruction. For example, among ethnically encapsulated students whose only contact with culturally different people has been through myths and cruel stereotypes, it may be helpful to begin with ethnically different people of similar backgrounds, values, and social class. Regional and class prejudices will then not have to be dealt with along with their ethnic bias. Dodds Stanford and Amin state that, "White middle-class students, even if they are from prejudiced backgrounds, should be able to empathize with the characters in *It's Good to Be Black, Mary McLeod Bethune,* and *and My Life with Dr. Martin King, Jr.* Working-class, urban, white students may find that they can identify with Althea Gibson, Connie Hawkins, or Gordon Parks."[47]

Lesson Plans That Develop Intercultural Competence

Faces, Families, and Friends

This lesson is designed for the multilingual primary-level classroom in which children differ in their English-language proficiency and academic progress. Some children are monolingual and speak only English, Spanish, or various Vietnamese dialects. Others are proficiently bilingual in both English and their mother tongue. Some have a limited proficiency in English but can read and write in their first language. Others have had no access to formal education and thus have not acquired basic academic skills.

Part of each day the children work in heterogeneous groups (cooperative teams) to strengthen oral language proficiency and develop creative problem-solving skills. A proficiently bilingual child is placed in each team, along with monolingual children (speakers of English and Spanish or Vietnamese dialects). Children have been taught cooperative teamwork and can effectively use the roles of group facilitator, translator, reporter, setup officer, and harmonizer. The children work for an hour each day in discussion groups to strengthen conceptual learning and oral language proficiency. They also work an hour each day in math and science learning centers to strengthen their creative problem-solving skills. The following lesson illustrates how the discussion groups work. Children become more interculturally competent as they learn about each other's verbal and nonverbal modes of communication.

Goals

- Increased language proficiency in two or three languages, one of which is English.
- Increased conceptual learning in two or three languages, one of which is English.
- Increased intercultural competence.

Objectives

1. The children will create a mask portrait of a member of their family (real or imagined) and describe the person to their group (using the bilingual interpreter as needed).
2. Teams write and act out a brief skit based on the characters created by the members.

Lesson Activities

1. The teacher gives each team facilitator a card that explains the task. Everyone in the group makes a mask. The mask is the face of a real or imaginary person in your family. Explain your mask (person) to your team. Help write a skit about all the people (masks) in your group.

(Continued)

2. The teams discuss the task card and the translator (who is bilingual) makes sure that everyone understands the task.
3. The setup officer gets the supplies needed to create the masks. (Supplies are clearly organized and identified with pictographs.)
4. Once the masks are finished (about thirty minutes), the facilitators and checkers work together to give everyone a chance to explain his or her mask. As the skit is being developed, they make sure that everyone has input and listens to the ideas of others. Reporters write words in two languages, aided by a bilingual pictionary (thirty minutes today, thirty to sixty minutes tomorrow).
5. The skits are acted out, videotaped, and discussed on the third day (thirty to sixty minutes).

Materials Needed

Task cards (trilingual and pictographs).

Team roles posted in room. These should be trilingual and include pictographs.

Paper plates, multicolored construction paper, scissors, glue sticks, and water-based markers for the masks.

Video camera and tape.

Recommended resource for teachers: Elizabeth G. Cohen, *Designing Groupwork: Strategies for the Heterogeneous Classroom*. Teachers College Press, New York, 1986. The theory and practice of groupwork are clearly explained, including the development of leadership roles that give everyone an essential part to play. Chapter 10 describes the "finding out" approach used in math and science. Teams discuss activity cards before they begin, as in the lesson above. Once everyone understands the task, they can move to the "interesting manipulative materials" that don't require English language proficiency. This approach has significantly enhanced higher-order thinking and problem-solving skills of young children and helps them to work at or well above grade level in math and science, whether or not they are highly proficient in English.

Nobody Speaks My Language   Pamela L. Tiedt and Iris M. Tiedt[48]

Give students a taste of what foreigners experience by setting up the classroom as a foreign country. For a brief period, everyone (including the teacher) will pretend that they cannot understand what anyone else says (or writes). Hide all written material so that students will not see anything in a familiar language. Students will have to communicate by pointing, gesturing, and acting out.

At the end of the specified time, discuss how everyone felt. How would this experience be similar to or different from that of a foreigner coming to this coun-

(Continued)

try for the first time? Was there anything they wanted to communicate but could not? How could they help someone in a similar situation?

A Local Language Survey

Do students know what languages are spoken in their area? Begin with the local place names. What languages have influenced local names? Ask families. What languages are spoken in the students' families? Do students know people who speak different languages?

Make a map or chart of the area on which to record the information students find. Have them research local history to see what the earliest languages were. Were there any Native American groups living nearby? What language did they speak and what happened to them? Ask who the first settlers were and what languages they brought with them. Trace the language history down to the present time. Students should be able to discover what the major local language groups are and how long their speakers have been in the area.

Once the major languages are identified, this can become an important resource for further study. Plan lessons around examples from these languages. Bring people in who speak various languages so that students can hear what the languages sound like.

Focusing on Spanish

Spanish is the most commonly spoken language in the United States other than English. Spanish-speaking Americans have their roots in Mexico, Spain, Puerto Rico, Cuba, and other countries. Most Spanish speakers are located throughout California and the Southwest. However, students may be surprised to learn that there are large groups of Spanish speakers in Colorado, Massachusetts, and Florida, for example. In addition, almost all major cities such as Chicago and New York have large Spanish-speaking communities. All children should be aware of the Spanish language and the variety of Spanish-speaking cultures represented in the United States.

The following activities are designed to acquaint all students with the Spanish language. They can be used with bilingual programs or classrooms in which only English is spoken. You can use these activities easily whether or not you know Spanish. Encourage Spanish-speaking students to contribute vocabulary and pronunciation information and reward them for their knowledge. If you have no Spanish-speaking students, bring in Spanish-language teaching tapes or records for the class to become accustomed to Spanish sounds. The activities given here are not intended to teach students Spanish. They are useful to make non-Spanish speakers aware of Spanish as an interesting and important language and to assure Spanish-speaking students that their ability to speak two languages is valued. Although the activities refer specifically to Spanish, they can be adapted for use with any language.

(Continued)

Comparing Alphabets

Show students how the Spanish alphabet is similar to the English alphabet. Show them how it differs. Write or print the letters on the board, circling the letters that are added, thus:

a	b	c	(ch)	d	e	f
g	h	i	j	k	l	(ll)
m	n	(ñ)	o	p	q	r
(rr)	s	t	u	v	w	x
y	z					

Explain that the letters *k* and *w* are used in the Spanish language only when words have been borrowed from other languages (kilómetro and Washington).

Letter Names

What are the names of the letters of the alphabet? English-speaking children will be interested in learning how Spanish-speaking children say the alphabet. Have a child who speaks Spanish say these letters slowly for the group. This is more effective than reading or saying them yourself, for it makes the students aware that knowledge of Spanish can be important in school.

Spanish Letter Names

a	ä	j	hōtä	r	ārā
b	bā	k	kä	rr	ārrā
c	sā	l	älä	s	äsä
ch	chä	ll	äyä	t	tä
d	dä	m	ämä	u	ü
e	ā	n	änä	v	bā
f	äffä	ñ	änyä	w	düblä bā
g	hä	o	ō	x	äkēs
h	ächä	p	pä	y	ē grē ägä (Greek i)
i	ē	q	kü	z	sätä

Comparing Phonemes and Graphemes

After examining the alphabet letters that are used in writing Spanish, show students the phonemes used in speaking Spanish, some of which are similar to English but none of which are exactly the same. Also show them corresponding graphemes for these phonemes. Here they will notice many differences between Spanish and English, as shown on the next page:

LESSON 8.9

(Continued)

Consonants	Spanish	English
b	también	rib
	abrir	like v, but with lips almost touching
c	casa	case (before a, o, u)
	nación	cent (before e, i)
ch	chico	church
d	donde	down
	madre	the
f	familia	family
g	gente	like exaggerated h (before e, i)
	gordo	game
h	hacer	silent
j	jugar	like exaggerated h
k	kilómetro	kitchen
l	làstima	little
ll	llena	yellow ⎫
		million ⎭ regional variation
m	mañana	morning
n	nada	nothing
ñ	niño	canyon
p	piña	supper
q	queso	key
r	pero	rich
	rico	trilled r
rr	perro	trilled r
s	sala	sad
t	trabajar	time
v	enviar	like b in también
	la vaca	like b in abrir
w	Wáshington	wash
x	examen	exam
	extranjero	sound
	México	hit
y	yo	yes
z	zapato	save

Vowels

a	padre	father
e	es	they
i	nida	police
o	poco	poem
u	luna	spoon
	querer	silent after q
ai, ay	traiga	nice
au	auto	mouse

(Continued)

(Continued)

Vowels	Spanish	English
ei, ey	aceituna	tr<u>ay</u>
eu	deuda	<u>ay</u> plus <u>oo</u>
ia, ya	hacia	<u>y</u>onder
ie, ye	nieve	<u>y</u>es
io, yo	dios	<u>y</u>olk
iu	ciudad	<u>y</u>ule
oi, oy	soy	b<u>oy</u>
ua	guante	<u>wa</u>nder
ue	vuelve	<u>wei</u>ght
y	y	<u>e</u>ven
ui, uy	muy	<u>we</u>
uo	cuota	<u>woe</u>

Spanish Pronunciation

Whether or not you have ever studied Spanish, it is important to be able to pronounce the Spanish that you introduce in your classroom as easily as possible. Use the chart of Spanish phonemes to become familiar with Spanish sounds. Ask Spanish-speaking students to share their knowledge of Spanish and contribute words or demonstrate pronunciations. There is no reason for you as the teacher to be afraid of making mistakes. You can help by making an effort to try Spanish words without having to speak Spanish fluently. Taking at least an introductory Spanish class is, of course, recommended for any teacher's professional development.

Varieties of Spanish

The information on Spanish presented in this book is very general. There are many varieties of Spanish spoken in the United States, depending on where the speakers live, how long they have lived in this country, and where they came from originally. Spanish in the Southwest is different from Spanish in the Midwest (Chicago), the Northeast, and Florida. Even in New York City, there are important cultural and linguistic differences between persons from Puerto Rico, Cuba, Dominican Republic, Colombia, Ecuador, Peru, Mexico, Venezuela, Bolivia, and other South American communities.

The differences in the Spanish of Latin America are primarily vocabulary and pronunciation. Some vocabulary differences are due to influence from local Indian languages, others to independent development of Spanish.

The following are examples of different words used in Latin America for boy.

Mexico—chamaco	Panama—chico
Cuba—chico	Colombia—pelado
Guatemala—patojo	Argentina—pibe
El Salvador—cipote	Chile—cabro

LESSON 8.9

(Continued)

Pronunciation also varies regionally. The following are some of the differences found: syllable final *s* becomes *h* or disappears—*estos* is [éhtoh] or [éto]; *ll* becomes the same, as *y*—*valla* and *vaya* are alike; and syllable final *r* sounds like *l*—*puerta* is [pwelta], *comer* is [komel].

Introduce vocabulary specific to local Spanish-speaking groups by having a variety of children's books available. Many books, written about members of particular groups, take pride in presenting common Spanish words that are special to that group.

From P. L. Tiedt and I. M. Tiedt, *Multicultural Teaching: A Handbook of Activities, Information, and Resources* (Boston: Allyn and Bacon, 1979), 84–88. Reprinted by permission.

The next multicultural lesson is for a high school choir and is primarily an introduction to the teaching of one or two Negro Spiritual selections to add to the choral repertoire. The plan, of course, would extend beyond one lesson.

Negro Spirituals for the School Choir   *Arlessa Barnes*

LESSON 8.10

Multicultural Goal

Developing culture consciousness and intercultural competence.

Objective

To understand and become aware of the unique characteristics evident in Negro Spirituals and to become aware of the contributions made to the Spiritual movement by several Black composers and artists. To develop skill in correct pronunciation of Black dialect used in the Spirituals.

Procedure

1. Listen to and discuss the characteristics of one or two Negro Spirituals that have been passed down from the African tradition.

   Suggested listening: any of the below or [any] selected from the Materials (discography)

   Note to teacher: Spirituals have certain distinctive features, syncopated rhythms, call and response technique (or leader and chorus), rich harmonies, etc. Spirituals are emotional expressions of Black individuals about their particular experiences (an example of an emotional Spiritual is "Sometimes I Feel Like a Motherless Child"). Spirituals also tell of biblical incidents, for example "Joshua Fought the Battle of Jericho." The call and response song form,

(Continued)

which is directly of African origin, is present throughout the African American repertoire. A song that employs the leader and chorus arrangement is "Swing Low, Sweet Chariot." Some of the Spirituals undoubtedly had hidden or double meanings and served as signals for escape purposes. "Steal Away to Jesus" is a classic example.

2. Select one or two Negro Spirituals to teach to your choir. Stress the importance that the Spiritual is a part of our American heritage.

   Suggested songs: see Materials (song collections)

   Note to teacher: Stress that your singers use proper Black dialect when singing Spirituals. Black dialect may present some difficulties to White people who have never lived in the South, but most of the Spirituals lose charm when they are sung in straight English. *Examples:*

   (dialect) "I ain't gonna study war no mo"
   (English) "I am not going to study war anymore"

   (dialect) "Gaud's go'nuh trouble duh watah"
   (English) "God's going to trouble the water"

3. Discuss the Fisk Jubilee Singers, who acquainted the masses with Spirituals during their American and European tours from 1871 to1878.
4. Discuss Marian Anderson, who perfected these songs with her skilled technique and culture.
5. Discuss J. Rosamond Johnson and Harry T. Burleigh (Spiritual composers).

Suggested Motivating Activities

1. Visit a Black church choir rehearsal or service. For those students who are unfamiliar with Black Gospel music, observing the emotional energy will help them relate to the Black aesthetic.
2. Attend a Black religious choral concert if one is scheduled nearby.
3. Have students attempt to harmonize by ear.
4. Allow students to move. Movement, such as foot tapping, swaying, facial expressions, and clapping, is an important part of the African American music culture and shows a true Black aesthetic.

Materials

1. Discography:

   Fisk Jubilee Singers (Folkways FA 2372)
   Tuskegee Institute Choir (Westminster 9633)
   He's Got the World, Marian Anderson (Victor LSC 2592)

LESSON 8.10

(Continued)

2. Song collections:

Chambers, H. A., ed. *The Treasury of Negro Spirituals*. New York: Emerson Books. 1963. The book is divided in two sections: "Traditional Spirituals" and "Modern Compositions." The Spirituals are tastefully arranged.

Johnson, James Weldon, and J. Rosamond Johnson. *The Book of American Negro Spirituals*. New York: Viking Press, 1954. Very useful and most recommended.

Landecks, Beatrice. *Echoes of Africa in Folk Songs of the Americas*. 2d rev. ed. New York: David McKay, 1969. Part Four, titled "Songs Roots of Jazz in the U.S.," has street cries, Spirituals, and shouts, work and minstrel songs, and blues. Good selections, with notes and suggestions for performance.

Lloyd, Ruth Norma, comp. and arr. *The American Heritage Songbook*. New York: American Heritage, 1969. Part Seven of this book, "Songs of the American Negro," contains thirteen Spirituals and folk songs with information about each one.

3. Suggested reading (for the teacher who may not be familiar with African American music):

Heilbut, Tony. *The Gospel Sound*. New York: Simon and Schuster, 1971. A solid contribution to the literature, good discography.

Marsh, J. B. T. *The Story of the Jubilee Singers: With Their Songs*. New York: Negro University Press, 1969.

Reeder, Barbara. "Getting Involved in Shaping the Sounds of Black Music." *Music Educators Journal* 59 (October 1972):80. This article delineates pertinent rhythmic aspects in Black music with activities to help students feel and respond.

Work, John Wesley. *American Negro Songs and Spirituals*. New York: Bonanza, 1940.

Evaluation

1. Listening exam(s): Test can be matching, multiple choice, and/or short essay. Construct tests whereby students would be required to pinpoint and describe various characteristics of the Negro Spiritual.

2. Ask students to prepare reports on one of the artists/composers studied.

3. If you have an opportunity to observe a live performance of a Black religious choir, instruct students to do a report, critiquing the performance and discussing various characteristics.

Reprinted with permission of the author.

Misunderstandings in Cross-Cultural Interactions: High School Level Spanish Class; Suburban Community Undergoing Sudden Increase in Hispanic Immigration   Delora Medina and Hilda Vazquez

Rationale

More than a means of verbal and nonverbal communication, language is itself the shaper of ideas.
—B.L. Whorf

We live in a diverse community that has undergone a rapid increase in our Hispanic population. It is important for the entire community to recognize that different cultures have different ways of looking at our world and interacting interpersonally. One of the most effective ways to reach the community is through our students. A better understanding of the way in which ethnic groups communicate consciously (such as language and gestures) and unconsciously (such as body language) can be taught in the classroom. In addition, it is important for the students to recognize how their *own* thoughts and behaviors might be misinterpreted by people from *other* cultures. Being unaware of these differences could undoubtedly result in conflicts. As foreign language teachers it is our responsibility to teach not just Spanish, but also the Hispanic culture. *Language is at the heart of culture*. The main goals of our lessons are to strengthen cultural consciousness and intercultural competence.

Objectives

Students will:
• Become aware that communication with others can be affected by their self-perception and their perception of others.
• Develop empathy toward interpreting the behavior of other cultural ethnic groups with a more positive attitude.
• Engage in group discussions about the feelings and emotions that occur when one is misunderstood.
• Sharpen their verbal and writing skills through discussions and compositions of a movie and skits.

Materials

• Video camera
• Videocassette of skits
• Television
• VCR
• Video "Fools Rush In"
  Romantic comedy of the relationship between a Mexican-American woman and an Anglo-Saxon man and the conflicts that arise because of their cultural differences

(Continued)

- Handouts of instructions for writing activities and assignment

Bennett, C. *Comprehensive Multicultural Education: Theory and Practice.* 4th ed. Boston: Allyn and Bacon, 1999.
Fools Rush In from Columbia Pictures, 1996 (~109 minutes).

Daily Lesson Plan and Activities

I. Introduction Lesson
  A. Show skits of interpersonal interactions (See Appendix A)
  B. Discussion of skits in class (See Appendix B)
II. Development Lesson
  A. Show video "Fools Rush In"
  B. Group discussion of movie
  C. Fill out worksheet while watching movie (See Appendix C)
  D. Composition assignment (See Appendix D)
III. Conclusion/Evaluation
  A. Students act out own skits in front of class (See Appendix E)

Skits of Interpersonal Interactions

- The skits portray interactions between two friends, one of Hispanic and the other of Anglo-Saxon backgrounds. Our high school students are beginning to form more complex social bonds and are dating. These are situations they may encounter and, possibly, misinterpret when interacting with a Hispanic person.
- Four sample skits (See Appendix A):
  — Guy and girl walking on sidewalk
  — Holding hands
  — Casual touching while talking
  — Kissing on the cheek
- Discussion Quesions (See Appendix B)

Video "Fools Rush In"

- The video provides an accurate portrayal of interracial relationship between Isabel Fuentes, a Mexican-American woman, and Alex Whitman, an Anglo-Saxon man. Problems arise between the couple and the respective families due to negative misconceptions about each other's cultures.
- Students are required to:

  1. Write a few Spanish sentences on key scenes during the movie (See Appendix C)
  2. Write a composition over the movie for homework (See Appendix D)

- Also, the class will have an open discussion in Spanish after watching the movie (sample questions below)

LESSON 8.11

(Continued)

Discussion Questions

- To what extent were these interactions simply misunderstandings rather than displays of ethnocentrism?
- What do you feel you have gained from this video?

Evaluation

Oral & Visual

- In groups of four, students will write their own skit to represent a misunderstanding between two different cultures. They do not need to portray a dating/friendship situation between the Hispanic and Anglo-Saxon cultures. Students may research other cultures, but they have to make sure they are not basing the skits on stereotypes. Each skit should be 3 to 5 minutes in length and in Spanish. All groups will perform the skit in class and will be videotaped.
- Handout with instructions on Appendix E.

Written

- Movie compositions will be peer-evaluated before they are turned in.
- Grades will be based on correct grammar, punctuation, and sentence structure.

Appendix A

Teacher Fact Sheet

Homemade Skits on Dating & Friendship
- When a guy and a girl are walking down a sidewalk, it is customary for the guy to walk on the 'street side' and for the girl to walk on the 'inside' of the sidewalk. It is a sign of security and protection toward the girl.
    Sample take: When a guy and a girl get to a sidewalk, the girl tries to move to the inside of the walk. He resists her attempt to cross in front of him and looks confused.
- Holding hands is very common among friends in Hispanic cultures. Friends can hold hands without it being a 'serious' move or sexual in nature.
    Sample take: While walking down a sidewalk the girl reaches out to hold the guy's hand. He instantly pulls his hand out of the way. She tries to hold his hand once more and he pulls it away again.
- Hispanic cultures are known for having very limited (or no) personal space. Ordinarily, Hispanic people will reach over and touch the person they are talking to without realizing it. A problem arises when a Hispanic person talks to someone from a different culture where personal space is well defined and respected. A small, unconscious touch can be misinterpreted as flirting, invasion of space, or disrespect.
    Sample take: The skit may involve a situation such as having a guy come over to watch TV at a girl's house.

(Continued)

Guy: Hi, how are you?

Girl: Fine, come on in. How are you?

Guy: What were you doing?

Girl: I was just sitting here flipping through the channels.
(They sit on the couch)

Guy: There's a football game on channel 2, if you want to watch that . . .

Girl: Oh really, who's playing?

Guy: The (team 1) vs. the (team 2).

Girl: Oh, I'm a big fan of the (team 1)! (reaching over and touching his leg)

Guy: (overreacts either by saying he has a girlfriend or taking the girl's touch as a sexual come-on)

- Hispanic friends and families kiss on the cheek when greeting each other hello and saying goodbye. It is not unusual for a Hispanic person to extend this expression to people from other cultures, unknowingly (possibly) invading their personal space.

  Sample take: The girl see her guy friend sitting at a table in the library and goes up to him to say hello. She leans in to kiss him on the cheek but he leans back trying to avoid getting 'too close.'

Appendix B

Discussion Questions Over Skits

- How does being aware of differences in personal interactions with people from other cultures help you become more aware of your own culture?
- Do you think that being unfamiliar with the Hispanic culture presented in the skits might lead you to make assumptions about their behavior (that may not necessarily be true)?
- How would you react to an unfamiliar action directed to you? Would you confront the person?
- What do you think you can do to resolve a situation of misunderstanding?

Appendix C

Nombre _____

Fecha _____

Película "Fools Rush In"

Instrucciones: Escribe de tres a cinco oraciones sobre cada una de las siguientes escenas de la película.

1. Cena de familia en casa de Isabel

_____

_____

_____

_____

(Continued)

2. Alex regresa a su casa y está decorada por la familia de Isabel

_____

_____

_____

_____

3. La visita inesperada de los padres de Alex

_____

_____

_____

4. Celebración del 5 de Mayo con los padres de Alex e Isabel

_____

_____

_____

_____

Appendix D

Nombre _____

Fecha _____

Composición sobre la película "Fools Rush In"

Instrucciones: Escribe tres o más párrafos sobre la película que vimos en clase. !Sé creativo! Cuenta la historia tal y como sucedió o describe lo que pasó después que nació el bebé de Alex e Isabel.

_____

_____

_____

_____

_____

_____

_____

_____

Appendix E

Nombre _____

Fecha _____

Actividad Especial

La última actividad de esta lección es una actividad en grupo. Tú y tres de tus compañeros de clase (grupos de cuatro personas) escribirán su propio 'dramita' de un malentendido entre dos culturas. Las culturas no tienen que ser las mismas que uti-

LESSON 8.11

(Continued)

lizamos en clase (Hispana y Anglo-Sajona). El dramita, de no más de 3 a 5 minutos de largo, va a ser actuado en español y grabado en clase. Piensa bien en lo que tú quieres hacer y trata de no representar estéreotipos negativos e innecesarios de las culturas que uses.

_____

_____

_____

_____

_____

_____

_____

_____

_____

_____

_____

_____

_____

Reprinted with permission from the authors.

This is a lesson plan for a sixth-grade social studies class.

LESSON 8.12

For the Good of the People   *Susan Goodman*

Objectives

Students will gain an understanding of Native American feelings about having to leave their land. Students will write a short paper comparing native peoples' feelings about the loss of their land to the simulation of the students' own loss of land.

Lesson Opener

Today we are going to use our time machine. First, we will visit the time period of the late 1700s to early 1800s. You will become a Cherokee. Next, we will use the time machine to move into the future and you will become a small farmer in Switz City.

Activity

Read the following and discuss in small groups.

Part 1: You are a Native American named White Horse. You and your ancestors have lived on this land for many years. It has supported your every need for food, shelter, and clothing. You respect and love the land. But now the white settlers are moving onto your land. They have built fences where you once freely traveled. They are killing the game—cutting the forests. The white men even complain

(Continued)

of your existence there. Finally, a treaty has been signed, and you are told you must move "for the good of your people." How do you feel?

Now reenter the time machine for your trip to the future:

Part 2: For several years your family has owned a small farm in Switz City. It has been passed from generation to generation. You have a deep feeling of home and security here. You have made an acceptable living for your family on this farm. Now the Department of Natural Resources is planning to construct a huge reservoir. Your property will be the middle of the lake. Your first angry inquiries are met by these facts:

Many of your neighbors are in the same position.

The state will pay you a fair price for your land. (The price actually turns out to be much less than a real estate agent said you could get.)

Your land has already been officially condemned.

Construction will begin in three months.

You have no appeal.

The state representative says he can do nothing to halt progress in the state.

The reservoir will "benefit all citizens of the state," says the governor in his form letter answering your angry telegram.

How do you feel? After fifteen to twenty minutes (or more) of discussion, write your paper, comparing your feelings as a farmer to those of the Native Americans. Point out any similarities and differences that you discover.

Evaluation

Observation of group work and the written papers of the students.

Materials

Handouts with parts 1 and 2 typed separately to hand out to different groups.

Enrichment

Have groups of the sixth graders do skits showing these two scenes to younger students in the early elementary school grades. The performers should do research and try to dress in authentic clothing. Then, another class member can lead the younger students in a discussion of feelings.

Reprinted with permission from the author.

Goal Four: Combating Racism, Sexism, Prejudice, and All Forms of Discrimination

Combating racism, sexism, prejudice, and discrimination means lessening negative attitudes and behavior which are based on gender bias and misconceptions about the inferiority of races and cultures different from one's own. Emphasis is on clearing up myths and stereotypes associated with gender, different races, and ethnic groups. Basic human similarities are stressed. The following lists several crucial assumptions that underlie this goal:

- It is worthwhile for educators to focus on the reduction of racial/ethnic prejudice and discrimination even though powerful sectors of the society and the world do not presently value this goal.
- It is appropriate for schools to teach certain humanistic and democratic values, such as the negative effects of racism and sexism.
- A reduction of racial/ethnic prejudice and discrimination is possible through appropriate educational experiences.

The goal is to develop antiracist, antisexist behavior based on awareness of historical and contemporary evidence of individual, institutional, and cultural racism and sexism in the United States and elsewhere in the world. It is directed at developing greater awareness of the existence and impact of racism, sexism, and ethnic prejudice and discrimination in U.S. society as well as within other nations and across national boundaries. Distinctions between cultural, individual, and institutional racism and sexism are important. Prejudice and discrimination are studied within the contexts of American and world history, science, literature, and the arts. Teaching efforts to reduce prejudice and discrimination are directed at clarifying students' values and at building moral reasoning skills. This, it is hoped, leads to understandings, attitudes, and behaviors that are consistent with basic democratic ideals, such as liberty, justice, and equal opportunity. Global issues related to Western colonialism and violations of human rights are also a focus.

Science and health teachers can debunk myths surrounding the concept of race and teach facts about the biological attributes shared by all humans. Scientists estimate that over 90 percent of one's genetic makeup is shared with all members of the human species, leaving only 6 to 7 percent related to gender and racial attributes and the remainder to individual variance. Misconceptions about the origins of the races and erroneous beliefs about the superiority of some races must be cleared up. Social studies educators can focus on the power dimension of racism. The fact that racial justice still eludes us must be made clear, and the possibility that our quest for racial justice has been misdirected (and needs to be redirected) must be considered.[49]

Teachers in all content areas can help students develop skills in detecting bias in texts and media. In math and general business classes, students can learn about racist loan shark practices that keep people in poverty while also learning percentages and interest rates. Typing teachers can include news articles that discuss racism in their typing skill assignments. Teachers in the humanities can use selected pieces of literature, art, and music to discuss themes related to racism and prejudice.

Positive interracial attitudes can also be fostered without modifying the curriculum extensively if the school population is racially and culturally diverse. Wherever students have a chance to work together to achieve a common goal, chances are excellent for improving mutual respect and appreciation. Sports and team efforts of every kind, musical or dramatic performances, and cooperative class projects are examples of activities many teachers use to develop positive interracial contact experiences. (The required ingredients for positive contact are provided in Chapters 1 and 9.)

A necessary first step in creating a revised curriculum is to face the facts of a racist past and present. It is essential to recognize the impact of racism on the oppressor as well as on the oppressed.

As painful as it may be, children and young adults must face facts about the racist past. Under the guidance of knowledgeable and caring teachers, minorities and nonminorities can gain insight into a social context that helps explain current patterns of poverty, protest, and apathy as well as interracial isolation, stereotypes, misconceptions, and conflict. These insights can help convert anger, rage, denial, guilt, and paternalism into the commitment and knowledge needed to combat racism and social injustice wherever it occurs.

Since racial equality and justice still elude us, an emphasis on combating racism is imperative. This necessity, however, must not blind us to other manifestations of prejudice and discrimination such as those directed at lower socioeconomic groups, the gay community, and certain religious groups (e.g., the BaHais, Universalists). The fight against racism can be extended into a broader fight for universal human rights and respect for human dignity.

Emphasizing unity through human similarities is one of the most positive and important ways to reduce racism and other types of prejudice and discrimination. Awareness of the common features of human life and the ways hu-

An appreciation of the fundamental unity of humankind can be learned during childhood.

mans are interconnected is vital to intergroup cooperation and harmony. Lee Anderson, a social scientist who is one of the founders of global education, vividly illustrates the possibilities of what might be achieved in his imaginary world-centered school, Terra.[50] The philosophy behind Terra school generates five overarching purposes:

- To develop students' understanding of themselves as individuals.
- To develop students' understanding of themselves as members of the human species.
- To develop students' understanding of themselves as inhabitants and dependents of planet Earth.
- To develop students' understanding of themselves as participants in global society.
- To develop within students the competencies requisite to living intelligently and responsibly as individuals, human beings, earthlings, and members of global society.[51]

The following list of questions captures how these purposes can be turned into classroom activity.

What do you know about being human?

1. How are human beings like all other living things?
2. How are human beings more like some living things than others? Are you more like animals than plants? How? Are you more like a jellyfish or a bird? How? Are you more like a bear or a lizard? How? Are you more like a monkey or a cow? How?
3. How are human beings unlike all other living things.[52]

In Anderson's school, the emphasis is on understanding human culture, and the curriculum is based on a program called The Human Way of Living. The curriculum at twenty-first century high school is organized around five major programs:

- Studies of individual development and behavior
- Studies of the human species
- Studies of humankind's planetary and cosmic environments
- Development of human competencies
- Social service, political action, and work-study[53]

How can we develop this world-centered perspective in the absence of adequate resources and curriculum materials? Considerations such as the following can be used as evaluative criteria with even the weakest materials.

- Look for evidence of ethnocentrism, the view that one's culture is the standard by which other cultures should be judged.
- Look for evidence that foreign countries are seen too simplistically, with no discussion of the various microcultures within each society. Make the same evaluation with respect to ethnic groups: Are all members of a particular

group assumed to share similar ideas, habits, and values, or is the diversity within each group recognized?

◼ Consider whether the text presents conflicts between groups, nations, or cultures in an overly simplified manner: White settlers versus Indians, the North versus the South during the American Civil War, labor versus management, the Communists versus the Free World.

◼ Watch for subtle suggestions that the so-called advanced civilizations are superior to, or must offer guidance to, less modern societies.

◼ Look for evidence of confusion arising from ignorance of specific cultures: for example, traditional Chinese women pictured in the dress of traditional Japanese women.

◼ Look for the erroneous use of Western assumptions to evaluate non-Western settings. For example, if an author states that "Many Islamic males are non-monogamous," does the word "nonmonogamous" itself carry overtones that may mislead the reader?

◼ Consider whether the learner is encouraged to imagine the world as others might see it, to understand the perceptions and interpretations of other cultures.

◼ Look for a recognition that, despite cultural differences, people in all societies share the basic similarities of being human.[54]

Lessons Plans That Combat Racism, Sexism, Prejudice, and Discrimination

Can You Recognize Racism?

Instructions

First work alone. Put a check before each statement you think is an example of racism. Then work with your small group and try to agree on the examples of racism. (Your group will receive a packet of statement cards to make the task easier.) Choose one member of your group to share your decisions with everyone.

1. Which of the following quotations or descriptive statements are examples of racism? Indicate these with a check (✔).

_____ "A Black family moved into our neighborhood this week."

_____ The principal interviewed two equally outstanding candidates, one Black and the other Latino. She selected the Black teacher because her school had several Latino teachers but no Black teachers.

_____ In 1882 immigration laws excluded the Chinese, and the Japanese were excluded in 1908.

LESSON 8.13

(Continued)

_____ During the 1960s civil rights movement, Mrs. Viola Liuzzo, a White civil rights worker from Michigan, was shot by White southern segregationists.

_____ Between 1892 and 1921 nearly 2,400 African Americans were lynched by vigilante mobs who were never brought to justice.

_____ "The best basketball players on our team this year are Black."

_____ The band director discouraged Black students from playing the flute or piccolo because he believed it was too difficult for them to excel on these instruments.

_____ When Mrs. Wallace, an African American woman from Detroit, visited a predominantly White university in northern Michigan to see her son play basketball, she was seriously injured in a car accident. She refused a blood transfusion because she was afraid of being contaminated by White blood.

_____ When Stacey Russell, an African American undergraduate, went through rush, the girls of an all-White sorority decided not to pledge her because several members threatened to move out if they did.

_____ The geography textbook described the peoples of Nigeria as primitive and underdeveloped.

_____ The children who attended an elementary school in southwest Texas spoke only Spanish at home. When they came to school all the books and intelligence tests were in English. Nearly all of the children were placed in remedial classes or in classes for the mentally retarded.

_____ Mr. Jones said, "It is true that Indians who still live on reservations live in extreme poverty. But this is because they refuse to give up their traditions and a culture which is obsolete in the modern world."

_____ The U.S. Constitution allowed each slave to be counted as three-fifths of a person.

_____ The reporter wrote that "Toni Morrison is a brilliant writer who accurately portrays much of the Black experience in America."

_____ When John brought home a new friend, his father was shocked and angry. Peter, the new friend, was of Japanese origin and John's father had been seriously wounded by the Japanese in World War II. John's father refused to allow Peter to visit again.

_____ In 1896 the Supreme Court ruled that separate facilities for the races were legal as long as they were *equal*. This resulted in separate schools, churches, restaurants, restrooms, swimming pools, theaters, doctors' offices, neighborhoods, Bibles used in court, and so forth.

_____ When Mary Adams wanted to find a place in the school cafeteria, the only vacant chair was at a table seating five Black girls. Mary, who is White, was afraid to join them.

_____ In California today, approximately 10 percent of the population is Black, while 41 percent of those in prison are Black. Blacks generally have more financial difficulty than Whites in hiring a lawyer and plea bargaining.

LESSON 8.13

(Continued)

2. Select one member to write your group's decisions below on the decision sheet and another person to share the results with the rest of us. Be prepared to explain your reasons if necessary.

   a. The following statements are examples of either individual or institutional racism: (Write numbers and a word or two for description, and arrange them according to those that refer to racist individuals or to racist policies and institutions.)

Individual Racism	Institutional Racism

   b. Our group's definition of racism is:

   _____

   c. The main difference between individual and institutional racism is:

   _____

   d. Examples of individual and institutional racism that we know about in our community are:

   Individual racism:

   _____
   _____
   _____

   Institutional racism:

   _____
   _____
   _____

The following Lesson 8.14 can be used at any grade level; the written decision-making sheet can be omitted for young children, and the wording made more appropriate for advanced high school youth. Eventually, the lesson could lead to an examination of ethnic bias in literature. Experience has shown that it is often most effective to begin with sex bias since everyone can identify with being either male or female. The lesson could fit into a variety of subjects. Possible units of study include images in literature or advertising, family relationships and sex role expectations, Title Nine and athletics, careers, and political behavior.

Hidden Messages in Children's Literature

Objectives

- Students will analyze how children's literature and other socialization agents work to shape the attitudes and behaviors of male and female children.
- Students will begin to develop strategies for detecting biased images in media.

Student Activity

Each class member is given one or more children's stories.

For Sexism	For Racism
Hansel and Gretel	*Mary Poppins*
Snow White	*Robinson Crusoe*
Little Red Riding Hood	*The Ugly Duckling*
Policeman Small	*The Slave Dancer*
Cinderella	*Pippi Longstocking*
Rumpelstiltzkin	*The Five Chinese Brothers*
Sleeping Beauty	*Charlie and the Chocolate Factory*
The Three Little Pigs	*Doctor Doolittle*
The Giving Tree	*Sounder*
I'm Glad I'm a Boy	*Magdalena*
I'm Glad I'm a Girl	
Pippi Longstocking	
Tamas Takes Charge	

1. I have examined the following books:

   _____

   _____

   I would like to include these other books:

   _____

   _____

2. Females tend to be described in these ways:

   _____

   Males tend to be described in these ways:

   _____

3. One or more of these books try to make children think and behave in these ways (list as many examples as possible):

   _____

   _____

(Continued)

4. The five most common characteristics associated with women and girls are:

_____

_____

_____

_____

_____

In what ways does our society support these images of females?

_____

_____

In what ways does our society reject these images of females?

_____

_____

_____

5. The five most common characteristics associated with men and boys are:

_____

_____

_____

_____

_____

In what ways does our society support these images of males?

_____

_____

In what ways does our society reject these images of males?

_____

_____

_____

6. Based on this evidence, what differences do you predict between the behavior of males and females in our society?

_____

_____

_____

Lesson 8.15 is designed for high school students. It takes approximately two class periods. Students should have had preliminary instruction on percents, elementary statistics, and the construction of bar, line, and circle graphs. The lesson will instruct students on constructing, reading, and interpreting graphs and tables while having them formulate ideas on discrimination based on racial prejudices.

Reading, Constructing, and Interpreting Graphs   Jean Seger[55]

LESSON 8.15

Performance Objectives

- The student will be able to correctly read Tables 1, 2, and 3. Upon looking at the tables the student will be able to answer orally or in writing questions concerning the information in the tables.

1. Given access to Table 1, the student will be able to construct a line graph comparing the income of Blacks to the total population with years of education completed.

TABLE 1
Estimated Income of Regularly Employed Persons over 18, by Race, Sex, and Schooling, 1980 (mean annual income in U. S. dollars)

	White Female	White Male	Black Female	Black Male
Elementary School				
0–8 years	8,353	14,142	7,757	11,574
High School				
1–3 years	9,208	15,845	8,678	12,360
4 years	10,374	17,648	9,916	13,726
College				
1–3 years	11,688	19,849	11,317	15,541
4 years	13,833	25,943	13,550	18,223
5 or more years	16,958	31,092	16,872	23,400

Source: Adapted from U. S. Bureau of the Census, *Statistical Abstracts of the United States, 1985,* 105th edition (Washington, DC, 1984).

2. Given access to Tables 2 and 3, the student will be able to choose three of six professions and the corresponding data and construct circle graphs for each one.
3. The student will be able to express his or her opinion either orally or in writing on the benefits that minority individuals receive by attending higher education institutions.
4. The student will be able to express his or her opinion either orally or in writing on the economic, social, and psychological ramifications for minority groups who are not adequately represented in higher education or the workforce.

(Continued)

TABLE 2
Occupation of Employed Persons 16 Years Old and Over, by Race and Sex, 1983 (percentage of total)

Occupation	Females	Blacks	Hispanic Americans
Managerial and Professional	40.9	5.6	2.6
Technical, sales, and administrative support	64.6	7.6	4.3
Service	60.1	16.6	6.8
Farming. forestry, and fishing occupations	16.0	7.5	8.2
Precision, production craft, and repair	8.1	6.8	6.2
Operators, fabrication, and laborers	26.6	14.0	8.3
All occupations combined	43.7	9.3	5.3

Source: Adapted from U.S. Bureau of Labor Statistics, *Employment and Earnings* (Washington, DC, January 1984).

TABLE 3
Profession of Employed Persons by Race and Sex, 1983, 50 States and District of Columbia (percentage of total)

Profession	Females	Blacks	Hispanic Americans
Dentists	6.7	2.4	1.0
Engineers	5.8	2.7	2.2
Lawyers and judges	15.8	2.7	1.0
Financial executives	38.6	3.5	3.1
Physicians	15.8	3.2	4.5
Teachers, college and university	36.3	4.4	1.8
Teachers, except college and university	70.9	9.1	2.7
All professions combined	40.9	9.3	5.3

Source: Adapted from U.S. Bureau of the Census, *Statistical Abstracts of the United States, 1985,* 105th edition (Washington, DC, 1984), pp. 402–403.

Strategy

In all lessons students will work in groups of two.

■ Day 1

Materials

1. Poster displaying the information in Table 1
2. Individual copies of the table
3. Rulers

(Continued)

Activities

1. Each group will receive a copy of Table 1 and a larger model of the table will appear on the front blackboard.
2. The teacher will direct students in the method for reading the table to find the median income of individuals based on education completed.
3. The teacher will ask students to orally *(a)* state the median income earned by individual; *(b)* compare the incomes of Blacks and Whites with same educational experience, and repeat for males and females; and *(c)* compare the incomes of Blacks and Whites with different educational experience.
4. Working in pairs, each group will construct a line graph based on the table.
5. Using the line graphs that students have constructed, the teacher will ask students to state their views on the following questions: Is there a correlation between education completed and median income earned? Is the discrimination in salaries between the total population and the Black population with equal educational experience fair? What about the income differences between males and females?

■ Day 2

Materials

1. Poster displaying the information in Tables 2 and 3
2. Individual copies of the table
3. Rulers, protractors, and compasses

Activities

1. Each group will receive a copy of Tables 2 and 3, and a larger model of these tables will appear on the front blackboard.
2. The teacher will direct students in the method of reading the chart to find the number and percent of population each racial group comprises in a profession.
3. The teacher will ask students to orally *(a)* state the percent of females, Whites, Blacks, and Hispanic Americans in each of the professions listed; *(b)* compare the percents between racial and gender groups; and *(c)* compare the percent of a race in each profession to the percent that race comprises of the U. S. population; repeat the comparison for gender.
4. Working in pairs, each group will construct circle graphs for three of the professions listed.
5. Using the circle graphs that groups have constructed, ask students to orally state their views on the following: Are Blacks and Hispanic Americans adequately represented in professions based on their population in the United States? Are females? What are the negative ramifications for groups who are not adequately represented in professions? Students should consider economic, social, and psychological ramifications. Will the percent of women and minority races in professions increase or decrease in the future?

Reprinted with permission from the author.

Women in the World   Georgia Duncan-Ladd[56]

Goal

To combat racism, prejudice, and discrimination perpetrated globally, nationally, and locally

Core Values

Respect for human diversity and universal human rights.

Educational Goals

Students will understand the global experiences of women and their contributions to their communities.

Objectives

Students will be able to identify, list, and compare the similarities and differences, the continuities and contrasts among women around the world.

Lesson Opener

Present the students with two exercises using the handouts: "Traits That Are Female or Male" and "Traits That Jobs Require." Compare the results upon completion of the lesson. (See lists below.)

Traits That Are Female or Male

Which traits do you believe are naturally female or male?

1. Emotional
2. Creative thinking
3. Dependent
4. Cruel
5. Forceful
6. Passive
7. Yielding
8. Aggressive
9. Gossipy
10. Natural leader
11. Desires to be protected
12. Selfish
13. Good in math
14. Intuitive
15. Caring
16. Creative
17. Intelligent
18. Dominant
19. Warm personality
20. Holds up in a crisis

Traits That Jobs Require

Using the twenty traits as a checklist, pick the two traits you consider most important for each of the occupations listed here. The jobs are suitable for women and men.

LESSON 8.16

(Continued)

1. U.S. senator
2. Nurse
3. Secretary
4. Electrician
5. Salesperson
6. Soldier
7. Banker
8. Cook
9. Librarian
10. Florist
11. Lawyer
12. Painter
13. Bartender
14. Mathematician
15. Nursery-school teacher
16. Engineer
17. Construction worker
18. Housekeeper
19. Interior designer
20. Social worker

Instructional Activities

Most women in the world, like most men, lead humble lives. What is striking, though, is how different women's ordinary lives are from men's ordinary lives. We cannot understand our world without understanding the everyday experiences of women. We cannot assume that all women are the same or in the same situation, but we can assume that women everywhere are worse off than men. They have less power, less autonomy, more work, less money, and more responsibility. Nowhere in the world are women [societally] equal to men.

For women, there are no developed countries. While many countries provide formally for sexual equality in law, very few governments have legislation to protect specific job and marriage rights. Nowhere do women have full equal rights with men. Women are biologically stronger, they live longer than men, and naturally outnumber them. In countries where they do not, it is only because of the effects of war, forced migration in search of work, or severe and systematic discrimination. (See the first section of Women in the World from *Women in the World Atlas,* Simon & Schuster Inc., New York, NY 10020, 1986.)

Women everywhere share primary responsibility for having and rearing children, for forming and maintaining families, and for contraception. Globally they share the fight for women's rights, for other civil rights, and for peace. They are victims of rape, health traumas from illegal abortions, and pornography. The fate of women is a critical detriment to human society.

1. Discuss one historian's view of the development of the traditional American life. (Adapted from "Backgrounds of the American Family" by Willystine Goodsell, from *Marriage and the Family* by Howard Becker and Reuben Hill, eds.)
2. Have students answer and discuss the following questions:
   a. What was the position of women in England and America in the 1700s?
   b. How does Goodsell think the American family has changed?
   c. What are the key factors that influenced the American family to change?
3. Have the students submit a brief analysis of their view of the following question: What do you think was gained by the changes in the American family just described? What may have been lost? What other conditions in the United States might have led to role changes?

(Continued)

4. Using the *Women in the World Atlas* (see above), present and discuss the following topics and data:

Marriage:	Young brides, domestic disorders, social surgery, single states
Motherhood:	Mothers, population policies, contraception and abortion, birth and death, birth care, families
Work:	Time budgets, agriculture, labor force, out to work, migrant workers, job ghettos, earnings, job protection
Resources:	Access to means, education, refugees
Welfare:	Illness and health, poverty
Authority:	The vote, government, crime, military service, body and mind, the media
Body politics:	Beauty contest, sex for sale, rape
Change:	Channels of change, protest.

Materials

Handouts "Traits That Are Female or Male" and "Traits That Jobs Require," *Male and Female in Today's World, Curriculum Development,* Harcourt Brace Jovanovich Inc., 757 Third Avenue, New York, NY, 10017, pp. 14–15, 20–21.
Copies of "What's the, Difference" trivia by Jane Barr Stump, in *How Men and Women Compare,* William Morrow, 1985.
Blackboard
Overhead projector

Practice Activities

Guided practice: The reading of graphs and tables to understand the data presented along with questions and discussions of the status of women in the world. (See above source *Women in the World Atlas.*)

Independent practice: Students will be divided into groups and asked to bring in evidence of male and female roles in other cultures. These will be presented to the class by the groups as a paper.

Evaluation

Based on student verbal and written demonstration of the objectives of the lesson.

Bibliography

Fry, Gladys-Marie. *Night Riders in Black Folk History.* University of Tennessee Press, Nashville 1975.
Gerson, Antell, and Walter Harris. *Current Issues in American Democracy.* Amsco School Publications, New York, 1982.

LESSON 8.16 *(Continued)*

Manning, Marable. *From the Grassroots, Social and Political Essays towards Afro-American Liberation.* South End Press, Boston, MA, 1980.

Meier, August, and Elliott Rudwick. *From Plantation to Ghetto.* McGraw-Hill Ryerson Ltd., Toronto, 1976.

Puttin' on Ole Massa. Edited by Gilbert Osofsky. Harper & Row Publishers, New York, 1969.

Sitkoff, Harvard. *The Struggle for Black Equality 1954–1980.* Hill and Wang, New York, 1981.

Reprinted with permission from the author.

Goal Five: Raising Awareness of the State of the Planet and Global Dynamics

An awareness of the state of the planet and global dynamics consists of the second and fourth dimensions of Hanvey's "attainable global perspective." Hanvey defines his second dimension as an "awareness of prevailing world conditions and developments, including emergent conditions and trends, e.g., population growth, migrations, economic conditions, resources and physical environment, political developments, science and technology, law, health, inter-nation and intra-nation conflicts, etc."[57]

■ The world can best be understood as a singular, complex global system.[58]

■ An individual's private and collective decisions and behaviors influence for better or worse the future of the world system.[59]

■ Multiple loyalties are possible, that is, humans can be committed to a series of concentric groups such as family, religion, nation, and all of humankind.[60]

■ Knowledge and understanding of problems facing the global ecosystem will enable and motivate students to participate effectively and responsibly in the world community.

Hanvey stresses examining the media and political thought when attempting to gain further awareness of global conditions and dynamics. What is important is not whether the information from these sources will shed any light on the subject but rather the recognition of the students that these sources lack and distort information and, in some cases, even withhold it. Typically, the media focus on extraordinary events, for example, an outbreak in influenza or a rapid decline on the stock exchange rather than on the long-standing poverty of hundreds of millions or endemic malaria. There are significant limits and distortions in what we can learn from the news media. Political ideology is another source of distortion since it limits access to information about certain nations, for example, the former Soviet Union, Cuba, South Africa, and China during the Cultural Revolution. Political ideology also distorts what we know about the testing of nuclear weapons, and the disposal of nuclear wastes.

Hanvey points out that the technical nature of much of the data about the world is another important deterrent to developing an awareness of the state of the planet. He illustrates his case with an example of the depletion of ozone in the stratosphere. Is this a problem that can be widely understood by the world's populace? Or is it destined to remain "within the private realms of specialists?" Hanvey makes a strong case for the former, provided that educators become involved. "If from the earliest grades on students examined and puzzled over cases where seemingly innocent behaviors—the diet rich in animal protein, the lavish use of fertilizer on the suburban lawn and golf course—are shown to have effects that were both unintended and global in scope, then there could be a receptivity for the kind of information involved in the ozone case."[61] The notion of global "unintended effects" brings us to dimension four, knowledge of global dynamics, which Hanvey defines as "some modest comprehension of key traits and mechanisms of the world system, with emphasis on theories and concepts that may increase intelligent consciousness of global change."[62]

Knowing both that causes and effects are complex and interactive and that "simple events ramify—unbelievably" is essential to an understanding of the world as a system.[63] There are often surprise effects. Hanvey illustrates this with descriptions of unanticipated results from adding new species to a pond, farm wagons to the Papago community, and the introduction of bottle feeding technology to Third World nations, which led to such surprise effects as infant mortality, poor growth and brain development, and economic loss. How can this goal be developed in the curriculum? Hanvey provides teachers with four targets to help students comprehend technological innovation and change:

1. Sensitize students to the global consequences of technological decisions, for example, stratospheric ozone depletion.
2. Help students imagine the unimaginable, for example, abolishing certain technologies such as nuclear energy because of the problem of nuclear wastes.
3. Examine our beliefs about the naturalness and goodness of technological change and the naturalness and goodness of economic growth.
4. Help students understand the dynamics of feedback and the characteristics of exponential growth.

A world system paradigm similar to Hanvey's is central to the work of most, if not all, global educators in the United States. (It is also an essential part of this book's vision of multicultural education!) Lee Anderson, for example, who is a founding leader in global education, identifies four characteristics of the world system paradigm that are essential to the curriculum:

1. Humankind as a biologically, historically, and culturally interlinked species of life
2. Planet Earth as a global ecosystem
3. The global social order as the basis for human social and ecological organization
4. Each member of the human species as responsible participatory citizens in the global social order[64]

Lesson Plans That Develop State of the Planet Awareness

The next lesson can be used in junior or senior high school during the study of North America and Europe.

Acid Rain   *Maureen Reynolds*

LESSON 8.17

Global Education Rationale

Acid rain is a form of environmental pollution caused by industrial activities. Because the acids that fall in acid rain can travel for hundreds of miles in the atmosphere, they cross national boundaries, causing pollution in countries that do not produce the acid pollution. Some of the damage done by acid rain is probably irreversible. Students need to be sensitive to the global consequences of technological and industrial activities on the environment and to consider the possibility that preserving the environment may mean that people, including Americans, may have to dramatically alter their lifestyles. The core values stressed in this lesson plan are responsibility to the world community and reverence for the earth.

Goals

- Students will become familiar with the causes and effects of acid rain.
- Students will consider which course of action should be taken with respect to acid rain.

Objective

All the students will participate in a values clarification lesson concerning acid rain and the environment.

Materials

Blackboard
Videocassette recorder
Television
Video "Acid Rain: More Bad News," NOVA, John D. & Catherine T. MacArthur
   Foundation Library Video Classics Project. New York: Ambrose Video Publishing, Inc., 1985. 57 minutes. The video shows damage done by acid rain to forests, lakes, and buildings in the United States, West Germany, and Sweden. It discusses how acid rain is formed and how it travels in the atmosphere. Scientists, public officials and private citizens are interviewed.

Activities

1. Ask the students what is acid rain and what does it do when it comes into contact with flesh, paints, animals, rocks, or soil. Based on their answers, have them guess what acid rain is.

(Continued)

2. Show the video "Acid Rain: More Bad News."

3. After the video is viewed, ask the students what things can be done to reduce acid rain or its effects. Have assigned students write each alternative with its resulting consequences on the blackboard (each alternative will have its own student).

4. Have students orally propose what they think are the economic, environmental, lifestyle, and health consequences for each listed alternative.

5. By hand, have all students vote for an alternative. Note who voted for what alternatives. Ask students why they voted for a particular alternative. If the class is unanimous, ask why they did not vote for the other alternatives.

6. Ask students how they feel about acid rain and their choice. Does acid rain scare them? Would they rather not think about it? Are they willing to give up material things and conveniences to reduce acid rain? Why do they feel that way? What is more important, a healthy environment or a productive economy? Why do they feel that way? Do they really think that their choice would help the acid rain problem? Do they feel that knowing about acid rain is important? Why?

7. Ask the students what they can do now about acid rain. If the students cannot think of anything, suggest that they write public officials and government agencies to find out their stand on acid rain and other environmental issues and to urge them to take action on such issues. Also, they may attend rallies and be more conscious of themselves as polluters.

Evaluation

• Through observation during the class, the teacher will determine whether most of the students are giving or are able to give reasons for their position.

• On their unit test, the students will be able to accurately discuss the effects of acid rain on lakes, forests, and buildings.

Reprinted with permission of the author.

Lesson 8.18 was written for a ninth-grade biology class.

Ecological Succession

Lisa M. Blank

On May 18, 1980, Mount Saint Helens exploded. The shock waves of that explosion leveled virtually all the fir trees in an area of approximately 18,000 hectares. The accompanying mudflows, traveling at speeds of up to 80 kilometers per hour, buried most of the remaining vegetation. The affected land is now in the process of resuming a state of growth and production. Those species first to appear, such as the plant Lupinus lepidus, have special features that allow them to flourish in this harsh environment. Such species will eventually yield to species better adapted for high-density communities; and so goes the process of ecological succession.

LESSON 8.18

(Continued)

The process of ecological succession can be altered by natural events, such as the eruption of Mount St. Helens, or by human activities. Human activities that result in incidents such as nutrient loading can speed up or alter ecological succession. It is important to understand such impacts of humanity on our environment, for the effects can be, and usually are, far more serious than the impact of the explosion of Mount St. Helens. By first understanding how our actions affect our environment, we can then begin to act in ways that promote a healthy environment, rather than a scarred and neglected one.

Goal

This lesson is designed to teach students about ecological succession. Multicultural/ global education will be addressed in the application phase of the lesson; specifically, appreciation of the interconnectedness of humans and the environment will be explored (awareness of the "State of the Planet" and global dynamics).

Objectives

1. Observe a pictorial record of an ecological succession that has occurred on the school grounds.
2. Define ecological succession and describe the process, including discussion of succession in at least two different ecosystems, for example, dunes and lakes.
3. Define eutrophication and list its effects on lakes and aquatic life.
4. Observe the effect of nutrient loading on plant communities.
5. Observe the effect of detergent on plant communities.
6. Participate in a group presentation where students will be given an environment where succession is being unnaturally sped up by anthropomorphic effects. Students will explain in general terms the effects of premature succession and their solutions to the given problem.

Materials Needed

Photographs of ecological succession
Overheads of the succession process
Four planters per group of students
Clean sand
Oats or wheat
Distilled water
Liquid plant food
Ruler
Pond or aquarium water
Two liter jars per group of students
Detergent
Styrofoam cups
Radish or beet seeds
Potting soil

(Continued)

Lesson Procedures

Lesson Opener/Exploration

1. Have the students list as many different ecosystems as they can think of. List these on the board and ask the students to guess which ecosystems are the oldest and which are the youngest.
2. Introduce the subject of succession and explain that ecologists now have a well-defined theory for understanding how old or young an ecosystem is.
3. Discuss a series of photographs taken on the school grounds that depict succession. At least ten different photographs should be used.

Concept Introduction

1. Define ecological succession and introduce the different stages of ecological succession using several different ecosystems—lakes, forests, grasslands, and so forth.
2. Discuss the fact that the natural succession is often sped up by human's interactions with the environment.
3. Introduce the concept of eutrophication and discuss its effects upon lake systems.

Concept Application

1. Split the class in half. Divide each half of the class into groups of two to four. Have one half of the class conduct an experiment on the effect of nutrient loading on plant communities and have the other half conduct an experiment on the effect of detergent on plant communities. (See Lab Investigations.)
2. Display the students' graphs and discuss the results with the class. Each group should turn in a lab report.
3. Using the same groups of students, give each group a scenario that describes a certain ecosystem. Have the group determine what stage of succession that ecosystem is in. Then introduce a human factor that has increased the rate of succession of the particular ecosystem. Have the group discuss the effect of the impact of this factor and their solutions to the problem. The group's comments should be presented in a five-minute group presentation. This will require the group to conduct outside research.

Lab Investigation: Effect of Detergent[65]

Materials (per setup)

two liter jars
detergent
soil
two Styrofoam cups
radish or beet seeds

(Continued)

Procedure

1. Fill two liter jars ¾ full with tap water.
2. Add 1 ml detergent to one jar.
3. Label the jars detergent water and tap water.
4. Put soil in two Styrofoam cups and label them the same way.
5. Plant 3 radish or beet seeds in each cup about 1 cm deep.
6. Place the cups in a sunny window.
7. Water each plant daily with 30 ml of solution labeled on the cup.
8. Record the growth of each plant for 3 weeks and see which germinates first and which grows faster.
9. Record your measurements on a graph.

Lab Investigation: Effect of Nutrient Loading[66]

Materials (per setup)

four planters
washed sand
oats or wheat
distilled water
liquid plant food
ruler

Procedure

1. Place approximately five inches of sand in four different pots. The sand needs to be washed to remove any salt or minerals.
2. Plant five oat or wheat seeds in each pot. Plant the seeds about one-half an inch below the surface of the sand.
3. Water two of the pots with distilled water and mark. Water the remaining two pots with the liquid plant food.
4. Keep all the pots in a cool, dark place until the seeds germinate. Then put the plants in the light.
5. Continue watering your plants as described. You may choose how often you wish to water your plants as long as you are consistent.
6. Record when you water the plants, the measurements of the plants' growth, and any other observations.
7. After three weeks, summarize what evidence you have that there are differences in the plants' growth.
8. Explain why there might be a difference in growth rates.
9. Make a graph to show the results of the lab. The horizontal axis should be marked in even intervals to correspond to those days the measurements were taken. The vertical axis should be marked off in inches for the plant height.

Reprinted with permission from the author.

LESSON 8.19

Chemical and Biological Warfare — *Lynn Bryan*

Grade Level

High school chemistry or biology

Rationale

The use of chemical weapons is both a technological and societal issue currently facing the world community. This lesson is intended to provoke students to reflect on the global consequences of decisions involved in chemical and biological warfare. Students will have an opportunity to reflect on their own ethical beliefs and values and make informed, hypothetical decisions about the research, production, and use of chemical weapons.

Goals

- To provide students with a basic understanding of how nerve gas affects the human motor system.
- To provide students with the skills and knowledge that they may intelligently predict and evaluate both the short-term and long-term impact (moral, ethical, and physical) of chemical and biological warfare on the human race.
- To acquaint students with perspectives from and by which various interest groups (scientists, politicians, peace activists, etc.) judge the issue of chemical and biological warfare research, production, and use.

Objectives

Students will be able to:
1. Successfully complete the laboratory activity;
2. Verbally formulate an explanation for his/her observations and actively partake in class discussions about the various student explanations;
3. Correctly define or give examples of the terms in Concept Introduction 3;
4. Actively participate in group activity to come up with a model of how nerve gases affect the human motor system and engage in the class discussion about the various group models;
5. Contribute to the round-table discussion concerning various perspectives of chemical and biological warfare.

Process Skills Used by Students

collecting information
communicating
critical thinking
identifying cause and effect
hypothesizing
inferring

9
1.
8
N
O
S
S
E
L

(Continued)

interpreting data
observing
predicting
problem solving
valuing

Materials

Article by David C. Tucker, "A Safe Lab on Nerve Gases." Laboratory activity and materials (listed under Laboratory Activity).
Article by Slesnick and Miller entitled "Difficult Decisions: Chemical Warfare" from *Science Teacher 55*, pp. 31–33, February 1988.
Discussion questions (copy attached)
Bibliography (copy attached)

Procedures

Concept Exploration

1. Review laboratory activity.
2. Prepare necessary solutions before students arrive for the laboratory activity.
3. Divide students into groups of two to four students per group.
4. Have students perform the laboratory activity.

Concept Introduction

1. Discuss the observations the students had during concept exploration. Record student responses on board or flip chart.
2. Brainstorm!! Have students formulate explanations for their observations.
3. Introduce or review the terms: neurotransmitters, neuron, synapse, synaptic cleft, postsynaptic cleft, enzyme, bromelain, acetylcholine, acetylcholinesterase, nerve gases, chemical and biological warfare.
4. Divide students into groups again. Allow time for each group to come up with a model of how nerve gases affect the enzyme acetylcholinesterase in the human body. The students may wish to use the library. Provide references as listed in attached bibliography.
5. Allow each group to present its proposed mechanisms. As a class, discuss and evaluate the proposals. Select as a class a mechanism that provides the most feasible explanation of how nerve gases work.
6. If time permits, review with the class the Questions for Further Thought listed at the end of the lab activity.

Concept Application/Evaluation

1. Have students read "Difficult Decisions: Chemical Warfare" by Irwin L. Slesnick and John A. Miller, *Science Teacher 55*, pp. 31–33, February 1988.
2. Lead a round-table discussion using the list of Questions to Consider to provoke discussion.

(Continued)

Chemical Warfare Laboratory Activity[67]

Materials

cheesecloth

one blender

hot plates for each lab group

seven test tubes for each lab group

one 200-mL beaker for each lab group

one box of gelatin for each lab group

two average-sized *fresh* pineapples

rock salt

50 mL of 6 M NaOH

50 mL of 6 M HCl

50 mL of 2% $CuSO_4$

500 mL of 0.1 M sodium phosphate buffer (Chemicals needed for buffer include 4.75 g of sodium monohydrogen phosphate, 1 g of cysteine, 6 M NaOH, 0.1 M NaOH, and 0.1 M HCl.)

safety goggles for each student

plastic gloves for each student

lab aprons for each student

copies of the article "The Neuron" by C. F. Stevens[68]

The instructor should prepare the following solutions before beginning the lab:

- *Sodium Phosphate Buffer, 0.1 M:* To prepare buffer, you will need 4.75 g of sodium monohydrogen phosphate, 1 g of cysteine, 6 M NaOH, 0.1 M NaOH, and 0.1 M HCl. Dissolve the sodium monohydrogen phosphate in 500 ml H_2O. Adjust pH of the buffer within range of pH 7.0 using the 6 M NaOH. Use the 0.1 M NaOH of 0.1 HCl to adjust the buffer pH to exactly pH 7.0. Add the cysteine.

- *Enzyme Solution:* Discard skin and core of pineapple. Cut the remainder into small pieces. Add 50 g of the fresh pineapple to 35 mL of the buffer. Homogenize this mixture in the blender for about 1 minute. Filter the slurry through the cheesecloth to remove the pulp. The juice obtained contains the enzyme bromeliad.

- *Ice Water—Salt Mixture:* Add rock salt to an ice-water slurry in a large tray until the temperature of the mixture reaches -10°C.

Procedure

Divide the class into groups of two to four students each. You may wish to have students read Charles F. Stevens's article "The Neuron" from *Scientific American* before beginning the experiment. This article provides an excellent review of the structure and function of neurons.

Each lab group will need seven test tubes in which to prepare the experimental solutions. Each lab group will do the following:

LESSON 8.19 *(Continued)*

1. Label test tubes as follows: Tube 1 control, Tube 2 untreated enzyme, Tube 3 heat, Tube 4 cold, Tube 5 base, Tube 6 acid, and Tube 7 heavy metal.
2. Add 1 mL H_2O to test tube 1.
3. Add 1 mL of juice to each of the other six tubes.
4. Set aside tubes 1 and 2.
5. Treat tubes 3 through 7 as follows:

   Tube 3: Heat sample in boiling water for 5 minutes.
   Tube 4: Freeze sample in ice-salt-water mixture for 10 minutes and then thaw.
   Tube 5: Add 5 drops of 6 *M* NaOH. Mix and let stand for 5 minutes. Add 5 drops of 6 *M* HCl and mix again.
   Tube 6: Add 5 drops of 6 *M* HCl. Mix and let stand for 5 minutes. Add 5 drops of 6 *M* NaOH and mix again.
   Tube 7: Add 5 drops of the 2% $CuSO_4$.

6. Prepare gelatin solution by dissolving contents of gelatin package in 125 mL of boiling H_2O. Remove the solution from the hot plate and stir constantly while it is cooling.
7. Carefully add 1 mL of the warm gelatin solution to each of the seven test tubes.
8. Mix each test tube thoroughly by inversion. This step is very important, as incomplete mixing will result in inconclusive results. If you notice any layering of colors in the test tubes, the ingredients are not adequately mixed.
9. Cool all of the test tubes in an ice-water bath (no salt), being careful not to freeze their contents.
10. Record all observations. The following results should be expected:

    Tube 1: Rapid gelation occurs; no bromelain present.
    Tube 2: Gelation does not occur; active bromelain present.
    Tube 3: Gelation occurs; bromelain denatured.
    Tube 4: Gelation does not occur; active bromelain present,
    Tube 5: Gelation occurs; bromelain denatured.
    Tube 6: Gelation occurs; bromelain denatured.
    Tube 7: Gelation occurs; bromelain inhibited.

The instructor may wish to refer to David C. Tucker's article for further information regarding the laboratory activity.

After students complete this activity, the instructor should discuss the groups' observations, possibly recording the different observations on the board. After a discussion of the results, allow students to brainstorm in groups and develop an explanation for what they observed in each of the test tubes. Then review with the students the article that they read before beginning the activity. Using what they have learned from their work in the laboratory and from their prelaboratory and postlaboratory work, students should be able to develop a model of how nerve gases affect the enzyme acetylcholinesterase. Allow students to work in groups. Give the students class time to research in the library if they wish to do so. One by one, have each group present its mechanisms to the class. Ask students to discuss, criticize, and evaluate each others' proposed mechanisms.

(Continued)

Questions For Further Thought

1. Directions on Jell-O gelatin packages state that fresh and frozen pineapple should not be used. Does this agree with your observations from the experiment?
2. Directions on Jell-O gelatin packages state that canned pineapple can be used. Explain why. (Hint—pineapple is heated during the canning process.)
3. Adolph's Meat Tenderizer contains the proteolytic enzyme papain (extract from papaya). Axion Detergent Presoak contains a mixture of proteolytic enzymes. What would happen if you added either of these substances to gelatin? Explain.
4. How does Axion remove bloodstains? Explain. (Hint—blood contains the protein hemoglobin.)[69]

Questions to Consider

1. The Germans discovered and produced nerve gas in the 1930s. They tested and used it on prisoners in concentration camps. They never used it against the Soviets or the British, even when their victory was threatened. Why do you think they did not use their nerve gas?[70]
2. Soldiers were ordered to attend the testing of nuclear weapons in the 1950s. Do you think the military should have the right to ask a soldier to volunteer or to order a soldier to participate in a test of an incapacitating agent?[71]
3. Suppose during World War II either Japan or the United States (but not both) had had highly effective nonlethal incapacitating agents. How might the war have been different?[72]
4. Do you think our military should be conducting research to develop nonlethal physically incapacitating agents? Why or why not?[73]
5. What are the ethical implications of using animals for such research? It has been documented that chemicals that incapacitate animals may have different effects on human subjects. What solutions, if any, can you provide researchers to overcome this dilemma?
6. The United States military expenditures for chemical warfare have exceeded $1 billion per year. Approximately 20 percent of the budget goes toward the research and development of physical incapacitants. How important do you feel it should be to allot some of the budget for the research and development of antidotes for existing incapacitating agents?
7. In South Korea, police broke up student riots with the use of tear gases and Mace. What are your thoughts about the use of nonlethal chemical agents? When, if ever, is their use ethical?
8. Assume that decades of high-priority research have produced incapacitating agents that can immobilize people as effectively as nerve gases can kill them. Under what conditions should these incapacitating agents be used? Should they be used strategically (against an enemy's ability to make war)?

LESSON 8.19

(Continued)

Tactically (on the battlefield)? Against terrorists? Against rioting prison inmates?[74]

9. How do you think other nations would react to the first use of incapacitating agents?[75]

10. Since the 1925 Geneva Protocol, chemical warfare has been used by the Italians against the Ethiopians, Japanese against the Chinese, and the Iraqis against the Iranians. What do you think should be done about countries who use chemical warfare even though the Geneva Protocol outlawed first-strike use of chemical and biological warfare? Who should enforce the rule and how?

11. Although the Geneva Protocol outlaws the use of chemical and biological weapons, it does not ban the production or the stockpiling of such weapons. Is this logical? Why or why not?

12. Suppose Country X unleashed mustard and cyanide gas on Country Y. It was reported by reliable sources that Country Z supplied component parts vital to the production of the poisonous gases to Country X. What are your feelings toward Country Z? Would your feelings differ depending on which countries are allies and which are enemies of your own country (e.g., if X is an enemy country and both Y and Z are allies, or if both X and Z are allies and Y is an enemy country)?

Bibliography

"Bad Chemistry." *New Republic* 190 (21 May 1984):7–9. Cookson, J., and J. Nottingham. *A Survey of Chemical and Biological Warfare.* New York: Monthly Review Press, 1969.

Hersh, S. *Chemical and Biological Warfare.* Indianapolis: Bobbs-Merrill, 1968.

Jones, M., et al. *Chemistry and Society.* Philadelphia: Saunders College, 1987.

Martin, D., and J. Sampugna. *Molecules in Living Systems: A Biochemistry Module.* New York: Harper & Row, 1978.

Morrisey, D. "The Return of Chemical Warfare." *The Progressive* 46 (February 1982):25–28.

Reigh, D. "Bromelain." *Journal of Chemical Education* 53 (June 1976):386.

Slesnick, I., and J. Miller "Difficult Decisions: Chemical Warfare." *Science Teacher* 55 (February 1988):31–33.

Smolowe, J. "The Search for a Poison Antidote." *Time* 133 (16 January 1989):22.

Stevens, C. "The Neuron." *Scientific American* 241 (September 1979):55–65.

Stockholm International Peace Research Institute. *The Problem of Chemical and Biological Warfare,* Vols. 1–6. New York: Humanities Press, 1971.

Tucker, D. "A Safe Lab on Nerve Gases." *Science Teacher* 55 (February 1988): 27–30.

Reprinted with permission of the author.

Global Conflict and Consequences

Alta Bertrand

Goals

- To promote global peace through knowledge and understanding.
- To sensitize students to the potential for human suffering when human rights are violated or denied.

Objectives

This unit should help students to:

1. Gain an understanding of the nature of the dual holocausts of World War II,
2. Develop an understanding of the moral issues in wartime;
3. Develop critical thinking skills through having to choose and defend a position on nuclear warfare; and
4. Appreciate the need for ethnic understanding on a global basis.

Rationale

Literature, drama, and film can, and should, play a prominent role in helping students develop principles and values. Racism and greed are destructive forces that often lead to oppression and war. If these evils are to be eradicated in the future, students must learn the lessons of history and philosophy. The arts provide a means to that end. The students of today will be the decision makers of tomorrow, and if we are to have global harmony, these future world citizens must acquire the knowledge and understanding that will enable them to reach that goal. The creative arts provide an excellent means for generating empathy, a vital component in successful multicultural interaction.

Performance Objectives

1. Students will read and be prepared to discuss a nonfiction account of the nuclear holocaust (see Materials, part C).
2. Students will view and be prepared to discuss a documentary on the Nazi Holocaust (see Materials, part D).
3. Students will read a play on the morality of nuclear warfare (see Materials, part E)
4. Students will perform the play for other English classes.
5. Students will write a position paper on use of nuclear weapons.

Procedures

1. Lectures
2. Films
3. Two discussion formats: full-class open discussion featuring I. S. (Inferential Strategy) questioning and small group (panel)
4. Supervised preparation and performance of dramatic presentation
5. Student participation: read assigned material, view films, discuss, take notes, evaluate information, present a play, and write an essay

(Continued)

Evaluation

1. Formative (periodic assessments of understanding and of affective manifestations)
2. Participation (open forum, group discussions, play)
3. Essay (Judgment will be made on the following criteria: development of position arguments, logic, coherence, structure, syntax, spelling, and punctuation.)

Materials

Lecture outlines (attached)

Lists of questions for class and group discussions (attached)

Hiroshima by John Hersey (New York: Bantam Books, 1946, 1986). The true story of six of the survivors of the atomic bomb attack on Hiroshima during World War II, this book enables students to view the holocaust from the perspective of those upon whom it was perpetrated. It also provides in-depth character studies of those involved, revealing the similarities and differences between individuals in the Japanese culture and our own. Its graphic descriptions of the horror of the aftermath are grim reminders of an event the world must never be allowed to forget.

Anne Frank: A Legacy for Our Time by Video Recording (New York: Anti-Defamation League, 1988).

Two filmstrips that explore the story of Anne Frank and her legacy:

The Story of Anne Frank. 19 minutes b/w.

The story of Anne Frank unfolds as portions of her diary reveal how the different periods of her life were shaped by world events: her early years in Germany, her childhood in Amsterdam, the two years spent in hiding in the "secret annex," and her tragic end in the Bergen-Belsen concentration camp.

The Lesson of Anne Frank. 19 minutes b/w.

Using the Anne Frank story as a catalyst, the filmstrip examines the relationship between prejudice and discrimination, identifies the elements of fascism, and describes the roles played by propaganda and scapegoating when they are exploited by fascists. It shows how Jews and other groups were treated by the Nazis and examines neofascist groups that exist today.

Dunbar's Bremen.: A Morality Play for the Nuclear Age by James A. Stengenga (Bloomington: Indiana Consortium for Security Studies, 1981). A morality play in one act on the use of tactical nuclear weapons. A NATO general, Frank Dunbar, is fired and arrested for refusing a direct presidential order to use tactical nuclear weapons against the Soviet forces during an escalation of a conventional war in Europe. The debate is between those who think it would be the most efficient means to an end, and those who believe in the principle of proportionality and discrimination. The fact that the United States was the only nation ever to have crossed the nuclear threshold complicates the situation, as does the notion of the "slippery slope" into all-out nuclear confrontation. General Dunbar's wife introduces the pacifist philosophy into the debate that then turns to the distinction between penultimate and ultimate values. (*Penultimate:* sovereignty; territorial boundaries; the existing political and economic order; defense of the state; national credibility; national "honor." *Ultimate:* life; liberty; justice; hap-

(Continued)

piness; dignity; well-being; human rights; human interests.) There is no resolution. The play ends as the newscaster reports that the Soviets are preparing to retaliate for our first use. This doomsday play should engender respect in the students for the awesome responsibility they are about to inherit.

Daily Lesson Plans

Sessions 1 and 2 (Preassigned Hiroshima)

I. Unit introduction lecture
  A. Format/Schedule
    1. Sessions 1 and 2: *Hiroshima* discussion
    2. Session 3: *Anne Frank* films viewing
    3. Sessions 4 and 5: *Dunbar's Bremen* and *Anne Frank* discussion
      a. discussion groups, assigned questions
      b. full-class discussion, share questions and responses
    4. Sessions 6 and 7: Assign parts and start rehearsal of play, *Dunbar's Bremen*
    5. Session 8: Present play to other English classes
    6. Session 9: Wrap-up discussion
    7. Session 10: In-class essay
  B. Explain evaluation (see Unit Plan)
II. Discussion on Hiroshima
  A. Unstructured, open forum (let students initiate topics and direction)
  B. I. S. questions to be used if needed to channel discussion:
    1. What are the cultural similarities between Japanese and Americans?
    2. What are the cultural differences?
    3. Is there diversity within Japanese culture?
    4. What are Japanese character traits? Individual and cultural?
    5. What are your feelings about dropping the bomb? On civilian targets?
    6. What is your assessment of Japanese/American interactions?
    7. What is the role of racism, if any? Institutionalized and individual?
    8. Should we use the bomb in future? Why?
  C. Homework
    1. Make notes on discussion for use in essay
    2. Start reading *Dunbar's Bremen*

Session 3

I. Show *Anne Frank* films
II. Homework
  A. Make notes on films
  B. Finish reading *Dunbar's Bremen*
  C. Makes notes on play for discussion and essay

Sessions 4 and 5

I. Discussion on *Anne Frank* films
  A. Unstructured, open forum (let students exchange ideas freely)

(Continued)

B. I. S. questions to be used to channel discussion if needed;
1. What was the role of racism in Germany?
2. What is the role of institutionalized racism in the United States?
3. What was the role of fascism in Nazi Holocaust?
4. Was the system or Hitler responsible for racism?
5. Is it ethical to use the results of medical experiments?
6. Could the same type of genocide occur here? Why? Why not?
7. Is there a comparable case of racism or genocide in our history?

II. Discussion on *Dunbar's Bremen* play
  A. Form six groups of three for discussion
1. Questions for Group 1:
   a. Is this hypothetical situation a real possibility?
   b. Could such a war begin in the future?
   c. What moral arguments does Frank use to justify his decisions, first to use some tactical nuclear weapons, but then to refuse?
   d. What was his dilemma?
   e. How did he resolve it?
2. Questions for Group 2:
   a. Whose arguments are the most convincing? Frank's or Vanderveen's? Frank's or Margaret's? The *New York Times*?
   b. How will history judge General Frank Dunbar?
   c. How will history judge President Vanderveen?
3. Questions for Group 3:
   a. As the play ends inconclusively, what do you imagine will happen next?
   b. Apocalypse? Surrender? Negotiated cease-fire?
   c. Will Frank become a hero?
   d. Will Frank be court-martialed?
   e. Will Frank be considered a martyr or a pariah?
4. Questions for Group 4:
   a. How does a religious person accommodate both the relatively permissive just war code (Frank's) and the more stringent Christian pacifism that Margaret expresses?
   b. How is the intellectual/moral tension between these two perspectives handled or reconciled, if at all?
5. Questions for Group 5:
   a. What do you think of Margaret's distinction between penultimate and ultimate values?
   b. How would you react if Margaret became a candidate for the U.S. Senate or the presidency?
   c. How would most Americans greet her candidacy? Why?
6. Questions for Group 6:
   a. Does the play work dramatically?
   b. Is it realistic and are the characters credible?
   c. Is the play too talky or too densely packed to play well?

(Continued)

   B. Open-forum discussion
     1. General questions for class discussion
        a. Is this play a good way to explore moral problems?
        b. What important lessons did you get from this play?
        c. What important lessons did you get from your group discussion?
     2. Groups share questions and responses
     3. Open debate—groups may challenge each other's views
   C. Homework
     1. Assign parts for play
        a. Three parts (two male, one female)
        b. Six English classes to perform for on Friday
        c. Assign parts for six entirely different casts (so that everyone will be included in performance)
        d. Students are to memorize their parts (assign a day)

Sessions 6 and 7

I. Rehearse play

Session 8

I. Perform play in auditorium (each group of three players to perform during the six consecutive English periods)

Session 9

I. Wrap-up discussion

Session 10

I. In-class Essay
   A. Position paper on use of nuclear weaponry
   B. Tie in *Hiroshima, Anne Frank* films, and *Dunbar's Bremen*
   C. Evaluation criteria: development of position arguments, logic, coherence, structure, syntax, spelling, and punctuation

Reprinted with permission of the author.

Goal Six: Developing Social Action Skills

Major problems threaten the future of the planet and the well-being of humanity. The aim of this goal is to give students the knowledge, attitudes, and skills that are necessary for active citizen participation. The emphasis is on thinking globally and acting locally and engendering a sense of personal and political efficacy and a participatory attitude, both of which are essential to the development of global responsibility among the citizens of the earth.

Underlying this goal are the following assumptions:

- The subjugation and unjust treatment of any cultural group dehumanizes everyone.
- Most people will, at some time in their lives, find themselves in the position of being a political minority.
- All groups in society should have equal opportunity to bring about social and political change.
- We value political access and participation for all citizens.
- The more learners can actively participate in decision-making activities and work on self-selected problems beyond the classroom, the more likely they are to increase their feelings of personal and political effectiveness.
- Citizens have a right to know about global crises that threaten human survival, and about actions that can be taken to lessen these problems.

This goal moves us beyond study, reflection, and analysis into a state of action. In view of the fact that certain ethnic groups and Third World nations are cut off from their fair share of the world's resources, suffer from poverty and starvation, serve as the world's dumping ground for toxic wastes, and are unable to gain, maintain, and effectively use political power, to ignore this goal would make the other goals meaningless.

The development of social action skills encompasses Hanvey's fifth dimension. He defines this dimension as "some awareness of the problems of choice confronting individuals, nations, and the human species as consciousness and knowledge of the global system expand."[76]

Decision-making skills are an integral part of these social action skills. This assumes that students can learn to identify alternative choices for themselves as well as for public policy-makers and that they can reflect upon the possible consequences of their choices.

There are special impediments to social action in the global arena that deserve attention. There is a lack of a global government and other appropriate institutions to carry out action plans at a global level. Joyce and Nicholson explain the situation this way:

> Although there are a number of agreed-on domains of international action in such fields as health, postal service, air traffic, weather observation, and international communications, most issues must be negotiated specifically in the absence of general policy. There is no universal language of learning comparable to Latin in the Middle Ages. The problem of creating international institutions, moreover, involves much more difficulty than merely extending existing national institutions to international dimensions. The deficiencies of the international monetary and legal systems point up this fact only too well. Added to this inherent difficulty are the differences in perceived self-interest among nations.[77]

Lack of mutual trust, cross-cultural misunderstandings, and differing world views compound the problem. A dramatic, if narrowly focused, incident concerning a novel written for young adolescents, *Monsoon: A Novel to End World Hunger,* illustrates the point.[78] The novel has received wide acclaim from American teachers and is thoroughly enjoyed by young American readers. But several visiting scholars from East Asian and Central African nations had a different reaction to the book. They found it offensive, patronizing, unrealistic, and misleading about the causes of world hunger. This criticism should not stop us from looking at this problem. Rather it should be a point of departure for discussing how people from different parts of the globe view the same problem. It could also lead to an examination of the necessary conditions for global collaboration for solving world hunger.

In her exemplary collection of teacher-designed curricula for peace education, Betty Reardon offers a variety of concepts and skills related to global responsibility.[79] Her book, *Educating for Global Responsibility,* contains thirty-five curricula plans for grades kindergarten through high school. The curricula cumulatively develop concepts, skills, and understandings related to peace education. Children begin with creative imagining in the early elementary grades and learn to express their fears about such things as nuclear war and share ways of coping with these fears. Teachers must be careful not to introduce materials that produce these fears in children. Children in grades four to six are introduced to problem-solving skills and learn that "people can and frequently do change society and resolve very grave, and overwhelming social problems."[80] Reardon stresses empowerment through the development of creative capacities and imagination via brainstorming, imaging, and model building. She urges that critical and analytical thinking skills be introduced during preadolescence, and high school students move on to ethical reflection and informed action. She writes

> Perhaps the most important attitude to be engendered [at this age level and above] is objectivity in the analysis of problems, an intention to examine all available evidence and views. It is also important to impart an understanding that to be objective is not to be neutral. One can hold values that have a direct bearing on an issue and still pursue objective knowledge of the facts. Ethical reflection is as important as consideration of the evidence.[81]

The case of apartheid in South Africa illustrates this point well. In examining the historical perspectives of Black South Africans, Coloreds, and White South Africans (both British and Dutch Afrikaans), students will better understand current events in South Africa. Knowledge about Afrikaner nationalism, which includes the belief in a God-given right to settle the land (similar to manifest destiny in the United States) and the racist socialization of young, White, South African children, will give students insight into the national government's actions. This understanding, however, is not the same as acceptance or approval of a system that violates the human rights of the Black population.

Although many educators feel schools should encourage students to be more effective agents of social change, the present curriculum is inadequate to meet this end.[82] Political socialization research, however, offers numerous insights into what kind of curricula and instructional strategies may be effective.[83] These insights range from simply encouraging class discussion of social issues, to political change case studies, small-group problem solving, and community action research. Writing in the early 1970s, an era of political activism, Bradbury Seasholes outlined the ingredients for teaching students to be active agents of change:

> Perhaps the greatest contribution educators can make to school-age . . . [youth] who will be tomorrow's adult citizens is to reorient their thinking about the de-

velopment and use of political strategy. This means spelling out with approval the various techniques of bargaining, forced demands, concession, and occasional retreat that are used by politically successful subgroups in our society. It means being candid on two scores when dealing with heterogeneous groups of students in the classroom—candid about the probable maximum of political potential that a given subgroup could have (just how successful groups can expect to be, given their total resources of numbers, money, effort, education, and so forth) and candid about the kind of political techniques that are in fact being used currently or may be used in the reasonably near future.

Political activity in this day and age, after all, involves not only voting, contributing money, and writing letters to congressmen. It sometimes involves street demonstrations and civil disobedience. These need talking out in the classroom too, not in normative terms but in terms of strategies which sometimes succeed or fail because they tread so close to the border of normatively acceptable political behavior.[84]

Today there may be a renewed interest in social activism, as seen in precollegiate service learning programs and revived interest in moral issues in education. Our students need opportunities to make choices and evaluate their decisions. They need to practice self-expression, decision-making skills, and problem resolution. This work practice can begin in kindergarten with opportunities to make simple choices, express opinions, set goals, and discuss classroom rules. Participatory learning can be expanded at the high school level to include simulations, service learning, and community or political action projects.

◼Lesson Plans That Develop Social Action Skills

The Cycle of Personal Alienation

LESSON 8.21

Socialization can be defined as a sociopsychological process, whereby the personality is created under the influence of educational institutions (and agents). Activities that help students understand this process should encourage students to use introspection to discover their own patterns of perception and work toward helping them become more empathetic. Thus the student begins within and moves outward. An examination of socialization processes, such as how people become who they are and learn to perceive and behave as they do, appears to be a valuable means of helping to break down perceptual and communication barriers between different ethnic and socioeconomic groups.

The possibilities for using this strategy in working toward the goals of cultural consciousness, intercultural competency, and eradication of ethnic and racial prejudice and discrimination are obvious. However, because of the impact of past behavior and experience on attitudes (including self-image) and future behavior, understanding of the socialization process is a crucial thread that ties the goal of social action skills to our conceptualization of multicultural education. If people are to become agents of change, they must understand the cycle of alienation (see

(Continued)

Figure 8.5), how they might be socialized into this cycle, how it might operate in their own lives, and how it might be broken.

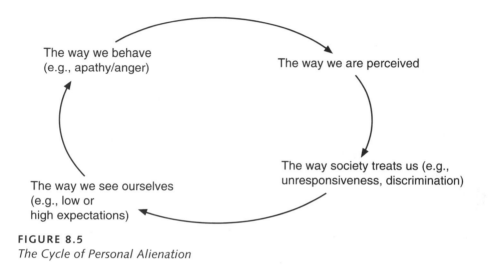

FIGURE 8.5
The Cycle of Personal Alienation

The activity that follows was designed specifically to develop students' understanding of this cycle. Although it focuses on attitudes about social or political issues, any feeling or belief can be substituted (for example, preferences in fashion, music, or food; concept of beauty; religion; attitudes toward different culture groups). When implemented among ethnically and socioeconomically diverse students, the exercise has proved to be a powerful means of enabling individuals to understand how they had been socialized politically, and the differences that exist in the political socialization of males, females, and different ethnic groups.

Students begin by examining their own values and attitudes, move on to analysis of how these attitudes and values developed (the socialization process), and are then asked to identify implications for their own lives. Once students have completed their individual reactions and recorded them on paper or tape, comparisons can be made across the lines of sex, race, and ethnicity.

Self-Analysis: How Did Your Attitudes Develop?

The topic of the next few activities is you. You will be exploring your own feelings and beliefs and attempting to discover how you developed them. The questions will help you begin. Answer them in a way that is meaningful to you; be as brief or as lengthy as you wish.

1. Describe your feelings and beliefs about the following (these may be modified according to student interest and knowledge background).
    School desegregation
    Capital punishment
    Voting in presidential elections
    Government welfare for unemployed mothers with dependent children

(Continued)

Participation in military service during time of war

Your city's police force

School prayer

Bilingual education in public schools

2. How important have each of the following been in influencing the feelings and beliefs you expressed above? (Just comment on the important ones and include specific examples.)

Your family (father, mother, other relatives)

Teachers

Friends

Church

Media (movies, TV, songs, books, newspapers)

Events and/or experiences

Other?

3. Considering the feelings and beliefs you have described, where would you place yourself on the following scales?

	Strongly Agree	Agree	Unsure	Disagree	Strongly Disagree
I am completely satisfied with how our society works.					
I feel that I can make a significant difference in how our society works if I want to change things.					
I believe most government officials and politicians can be trusted to do what's best.					

4. How will these attitudes affect your life?

To Take a Stand or to Not to Take a Stand

Students can develop decision-making skills if they are given an opportunity to act out a problematic situation in role play before they actually encounter it. Young children can use dolls, puppets, or masks made of decorated paper plates during the role play. Older students can be given role cards that define their new personality or they can be asked to empathize with a person in an open-ended situation. Examples of role playing that help build decision-making skills related to multicultural education goals are listed below. Students can be asked whether they would take a stand or not, depending on who they are (themselves, another actual

LESSON 8.22

(Continued)

person, or a contrived character). Wording would be modified according to students' grade level.

1. Your best friend uses a racial slur to insult a classmate.
2. You feel that your teacher is racist because Black/White/Latino students get away with murder in the classroom and you get punished for much less.
3. Your parent tells a cruel ethnic joke that cuts down _____ (insert name) at a family gathering.
4. You find out that the sorority/fraternity you want to join will not pledge anyone from a different race. You are/are not a member of the same race.
5. You are White and have a new job in a sporting-goods store. Your boss asks you to make a note of any Black person who cashes a check in the store.
6. One of your best friends in school is Black/Latino/White. You want to invite this friend to your birthday party but your parent(s) says no.
7. You catch a classmate cheating on an exam. The cheater is of a different race from you and you are afraid of being called prejudiced. Yet you know the cheater shared the exam with a small group of close friends, which raised the class curve, causing you and others to do poorly.
8. A teacher's purse was stolen by a tall Black person wearing an Afro. You are innocent, but because you fit the description you are called in for questioning and accused of the crime.
9. You have just learned that you will be transported by bus to a new school next year in a distant part of town. You hear that the parents in that neighborhood are angry and upset that you and classmates from your neighborhood are being brought in.
10. Before you came to the United States you loved school and were a good student. Now you understand little of what the teacher and classmates say, and you have been placed in a classroom for the mentally retarded.

No Man Is an Island: The Importance of Perspective in Decision Making

Karen Kulp

LESSON 8.23

Topic

An introduction to *jury selection* from a multicultural perspective for a unit on the *American Legal System*, Senior High School, Government class, 1 to 2 days.

Rationale for Multicultural and Global Education

The making of decisions and facing the consequences of decisions made by others will occur in many contexts and at all levels throughout a student's life: global, national, local, and family. It is therefore crucial that the student understand that de-

(Continued)

cisions are rarely made in a vacuum. Just as one's own life history influences one's judgment and perspective when faced with decision, so too does personal history influence the judgment and perspective of every person involved in a decision-making process.

The concept of a jury is a particularly interesting way to illustrate the above point. Because all U.S. citizens of voting age, who are of sound mind and who have not committed a felony, may be called to serve on a jury, the verdict reached by a jury will necessarily reflect the multitude of experiences and attitudes of those who serve.

In the course of this lesson, the student will find it necessary to exercise critical thinking skills by taking into account the variety of factors that may influence an individual's attitude, as well as demonstrate the ability to negotiate with a partner whose interest in the outcome of the case is diametrically opposed to his or her own. The above named factors make this lesson particularly suitable for use by a teacher interested in multicultural and global education.

Objective

Students will demonstrate critical thinking/inquiry skills by choosing prospective jurors for a court case involving drunk driving. In making their choices, students will be asked to consider the possible impact and interplay of various factors on the jurors' reaction to the case. Among these factors are race, sex, age, religious belief, and life history.

Procedure

Prepare the students' minds for learning by posing the following questions:

1. How many of you know someone who has ever driven a car while under the influence of alcohol?
2. How many of you know anyone who has suffered injury or death as a result of a driver who was under the influence of alcohol? How do, or would, you feel if this happened?

Allow time for discussion.

Introduce the lesson by explaining that you want the class to simulate the selection of a jury in a drunk driving case.

Hand out the Student Information Sheet and the list of prospective jurors.

Present the following information to the students:

1. Read your Student Information Sheet carefully. While reading it consider the impact (if any) that a prospective juror's race, sex, religious beliefs, and life history might have on his or her attitudes toward the defendant.
2. Each student will select his or her prospective jurors from the perspective of an attorney either for the prosecution or defense. (Teacher should assign roles and opposition partners at this time.)

(Continued)

3. Students should write down the three potential jurors they wish to eliminate, giving their reasons. They then join their partner who is playing an attorney for the opposing side. The two attorneys must negotiate in order to seat a jury of twelve. When they have come to an agreement, each attorney will explain the decisions and compromises that were made in writing (on a separate sheet of paper).

4. Students will staple and hand in all three sheets. They should be sure their individual sheet had their name on it as well as whether they are a prosecution or defense attorney. The joint sheet should also have both names on it.

Materials

Student Information Sheet
List of prospective jurors
Pencils and paper

Evaluation

Evaluation will be on the basis of students' active participation in the exercise and on the basis of their written responses to the exercises. Particular attention should be paid to the reasoning the student used in his or her choices for elimination.

Student Information Sheet

You will be assigned to play the role of either an attorney for the prosecution or attorney for the defense. Your job in this exercise will be to select a jury that will be impartial, if not sympathetic, to the side of the case you represent.

Attached to this information sheet is a list of fifteen potential jurors. You will need to eliminate three, but remember that you will need to negotiate with another attorney in order to complete the exercise.

Instructions

1. Read the case below and the attached sheet with descriptions of the prospective jurors. Keep in mind any factors such as race, age, sex, religious persuasion, and attitude toward alcohol that you believe may influence a prospective juror's attitude.

2. On a sheet of paper write your name and the side of the case you represent.

3. List those jurors you are inclined to challenge and your reasons. Then list those jurors that you definitely want on the jury and again your reasons.

4. When you have completed your list, join your assigned partner and negotiate to set a jury of twelve.

5. On a separate sheet of paper, name the three jurors that you and the other attorney eliminated as a team. Explain the decisions and compromises that you each made in order to come to an agreement. Staple all three sheets together and hand them in.

(Continued)

People versus Robin Carusa

The defendant, Robin Carusa, is Caucasian, 43 years old, and a resident of Bloomington, Indiana. He is Catholic. Upon graduation from Bloomington High School North, Carusa joined the Marines and served for three years in Vietnam. He is single, has one noncustodial child, and is an attorney.

On the night of October 3, 19—, Carusa and his fiancee, Cindy Freitag, went to a popular nightclub called The Island to hear the local band Voyage. According to the deposition taken from John Donne who is a bouncer at The Island, Carusa and Freitag arrived sometime after 9:00, but before 9:30 P.M. Again, according to Donne, Carusa and Freitag left the nightclub at around 1:00 A.M.

At approximately 2:30 A.M., Carusa's Mercedes crossed the center line on College Avenue and struck an oncoming Volkswagen head-on, killing both occupants instantly. The deceased have been identified as Lilly Mitchell and her 2-year-old son, Damon. Mitchell was Black, 35 years old, and the mother of three children. According to her husband Robert Mitchell, Lilly Mitchell was taking Damon to the emergency room of Bloomington Hospital for a severe case of the croup. Neither Carusa nor Freitag was seriously injured.

Carusa was given a Breathalyzer test at the scene, and his blood alcohol level registered 0.12 percent (1 percent is considered legally intoxicated under Indiana State law). According to Carusa, he drank three beers while at The Island and for the next hour while he and Freitag sat talking in his car, he claims he did not drink at all. Freitag substantiates his statement. However, five empty beer cans and one unopened can were found on the floor of Carusa's car. Carusa claims that he had a cold that could have skewed the test. He also claims that due to a recent rainfall the road was wet, and his car hydroplaned causing him to lose control.

Carusa is being charged with one count of operating a motor vehicle while intoxicated resulting in death, and two counts of reckless homicide. Both counts are considered Class C felonies under Indiana State law.

Prospective Jurors

- *Harlan Curry,* Caucasian, age 66, retired auto mechanic. Married, 3 children, 7 grandchildren. World War II veteran, no active church affiliation, recovered alcoholic.
- *Susan Andros,* Caucasian, age 40, office manager. Married (spouse is a local attorney), two children at home. Member of local Episcopal church, social drinker.
- *John Davis,* Black, age 33, assistant professor in the Indiana University School of Business. Single, no children. Member of Unitarian-Universalist Church. Davis does not drink because his father, a retired police officer from Detroit, is an alcoholic.
- *Mark Sampson,* Caucasian, age 29, high school drop-out, employed at Kinser Lumber four years. Divorced, two noncustodial children. One previous arrest DWI (no conviction). No church affiliation.

(Continued)

- *Jane Long,* Caucasian, age 20, Indiana University student (School of Education). Graduated from Bloomington High School North, active in Youth for Christ, does not drink.
- *Alice Murray,* Black, age 71, retired to Bloomington after teaching school in Georgia for 35 years. Widowed, one child (died of scarlet fever at age two). Member local Baptist Church, does not drink.
- *James Fanelli,* Caucasian, age 45, sales manager Tom O'Daniel Ford. Married, four children at home. College graduate, Vietnam veteran, active member of St. Charles Catholic Church, social drinker.
- *Julie Chase,* Caucasian, age 36, doctor, Bloomington Hospital, Emergency Room. Divorced, one child at home. Member of and medical consultant to Alcoholics Anonymous. No church affiliation.
- *Shelly Arno,* Caucasian, age 28, unemployed. Widowed (husband killed in a car accident), two children at home. Engaged to Assistant Minister at the Bloomington Pentecostal Church. Does not drink.
- *Jack Allen,* Black, 33, graduate student at Indiana University. Married (wife Caucasian), one child at home. Worked as an insurance investigator before returning to school. No church affiliation, social drinker.
- *Joe Chin,* Vietnamese-American, age 52, teacher, elementary school. Married, one child (deceased). Member of St. Charles Catholic Church, does not drink.
- *Sally Frank,* Caucasian, age 69, owner of local bookstore. Widowed (deceased husband was career military), two children, one grandchild. No church affiliation, social drinker.
- *Edward Said,* Lebanese-American, age 40, Professor of Arabic at Indiana University. Single, no children. Moslem, does not drink.
- *John Marks,* Caucasian, age 23, musician in a local rock band. Single, no children. No church affiliation, social drinker.
- *Maya Davis,* Black, age 32, novelist. Married, one child at home. No church affiliation, social drinker.

Reprinted with permission of the author.

Global Economics and the U.S. Consumer: Nike Goes Global

Kathy Ellis

Objectives

1. The student will be able to give specific details concerning one company's (Nike's) move of production out of the country.
2. The student will examine his or her feelings and attitudes as to the buying power and decisions to be made by an informed consumer.
3. The student will exercise consumer power by writing a letter to Nike headquarters requesting further information, voicing support, or criticizing Nike's

◄ ■ ■ N Z O S S W J LESSON 8.24

(Continued)

decision to move production elsewhere. (If a student does not wish to communicate with Nike, the student may write a one- to two-page essay on "A Company's Right to Move Production.")

Method/Activities

1. Gain student attention by showing a Nike commercial. (Kathy created her own 15-minute video using Nike's television commercials.) Ask the students these three questions and have someone write the answers on the board:
   a. What do you think the commercial was trying to establish?
   b. What do you know about the Nike company?
   c. What does it mean to be an informed consumer? (Does it mean that you base decisions on the information learned?) (This should take approximately 20 minutes.)
2. Pass out the article from *Harper's* magazine: "The New Free-Trade Heel."
3. Ask the students to read the article and answer the reading guide questions. The article is short, so it could be easily read out loud in class.
4. Then have the students, working in groups, answer the following two questions on overhead transparencies:
   a. List two or three concerns or questions that a U.S. consumer/citizen might have regarding the Nike company.
   b. What are some options for citizens/consumers who question a company's business practices? (This should complete the first period.)
5. Pass out paper to the students. Their assignment is to write a letter to Nike headquarters supporting Nike's decision to move production out of the country, criticizing the decision, or asking questions about the decision. Each letter should contain at least two questions to the Nike company. The letter will be graded on logical reasoning and application of knowledge of global economics. It will not be graded on grammar, but since these letters will be actually mailed, the students might edit each other's letters.

Materials

Video of a Nike commercial
Article: "The New Free-Trade Heel," *Harper's*, August 1992, pp. 46–47.
Reading guide with questions

Assessment

The object of this lesson is for students to see that they actually are a part of global economics and that the decisions that people of their age group make might possibly have an effect. Another part of the lesson is that being an informed consumer does not necessarily make decisions easier. There are no right or wrong "answers" in the students' letter-writing assignment just as there are sometimes no right or wrong decisions regarding consumer decisions. The real assessment of the lesson will be whether or not the students showed any critical thinking about the Nike company's move of operation.

(Continued)

Reading Guide for "The New Free-Trade Heel" Name:

1. Answer these questions as you read "The New Free-Trade Heel," *Harper's,* August 1992.
   a. What product does Nike produce?
   b. In what state is Nike based?
   c. How many Nike footwear factories are currently operating in the United States?
   d. Between 1982 and 1989, how many footwear jobs did the United States lose?
   e. How many pairs of shoes does Nike produce annually?
   f. List the five countries in which Nike contracts to have shoes made.
   g. What was Nike's net profit in 1991?
   h. How much is Sadisah paid *per day?*
   i. How much is Sadisah paid *per hour?*
   j. What are Sadisah's living conditions?
   k. What is the labor cost for a pair of Nike's that sells in the United States for $80.00?
2. Think about this question: How would a U.S. shoeworker be affected by Nike's decision to move its factories out of the country?
3. Working in groups, answer these two questions using overhead transparencies.
   a. List some concerns or questions that a U.S. citizen/consumer might have regarding the Nike company.
   b. What are some options for citizens/consumers who question a company's business practices?

Assignment

First assignment of this six weeks.
Write a letter to the Nike company expressing your support of its decision to move production out of the country, criticizing its decision to move production out of the country, or asking questions for more information. Every letter should be at least a page long and should include a couple questions relating to global economics.

We are hopeful that Nike will respond. A response might be more likely if you include a little information about yourself.

(If you are opposed to writing a letter to Nike, the alternative assignment is to write a one- or two-page essay on the subject of "A Company's Right to Move Production out of the Country.")

Grading

This assignment is worth 25 points. There are no right or wrong opinions but points will be awarded on the basis of logical reasoning and depth of explanation. Extra-credit points will be issued to a person who receives a response from Nike.

■*Implementing the Model through an Interdisciplinary Unit*

Historical Fiction and Multicultural Education in a World War II Unit— John Kornfeld

Goals

■ Students will learn that World War II—and any historical event—should be examined and understood from a variety of perspectives.

■ Students will develop myriad reading, language arts, art, and social studies skills in an interdisciplinary unit.

Introduction

Students in the United States studying World War II in school usually learn about the war from the Allied perspective, in terms of black and white: Hitler bombed England, which was bad, and we bombed Japan, which was good; the Allies won and the Axis lost, which was good. Obviously, no historical period is that simple. Students need to learn that different societies viewed World War II in a variety of ways, and that regardless of who won or lost, there were ramifications of the war that textbooks cannot adequately communicate to students. Historical fiction offers one way to introduce and reinforce these ideas. Stories of earlier times are intriguing to people of all ages, and they can provide a kaleidoscopic picture of the world in all its diversity and commonalities. It is up to the teacher to help students interpret these stories and, in doing so, provide a coherent, global picture for the students.

World War II has spawned a rich profusion of historical fiction with which to create a powerful multicultural unit of study. A tantalizing variety of books presents perspectives from all over the world—of soldiers throughout Europe and the Pacific, of Jews caught in the Holocaust, of orphaned and abandoned children in Eastern Europe, of Dutch, Danish, and French resisting the Nazis, of Japanese Americans interned in relocation camps, of ordinary people helplessly watching bombs fall on their homes in England, Poland, Italy, Germany, Japan, and the U. S. S. R. (See Appendix for an annotated list of representative titles.)

This unit explains how to use historical fiction in an interdisciplinary multicultural unit on World War II. Obviously, the methods described could be used in any number of multicultural units at almost any grade level.

Preparing for the Unit

Gather as many books about World War II as possible from your school library, the public library, garage sales, and the like. Be sure to include books for every reading level, from easy picture books to adult level. There are literally hundreds of World War II historical fiction books available, told from every conceivable perspective. In addition to works of fiction, bring in lots of nonfiction books for reference. Finally, choose a few titles of varying difficulty that present different points of view, and order them in sets of 6 to 8 books for reading groups.

Now comes the best part: read as many of the books as you can before starting the unit!

Getting Started

To begin the unit, divide students into groups and assign each group a book to read. You might begin, for example, with *The Devil's Arithmetic, The Machine Gunners, The Road to Memphis, Journey to Topaz,* and *Maus.* Give them reading assignments as you would for any other book. You may want to assign a minimum number of pages per night, but allow students to read more if they wish. Daily meetings with reading groups will enable you to monitor students' progress, clarify ideas in the books, and answer any questions they might have about events in the book.

As soon as the students start reading the books, they will begin asking questions. Why were the Nazis rounding up Jews in *The Devil's Arithmetic?* Where were the bombers coming from in *The Machine Gunners?* What were they hoping to accomplish? Why did the Japanese bomb Pearl Harbor (*Journey to Topaz*)? Thus, the stories the students read will stimulate their curiosity, motivating them to find out more historical information than the books provide. By helping students find the answers to their questions, you will help them make connections between the stories they are reading and the historical events surrounding the stories. Here are a few suggestions:

Assign readings in the textbook.
Direct students to encyclopedias, atlases, and other reference books.
Create vocabulary lists based on words common to many of the stories
(Nazi, Gestapo, Allies, Axis, resistance, refugee, concentration camp, etc.).
Teach geography skills to help students understand the stories' settings.
Assign research exercises to assess the historical accuracy of events in the books.

Discussions

Class discussions are an integral part of this unit. Students will want to share with one another the stories they have been reading. Each book offers only a narrow perspective of a global conflict; listening to one another will help everyone understand that many events were happening at the same time in different places, that the war was a different experience for different people. While Japanese Americans in *Journey to Topaz* were being interned in the western United States, Artie's father in *Maus* was hiding from the Nazis in Poland, and the Soviets were deporting Esther and her family to Siberia in *The Endless Steppe.* Resulting conversations about racism, prejudice, and discrimination are inevitable.

Discussion should also reveal differences and commonalities among different peoples. Most of the books give us a sense of the unique character of a particular culture, from the food they eat, to their family life, to their beliefs and hopes. But in comparing different people's experiences in the war, students will also discover that people on both sides, in many different places, suffered similar tragedies in this War. At the same time that the Allies were enduring bombing attacks (*The Machine Gunners, Along the Tracks,* etc.), the people in the Axis countries (*The Little Fishes, Faithful Elephants, Hiroshima No Pika,* etc.) were suffering bombing raids as well.

What and How Much Should Students Read?

Some of the best works of children's historical fiction happen to be "easy" books (for example, *Hiroshima No Pika, Faithful Elephants,* and *Rose Blanche*). Read some of them to the class and encourage everyone to read them; in this way, everyone benefits from these excellent books, and the stigma of reading "baby books" will be removed as well for those who are unable to read anything more difficult. As your students will soon learn, there is nothing childish about the subject matter in these books.

While a few students will read at the minimum pace you assign, most will simply devour their books and ask for more; encourage students to read as many different books as possible, and ask them to share the different perspectives that the stories depict. Soon the original groups will have disappeared, but you may want to continue to meet with groups of students who are reading or have read particular books.

Open-ended Activities That Grow out of the Books

Good historical fiction is about poverty, disagreement, oppression, cowardice, and hatred, as well as kindness, camaraderie, compassion, joy, and love. Reading an array of World War II fiction will not just teach students "facts"; it will also induce rage, laughter, sadness, guilt, and hope. The stories will cause the students to care deeply about people all over the world whose lives were changed by the war; they will elicit questions, arguments, confusion, and discussion. Plan a variety of activities which allow students to consider the many issues the books raise and to express their thoughts and values about the events of the war. Here are some activities you could assign to your students:

> Write a fictional diary, letter, or story that relates events in the book from a particular point of view.
> Write or record (video or audio) a fictionalized interview or news story related to the book.
> Create a newspaper, including editorials, on "current events" from the book.
> Paint pictures based on the story.
> Compose poetry expressing your reactions to events in the story.
> Perform skits or spontaneous role-plays based on events in the book.

Using Excerpts

What about the students who are slow readers and those who are only able to read only the easiest books? How will they benefit from all the books you brought into the classroom? And what if you have only one copy of a book that you feel everyone should read?

You can use excerpts from the books to familiarize the whole class with issues and perspectives that you feel everyone should examine. For example, you might want all students to learn about the fate of vagabond children around the world orphaned and made homeless by nightly bombings. You could read aloud short sections from *Along the Tracks* or *The Little Fishes* and generate discussion or an assignment related to this topic. Or you could arrange the class in heterogeneous groups—low readers with higher readers—and have them read the passage together before doing the related assignment. In this way, every student can become conversant with many different perspectives, even if they do not actually finish many books.

Completing the Unit

This unit could go on for months. With the number of books available, the complexity of the events and issues involved, and sheer number and variety of people affected by World War II, a class could conceivably spend an entire semester studying it. You will never be able to "finish" the war, but when you are ready to move on to another topic, individual or group projects are a wonderful way to complete the unit. Possible projects include:

> Write a historical novella or a children's picture book about the war from a particular perspective.
> Complete a project that illuminates the war experiences of a particular group of people (African Americans, German citizens, Italian children, American women, etc.).
> Write and film a video play about the war.
> Conduct a research project on any aspect of the war.
> Create dioramas, murals, or other art projects.
> Design maps, charts, time lines, etc.

When the projects are completed, plan some kind of culminating event in which students can share what they have created and learn from each other. With a variety of projects about people from all over the world, this event will not only be a retrospective on the war, but it also should be a celebration of global diversity as well.

Selected World War II Historical Fiction

> * = picture book
> + = easy reading
> ^ = intermediate reading
> # = more difficult reading

> * Ahlberg, Janet and Allan. *Peek-A-Boo!* Puffin Books, 1981. A day in the life of a British toddler during World War II.
> # Bergman, Tama. *Along the Tracks,* translated from the Hebrew by Michael Swirsky. Boston: Houghton Mifflin, 1991. The true story of a young Jewish boy who flees Nazi-occupied Poland with his family, then is separated from his family and becomes one of the thousands of abandoned children wandering through Russia.

+ Bishop, Claire Huchet. *Pancakes-Paris*. New York: Viking Press, 1947. In postwar Paris, a poor French family is befriended by American soldiers, who help make Mardi Gras a festive occasion, complete with American pancakes.
+ Bishop, Claire Huchet. *Twenty and Ten*. New York: Viking Press, 1952. In occupied France twenty Gentile children bravely hide and protect ten Jewish children from the Nazis.
+ Coerr, Eleano, *Sadako and the Thousand Paper Cranes*. New York: Dell Publishing, 1977. Ten years after the Allies dropped the atom bomb on her home in Hiroshima, Sadako comes down with leukemia, caused by the bomb's radiation.
^ Dahl, Roald. *Going Solo*. London: Penguin Books, 1986. Dahl relates his experiences as a fighter pilot in Africa, Greece, and the Middle East. This true story is as amazing and almost as surreal as Dahl's fiction.
^ Degens, T. *Transport 7-41-R*. New York: The Viking Press, 1974. A thirteen-year-old girl traveling alone describes her journey from the Russian sector of defeated Germany to Cologne on a train carrying returning refugees in 1946.
# Forman, James. *Ceremony of Innocence*. New York: Hawthorne Books, 1970. This is the story of Hans and Sophie Scholl, German citizens who produced the "White Rose" leaflets denouncing Nazism until they were caught and executed by the Gestapo.
^ Garrigue, Sheila. *The Eternal Spring of Mr. Ito*. New York: Bradbury Press, 1985. A young girl sent from London to stay with relatives in Canada during the blitz learns about racism and hysteria toward Japanese citizens.
# Greene, Bette. *Summer of My German Soldier*. New York: The Dial Press, 1973. In Arkansas a Jewish teenage girl befriends and protects a German soldier who has escaped from a nearby prisoner-of-war camp.
# Haugaard, Erik Christian. *The Little Fishes*. Boston: Houghton Mifflin, 1967. This story traces the odyssey of three homeless orphan children from Naples to Cassino in war-ravaged Italy.
# Hautzig, Esther. *The Endless Steppe*. New York: Thomas Y. Crowell Co., 1968. A Jewish family, exiled from Poland to Siberia, endures bitter hardships in its struggle for survival.
* Innocenti, Roberto. *Rose Blanche*. Mankato, Minnesota: Creative Education Inc., 1985. Rose Blanche lives in a small German town. At first, the war seems to cause little change in her life. Then she discovers the concentration camp outside of town.
^ Kerr, Judith. *When Hitler Stole Pink Rabbit*. New York: Coward, McCann & Geoghegan, Inc., 1972. Nine-year-old Anna must leave the protected world she knows and loves because of the articles her father, a well-known Jewish journalist, writes about the Nazis. As a refugee, she grows in many ways as her family moves from Berlin to Switzerland, Paris, then London.
+ Leitner, Isabella. *The Big Lie*. New York: Scholastic, 1992. Isabella and her family are taken to Auschwitz, but not all of them survive the ordeal.

^ Levitin, Sonia. *Journey to America.* New York: Atheneum, 1970. In 1938 Lisa and her family leave Berlin to escape the Nazis. After many hardships and separations, they are reunited in America.

+ Levoy, Myron. *Alan and Naomi.* New York: Harper and Row, 1977. In New York City, Alan befriends and tries to help Naomi, who is haunted by her recent experiences in France at the hands of the Nazis.

^ Lowry, Lois. *Number the Stars.* New York: Dell Publishing, 1989. In German-occupied Denmark, a ten-year-old girl and her family use courage and cunning to help their Jewish friends escape the Nazis.

* Maruki, Toshi. *Hiroshima No Pika.* New York: Lothrop, 1980. Young Mii is eating breakfast at home in Hiroshima when the atom bomb hits. This story chronicles her ordeal.

^ Maser, Harry. *The Last Mission.* New York: Delacorte Press, 1979. Young Jack falsifies his age so that he can fight the Germans. He learns the horrors and the futility of war.

Murray, Michele. *The Crystal Nights.* New York: Seabury Press, 1973. Elly and her family must adjust to the arrival of Jewish relatives fleeing Nazi Germany.

^ Reiss, Johanna. *The Upstairs Room.* New York: Harper Collins, 1972. Annie must hide for the entire war in an upstairs room, protected by a courageous Dutch family.

^ Shemin, Margaretha. *The Empty Moat.* New York: Coward, McCann & Geoghegan, 1969. In German-occupied Holland, Elizabeth must decide whether or not to overcome her fears and help the Dutch underground hide Jewish refugees from the Nazis.

+ Shemin, Margaretha. *The Little Riders.* New York: Coward-McCann, Inc., 1963. In a small Dutch town, Johanna saves the "Little Riders," metal figures that have come to represent resistance to the Germans who occupy the town.

+ Spiegelman, Art. *Maus I: A Survivor's Tale.* New York: Scholastic, Inc., 1986. Written in comic book form, with Polish mice and Nazi cats, an old Jewish mouse tells his son the story of his life during the war, of Nazi persecution and his family's attempts to avoid capture.

^ Taylor, Mildred. *The Road to Memphis.* New York: Dial Books, 1990. This is the fifth book about the Logans, a close-knit African American family faced with White hatred and bigotry in the South. The year is 1941 and Stacy Logan is old enough to join the army. Although far away, the war is never far from anyone's mind.

^ Taylor, Theodore. *The Cay.* New York: Doubleday, 1969. In 1942, young Phillip's ship is torpedoed by a German U-Boat. He and an old Black man drift to a deserted island, where they develop an unexpected friendship.

* Tsuchiya, Yukio. *Faithful Elephants: A True Story of Animals, People, and War,* translated by Tomoko Tsuchiya Dykes. New York: Trumpet Club, 1988. In Tokyo, zoo keepers must kill the wild animals because the army fears that bombs may hit the zoo and permit the animals to escape.

\# Tunis, John. *His Enemy, His Friend*. New York: William Morrow and Co., 1967. A German soldier stationed in occupied France befriends the French villagers until he is ordered to kill six of them.

^ Uchida, Yoshiko. *Journey to Topaz: A Story of the Japanese-American Evacuation*. New York: Charles Scribner's Sons, 1971. After the Japanese attack on Pearl Harbor, Japanese-American families, although loyal to the United States, must move to internment camps far from home.

\# Westall, Robert. *The Machine Gunners*. New York: William Morrow and Co., 1976. In a northern English town which suffers from nightly bombing raids, Chas and his friends make a game of collecting souvenirs from enemy war planes that have been shot down. But when they find a machine gun, build their own bunker, and capture an enemy flier, the game becomes very real.

^ Yolen, Jane. *The Devil's Arithmetic*. New York: Viking Kestrel, 1988. Hannah wishes her Jewish parents would forget the Holocaust: after all, those things happened years ago. But one Passover, she opens the door and finds herself in a Polish village during the war. As she is relocated to the concentration camp, she begins to understand why no one should ever forget what happened.

Historical Fiction Activities

Write a diary from a character's point of view.

Write a letter from one character to another describing important events in the book.

Write a poem about one of the characters or events in the story.

Based on the story and on what you have learned about this period in history, write a sequel to the book.

Write about a character with whom you identify strongly. How are you and the character alike? How are you different?

Produce a news feature on a character in the story.

Pretend you are a reporter (newspaper, radio, or TV) summarizing the events in the book.

Write a news editorial discussing events or actions in the story.

Draw a political cartoon commenting on an event in the story from your point of view, or from a character's perspective.

Perform a "Newscast from the Past" depicting events from this story, along with events that were going on elsewhere at the same time.

Pretend that you are a book reviewer and write a critique of the book.

Re-create the clothes of one of the characters and come to class dressed as that character.

Prepare a meal that the people in the story might have eaten.

Describe a typical day in the life of a character in the story. Compare it (using words or pictures) to a typical day of a character in another time or country.

Compare (using words or pictures) events, settings, customs, etc. portrayed in this book to those in other books.

Choose a character and explain how that person makes a living in the story.

Choose five examples of the latest technology in the story, draw a picture of each, tell how each was made, and explain its use.

List all the places mentioned in the book which could be put on a map, and make a map using this list.

Make a map of the world and show the location(s) of this story, as well as the settings of related stories and historical events.

Make a time line of the book's main events, or of historical events happening while the story takes place.

Choose some real (as opposed to fictional) characters and events in the story and do some research to find out more about them.

List all the historical "facts" that you learned in this book.

Write or record an interview with one of the historical characters in the book.

Make a list of important vocabulary words you learned from reading this book.

Make a picture time line of the book's main events.

Draw or paint pictures, make dioramas, create a poster or mural, or make a collage of some or all of the events in the book.

Take a series of photographs that represents your response to events in the book.

Make a book cover, complete with picture on the front and blurb on the back.

Draw a picture of or build a character's house.

Make a mobile about the book.

Make a diorama or draw a picture that shows details of the story's setting.

Write music that evokes the mood of part or all of the book.

Perform a pantomime of certain events in the story.

Perform some music or a dance that the characters may have enjoyed at the time they lived.

Make puppets of characters in the story and perform a puppet show about them.

Stage a debate between characters in the story who represent opposing viewpoints.

Choose the most important or moving section of the book and give an oral reading of this excerpt.

Make a video dramatizing some or all of the story.

Analyze or debate the ethics or morality of a character's actions.

Examine the author's perspective in this story. What do you think is the author's opinion of events in the story? Does the author seem to have any biases that affect the way that the story is told?

CONCLUSIONS

The curriculum model described in this chapter provides a rationale for multicultural education (i.e., the core values and goals) that gives teachers the support they may need when they face pressures and questions from colleagues, the community, and students. The chapter's instructional units and lessons breathe life into the model and illustrate how teachers have used it to create both interdisciplinary and single-discipline plans for teaching.

If teachers are to include multicultural perspectives in their curriculum, they will need to develop new plans for instruction. A curriculum model such as the one proposed here can guide us as we gather sources of information (media, texts, speakers, etc.); select subject matter content, resources, and materials; identify instructional goals and objectives; and decide on teaching strategies and learning activities.

We can see that a multicultural curriculum is inclusive of diverse cultural perspectives and histories, and also fosters fair-minded critical thinking, compassion, and social action. Furthermore, it is based on the belief and assumption that teachers can make a difference in students' lives and that students can eventually make a difference in society. Thus, a multicultural curriculum is highly interactive with the three other dimensions of multicultural education identified in Chapter 1: the movement toward educational equity, the process of becoming interculturally competent, and the commitment to combat racism, sexism, as well as all forms of prejudice and discrimination.

COMPARE AND CONTRAST

1. The curriculum goals of multicultural education based on the learner, society, and the discipline
2. Informed empathy and intercultural competence
3. Historical perspectives and cultural consciousness
4. Combating racism and social action skills
5. The curriculum goals of multicultural education and the core values
6. Social action skills and responsibility to a world community
7. Awareness of state of the planet and global dynamics, and reverence for the earth
8. Fair-minded critical thinking and the core values of multicultural education

ACTIVITIES AND QUESTIONS

1. Develop a multicultural calendar with other members of your class or let your students help you. Individuals or small groups could focus on a different ethnic group and research people and events to be included in the calendar. At least one entry per month per ethnic group could be the initial goal, with the number expanding as the database increases over the years. Both minority perspectives and ethnic group diversity should be reflected

in the calendar as it emerges. The calendar's people and events could be related to a specific subject, sports and athletics, music, art, literature, government, and so on.

2. Why does Black History Month sometimes trigger resentment among non-Black students? How might the goals and philosophy behind Black History Month be best achieved?

3. What are the arguments for and against school programs that include Christian beliefs, music, and traditions, as, for example, at Christmas or Easter? How should schools handle the controversy?

4. What are some ways courses outside the humanities and social sciences (specifically physical sciences, mathematics, and physical education) can help develop informed empathy? Brainstorm in small groups to generate lists of ideas and share the results with the other participants in your class.

5. Sometimes freedom of thought and expression, as well as the desire to eliminate racism from the curriculum, conflicts with school censorship policies. Answer and discuss the following questions:

   a. Should racist books be eliminated from schools, including the library shelves?

   b. Can books that contain profanity and ethnic dialects be used without reinforcing negative stereotypes? Should they be used?

6. Consider the multicultural curriculum model presented in this chapter. Explain which areas of the elementary, middle, and secondary school curriculum are most compatible with each goal. Provide specific reasons and illustrations.

7. Explain how the model's core value concepts can help teachers deal with the issues such as apartheid and affirmative action. Be specific in your reasoning and illustrations.

8. What are some of the most important issues of human rights that teachers in your field need to deal with? What have you learned about the nature of the learner and about guidelines for interpersonal communications that will help you conduct effective classroom discussions on human rights issues?

9. You are part of an interdisciplinary team of elementary-middle-secondary school teachers charged with developing a curriculum unit on one of the following global issues: nuclear weapons, world hunger, or destruction of the environment. Explain your contribution to the team. Be specific.

10. Imagine that you are infusing multicultural education into your regular curriculum, in a fashion similar to Sam Jones's. The parents in your school become very upset with you. What do they say? What actions do they take? How do you respond?

11. Let's assume that you do want to include comprehensive multicultural education in your teaching. What are the five most difficult problems you anticipate? What will you do to overcome these problems?

NOTES

1. G. J. Posner and A. N. Rudnitsky, *Course Design: A Guide to Curriculum Development for Teachers,* rev. ed. (New York: Longman, 1982), 50.
2. Ibid., 45.
3. Richard Paul, Critical *Thinking: What Every Person Needs to Survive in a Rapidly Changing World* (Santa Rosa, CA: Foundation for Critical Thinking, 1993).
4. Ibid., 139.
5. Ibid., 136.
6. Edward W. Cassidy and Dana G. Kurfman, "Decision Making as Purpose and Process," *Developing Decision Making Skills,* 47th Yearbook, 1977. National Council for the Social Studies, 1–28.
7. K. Y. Chun-Hoon, "Teaching the Asian-American Experience" in *Teaching Ethnic Studies: Concepts and Strategies,* J. A. Banks, ed. (Washington, DC: National Council for the Social Studies, 1973), 139. Quotations from this source, the NCSS 43rd Yearbook, are reprinted by permission of the publisher.
8. Ibid., 122.
9. L. Tiedt and I. M. Tiedt, *Multicultural Teaching: A Handbook of Activities, Information, and Resources* (Boston: Allyn and Bacon, 1979), 84–88.
10. F. Berry and J. W. Blassingame, *Long Memory: The Black Experience in America,* (New York: Oxford University Press, 1982). Quotations from this source are reprinted with permission.
11. Ibid.
12. Ibid., 31.
13. C. V. Hamilton, "Race and Education: A Search for Legitimacy." in *Issues in Race and Ethnic Relations,* J. Rothman, ed. (Itasca, IL: F. E. Peacock, 1977), 101–115. Originally published in *Harvard Educational Review* 38, no. 4:669–684. Copy-

right © by President and Fellows of Harvard College. Reprinted by permission.
14. J. O. Killens, *Black Man's Burden* (New York: Trident Press, 1965), 14–15.
15. Ibid., 17.
16. L. Bennett, "Was Abe Lincoln a White Supremacist?" *Ebony* 23, no. 4 (February (1968), 35.
17. *More Than Bows and Arrows* (Seattle, WA: Cinema Associates, 1978), A. Hirschfelder, *Happily May I Walk: American Indians and Alaska Natives Today* (New York: Scribner, 1986), and Jack Weatherford, *Indian Givers: How The Indians of the Americas Transformed the World* (New York: Fawcett Columbine, 1988).
18. Adapted from J. D. Forbes, "Teaching Native American Values and Cultures," in *Teaching Ethnic Studies: Concepts and Strategies,* J. A. Banks, ed. (Washington, DC: National Council for the Social Studies, 1973), 218–219. Reprinted by permission of the author and publisher.
19. D. Johnson, "The Contribution of the Humanities to a Global Perspective in Teacher Education," ERIC ED 265 114, 1987.
20. D. Levering Lewis, *When Harlem Was in Vogue* (New York: Knopf, 1981), 15.
21. *Chinese Americans, Realities and Myths,* multimedia kit, The Association of Chinese Teachers (TACT) Curriculum Materials, 74–6A Ninth Avenue, San Francisco, CA 94118; and S. Steiner, *Fusang: The Chinese Who Built America* (New York: Harper & Row, 1979).
22. L. W. Levine, *Black Culture and Black Consciousness* (Oxford, England: Oxford University Press, 1977), 397.
23. C. E. Cortez, "Teaching the Chicano Experience," *in Teaching Ethnic Studies: Concepts and Strategies,* J. A. Banks, ed. (Washington, DC: National Council for the Social Studies, 1973), 191.

24. Denis Wood, "The Power of Maps," *Scientific American,* May 1993, 90.

25. R. Hanvey, *An Attainable Global Perspective* (New York: Center for War/Peace Studies, 1975), 4.

26. Ibid., 8.

27. Ibid., 10.

28. Ibid., 11.

29. Ibid.

30. S. P. Huntington, "The Clash of Civilizations?" *Foreign Affairs* (Summer 1993): 26.

31. Ibid., 31.

32. Ibid., 31.

33. Ibid., 40.

34. Copyright 1926 by Alfred A. Knopf, Inc., and renewed 1954 by Langston Hughes. Reprinted from *Selected Poems of Langston Hughes,* by permission of Alfred A. Knopf, Inc.

35. A. J. Kraemer, "A Cultural Self-awareness Approach to Improving Intercultural Communication Skills," ERIC ED 079 213 (April 1975):2.

36. Hanvey, *An Attainable Global Perspective,* 12.

37. W. B. Gudykunst and Y. Y. Kim, *Communicating with Strangers: An Approach to Intercultural Communication* (Reading, MA: Addison-Wesley, 1984), 230.

38. Ibid., 231.

39. Ibid.

40. D. Dufty, S. Sawkins, N. Pickard, J. Power, and A. Bowe, *Seeing It Their Way: Ideas, Activities, and Resources for Intercultural Studies* (London, England: Reed Education, 1976).

41. Ibid.

42. Wolsk, "An Experience Centered Curriculum: Exercises in Personal and Social Reality," United Nations Education, Scientific and Cultural Organization (Paris), ERIC ED 099 269, 1974; and see also D. Casteel, *Cross-cultural Models of Teaching: Latin American Example* (Gainesville, FL.: University of Florida Press, 1976).

43. H. C. Triandis, "Culture Training, Cognitive Complexity and Interpersonal Attitudes," in *Cross-cultural Perspectives on Learning,* R. W. Brislin, S. Bochner, and W. J. Lonner, eds. (New York: Wiley, 1975), 70–71.

44. Rivera, "The Teaching of Chicano History," in *The Chicanos: Mexican American Voices,* E. W. Ludwig and J. Santibanez, eds. (New York: Penguin, 1971), 200.

45. M. Miles, *Annie and the Old One,* illustr. Peter Parnall (Boston: Little, Brown, 1971).

46. B. Dodds Stanford and K. Amin, *Black Literature for High School Students* (Urbana, IL: National Council of Teachers of English, 1978), 10.

47. Ibid., 11–12.

48. Excerpt from P. L. Tiedt and I. M. Tiedt, *Multicultural Teaching: A Handbook of Activities, Information, and Resources* (Boston: Allyn and Bacon, 1979), 84–88. Reprinted by permission.

49. See R. M. Young, "Racist Society, Racist Science," *Multicultural Teaching,* 5.3 (Summer 1987):43–50. See also D. Bell, *And We Are Not Yet Saved: The Elusive Quest for Racial Justice* (New York: Basic Books, 1987).

50. L. Anderson, *Schooling and Citizenship in a Global Age: An Exploration of the Meaning and Significance of Global Education* (Bloomington, IN: Social Studies Development Center, 1979).

51. Ibid., 438–439.

52. Ibid., 447.

53. Ibid., 464.

54. This list is based in part on Dufty et al., *Seeing It Their Way,* 149.

55. Tables expanded and updated by C. Bennett.

56. This lesson plan has been field tested in two classes of eleventh-grade American Literature students at a large suburban high school in Indiana.

57. Hanvey, *An Attainable Global Perspective,* 6.

58. L. Anderson, "Some Propositions about the Nature of Global Studies," Northwestern University, u.d. ms., 6.

59. Ibid.

60. D. Lasswell "Multiple Loyalties in a Shrinking World," paper presented at the National Council of the Social Studies conference, Washington, DC, November 29,

1968. Also see G. Allport, *Nature of Prejudice* (Reading, MA: Addison-Wesley, 1979).

61. Hanvey, *An Attainable Global Perspective,* 7.

62. Ibid., 13.

63. Ibid.

64. Anderson, "Some Propositions," 6.

65. This lab procedure was adapted from P. Brandwien, *Science and Technology* (Chicago: Coronado, u.d.)

66. Ibid.

67. D. C. Tucker, "A Safe Lab on Nerve Gases," *Science Teacher* 55 (February 1988):27–30.

68. C. F. Stevens, "The Neuron," *Scientific American* 241 (September 1979):55–65.

69. Tucker, "A Safe Lab."

70. I. Slesnick and J. Miller, "Difficult Decisions: Chemical Warfare, " *Science Teacher* 55 (February 1988):31–33.

71. Ibid.

72. Ibid.

73. Ibid.

74. Ibid.

75. Ibid.

76. Hanvey, *An Attainable Global Perspective,* 22.

77. R. Joyce and A. M. Nicholson, "Imperatives for Global Education," in *Schooling for a Global Age,* J. A. Becker, ed. (New York: McGraw-Hill, 1979).

78. Ballard, *Monsoon: A Novel to End World Hunger* (Marina Del Rey, CA: New Horizons, 1986).

79. B. A. Reardon (ed.), *Teaching for Global Responsibility,* (New York: Teachers College Press, 1988).

80. Ibid., 24.

81. Ibid., 81–82.

82. See, for example, "Education for Racial Equality under Attack," *Multicultural Teaching* 5, no. 3 (Summer 1987):4–7; and C. Grant and C. Sleeter, "The Literature on Multicultural Education: Review and Analysis," *Educational Review* 37, no. 2 (1985):97–118.

83. See, for example, R. D. Hess and F. M. Newman, "Political Socialization in the Schools," *Harvard Education Review* 38 (Summer 1968):528–545; B. Seasholes, "Political Socialization of Blacks: Implications for Self and Society," in *Black Self-Concept,* J. A. Banks and J. D. Grambs, eds. (New York: McGraw-Hill, 1972); L. H. Ehman, "Political Socialization and the High School Social Studies Curriculum," unpublished Ph.D. diss., University of Michigan, 1970; and C. Bennett Button, "Political Education and Minority Youth," in *New Views of Children and Politics,* R. G. Niemi, ed. (San Francisco: Jossey-Bass, 1974). See also R. Muller, *New Genesis, Shaping a Global Spirituality,* (Garden City, NY: Doubleday, 1982) and N. van Oudenhoven, "Act Locally, Think Globally: Some Comments on Prosocial Behavior, Information Processing and Development Education" (New York: UNICEF, Information Division, "Development Education Paper No. 24," September 1982).

84. B. Seasholes, "Political Socialization of Blacks: Implications for Self and Society," in *Black Self Concept,* J. A. Banks and J. D. Grambs, eds. (New York: McGraw-Hill, 1972).

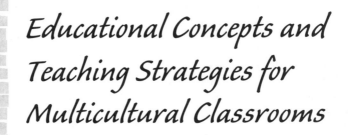

chapter 9

Educational Concepts and Teaching Strategies for Multicultural Classrooms

*T*he previous chapter described a curriculum development model teachers can use to develop multicultural perspectives in the curriculum. Chapter 8 emphasized the model's core values, goals, and content. In this chapter we will focus on concepts and teaching strategies which are also an important aspect of the model. It includes a range of teaching concepts and strategies known to be effective in working with the cultural and individual differences students bring to the classroom.

The chapter begins with culturally relevant teaching, an idea that has emerged from nearly two decades of research with teachers who are especially effective with students of color, as well as low-income White students who are ill-served by our schools. It continues with the idea of individualizing instruction and describes the concepts of mastery learning, experiential learning, and bilingual education programs. It then defines and illustrates five strategies to individualize instruction: (1) learning activity packets, (2) learning centers, (3) independent study, (4) cooperative team learning, and (5) peer and crossage tutoring.

The Promise of Culturally Relevant Teaching

The idea of culturally relevant teaching has developed primarily from studies of excellent teachers who work with African American students.[1] However, culturally relevant teaching is appropriate for *all* students, including those who are ill-served by the school because of their ethnicity or low-income background. It originated in research aimed at understanding and mediating mismatches between students' home culture and the culture of the school through teaching that has been labeled "culturally appropriate," "culturally congruent," "culturally compatible," or "culturally responsive." The work of Gloria Ladson-Billings, a former teacher in Philadelphia Public Schools who is now a professor at the University of Wisconsin, is among the most important on this topic and uses the term "culturally relevant teaching."[2] Let's consider her award-winning research based on three years of qualitative inquiry in a California school district that serves primarily African American families.

The first step in the Ladson-Billings research was the identification of successful teachers of African American children. She asked both the parents and principals in four schools to nominate "excellent teachers." What the parents and principals looked for differed dramatically. The parents' criteria included: (1) Enthusiasm their *children* showed in learning while in the teacher's classroom; (2) Consistent levels of respect they (the parent) felt from the teacher; and (3) Their perception that the teachers "understood the need for the students to operate in the dual worlds of their home community and the White community."[3] Principals, on the other hand, used the following criteria: (1) Low number of discipline referrals; (2) High attendance rates; and (3) Standardized test scores. Nine teachers were on both the parents' and the principals' lists. Eight agreed to participate in the study.

A discussion of "Funds of Knowledge" research and the importance of culturally relevant teaching.

Funded for two years, the Ladson-Billings study included in-depth ethnographic interviews with each teacher, unannounced classroom visitations, extensive videotaping of classroom instruction, and collaborative reflection and inquiry with all the teachers in the study. She extended her study for a third year to focus on literacy teaching.

At first this researcher despaired of discovering any patterns or themes that could help her identify some principles that would explain why these teachers were so outstanding. Her teachers differed dramatically in terms of structure, style, strategies, and personality. Eventually, however, it became clear that these teachers (who were either African American or White) were very similar in how they viewed themselves as teachers and how they viewed their students, parents, and others in the community; in how they structured social relations inside and outside their classrooms; and in how they viewed knowledge. First of all, they were proud of teaching as a profession and had chosen to teach in this low-income, primarily African American community. Each of these teachers felt a strong sense of purpose and believed it was his or her responsibility to ensure the success of each student. Second (whether African American or White), they were aware of the societal conditions of discrimination and injustice for African Americans and understood how this influenced the school's academic expectations for students of color. Third, they avoided "assimilationist" approaches to teaching and wanted to prepare their students to become change agents, not just to fit into mainstream society. And fourth, they capitalized on their students' home and community culture by creating a flexible, fluid, and collaborative learning climate where everyone (including the teacher) learned from everyone else. From these "similarities and points of convergence" the theoretical framework of culturally relevant teaching emerged.

Principles of Culturally Relevant Teaching

Three promising principles of culturally relevant teaching have developed from the Ladson-Billings research. Some educators describe it as "just good teaching," which leads us to wonder why it is so rare among students of color, as well as among rural and low-income White students.

1. Students must experience academic success, including literacy; numeracy; and the technological, social, and political skills they need to be active participants in a democracy. This is not false self-esteem building. Rather, self-esteem accompanies genuine academic success.

2. Students must develop and/or maintain cultural competence, and the student's home culture becomes a vehicle for learning. For example, one of the teachers in the study whose teenaged son was an avid rap fan encouraged her second graders to write and sing rap as a tool for writing poetry and for becoming bilingual and bidialectical. (The students' raps had to be something they would sing at home!)

3. Students must develop a "critical consciousness" through which they may challenge social injustice. Some of the teachers studied engaged

their students in rewriting out-of-date textbooks; others got involved in community information drives and community problem solving.

Examples of Culturally Relevant Teaching

In *The Dreamkeepers: Successful Teachers of African American Children*, Ladson-Billings presents vivid portraits of the eight teachers in her study. One of them, Ann Lewis, is a 44-year-old Italian American woman who has taught sixth grade in a low-income, predominantly African American community for 14 years.[4] Most of Ann's African American boys have a history of "misbehavior" and are considered to be "at risk" of school failure. Ann encouraged them to lead discussions and other class activities, to initiate inquiry, and to challenge the status quo. In her class it was "cool" or "hip" to be academically excellent. She emphasized a learning community based on cooperation and collaboration, rather than competition, and encouraged her students to rely on and support each other. Ann included the students' real-life experiences as legitimate parts of the "official curriculum," and often learned from her students. Although she selected literature for her students, such as *Charlie Pippin* (a story about a young African American girl who launches an antinuclear war protest), she allowed her students to ask their own questions and search for their own answers. She relied on her students' own lives to build and extend the curriculum. For example, the discussion of Charlie Pippin led a student to comment that he lived in a "war zone," which led to discussion and writing about living in a community plagued by violence. On another occasion Ann used her students' fears about attending an integrated camp as an opportunity to read, write, and talk about threatening social conditions. When some of her students did encounter a racial incident at the camp, they were better prepared to deal with it without violence.

Another powerful example of culturally relevant teaching is Martha Demientieff, a Native Alaskan teacher of Athabaskan Indian students, who is described in Lisa Delpit's book, *Other People's Children: Cultural Conflicts in the Classroom*. Martha's students live in a small, isolated village of about 200 people. Martha builds upon her students' knowledge of their own language and culture to help them understand the language of power in our society; her goal is intercultural competence, not assimilation through eradication of the village culture. For example, she analyzes their writing for examples of "Village English" and writes them on the blackboard under the heading "Our Heritage Language." Opposite each example she writes an "equivalent statement" under the heading "Formal English." Delpit describes what happens next in Martha's classroom:

> She and the students spend a long time on the "Heritage English" section, savoring the words, discussing the nuances. She tells the students, "That's the way we say things. Doesn't it feel good? Isn't this the absolute best way of getting that idea across?" Then she turns to the other side of the board. She tells the students that they are people, not like those in the village, who judge others by the way they talk or write."[5]

Martha tells them,

> We listen to the way people talk, not to judge them, but to tell what part of the river they come from. These other people are not like that. They think everybody needs to talk like them. Unlike us, they have a hard time hearing what people say if they don't talk exactly like them. Their way of talking and writing is called "Formal English."
>
> We have to feel a little sorry for them because they have only one way to talk. We're going to learn two ways to say things . . . One will be our Heritage way. The other will be Formal English. Then, when we go to get jobs, we'll be able to talk like those people who only know and can only listen to one way. Maybe after we get the jobs we can help them to learn how it feels to have another language, like ours, that feels so good. We'll talk like them when we have to, but we'll always know our way is best.[6]

Martha does many follow-up activities to help students understand informal or Heritage English and Formal English. She also helps them see differences between "wordy" academic language and the metaphoric style of Athabaskan. The students are helped to see how "book language always uses more words" while in Heritage language "the shorter way is always better."[7] Martha encourages her students to write enough to "sound like a book" and then to reduce the message to a "saying" brief enough to fit on a T-shirt!

A third example of culturally relevant teaching is seen with Kathy, a Head Start teacher who works in a rural school in Northern Michigan that serves low-income White students.[8] In contrast to most Head Start teachers who follow curriculum guidelines provided by their Head Start coordinator, Kathy builds her teaching around her children's interests and questions. Like Ann and Martha, Kathy chooses to teach in a low-income community and believes it is necessary to connect her teaching with the lives of her children. Kathy, too, is an advocate for her children and their families. She rejects the idea that her role as an "at-risk" teacher is to instruct the children and families in how fit into middle-class society. She said:

> I believe that it is my responsibility to learn as much as I can about the child's family and their culture and then implement that into my classroom, so that the child can see that his/her culture is a part of our classroom and that I respect them and their family and their culture. It can be hard, I don't want to present any new stereotypes to these kids, so I ask the parents a lot of questions. Sometimes I get the answers and sometimes I don't, but at least they can see I am trying.[9]

Kathy watches her children to discover what interests them. For example, one warm winter day a fly was in the classroom, and her students were fascinated. "They talked about and followed that fly all day!"[10] That evening Kathy gathered books and other materials about flies and insects, and she and the children spent two weeks on bugs.

Kathy does not find much collegial support for her approach to teaching and is likely to lose her current job with Head Start. She might find encouragement in the collaborative research among a team of teacher-researchers who, like herself, want to know and understand their students' funds of knowledge.

Funds of Knowledge Research and Teaching

A team of educators and anthropologists working with schools and communities in southern Arizona is developing another promising line of research that is compatible with culturally relevant teaching. Through their study of household and classroom practices within working-class, Mexican-origin communities in Tucson, Arizona, they are developing "innovations in teaching that draw upon the knowledge and skills found in local households."[11] Although this research has focused on Mexican origin and Yaqui families living in the borderlands, it has exciting implications for multicultural teaching throughout the country.

In the original study, ten teachers each conducted research in three households of children in their classroom. In partnership with an anthropologist skilled in ethnographic inquiry, the teachers entered these households as *learners,* or ethnographers who wanted to know and understand their students and their students' households' "funds of knowledge."[12] This term refers to "historically accumulated and culturally developed bodies of knowledge and skills essential for household or individual functioning and well-being."[13] (A basic assumption of this research is that students will learn more in classrooms where teachers know and understand these funds of knowledge.) To discover these funds of knowledge, the teachers interviewed family members and served as participant observers, keenly listening and watching, and learned about the lived practices of their students' households.

> As they approached the households, they noted gardens, recreational areas, tools, equipment, physical and spatial layouts of the homes, books, toys, and any other material clues that might lead to the discovery of household strategies and resources. They engaged in a series of open-ended interviews with parents that focused on family histories and social networks, labor histories of households, and language and child-rearing ideologies. In this way, teacher-researchers came to appreciate the repertoire from which households draw in order to subsist and validated household knowledge as worthy of pedagogical notice.[14]

The household funds of knowledge they initially gathered are based on a sample of about 100 families and embrace areas such as ranching and farming, including horse and riding skills, animal management, soil and irrigation systems; mining and timbering, including minerals and blasting; business, such as market values, appraising, renting and selling, loans, labor laws, building codes, accounting, and sales; household management, like budgeting, child care, cooking, and appliance repairs; home construction, design, and maintenance; repair of airplanes, automobiles, and heavy equipment; contemporary and folk medicine; and religion, such as catechism, babtism, Bible stories, moral knowledge, and ethics.[15]

While they were engaged in this research, the teachers worked together in after-school study groups to develop innovative teaching practices that made strategic connections between homes and classrooms. The authors of this research emphasize that their approach avoids ill-founded attempts at teaching a "culture-sensitive curriculum" that is based on "folkloric displays, such as storytelling, arts, crafts, and dance performance."[16] Instead, the students' funds of knowledge are drawn upon to enhance student learning in all the content areas, such as mathematics, language arts, science, social studies, and physical education. For example, one teacher-researcher built upon her students' households' knowledge of the medicinal value of plants and herbs, and created a unit on the curative properties of plants. Another teacher developed an inquiry-based unit on candy that explored nutritional content, production, marketing, and a cross-national preference survey report, when she learned that one of her students regularly participated in trans-border activities and often returned from northern Mexico with candy to sell.[17]

The research described above is inspiring. Hopefully it will be replicated in schools and communities across the country.

In the remainder of this chapter we will consider concepts and strategies that are appropriate in classrooms that serve culturally diverse groups of students as well as students who are relatively homogenous, culturally speaking. In both situations there exists tremendous diversity in terms of the individual differences discussed in Chapters 6 and 7.

Individualizing Instruction: A Response to Cultural and Individual Differences

Is it possible to create a flexible learning environment without classroom chaos? Is it possible to allow students to learn in different ways and still maintain high standards of achievement? If so, is it possible to accomplish this without becoming exhausted over excessive lesson planning and record keeping? The purpose of this section of the chapter is to provide some affirmative answers to these questions.

Most teachers are in favor of individualizing instruction, even though they feel it is possible only with small numbers of students. Part of the problem is misunderstanding what the concept means. "During the 1960s, individualized instruction was associated with teaching machines and programmed texts, and conjured up images of a single learner alone in timeless space, facing a panel board with several control knobs, and responding to lists of stimuli that had been previously tested and sequenced in a manner than ensured successful learning."[18] Most recently, individualized instruction may be defined as "any steps taken in planning and conducting programs of studies and lessons that suit . . . the individual student's learning needs, learning readiness, and learner characteristics or 'learning style.' "[19]

Eric Jones's classroom illustrates the possibilities. Jones, a Los Angeles high school teacher, has implemented individualization and established a pluralistic learning environment in his classroom. The following describes and analyzes his key concepts and strategies as well as proposes how they can be implemented in other classroom settings. A key to Eric Jones's success is the flexible learning environment that allows for individualized instruction. Mastery learning, experiential learning, and bilingual education are combined to provide the basic framework for individualized instruction in his classroom. They are implemented through a variety of teaching strategies including peer and cross-age tutoring, independent study, learning centers, and learning activity packets. Other strategies not discussed but present nevertheless include student team learning, lecture, and small-group discussion.

ERIC JONES'S CLASSROOM

It is Thursday morning in November. Eric Jones, a tenth-grade English teacher in Los Angeles, arrives early to set up his classroom before the arrival of his first-period students.

Today, Eric is following up Monday and Tuesday's large-group activity, *Bafá Bafá*, a cross-cultural simulation.[20] Eric's classroom arrangement (Figure 9.1) differs sharply from most of the others in Green Grove High.

Eric's plan includes areas for quiet study. Cubicles are set up with large painted cardboard boxes lined with Styrofoam egg cartons to absorb sound. These are placed on individual small tables, or several together on a long one. Eric creates other areas conducive to group work by arranging circles of desks or tables and chairs. His equipment is accessible and the students know how to operate it themselves. He stores student folders and answer keys for his self-directed learning centers in labeled boxes covered with brightly colored contact paper. These files are conveniently located since the students refer to them often.

Eric uses few partitions. He prefers to keep the classroom open so that he can keep an eye on what is going on and be available to help when students raise their hands or become frustrated with malfunctioning equipment. He

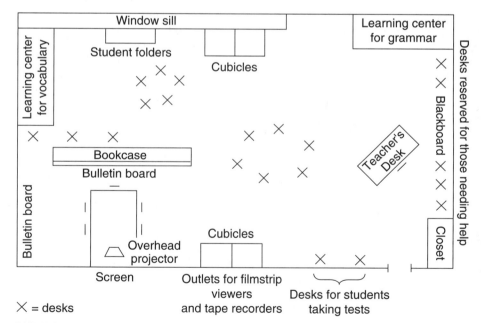

FIGURE 9.1

Basic Floor Plan of Tenth-grade English Classroom Arrangement

Adapted from Christine Bennett, "Individualized Instruction in the Secondary Schools," *Viewpoints in Teaching and Learning* 55, no. 20 (Spring 1979):77.

uses movable bookcases set on wheels for placement of alternative textbooks and a good-sized paperback library. The bookcase can be swung around to quickly create more private areas for tutoring or small-group discussion.

Eric's students are a heterogeneous group in terms of ethnicity, family income level, values, interests, learning-style preferences, and achievement. He prefers this. Experience has taught him that human diversity in the classroom can be in itself motivating for students and can assist the teacher in reaching students who might otherwise be unteachable.

Take Tony Castillo and Tomás Cortez as examples. Neither speaks more than a few words of English. Although Eric has had two years of college Spanish at UCLA, he lacks the necessary fluency in oral Spanish to fully assist Tony and Tomás. The school does have a bilingual education program, but it is already overcrowded and understaffed. Neither Tomás nor Tony has been able to get into the program. Fortunately, Eric was able to schedule a bilingual student, Ricardo Juarez, into this class. In addition to benefiting Tony and Tomás, Ricardo's overall school achievement and attitude have improved markedly since he assumed the role of peer instructor.

The simulation Eric used on Monday was designed to enable his students to feel what it's like to visit another culture. The students were physically separated into two different cultures, the Alphas and Betas, and then were given approximately twenty minutes to learn and practice their new culture. Each culture had its own unique traditions, customs, language, and assumptions. Observers and visitors moved back and forth between the two cultures until everyone had an opportunity to visit the other culture.

Eric then allowed the class time to discuss what happened. Students were amazed to discover that a mere twenty minutes in their new culture had helped shape their perceptions and assumptions, and had made them rather ethnocentric. Alphas and Betas both felt strange, uncomfortable, unwelcome, confused, and even afraid when they visited each other. Each perceived the other as rude, stupid, and either greedy or nosy. Each made incorrect assumptions about the other, and the reporters made many errors in their interpretations of what they saw.

In the follow-up discussion on Tuesday, the class eagerly discussed what it felt like to visit another culture, to be misperceived by others, and to discover their own misperceptions and erroneous assumptions. They analyzed causes of the misperceptions and cultural conflicts that occurred. Implications for American society were analyzed, particularly those associated with ethnicity in Los Angeles, their school, and in their own classroom. Media coverage of two historic incidents in Los Angeles, the zootsuit riots during World War II and the shooting of Rubin Salazar, were described, analyzed, and discussed. Both incidents involved conflict between the Anglo and Chicano communities.

Several days after the introductory simulation, Eric's students gather in small groups and begin independent learning activities that have grown out of Monday's experience (Figure 9.2). These activities have been carefully selected for each student on the basis of the student's mastery level of common core learnings (or mastery level of a student's self-selected learning) and the student's preferred style of learning.

Eric labels common core learnings those skills and understandings that everyone is expected to master. Examples of common core learnings for his course as a whole are basic vocabulary and acquisition of key concepts, plus interpersonal communication, decision making, and thinking skills. An example of common core learnings for the unit on "The News Media: Believe It or Not?" is the ability

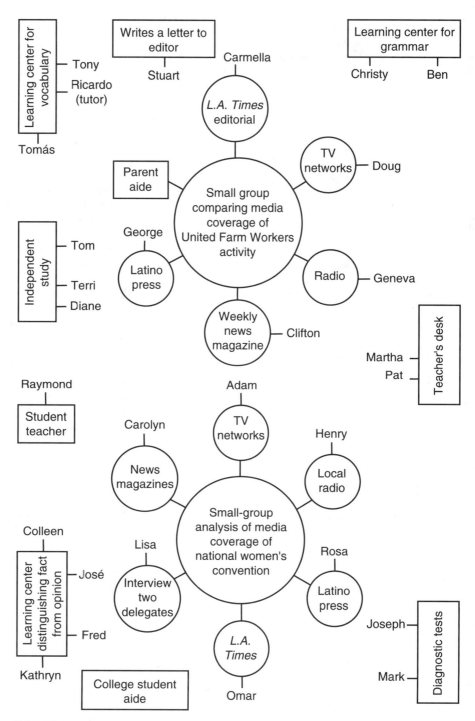

FIGURE 9.2
Classroom Floor Plan in Use by Students
Adapted from Christine Bennett, "Individualized Instruction in the Secondary Schools," *Viewpoints in Teaching and Learning* 55, no. 20 (Spring 1979):80.

to distinguish facts from opinion in selected samples of printed, visual, and aural news media. Students who have achieved mastery of the unit's common core learning objectives are free to work toward mastery of self-selected learnings. Today, Stuart, Martha, Pat, Tom, Terri, and Diane are working in self-selected areas according to a contract set up with Eric. Ricardo has developed an original activity for Tomás and Tony to supplement Eric's vocabulary learning center. Everyone else is working toward common core mastery learning, although the methods and/or materials vary.

Eric has gathered diagnostic information on most of his students (approximately 140 in his five classes) during the past few months. He maintains a file for each student. These files contain information on the student's reading level, cognitive style (abstract or concrete), preferred mode of learning (visual, auditory, kinesthetic, mixed), need for structure, preferred mode of instruction (independent, one to one, small group, large group), and interests.

At first Eric found the gathering and storing of student information overwhelming, and he nearly gave up. Although the first month of each year is still demanding, he has worked out an efficient and effective system of record keeping that runs smoothly and assists each student in understanding his or her progress.

Eric makes excellent use of aides from the community and participants from local schools. He finds that most of these people can come only one day a week for approximately three hours, and some valuable community resource people are free only one hour a week or less. To avoid confusion and the possible distraction of new people moving in and out of the room, he has developed a master schedule illustrating who comes when and for what purpose. He insists that his regular participants and volunteers be reliable and punctual, and participate in at least one class at the same time each week for one school semester. He categorizes his aides according to their areas of skill and interest and develops tasks accordingly. Every aide has a specific job to do whenever she or he is present in the classroom. Some of the tasks many aides, especially senior citizens, can do include typing or writing as the pupil dictates an original story, vocabulary card games, Scrabble, conversing in Spanish and standard English, grading and recording tests, and discussing literature. Those participants who serve as tutors go through a twelve-hour training program that is coordinated by another teacher at school.

Occasionally, he sets up pot-luck or brown-bag lunches to allow his students to meet and talk with busy resource people from the community. This semester each of his five classes has a minimum of one aide for two days every week; some classes have an aide every day. Eric uses a grandmother, a former fifth-grade teacher, to help organize and coordinate the activities of all the other aides.

Involvement of outside people might be more than many teachers can take, at least all at once. Eric has developed his organization and network of people over several years so that community people from the neighborhoods of all his students are an integral part of his classroom environment. And it isn't a one-way street. Many of his students voluntarily reciprocate with neighborhood clean-up, gardening projects, grocery shopping, and yard care.

This classroom exemplifies the use of a cluster of basic strategies for individualized instruction. First, in the simulation activity the teacher uses experiential learning in the large group to motivate students and introduce a new unit or topic. Teachers who use the experiential or do-look-learn approach select an experience situation as a springboard to discussion, analysis, and follow-up activities, which lead into the ongoing curriculum. Typical experience situations are simulations, role playing, or contrived activities that involve every student.

Second, the teacher's program includes mastery learning. Mastery learning is based on the premise that all but a few students are capable of learning the basic concepts and skills of a subject if they are given appropriate instruction. In this classroom, a common core of learning objectives is identified for each unit. With a few exceptions, no student moves on to a new unit until mastery (usually 85 percent correct on unit test) has been achieved. Rapid learners may spend most of their time working on self-selected objectives that allow them to pursue special interests related to the topic. Learners who are slow to master the first few units often begin to speed up as they experience learning success, many for the first time.

Third, the teacher has set up an extensive tutoring program that involves peers and community aides. Tutoring, especially cross-age tutoring, appears to be an effective strategy for raising student achievement levels. Research on the impact of tutoring programs concludes the following:

1. Training is necessary. Tutors must receive training in basic human relations and techniques appropriate for the content to be taught.
2. Tutors generally benefit more than tutees; however, tutees also benefit in terms of achievement gains.
3. Students who are failing in their own classwork can be helped to instruct younger learners in their regular schoolwork.

Finally, the teacher is also making effective use of the learning activity package (LAP), learning centers or stations, and independent study. These strategies are basic ways of building a more flexible learning environment.

The remainder of this chapter provides a description and analysis of each of these concepts and strategies. It also presents student team learning, a strategy not evident in Eric's classroom. Sample lessons created by practicing teachers are included to illustrate how a variety of teachers have moved to create more flexible learning environments.

Mastery Learning

Mastery learning refers to a teaching concept that breaks subject matter down into a series of units to be learned sequentially. The learner must achieve a high level of competency in one unit before moving on to the next unit in the sequence.

Proponents of mastery learning contend that the vast majority of students (90 to 95 percent) are capable of mastering most learning tasks in the school's basic curriculum if given sufficient time and appropriate instruction.[21] They believe that high standards (at least as high as the traditional grade levels) can be expected and achieved if the quality of instruction is adequate. Quality of instruction depends on factors such as the clarity of the learning task, appropriate sequencing of instructional materials, and effective use of tests to provide corrective feedback and motivational support. How quickly a student will learn new tasks depends on prior learning, aptitude, the task's complexity, perseverance, and the learner's ability to understand instructions, as well as the quality of teaching. The major point is, however, that nearly all students can eventually learn if they have good instructors.

Patricia Cross, a scholar who has focused on nontraditional students (those outside the White middle class), believes that mastery learning is the missing link needed to foster academic success among those who have been overrepresented among the students who fail in school or drop out.[22] For one thing, mastery learning assumes that virtually all students can learn. For another, it helps school failures—those who have not mastered basic essentials—catch up.

For a variety of reasons many students are not ready to learn certain concepts or skills when they are introduced, or they are unable to master them as taught by a particular teacher. Yet these students are rushed through the curriculum, and the gap between school achievers and nonachievers widens every year. Proponents of mastery learning argue that the concept provides a solution to these problems because it lays the foundation for future learning by insisting that one unit must be mastered before the learner tackles the next. Furthermore, poor students discover that they are, in fact, capable of doing good work.

Some critics of the mastery learning approach fear that the overall levels of student achievement will decline because teachers will put most of their efforts into getting everyone up to a minimum standard. Other critics argue that it places too much burden on teachers by blaming them for student failures. Proponents, on the other hand, argue that the schools often do contribute to failure. In his introduction to *Schools without Failure,* for example, Glasser writes:

> Much has been written on the difficulties of improving education in the central city. From personal experience, I believe that most people who write about these schools have not raised the critical issue They have been so obsessed with the social, environmental and cultural factors affecting students that they have not looked deeply enough into the role education itself has played in causing students to fail, not only in the central city but in all schools. . . . Very few children come to school failures, none come labeled failures; it is school and school alone which pins the label of failure on children.[23]

Mastery learning's proponents believe they can provide at least a partial antidote to school failure. Benjamin Bloom claims, for example, that with appropriate instruction 95 percent of students can attain mastery and a grade of A. For Bloom, the notion of grading by the bell-shaped normal curve makes no sense in the classroom because it is a statistical tool designed to reflect random processes. To the degree that the teacher has purposeful impact on learners, the grading curve should depart from a chance distribution; thus Bloom asserts that the closer student achievement follows a normal distribution, the more unsuccessful are the teacher's efforts.[24]

The mastery learning literature has grown dramatically since the seminal works of John Carroll in 1963 and Bloom in 1968.[25] James Block has probably done more than anyone to date in helping educators transfer the theories of mastery learning into practice.[26] Typically, a course based on Bloom's mastery learning is developed according to the following steps:

1. The course or subject is broken down into a series of learning units covering one or two weeks of instruction.
2. The instructional objectives, representing a wide range of learning outcomes (e.g., knowledge, comprehension, and application), are clearly specified for each unit.
3. The learning tasks within each unit are taught using regular group-based instruction.
4. Diagnostic-progress tests (formative tests) are administered at the end of each learning unit.
5. The results of the end-of-unit tests are used to reinforce the learning of students who have mastered the unit and to diagnose the learning errors of those who fail to demonstrate mastery.
6. Specific procedures for correcting learning deficiencies (e.g., rereading particular pages, using programmed materials, and using audiovisual aids) and additional learning time are prescribed for those who do not achieve unit mastery. Pretesting may be done after the corrective study. (See Table 9.1 for types of correctives.)
7. Upon completion of all the units, an end-of-course (summary) test is administered to determine students' course grades. All students who perform at or above the predetermined mastery level (set at course's outset) receive a grade of A in the course. Lower grades are also assigned an the basis of absolute standards that have been set for the course.
8. The results of the unit tests (formative tests) and the final examination (summary tests) are used as a basis for improving the methods, materials, and sequencing of instruction.[27]

TABLE 9.1
Block and Anderson's Summary of General Types of Correctives

Corrective	Individual	Group	Presentation	Involvement
Alternative textbooks	X		X	
Workbooks	X		X	
Flashcards	X		X	
Reteaching		X	X	
Audiovisual materials[a]		X	X	
Token economies	X			X
Academic games		X		X
Group affective exercises[a]		X		X
Programmed instruction	X		X	X
Tutoring	X		X	X
Small group study sessions		X	X	X

Source: Reprinted with permission of Macmillan Publishing Company from *Mastery Learning in Classroom Instruction* by James H. Block and Lorin W. Anderson. Copyright © 1975 Macmillan Publishing Company.

[a]These correctives might also be used on an individual basis in some situations.

Eric used a modified version of Bloom's mastery learning (see Figures 9.3 and 9.4). He identifies the learning goals and objectives in the common-core area, and divides his course into a sequence of cumulative units (Figure 9.3) designed to help students master the overarching objects for the course. With a few exceptions, no student moves on to a new unit until mastery has been achieved. However, enrichment learning objectives also become a systematic part of his planning. These are developed, or emerge, in each unit for students who have already mastered the core material or who will learn it very quickly.

In contrast to the core learning objectives, which are spelled out in advance, the enrichment learning objectives need not follow a cumulative sequence from unit to unit and are relatively open-ended to encourage student creativity and divergent thinking. In the case of short-term enrichment objectives, contracts are used, and they match the student's need for structure as well as the amount of time likely to be available before the entire class moves on to the next unit. It is possible, however, for some students to pursue enrichment learning objectives that span two or more common-core learning units.

Rapid learners may spend most of their time working on enrichment objectives. Students like Tony and Tomás, however, will also have some opportunity to work on student-selected enrichment objectives. A key to the success of Eric's program is the fact that the enrichment objectives are, in fact, enriching. Students do not regard them as extra or busy work.

In addition to including the student-selected enrichment objectives, Eric has modified Bloom's mastery learning in a second important way. Rather than

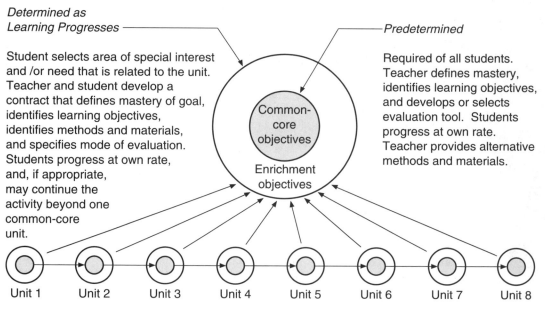

FIGURE 9.3
Overview of Learning Objectives for Entire Course

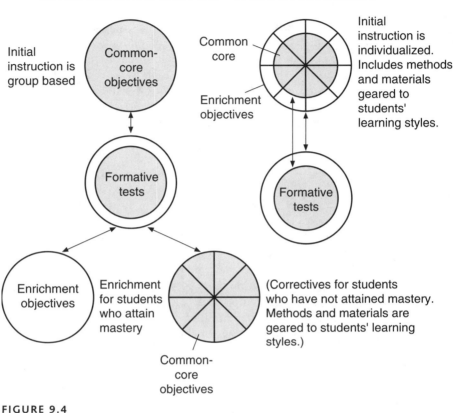

BLOOM'S MASTERY LEARNING   ERIC'S MODIFICATIONS

FIGURE 9.4
Mastery Learning Modified

using correctives to reteach students who do not achieve mastery on the unit test, he *continually* builds the correctives into his learning program. He uses group-based instruction largely for motivation, basic instructions, and occasional lectures. He feels this greater flexibility is necessary because of the strong cultural diversity and numerous individual differences among his students. Because he knows the students cannot all master the objectives in the same way with ease, he does not wait until a unit test has identified students who need different strategies (see Figure 9.4). Eric's floor plan illustrates how he organizes his classroom so that many of these correctives can be used throughout the unit as part of his original instructional plan.

One of the most important advantages of mastery learning is that it provides learners with a feeling of success and accomplishment. Furthermore, the feeling is based on actual achievement and new competence. These achievements generate feelings of confidence that are necessary for school success; because students are actually mastering the expected learning objectives, problems of social promotion are minimized or eliminated. It is no longer acceptable to cover material and move on if students have not learned.

As conceptualized by Bloom and Block and Anderson, mastery learning is well suited for the constraints most teachers face—for example, large groups, required textbooks, grade-level groupings, and strict time schedules.[28] Mastery learning allows us to teach a group of students in whatever way we wish. We are required to modify the large group plan by using one or more correctives (see Table 9.1) only for those students who did not learn during the initial group-based instruction. Furthermore, mastery learning is not all that new. Many textbooks and supplementary materials in all areas of the curriculum are already based on the mastery learning concept. Teachers just have not been expecting mastery on the part of most students.

The approach is not without problems, however. Teachers worry that too much time will be spent waiting for slower learners to catch up. (Actual experience shows that once the fundamentals are learned in early units, high levels of mastery are achieved more quickly in subsequent units.) Parents and high-achieving students under the traditional approach often resent the lack of recognition and the fact that everyone can get As. If mastery learning is to be successful, a careful orientation is necessary for students, parents, and teachers. Competition for grades must be replaced by shared responsibility for achievement and the recognition that everyone benefits when the overall level of learning is significantly improved. There is still room for the development of individual talents and gifts, however, and this must be part of the plan.

Students who are accustomed to failure must be given encouragement, support, and the experience of success. Students who are accustomed to school success must continue to experience it. When genuine enrichment opportunities are available, learning expands and students need not suffer through redundant material. Report cards can be modified to record students' special achievements beyond the basic course requirements.

Teachers will need to rely on their common sense as they implement mastery learning in their own classrooms. Eric, for example, believes that mastery learning works best for those portions of the course in which concepts and skills are typically learned sequentially, complex behaviors depend on the previous learning of less complex behaviors, and students use convergent thinking (recall) rather than divergent thinking (synthesis). This is a clue that students who tend to be highly intuitive, approach learning holistically, or prefer inductive learning might become frustrated or uncomfortable with a total program comprised of performance-based sequential and convergent learning tasks. Higher-order thinking skills—including application, analysis, synthesis, and evaluation—can, however, be taught through the mastery learning approach.

Furthermore, there are important areas in Eric's course where predetermination of objectives and methods of evaluation associated with mastery learning are inappropriate because they cannot be specified prior to knowing the students personally: areas related to personal creativity and expression, special knowledge interests, and attitudes and behavior such as cooperation, empathy, and respect. Finally, some students with high aptitudes may lack requisite entry-level knowledge skills such as (for this classroom) standard English.

■*Experiential Learning*

Experiential learning uses personal experience to engage the learner totally (physically, emotionally, and intellectually) in the discovery of new knowledge. Experiential learning is a teaching concept that is different from mastery learning. The two approaches of teaching can be compatible, as is the case in Eric's classroom.

Some make a distinction between the two concepts on the basis of the humanist-behaviorist controversy. To the degree that mastery learning is based on behavioral objectives and behavior modification, it falls into the psychological school of behaviorism. Experiential learning, on the other hand, falls into the school of humanism.

With mastery learning the knowledge goals and learning objectives are centered in the subject matter. With experiential learning, knowledge is centered in the pupil's behavior and personal and social reality. Knowledge is valued most when it is personally discovered, analyzed, and assimilated. The teacher acts as a fellow investigator rather than as an expert, but encourages students to observe and analyze their experiences.

Eric uses experiential learning to introduce traditional subject matter. His students are engaged in a variety of learning activities that have grown out of the simulation *Bafá Bafá*.[29]

An outstanding resource on the experience-centered curriculum has been developed by an international group of teachers from eight different countries who have worked with David Wolsk as part of a UNESCO-sponsored project for developing international understanding. These teachers have developed a total of fifty-eight units intended mainly for students between the ages of eleven and eighteen. They have also developed guidelines for applying the units to specific subject areas, including biology; mathematics; literature, writing, and language; social studies; physical sciences; physical education; and the arts.[30] There are four required stages:

Stage One: The experience situation
Stage Two: Development of observation and description skills
Stage Three: Development of analysis and decision-making skills
Stage Four: Follow-up activities that link the experience situation and discussion with the ongoing curriculum

Typically, the teacher creates or selects an experience situation to introduce a new concept or unit. These experiences are designed to involve and stimulate students physically, emotionally, and intellectually, for example, a simulation or contrived incident. A carefully developed discussion and appropriate follow-up activities are necessary bridges to the common-core learning objectives of the course; otherwise, the experience situation can degenerate into fun-and-games.

For example, the UNESCO project developed one simple exercise to illustrate the process of stereotyping. Students were asked to discuss their own answers to the question, "What is a (*Dane*)?"

One Danish class recorded their discussion of "What is a Dane?" and exchanged it with a Hungarian class that had written their answers to "What is a Hungarian?" as well as their ideas about Danes. In the follow-up to the exchange, both classes were able to see how they look to others, how they tend to stereotype themselves, how misinformed were their expectations of national differences, and how it feels to be "judged" by others. This judging is what caused their biggest reaction.[31]

Another unit, Blind Trust, is based on a trust walk. Half the students are blindfolded and then led throughout the school and/or outdoors on a ten-minute walk by an unknown partner. Talking is not permitted. Later, the students exchange roles so that each experiences leadership and dependency. A third unit, Four Hands on the Clay, illustrates some of the practices involved in cooperative decision making. Students work in pairs on a large block of clay, with their eyes closed. After the students have removed watches and jewelry and have rolled up their sleeves, they are lined up along the walls; then they are instructed to close their eyes and keep them closed throughout the exercise. The students are instructed not to talk or laugh or make any noise that would allow others to identify them. Partners are then led one by one over to chairs next to large blocks of clay that have been distributed around the desks or tables so that partners can sit opposite each other with the clay between them. The partners are instructed to create something out of the clay, working and communicating only with their hands.[32]

Even if experience situations such as these do not turn out as the teacher expected, the activity cannot fail. Whatever happens should become the basis of the follow-up discussion in stage two. Once class members have discussed their observations of what happened, they should move to a discussion of their feelings and analyses in stage three.

After a trust walk, students might be asked what influenced them to trust or not trust the other person. What cues from the other person did they tune into? How did the other person feel? Would it have helped to know who their partner was, or not? During the exercise Four Hands on the Clay, students could explain how they decided what would be created. Without the use of eyes and ears, how did communication take place? What was your partner feeling?

In the fourth stage, follow-up activities are needed to link the experience situation and discussions with important course objectives. Students should not regard these activities as just fun and frills. Independent study or small-group projects are possible follow-ups, as well as large-group instruction and lectures. Four Hands on the Clay, for example, could introduce students to a study of the nervous system. What was going on in the brain during their activity? All students experienced a visual image as they worked. How can this occur? Four Hands on the Clay could also motivate students to explore nonverbal communication, to develop their own creative expressions, or to increase their decision-making skill. (How did the partners communicate? Or did they? Could they cooperate?) Students might build upon their experiences in the trust walk to examine the role of trust in cross-cultural communication, international agreements, and the role of spotters in physical education classes.

The curriculum developed by Wolsk and his team has been found to significantly increase pupils' readiness to associate with students and families of different nationalities. Positive impact has also been noted on students' feelings of acceptance by the teacher and other pupils, attitudes toward school learning, decreased levels of school and general anxiety, and increased social sensitivity through greater empathy, acceptance, respect, and genuineness. Thus, the approach clearly has implications for any teacher who wishes to decrease interpersonal and group barriers based on ethnic differences, and to increase empathy.

Wolsk's curriculum has also been found to enhance student achievement. The experiences of one eighth- and ninth-grade English teacher in the rural Midwest is typical of teachers everywhere who decide to implement experiential learning. In this teacher's classes, the students' writing skills improved dramatically during the program, particularly when compared with the skills of classmates who did not have an opportunity to discuss and write about experience situations. The teacher happened to be exceptionally creative in developing ingenious experience situations. Other teachers in his school tended to be suspicious and even ridiculing of his approach until the student achievement results became obvious by the end of the year.

An experiential approach is especially effective with culturally diverse groups of students because (with the important exception of language) there are no specific knowledge, attitude, or skill prerequisites for the initial involvement. Students can participate in the introductory activity regardless of their achievement levels or cultural orientations. In fact, the greater the diversity of experiences among the students who participate, the richer the follow-up discussion and activities will be for all the students. As happened in Eric's second-period class, cultural patterns often emerge spontaneously and can be examined with less risk of stereotyping because these patterns coexist with individual variability.

The experience-centered curriculum is an approach to individualized instruction that works well in conjunction with mastery learning because it injects the motivation that is often necessary to move learners on to mastery.

> A class learning from a textbook and the teacher's lessons uses much of their time and energy in adjusting the structures of their own information processing systems, their individual classification structures, to the teacher's and textbook's classifications. Alternatively, when an experience situation is used as a starting point, and an open-ended discussion follows, the pupils are, in a sense, being left alone to learn in their own style. They individually put in and take out of the situation what they are ready for. When they follow this up with textbooks and teachers' lessons, it is with a series of questions stated in their own terms and linked to their own reactions to the experience situation and to individual views of their own past, present and future lives.[33]

Bilingual Education

Multicultural schools are environments where all children of every ethnic and socioeconomic background feel welcome and are encouraged to reach their highest potential. In linguistically diverse societies such as the United States,

Multicultural schools help prepare students for life in an interconnected world.

bilingual education is a necessary component of multicultural schools. Children are taught in two languages: English and the native language.

It is common sense that students will learn better if they understand what is being taught, an assumption that is backed up by research. In their book *Learning in Two Worlds: An Integrated Spanish/English Biliteracy Approach,* Perez and Torres-Guzmán write:

> For children who come to our schools speaking Spanish, developing literacy in the language for which they have oral forms is essential. Children who use their first language to solve problems and discuss abstract ideas also learn to use a second language in similar ways. A substantial amount of research . . . has shown that the most effective route to English language literacy for language minority students is through their first language.[34]

This is true for all language minority students, such as those who speak an African American dialect, as well as the myriad American Indian and Asian languages.

As shown in the discussion in Chapter 2 of high- and low-context culture, world view, and scholastic ethnicity, language is at the heart of culture. More than a means of verbal and nonverbal communication, language is itself a shaper of ideas.[35] Members of a speech community develop shared standards for ways of thinking, feeling, acting, and judging.[36]

By the age of three, a child has begun to master the phonological, semantic, and syntactic components that all languages must have.[37] These sound, meaning, and grammar systems develop in generative stages referred to as *holophrastic* (one-word utterances), *telegraphic* ("me go home"), and *pivo-*

topen grammar ("allgone egg"). The vocabulary, intonation patterns, and non-verbal gestures that accompany language production are learned from models (parents, siblings, and neighbors) and are culture bound. World view, perception, and intuition are interactive in the language learning process.

Students with limited English proficiency are often caught up in conflicts between personal language needs—for example, the need to consolidate cognitive skills in the native language—and a sociopolitical climate that views standard English as most desirable and prestigious. Cultural conflict with the school occurs in crucial areas that require English language proficiency: textbooks and tools for assessing language skills, cognitive abilities, achievement level, and academic potential, not to mention ongoing interpersonal communication during classroom instruction.

According to the 1990 census, 14 percent of Americans five years old and over are from non-English-speaking homes.[38] During the past decade the number of residents for whom English is a foreign tongue jumped by more than a third to 31.8 million in the 1980s, due largely to a wave of immigration from Latin America, Asia, and Europe. About 7.5 percent of the population over age five speak Spanish, and another 3.9 percent speak one of nine other languages at home. Furthermore, families with limited or no proficiency in English are found in virtually every state. These trends are not new. "The history of American education is marked by attempts to grapple with our 'polyglot' heritage.' "[39]

The United States is not the first country to formulate policy for a polyglot or multilingual society. National strategies for language policy tend to fall into three categories: (1) emphasis on a national language at the expense of indigenous languages, such as in Australia, Canada, and the former Soviet Union; (2) elevation of a local language (vernacular) that symbolizes sociocultural, religious, or political unity to the status of national language, as in Quebec (French) and India (Hindi); or (3) retention of the language of a previously occupying nation, or colonial languages, as the official language when there are numerous traditional language groups competing for power, as in Nigeria. The history of language policy in the United States is best described by the first strategy, emphasis on national language at the expense of indigenous languages.

The nineteenth- and early twentieth-century waves of immigration from Europe, China, and Japan prior to World War I led initially to the establishment of private and public schools that used native languages as the primary mediums of instruction.[40] These multilingual education programs and a national tolerance for cultural diversity were soon submerged by Americanization programs in the schools. By 1923, thirty-two states had adopted English-only instruction for the schools. Some school systems attempted to prohibit any kind of foreign language instruction. This step, however, was ruled unconstitutional by the Supreme Court (*Meyer v. Nebraska*) in 1923. In part a reaction to World War I, these English-only laws still exist in a few states today. Assessing their intent, Arnold Leibowitz states that they were designed "to limit access to economic and political life."[41] Although educational trends have moved away from the banning of foreign language instruction, an effort is being made to politically establish English as the official language of the United States. Although this type of bill has failed in Congress on numerous occasions, individual states have begun to investigate such legislation. In 1984 the state senates passed a bill that established English as the official language in Indiana, Kentucky, and Tennessee. Since then over thirty states have had legislation introduced. It has passed in eight states, including California, Florida, and Arizona. By 1988 there were sixteen "official-English" states in the United States.[42]

World War II led to the realization that the trend toward educational monolingualism had left the United States at a global disadvantage. It was not until 1958, however, after the Russians launched *Sputnik,* that the United States realized the disadvantage of a policy of linguistic isolation. The National Defense Education Act, passed that year, had as its primary goal the facilitation of foreign language instruction in the United States. One ramification of this act came in the form of assertive efforts on behalf of linguistic minorities during the 1960s.

The concept of bilingual education has steadily gained momentum in this society since the formation of Miami's Coral Way School in 1963. Established by the wave of Cuban immigrants who entered Florida in the early 1960s—most of whom were highly educated, skilled professionals who held social and educational values compatible with Miami's mainstream—the school provided Spanish-language-dominant and English-language-dominant children proficiency in two languages and an appreciation of knowledge of two cultures. The success of this Dade County, Florida, school greatly influenced language education policy over the next twenty years. A chronology follows:

1963 Dade County, Florida, initiated a bilingual program for Spanish-speaking Cuban children and English-dominant children who want to become bilingual.

1965 The Elementary and Secondary Education Act (ESEA) granted funds to schools to upgrade education, including the areas of languages and linguistics.

1966 The first Navajo/English school was created in Rough Rock, Arizona.

1967 The Elementary and Secondary Education Act provided funds for schools that wished to implement bilingual education designed for language-minority students. Seventy-two bilingual programs started in 1969.

1968 The Bilingual Education Act was passed by Congress. The act was reauthorized in 1974, 1978, 1984, 1988, and 1990.

1971 Massachusetts became the first state to pass a law mandating bilingual education for limited-English-proficient students.

1973 The Bilingual Education Reform Act updated the 1968 law and mandated the study of history and culture in bilingual programs.

1974 The United States Supreme Court decision, *Lau v. Nichols,* decreed that limited-English-proficient students have a legal right to special assistance as part of equal educational opportunity.

1974 The National Council of Teachers of English (NCTE) affirmed the right of a student to use his or her own language.

1979 Ann Arbor, Michigan, court decision on dialects stated that use of Black English vernacular is not an indication of intellectual inferiority or learning disability.

1979 The President's Commission on Foreign Language and International Studies reported, "The inability of most Americans to speak or understand any language except English and to comprehend other cultures handicaps the U.S. seriously in the international arena."

1983 The National Commission on Excellence in Education called for renewed efforts in teaching foreign languages.

1988 The Bilingual Education Act was reauthorized and amended by the three-year enrollment rule, implying that three years of bilingual education was sufficient for most students with limited English proficiency.

In adding the three-year enrollment rule to the Bilingual Education Act in 1988, Congress accepted the myth that prolonged reliance on the native language hinders English language development. Two decades of research appear to have been ignored.[43]

Some of the most important research on second-language acquisition has been carried out by Stephen Krashen, of the University of Southern California, and Jim Cummins, of the Ontario Institute for Studies in Education.[44] According to Krashen, children do not learn a second language through direct instruction. Instead, proficiency in a second language is acquired in the same way the first language was acquired, when it is understood. Therefore, Krashen recommends that teachers provide background knowledge in the native tongue to make English instruction more comprehensible. Native-language instruction also helps penetrate the child's *affective filter*, such as "anxiety, lack of self-confidence, and inadequate motivation to speak the second language."[45]

Cummins hypothesizes that thinking skills developed in the first language will transfer to the second language. However, if the transfer from the first to second language occurs prematurely, prior to the five to seven years typically required to reach the "threshold level," the child "is likely to be cognitively retarded in both languages."[46] Cummins criticizes quick-exit transitional bilingual education programs that don't allow children time to develop beyond basic interpersonal communication skills (BICS), sometimes called "playground English." Cummins believes that children must attain cognitive academic language proficiency (CALP) in their first language in all the school subjects before they are ready to learn these subjects in English. He advocates five to seven years of native language instruction in reading, writing, mathematics, and social studies, along with communication-based ESL and sheltered English classes. (In sheltered English classes the teacher bases instruction on the English vocabulary students already know. Students are "sheltered" from words and phrases they cannot understand.)

The design of bilingual/multicultural education programs varies according to the underlying philosophy of a local community or state. These philosophies fall along the continuum of cultural assimilation at one end and cultural pluralism on the other.

Transitional programs focus on the goal of mainstreaming students with limited English language skills into English-only classes as soon as they have the English proficiency to succeed, and cultural assimilation is often stressed. Transitional programs provide instruction in the children's native language "to help them keep up in school subjects, while they study English in programs designed for second-language learners."[47] The goal is to prepare for English-only classrooms, typically within two to three years.[48] Unfortunately, transference is often expected prior to the consolidation of language skills in the native language, which typically occurs around the age of ten or eleven. This premature transference may harm children's cognitive development by disallowing use of the home language as a cognitive tool.

Maintenance or developmental programs, on the other hand, are designed to help children develop cognitive skills in both their native language and English. Maintenance of the native language is believed to support and facilitate transition into English while strengthening a sense of ethnic identity. An ideal maintenance program provides dual-language instruction for students from kindergarten through twelfth grade, although few exist at the secondary level. The student develops cognitively in both languages and is instructed in the history and culture of his or her ethnic group, as well as that of the dominant culture. Students retain and expand the home language while also becoming proficient in standard English.

Two-way bilingual education is another way to approach maintenance or developmental bilingual programs. Children who speak different home languages are placed together in a bilingual classroom. They learn each other's languages and work academically in both languages.[49]

There are also English as a Second Language (ESL) programs, which use only English as a medium of English-language instruction. The goal is to assimilate learners into the English language as quickly as possible. The ESL programs may be found as a language arts component of a bilingual education program or used alone to simultaneously teach English to a variety of students with different native-language backgrounds. ESL programs seem most effective when more than one home language is represented in a classroom. They provide English-only instruction but may include a multicultural emphasis. According to Troike, research indicates that an English-only classroom is not as cognitively effective as a sound bilingual program.[50] ESL programs, however, can be highly effective and appropriate for students who are motivated to learn the new language in a mainstream English-only classroom. There are also enrichment immersion programs widely successful among language majority children who wish to acquire a second language, as in the French immersion language program in Quebec and the Chinese language immersion program in Indiana.

Whatever approach is used, motivation is the key to successful language learning. Gardner and Lambert described integrative and instrumental motivation as being the determining factors in language learning.[51] Integrative motivation exists when the learner wants to incorporate both the new language and aspects of the new culture into his or her lifestyle. Instrumental motivation, however, is more single-goal oriented—learning the language to enhance career goals or academic success, for example.

A variety of factors affects the motivation of students' desire to learn the English language, as well as their motivation to retain their original language. Table 9.2 summarizes major factors that encourage language retention and lan-

TABLE 9.2
Factors Encouraging Language Retention and Loss

Language Retention	Language Loss
Political, Social, and Demographic Factors	
Large number of speakers living in concentration (ghettos, reservations, ethnic neighborhoods, rural speech islands)	Small number of speakers, dispersed among speakers of other languages
Recent arrival and/or continuing immigration	Long, stable residence in the United States
Geographical proximity to the homeland; ease of travel to the homeland	Homeland remote and inaccessible
High rate of return to the homeland; intention to return to the homeland, homeland language community still intact	Low rate or impossibility of return to homeland (refugees, Indians displaced from their tribal territories)
Occupational continuity	Occupational shift, especially from rural to urban
Vocational concentration, i.e., employment where co-workers share language background; employment within the language community (stores serving the community, traditional crafts, homemaking, etc.)	Vocations in which some interactions with English or other languages is required; speakers dispersed by employers (e.g., African slaves)
Low social and economic mobility in mainstream applications	High social and economic mobility in mainstream occupations
Low level of education, leading to low social and economic mobility; *but* educated and articulate community leaders, familiar with the English-speaking society and loyal to their own language community	Advanced level of education, leading to socioeconomic mobility; education that alienates potential community leaders.
Nativism, racism, and ethnic discrimination as they serve to isolate a community and encourage identity with the ethnic group rather than the nation at large.	Nativism, racism, and ethnic discrimination, as they force individuals to deny their ethnic identity in order to make their way in society
Cultural Factors	
Mother-tongue institutions, including schools, churches, clubs, theaters, presses, broadcasts	Lack of mother-tongue institutions, from lack of interest or lack of resources
Religious and/or cultural ceremonies requiring command of the mother tongue	Ceremonial life institutionalized in another tongue or not requiring active use of mother tongue
Ethnic identity strongly tied to language; nationalistic aspirations as a language group; mother tongue, the homeland national language	Ethnic identity defined by factors other than language, as for those from multilingual countries or language groups spanning several nations; low level of nationalism
Emotional attachment to mother tongue as a defining characteristic of ethnicity, of self	Ethnic identity, sense of self derived from factors such as religion, custom, race rather than shared speech

Continued

TABLE 9.2
Factors Encouraging Language Retention and Loss *(Continued)*

Language Retention	*Language Loss*
Emphasis on family ties and position in kinship or community network	Low emphasis on family or community ties, high emphasis on individual achievement
Emphasis on education, if in mother-tongue or community-controlled schools, or used to enhance awareness of ethnic heritage; low emphasis on education otherwise	Emphasis on education and acceptance of public education in English
Culture unlike Anglo society	Culture and religion congruent with Anglo society
Linguistic Factors	
Standard, written variety is mother tongue	Minor, nonstandard, and/or unwritten variety as mother tongue
Use of Latin alphabet in mother tongue, making reproduction inexpensive and second-language literacy relatively easy	Use of non-Latin writing system in mother tongue, especially if it is unusual, expensive to reproduce, or difficult for bilinguals to learn
Mother tongue with international status	Mother tongue of little international importance
Literacy in mother tongue, used for exchange within the community and with homeland	No literacy in mother tongue; illiteracy
Some tolerance for loan words, if they lead to flexibility of the language in its new setting	No tolerance for loan words, if no alternate ways of capturing new experiences evolve, too much tolerance of loans, leading to mixing and eventual language loss

Source: Reprinted with permission of The Free Press, a Division of Macmillian, Inc., from *A Host of Tongues* by Nancy Faires Conklin and Margaret A. Lourie. Copyright © 1983 The Free Press.

guage loss. It is essential for teachers to recognize that some ethnic groups tend to be more motivated than others to learn standard English. The Spanish-speaking communities of the Southwest, for example, were guaranteed the right to retain the Spanish language under the conditions of the Treaty of Guadalupe Hidalgo, and fluency in the Spanish language is essential to maintaining family and community bonds on both sides of the border. Newly arrived Vietnamese, on the other hand, who are eager to build a new life in the United States, may also be eager to master English. When family members encourage the acquisition of English or are themselves bilingual, the child's acquisition of the new language is enhanced. The mastery of standard English need not result in the loss of the home language. The knowledge of two or more languages or the ability to code switch from one variety of English grammar, pronunciation, and usage to another (bidialectalism) is very desirable in a pluralistic society.

Obviously, the best teachers for students with limited proficiency in English are bilingual teachers who can use the home language as well as English. Yet bilingual teachers for some languages are difficult to find. Therefore, more monolingual teachers will at some time experience language diversity in their classroom. What can these teachers do? The full answer is beyond the scope of this book and may be pursued in the sources listed in the notes at the end of this chapter. Strategies for improving reading skills among dialect-dominant students illustrate how bilingual education strategies have emerged out of foreign language pedagogy. These guidelines also provide a sample of what is available. The teaching strategies may be modified to reach students with limited proficiency in English, whether or not the teacher is bilingual.

Guidelines for Teachers with Dialect-Dominant Students[52]

1. Become familiar with features of the students' dialect. This will allow the teacher to better understand students and to recognize a reading miscue (a noncomprehension feature) from a comprehension error. Students should not be interrupted during the oral reading process. Correction of comprehension features is best done after the reading segment.

2. Allow students to listen to a passage or story first. This can be done in two ways: (a) finish the story and then ask comprehension questions or (b) interrupt the story at key comprehension segments and ask students to predict the outcome.

3. Use predictable stories, which can be familiar episodes in literature, music, or history. They can be original works or experiential readers.

4. Use visual aids to enhance comprehension. Visual images, whether pictures or words, will aid word recognition and comprehension.

5. Use cloze procedure deletions to focus on vocabulary and meaning. Cloze procedures are simply selected deletions of words from a passage in order to focus on a specific text feature. EXAMPLES:
   The little red hen found an ear of corn. The little red —— said, "Who will dry the ear of ——?" (vocabulary focus)
   Today I feel like a *(noun)*. (grammar focus)
   There was a *(pain)* in the pit of his stomach. (semantic focus)

6. Allow students to retell the story or passage in various speech styles. Have students select different people to whom they would like to retell the story (family member, principal, friend) and assist them in selecting synonyms most appropriate to each audience. This allows both teacher and student to become language authorities.

7. Integrate reading, speaking, and writing skills whenever possible.

8. Use the personal computer (if available) as a time-on-task exercise. The personal computer can effectively assist in teaching the reading techniques of skimming (general idea), scanning (focused reference), reading for comprehension (master total message), and critical reading (inference and evaluation). Time on task is extremely important to skills development.

■ *Learning Activity Packets and Learning Centers*

Learning activity packets (LAPs) and learning centers are useful strategies for providing help to supplement large-group instruction. Both strategies are self-contained learning units for one or a small group of students that require a minimum of teacher guidance if designed and implemented properly. Both can be designed as a single lesson or a series of lessons, or they may be integrated into an entire instructional program as part of the overall classroom organization plan. Learners are usually permitted to progress at their own rate.

The main difference between the two strategies is format. LAPs are typically designed for a single student and are usually packaged in a folder, envelope, or booklet. Centers, on the other hand, involve the creative use of some designated space to develop one or more stations that can be used by one student or a small group of students. For some it "may be a designated area of a room; on a wall, on a shelf, hanging from the ceiling, free standing in the room, or in folders in a box for portability. For others it may engulf the entire physical confines of an area allowing complete freedom of movement and encouraging all manner of learning modes."[53]

A second difference is that LAPs, sometimes referred to as modules or unipacs, represent mastery learning in microcosm, especially if they are performance based. The rationale underlying mastery learning and performance-based packets is identical: Simple concepts must be learned as a foundation for future complex learning, and most students are capable of high achievement although the rate of learning and approach may be different. LAPs are a useful tool for providing instructional alternatives because teachers can create or select LAPs to match the learning needs of an individual or a small group of students. Theoretically, it is possible to imagine thirty students in a self-contained classroom working independently in thirty different LAPs. One of the dangers of LAPs is an underemphasis on affective objectives since the necessary measurement techniques are less readily available.

LAPs are used at all age levels (kindergarten to adult) and can be implemented in any subject area. Some are based primarily on the written word; others take the form of skill centers (such as physical education) or may even be extended into learning centers that include a variety of pictures and instructional media. Whatever the format, these learning units should contain the following components.

1. *Title.* This should arouse student interest.
2. *Motivating Rationale.* Often this is a very brief statement of purpose that tells why the unit is worth studying. Many teachers include some kind of motivational set or attention grabber.
3. *One or More Learning Objectives.* These objectives tell the learner what she or he must do to master the unit. Objectives should focus on the thinking, feeling, and acting dimensions of the learner. Too often, LAPs contain objectives aimed solely at knowledge recall.
4. *Pretest.* This activity enables the teacher to determine the learner's readiness for the unit. It also allows learners to see where they stand in relation to what they are expected to master. The pretest helps avoid redundancy for students who have already mastered the unit or portions of it. It also helps avoid a mismatch for students who lack prerequisite background of skill and information.

5. *Learning Activities.* Experiences and materials are selected or developed to assist the learner in achieving the unit objective(s). In some units students are expected to complete the same assignments in the same way, and the learning activities section might be relatively brief. Usually, it is desirable to provide alternative materials and activities to allow for differences in learning style and language. Gronlund suggests that the following list of activities be considered in planning assignments.

> Read books
> Read magazine articles
> Read newspaper articles
> Use programmed materials
> View film or filmstrips
> Listen to tapes
> Conduct experiments
> Do projects
> Play games
> Take field trips
> Practice communication skills
> Practice physical skills
> Discuss questions with teacher or peers
> Take self-test on unit activities[54]

Special attention must be given to the level of the reading material. It may be necessary to write special instructional materials that can be read by everyone, including learners whose first language is not standard English.

6. *Posttest.* The posttest measures learner attainment of the unit objective(s) and is usually an alternate form of the pretest. Unless it is used as a self-test, the posttest is not included in the packet itself and may be obtained from the teacher when the learner feels ready. Except for certain attitudinal and valuing measures, the posttest is typically criterion referenced (that is, absolute standards of mastery are established, usually 85 percent correct).

Learning centers may be modeled after mastery learning, depending on the purpose of the center, but typically they are not. Each station usually contains all the components needed in a LAP: title, rationale, learning objectives, pretest, learning activities (methods and materials), and means for determining student achievement. Rather than receiving a printed package from the instructor, as with the LAP, the student moves to a center and can receive audio or pictorial instructions and a variety of learning materials and activities. The amount of written explanation can vary from none to extensive. Up to six different learning centers might exist simultaneously in a self-contained classroom, and students might be required to complete any number of them.

> Centers can be developmental, presenting new understandings and skills; functional, providing opportunities to use newly acquired skills and understandings; and/or recreational, providing opportunities to engage in activities for the sake of creativity and pleasure. They should allow for exploration through open-

endedness and afford opportunities to pursue the solution to problems in the learner's own way and should provide the child with the option of manipulating ideas and materials and sharing reactions of such manipulations with their peers and teachers.[55]

Whatever the purpose, successful centers contain three components. The first, clear directions, must tell the student where to place completed work and should guide self-evaluation an assessment. They may be written, flow charted, tape recorded, or given by the teacher or another student. The second component is alternative activities for learning, with emphasis on different learning styles. The third is a method of assessing and recording the learner's involvement in the center.

Both LAPs and learning centers are available commercially, although many teachers prefer to create their own materials. Two samples of teacher-created lessons follow. The first is an excerpt from a LAP created by Teresa Hogue, a high school literature teacher (see Lesson 9.1). The second, by Janice Bristow, describes an eighth-grade foreign language teacher's experiences with learning centers (see Lesson 9.2). Before presenting these examples, this section concludes with a listing of major advantages and disadvantages associated with LAPs and centers.

Both LAPs and learning centers offer advantages such as these:

- They allow students to work in their own learning styles and at their own levels of ability in achieving an objective.
- They enable students to work at their own rates.
- They permit self-pacing and self-evaluation without comparison with others.
- They encourage teachers to assess the interests, needs, and abilities of students before and during the learning activity.
- They help remove the fear of failure from the learning environment. Students can continue working until the desired competency has been reached.
- They encourage the student to take responsibility for learning and yet provide specific feedback and guidance through self-checking activities.
- They help teachers monitor student learning as it progresses, allowing modifications of instruction when required.
- They encourage teacher and student creativity in developing new centers and LAPs and in making existing ones more effective. Teachers can collaborate in creating and sharing new LAPs and centers.

These strategies are not free from problems, however:

- LAPs are sometimes viewed by students, colleagues, parents—and even teachers—as a factory-line approach to instruction that is inconsistent with the traditional role of the teacher as the sole distributor of knowledge. Centers are sometimes perceived to foster student socializing at the expense of learning.
- Students who are not accustomed to self-paced instruction and self-evaluation may feel uncomfortable or be unaccepting.
- Both strategies require a considerable amount of development and preparation time from teachers. Additional teacher time is also spent in supervising and orienting students, particularly during the introduction of the strategy.
- Because of time constraints teachers might be discouraged from doing the revision necessary to meet the changing needs and interests of new students.

Learning Activity Packet   *Teresa Hogue*

SHORT STORY PACKET II

SNEAKING A PEEK
at
Setting

by Teresa Hogue

I. INTRODUCTION

Congratulations!! You are about to embark upon another thrill-packed adventure into the realm of "literature." (Now don't get too excited. . . .) By now you are a veteran user of LAPs because you have survived the activities outlined for you in Short Story Packet I: The Plot Sickens. Remember that in Packet II the learning activities branch out. Our discussion will go beyond a simple definition of *SETTING* and how it aids in understanding the short story. We will examine a broader definition of *SETTING* and think about how an individual's surroundings or environment can shape the person he becomes.

Let's review the rules for using LAPs. Using the tape is optional. If it helps you with your reading, continue to listen to the tape as you read. If it bothers you, don't use it. Different people learn in different ways, so choose the way that you learn best.

If you run across a word that you do not know the meaning of—STOP—grab a copy of Brother Webster and look it up!

If you don't understand an activity in the LAP—STOP—get your hand in the air and I will come running. Together we will clear up your problem.

If you can think of an alternate activity that would be more meaningful for you to do—STOP—get your hand in the air and we will talk about it.

When you are through working with this packet, return it to the shelves INTACT—that means complete, the way you got it, and

(Continued)

with no pieces missing!! Failure to comply will result in death by slow torture. . . . **NEED I SAY MORE?**

II. INSTRUCTIONS

Short Story Packet II: Sneaking a Peek at *SETTING* contains two major objectives. For each objective there are a variety of learning activities designed to help you achieve that objective. In this packet, you will be required to complete <u>all</u> activities unless you are told otherwise.

In addition to this packet, you will need your <u>Self Journal</u>, probably another notebook, and writing implements. Unless a formal writing assignment is indicated, you may use any color of pen you like. (Am I nice, or what?) Creativity in the completion of LAP activities will be rewarded with higher grades.

After you have completed all the activities in <u>Packet II</u>, it will be time for a conference with Ol' Lady Hogue. At that time we will evaluate your work and discuss moving on to the next packet.

All writing assignments, to the activity, may be Remember that an outline accompany the tape!

unless they appear next taped on cassette. of your work must

III. OBJECTIVES

1. You will review the definition of *SETTING* and understand why it is an important element in the study of the short story. The following activities will help you achieve this objective:

   (a) Organizing a chapter in your <u>Self Journal</u> entitled *SETTING*; this will serve as the "vehicle" we'll use to present your work from <u>Packet II</u>.

Don't Panic! Turn the Page!

LESSON 9.1

(Continued)

       (b) Demonstrating your understanding of *SETTING* by reading two stories and analyzing their settings, and by making up your own settings from pictures that suggest a story.

       (c) Reading a third story and deciding why *SETTING* is crucial to that story and how the story would be different if either element of setting were changed.

2. You will broaden your definition of *SETTING* and think about how surroundings and environment affect people. These activities will help you achieve this objective:

       (a) Brainstorming as many broad definitions of *SETTING* as you can with your friends. This will be the springboard we'll use to understand ourselves in relation to our surroundings.

       (b) Researching (in the library!!) the life of a person whom you admire and deciding how environment shaped his or her achievements.

       (c) Outlining an assignment to demonstrate how your environment both stops you from doing some things and offers a wide variety of things you can do.

       (d) Writing (oh, boy!) a formal composition that discusses how your environment has affected you in the past and how it affects you at the present, and what your goals are for the future.

IV.   <u>ACTIVITIES—1</u>

A. In your journal, begin a chapter on *SETTING*. This chapter will include a title page, a definitions page, and several activities pages.

    (1) <u>Title Page</u>. The word *SETTING* should be displayed in bold letters somewhere on the page. (Doesn't freedom make you feel giddy?) Persons in search of brownie points will want to tastefully illustrate the page.

    (2) <u>Definitions Page</u>. In the glossary of your lit book, look up the definition of *SETTING*. Copy it into your journal. This will be definition "A."

| Definitions: |
| A. *wwwwww wwww* |
| *wwww wwwww* |
| B. *wwwww pwww wwww* |
| *wwww www wwwww www* |
| *wwww wwww wwww www* |
| *www wwww* |
| My ideas: *www www* |
| *w wwwwwww w w* |
| *wwww wwww ww* |

(Continued)

Walk, don't run, to the bookshelves and latch onto a copy of Brother Webster. You'll find five definitions. Which one applies most closely to the study of literature? Copy it into your journal. This will be definition "B."

(3) Congratulations. You have just completed Activity A.

B. Firming It Up: Are you ready to continue? Of course you are! In your literature text, your assignment is to read "The Day We Flew the Kites" on p. 103 and "The Hunchback Madonna" on p. 156. Stop and Execute.

Welcome back. I'd suggest a piece of scrap paper and finished product into your . . . First, I want you to ting is for each story. If you now! Okay. Then tell me in think setting is most impor- setting is not as important story. Stop and Execute.

READ AT YOUR OWN RISK

doing this activity on then copying the journal. Listen up. decide what the set- need help ask for it which story you tant. Explain why or vital in the other

REMEMBER: SETTINGS CAN CHANGE WITHIN A STORY!!!!

C. Story Starters: In pocket 1 of the LAP folder, you will find three pictures.

⇨ ⇨ If these pictures were short story illustrations, what do you think the setting of each story might be?

Choose one of the pictures. Write the opening paragraphs of a short story suggested by the picture. You should establish or explain the setting of the story in those two paragraphs. This assignment should be about 200 words long.
—OR—
You may find your own picture and do the same assignment.
—OR—
You may draw or illustrate your own picture.
—OR—
You may creatively illustrate the setting of your story starter by sculpting a statue.
—OR—
You may illustrate your started story with a ten-frame storyboard. ★ Stop and Execute.

(Continued)

D. <u>The Wizard of Frank</u>

(1) In your literature text, turn to p. 308 and read "The Diary of Anne Frank."

"Diary" is <u>NOT</u> a short story because it is non-fiction.

If it will help or entertain you, I have taped the story on cassette 6 under Autobiography.

(2) What is the setting of this story?

(3) You may want to scribble the rest of this assignment on scrap paper and then recopy it into your journal, because it is a formal writing assignment. I want you to tell me about how time and place—or Anne's environment—affected her life. What political events were going on around Anne as she wrote in her diary? How did these events affect Anne and her family? Why were they especially vulnerable to the situation in Europe? In spite of the turmoil of Anne's surroundings, what were her major concerns? Are they like or unlike the things that are important to you?

(4) You will relish this exercise because it means you get out of class to go to the library!! Listen carefully to the assignment and take any notes you may need. Remember that LAPs stay in the room.

Imagine that you are a wizard. You have the power to change time and place. See options for completing this activity below:

(a) <u>Change Place</u>: You magically place Anne Frank in another city during World War II. Use at least two sources for a 300-word written report on what life would be like for a young person in that city. For example, you could describe Anne's life if she lived in London during the Blitz.

(b) <u>Change Time</u>: This one is a little more difficult but can be fun—especially if you are a history buff. You will magically place Anne in Amsterdam during another period in history. For example, you could describe what life was like for a young Jewish girl in Amsterdam during World War I or during the Napoleonic Wars.

The librarian is expecting you and can help you with questions you might have on research. You will be allowed <u>one</u> class period in the library to research this assignment. ✰

LESSON 9.1

(Continued)

V. ACTIVITIES—2

A. <u>Brainstorming</u>: With your friends, your relatives, and any stranger you meet on the street who is as excited about broad definitions of *SETTING* as you are, brainstorm as many definitions of *SETTING* as you can. Dedicate a page in your journal to the fruits of your labors.

B. <u>Mirror, Mirror</u>: In pocket 1, you will discover a mirror. . . . After you have admired yourself, take a serious look at the person staring back at you.

Consider the limits your environment places on what you can do. Think also about the opportunities your environment offers you.

There are limits to what we can do because of when and where we live, but there are also endless possibilities. In Central Indiana it is not possible to pile in the car after school and go to the ocean or the mountains. Nor can we visit with King Henry VIII or vacation on Mars. But there are many opportunities available to us in our place and time. Ten years ago, you could not enroll in computer class. Fifty years ago, you would not be listening to this tape.

In your journal, introduce yourself and describe your environment. You may be very specific or very general. On the back of the page, make three columns. In column I, list five things you can't do because your environment doesn't offer them. Then list five things you <u>can</u> do. In the third column, list four goals or things that you would like to do sometime during your lifetime.

(Continued)

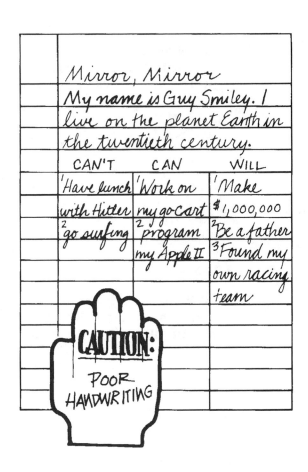

Mirror, Mirror

My name is Guy Smiley. I live on the planet Earth in the twentieth century.

CAN'T	CAN	WILL
¹Have lunch with Hitler	¹Work on my go-cart	¹Make $1,000,000
²go surfing	²program my Apple II	²Be a father
		³Found my own racing team

CAUTION: POOR HANDWRITING

C. <u>Hero at Large</u>: In a magazine, find a picture of your favorite sports hero, rock star, actor, etc. Read about that person's life in newspapers and magazines, or call for an interview if you can arrange it. (You may have a study hall pass, if you need one.)

What happened early in life that led this person to success in his or her field? Did the environment offer special opportunities or obstacles that had to be overcome? After researching this person's life, do you admire him or her more, or are you disappointed? Record your ideas and reactions in a 200-word journal entry. ✭

LESSON 9.1

(Continued)

D. In a formal composition, discuss the environment you are growing up in. Talk about its effect on your past and your present. What are your goals for the future and how do your surroundings affect those goals? ☆

Further Instructions: After you have finished all of the activities in this packet, prepare to turn in your journal. Make an appointment with your teacher for evaluation.

Speaking of Evaluation: Your grade will be based on how neatly, creatively, and completely you have completed the packet activities. Each LAP will count as a test grade.

This lesson is reprinted with the permission of the author.

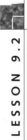

Learning Centers in a Foreign Language Classroom

LESSON 9.2

I have always pictured learning centers as places to go when finished with work, a place for extra information and enjoyment. Naturally, I decided to create a learning center for recreation and enrichment. I never had enough time to present the cultural information I should, so I decided the emphasis of my center would be daily life in Germany. I planned the center to be used specifically with my German 8B class, which is the class for all eighth graders who did not make it into the two-year language program.

(Continued)

There were many problems. Even with the center stuck in a corner, there was always too much noise and confusion. Many students would want to use the center at the same time, and only students who finish work quickly could get a chance. There were no evaluations, as the material was intended for enjoyment, so students did not take the center seriously. Generally, the center became a place for conversation and discipline problems.

My solution was drastic. I threw out the center and started over. I felt I needed a clear plan with clear objectives. I decided upon a learning center to be used for reinforcement of skills taught through lecture and through the text. All students would use the center; in fact, it would become part of the regular class work. Students would be evaluated by the quizzes and tests I normally give after lecture and text exercises. There were again many problems. Since I share a room with another teacher, and since I teach four different classes, the center for German 8B had to be portable—easily assembled and taken apart, as well as easily stored. (See Figure 9.5 for room plans for the arrangements made.) Since I wanted to use the center with each chapter of the book, the materials had to be simple and easily changed:

Station A: Classroom Vocabulary

Materials:

Flashcards with a picture, the English and German words
Blank cards, markers, tape
White 9" × 12" paper, crayons
Textbooks
Cassette player with tape of vocabulary
Large sign with instructions

Students are instructed to choose between:

Memorizing vocabulary with cards
Making labels and placing them around the room on classroom objects
Drawing and labeling vocabulary
Listening and repeating tape presentation of vocabulary

Station B: Verb Conjugation

Materials:

Chalkboard
Colored chalk, eraser
Answer key
Large sign with instructions

Students are instructed to:

Follow step-by-step instructions to write the different parts of several verbs in different colored chalk. They then check their work with the answer key.

(Continued)

Station C: German Schools

Materials:

A description of German schools written on tagboard with pictures and photographs
Notebook paper and pencils
Large sign with instructions

Students are instructed to:

Read the description
Pretend they are a German student and write a brief report or skit about their typical day at school. These may be read or performed if the student desires.

Station D: Listening, Comprehension, Pronunciation

Materials:

Reel-to-reel tape player
Tape of dialogue with native German speakers
Textbook
Dittoes for dictation exercises
Large sign with instructions

Students are instructed to:

Follow the tape presentation with their text, repeating in the appropriate places. Then they are to close their books and write what is spoken on their dittoes. They then open the book and check their work.

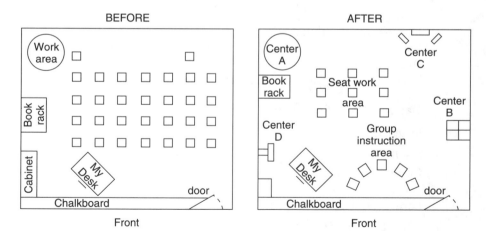

FIGURE 9.5
Room Plans

(Continued)

The next problem was dealing with twenty-one students using the center. To solve this, I first divided the class into three ability groups. Then, I divided class time into three sections. Then, instead of one center, I created four centers. Each center deals with a component of the text chapter—for instance, grammar, vocabulary, culture, and oral comprehension. I made a rotation chart (see Figure 9.6), so that during a class period each group would work with the centers, work on assignments at their seats, and work with me on reinforcement of class lecture. Working with seven students at a time, I felt I could better meet their needs. This way, with four centers, there would only be two students per center per time unit. In one day each student only gets to one center, so I have included a rotation of centers to my chart. We spend three weeks on each unit. During those three weeks, we spend four days on this new schedule so that everyone gets to all centers and gets four days of small-group work with me.

DAY ➡	1	2	3	4
Eva C Jeff Elaine Kim Brian E➡ Stephen	A	B	C	D
Steve N Jim R. Mingo Chris S. Missy T Ernest	B	C	D	A
Jenny E Jill William Mark Kerry R Chris B.	C	D	A	B
Ihab S Jim D. John ⬇	D	A	B	C
Today's order of instruction	group purple red orange	seatwork red orange purple	LC's orange purple red	

Purple: Eva, Steve, Jenny, Ihab, Jeff, Jim R., Jill

Red: Elaine, Mingo, William, Jim D., Brian, Ernest, Kerry

Orange: Kim, Missy, Mark, John, Stephen, Chris S., Chris B.

(Names are color coded on chart.)

FIGURE 9.6
Rotation Chart and Ability Groups

(Continued)

There are still a few details to be worked on, but so far the plan is working well. I get a chance to work with seven students instead of twenty-one, and each student gets a chance to become more responsible for his or her own learning at my four centers. The centers are simple enough to be set up before class, and simple enough to adapt for each chapter. I am also getting students involved with the setting up of the centers, which adds to their sense of responsibility and helps them understand that they are their centers, not the teacher's centers.

This lesson is reprinted with the permission of the author.

Independent Study

Independent study means much more than simply allowing students to work alone on assignments. In its truest sense, independent study refers to that portion of the teacher's instructional program that permits students to choose their own learning objectives, as well as methods and materials of study. It is the strategy for individualized instruction that best satisfies a student's own interests, learning style, and learning rate.

Independent study is a necessary component of Eric Jones's instructional plans. It encourages students to pursue enrichment learning activities and provides the teacher with guidelines for classroom management through the use of contracts.

Independent study allows advanced students to explore a topic as deeply as they wish, and to be as creative as possible. Students are enabled to develop knowledge and skills that go far beyond what is possible in the large-group instructional setting. Their learning and experiences should be shared with other members of the class, during the study and after its completion.

Typically, independent study has been used only with students believed to be the most able; where accelerated courses are not available, independent study is essential. Even though students differ in their readiness to study and investigate on their own, every student can and should be encouraged to pursue independent study to some degree.

The rationale underlying independent study is the assumption that if students can learn how to learn in school, they will become lifelong learners as adults. Independent study develops the sense of responsibility, direction, and self-motivation requisite to lifelong learning. It also helps develop the requisite skills of inquiry.

It has been shown that independent study can be plugged into the ongoing curriculum as an outgrowth of experience situations. Furthermore, independent study projects can enhance students' motivation by allowing them to delve more deeply into topics that hold their interest. One of the advantages of independent study is that it can be extended beyond the classroom into the community itself. The approach can be used in any school, in any community, and in any subject area.

Independent study is most effective when teachers include the following activities:

■ Identify individual students' interests and abilities through interviews, inventories, and tests.

■ Make available materials and experiences that correspond to students' interests and abilities.

■ Know the amount of structure each student needs. (David Hunt's description of students who require high, moderate, or low degrees of structure offers helpful guidelines; see Chapter 6.)

■ Develop contracts and use progress reports that match the learner's need for structure and strengthen self-evaluation skills.

■ Realize that some students do not understand contracts and the notion that they are responsible for meeting their commitment. Start small with these students.

■ Do not expect the same type of contract to work with all students. It may take several years of trial and error to develop a repertoire of contracts that satisfy teacher and students.

■ Do not use independent study as the only strategy for any student. All students need social interaction, especially recluses and shrinking violets who are most apt to enjoy independent work.

The following example was developed by an algebra teacher and includes two contracts providing different degrees of structure.

Contracts can also be used in the primary grades, as illustrated in Figure 9.9.

Independent Study   Debra York-Heck

LESSON 9.3

Because I was planning a unit on graphs/graphing in my algebra classes, I planned the following independent study project: Each student was supposed to select a topic of interest and study the relationship between a constant and some related variable. Then they were instructed to illustrate their results on a graph of their choice and supply a typed explanation of their procedures. This was the basis of evaluation. As an example, one student chose to determine what school fundraiser earned the most money. To illustrate the results, she constructed a broken line graph and attached to it a description of her procedures. The purpose of these projects was to strengthen the students' abilities in drawing information from graphs. By creating their own, I believed it would enable them to decipher information from graphs more easily. Once I decided on this project, I thought a contract between each student and myself would be of great convenience (see Figures 9.7 and 9.8). Because each student's project would be different, I felt this would be the most practical method of recording their learning agreements, which we had discussed. I was right.

LESSON 9.3

(Continued)

Name _____

Project beginning October 24, 19—, and ending November 21, 19—.

Purpose
To further the student's understanding of graph representations.

Criterion Performance
Create a graph illustrating the correlation between any constant and one or more variables. There must be a typed explanation of your procedures and the results illustrated on a poster unless negotiated otherwise.

Method
You may work alone or with a partner. Topics are optional. The following are only suggestions: mileage of various cars, number of various sandwiches sold at fast-food chains, food prices at different stores, clothing sales, basketball scores, couples vs. single guests at a restaurant, number of people attending movies on various nights and/or afternoons, annual snow/rainfall, average temperatures for various months, number of songs played in an hour on different radio stations, number of drunk-driving arrests since new law.

Resources
There will be three other sources available at the Resource Service Desk if you choose to utilize them.

   1. *Career Mathematics: Industry and the Trades*
      Lying, Merwin J., Meconi, L. J., Zurck, Earl J.
   2. *Essentials of Basic Mathematics*, 3d ed.
      Edmond, Carolyn E., Plotkin, Samuel H., Washington, Allyn J.
   3. *Math Squared*
      Stern, David.

Student's choice of topic, working situation, and evaluation

                             Signed _____
                                             (student)

                             Signed _____
                                         (teacher)

FIGURE 9.7
Algebra II—Contract 1 (Highly Structured)

    This project began October 24 and was not due until November 21. The results throughout were terrific. First of all, they loved the idea of having a contract. I thought it might make them uneasy since the use of one was foreign to them, but it didn't. It made them feel more responsible (and none of their friends ever used a contract before so they "had one on them"). By conferencing with each student

(Continued)

Name _____

Project beginning October 24, 19—, and ending November 21, 19—.

Purpose
To further the student's understanding of graph representations.

Criterion Performance
Create a graph illustrating the correlation between any constant and one or more variables. There must be a typed explanation of your procedures and the results illustrated on a poster unless negotiated otherwise.

Method
You may work alone or with a partner. Topics are optional.

Resources
The use of other resources is optional.

Student's choice of topic, working situation, and evaluation

Signed _____
(student)

Signed _____
(teacher)

FIGURE 9.8
Algebra Ii—Contract 2 (Less Structured)

at least once a week, I was able to determine their progress. I did not have to push any of them to begin, and they always had new results to report to me. They conducted their studies, the results of which were to be put into the required evaluative format. It was a new and welcome experience to see them so involved.

This lesson is reprinted with the permission of the author.

Cooperative Learning: Student Team Learning

Student team learning has emerged recently as one of the most promising strategies for working with diverse groups of students. Developed originally for racially desegregated schools, the approach has been extended to virtually all types of schools. Most recently, student team learning techniques have been used to help integrate mainstreamed learners into the "least restrictive environments" with "normal-progress" classmates, and with language-minority at-risk students.[56]

Topic chosen by student:
What If I Had Been Born Fifty Years Ago?

I want to find out what it was like to live fifty years ago. This week I will do one/two/three things (pupil circles one) to find some answers.

_____ 1. I will talk to these people:

_____

_____

_____

_____ 2. I will read this book:

_____

_____ 3. I will watch this television program:

_____

_____ 4. I will visit this place:

_____

_____ 5. I will write a letter to:

_____

I will ask this question:

_____

On _____(day)_____ I will share what I find out. I will (pupil checks one):

_____ Write a paragraph   _____ Draw a picture

_____ Speak on a tape   _____ Speak to the class

_____ Put on a skit with these friends:

_____

_____

Signed _____
(pupil)

_____
(teacher)

Date _____

FIGURE 9.9
Sample Contract, Grades 2 to 4 (teacher can fill in if necessary)

Various learning techniques have been developed as alternatives to the competitive incentive structure and individualistic task structure of traditional classrooms. The success of the student team learning approach developed by Robert Slavin, David DeVries, and Keith Edwards at Johns Hopkins University, however, has been most fully documented.[57]

Research results show that student team learning improves both academic achievement and students' interpersonal relationships. All students (including high, average, and low achievers) appear to benefit. One of the most consistent findings is that African American students, and possibly Chicanos, "gain outstandingly in cooperative learning."[58] Further research is needed before these race-X treatment interactions can be fully explained. There is some evidence to support the possibility that children raised in Black and Hispanic communities tend to be more motivated by cooperation than competition, while the reverse is often true for those raised in the White middle-class milieu.[59] In contrast to the orientations of many Black and Hispanic students, the traditional classrooms in United States society stress competition and individual achievement. This emphasis can be stressful when students are faced with the situation of "attempting to excel academically and risk alienating their peers, or to do the minimum needed to get by."[60] Given the fact that disproportionate numbers of African American and Chicano students are low achievers, Slavin suggests that student team learning may help close the school success gap between minority and nonminority students. This is not to imply that the needs of White students are overlooked in the process. Although the achievement gains among nonminority White students tend to be less dramatic, says Slavin, their school achievement is not hindered by cooperative learning, and they reap many benefits in intergroup relations.

> For improving race relations, our results have been phenomenal. In seven field studies in desegregated schools, most of them inner-city Baltimore junior high schools, we found out team learning classes had much better racial attitudes and behaviors than traditional classes. In many cases, when we asked students to name their friends, they named as many or almost as many friends of other races as they would have if race were not a criterion. This was quite different from our pretests in these classes and in our control classes; in fact, in most of our control classes there were fewer cross-racial friendships on the posttest than there were on the pretest.
>
> In addition to positive effects on race relations the team classes learned as much or more than the traditional classes. In five of the seven studies in desegregated schools, the team classes learned significantly more language arts and mathematics than did the traditionally taught students. In many of the studies, students in the team classes engaged in less off-task behavior than did control students. This indicates that team learning techniques may also improve discipline in desegregated schools. Team learning techniques don't have to cost anything, and they are easy to learn and use. Instead of the usual one-day workshop in which speakers try to reduce teachers' prejudice, we can spend the same time to teach teachers to use an instructional system that is far more likely to improve students' racial attitudes and behaviors as well as their achievement.[61]

The three student team learning methods used most widely are: Student Teams–Achievement Divisions (STAD), Teams–Games–Tournaments (TGT), and Jigsaw II. The following descriptions are taken from the teacher's manual available from the Johns Hopkins Team Learning Project.

> In the *Jigsaw,* students are assigned to six-member teams. Academic material is broken down into as many parts as there are students on each team. For example, a biography might be broken into early life, first accomplishments, major setbacks, and so on. Members of the different teams who have the same section form "experts groups" and study together. Each then returns to his or her team and teaches the section to the team. Often, the students take a quiz on the entire set of material. The only way students can do well on this quiz is to pay close attention to their teammates' sections, so students are motivated to support and show interest in each other's work.
>
> *Teams–Games–Tournaments* (TGT) is the best researched of the classroom techniques that use teams. In TGT, students are assigned to four- or five-member learning teams. Each week, the teacher introduces new material in a lecture or discussion. The teams then study work sheets on the material together, and at the end of the week, team members compete in "tournaments" with members of other teams to add points to their team scores. In the tournaments, students compete on skill-exercise games with others who are comparable in past academic performance. This equal competition makes it possible for every student to have a good chance of contributing a maximum number of points to his or her team. A weekly newsletter, prepared by the teacher, recognizes successful teams and students who have contributed outstandingly to their team scores. The excitement and motivation generated by TGT is enormous. Teachers using this method have reported that students who were never particularly interested in school were coming in after class to get materials to take home to study, asking for special help, and becoming active in class discussions. In one project in a Baltimore junior high school that contains a large number of students bused from the inner city, almost every student in two classes stayed after school (and missed their buses) to attend a tie-breaker playoff in the TGT tournament competition [see Figure 9.10].
>
> *Student Teams–Achievement Divisions* (STAD) is a simple team technique in which students work in four- or five-member teams, and then take individual quizzes to make points for their team. Each student's score is compared to that of other students of similar past performance, so that in STAD, as in TGT, students of all ability levels have a good chance of earning maximum points for their teams. Thus, STAD is like TGT, except that it substitutes individual quizzes for the TGT game tournament.[62]

A fourth technique, Team-Assisted Individualization (TAI), has been developed and evaluated more recently. Developed originally for math, TAI is a unique form of cooperative learning in that it uses individualized rather than class-paced instruction. TAI is designed especially for classrooms where students are too heterogeneous to progress at similar rates. In TAI, students are assigned to four- to five-member heterogeneous teams as in other forms of team learning. After diagnostic testing, each team member works through the appropriate set of programmed mathematics units at his or her own pace.[63]

TEAM A

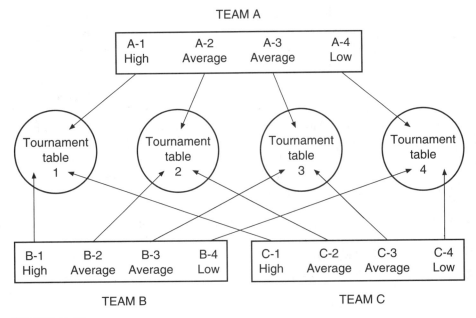

FIGURE 9.10
Assignment of Tourament Tables
From Robert E. Slavin, *Teacher Manual for Student Team Learning* (Baltimore, MD: Center for Social Organization of Schools, Johns Hopkins University, 1978), p. 10. Reprinted by permission of the author.

Why is student team learning so successful? For one thing, the strategy avoids problems due to diffusion of responsibility often associated with small-group work. Many people have worked in groups where some individuals were rewarded even if they contributed little or nothing to the group and where those who contributed most, or who worked to their fullest potential, received no recognition. Team learning avoids these problems because *group rewards are based on each individual member's learning.* The strategy is structured so that "the achievement of all group members does in fact contribute to group success. . . . [Furthermore] the contributions of each group member can be easily seen, so that praise or blame among group members can be correctly applied.[64]

An important aspect of student team learning is equal-opportunity scoring. Team scores are derived from the improvement on test scores of individual members in STAD and Jigsaw II and from game competition with equals in TGT. This enables all students, no matter what their entry-level skills, to contribute to the team if they do their best. This scoring system is believed to increase student achievement and is necessary for several reasons. First, it avoids the problem of low student motivation under traditional grading systems, in which some students are virtually guaranteed high marks while others do poorly no matter how hard they try. When grades correspond to ability rather than effort, high-ability students can often take things easy, while lower-ability students become discouraged over too difficult tasks. When improvement is the criterion for success, both success and failure are within the reach of all students. This is believed to enhance motivation and personal responsibility.

A second advantage of equal-opportunity scoring is that it lessens the chances that the less able group members will be devalued by their group mates. A system that rewards performance increases makes every team member a potential contributor. Experience shows that more able team members often become motivated to tutor the less able students who might otherwise be ignored or resented because they are perceived as a liability to the group.

Because equal-opportunity scoring is embedded in the student team learning strategies, its separate effect is difficult to determine. The results to date do suggest, however, that it may have a positive effect on student achievement.[65]

The effectiveness of task specialization, whereby each team member becomes an expert on one piece of the puzzle (e.g., Jigsaw) is not conclusive either. Positive results have been obtained in courses like social studies, science, and literature when content can be broken into subtopics. When the learning task requires mastery of a specific set of skills, concepts, or facts, as in a language, then group study (i.e., STAD and TGT) is more effective than task specialization.

Cooperative team learning is not without problems, however. One of the most serious arises from the differences in students' academic status (e.g., entry-level skills and knowledge, language proficiency), social status as ascribed by the outside society (e.g., ethnicity and sex), and peer status (e.g., friendship network).[66] The extensive research and curriculum development work by Cohen and associates at Stanford University has identified ways of treating status problems in cooperative classrooms, grades two through five. Successful treatments include

- Training students to use cooperative behaviors, such as listening, giving everyone a chance to talk, and asking for assistance.
- Assigning of rotating roles, such as facilitator, to each group member.
- Using rich, stimulating, learning materials that are intrinsically motivating and not entirely dependent on reading materials.
- Including tasks that are open-ended so that "precocious students can carry them further, while less mature students can complete them on a simpler level."[67]
- Introducing each set of activities as requiring multiple abilities.
- Assigning competence to low-status students through specific and public praise of behaviors such as reasoning or imagining, or of skills that require spatial ability or activities that require precision.[68]

Cohen's text, *Designing Groupwork: Strategies for Heterogeneous Classrooms*,[69] is an invaluable source for teachers. She clearly explains the theoretical framework for small-group instruction in terms of students' gains in academic learning (e.g., conceptual learning and improved oral language proficiency) and social development, as well as the benefits for classroom management. The theory is translated into practice by means of classroom examples

Teachers can also experience cooperative team learning as they develop multicultural lessons and practice a strategy they plan to use in their own classrooms.

at the elementary, middle, and high school level, and can include multilingual classrooms. The book's appendix contains team-building activities and suggestions for helping students learn the various team roles.

Peer and Cross-Age Tutoring

Tutoring can be another effective strategy for providing individualized help to supplement large-group instruction. Peer tutoring involves students teaching students their same age, while cross-age tutoring involves older children teaching younger children. It is also conceivable for children to teach adults or older children when they have special skills or knowledge. Bilingual-bicultural individuals of any age, for example, can be invaluable in helping monolingual learners understand course content and make transitions between home environments and culturally different school environments.

Peer tutoring can be used at all levels above grades three or four in any subject area where one or more students are at a relatively advanced level of skill or understanding as compared with their classmates. Advanced students help instruct less advanced students. This is the simplest and most direct form of tutoring and can be monitored by one teacher. Typically, tutoring is one-on-one, but small groups are possible. Imagine a large class in tennis or gymnastics in which four or five highly skilled students are used to help instruct students grouped according to their skill level. Imagine a fifth-grade math class that has, instead of students in groups labeled high, average, or low, heterogeneous (mixed abilities) children grouped by modality strengths and working on fractions under the direction of a classmate who has mastered the concepts. Imagine a compulsory Spanish class in which native speakers of Spanish are helping small groups of non-Spanish-speaking classmates improve their conversational skill.

Although tutoring is conceived as a remedial measure designed to help low achievers, research shows that tutors are likely to improve their own learning and emotional development in the process. Being in the instructor role has obvious benefits that need not be limited to high achievers. Through cross-age tutoring, students who are failing in their own class work can be helped to effectively instruct younger children in their schoolwork. The personal achievement gains of these tutors are sometimes dramatic.

Cross-age tutoring requires the cooperation of at least two teachers and therefore involves more complex management. One exemplary cross-age tutoring program has been developed by Lippitt and her associates at the University of Michigan, and it is available to teachers.[70]

Effective tutoring programs do not happen automatically. They are effective only under proper conditions. First of all, teachers must accept the idea. Often it is difficult to give up the teacher role and admit that sometimes our students are better able to communicate a concept or an idea than we are. This is particularly true among peer-oriented learners. Second, the competitive structure of schools needs to be modified so that education can become what Bruner calls a "communal undertaking." Bruner proposes that teachers give students more responsibility for the education of their fellow students, especially younger students, as one means of controlling the psychological problems associated with prolonged adolescence.[71] Under the conditions of communal learning, advanced students do not resent sharing their expertise and parents do not feel their children are being exploited or held back. Even when little can be done to change the school's competitive structure, the classroom environment can become relatively cooperative and accepting, and some degree of tutoring is possible.

In addition to these general theoretical considerations, there are the following specific conditions, which are discussed more fully in the excellent monograph *Peer and Cross-Age Tutoring in the Schools* by Bloom.

1. There is a structured situation in terms of a clearly specified task, time, material, and procedures.
2. There is a supportive teacher or supervisor—the tutor as well as the tutee needs sustained and continuous direction and encouragement.
3. The tutors and tutees support and reinforce each other.
4. While tutors do not need elaborate training, they do need clear directions and a model of appropriate behavior.
5. Both tutors and tutees need feedback and correction, and both need clearly perceived learning gains.[72]

Research into the effectiveness of tutoring programs in the schools underscores the importance of orientation and training of tutors. We cannot assume that untrained tutors, be they children or adults, will automatically use effective strategies; research and observation show the opposite.[73] On the other hand, research also shows that effective and manageable training programs have been developed and are available.[74] These programs have a dual focus. First, tutors need training in the content area they are teaching and knowledge of the most effective techniques for the subject matter. Knowledge about the tutees' modality strengths may also prove helpful; for example, multiplication facts could be taught using flash cards, oral response, games, manipulatives, worksheets, or some combination of these. Second, tutors need to develop human relations skills to help them relate constructively to the learner. Tutors (including adults) may feel frustrated when learning progresses at a slow pace, and they need to avoid using ridicule or doing the work for the learner.

On the basis of his own research as well as that of others, Von Harrison has asserted that "almost all upper-grade elementary children can be trained to use effective teaching skills when tutoring."[75] He found that the most effective procedure for training tutors consists of three steps: "First, the tutor reads instructions in simple expository text form concerning the task; second, the skills described by the written text are discussed and clarified; and, third, a role playing session follows with the trainer playing the part of the learner and tutors taking turns practicing the tutoring skills."[76]

In contrast to cooperative team learning, there is very little research to date on the effectiveness of peer tutoring in culturally pluralistic classrooms. It seems obvious, however, that an effective tutoring program must consider cultural differences based on language, nonverbal communication, social values, and learning styles. Where cultural traditions emphasize the authority of males or seniority, for example, female tutors for males or younger tutors are likely to be unacceptable.

Under the proper conditions, tutoring is an indispensable and effective resource for the teacher, tutor, and tutee; however, it is not without drawbacks. Perhaps the greatest of these are the burdens of training tutors and managing the program. Unless the school has a tutoring program managed by a supervisor available to all teachers, these burdens are likely to fall on the classroom teacher. In some cases, such as in the classroom of Eric Jones, it is possible to organize outside help. Sometimes only a few students in class require tutoring. Other times, particularly when students are tracked into low-achievement groups, an entire group of students would benefit. How one eighth-grade math teacher developed a tutoring program tailored to his particular situation is presented in the following illustration, which the teacher subtitled "A Sneaky Way to Identify and Train Peer Tutors for Interclass Tutoring."

Individualization through Use of Partners   E. Van Campbell

LESSON 9.4

Purpose

To use partners to develop tutor-tutee relationships in order to satisfy more of the individual needs of the students in attaining mastery of some basic math skills.

Rationale

Due to the shortcomings of group instruction in my classroom and the limits of my time and energy, some of my students need help that I alone cannot give them. I have found in the past that many students are willing to help their classmates

(Continued)

learn a task. Research indicates that a tutor's knowledge alone does not yield positive effects. Successful tutors must have appropriate communication skills. Training has been effective in developing a positive tutor-tutee relationship. Intraclass peer tutoring fits my situation best, but I believe it would be counterproductive to formalize tutor-tutee roles. Training partners to use appropriate communication techniques should be good for both the tutor and tutee and enable each student to assume either role. Then, as my students naturally space themselves in the self-paced materials we use they will be more prepared to help their slower-paced classmates or work cooperatively with a partner.

Training of Tutors

Ideally, the tutors learn as the trainer models the procedures. Each tutor is then given an opportunity to role-play the procedures once, twice, or as many times as necessary. Tutors need to rehearse the specific material they will use in the tutoring session.

The minimum training would include the following subjects.

- How to begin the tutoring session and set a positive tone.
- A step-by-step procedure for the learning, practice, and application of a skill, using specific materials.
- What to do when the answer is right: praise and reward.
- What to do when the answer is wrong: For incomplete answers, repeat the question in different words. For incorrect answers, model the correct answer by saying "my turn" and telling the answer; then say "your turn" and let the tutee repeat the correct answer. If the tutee almost knows the answer, contrast tutee's answer with the correct answer and let tutee discover the difference. Don't let tutee struggle too long to get the right answer. It wastes time and frustration sets in.
- What to do if the tutoring goes very badly: Ask the teacher or supervisor for suggestions.
- How to vary the tutoring session with suggestions for keeping high interest and good attention.
- How to end the session with a brief game, story, joke, riddle, or some other way of reducing the tension of intensive work.
- How to keep a simple checklist or other record form.[77]

Sample Tutoring Activity: An Introductory Activity to Number Theory

Objective: to have all students master the following task. Mastery will be defined as 95 percent correct with a two-minute limit.

Task: to write the whole numbers one to sixty as the product of two whole numbers, using the number one only when necessary.

Required materials: pencil with eraser and then a worksheet (see Figures 9.11 and 9.12). Since this is a speed drill, notice all cumbersome symbols are already provided on the worksheet.

Suggested practice modes: using a designated partner.

LESSON 9.4

(Continued)

Name _____	Date _____	Period _____
1 =	21 =	41 =
2 =	22 =	42 =
3 =	23 =	43 =
4 =	24 =	44 =
5 =	25 =	45 =
6 =	26 =	46 =
7 =	27 =	47 =
8 =	28 =	48 =
9 =	29 =	49 =
10 =	30 =	50 =
11 =	31 =	51 =
12 =	32 =	52 =
13 =	33 =	53 =
14 =	34 =	54 =
15 =	35 =	55 =
16 =	36 =	56 =
17 =	37 =	57 =
18 =	38 =	58 =
19 =	39 =	59 =
20 =	40 =	60 =

FIGURE 9.11
Worksheet for Task in Number Theory

Oral–Oral Practice

- Quizzer states number, quizzee responds with a product.
- Quizzer says "ok" after each correct response.
- Quizzer says "again" when an incorrect response is received.
- Quizzee should never guess; appropriate options are to say "help" or "skip" or be silent.
- Quizzer responds to "help" by repeating number, pausing, giving a correct response, and then repeating number for quizzee.
- Quizzer responds to "skip" by making a note and then repeating at end of the list.
- Quizzer also makes note of any number on which help was given.
- Quizzer reacts to a pause by saying "my turn," giving number, product, and repeating number to tutee.

Oral–Oral/Written Practice

- Quizzer gives orally.
- Quizzee answers both orally and in writing.
- Only the expressed product is written.

(Continued)

Name _____   Date _____   Period _____

1	$= 1 \times 1$	C21 $= C \times 7$	P41	$= 1 \times 41$
P2	$= 1 \times 2$	C22 $= 2 \times 11$	C42	$= 2 \times 21$
P3	$= 1 \times 3$	P23 $= 1 \times 23$	P43	$= 1 \times 43$
C4	$= 2 \times 2$	C24 $= 2 \times 12, 3 \times 8,$	C44	$= 2 \times 22, 4 \times 11$
P5	$= 1 \times 5$	$\quad\quad 4 \times 6$	C45	$= 3 \times 15, 5 \times 9$
C6	$= 2 \times 3$	C25 $= 5 \times 5$	C46	$= 2 \times 23$
P7	$= 1 \times 7$	C26 $= 2 \times 13$	P47	$= 1 \times 47$
C8	$= 2 \times 4$	C27 $= 3 \times 9$	C48	$= 2 \times 24, 3 \times 16,$
C9	$= 3 \times 3$	C28 $= 2 \times 14, 4 \times 7$		$\quad\quad 4 \times 12, 6 \times 8$
C10	$= 2 \times 5$	P29 $= 1 \times 29$	C49	$= 7 \times 7$
P11	$= 1 \times 11$	C30 $= 2 \times 15, 3 \times 10,$	C50	$= 2 \times 25, 5 \times 10$
C12	$= 2 \times 6, 3 \times 4$	$\quad\quad 5 \times 6$	C51	$= 3 \times 17$
P13	$= 1 \times 13$	P31 $= 1 \times 31$	C52	$= 2 \times 26, 4 \times 13$
C14	$= 2 \times 7$	C32 $= 2 \times 16, 4 \times 8$	P53	$= 1 \times 53$
C15	$= 3 \times 5$	C33 $= 3 \times 11$	C54	$= 2 \times 27, 3 \times 18$
C16	$= 2 \times 8, 4 \times 4$	C34 $= 2 \times 17$		$\quad\quad 6 \times 9$
P17	$= 1 \times 17$	C35 $= 5 \times 7$	C55	$= 5 \times 11$
C18	$= 2 \times 9, 3 \times 6$	C36 $= 2 \times 18, 3 \times 12,$	C56	$= 2 \times 28, 4 \times 14$
P19	$= 1 \times 19$	$\quad\quad 4 \times 9, 6 \times 6$		$\quad\quad 7 \times 8$
C20	$= 2 \times 10, 4 \times 5$	P37 $= 1 \times 37$	C57	$= 3 \times 19$
		C38 $= 2 \times 19$	C58	$= 2 \times 29$
		C39 $= 3 \times 13$	P59	$= 1 \times 59$
		C40 $= 2 \times 20, 4 \times 10,$	C60	$= 2 \times 30, 3 \times 20,$
		$\quad\quad 5 \times 8$		$\quad\quad 4 \times 15, 5 \times 12,$
				$\quad\quad 6 \times 10$

FIGURE 9.12
Answers to Problems in Figure 9.11

Written Practice

- Quizzee to be provided with a worksheet test.
- Quizzer watches as quizzee works on worksheet.
- Quizzer says correct answer when quizzee says "help."
- Quizzer, when seeing an incorrect response, says "my turn," erases incorrect response, and writes correct response.

Timed Practice

- Quizzer works as a timer.
- Quizzee skips any number that cannot be answered immediately.
- Quizzee is allowed to go back at end.
- Quizzee says "stop" when finished.

LESSON 9.4

(Continued)

- Quizzer responds with a positive statement, such as: "Your time really improved." "Wow, you really zipped through the first twenty." "Hey, you're almost there." "That'll be hard for me to beat."
- Quizzer and quizzee check work together.

Evaluation of task:

Students will be given a timed test (same as worksheet) by the teacher in a group situation. Those who demonstrate mastery will be able to move into individually paced workbooks. Those who do not demonstrate mastery will consult with the teacher about a practice partner. The practice partner could be a student who has attained mastery. All students will be expected to demonstrate mastery on subsequent days before beginning workbooks.

Some suggested partner and helping techniques:
- Cross out the twenty most difficult—time yourself.
- Practice the twenty most difficult—time yourself.
- Practice the 30s only.
- Practice the rough spots,
- Tutor could write one factor as a hint.
- Tutee could practice the 2s, 3s, etc.
- Tutee could orally note the problem numbers before being timed.
- Don't race; speed up only when comfortable.

This lesson is reprinted with the permission of the author.

Connections with Multicultural Education

How do these concepts and strategies relate to multicultural education? Aren't these examples of good approaches to teaching in any classroom?

First of all, it is true that what is effective in culturally diverse classrooms is generally effective in most if not all classrooms. Multicultural teaching, with its emphasis on equity and development of the learner's potential, is good for *all* students. In fact, the reforms suggested by multicultural educators are likely to bring about the educational excellence many nonadvocates of multicultural education are demanding. However, the opposite is not true. What often appears to be effective teaching in relatively homogeneous classrooms, where students learn and behave in similar ways and master a monocultural curriculum, is not likely to be effective in multicultural classrooms.

This chapter addresses the need for multicultural learning environments that accommodate cultural and personal differences among students (Chapter 8 addressed changes in the curriculum). Several of the strategies, for example, cooperative team learning, were originally developed for desegregated classrooms. Together they represent ways of avoiding resegregation through tracking and provide ways of fostering the necessary conditions for positive inter-group contact.

Mastery learning is based on the assumption that virtually all students are capable of learning. Experiential learning helps motivate students by engaging them in activities that relate to their personal and cultural experience. It then provides connections with the ongoing program. Learning centers and learning activity packets allow students to progress at their own rate without being compared with others. Peer and cross-age tutoring provide all students an opportunity to learn through teaching, which in turn fosters a communal learning environment. Small groups and team learning create the conditions of positive intergroup contact and have been shown to increase both academic achievement and positive interracial attitudes. Independent study allows students to pursue individual interests related to their personal and cultural backgrounds. Any one or all of these teaching concepts and strategies can be included in culturally relevant teaching. Overall, the goal is a supportive non-competitive communal learning environment where individual students are encouraged to put forth their best efforts and achieve their highest potential. Student diversity is accommodated without sacrificing quality in what students are learning.

CONCLUSIONS

A small proportion of students can learn well no matter what teachers do. Most students, however, seem to require some form of individualized help beyond regular classroom instruction if they are to maximize their learning and development. The challenge to teachers of culturally diverse groups of students is tremendous, for added to the variety of individual differences always present is the factor of ethnicity.

This chapter has focused on teaching concepts and strategies that are known to be most effective with diverse groups of students. Culturally relevant teaching, experiential learning, bilingual education, and student team learning were developed especially to meet student needs based on cultural differences. Each of the five strategies presented offers a distinct way of supplementing large-group instruction to create greater flexibility in the learning environment. Some strategies will appeal to teachers and students more than others. None of the strategies represents a panacea; none would be effective and appropriate for all students all of the time. It is up to teachers to create clusters of strategies for a given group of students at a particular point in the curriculum.

Few teachers would feel comfortable with the degree of flexibility evident in Eric Jones's classroom. The idea of managing, monitoring, and keeping records of students' learning can be overwhelming. The key is to start small. This chapter concludes with two approaches to getting started. Some teachers may prefer to begin with a small group of learners, those who are having the most difficulty or those who are far beyond their peers. Others may prefer to start with the total classroom environment. Still others may prefer some combination of the two.

Approach A: Focus on the Learner

1. Identify the students who are not achieving well under the present classroom conditions or who are exceptionally advanced.
2. Identify reasons for the students' difficulties. The list of twelve individual differences that affect student learning, discussed in Chapters 5 and 6, can provide guidelines.
3. Identify the most essential learning goals and objectives for those students.
4. Select strategies to supplement large-group instruction, which are likely to meet students' learning needs.
5. Gather and assemble the needed materials and/or select necessary persons.
6. Plan the schedule, place, location of assembled materials, and record keeping strategy.
7. Monitor students' progress and evaluate their success.
8. Revise the instructional plan as necessary.

Approach B: Focus on the Total Classroom Environment

1. Select one of the strategies presented in this chapter as a means of supplementing large-group instruction.
2. Based on the organization of the course, identify points at which to introduce the strategy.
3. Select one point and fully develop the strategy. Implement, evaluate, and revise your strategy as necessary.
4. Attempt to develop, implement, and revise one new version of the strategy each semester.
5. When possible, work with other teachers in the development, evaluation, and revising process. This can add depth to any one strategy, as, for example, when each teacher develops materials for a specific modality preference or for a different subtopic to be included in a LAP, learning center, or tutoring session. Interteacher cooperation can also expand the strategy repertoire of everyone in the group. Teachers can request that inservice days, or college course projects, be designed for this purpose.
6. Once the strategy is fully integrated into the instructional plan, select another strategy and repeat the process.

COMPARE AND CONTRAST

1. Culturally Relevant Teaching and Funds of Knowledge
2. Core values in MCE and Culturally Relevant Teaching
3. Culturally Relevant Teaching and "Cultural Deficit" approaches to teaching (Chapter 7)
4. Mastery learning and experiential learning
5. Peer tutoring and cooperative team learning
6. Independent study and individualized instruction
7. Bilingual education and multicultural education
8. Learning centers and learning activity packets

ACTIVITIES AND QUESTIONS

1. Consider the case of Eric Jones. What do you like and dislike about his classroom? In what ways is he responding to individual and/or cultural differences? To what degree, if any, would you be comfortable teaching in his classroom? What problems would you anticipate? How could you attempt to deal with them?

2. Compare and contrast the classrooms of Warren Benson and Eric Jones. What are the similarities? What are the differences?

3. Imagine that you are working with Warren Benson's students in your own area of specialization. Explain how you could structure the learning environment to individualize student learning to a greater degree. Be sensitive to the possibilities of both individual and cultural diversity. Would you reorganize your formal curriculum in any way? Explain. Would equal-opportunity scoring, as used in cooperative team learning, work in this classroom setting? Explain.

4. This book takes the position that the teacher's major goal is to foster the intellectual, social, and personal development of students to their highest potential. Furthermore, this position is based on the assumption that virtually all students are capable of growth, development, and academic success. Would you qualify these assumptions in any way? Explain.

5. The following activity helps clarify the sources of individualized instruction. Here is the scenario. This year you have several students who are having great difficulty learning in your class. At least a few of them, you believe, are achieving far below their capabilities. You decide to restructure your learning environment to enable you to individualize instruction to a greater degree. Listed below are twelve sources that you could use as you develop plans for individualizing student learning. Work alone in part one and rank these from the information source you believe would be most helpful (1) to the source you believe would be least helpful (12). Complete part two with other members of your group. You may modify any of the source statements if necessary.

PART ONE

_____ 1. Measures that indicate each student's learning style.

_____ 2. Community goals and competency expectations for students.

_____ 3. Your own view of the needs of your students, which may be due in part to the views of previous teachers and cumulative records.

_____ 4. Inventories that measure students' personal values, goals, and attitudes.

_____ 5. Key concepts, generalizations, and skills that are germane to the subject area(s).

_____ 6. Knowledge about personal family problems your students face.

_____ 7. Measures of student learning rate.

_____ 8. Pretests of student knowledge background.

_____ 9. Knowledge about the social climate (human dynamics) of your classroom and school.

_____ 10. The school district's curriculum guide, which lists knowledge and skills students are expected to attain.

_____ 11. Knowledge about students' ethnicity.

_____ 12. Other? Specify _____

PART TWO

A. The three information sources we believe would be helpful in planning for individualizing instruction are the following.
   1. _____
   2. _____
   3. _____
   Our reasons are: _____
   _____

B. The three sources we believe would be least helpful are
   1. _____
   2. _____
   3. _____
   Our reasons are: _____
   _____

6. Assume that you plan to include more individualized instruction in your classroom next year. What do you see as your major challenges? How could you meet them?

7. Given a situation where mastery learning is implemented in its classic form (that presented by Benjamin Bloom), which students are likely to benefit most—gifted, average, or low achievers? Would the result be different with the modified approach used by Eric Jones? Explain fully.

8. Read *Hunger of Memory* by Richard Rodriguez. In what ways did he experience transitional trauma between home and school, between the Mexican Catholic church and the Irish Catholic church, and within his family and neighborhood? What have been his deepest pains in growing up? His greatest joys? What does his life reveal about life in America? What are his views on bilingual education? Who finds his views controversial and why?

NOTES

1. Gloria Ladson-Billings, "But That's Just Good Teaching! The Case for Culturally Relevant Pedagogy," *Theory Into Practice,* Volume 34, Number 3, Summer 1995, pp. 161–165, *The Dream Keepers* (San Francisco: Jossey-Bass), 1994; and "Liberatory Consequences of Literacy: A Case of Culturally Relevant Instruction for African-American Students," *Journal of Negro Education,* 61, 378–391.
2. Ibid.
3. Ibid., op cit., *Theory into Practice* p. 162.
4. *Journal of Negro Education,* p. 383.
5. Lisa Delpit. *Other People's Children: Cultural Conflict in the Classroom* (New York: The New Press) 1995, 41.
6. Ibid.
7. Ibid., 42.
8. Julie Chlebo (1998, in press) "There Is No Rose Garden: A Second Generation Rural Head Start Program. "Unpublished doctoral dissertation, Indiana University.
9. Ibid., 169.
10. Ibid., 171.
11. Luis C. Moll, Cathy Amanti, Deborah Neff, and Norma Gonzalez, "Funds of Knowledge for Teaching: Using a Qualitative Approach to Connect Homes and Classrooms," *Theory Into Practice,* 31, 2, 1992, 132–140.
12. Norma Gonzalez, "Processual Approaches to Multicultural Education." *Journal of Applied Behavioral Science,* 31, 2, 1995, 234.
13. Moll, et. al. op cit., 133.
14. Ibid., 238.
15. Moll, et. al. op.cit., 133.
16. Moll, et. al., op.cit., 139.
17. Gonzalez, op.cit., 240.
18. H. H. Talmage (ed.), *Systems of Individualized Education* (Berkeley, CA: McCutchan, 1975), 36.
19. G. Heathers, "A Working Definition of Individualized Instruction," *Educational Leadership* 34, no. 5 (February 1977):342.
20. R. G. Shirts, *Bafá Bafá: A Cross Culture Simulation* (Simile 11, 218 Twelfth Street, P.O. Box 910, Del Mar, CA 92014, 1977).
21. B. S. Bloom, "Mastery Learning," in *Mastery Learning: Theory and Practice,* J. H. Block, ed. (New York: Holt, Rinehart and Winston, 1971).
22. K. P. Cross, *Accent on Learning* (San Francisco; Jossey-Bass, 1976).
23. W. Glasser. *Schools without Failure* (New York: Harper & Row, 1969), 26.
24. Bloom, "Mastery Learning."
25. J. B. Carroll, "A Model of School Learning," *Teachers College Record* 64 (May 1963):723–733; and B. S. Bloom, "Learning for Mastery," *Evaluation Comment* 1, no. 2 (1968).
26. J. H. Block (ed.), *Mastery Learning: Theory and Practice* (New York: Holt, Rinehart and Winston, 1971).
27. N. E. Gronlund, *Individualizing Classroom Instruction* (New York: Macmillan, 1974), 10. The list of steps reprinted with permission of Macmillan Publishing Company from *Individualizing Classroom Instruction* by Norman E. Gronlund. Copyright © 1974 by Norman E. Gronlund.
28. See J. H. Block and L. W. Anderson, *Mastery Learning in Classroom Instruction* (New York: Macmillan, 1975), 38.
29. Shirts, *Bafá Bafá.*
30. D. Wolsk, *An Experience Centered Curriculum: Exercises in Personal and Social Reality* (Paris; United Nations Educational, Scientific and Cultural Organization,1974), ERIC ED 099 269.
31. Ibid., 2.
32. Ibid., 3.
33. Ibid., 8.
34. Bertha Perez and Maria E. Torres-Guzmán, *Learning in Two Worlds: An Integrated Spanish/English Biliteracy Approach* (New York: Longman, 1992), p. xxiii.
35. B. L. Whorf, *Language, Thought, and Reality* (New York: Wiley, 1956).
36. W. Goodenough, *Culture, Language and Society,* 2nd ed. (Menlo Park, CA: Benjamin Cummings, 1981).
37. This paragraph is based on Karen Shuster Webb's section on bilingual education that appeared in my previous editions.

38. Felicity Barringer, "Immigration in 80's Made English a Foreign Language for Millions." *New York Times,* Wednesday, April 28, 1993, 1, 10.

39. M. Brisk, "Language Policies in American Education: A Historical Overview," in *Bilingual Education Teacher Handbook,* Martha Montero, ed. (Cambridge, MA: Evaluation, Dissemination and Assessment Center for Bilingual Education, 1982).

40. R. Garcia, *Learning in Two Languages* (Bloomington, IN: Phi Delta Kappa Educational Foundation, 1976).

41. A. H. Leibowitz, "Language, a Means of Social Control: The United States Experience" (unpublished manuscript, August 1974).

42. James Crawford, *Bilingual Education: History, Politics, Theory and Practice* (Trenton, NJ: Crane Publishing Co., 1989), 53.

43. Ibid., 84.

44. Ibid., 97–111.

45. Ibid., 104.

46. Ibid., 106.

47. Ibid., 175.

48. Ibid.

49. Carlos J. Ovando and Virginia P. Collier, *Bilingual and ESL Classrooms: Teaching in Multicultural Contexts* (New York: McGraw-Hill Book Co., 1985).

50. R. C. Troike, "Synthesis of Research on Bilingual Education," *Educational Leadership* 38 (March 1981):498–504.

51. R. C. Gardner and W. E. Lambert, *Attitudes and Motivation in Second-Language Learning* (Rowley, MA: Newbury House, 1972).

52. Karen Shuster Webb contributed this section in the first two editions of *Comprehensive Multicultural Education.*

53. C. Compton, "Learning Centers" (Alachua County Public Schools, Gainesville, FL, unpublished and undated reprint).

54. Gronlund, *Individualizing Classroom Instruction,* 46–47. The list is reprinted with permission of Macmillan Publishing Company from *Individualizing Classroom Instruction* by Norman E. Gronlund. Copyright © 1974 by Norman E. Gronlund.

55. Compton, "Learning Centers."

56. R. Slavin, D. DeVries, and K. Edwards, *Cooperative Learning* (New York; Longman, 1983); E. G. Cohen and M. B. Arias, "Accelerating the Education of Language Minority At-risk Students" (paper presented at Conference on Accelerating the Education of At-risk Students, Stanford University, November 17–18, 1988).

57. Ibid.

58. Ibid., 61.

59. Ibid., 62.

60. Ibid.

61. R. Slavin, *Using Student Team Learning,* rev. ed. (Baltimore: Center for Social Organization of Schools, Johns Hopkins University, 1980), 2–3. Reprinted by permission of the author.

62. R. Slavin, *Teacher Manual for Student Team Learning* (Baltimore: Center for Social Organization of Schools, Johns Hopkins University, 1978), 6–7. Reprinted by permission of the author.

63. Slavin, *Cooperative Learning,* 27.

64. Ibid., 32–33.

65. Ibid., 52–53.

66. E. G. Cohen, "Restructuring the Classroom: Conditions for Productive Small Groups," *Review of Educational Research* 64 (Spring 1994):1–35.

67. E. G. Cohen and M. B. Arias. "Accelerating the Education of Language Minority At-risk Students" (paper presented at Conference on Accelerating the Education of At-risk Students, Stanford University, November 17–18, 1988).

68. Cohen, Loten, and Catanzarite, "Treating Status Problems."

69. E. Cohen, *Designing Groupwork: Strategies for Heterogeneous Classrooms* (New York: Teachers College Press, 1986).

70. P. Lippitt, J. Eiseman, and D. Lippitt, *Cross-Age Helping Program: Orientation, Training, and Related Materials* (Ann Arbor: University of Michigan, Center for Research on Utilization of Scientific Knowledge, Institute for Social Research, 1969). A cross-age helping package of dissemination materials is published by Xicom, RFD #1, Sterling Forest. Tuxedo, NY.

71. J. Bruner, "Immaturity—Its Uses, Nature and Management," *Times Educational Supplement* (London), October 27, 1972:62–63.

72. S. Bloom, *Peer and Cross-age Tutoring in the Schools* (Washington, DC: National Institute of Education, December 1976).

73. G. Von Harrison, "Structured Tutoring: Antidote for Low Achievement," in *Children as Teachers,* Vernon L. Allen, ed. (New York: Academic Press, 1976), 169–177.

74. Ibid.

75. Ibid., 171.

76. Ibid.

77. Bloom, *Peer and Cross-age Tutoring,* 30.

Index

435